# ROUTLEDGE INTERNATIONAL HANDBOOK OF DELINQUENCY AND HEALTH

The *Routledge International Handbook of Delinquency and Health* presents state-of-the-art research and theorizing on the intersections between health, delinquency, and the juvenile justice system. Organized into three parts—Theoretical and Empirical Foundations; Behavioral, Mental, and Physical Health Conditions; and Prevention, Policy, and Health Promotion Systems—it is the largest and most comprehensive work of its kind, featuring contributions from scholars from multiple nations and global regions.

A growing number of researchers, practitioners, and policymakers from criminology and criminal justice, social work, medicine, psychiatry and psychology, and other health science disciplines engage with marginalized adolescent populations who are at elevated risk for violence and delinquency, alcohol and other drug use, health and mental health problems, and other difficulties directly related to public safety and well-being. These risk factors often lead to short-term (e.g., detention, juvenile residential treatment facilities) and long-term (e.g., prison, parole) contact with the criminal justice system. As these fields increasingly overlap, the distinctions between them are blurred. Sound decision-making in the juvenile justice system depends on adequate research and policy at the intersection of delinquency and health.

This volume represents an agenda-setting scholarly resource for the expansion of research and policymaking across the international delinquency and health continuum, and will be an essential resource for all who study or work in the field.

**Michael G. Vaughn**, PhD, is Professor in the School of Social Work, College for Public Health and Social Justice, at Saint Louis University where he also is the founder and Director of the Health Criminology Research Consortium. He is a fellow of the American Academy of Social Work and Social Welfare and the Society for Social Work and Research. Professor Vaughn is an internationally recognized scientist who has published more than 400 scholarly works.

**Christopher P. Salas-Wright**, PhD, is Assistant Professor in the Boston University School of Social Work and a Research Fellow with the National Hispanic Science Network's (NHSN) Early Stage Career Mentoring for NIDA Research program. He is also a holder of an NIH (K01) early career award. Since 2012, Dr. Salas-Wright has authored more than 125 scholarly publications.

**Dylan B. Jackson**, PhD, is Assistant Professor in the Department of Criminal Justice (College of Public Policy) at the University of Texas at San Antonio (UTSA), and an Associate of UTSA's Institute for Health Disparities Research. As a developmental and health criminologist, Dr. Jackson's research is integrative, bridging empirical and theoretical developments from multiple social and health science fields.

# ROUTLEDGE INTERNATIONAL HANDBOOK OF DELINQUENCY AND HEALTH

*Edited by Michael G. Vaughn,
Christopher P. Salas-Wright, and Dylan B. Jackson*

NEW YORK AND LONDON

First published 2020
by Routledge
52 Vanderbilt Avenue, New York, NY 10017

and by Routledge
2 Park Square, Milton Park, Abingdon, Oxon, OX14 4RN

*Routledge is an imprint of the Taylor & Francis Group, an informa business*

© 2020 Taylor & Francis

The right of Michael G. Vaughn, Christopher P. Salas-Wright & Dylan B. Jackson to be identified as the authors of the editorial material, and of the authors for their individual chapters, has been asserted in accordance with sections 77 and 78 of the Copyright, Designs and Patents Act 1988.

All rights reserved. No part of this book may be reprinted or reproduced or utilized in any form or by any electronic, mechanical, or other means, now known or hereafter invented, including photocopying and recording, or in any information storage or retrieval system, without permission in writing from the publishers.

*Trademark notice*: Product or corporate names may be trademarks or registered trademarks, and are used only for identification and explanation without intent to infringe.

*Library of Congress Cataloging-in-Publication Data*
Names: Vaughn, Michael G., author. | Salas-Wright, Christopher P., author. | Jackson, Dylan, author.
Title: Routledge international handbook of delinquency and health / Michael G. Vaughn, Christopher P. Salas-Wright & Dylan B. Jackson.
Description: 1 Edition. | New York : Routledge, 2020.
Identifiers: LCCN 2019014159 (print) | LCCN 2019016464 (ebook) | ISBN 9780429289194 (Ebook) | ISBN 9780367256920 (hardback) | ISBN 9780429289194 (ebk)
Subjects: LCSH: Juvenile justice, Administration of. | Juvenile delinquency. | Discrimination in juvenile justice administration.
Classification: LCC HV9069 (ebook) | LCC HV9069 .V378 2020 (print) | DDC 364.36–dc23
LC record available at https://lccn.loc.gov/2019014159

ISBN: 978-0-367-25692-0 (hbk)
ISBN: 978-0-429-28919-4 (ebk)

Typeset in Bembo
by Swales & Willis, Exeter, Devon, UK

# CONTENTS

*Preface* — viii
*List of Contributors* — x

**PART I**
**Theoretical and Empirical Foundations** — 1

1. Theorizing the Role of Health and Health Disparities in the Life-Course Criminological Paradigm — 3
   *Dylan B. Jackson and Michael G. Vaughn*

2. Evidence on Prenatal and Perinatal Health Factors Associated with Juvenile Delinquency — 16
   *Stacy Tzoumakis and Jesse Cale*

3. Racial Disparities in Health and Justice System Exposure: Patterns and Explanations — 33
   *Graham C. Ousey and Tracy W.P. Sohoni*

4. Influences of Early Nutrition on Child and Adolescent Antisocial Behavior — 50
   *Phoebe Um and Jianghong Liu*

5. What Becomes of the Problem Child?: The Foundational Role of Temperament in Health and Juvenile Offending — 61
   *Matthew DeLisi*

6. The Stress Mechanisms of Adolescent Physical, Mental, and Behavioral Health — 74
   *Lisa A. Kort-Butler*

7   Adverse Childhood Experiences, Delinquency, and Health: Implications for Juvenile Justice Systems  90
    *Michael Baglivio*

8   The Health Consequences of Incarceration for Families  104
    *Kristin Turney and Martha Morales Hernandez*

## PART II
## Behavioral, Mental, and Physical Health Conditions  117

9   Traumatic Brain Injury and Justice-Involved Youth: Assessment and Intervention  119
    *Christopher A. Veeh and Tanya Renn*

10  Sleep and Delinquency: An Emerging Area of Research  132
    *Samantha S. Clinkinbeard and Pete Simi*

11  The Impact of Youth with Psychopathic Traits on Health: A Social-Ecological Perspective  145
    *Dennis E. Reidy, Katherine W. Bogen, and Scott O. Lilienfeld*

12  Alcohol and Drug Misuse, Delinquency, and Health  160
    *Christopher P. Salas-Wright*

13  Key Health Behaviors Across the Life Course: The Salience of Comorbid Substance Use and Depression  169
    *Abby K. Johnson and Megan Bears Augustyn*

14  The Health Consequences of Victimization  185
    *Chad Posick and Kalynn Gruenfelder*

15  The Prevalence and Dynamics of Teen Dating Violence  197
    *Vithya Murugan, Annah K. Bender, Elise Trombetta, and Caroline Dilts*

16  Health Focused Criminology: Lead, Crime, and the Use of Quantitative Genetics to Examine Causality  209
    *Brian B. Boutwell and Stephen J. Watts*

## PART III
## Prevention, Policy, and Health Promotion Systems  219

17  Early Childhood Risk Factors, Prevention and Intervention  221
    *Ruth Paris, Jessica Dym Bartlett, and Corinne Beaugard*

18  Mobilizing Communities to Prevent Adolescent Substance Use and Delinquency   244
    *Abigail A. Fagan and C. Cory Lowe*

19  Behavioral Health and Treatment Utilization among Youth involved in the
    Juvenile Justice System   257
    *Matthew C. Aalsma and Katherine Schwartz*

20  Restorative Justice in K–12 Schools as a Structural Health Equity Intervention   269
    *Jelena Todic, Catherine Cubbin, and Marilyn Armour*

21  The Role of Occupational Science and Occupational Therapy in the Juvenile
    Justice System   291
    *Lisa A. Jaegers, Karen F. Barney, and Rebecca M. Aldrich*

22  Qualitative Research at the Intersections of Youth Justice and Health   305
    *Laura S. Abrams and Elizabeth S. Barnert*

23  Drugs, Health and Juvenile Delinquency in Latin America: Trends, Policies
    and Actions   315
    *Augusto Pérez-Gómez, Juliana Mejía-Trujillo, Mónica Pérez-Trujillo, and Jessica Orr*

24  Delinquency and Health in Australian Youth   329
    *Sheryl A. Hemphill and Jessica A. Heerde*

25  Delinquency and Health: Future Directions   341
    *Michael G. Vaughn, Christopher P. Salas-Wright, and Dylan B. Jackson*

Index   347

# PREFACE

A growing number of researchers, practitioners, and policy-makers from criminology and criminal justice, social work, medicine, psychiatry and psychology, and other health science disciplines engage with marginalized adolescent populations who are at elevated risk for violence and delinquency, alcohol and drug use, health and mental health problems, and other difficulties directly related to public safety and well-being. The life-course risk factors experienced often lead to short-term (e.g., detention, juvenile residential treatment facilities) and long-term (e.g., prison, parole) contact with the criminal justice system. As the fields of health and criminology increasingly overlap, the distinctions between the research foci are blurred. Sound decision-making in the juvenile justice system depends on adequate research and policy at the intersection of delinquency and health. Juvenile justice populations often have extensive health needs including chronic disease, notable mental health and substance use disorders, and educational and behavioral rehabilitation needs. Many of these health conditions have deep causal roots which are also shared with the behaviors that have let to justice-system involvement.

Our goal with this volume is to present the state-of-the-art research and theorizing on the intersections between health, delinquency, and the juvenile justice system. To our knowledge, this volume represents the largest and most comprehensive work of its kind, and includes contributions from scholars from multiple nations and global regions. Our hope was to begin to call attention to these research intersections and provide an agenda-setting scholarly resource for the expansion of research and policy-making across the international delinquency and health continuum.

The volume is divided into three parts that collectively span the terrain of health and its intersection with delinquency and the juvenile justice system. Part I, "Theoretical and Empirical Foundations," examines core theoretical/conceptual issues and major empirical findings at the intersection of health and delinquency research including the key relationships between health nascent health criminology and traditional criminological theorizing, research on health disparities, the life course, nutrition, health behavior and temperament theories, stress mechanisms, adverse childhood experiences, and health consequences of incarceration for families. Next, Part II, "Behavioral, Mental, and Physical Health Conditions," includes chapters on traumatic brain injury, sleep, psychopathy and public health, substance use and its comorbidity with depression, victimization, and lead poisoning and quantitative genetics. This section essentially examines the behavioral health, mental health, and physical health conditions among at-risk populations that are on life-course pathways to delinquency, or who are already juvenile offenders at risk for future contact with the criminal justice system. Finally, Part III, "Prevention, Policy, and Health Promotion Systems," involves the application of prevention science over the early sections of the life course, health policy matters, and coverage of health promotion systems in and applied to the juvenile justice system. More specifically, this final section includes chapters on community level prevention, treatment utilization, occupational therapy, the use of restorative justice in schools, employment of qualitative methods, and delinquency and health in Latin American and Australia. Finally, a brief chapter on future directions is included to highlight some missing gaps and identify areas where these exists some unique research opportunities.

Health criminology is an emerging area, many criminology and criminal justice programs are considering or developing courses that span the intersection of health and mental health and the criminal justice system, and/or have introduced health criminology material into their curricula. We think the present volume can be used with advanced undergraduate or graduate courses and provide a useful reference for researchers. Our hope is that scholars can build on the foundation laid forth in the volume. New theorizing and research is certainly needed.

*Michael G. Vaughn, PhD*
*Christopher P. Salas-Wright, PhD*
*Dylan B. Jackson, PhD*

# CONTRIBUTORS

**Matthew C. Aalsma,** PhD, is a Professor of Pediatrics and Psychology and the Director of the Adolescent Behavioral Health Research Program at the Indiana University School of Medicine. His research focuses on interdisciplinary approaches to improve outcomes among vulnerable youth, including young people involved in the juvenile justice system.

**Laura S. Abrams**, PhD, MSW, is Professor and Chair of the Department of Social Welfare at UCLA Luskin School of Public Affairs. Her scholarship examines juvenile justice institutions, transitions, and reentry.

**Rebecca M. Aldrich,** PhD, OTR/L, is an Associate Professor of Clinical Occupational Therapy in the Mrs. T.H. Chan Division of Occupational Science and Occupational Therapy at the University of Southern California.

**Marilyn Armour,** PhD, MSW, is a University Distinguished Teaching Professor in the Steve Hicks School of Social Work, and director of the Institute for Restorative Justice and Restorative Dialogue, The University of Texas at Austin. Armour's work focuses on the healing of victims, offenders and the community related to crime and wrongdoing.

**Megan Bears Augustyn,** PhD, is an Assistant Professor in the Department of Criminal Justice at the University of Texas at San Antonio. Her research interests include the causes and consequences of crime and victimizations over the life course, help-seeking behaviors, intimate and family violence, and gender and crime.

**Michael Baglivio,** PhD, serves as Chief Executive Officer for Analytic Initiatives, LLC. He is responsible for evaluating the effectiveness of treatment programming on short- and longer-term performance measures and outcomes. For over ten years he has focused research on evaluation of juvenile justice reform initiatives, including assessing the predictive validity of risk/needs assessment, reducing recidivism through a disposition recommendation matrix, examining changes in dynamic risk and protective factors, and the significance of Adverse Childhood Experiences (ACEs) in juvenile outcomes.

**Elizabeth S. Barnert,** MD, MPH, MS, is an Assistant Professor of Pediatrics at The David Geffen School of Medicine at UCLA. Dr. Barnert's clinical work is in general pediatrics and her research scholarship focuses on addressing the health needs of youth involved in the juvenile justice system.

**Karen F. Barney**, PhD, OTR/L, FAOTA, Professor Emerita, Department of Occupational Science and Occupational Therapy, Saint Louis University, is an occupational therapist with over 50 years of experience in practice and higher education.

**Jessica Dym Bartlett**, MSW, PhD, is Co-Director of Early Childhood Research at Child Trends, a non-profit, non-partisan institution dedicated to improving the lives of all children through rigorous research. She conducts research on early childhood trauma and adversity, with a focus on identifying protective factors at the parent, family, contextual, and program level that contribute to resilience among young children and their families.

**Corinne Beaugard**, MSW, is a PhD student at Boston University School of Social Work. She assists in research broadly related to substance use disorders and medication assisted treatment, as well as research on pregnant and parenting women with a history of substance use.

**Annah K. Bender**, PhD, is a Research Associate in the College of Nursing at the University of Missouri-St. Louis. She researches intimate partner violence among under-resourced populations and formerly worked in domestic violence and community mental health settings.

**Katherine W. Bogen** is a Clinical Research Program Coordinator for the Department of Psychiatry at Rhode Island Hospital, where she implements and evaluates dating violence and sexual assault prevention programming. Her areas of interest include violence prevention program design and evaluation; patterns of online violence disclosure and response; and social media analysis.

**Brian B. Boutwell**, PhD, is an Associate Professor and Associate Dean of Research in the College for Public Health and Social Justice at Saint Louis University. He is interested in the evolution of various human traits, the environmental and genetic underpinnings of human violence and aggression, and the intersection of general intelligence with various public health and behavioral outcomes.

**Jesse Cale**, PhD, is an Associate Professor of Criminology at the University of New South Wales in Sydney, Australia. His main areas of research involve the causes and consequences of sexual violence, developmental criminology, and criminal justice policy and evaluation.

**Samantha S. Clinkinbeard**, PhD, is an Associate Professor and Undergraduate Program Coordinator in the School of Criminology and Criminal Justice at the University of Nebraska at Omaha. Her research focuses on gendered self-concepts, future orientation, self-control, and risk-behavior among adolescents.

**Catherine Cubbin**, PhD, is Professor and Associate Dean for Research in the Steve Hicks School of Social Work, and a faculty research associate at the Population Research Center, The University of Texas at Austin. Cubbin's research focuses on using epidemiological methods to better understand socioeconomic and racial/ethnic inequalities in health for the purpose of informing policy.

**Matthew DeLisi**, PhD, is College of Liberal Arts and Sciences Dean's Professor, Coordinator of Criminal Justice Studies, Professor in the Department of Sociology, and Faculty Affiliate of the Center for the Study of Violence at Iowa State University. A renowned scholar, Professor DeLisi is one of the most prolific and highly cited criminologists in the world with approximately 400 scholarly publications on an array of topics in the social, behavioral, and forensic sciences.

**Caroline Dilts**, MSW, is a recent MSW graduate from Saint Louis University. She currently works as an in-home therapist at Eliot Community Human Services in Massachusetts.

**Abigail A. Fagan**, PhD, is an Associate Professor at the University of Florida. Dr. Fagan's research focuses on the etiology and prevention of adolescent substance use, delinquency, and violence, with an emphasis on examining the ways in which scientific advances can be successfully translated into effective crime and delinquency prevention practices.

**Kalynn Gruenfelder** is a Doctoral Student in Clinical Psychology at Georgia Southern University. Her research interests include perceptions of childhood sexual abuse and the various factors affecting those perceptions. Her clinical interests include child and adult psychotherapy. She teaches Introduction to Psychology and participates in leadership roles on campus.

**Jessica A. Heerde**, PhD, is a Research Fellow and adolescent health researcher in the Department of Paediatrics at the University of Melbourne. She conducts qualitative and quantitative research focusing on the influence of modifiable factors on the health and behavior of young Australians, with a specialized focus on homelessness and social marginalization. Her research seeks to inform prevention and early intervention programs leading to improving the lives of young Australians and their families. Dr. Heerde is supported by a Westpac Bicentennial Foundation Research Fellowship (2017–2020).

**Sheryl A. Hemphill**, PhD, is currently self-employed as a research consultant. She is an Adjunct Professor at La Trobe University, an Honorary Principal Research Fellow at the University of Melbourne, and an Honorary Fellow at Murdoch Children's Research Institute. Professor Hemphill has conducted research on the development and prevention of externalizing behaviors including violence, bullying, and antisocial behavior in young people for over 25 years.

**Martha Morales Hernandez** is a PhD student in the Department of Sociology at the University of California, Irvine. Her research interests are broadly within the fields of immigration, health, and education. Her current research investigates the role of immigration status in shaping the educational experiences and well-being of undocumented youth in institutions of higher learning.

**Dylan B. Jackson**, PhD, is Assistant Professor in the Department of Criminal Justice (College of Public Policy) at the University of Texas at San Antonio (UTSA), and an Associate of UTSA's Institute for Health Disparities Research.

**Lisa A. Jaegers**, PhD, is Assistant Professor in the Department of Occupational Science & Occupational Therapy, Doisy College of Health Sciences, and holds a secondary appointment in the School of Social Work and Criminology, College for Public Health and Social Justice at Saint Louis University. Jaegers' research explores the collaborative intersection of correctional workplace health promotion with diversion, transition, and community integration models of service to address solutions towards transformative justice.

**Abby K. Johnson** is a second year graduate student in the Applied Social and Health Psychology program at Colorado State University. She studies substance use, mental health, and health disparities among marginalized populations. She hopes to use her degree to better mental health care at the system, community, and individual levels.

**Lisa A. Kort-Butler**, PhD, is an Associate Professor of Sociology at the University of Nebraska-Lincoln. Her research focuses on adolescent and young adult well-being, including physical, mental, and behavioral health. She is interested in the role of social psychological factors in the social processes that influence well-being.

**Scott O. Lilienfeld**, PhD, is Samuel Candler Dobbs Professor of Psychology at Emory University in Atlanta, Georgia and visiting Professor at the University of Melbourne in Australia.

*Contributors*

**Jianghong Liu**, PhD, is currently an Associate Professor in the Schools of Nursing and Public Health at the University of Pennsylvania. She is also the director of the NIH-funded China Jintan Child Health Project, where she is following more than 1,000 children in Jintan city from pre-school into adolescence to understand the influence of exposure to lead and micronutrient deficiency on their behavior.

**C. Cory Lowe**, MA, is a PhD student and Graduate School Fellow in the Department of Sociology and Criminology & Law at the University of Florida. He received his MA in the Social Sciences from Georgia Southern University in 2015. His research interests include risk and protective factors for crime, delinquency, and substance use; communities and crime; criminological theory; and juvenile delinquency and prevention.

**Juliana Mejía-Trujillo** is a social worker with a Master's degree on Anthropology, with a large experience working with vulnerable communities. She is Director of Prevention at Corporación Nuevos Rumbos and is also the person in charge of training processes at a national as well as international level (Chile, Panama, Mexico).

**Vithya Murugan**, PhD, is an Assistant Professor of Social Work at Saint Louis University. Her research interests include violence against minority women, including immigrants and refugees; gender empowerment; and cross-cultural research.

**Jessica Orr** has a Bachelor of Arts in Spanish Literature and Art from the University of Puget Sound, with a professional background in clinical care coordination. She is currently a graduate candidate for the Master of Public Health and Master of Arts in Latin American Studies program from the University of Miami for 2019

**Graham C. Ousey**, PhD, is a Professor and Chair of the Department of Sociology at the College of William & Mary in Virginia. His current research interests include the confluence of crime and negative health outcomes, racial disparities in crime and justice, stability and change in criminal offending and victimization, immigration and crime, and cultural explanations of crime across places. His research on these and other issues has been published in outlets including *Criminology, Social Problems, Social Forces, Rural Sociology, Journal of Research in Crime and Delinquency, Justice Quarterly, Journal of Quantitative Criminology*, and *Journal of Criminal Justice*.

**Ruth Paris**, PhD, LICSW, is an Associate Professor of Clinical Practice at Boston University School of Social Work where she serves as the Chair of the Clinical Practice Department. Her program of research focuses on attachment-based interventions for vulnerable families with young children. With support from SAMHSA, DOD, NIH, HRSA and private foundations, she has developed and evaluated multiple interventions implemented in a variety of community settings focused on families at-risk.

**Augusto Pérez-Gómez**, PhD, is a Professor (r) of Clinical Psychology, Universidad de los Andes, Colombia; Director of Corporación Nuevos Rumbos since 2002; Visiting Professor at the School of Medicine at Chelsea and Westminster, London University (1994–1995) and at the School of Medicine and Dentistry, University of New Jersey (2003–2006). He has published 176 papers in Spanish, English, French, German and Portuguese, and 14 books

**Mónica Pérez-Trujillo**, PhD, is an Associate Professor at the University of Los Andes, Colombia. She received her MA and PhD in Criminology from the University of Melbourne. Her main research interests focus on domestic and sexual violence, alcohol-related violence, institutional responses to victims and offenders, and situational crime prevention.

**Chad Posick**, PhD, is an Associate Professor of Criminal Justice and Criminology at Georgia Southern University. His research interests include the causes and consequences of victimization, violence prevention and intervention, and biopsychosocial perspectives in criminology. He teaches in the area of statistics, criminological theory, and victimology. He is a member of the Scholars Strategy Network and member of the Health Criminology Research Consortium.

**Dennis E. Reidy**, PhD, is an Assistant Professor in the School of Public Health at Georgia State University. He received his PhD in Clinical Psychology from the University of Georgia in 2008. Prior to joining the faculty at GSU he worked as a behavioral scientist in the Division of Violence Prevention at the Centers for Disease Control and Prevention for eight years where he oversaw etiological prevention outcome research at multiple levels of the social ecology.

**Tanya Renn**, PhD, MSSW, MPH, is an Assistant Professor in the College of Social Work and the Assistant Director of the Institute for Justice Research and Development at Florida State University. As a criminal justice and addictions researcher, Dr. Renn focuses on understanding the relational pathways that exist between trauma/stress, high-risk behaviors (i.e. substance use and high-risk sexual behavior), and well-being among those involved in the criminal justice system.

**Christopher P. Salas-Wright**, PhD, is Assistant Professor in the Boston University School of Social Work and a Research Fellow with the National Hispanic Science Network's (NHSN) Early Stage Career Mentoring for NIDA Research program. He is also an inaugural Research Fellow with Saint Louis University's Health Criminology Research Consortium.

**Katherine Schwartz**, JD, MPA, is a Research Associate at the Indiana University School of Medicine. Her research focuses on program development and evaluation for justice-involved populations and their families.

**Pete Simi**, PhD, is an Associate Professor of Sociology and Director of the Earl Babbie Research Center at Chapman University. His research focuses on political violence, life course criminology, street gangs, and juvenile delinquency.

**Tracy W. P. Sohoni**, PhD, is an Assistant Professor in the Department of Sociology and Criminal Justice at Old Dominion University in Norfolk, Virginia. Her research interests focus on the intersection of race, ethnicity, and crime, and also include research on perceptions of criminality, as well as the collateral consequences of crime. Her work has been published in such journals as *The Sociological Quarterly*, the *Journal of Crime and Justice*, and the *Journal of Research in Crime and Delinquency*.

**Jelena Todic**, PhD, MSW, is an Assistant Professor at The University of Texas at San Antonio College of Public Policy, Department of Social Work. Todic's research broadly focuses on structural interventions which aim to eliminate health inequities by targeting social determinants of health and their fundamental drivers. More specifically, she is interested in large organizations as potential hosts of such interventions as well as the role that critical and relational theories can play in guiding interventions aimed at eliminating health inequities.

**Elise Trombetta** is a first year MSW student at Saint Louis University. She hopes to continue her education to research childhood trauma, women's issues, food insecurity, and mental and physical health.

**Kristin Turney**, PhD, is an Associate Professor in the Department of Sociology at the University of California, Irvine. Her research investigates the complex and dynamic role of families in creating and exacerbating social inequalities. Existing research examines the consequences of criminal justice contact for individuals, families, and children. In the related ongoing Jail &

Family Life Study, she is interviewing jailed fathers and their family members—including current and former romantic partners, children, and mothers—during incarceration and after release.

**Stacy Tzoumakis**, PhD, is a lecturer in Criminology at the University of New South Wales in Sydney, Australia. Her research focuses on understanding the development of aggressive and antisocial behavior over the life course.

**Phoebe Um** is currently a medical student at the Ohio State University College of Medicine after graduating summa cum laude from the University of Pennsylvania with a degree in neuroscience. Her research interests are in the effects of early childhood stressors on neurodevelopment, particularly regarding the underlying biological mechanisms.

**Michael G. Vaughn**, PhD, is Professor in the School of Social Work, College for Public Health and Social Justice, at Saint Louis University where he also is the founder and Director of the Health Criminology Research Consortium.

**Christopher A. Veeh**, PhD, MSW, is Assistant Professor in the School of Social Work at the University of Iowa. His research interests include traumatic brain injury and well-being development within adolescents and emerging adults in the criminal justice system.

**Stephen J. Watts**, PhD, is an Assistant Professor in the Department of Criminology and Criminal Justice at the University of Memphis. His research focuses on integrating traditional theories of crime into a biosocial framework.

# PART I

# Theoretical and Empirical Foundations

# 1

# THEORIZING THE ROLE OF HEALTH AND HEALTH DISPARITIES IN THE LIFE-COURSE CRIMINOLOGICAL PARADIGM

*Dylan B. Jackson and Michael G. Vaughn*

Life-course criminology is a major criminological paradigm that acknowledges stability/continuity of behavior as well as change in behavior at different points in the life course as the result of various life-altering events (Sampson & Laub, 2003). This perspective acknowledges the possibility that the factors that influence the timing of the onset of crime may or may not be the same factors that influence criminal persistence, desistance, or intensity. Consequently, the perspective considers the whole stretch of the human life as potentially relevant to the explanation of criminal behavior, not solely the adolescent or young adult years. This approach to the study of crime is developmental in nature and encompasses a number of theories. Two of the most well-known life-course theories in criminology are Moffitt's developmental taxonomy of offenders (1993) and Sampson and Laub's age-graded theory of informal social control (1993, 2003). Life-course theorizing has much to offer if thoughtfully integrated with extant health disparities frameworks for better elucidating the intersections between delinquency and health. In this chapter, we discuss the untapped potential of these intersections and reveal ways in which health disparities and related public health reasoning can enrich the criminological life-course paradigm.

## Moffitt's Developmental Taxonomy

Moffitt's (1993) developmental taxonomy proposes that the causes of criminality differ depending on the nature and duration of the offending. Specifically, she posits that there are two distinct types of offenders: life-course-persistent (LCP) and adolescence-limited (AL) offenders. Moffitt theorizes that the offending of these two groups is distinct, both in its patterns and etiology. She proposes that LCP offenders consist of a small group of offenders who demonstrate substantial continuity in offending behaviors (i.e., offending begins prior to adolescence and continues into adolescence and adulthood). According to the theory, the origins of LCP offending is an amalgam of childhood neuropsychological deficits, negative/impulsive temperament, and adverse familial environments across development, resulting in a stable propensity for antisocial behavior. The early, multifaceted origins of LCP offending are thought to place individuals on a path of cumulative disadvantage and social dysfunction across the life course. As a result, they are at risk of more severe and/or violent criminal behaviors. AL offenders, on the other hand, have (1) shorter offending trajectories, and (2) consist of the majority of offending individuals. The cause of their offending is rooted in a social group phenomenon that Moffitt called the 'maturity gap' (Moffitt, 1993). Moffitt described this gap as a disjuncture between biological and social maturity, where youth are biologically 'adults', but are denied the autonomy or legal permission to make many adult decisions. As a result, AL offenders are temporarily compelled to engage in rebellious delinquency that can take the form of 'adult-like' behaviors, such as drinking and smoking, in an effort to attain power and status. However, by the time they reach early adulthood, the motivation behind their offending dissipates and they no longer offend. In sum, AL offending is short-term and is explained by an age-dependent motivational state (i.e., the maturity gap), whereas LCP offending is more severe, more chronic, and is rooted in biological and social risks that are compounded early in life (Moffitt, 1993). Overall, Moffitt's theory has received a substantial degree of empirical support (for a review, see Jennings & Reingle, 2012), despite some evidence that Moffitt's conceptualization of persistent offending may be too narrow (Blokland, Nagin, & Nieuwbeerta, 2005; Gunnison, 2015; Odgers et al., 2008). Some studies also suggest that race/ethnicity and social class may moderate associations between neuropsychological deficits, adverse parenting, and offending behaviors (Jackson & Beaver, 2016; Turner, Hartman, & Bishop, 2007).

## Sampson and Laub's Age-Graded Theory of Informal Social Control

Another seminal life-course theory in criminology is Sampson and Laub's Age-Graded Theory of Informal Social Control (1993). Sampson and Laub's theory is similar to Moffitt's in that it emphasizes life trajectories and divergent pathways. Even so, the theories differ in many respects. The age-graded theory of informal social control is rooted in the theoretical developments of Elder (1995, 1998) and underscores the importance of two distinct, yet co-occurring phenomena: state dependence and population heterogeneity. Sampson and Laub argue that future behavior is both a reflection of (a) the social consequences of past experiences and behaviors, and (b) individual differences in propensity towards that behavior. To illustrate, Sampson and Laub recognize that delinquency and social bonds (to conventional persons and institutions) have a reciprocal relationship over the life course, such that early childhood and adolescent bonds diminish the likelihood of adolescent offending, but that such offending (as well as a criminal record) can also interfere with future adult bonds, like marriage and employment. Thus, the mutual reinforcement of attenuated social bonds and delinquency over time is a potent explanation of stability. Nevertheless, to explain change, they also make room in their theory for various serendipitous, fortunate life occurrences that can serve as turning points that deflect individuals off of the criminal course and 'knife off' the past from the future. For example, important life transitions like marriage, serving in the military, and access to gainful employment, may all operate as mechanisms of informal social control that place individuals on a law-abiding path. Sampson and Laub also contend that elements of luck/randomness and human agency can play a role in criminal desistance (Sampson & Laub, 2003). Thus, the theory is an age-graded theory of informal social control in that different sources of informal control have the potential to be turning points at different points during the life course. A number of studies support Sampson and Laub's postulations (Doherty, 2006; Sampson, Laub, & Wimer, 2006; Wright & Cullen, 2004), though many scholars have emphasized that properly accounting for social selection (i.e., environmental selection on the basis of preexisting traits, like self-control) tends to attenuate support for social causation (see Barnes & Beaver, 2012; Barnes et al., 2014; Wright et al. 2001).

# The Untapped Relevance of Health Disparities Research for Life-Course Criminological Theorizing

Despite the impact that the life-course perspective has had on the field of criminology over the past two decades (Barnes & Beaver, 2012; Barnes et al., 2014; Blokland, Nagin, & Nieuwbeerta, 2005; Doherty, 2006; Gunnison, 2015; Jennings & Reingle, 2012; Odgers et al., 2008; Sampson, Laub, & Wimer, 2006; Wright et al., 2001; Wright & Cullen, 2004), the most influential theories under this paradigm adhere to a somewhat limited scope of potentially criminogenic variables, such as attenuated social bonds (e.g., marriage, employment), negative childhood temperament, and neuropsychological deficits (Laub & Sampson, 1993; Moffitt, 1993; Sampson & Laub, 2003). The theoretical emphasis on a fairly narrow range of risk factors has prevented life-course criminologists from systematically integrating relevant research and theoretical developments from related fields into this criminological perspective. For instance, scholars from fields such as sociology (e.g., sociology of health and illness, medical sociology), demography, epidemiology, and public health have frequently engaged in cross-disciplinary efforts to examine health disparities, or the existence of heightened health risks (and diminished health status) in the context of social disadvantage (Adler & Newman, 2002; Amone-P'Olak et al., 2009; Cerdá et al., 2014; Skalamera & Hummer, 2016; White & Borrell, 2011). At the turn of the twenty-first century, the reduction of socioeconomic and racial/ethnic disparities in health was identified as a major priority for public health practice and scholarship by the U.S. Public Health Service and the National Institute of Health (House & Williams, 2000; U.S. Department of Health and Human Services, 1999 see also House, 2002). Consequently, this area of research has the potential to significantly enhance the criminological life-course paradigm, and render it increasingly relevant to cross-disciplinary evidence-based prevention and intervention efforts, particularly in light of the well-established associations between the socioeconomic status, race/ethnicity, and involvement in violent crime (Heimer, 1997; Markowitz, 2003; McNulty & Bellair, 2003; Stewart & Simons, 2006), early-onset delinquency (Aguilar et al., 2000; Staff et al., 2015), and LCP offending (Moffitt & Caspi, 2001; Piquero, Moffitt, & Lawton, 2005). In short, while criminologists acknowledge that racial/ethnic minorities and lower class individuals are exposed to early, criminogenic conditions more consistently, they do not systematically examine the criminogenic effects of racial and socioeconomic disparities in high-risk health conditions/behaviors or diminished health resources, particularly during the early life course. Instead, when criminologists study health, they typically examine it as an *outcome* of criminal justice involvement and/or involvement in chronic offending (Manninen et al., 2015; Moffitt et al., 2002; Odgers et al., 2007; Piquero et al., 2007; Piquero et al., 2014; Shepherd, Farrington, & Potts, 2004; Vaughn et al., 2014). This is an unfortunate gap in the literature that, if addressed, can greatly enhance the theoretical and practical contributions of life-course criminological research.

To date, research has yielded substantial evidence for the existence of health disparities among individuals with varying social identities and/or positions within the social structure. For instance, research has revealed that inequalities in income, education, and employment widen the gap in physical and mental health between the haves and the have-nots (Adler & Newman, 2002; Amone-P'Olak et al., 2009; Schreier & Chen, 2013; Skalamera & Hummer, 2016; Quon & McGrath, 2015). To illustrate, research has provided evidence for socioeconomic disparities in depression (Zimmerman & Katon, 2005), asthma (Schreier & Chen, 2013), obesity (Schreier & Chen, 2013), hypertension (Quon & McGrath, 2015), and LDL cholesterol (Quon & McGrath, 2015). This process can occur in various contexts and through several mediating mechanisms, including adverse housing conditions (Krieger & Higgins, 2002), neighborhood disadvantage or disorder and associated deficits in social capital (Ross & Mirowsky, 2001; Vyncke et al., 2013), school physical activities practices (Carlson et al., 2014), and diminished access to fundamental health resources, including food (Cook & Frank, 2008) and medical care (Alder & Newman, 2002; Larson & Halfon, 2010). In general, explanations of socioeconomic disparities in health are rooted in the understanding of socioeconomic disparities in exposure to sources of chronic stress (Adler & Newman, 2002; Brunner, 1997; Lantz et al., 2005) and the capacity to manage or cope with chronic stress (Gallo & Matthews, 2003). Research has also indicated socioeconomic disparities in behaviors associated with health and wellbeing. Results from a sample of 2,071 Australian children indicated that higher income children spend significantly more time playing sports and music, whereas low-income individuals spend significantly more time watching television and playing video games (Ferrar, Olds & Walters, 2012). The researchers propose that differential engagement in these behaviors may be an important source of health inequalities between socioeconomic groups across development. A study examining a Finnish sample of adolescents yielded similar findings, as youths engaging in more health-protective behaviors (e.g., physical exercise, hygiene, seatbelt use, abstention from smoking, limited TV viewing) were on a more advanced educational track than adolescents who did not engage in health-protective behaviors (Koivusilta, Rimpelä, & Rimpelä, 1999; see also Skalamera & Hummer, 2016). Research also suggests that dietary behaviors among adolescents are stratified by household SES (Quon & McGrath, 2015).

Apart from socioeconomic disparities in health, research has also provided evidence for racial/ethnic disparities in health, particularly in the U.S. (for a review, see Williams & Sternthal, 2010). In general, this body of research suggests that racial disparities in health status and exposure to health risks may be partly explained by four interrelated phenomena: (1) differential access to social capital (Ard et al., 2016), (2) de facto residential segregation into unequal neighborhoods (Cerdá et al., 2014; Kravitz-Wirtz, 2016; Williams & Collins, 2001), (3) an ongoing history of racial discrimination (Keene, Lynch & Baker, 2014; Saegert, Fields, & Libman, 2011; Tobler et al., 2013), and (4) differential engagement in high-risk health behaviors by minority groups, particularly blacks (Block, Scribner & DeSalvo, 2004; Bowman et al., 2004). For instance, a recent study of a U.S. sample by Ard and colleagues (2016) revealed a significant gap in self-rated health between African Americans and Whites, as well as Hispanics and Whites. The study also indicated that social capital (e.g., community cohesion, trust of individuals outside of their social group) explained a significant portion of these gaps (84% and 54% respectively). A recent study by Kravitz-Wirtz (2016) revealed that racial disparities between blacks and whites in exposure to concentrated disadvantage during childhood and adolescence (e.g., education, poverty, female-headed household) predicted disparities in health status by early adulthood. Similar studies suggest that, to the extent that minorities are overrepresented in disadvantaged or underresourced neighborhoods, fear of crime (see Chandola, 2001) and exposure to neighborhood violence (Zimmerman & Messner, 2013) may also contribute to racial disparities in mental and physical health.

Health disparities research has also indicated that race and SES can intersect in ways that have complex implications for the health and wellbeing of these subsets of the population (Do, Frank & Finch, 2012; Williams & Sternthal, 2010). To illustrate, recent research suggests that racial disparities in health can have important implications for life chances, including housing/mortgage strain, foreclosure, and broader financial strain, particularly in the absence of personal/public safety nets that might buffer the functional impairments caused by chronic illness (Keene, Lynch, & Baker, 2014; Saegert, Fields, & Libman, 2011). Thus, to the extent that health impairments in racial/ethnic minorities increase the financial fragility and strain of the household, racial disparities in health might also engender socioeconomic disparities in health and continuing residential segregation into fundamentally unequal neighborhoods (which only serves to reinforce racial disparities in health; see Cerdá et al., 2014; Kravitz-Wirtz, 2016).

## Historical Focus on the Health Consequences of Crime and Criminal Justice Involvement

In general, research on crime, criminal justice involvement, and health has largely taken a 'back end' focus that prioritizes consequences in adulthood. This is, in part, due to a newer hypothesis derived from Moffitt's taxonomy of offenders that 'life-course-persistent offenders will be at risk for adverse physical and mental health outcomes' (Piquero et al., 2007, p. 189). To date, most criminological research that has explored potential links between health and crime is (1) divorced from broader research developments on racial and socioeconomic health disparities and (2) tends to prioritize the study of either the negative health consequences of chronic/severe offending among adolescents and adults (Manninen et al., 2015; Moffitt et al., 2002; Odgers et al., 2007; Piquero et al., 2014; Piquero et al., 2007) or the negative health consequences of incarceration or criminal justice system involvement for offenders and their families (Jackson & Vaughn, 2017a; Massoglia, 2008; Porter, 2014; Turney, 2014; Vaughn et al., 2014). That is, the focus is on correctional health or health consequences of incarceration. Meanwhile, research examining the role of early health risks in early involvement in offending is much less common and much more limited in scope (McGloin & Pratt, 2003; Tibbetts & Piquero, 1999), and existing research has yet to explore racial and socioeconomic disparities in health during the early life course for early-onset offending.

Research on the link between incarceration and health with a 'back end' focus has indicated that incarcerated youth experience higher mortality and morbidity compared to non-incarcerated youths (Barnert, Perry, & Morris, 2016), in part due to the effect of juvenile incarceration on later health, exposure to violence, and social wellbeing (Barnert, Perry, & Morris, 2016). A related study of a nationally representative sample of U.S. young adults recently revealed that incarceration increases the likelihood of functional limitations, poor general health, depression, and suicidality during adulthood (Barnert et al., 2017), with one study suggesting that these processes might also explain racial disparities in health (see Massoglia, 2008). Criminal justice involvement (i.e., arrested and booked for an offense) among adults age 18–64 is also associated with a hosts of health risks among males and female participants, including pancreatitis, hepatitis, and STDs (Vaughn et al., 2014). Research has also indicated a higher incidence of traumatic brain injury among incarcerated youth across multiple jail systems (Fareer et al., 2013; Kaba et al., 2014). Incarceration experiences, moreover, have been found to increase the risk of disease by limiting access to health resources and diminishing the quality of care (Galea & Vlahov, 2002). Incarceration may also diminish health status by increasing engagement in risky health behaviors. A recent study by Porter (2014) indicated that former young-adult inmates engage in more high risk health behaviors (e.g., fast food consumption, smoking) than their similarly situated peers without a history of incarceration.

Some criminological studies employing adolescent or adult samples have also explored the health consequences of criminogenic traits (Beaver et al., 2014; Miller, Barnes, & Beaver, 2011), LCP offending (Moffitt et al., 2002; Piquero et al., 2014; Piquero et al., 2007), and violence (Stogner, Gibson, & Miller, 2014). Young adults with psychopathic personality traits, for instance, have been found to incur a greater health burden (Beaver et al., 2014). LCP offenders, moreover, have been found to be at greater risk of mental illness and substance use (Moffitt et al., 2002). A seminal study by Odgers and colleagues (2007) indicated that LCP offenders, at 32 years of age, had the worst health burden (relative to low-level offenders and adolescent-limited offenders). The health burdens examined included indicators of poor mental health (e.g., depression, anxiety, and PTSD) and poor physical health (e.g., cardiovascular disease, injuries, and respiratory function). Similar criminological research by Piquero and colleagues (2007) and Reingle and colleagues (2014) has indicated that LCP offenders and offenders who exhibit violence continuity into adulthood are at higher risk of chronic illness and/or one or more of various health problems, including heart trouble, hypertension, diabetes, ulcers, and kidney problems. A follow-up study by Piquero and colleagues (2014) also found that LCP offenders, particularly those engaging in chronic offending at a high rate, are at the highest risk of early death. Collectively, these studies suggest that the most serious offenders appear to exhibit a number of health risks during adulthood that may increase their likelihood of early death.

Collateral health consequences for family members of men and women who have been incarcerated has also been explored in the literature (Jackson & Vaughn, 2017a; Wakefield & Wildeman, 2011; Wildeman, Goldman, & Turney, 2018; Turney, 2014). For instance, a study by Turney (2014) revealed that children whose parents had been incarcerated were at greater risk of behavioral problems, speech problems, and developmental delays. A recent study also indicated that high-risk health behaviors, such as poor sleep and eating behaviors, also appear to be more common among children with incarcerated parents (Jackson & Vaughn, 2017a). A recent review of the literature (Wildeman, Goldman, & Turney, 2018) revealed, among other things, that incarceration of a parent (particularly a father) is negatively associated with a wide variety of indicators of child health and wellbeing. Thus, the role of criminal justice involvement, particularly incarceration, in mental and physical health outcomes of family members (including children) is well established.

## Incorporating Health and Health Disparities Research into Developmental Crime Prevention

As illustrated, a sizeable body of research has focused on the 'back end' health effects of chronic offending and criminal justice involvement. Even so, the application of a health disparities framework, with particular emphasis on racial and socioeconomic disparities in health, to 'front end' criminological research is sorely lacking. It should be noted, however, that some scholars have advocated for the methodological and theoretical integration of sociology of health and illness, epidemiology, and criminology, but not within the life-course framework (Timmermans & Gabe, 2002; Akers & Lanier, 2009). Furthermore, prior efforts to integrate the theories, methods, and findings of these fields have been limited in other respects. Specifically, efforts at cross-fertilization are not typically 'front end' focused, but are 'back end' focused, emphasizing drug use/addiction and/or HIV among incarcerated individuals (Lanier, Zaitzow, & Farrell, 2015) or those under community supervision, probation, or parole (Potter & Akers, 2010). While this work is an important step in the effort to foster cross-fertilization of associated fields of study, it does not explore the etiological relevance of early health risks for crime and delinquency across the early stages of the life course, nor does it apply extant knowledge concerning early health disparities to enhance the effectiveness of crime prevention efforts.

Despite prior attempts to incorporate current knowledge concerning health disparities into criminological theory and research, life-course criminology and its accompanying seminal theories have not been evaluated, analyzed, or understood in the context of racial and socioeconomic disparities in health. Again, this oversight is important for criminologists to consider, as subsets of the work already conducted by medical sociologists, public health scholars, demographers, and epidemiologists may have direct relevance to criminological theorizing, but are often overlooked due to stifling disciplinary boundaries.

Although research testing life-course theories in criminology has examined racial/ethnic and socioeconomic disparities in violence, it has yet to carefully explore the role of broader disparities in health conditions, behaviors, and resources in such disparities in violence (see Sampson, Morenoff, & Raudenbush, 2005). Although Moffitt's theory is consistent with the notion that early neurological health structures sensitivity to adverse familial socialization, its emphasis on early neurological health remains quite limited in scope (i.e., alternative indicators of health among at-risks populations are overlooked). Emergent research by criminologists and others is beginning to suggest that other dimensions of health – including health behaviors and health resources – might also have important implications for violence and misconduct (Jackson, 2016; Jackson, Newsome, & Lynch, 2017; Jackson et al., 2018).

Furthermore, Moffitt's (1993) theory does not address the implications of broader socioeconomic or racial disparities in health at the earliest stages of the life for early-onset or LCP offending. Sampson and Laub's (1993) theory, moreover, does not explicitly consider the ways that social bonds and social control over the life course might be linked to individual health across various stages of the life course, and the implications these associations might have for criminal involvement across different portions of the social structure and across individuals with varying social identities. In short, while racial/ethnic and socioeconomic stratification of crime and delinquency is widely acknowledged by life-course criminologists (Sampson & Lauritsen, 1997; Sampson, Raudenbush, & Earls, 1997; Sampson, Morenoff, & Raudenbush, 2005), such stratification is not explored as a function of early stratification in individual health – including health conditions, behaviors/lifestyles, and/or resources.[1]

Ultimately, we propose that a health disparities framework can elevate the current theorizing concerning the developmental origins of crime. This assertion is rooted in empirical developments in sociology, epidemiology, and public health that have yielded evidence for socioeconomic and racial disparities in health among very young populations, including neonates/infants (Blumenshine et al., 2010; Lu & Halfon, 2003) and young children (Priest et al., 2013; Reiss, 2013; Taveras et al., 2010). Some of these studies have even examined ways that these health disparities might be transmitted intergenerationally though exposure to prenatal health risks (Dominguez et al., 2008; Kramer et al., 2000). Additionally, health sociologists and public health scholars have long noted that individuals of less privileged status have higher exposure to health-related stressors or traumas at early stages of life (even at or before birth), and that these processes might underpin disparities in later morbidity and mortality at later life stages (Pearlin et al., 2005; Shonkoff, Boyce, & McEwen, 2009). Some have also highlighted the ways in which improving health during developmentally sensitive periods (e.g., infancy and early childhood) likely yields greater benefits than attempts to alter health-related behaviors or improve access to healthcare during adulthood (Shonkoff, Boyce, & McEwen, 2009). This body of health disparities research is decidedly developmental, or 'front end', and, as noted, has important implications for assessment of health risks early in the life course and disease prevention among socially disadvantaged subsets of the population.

This body of health disparities research also has tacit implications and clear relevance for the emergent body of life-course criminological research that examines health risks as predictors of crime and criminal violence. A growing body of life-course criminological research has explored the link between various prenatal, infant, and childhood health risks and problem/delinquent behaviors (Beaver & Wright, 2005; Gibson, Piquero, & Tibbetts, 2000; Jackson & Beaver, 2016; Jackson, 2016; Jackson & Newsome, 2016; Jackson & Vaughn, 2017b, 2018; Tibbetts & Piquero, 1999; Vaske, Newsome, & Boisvert, 2013; Vaske et al., 2015). For instance, a diverse range of health risks during pregnancy, infancy, and early childhood have been found to increase involvement in problem and delinquent behaviors, including maternal prenatal medical conditions (Jackson & Vaughn, 2018), low birth weight (Vaske, Newsome, & Boisvert, 2013; Vaske et al., 2015), birth complications (Beaver & Wright, 2005), neonatal health problems (Jackson & Newsome, 2016), poor diet quality during childhood (Jackson, 2016), and household food insecurity during childhood (Jackson & Vaughn, 2017b). Even so, these studies do not systematically examine early health risks for delinquency through the lens of racial and/or socioeconomic disparities in health, despite clear evidence of racial and socioeconomic differences in early problem behaviors, delinquency, and violence (Aguilar et al., 2000; Heimer, 1997; Markowitz, 2003; McNulty & Bellair, 2003; Stewart & Simons, 2006; Staff et al., 2015).

To be more precise, extant criminological studies exploring health factors as predictors of problem and delinquent behaviors are limited in key respects. Criminological research exploring early health risks as predictors of problem behaviors and early delinquency are (1) relatively infrequent, (2) disconnected and non-systematic (specific health risks often examined in isolation), and (3) outside of the framework of existing, cross-disciplinary health disparities research. Limitation 2 is partly a function of limitation 3, as the incorporation of a guiding health disparities framework into this body of life-course criminological research would diminish non-systematic approaches to the study of early health risks and the development of delinquent behaviors. To date, criminologists have only rarely considered whether racial and/or socioeconomic disparities in early health risks might explain racial and/or socioeconomic disparities in the development of problem behaviors and early-onset delinquency (Barnes et al., 2016). This is especially important, as race/ethnicity and socioeconomic status can play a significant role in childhood developmental ecologies that at least partially determine exposure to a variety of health risk during the early life course (see Mollborn, 2016). Furthermore, criminologists have generally overlooked the context of social privilege when studying early health risks, and whether or not social privilege buffers the influence of early health risks on problem behaviors and delinquency (however, see Jackson & Beaver, 2016; Turner, Hartman, & Bishop, 2007).

One recent study, however, by a group of life-course criminologists did examine prenatal and perinatal health disparities as explanations of the differences in childhood self-control (and important risk factor for crime and delinquency) across racial groups (Barnes et al., 2016). The findings lend credence to the potential for racial disparities in early health risks to explain racial disparities in the development of criminogenic traits among children. Even so, the study was not couched within a health disparities framework, although the authors briefly mentioned racial disparities in access to medical care during the first trimester as a potential explanation of the findings that was not explicitly tested. The limited attention given to the expansive health disparities research highlights the existing gulf between developmental crime prevention research and broader knowledge concerning health disparities from fields like sociology, epidemiology, and public health. Moreover, the study addressed health risks at only one life stage and did not examine early-onset delinquency as an outcome, both of which would hasten the integration of health disparities research into the life-course framework within criminology.

## Conclusion

In conclusion, we propose that a more complete integration of health disparities research into life-course criminological theorizing is long overdue, and that doing so will contribute to a more holistic approach to developmental crime prevention that assesses the mental and physical well-being of children, as well as better alignment in criminal justice and health policy. We contend that, while an early life-course perspective on health disparities has been proposed by sociologists and public health scholars, it has not been systematically integrated into life-course research on the study of crime and delinquency. Life-course explanations of crime often refer to differences in macro and micro levels of social control across less privileged subsets of the population, but only rarely do they explore socioeconomic and/or racial disparities in early-life health as predictors of later involvement in delinquency and the development of criminogenic traits. Sociological research suggests that, couched within a life-course framework, a health disparities approach to the study of early behavioral development (including childhood behavioral problems) is legitimate and likely promising. For instance, economic and occupational success, educational attainment, and life chances more generally are impaired among children who experience an accumulation of developmental health risks (Braveman, 2014), intimating that crime could stem from similar developmental processes. Additionally, Mollborn and colleagues (2014) recently found that preschool health lifestyles (diet, sleep, secondhand smoke, safety, and violence exposure) were predictive of multiple components of children's development. In light of these results, Mollborn and her colleagues advocate for more research that examines health behaviors and health lifestyles among children as predictors of behavioral development, particularly in the context of SES and household resources (see also Pinquart & Shen, 2011). This work can inform and be closely aligned with the work of developmental criminologists who want to cross-fertilize the wealth of knowledge at the intersection of life-course criminology and public health.

Ultimately, we argue that there is a pressing need to expand the boundaries of life-course criminological theorizing – and criminological theorizing more generally – by integrating a health disparities framework into the study of early delinquent involvement, as this will likely improve crime prevention efforts during early life stages. We hope that this integration will yield insights upon which developmental and life-course criminologists who study the link between early health risks and early-onset offending can build. We anticipate that such integration will also result in initial, evidence-based recommendations for early intervention and prevention efforts of crime and delinquency that will be of interest to policymakers, a diverse set of practitioners (e.g., social workers, pediatricians), and scholars across the social and health sciences. Ultimately, our hope is that seminal work at this intersection will inspire scholars across the health and social sciences to work together and employ multiple bodies of knowledge and theoretical developments in our efforts to find solutions to violence, health disparities, and associated social problems.

## Note

1 While health conditions refer to bodily manifestations, whether mental or physical, of suboptimal health, health behaviors refer to an individual's actions (and associated beliefs) concerning their health and wellbeing. Health resources, on the other hand, refer to a readily accessible supply of health promoting goods or assets.

## References

Adler, N. E., & Newman, K. (2002). Socioeconomic disparities in health: Pathways and policies. *Health Affairs*, *21*(2), 60–76.

Aguilar, B., Sroufe, L. A., Egeland, B., & Carlson, E. (2000). Distinguishing the early-onset/persistent and adolescence-onset antisocial behavior types: From birth to 16 years. *Development and Psychopathology*, *12*(2), 109–132.

Akers, T. A., & Lanier, M. M. (2009). "Epidemiological criminology": Coming full circle. *American Journal of Public Health*, *99*(3), 397–402.

Amone-P'Olak, K., Burger, H., Ormel, J., Huisman, M., Verhulst, F. C., & Oldehinkel, A. J. (2009). Socioeconomic position and mental health problems in pre-and early-adolescents. *Social Psychiatry and Psychiatric Epidemiology*, *44*(3), 231–238.

Ard, K., Colen, C., Becerra, M., & Velez, T. (2016). Two mechanisms: The role of social capital and industrial pollution exposure in explaining racial disparities in self-rated health. *International Journal of Environmental Research and Public Health*, *13*(10), 1025.

Barnert, E. S., Dudovitz, R., Nelson, B. B., Coker, T. R., Biely, C., Li, N., & Chung, P. J. (2017). How does incarcerating young people affect their adult health outcomes? *Pediatrics*, *139*(2), e20162624.

Barnert, E. S., Perry, R., & Morris, R. E. (2016). Juvenile incarceration and health. *Academic Pediatrics*, *16*(2), 99–109.

Barnes, J. C., & Beaver, K. M. (2012). Marriage and desistance from crime: A consideration of gene–environment correlation. *Journal of Marriage and Family*, *74*(1), 19–33.

Barnes, J. C., Boutwell, B. B., Miller, J. M., DeShay, R. A., Beaver, K. M., & White, N. (2016). Exposure to pre-and perinatal risk factors partially explains mean differences in self-regulation between races. *PloS One*, *11*(2), e0141954.

Barnes, J. C., Golden, K., Mancini, C., Boutwell, B. B., Beaver, K. M., & Diamond, B. (2014). Marriage and involvement in crime: A consideration of reciprocal effects in a nationally representative sample. *Justice Quarterly*, *31*(2), 229–256.

Beaver, K. M., Nedelec, J. L., Da Silva Costa, C., Poersch, A. P., Stelmach, M. C., Freddi, M. C., ... & Boccio, C. (2014). The association between psychopathic personality traits and health-related outcomes. *Journal of Criminal Justice, 42*(5), 399–407.

Beaver, K. M., & Wright, J. P. (2005). Evaluating the effects of birth complications on low self-control in a sample of twins. *International Journal of Offender Therapy and Comparative Criminology, 49*(4), 450–471.

Block, J. P., Scribner, R. A., & DeSalvo, K. B. (2004). Fast food, race/ethnicity, and income: A geographic analysis. *American Journal of Preventive Medicine, 27*(3), 211–217.

Blokland, A. A., Nagin, D., & Nieuwbeerta, P. (2005). Life span offending trajectories of a Dutch conviction cohort. *Criminology, 43*(4), 919–954.

Blumenshine, P., Egerter, S., Barclay, C. J., Cubbin, C., & Braveman, P. A. (2010). Socioeconomic disparities in adverse birth outcomes: A systematic review. *American Journal of Preventive Medicine, 39*(3), 263–272.

Bowman, S. A., Gortmaker, S. L., Ebbeling, C. B., Pereira, M. A., & Ludwig, D. S. (2004). Effects of fast-food consumption on energy intake and diet quality among children in a national household survey. *Pediatrics, 113*(1), 112–118.

Braveman, P. (2014). What is health equity and how does a life-course approach take us further toward it? *Maternal and Child Health Journal, 18*(2), 366–372.

Brunner, E. (1997). Socioeconomic determinants of health: Stress and the biology of inequality. *BMJ, 314*(7092), 1472.

Carlson, J. A., Mignano, A. M., Norman, G. J., McKenzie, T. L., Kerr, J., Arredondo, E. M., ... & Sallis, J. F. (2014). Socioeconomic disparities in elementary school practices and children's physical activity during school. *American Journal of Health Promotion, 28*(3_suppl), S47–S53.

Cerdá, M., Tracy, M., Ahern, J., & Galea, S. (2014). Addressing population health and health inequalities: The role of fundamental causes. *American Journal of Public Health, 104*(S4), S609–S619.

Chandola, T. (2001). The fear of crime and area differences in health. *Health & Place, 7*(2), 105–116.

Cook, J. T., & Frank, D. A. (2008). Food security, poverty, and human development in the United States. *Annals of the New York Academy of Sciences, 1136*(1), 193–209.

Do, D. P., Frank, R., & Finch, B. K. (2012). Does SES explain more of the black/white health gap than we thought? Revisiting our approach toward understanding racial disparities in health. *Social Science & Medicine, 74*(9), 1385–1393.

Doherty, E. E. (2006). Self-control, social bonds, and desistance: A test of life-course interdependence. *Criminology, 44*(4), 807–833.

Dominguez, T. P., Dunkel-Schetter, C., Glynn, L. M., Hobel, C., & Sandman, C. A. (2008). Racial differences in birth outcomes: The role of general, pregnancy, and racism stress. *Health Psychology, 27*(2), 194.

Elder Jr, G. H. (1995). The life course paradigm: Social change and individual development. In P. Moen, G. H. Elder, Jr., & K. Lüscher (Eds.), *Examining lives in context: Perspectives on the ecology of human development* (pp. 101–139). Washington, DC: American Psychological Association.

Elder Jr, G. H. (1998). The life course as developmental theory. *Child Development, 69*(1), 1–12.

Farrer, T. J., Frost, R. B., & Hedges, D. W. (2013). Prevalence of traumatic brain injury in juvenile offenders: A meta-analysis. *Child Neuropsychology, 19*(3), 225–234.

Ferrar, K. E., Olds, T. S., & Walters, J. L. (2012). All the stereotypes confirmed: Differences in how Australian boys and girls use their time. *Health Education & Behavior, 39*(5), 589–595.

Galea, S., & Vlahov, D. (2002). Social determinants and the health of drug users: Socioeconomic status, homelessness, and incarceration. *Public Health Reports, 117*(Suppl 1), S135.

Gallo, L. C., & Matthews, K. A. (2003). Understanding the association between socioeconomic status and physical health: Do negative emotions play a role? *Psychological Bulletin, 129*(1), 10.

Gibson, C. L., Piquero, A. R., & Tibbetts, S. G. (2000). Assessing the relationship between maternal cigarette smoking during pregnancy and age at first police contact. *Justice Quarterly, 17*(3), 519–542.

Gunnison, E. (2015). Investigating life course offender subgroup heterogeneity: An exploratory latent class analysis approach. *Women & Criminal Justice, 25*(4), 223–240.

Heimer, K. (1997). Socioeconomic status, subcultural definitions, and violent delinquency. *Social Forces, 75*(3), 799–833.

House, J. S. (2002). Understanding social factors and inequalities in health: 20th century progress and 21st century prospects. *Journal of Health and Social Behavior, 43*, 125–142.

House, J. S., & Williams, D. R. (2000). Understanding and reducing socioeconomic and racial/ethnic disparities in health. *Promoting Health: Intervention Strategies from Social and Behavioral Research, 81*, 125.

Jackson, D. B. (2016). The link between poor quality nutrition and childhood antisocial behavior: A genetically informative analysis. *Journal of Criminal Justice, 44*, 13–20.

Jackson, D. B., & Beaver, K. M. (2016). The interplay between neuropsychological deficits and adverse parenting in the prediction of adolescent misconduct: A partial test of the generalizability of Moffitt's theory. *Criminal Justice and Behavior, 43*(11), 1505–1521.

Jackson, D. B., & Newsome, J. (2016). The link between infant neuropsychological risk and childhood antisocial behavior among males: The moderating role of neonatal health risk. *Journal of Criminal Justice, 47*, 32–40.

Jackson, D. B., Newsome, J., & Lynch, K. R. (2017). Adverse housing conditions and early-onset delinquency. *American Journal of Community Psychology, 60*(1–2), 160–174.

Jackson, D. B., Newsome, J., Vaughn, M. G., & Johnson, K. R. (2018). Considering the role of food insecurity in low self-control and early delinquency. *Journal of Criminal Justice, 56*, 127–139.

Jackson, D. B., & Vaughn, M. G. (2017a). Parental incarceration and child sleep and eating behaviors. *The Journal of Pediatrics, 185*, 211–217.

Jackson, D. B., & Vaughn, M. G. (2017b). Household food insecurity during childhood and adolescent misconduct. *Preventive Medicine, 96*, 113–117.

Jackson, D. B., & Vaughn, M. G. (2018). Maternal medical risks during pregnancy and childhood externalizing behavior. *Social Science & Medicine, 207*, 19–24.

Jennings, W. G., & Reingle, J. M. (2012). On the number and shape of developmental/life-course violence, aggression, and delinquency trajectories: A state-of-the-art review. *Journal of Criminal Justice, 40*(6), 472–489.

Kaba, F., Diamond, P., MacDonald, R., & Venters, H. (2014). Traumatic brain injury among newly admitted adolescents in the New York City jail system. *Journal of Adolescent Health, 54*(5), 615–617.

Keene, D. E., Lynch, J. F., & Baker, A. C. (2014). Fragile health and fragile wealth: Mortgage strain among African American homeowners. *Social Science & Medicine, 118*, 119–126.

Koivusilta, L. K., Rimpelä, A. H., & Rimpelä, M. K. (1999). Health-related lifestyle in adolescence – origin of social class differences in health? *Health Education Research, 14*(3), 339–355.

Kramer, M. S., Seguin, L., Lydon, J., & Goulet, L. (2000). Socio-economic disparities in pregnancy outcome: Why do the poor fare so poorly? *Paediatric and Perinatal Epidemiology, 14*(3), 194–210.

Kravitz-Wirtz, N. (2016). Cumulative effects of growing up in separate and unequal neighborhoods on racial disparities in self-rated health in early adulthood. *Journal of Health and Social Behavior, 57*(4), 453–470.

Krieger, J., & Higgins, D. L. (2002). Housing and health: Time again for public health action. *American Journal of Public Health, 92*(5), 758–768.

Lanier, M. M., Zaitzow, B. H., & Farrell, C. T. (2015). Epidemiological criminology: Contextualization of HIV/AIDS health care for female inmates. *Journal of Correctional Health Care, 21*(2), 152–163.

Lantz, P. M., House, J. S., Mero, R. P., & Williams, D. R. (2005). Stress, life events, and socioeconomic disparities in health: Results from the Americans' Changing Lives Study. *Journal of Health and Social Behavior, 46*(3), 274–288.

Larson, K., & Halfon, N. (2010). Family income gradients in the health and health care access of US children. *Maternal and Child Health Journal, 14*(3), 332–342.

Laub, J. H., & Sampson, R. J. (1993). Turning points in the life course: Why change matters to the study of crime. *Criminology, 31*(3), 301–325.

Lu, M. C., & Halfon, N. (2003). Racial and ethnic disparities in birth outcomes: A life-course perspective. *Maternal and Child Health Journal, 7*(1), 13–30.

Manninen, M., Pankakoski, M., Gissler, M., & Suvisaari, J. (2015). Adolescents in a residential school for behavior disorders have an elevated mortality risk in young adulthood. *Child and Adolescent Psychiatry and Mental Health, 9*, 46.

Markowitz, F. E. (2003). Socioeconomic disadvantage and violence: Recent research on culture and neighborhood control as explanatory mechanisms. *Aggression and Violent Behavior, 8*(2), 145–154.

Massoglia, M. (2008). Incarceration, health, and racial disparities in health. *Law & Society Review, 42*(2), 275–306.

McGloin, J. M., & Pratt, T. C. (2003). Cognitive ability and delinquent behavior among inner-city youth: A life-course analysis of main, mediating, and interaction effects. *International Journal of Offender Therapy and Comparative Criminology, 47*(3), 253–271.

McNulty, T. L., & Bellair, P. E. (2003). Explaining racial and ethnic differences in serious adolescent violent behavior. *Criminology, 41*(3), 709–747.

Miller, H. V., Barnes, J. C., & Beaver, K. M. (2011). Self-control and health outcomes in a nationally representative sample. *American Journal of Health Behavior, 35*(1), 15–27.

Moffitt, T. E. (1993). Adolescence-limited and life-course-persistent antisocial behavior: A developmental taxonomy. *Psychological Review, 100*(4), 674–701.

Moffitt, T. E., & Caspi, A. (2001). Childhood predictors differentiate life-course persistent and adolescence-limited antisocial pathways among males and females. *Development and Psychopathology, 13*(2), 355–375.

Moffitt, T. E., Caspi, A., Harrington, H., & Milne, B. J. (2002). Males on the life-course-persistent and adolescence-limited antisocial pathways: Follow-up at age 26 years. *Development and Psychopathology, 14*(1), 179–207.

Mollborn, S. (2016). Young children's developmental ecologies and kindergarten readiness. *Demography, 53*(6), 1853–1882.

Mollborn, S., James-Hawkins, L., Lawrence, E., & Fomby, P. (2014). Health lifestyles in early childhood. *Journal of Health and Social Behavior, 55*(4), 386–402.

Odgers, C. L., Caspi, A., Broadbent, J. M., Dickson, N., Hancox, R. J., Harrington, H., ... & Moffitt, T. E. (2007). Prediction of differential adult health burden by conduct problem subtypes in males. *Archives of General Psychiatry, 64*(4), 476–484.

Odgers, C. L., Moffitt, T. E., Broadbent, J. M., Dickson, N., Hancox, R. J., Harrington, H., ... & Caspi, A. (2008). Female and male antisocial trajectories: From childhood origins to adult outcomes. *Development and Psychopathology, 20*(2), 673–716.

Pearlin, L. I., Schieman, S., Fazio, E. M., & Meersman, S. C. (2005). Stress, health, and the life course: Some conceptual perspectives. *Journal of Health and Social Behavior, 46*(2), 205–219.

Pinquart, M., & Shen, Y. (2011). Behavior problems in children and adolescents with chronic physical illness: A meta-analysis. *Journal of Pediatric Psychology, 36*(9), 1003–1016.

Piquero, A. R., Daigle, L. E., Gibson, C., Piquero, N. L., & Tibbetts, S. G. (2007). Research note: Are life-course-persistent offenders at risk for adverse health outcomes? *Journal of Research in Crime and Delinquency, 44*(2), 185–207.

Piquero, A. R., Farrington, D. P., Shepherd, J. P., & Auty, K. (2014). Offending and early death in the Cambridge Study in Delinquent Development. *Justice Quarterly, 31*(3), 445–472.

Piquero, A. R., Moffitt, T. E., & Lawton, B. (2005). Race and crime: The contribution of individual, familial, and neighborhood-level risk factors to life-course-persistent offending. In D. F. Hawkins & K. Kempf-Leonard (Eds.), *Our children, their children: Confronting racial and ethnic differences in American juvenile justice* (pp. 202–244). Chicago, IL: University of Chicago Press.

Porter, L. C. (2014). Incarceration and post-release health behavior. *Journal of Health and Social Behavior, 55*(2), 234–249.

Potter, R. H., & Akers, T. A. (2010). Improving the health of minority communities through probation-public health collaborations: An application of the epidemiological criminology framework. *Journal of Offender Rehabilitation, 49*(8), 595–609.

Priest, N., Paradies, Y., Trenerry, B., Truong, M., Karlsen, S., & Kelly, Y. (2013). A systematic review of studies examining the relationship between reported racism and health and wellbeing for children and young people. *Social Science & Medicine, 95*, 115–127.

Quon, E. C., & McGrath, J. J. (2015). Community, family, and subjective socioeconomic status: Relative status and adolescent health. *Health Psychology, 34*(6), 591.

Reingle, J. M., Jennings, W. G., Piquero, A. R., & Maldonado-Molina, M. M. (2014). Is violence bad for your health? An assessment of chronic disease outcomes in a nationally representative sample. *Justice Quarterly, 31*(3), 524–538.

Reiss, F. (2013). Socioeconomic inequalities and mental health problems in children and adolescents: A systematic review. *Social Science & Medicine, 90*, 24–31.

Ross, C. E., & Mirowsky, J. (2001). Neighborhood disadvantage, disorder, and health. *Journal of Health and Social Behavior, 42*, 258–276.

Saegert, S., Fields, D., & Libman, K. (2011). Mortgage foreclosure and health disparities: Serial displacement as asset extraction in African American populations. *Journal of Urban Health, 88*(3), 390–402.

Sampson, R. J., & Laub, J. H. (2003). Life-course desisters? Trajectories of crime among delinquent boys followed to age 70. *Criminology, 41*(3), 555–592.

Sampson, R. J., Laub, J. H., & Wimer, C. (2006). Does marriage reduce crime? A counterfactual approach to within-individual causal effects. *Criminology, 44*(3), 465–508.

Sampson, R. J., & Lauritsen, J. L. (1997). Racial and ethnic disparities in crime and criminal justice in the United States. *Crime and Justice, 21*, 311–374.

Sampson, R. J., Morenoff, J. D., & Raudenbush, S. (2005). Social anatomy of racial and ethnic disparities in violence. *American Journal of Public Health, 95*(2), 224–232.

Sampson, R. J., Raudenbush, S. W., & Earls, F. (1997). Neighborhoods and violent crime: A multilevel study of collective efficacy. *Science, 277*(5328), 918–924.

Schreier, H., & Chen, E. (2013). Socioeconomic status and the health of youth: A multilevel, multidomain approach to conceptualizing pathways. *Psychological Bulletin, 139*(3), 606.

Shepherd, J., Farrington, D., & Potts, J. (2004). Impact of antisocial lifestyle on health. *Journal of Public Health, 26*(4), 347–352.

Shonkoff, J. P., Boyce, W. T., & McEwen, B. S. (2009). Neuroscience, molecular biology, and the childhood roots of health disparities: Building a new framework for health promotion and disease prevention. *Jama, 301*(21), 2252–2259.

Skalamera, J., & Hummer, R. A. (2016). Educational attainment and the clustering of health-related behavior among US young adults. *Preventive Medicine, 84*, 83–89.

Staff, J., Whichard, C., Siennick, S. E., & Maggs, J. (2015). Early life risks, antisocial tendencies, and preteen delinquency. *Criminology, 53*(4), 677–701.

Stewart, E. A., & Simons, R. L. (2006). Structure and culture in African American adolescent violence: A partial test of the "code of the street" thesis. *Justice Quarterly, 23*(1), 1–33.

Stogner, J., Gibson, C. L., & Miller, J. M. (2014). Examining the reciprocal nature of the health-violence relationship: Results from a nationally representative sample. *Justice Quarterly, 31*(3), 473–499.

Taveras, E. M., Gillman, M. W., Kleinman, K., Rich-Edwards, J. W., & Rifas-Shiman, S. L. (2010). Racial/ethnic differences in early-life risk factors for childhood obesity. *Pediatrics, 125*(4), 686–695.

Tibbetts, S. G., & Piquero, A. R. (1999). The influence of gender, low birth weight, and disadvantaged environment in predicting early onset of offending: A test of Moffitt's interactional hypothesis. *Criminology, 37*(4), 843–878.

Timmermans, S., & Gabe, J. (2002). Introduction: Connecting criminology and sociology of health and illness. *Sociology of Health & Illness, 24*(5), 501–516.

Tobler, A. L., Maldonado-Molina, M. M., Staras, S. A., O'Mara, R. J., Livingston, M. D., & Komro, K. A. (2013). Perceived racial/ethnic discrimination, problem behaviors, and mental health among minority urban youth. *Ethnicity & Health, 18*(4), 337–349.

Turner, M. G., Hartman, J. L., & Bishop, D. M. (2007). The effects of prenatal problems, family functioning, and neighborhood disadvantage in predicting life-course-persistent offending. *Criminal Justice & Behavior, 34*(10), 1241–1261.

Turney, K. (2014). Stress proliferation across generations? Examining the relationship between parental incarceration and childhood health. *Journal of Health and Social Behavior, 55*(3), 302–319.

U.S. Department of Health and Human Services. (1999). *Health People 2010: Objectives: Draft for Public Comment.* [http://web.health.gov/healthypeople/2010Draft/object.htm].

Vaske, J., Newsome, J., & Boisvert, D. (2013). The mediating effects of verbal skills in the relationship between low birth weight and childhood aggressive behaviour. *Infant and Child Development, 22*(3), 235–249.

Vaske, J. C., Newsome, J., Boisvert, D. L., Piquero, A. R., Paradis, A. D., & Buka, S. L. (2015). The impact of low birth weight and maternal age on adulthood offending. *Journal of Criminal Justice, 43*(1), 49–56.

Vaughn, M. G., Salas-Wright, C. P., Delisi, M., & Piquero, A. R. (2014). Health associations of drug-involved and criminal-justice-involved adults in the United States. *Criminal Justice & Behavior, 41*(3), 318–336.

Vyncke, V., De Clercq, B., Stevens, V., Costongs, C., Barbareschi, G., Jónsson, S. H., ... & Maes, L. (2013). Does neighbourhood social capital aid in levelling the social gradient in the health and well-being of children and adolescents? A literature review. *BMC Public Health, 13*(1), 65.

Wakefield, S., & Wildeman, C. (2011). Mass imprisonment and racial disparities in childhood behavioral problems. *Criminology & Public Policy, 10*(3), 793–817.

White, K., & Borrell, L. N. (2011). Racial/ethnic residential segregation: Framing the context of health risk and health disparities. *Health & Place, 17*(2), 438–448.

Wildeman, C., Goldman, A. W., & Turney, K. (2018). Parental incarceration and child health in the United States. *Epidemiologic Reviews, 40*(1), 146–156.

Williams, D. R., & Collins, C. (2001). Racial residential segregation: A fundamental cause of racial disparities in health. *Public Health Reports, 116*(5), 404.

Williams, D. R., & Sternthal, M. (2010). Understanding racial-ethnic disparities in health: Sociological contributions. *Journal of Health and Social Behavior, 51*(1_suppl), S15-S27.

Wright, B. R. E., Caspi, A., Moffitt, T. E., & Silva, P. A. (2001). The effects of social ties on crime vary by criminal propensity: A life-course model of interdependence. *Criminology, 39*(2), 321–348.

Wright, J. P., & Cullen, F. T. (2004). Employment, peers, and life-course transitions. *Justice Quarterly, 21*(1), 183–205.

Zimmerman, F. J., & Katon, W. (2005). Socioeconomic status, depression disparities, and financial strain: What lies behind the income-depression relationship? *Health Economics, 14*(12), 1197–1215.

Zimmerman, G. M., & Messner, S. F. (2013). Individual, family background, and contextual explanations of racial and ethnic disparities in youths' exposure to violence. *American Journal of Public Health, 103*(3), 435–442.

# 2

# EVIDENCE ON PRENATAL AND PERINATAL HEALTH FACTORS ASSOCIATED WITH JUVENILE DELINQUENCY

*Stacy Tzoumakis and Jesse Cale*

There is an abundance of empirical research in the fields of public health, psychiatry, and psychology demonstrating that prenatal and perinatal risk factors are associated with a wide range of adverse physical and mental health outcomes over the life course (Cannon, Jones, & Murray, 2002; Mwaniki, Atieno, Lawn, & Newton, 2012; Williams & Ross, 2007). This line of research has not been paralleled in criminology where the investigation of early health factors associated with criminality has been comparatively limited (Jackson & Vaughn, 2018b). Since the early-to-mid-twentieth century, the emphasis in criminology on understanding cultural and sociological factors associated with crime has meant that far less attention has been paid to investigating potential health factors associated with the development of antisocial behavior. Only since around 2000 has there been increasing interest in examining the relationship between early health predictors and antisocial behavior and offending (Tibbetts, 2014). In terms of prenatal and perinatal risk factors, it is well established that fetal development can be hindered by prenatal exposures to teratogenic substances, and related birth complications can cause fetal injury, both of which can adversely influence brain development. Furthermore, prenatal health risks can also cause epigenetic alterations that influence fetal growth and development (Knopik, Maccani, Francazio, & McGeary, 2012). Whether the effects of prenatal and perinatal factors directly impact the brain or are epigenetic in nature, they can affect cognitive functioning, temperament, and behavioral problems that can eventually result in juvenile delinquency, antisocial behavior and offending in adulthood for some. From a criminological perspective, the leading theoretical paradigm accounting for prenatal and perinatal risk factors is Moffit's(1993) developmental taxonomy (McGloin, Pratt, & Piquero, 2006; Piquero, Gibson, Tibbetts, Turner, & Katz, 2002). One key tenet of Moffitt's developmental taxonomy is that deficits in neuropsychological functions of the infant nervous system place some individuals at risk of developing a difficult temperament and behavioral problems early in life (see also, DeLisi & Vaughn, 2014). In turn, this can place stress on parents, for example, some of whom may experience broader social stressors such as a low socioeconomic status. Since infant neurological development can be impacted by prenatal and perinatal insults, these health risk factors and associated behavioral outcomes can accumulate and cascade across developmental periods, increasing the likelihood of involvement in antisocial behavior and offending later in life. In effect, if the brain can be considered as one of the mediating mechanisms between prenatal and perinatal risk factors and antisocial behavior (Liu, 2011), then environmental factors play a role in moderating this relationship.

This chapter reviews the empirical research evidence on some of the most common prenatal and perinatal risk factors associated with juvenile delinquency, including prenatal substance exposure (i.e., alcohol, smoking, illicit drugs), maternal stress during pregnancy, prematurity, low birth weight, and other pregnancy and birth complications. We examine the evidence around the association between these risk factors and adolescent antisocial/juvenile delinquency, but also childhood outcomes such as externalizing, conduct, or aggressive behavioral problems, as these are typically precursors to delinquency (Broidy et al., 2003). Finally, other prenatal and perinatal risk factors associated with behavioral development over the life course that have not been emphasized in the criminological research are also explored, including exposure to licit drugs and maternal infection during pregnancy. The evidence for these early health risk factors is discussed to determine the viability of integrating prenatal and perinatal health into broader multimodal prevention strategies.

## Prenatal Exposures as Risk Factors for Delinquency

From the time of conception up until birth, a wide range of factors can adversely influence fetal development including the genes of the fetus itself, maternal biological and psychological characteristics, maternal experiences, and interactions between all of these factors (Hodgins, Kratzer, & McNeil, 2001, 2002). Perturbations in fetal development during pregnancy (i.e., prenatal insults) are associated with a wide range of adverse physical, mental, cognitive, and behavioral developmental outcomes in offspring. Furthermore, the amount of exposure to, and timing of, prenatal insults are also hypothesized to differentially influence fetal development and can also set the stage for perinatal complications (i.e., complications just prior to, during, and immediately following birth) that can further increase the likelihood of adverse developmental outcomes in offspring, including delinquency and antisocial behavior later in life.

### *Prenatal Alcohol Exposure*

Heavy alcohol consumption (i.e., two or more drinks per day or five to six drinks per occasion) during pregnancy can impact the developing brain of a fetus leading to Fetal Alcohol Spectrum Disorder (FASD) in offspring. The global prevalence of maternal prenatal alcohol use is estimated at approximately 10%; among the approximately 10% of infants exposed to alcohol prenatally, it is estimated that nearly one in 70 develop FASD (Popova, Lange, Probst, Gmel, & Rehm, 2017). FASD involves a range of adverse neuropsychological impacts on intelligence, learning and memory, executive function, attention and activity levels, and behavior (Mattson, Crocker, & Nguyen, 2011; Popova et al., 2017). Furthermore, the impact on neurological development varies not only in terms of the quantity of alcohol exposure but also the timing (Sokol, Delaney-Black, & Nordstrom, 2003). For example, Sayal, Heron, Golding, and Emond (2007) showed that even low levels of alcohol exposure early on in pregnancy can result in adverse mental health outcomes in offspring.

Given the range of neuropsychological impacts maternal alcohol use can have on a developing fetus, it is not surprising that prenatal alcohol exposure is consistently associated with a higher likelihood of conduct problems in offspring compared to those who are not exposed (Disney, Iacono, McGue, Tully, & Legrand, 2008). A recent meta-analysis including nine studies estimated that the summary odds ratio for prenatal alcohol use and conduct problems in childhood and adolescence was over two (Ruisch, Dietrich, Glennon, Buitelaar, & Hoekstra, 2018). While the relationship between alcohol exposure during pregnancy and subsequent poor offspring mental health outcomes in young children is robust (O'Connor, 2014), comparatively less research has considered later outcomes such as juvenile delinquency. Nonetheless, there is fairly strong evidence to suggest the impacts of FASD extend beyond mental health outcomes in childhood. For example, there is evidence for a range of poor outcomes among adolescents exposed to heavy alcohol use during pregnancy including poor school performance, alcohol and drug problems, inappropriate sexual behaviors, and involvement with the criminal justice system (Streissguth et al., 2004). In terms of involvement in the justice system, there is also evidence to suggest there is an overrepresentation of FASD among youth incarcerated in detention centers (e.g., approximately 11–20% compared to 1–5% in the general population), despite the fact there are substantial difficulties accurately diagnosing FASD retrospectively (Flannigan, Pei, Stewart, & Johnson, 2018; Hughes, Clasby, Chitsabesan, & Williams, 2016). Findings from a recent Australian study suggested that the rates of FASD might be even higher among incarcerated youth; Bower et al. (2018) diagnosed over one-third (36%) of youth in an Australian youth detention center with FASD after conducting comprehensive assessments.

## *Maternal Prenatal Smoking*

The global prevalence of smoking during pregnancy is estimated to be less than 2%; however, among mothers who smoke while pregnant, it is estimated that approximately three quarters are daily smokers and over half of daily smokers do so throughout their entire pregnancies (Lange, Probst, Rehm, & Popova, 2018). Prenatal smoking exposure can impair brain growth and result in structural deficits in the brain due to nicotine and carbon monoxide exposure (Liu, 2011). There is also evidence of teratogenic effects of prenatal smoking on the placenta's anatomy, and epidemiological studies have provided evidence that prenatal smoking is causally linked to several pregnancy and birth complications, including placental abruption and poor fetal growth (Jauniaux & Burton, 2007; Salihu & Wilson, 2007). Compared to other early health risk factors, the impact of maternal smoking on delinquency outcomes has been relatively well studied in criminological research (Pratt, McGloin, & Fearn, 2006).

At the individual level, maternal prenatal smoking is associated with the development of a range of adverse offspring behavioral outcomes including inattention, hyperactivity, conduct and substance use problems, conduct disorder, and delinquency (Button, Maughan, & McGuffin, 2007; Ruisch et al., 2018; Wakschlag, Pickett, Cook Jr., Benowitz, & Leventhal, 2002). Prospective longitudinal studies have further established links between maternal prenatal smoking and adolescent externalizing problems, antisocial behavior and delinquency (Ashford, Van Lier, Timmermans, Cuijpers, & Koot, 2008; Cornelius, Goldschmidt, De Genna, & Larkby, 2012; Gibson, Piquero, & Tibbetts, 2000). For example, Obel et al. (2008) found evidence of a dose-response relationship between prenatal smoking and offspring hyperactivity-inattention in childhood, and Brennan, Grekin, and Mednick (1999) uncovered a similar dose-response pattern in terms of its relationship to offending outcomes in adulthood.

Using data on over 6,000 offspring from the National Longitudinal Survey of Youth, D'Onofrio, Van Hulle, Goodnight, Rathouz, and Lahey (2012) examined the association between maternal prenatal smoking and juvenile delinquency among offspring. They found that exposure to prenatal smoking was robustly associated with delinquency controlling for other important covariates such as maternal alcohol use during pregnancy, maternal education, maternal antisocial behavior, and maternal substance use, among others. Comparable studies have found similarly robust results (e.g., Fergusson, Woodward, & Horwood, 1998). However, when controlling for correlated genetic and environmental factors using sibling comparisons, D'Onofrio et al. (2012)

found that the link between maternal prenatal smoking and delinquency disappeared. Others have provided similar evidence along these lines with different childhood and adolescent behavioral outcomes (D'Onofrio et al., 2008; Maughan, Taylor, Caspi, & Moffitt, 2004; Roza et al., 2008; Skoglund, Chen, D'Onofrio, Lichtenstein, & Larsson, 2014). In effect, the association between maternal prenatal smoking on offspring externalizing and conduct problems and delinquency is confounded by familial and other social factors such as socioeconomic disadvantage. For example, mothers who smoke during pregnancy often experience additional risk factors (e.g., younger, more likely to be involved in antisocial behavior, low education). As a result, they are also likely in some cases to delay and/or limit contact with healthcare service providers, which in turn limits opportunities for healthcare workers to assist with challenges such as smoking cessation and other developmental/familial issues (Schneider, Huy, Schuetz, & Diehl, 2010; Tzoumakis et al., 2018).

## *Prenatal Exposure to Illicit Drugs*

The prevalence of illicit substance use during pregnancy in the US is estimated to be less than 5% according to a national survey of women (Substance Abuse and Mental Health Services Administration, 2011), with marijuana possibly the most commonly used drug among women of reproductive age. There is a paucity of criminological research investigating the impact of illicit drugs on fetal development, and whether and to what extent prenatal exposure to different illicit drugs is associated with longer term behavioral outcomes such as delinquency (Forman et al., 2017; Irner, 2012). As with alcohol, the biological impact of prenatal marijuana consumption on the fetal development is hypothesized to vary in terms of timing and degree of exposure as it can result in hypoxia due to carbon monoxide exposure (Barthelemy, Richardson, Cabral, & Frank, 2016). However, the extent of transfer and overall impact of tetrahydrocannabinol (THC; the psychoactive ingredient in marijuana) to the fetus through the placenta in humans in not currently known (Barthelemy, Richardson, Cabral, & Frank, 2016). In their review of the consequences of prenatal marijuana exposure in children, Fried and Smith (2001) concluded that there is some evidence across studies that prenatal marijuana exposure is associated with the development of certain executive function deficits. Other studies have uncovered associations between marijuana exposure during pregnancy and broader childhood and adolescent behavioral outcomes such as the development of externalizing problems and deficits in inhibitory control (Banz, Wu, Crowley, Potenza, & Mayes, 2016; Bridgett & Mayes, 2011; Buckingham-Howes, Berger, Scaletti, & Black, 2013; Min et al., 2014). Day, Leech and Goldschmidt (2011) found that marijuana use during pregnancy, and particularly heavy use (i.e., one or more joints per day), was linked to offspring self-reported delinquency in adolescence; however, this association was mediated by neurocognitive functioning.

Exposure to cocaine in utero is associated with the development of altered stress responses, deficits in attention regulation, and abnormal arousal patterns in offspring (Mayes, 1999, 2002). In terms of early childhood behavioral development, Accornero et al. (2011) found that pre-natal cocaine exposure was associated with difficulties in child behavioral regulation at age seven, after statistically controlling for demographic characteristics and prenatal exposure to other substances (e.g., alcohol, tobacco, marijuana). Other studies have also produced evidence that prenatal cocaine exposure is associated with elevated levels of aggression in boys (Bennett, Bendersky, & Lewis, 2007). However, these associations are influenced by both individual differences and environmental contexts. In their review of the effects of prenatal cocaine exposure among school-aged children, Ackerman, Riggins, and Black (2010) concluded that prenatal cocaine exposure was negatively associated with sustained attention and behavioral self-regulation, but that the impact of prenatal cocaine exposure on cognitive ability, academic achievement, and language functioning was attenuated by environmental variables.

Not surprisingly then, there is mixed evidence in terms of the association between prenatal cocaine exposure, childhood behavioral problems, and, later, delinquency. Some studies have uncovered positive associations between prenatal cocaine exposure and self-reported delinquency (e.g., Lambert et al., 2013; Richardson, Goldschmidt, Larkby, & Day, 2015), while others have not (e.g., Gerteis et al., 2011). In effect, prenatal exposure to cocaine, as with other drugs, is one of numerous interacting factors that include, but are not limited to: genetics, parenting styles, environment, and sociodemographic characteristics (Lambert & Bauer, 2012). Similar patterns of findings can be observed in research on the impact of prenatal methamphetamine exposure.

Studies have produced mixed results in terms of the impact of prenatal methamphetamine exposure and offspring behavioral outcomes in childhood and adolescence. An early Swedish prospective longitudinal study produced evidence that prenatal methamphetamine exposure was associated with lower IQ scores than non-exposed children by age four (Billing, Eriksson, Steneroth, & Zetterström, 1988), peer problems and aggression at age eight (Billing, Eriksson, Jonsson, Steneroth, & Zetterström, 1994), and poor school performance by age 14 (Cernerud, Eriksson, Jonsson, Steneroth, & Zetterstrom, 1996). All of these outcomes typically share some of the variance in explaining delinquency in childhood and adolescence. More recently, the Infant Development, Environment, and Lifestyle (IDEAL) study, which is a prospective multi-site longitudinal study of 412 mother-infant pairs, approximately half of which were identified with prenatal methamphetamine exposure, examined a wide range of offspring outcomes among prenatal methamphetamine exposed infants. The results showed prenatal methamphetamine exposed infants displayed higher levels of emotional reactivity, anxiety and depression up to five years of age compared to controls (LaGasse et al., 2012). Furthermore, by age five, prenatal methamphetamine exposed infants also displayed more externalizing and attention deficit and hyperactivity problems than matched controls. Using the same data, a study by Diaz et al. (2014) provided evidence that prenatal methamphetamine exposure was associated with the development of early cognitive problems in infants. However, Smith et al. (2015) reported that home environments responsive to developmental and emotional needs of children significantly reduced the risks for internalizing and externalizing behaviors among prenatal methamphetamine exposed infants. In terms of school-aged outcomes, Eze et al. (2016) reported that prenatal methamphetamine exposure was associated with externalizing, rule-breaking, and aggressive behavior at age 7.5 years, and that early environmental adversity attenuated this relationship. Importantly, this relationship stood also controlling for polysubstance abuse profiles (specifically, tobacco, alcohol, and marijuana exposure) of pregnant mothers.

## *Maternal Stress during Pregnancy*

High levels of maternal stress during pregnancy can result in fetal exposure to increased levels of cortisol in-utero resulting in low birth-weight, prematurity, and increased cortisol levels in infants (Cottrell & Seckl, 2009; Field & Diego, 2008). Furthermore, there is empirical evidence linking maternal prenatal stress levels to impediments in the development of behavioral and emotional regulation among offspring, including temperament difficulties during infancy (e.g., Bergman, Sarkar, O'Connor, Modi, & Glover, 2007), negative emotionality and inhibition in the preschool years (e.g., Martin, Noyes, Wisenbaker, & Huttunen, 1999), and internalizing and externalizing problems in childhood and adolescence (e.g., Davis & Sandman, 2012). Using data on over 10,000 mother-offspring pairs from the AVON longitudinal study based in the United Kingdom, MacKinnon, Kingsbury, Mahedy, Evans, and Colman (2018) showed that offspring exposure to the highest levels of maternal stress during pregnancy was associated with membership in high symptom hyperactivity and conduct disorder trajectories up to age 16 after controlling for parental demographic characteristics as well as other prenatal risk factors such as maternal substance use. In a recent systematic review that summarized key findings from prospective longitudinal studies on the link between maternal prenatal stress and behavioral and mental health outcomes in offspring, Van den Bergh et al. (2017) found general consensus across epidemiological and case-control studies that maternal prenatal stress is associated with adverse outcomes among offspring neurodevelopment, cognitive development, affectivity, temperament and psychiatric well-being. They also found evidence for differential impact of prenatal stress across these domains between male and female offspring. Along these lines, in a large epidemiological study based in Finland, Mäki et al. (2003) showed male offspring of antenatally depressed mothers displayed slightly higher non-violent and violent criminal activity in adulthood compared to their female counterparts. The empirical evidence suggests that both inherited factors and post-natal environmental factors play a role in the link between prenatal stress and aggression (e.g., Buchmann et al., 2014), antisocial behavior in childhood and adolescence (Hay, Pawlby, Waters, Perra, & Sharp, 2010) and criminal outcomes later in life (e.g., Mäki et al., 2003).

## *Overview of Prenatal Exposures as Risk Factors and Juvenile Delinquency*

Taken together, there is an absence of strong evidence suggesting any direct relationship exists between prenatal exposure to substances such as tobacco, alcohol, and common illicit drugs and delinquency later in life. The link between these phenomena are far more complex. First, exposure to prenatal complications such as those discussed above are associated with the development of structural deficits in different parts of the developing brain such as those that govern executive functioning, cognitive functioning, and emotional regulation, among others. However, there is increasing empirical evidence showing that the degree of exposure as well as the timing of exposure play a role, to some extent, on the impact these factors have on neurological development of the fetus. Second, it is necessary to understand the nature and extent of structural damage caused by prenatal exposures and how these are related to the development of different physical and mental health, and behavioral problems in infancy and early childhood among different children. This is critical because these infancy and early childhood outcomes are well-known precursors to antisocial behavior and juvenile delinquency. Third, these same infancy and early childhood adverse outcomes are attenuated, at least to some extent, by environmental factors such as the sociodemographic characteristics of parents and parenting practices among others. Fourth, individual differences among offspring and early environmental factors set the stage for the nature and extent of interactions with peers and performance in school from early childhood through adolescence. Finally, deficits in these domains (e.g., having delinquent peers, poor performance in school) are also associated with the development of juvenile delinquency and antisocial behavior later in life.

When considering these and other possible developmental pathways beginning in-utero through infancy, childhood, adolescence, and adulthood leading to delinquency and antisocial behavior, it becomes less surprising that studies examining prenatal risk factors for juvenile delinquency have produced discrepant findings. These discrepancies across studies can largely be attributed to differences in methodological designs and samples, in addition to the nature and extent of covariates considered in different analyses. Furthermore, the prenatal risk factors discussed above, among others, often result in perinatal complications that can also adversely impact neurological development in early infancy and beyond. As such, several studies utilize perinatal complications as markers for prenatal exposures; one reason for this is that data on perinatal complications are typically more reliably recorded (e.g., in birth records) than retrospective, self-reported data on substance use or maternal stress during pregnancy, for example. However, perinatal complications can also occur in the absence of those prenatal insults discussed above, and also adversely influence early neurological development in early infancy and through the life-course. Below we review some of the most common perinatal complications that have been examined in the context of the development of delinquency and antisocial behavior.

## Pregnancy and Birth Complications as Risk Factors for Delinquency

### *Prematurity and Low Birth Weight*

Prematurity (approximately 11% of all live births globally) is typically defined as birth at less than 37 weeks of gestation; however, more specific distinctions include preterm (37 weeks), moderate preterm (32 to <37), very preterm (28 to <32 weeks), and extremely preterm (<28 weeks) infants (Blencowe et al., 2012). Low birth weight (approximately 7% prevalence in industrialized countries) is typically considered less than 2,500 grams, very low birth weight is <1,500 grams, and extremely low birth weight is <1,000 grams (United Nations Children's Fund and World Health Organization, 2004). Both prematurity and low birth weight are linked to infant mortality as well as to numerous other poor infant health outcomes, and in general, the lower the birth weight or the more premature, the poorer these outcomes tend to be (Jarjour, 2015; Wilcox, 2001). Due to the fact that prematurity is typically closely tied to birth weight, some health researchers operationalize birth weight by gestational age to identify whether the infant is small for their gestational age. Small for gestational age is typically calculated using population data and defined as: (1) birth weight and/or length of at least two standard deviations below the mean for gestational age; or (2) birth weight that is below the 10th percentile for gestational age (Lee, Chernausek, Hokken-Koelega, & Czernichow, 2003).

While there is extensive research examining the link between low birth weight and prematurity on health outcomes, research on the link to delinquency and antisocial outcomes in adolescence and over the life-course is much scarcer. Criminological studies have employed very broad measures indicative of birthweight; these studies typically dichotomize birth weight (i.e., low birth weight or not) rather than account for more specific birthweight categories (e.g., very low, extremely low). Critically, no criminological studies have specifically operationalized and examined small for gestational age. One study that examined a range of maternal and perinatal risk factors, found no link between low birth weight, prematurity and risk for delinquency, but found that young motherhood was an important risk factor chronic juvenile offending (Conseur, Rivara, Barnoski, & Emanuel, 1997). In fact, very or extremely low birth weight and extremely preterm children are likely to display adolescent internalizing behavioral problems, but this same pattern is not clearly evident for externalizing behaviors and conduct problems (Gardner et al., 2004; Hille et al., 2001; Samuelsson et al., 2017). For example, some studies have even found lower levels of delinquent behavior among very low birth weight infants compared to those with normal birth weights (Dahl et al., 2006; Hack et al., 2004).

In line with the research on the link between prenatal risk factors and delinquency, it is not clear that the relationship between perinatal risk factors and poor offspring outcomes is causal by any means (Wilcox, 2001). For example, mothers living in the most disadvantaged neighborhoods are at higher risk of having preterm and low birth weight infants (Ncube, Enquobahrie, Albert, Herrick, & Burke, 2016). This suggests the likely possibility that, as with other prenatal risk factors, indirect relationships characterize any associations between low birth weight and delinquency. For instance, Tibbetts and Piquero (1999) found that low birth weight, which was used a proxy measure for neuropsychological deficits, interacted with environmental disadvantage to predict early onset of offending (but not late onset of offending). Another study of male adolescents found that very low birth weight alone was not linked to affiliation with delinquent peers, but when high genetic risk was accounted for very low birth was a significant risk factor for delinquency (Jackson & Beaver, 2016). Taken together, the balance of evidence indicates that low birth weight and prematurity do not directly influence delinquent behavior but do play a role in the context of other risk factors.

## *Pregnancy and Birth Complications*

There are a range of pregnancy (e.g., gestational diabetes, preeclampsia/eclampsia, placenta previa, uterine bleeding, anemia) and birth complications (e.g., use of forceps, fetal distress, anoxia, low Apgar scores) that are associated with poor offspring outcomes. Individually, these types of complications are relatively rare. As such empirical studies often include indices or composite scales that reflect the severity of complications or a higher risk pregnancy and delivery (Jackson & Vaughn, 2018a; Liu, Raine, Wuerker, Venables, & Mednick, 2009). However, this can be problematic because it then becomes difficult to disentangle the role of specific pregnancy and/or birth complications with broader behavioral outcomes at different points over the lifecourse; findings on the association between pregnancy and birth complications, and delinquency and offending later in life have produced conflicting results. For example, there is some evidence that pregnancy and birth complications have different impacts on offending behavior (Raine, 2013; Tibbetts & Rivera, 2015). On the one hand, results from a prospective longitudinal Canadian study of mothers and their offspring provided evidence that pregnancy (but not birth) complications were associated with offspring aggression in early childhood (Lussier, Tzoumakis, Healey, Corrado, & Reebye, 2011). On the other hand, looking into adulthood, Kandel and Mednick (1991) found that birth and not pregnancy complications were linked to offending in a sample of young adults in their early twenties. One possibility is that pregnancy and birth complications may have differential associations with childhood externalizing behaviors (Beaver & Wright, 2005; Beck & Shaw, 2005) and adult offending outcomes (Hodgins, Kratzer, & McNeil, 2001; Raine, Brennan, & Mednick, 1997). However, at the same time, pregnancy and birth complications are likely also moderated by other prenatal and perinatal factors, and postnatal family and social factors early in life such as parenting styles and socioeconomic status.

Pregnancy and birth complications both can emerge from prenatal risk factors such as substance use, among other factors (e.g., stress, malnutrition), and there is evidence of interactive and multiplicative effects of these early health risk factors (Liu, 2011). For instance, mothers who smoke during pregnancy tend to produce low birth weight babies (Wilcox, 2001). Another study found that birth complications (i.e., low Apgar score) interacted with maternal prenatal smoking to predict offending in early adulthood, but individually, neither of these two factors predicted offending (Gibson & Tibbetts, 1998). Therefore, the link between birth complications and delinquency is also likely influenced by social disadvantage and family adversity, as is low birth weight and prematurity. For example, a longitudinal Canadian study that followed 849 boys from birth to age 17 found that serious birth complications increased the risk of violence between ages 6 and 17 years, but only for those from the most disadvantaged environments (Arseneault, Tremblay, Boulerice, & Saucier, 2002).

## *Consideration of Other Early Health Risk Factors for Delinquency*

There are several early health risk and protective factors associated with mental health, cognitive, and behavioral outcomes in offspring that may be useful to consider in future research on the development of delinquency. For instance, in health research, prenatal nutrition is increasingly being examined in terms of its relationship to child development. A recent meta-analysis provided evidence suggesting there is at least a small positive association between good quality maternal diet and cognitive outcomes early in life (Borge, Aase, Brantsæter, & Biele, 2017). In addition, prenatal exposure to licit drugs has not been considered in criminological research in terms of any possible associations with the development of delinquency. This is despite some evidence that licit drugs can have adverse implications for developing fetuses. Some recent population-based studies have linked prenatal use of licit substances, such as anti-depressants and acetaminophen, to mental health and behavioral problems in offspring (Liew, Ritz, Rebordosa, Lee, & Olsen, 2014; Liu et al., 2017). One study of 190,000 children in Hong Kong found evidence of an association between antidepressant use in pregnancy and ADHD among offspring; however, this relationship was confounded by mothers' pre-existing mental health disorders (Man et al., 2017). Another study found associations between prenatal acetaminophen use and offspring conduct problems in childhood (Stergiakouli, Thapar, & Davey Smith, 2016). Despite this preliminary evidence, the potential intrauterine mechanisms explaining this relationship are not currently known, nor whether any clear associations are evident with delinquency and antisocial behavior later in life.

Another prenatal risk factor that merits careful consideration is lead exposure; while there are few studies have examined prenatal lead exposure specifically (Dietrich, Douglas, Succop, Berger, & Bornschein, 2001), some recent evidence suggests that increased blood lead levels (not limited to prenatal exposure) possibly have a causal relationship with adolescent antisocial behavior (Sampson & Winter, 2018). Again, however, the empirical evidence is mixed; another study found that the relationship between blood lead levels and adult offending was weak (Beckley et al., 2018). Increasing attention is also being paid to prenatal exposure to maternal diseases and offspring developmental functioning in early childhood and subsequent serious mental illness in adulthood (Green et al., 2018; Khandaker, Zimbron, Lewis, & Jones, 2013). While the biological mechanisms underpinning these potential links are unclear, one current hypothesis is that infection activates the maternal immune system, which in turn influences fetal brain development and gene regulation (Green et al., 2018). For example, there is some evidence that maternal prenatal infection is linked to attention deficit and behavioral problems in childhood (Green et al., 2018; Parker et al., 2016; Werenberg Dreier et al., 2016). Maternal infection during pregnancy could therefore be another way in which early neuropsychological deficits are transmitted to offspring. However, these early health risk factors require further investigation, particularly in terms of delinquency and antisocial behavioral outcomes over the life-course.

## Consideration of Prenatal and Perinatal Factors in Long-Term Delinquency Prevention Strategies

Targeting a specific prenatal or perinatal risk factor is unlikely to succeed in reducing delinquency since these factors interact with broader psychological and social factors (Jackson & Newsome, 2016; Mason et al., 2016; Tibbetts, 2014). Moreover, the evidence reviewed in this chapter suggests that while many prenatal and perinatal factors are associated with delinquency as well as with behavioral precursors to delinquency, children exposed to prenatal and perinatal risk factors also experience several other risk factors, such as family adversity and social disadvantage, that also need to be addressed through multimodal prevention and intervention strategies. For example, although the rates of smoking cessation during pregnancy continue to increase, younger and more disadvantaged mothers still have some of the lowest smoking cessation rates during pregnancy (Graham, Hawkins, & Law, 2010; Passmore, McGuire, Correll, & Bentley, 2015). Qualitative research on smoking cessation during pregnancy reveals that intervention among these vulnerable groups poses a number of challenges. Most mothers recognize that continuing to smoke during pregnancy may harm the fetus, but smoking was perceived as a source of relaxation, stress reduction, and relief from the chronic stressors and multiple disadvantages that they experience (Flemming, McCaughan, Angus, & Graham, 2015). Considering the life circumstances of some mothers who continue to smoke and use other substances during pregnancy, it is unlikely that public health prevention programs targeted at the use of specific substances in isolation will be effective. Successful interventions need to address broader health and social issues (e.g., disadvantage, education/employment, mental illness, poor physical health, and involvement in offending) that some of these women experience over the life course. In line with this, we know from research on interventions targeted for young people at risk of persistent delinquency that the most beneficial programs tend to be those that are intensive, target multiple problems (i.e., are multimodal), and include the family (de Vries, Hoeve, Assink, Stams, & Asscher, 2015).

Nonetheless, this does not mean that knowledge on prenatal and perinatal risk factors are of no use to practitioners and policymakers. They could potentially serve as 'flags' or proxy indicators for women requiring more intensive targeted services. However, we should be prepared to offer intensive multi-faceted services to these women and not simply a substance use cessation program for example. A better approach to preventing future delinquency is to support vulnerable young women prior to and during pregnancy to prevent the development of early deficits and the accumulation of risk factors their children may experience, which can, in turn, lead to behavioral problems in childhood and eventually to juvenile delinquency and antisocial behavior. Since many of the prenatal and perinatal risk factors reviewed here influence childhood outcomes, there is also a need to intervene early, if not prior to or during pregnancy, then prior to school entry, to prevent the possibility of juvenile delinquency. This is especially important considering the increasing volume of empirical evidence indicating that developmental prevention initiatives are effective in reducing delinquency (Farrington, Gaffney, Lösel, & Ttofi, 2017).

## Conclusion

This chapter reviewed the empirical evidence on some of the most common prenatal and perinatal risk factors linked to delinquency or to childhood precursors to delinquency. The literature reviewed indicated that it is relatively well-established that frequent alcohol consumption during pregnancy can cause FASD, and that young people with FASD are overrepresented in offending and custody. Moreover, while there are clear associations between prenatal smoking and antisocial behavior/delinquency, this relationship is typically confounded by social factors. There is far less research evidence on the impact of exposure to other types of illicit (and licit) substances on behavioral problems and delinquent outcomes; much more research is needed in this area. It is also crucial to account for the co-occurrence and interaction of prenatal and perinatal risk factors, since these typically do not occur in isolation. Furthermore, these need to be considered against the backdrop of broader health, family, and social risk factors considering that women who experience prenatal and perinatal risk can be considered an at-risk population. Where possible studies need to disentangle the synergistic nature of complex relations between prenatal and perinatal risk factors, family, social, and other environmental factors. This highlights the importance of cross-disciplinary research in this area that merges health, criminology, and psychology, for example. Criminological research should continue to increasingly examine early health risk factors to provide additional insight into some of the underlying mechanisms explaining delinquency and offending, while also recognizing the interrelationships between many of these factors and that social disadvantage will continue to play a critical role.

## Acknowledgments

Stacy Tzoumakis was supported by a NARSAD Young Investigator Grant from the Brain & Behavior Research Foundation.

## References

Accornero, V. H., Anthony, J. C., Morrow, C. E., Xue, L., Mansoor, E., Johnson, A. L., ... Bandstra, E. S. (2011). Estimated effect of prenatal cocaine exposure on examiner-rated behavior at age 7 years. *Neurotoxicology and Teratology, 33*(3), 370–378. doi:10.1016/j.ntt.2011.02.014.

Ackerman, J. P., Riggins, T., & Black, M. M. (2010). A review of the effects of prenatal cocaine exposure among school-aged children. *Pediatrics, 125*(3): 554–565 peds. 2009-0637.

Arseneault, L., Tremblay, R. E., Boulerice, B., & Saucier, J. F. (2002). Obstetrical complications and violent delinquency: testing two developmental pathways. *Child Development, 73*(2), 496–508. doi:10.1111/1467-8624.00420.

Ashford, J., Van Lier, P. A. C., Timmermans, M., Cuijpers, P., & Koot, H. M. (2008). Prenatal smoking and internalizing and externalizing problems in children studied from childhood to late adolescence. *Journal of the American Academy of Child & Adolescent Psychiatry, 47*(7), 779–787. doi:10.1097/CHI.0b013e318172eefb.

Banz, B. C., Wu, J., Crowley, M. J., Potenza, M. N., & Mayes, L. C. (2016). Gender-related differences in inhibitory control and sustained attention among adolescents with prenatal cocaine exposure. *Yale Journal of Biology and Medicine, 89*(2), 143–151.

Barthelemy, O. J., Richardson, M. A., Cabral, H. J., & Frank, D. A. (2016). Prenatal, perinatal, and adolescent exposure to marijuana: relationships with aggressive behavior. *Neurotoxicology and Teratology, 58*, 60–77. doi:10.1016/j.ntt.2016.06.009.

Beaver, K. M., & Wright, J. P. (2005). Evaluating the effects of birth complications on low self-control in a sample of twins. *International Journal of Offender Therapy and Comparative Criminology, 49*(4), 450–471. doi:10.1177/0306624X05274687.

Beck, J. E., & Shaw, D. S. (2005). The influence of perinatal complications and environmental adversity on boys' antisocial behavior. *Journal of Child Psychology and Psychiatry, 46*(1), 35–46. doi:10.1111/j.1469-7610.2004.00336.x.

Beckley, A. L., Caspi, A., Broadbent, J., Harrington, H., Houts, R. M., Poulton, R., ... Moffitt, T. E. (2018). Association of childhood blood lead levels with criminal offending. *JAMA Pediatrics, 172*(2), 166–173. doi:10.1001/jamapediatrics.2017.4005.

Bennett, D., Bendersky, M., & Lewis, M. (2007). Preadolescent health risk behavior as a function of prenatal cocaine exposure and gender. *Journal of Developmental & Behavioral Pediatrics, 28*(6), 467–472. doi:10.1097/DBP.0b013e31811320d8.

Bergman, K., Sarkar, P., O'Connor, T. G., Modi, N., & Glover, V. (2007). Maternal stress during pregnancy predicts cognitive ability and fearfulness in infancy. *Journal of the American Academy of Child & Adolescent Psychiatry, 46*(11), 1454–1463.

Billing, L., Eriksson, M., Jonsson, B., Steneroth, G., & Zetterström, R. (1994). The influence of environmental factors on behavioural problems in 8-year-old children exposed to amphetamine during fetal life. *Child Abuse & Neglect, 18*(1), 3–9.

Billing, L., Eriksson, M., Steneroth, G., & Zetterström, R. (1988). Predictive indicators for adjustment in 4-year-old children whose mothers used amphetamine during pregnancy. *Child Abuse & Neglect, 12*(4), 503–507.

Blencowe, H., Cousens, S., Oestergaard, M. Z., Chou, D., Moller, A.-B., Narwal, R., ... Lawn, J. E. (2012). National, regional, and worldwide estimates of preterm birth rates in the year 2010 with time trends since 1990 for selected countries: a systematic analysis and implications. *The Lancet, 379*(9832), 2162–2172. doi:10.1016/S0140-6736(12)60820-4.

Borge, T. C., Aase, H., Brantsæter, A. L., & Biele, G. (2017). The importance of maternal diet quality during pregnancy on cognitive and behavioural outcomes in children: a systematic review and meta-analysis. *BMJ Open, 7*(9), e016777. doi:10.1136/bmjopen-2017-016777.

Bower, C., Watkins, R. E., Mutch, R. C., Marriott, R., Freeman, J., Kippin, N. R., ... Giglia, R. (2018). Fetal alcohol spectrum disorder and youth justice: a prevalence study among young people sentenced to detention in Western Australia. *BMJ Open, 8*(2), e019605. doi:10.1136/bmjopen-2017-019605.

Brennan, P. A., Grekin, E. R., & Mednick, S. A. (1999). Maternal smoking during pregnancy and adult male criminal outcomes. *Archives of General Psychiatry, 56*(3), 215–219. doi:10.1001/archpsyc.56.3.215.

Bridgett, D. J., & Mayes, L. C. (2011). Development of inhibitory control among prenatally cocaine exposed and non-cocaine exposed youths from late childhood to early adolescence: the effects of gender and risk and subsequent aggressive behavior. *Neurotoxicology and Teratology, 33*(1), 47–60. doi:10.1016/j.ntt.2010.08.002.

Broidy, L. M., Nagin, D. S., Tremblay, R. E., Bates, J. E., Brame, B., Dodge, K. A., ... Laird, R. (2003). Developmental trajectories of childhood disruptive behaviors and adolescent delinquency: a six-site, cross-national study. *Developmental Psychology, 39*(2), 222–245. doi:10.1037/0012-1649.39.2.222.

Buchmann, A. F., Zohsel, K., Blomeyer, D., Hohm, E., Hohmann, S., Jennen-Steinmetz, C., ... Schmidt, M. H. (2014). Interaction between prenatal stress and dopamine D4 receptor genotype in predicting aggression and cortisol levels in young adults. *Psychopharmacology, 231*(16), 3089–3097.

Buckingham-Howes, S., Berger, S. S., Scaletti, L. A., & Black, M. M. (2013). Systematic review of prenatal cocaine exposure and adolescent development. *Pediatrics*, e1917–e1936. doi:10.1542/peds.2012-0945.

Button, T. M. M., Maughan, B., & McGuffin, P. (2007). The relationship of maternal smoking to psychological problems in the offspring. *Early Human Development, 83*(11), 727–732. doi:10.1016/j.earlhumdev.2007.07.006.

Cannon, M., Jones, P. B., & Murray, R. (2002). Obstetric complications and schizophrenia: historical and meta-analytic review. *American Journal of Psychiatry, 159*(7), 1080–1092. doi:10.1176/appi.ajp.159.7.1080.

Cernerud, L., Eriksson, M., Jonsson, B., Steneroth, G., & Zetterstrom, R. (1996). Amphetamine addiction during pregnancy: 14-year follow-up of growth and school performance. *Acta Paediatrica, 85*(2), 204–208.

Conseur, A., Rivara, F. P., Barnoski, R., & Emanuel, I. (1997). Maternal and perinatal risk factors for later delinquency. *Pediatrics, 99*(6), 785–790. doi:10.1542/peds.99.6.785.

Cornelius, M. D., Goldschmidt, L., De Genna, N. M., & Larkby, C. (2012). Long-term effects of prenatal cigarette smoke exposure on behavior dysregulation among 14-year-old offspring of teenage mothers. *Maternal and Child Health Journal, 16*(3), 694–705. doi:10.1007/s10995-011-0766-0.

Cottrell, E. C., & Seckl, J. (2009). Prenatal stress, glucocorticoids and the programming of adult disease. *Frontiers in Behavioral Neuroscience, 3*, 19.

D'Onofrio, B. M., Van Hulle, C. A., Goodnight, J. A., Rathouz, P. J., & Lahey, B. B. (2012). Is maternal smoking during pregnancy a causal environmental risk factor for adolescent antisocial behavior? Testing etiological theories and assumptions. *Psychological Medicine, 42*(7), 1535–1545. doi:10.1017/S0033291711002443.

D'Onofrio, B. M., Van Hulle, C. A., Waldman, I. D., Rodgers, J. L., Harden, K. P., Rathouz, P. J., & Lahey, B. B. (2008). Smoking during pregnancy and offspring externalizing problems: an exploration of genetic and environmental confounds. *Development and Psychopathology, 20*(1), 139–164. doi:10.1017/S0954579408000072.

Dahl, L. B., Kaaresen, P. I., Tunby, J., Handegård, B. H., Kvernmo, S., & Rønning, J. A. (2006). Emotional, behavioral, social, and academic outcomes in adolescents born with very low birth weight. *Pediatrics, 118*(2), e449–e459. doi:10.1542/peds.2005-3024.

Davis, E. P., & Sandman, C. A. (2012). Prenatal psychobiological predictors of anxiety risk in preadolescent children. *Psychoneuroendocrinology, 37*(8), 1224–1233.

Day, N. L., Leech, S. L., & Goldschmidt, L. (2011). The effects of prenatal marijuana exposure on delinquent behaviors are mediated by measures of neurocognitive functioning. *Neurotoxicology and Teratology, 33*(1), 129–136. doi:10.1016/j.ntt.2010.07.006.

de Vries, S. L. A., Hoeve, M., Assink, M., Stams, G. J. J. M., & Asscher, J. J. (2015). Practitioner review: effective ingredients of prevention programs for youth at risk of persistent juvenile delinquency – recommendations for clinical practice. *Journal of Child Psychology and Psychiatry, 56*(2), 108–121. doi:10.1111/jcp.12320.

DeLisi, M., & Vaughn, M. G. (2014). Foundation for a temperament-based theory of antisocial behavior and criminal justice system involvement. *Journal of Criminal Justice, 42*(1), 10–25. doi:10.1016/j.jcrimjus.2013.11.001.

Diaz, S. D., Smith, L. M., LaGasse, L. L., Derauf, C., Newman, E., Shah, R., ... Lester, B. M. (2014). Effects of prenatal methamphetamine exposure on behavioral and cognitive findings at 7.5 years. *The Journal of Pediatrics, 164*(6), 1333–1338. doi:10.1016/j.jpeds.2014.01.053.

Dietrich, K. N., Douglas, R. M., Succop, P. A., Berger, O. G., & Bornschein, R. L. (2001). Early exposure to lead and juvenile delinquency. *Neurotoxicology and Teratology, 23*(6), 511–518. doi:10.1016/S0892-0362(01)00184-2.

Disney, E. R., Iacono, W., McGue, M., Tully, E., & Legrand, L. (2008). Strengthening the case: prenatal alcohol exposure is associated with increased risk for conduct disorder. *Pediatrics, 122*(6), e1225–e1230. doi:10.1542/peds.2008-1380.

Eze, N., Smith, L. M., LaGasse, L. L., Derauf, C., Newman, E., Arria, A., ... Neal, C. (2016). School-aged outcomes following prenatal methamphetamine exposure: 7.5-year follow-up from the Infant Development, Environment, and Lifestyle Study. *The Journal of Pediatrics, 170*(34–38), e31. doi:10.1016/j.jpeds.2015.11.070.

Farrington, D. P., Gaffney, H., Lösel, F., & Ttofi, M. M. (2017). Systematic reviews of the effectiveness of developmental prevention programs in reducing delinquency, aggression, and bullying. *Aggression and Violent Behavior, 33*, 91–106. doi:10.1016/j.avb.2016.11.003.

Fergusson, D. M., Woodward, L. J., & Horwood, L. J. (1998). Maternal smoking during pregnancy and psychiatric adjustment in late adolescence. *Archives of General Psychiatry, 55*(8), 721–727.

Field, T., & Diego, M. (2008). Cortisol: the culprit prenatal stress variable. *International Journal of Neuroscience, 118*(8), 1181–1205.

Flannigan, K., Pei, J., Stewart, M., & Johnson, A. (2018). Fetal alcohol spectrum disorder and the criminal justice system: a systematic literature review. *International Journal of Law and Psychiatry, 57*, 42–52. doi:10.1016/j.ijlp.2017.12.008.

Flemming, K., McCaughan, D., Angus, K., & Graham, H. (2015). Qualitative systematic review: barriers and facilitators to smoking cessation experienced by women in pregnancy and following childbirth. *Journal of Advanced Nursing, 71*(6), 1210–1226. doi:10.1111/jan.12580.

Forman, L. S., Liebschutz, J. M., Rose-Jacobs, R., Richardson, M. A., Cabral, H. J., Heeren, T. C., & Frank, D. A. (2017). Urban young adults' adaptive functioning: is there an association with history of prenatal exposure to cocaine and other substances? *Journal of Drug Issues, 47*(2), 261–276. doi:10.1177/0022042616684679.

Fried, P., & Smith, A. (2001). A literature review of the consequences of prenatal marihuana exposure: an emerging theme of a deficiency in aspects of executive function. *Neurotoxicology and Teratology, 23*(1), 1–11. doi:10.1016/S0892-0362(00)00119-7.

Gardner, F., Johnson, A., Yudkin, P., Bowler, U., Hockley, C., Mutch, L., & Wariyar, U. (2004). Behavioral and emotional adjustment of teenagers in mainstream school who were born before 29 weeks' gestation. *Pediatrics, 114*(3), 676–682. doi:10.1542/peds.2003-0763-L.

Gerteis, J., Chartrand, M., Martin, B., Cabral, H. J., Rose-Jacobs, R., Crooks, D., & Frank, D. A. (2011). Are there effects of intrauterine cocaine exposure on delinquency during early adolescence? A preliminary report. *Journal of Developmental and Behavioral Pediatrics, 32*(5), 393–401. doi:10.1097/DBP.0b013e318218d9f2.

Gibson, C. L., Piquero, A. R., & Tibbetts, S. G. (2000). Assessing the relationship between maternal cigarette smoking during pregnancy and age at first police contact. *Justice Quarterly, 17*(3), 519–542. doi:10.1080/07418820000094651.

Gibson, C. L., & Tibbetts, S. G. (1998). Interaction between maternal cigarette smoking and Apgar scores in predicting offending behavior. *Psychological Reports, 83*(2), 579–586. doi:10.2466/pr0.1998.83.2.579.

Graham, H., Hawkins, S. S., & Law, C. (2010). Lifecourse influences on women's smoking before, during and after pregnancy. *Social Science & Medicine, 70*(4), 582–587. doi:10.1016/j.socscimed.2009.10.041.

Green, M. J., Kariuki, M., Dean, K., Laurens, K. R., Tzoumakis, S., Harris, F., & Carr, V. J. (2018). Childhood developmental vulnerabilities associated with early life exposure to infectious and noninfectious diseases and maternal mental illness. *Journal of Child Psychology and Psychiatry, 59*(7), 801–810. doi:10.1111/jcp.12856.

Hack, M., Youngstrom, E. A., Cartar, L., Schluchter, M., Taylor, H. G., Flannery, D., ... Borawski, E. (2004). Behavioral outcomes and evidence of psychopathology among very low birth weight infants at age 20 years. *Pediatrics, 114*(4), 932–940. doi:10.1542/peds.2003-1017-L.

Hay, D. F., Pawlby, S., Waters, C. S., Perra, O., & Sharp, D. (2010). Mothers' antenatal depression and their children's antisocial outcomes. *Child Development, 81*, doi:10.1111/j.1467-8624.2009.01386.x.

Hille, E. T., Den Ouden, A. L., Saigal, S., Wolke, D., Lambert, M., Whitaker, A., ... Feldman, J. F. (2001). Behavioural problems in children who weigh 1000 g or less at birth in four countries. *The Lancet, 357*(9269), 1641–1643. doi:10.1016/S0140-6736(00)04818-2.

Hodgins, S., Kratzer, L., & McNeil, T. F. (2001). Obstetric complications, parenting, and risk of criminal behavior. *Archives of General Psychiatry, 58*(8), 746–752. doi:10.1001/archpsyc.58.8.746.

Hodgins, S., Kratzer, L., & McNeil, T. F. (2002). Are pre and perinatal factors related to the development of criminal offending? In R. R. Corrado, R. Roesch, S. Hart, & J. Gierowski (Eds.), *Multi-problem violent youth: a foundation for comparative research on needs, interventions and outcomes* (pp. 58–80). Amsterdam: IOS Press.

Hughes, N., Clasby, B., Chitsabesan, P., & Williams, H. (2016). A systematic review of the prevalence of foetal alcohol syndrome disorders among young people in the criminal justice system. *Cogent Psychology*, 3(1), 1214213. doi:10.1080/23311908.2016.1214213.

Irner, T. B. (2012). Substance exposure in utero and developmental consequences in adolescence: a systematic review. *Child Neuropsychology*, 18(6), 521–549. doi:10.1080/09297049.2011.628309.

Jackson, D. B., & Beaver, K. M. (2016). Evidence of a gene × environment interaction between birth weight and genetic risk in the prediction of criminogenic outcomes among adolescent males. *International Journal of Offender Therapy and Comparative Criminology*, 60(1), 99–120. doi:10.1177/0306624x14547494.

Jackson, D. B., & Newsome, J. (2016). The link between infant neuropsychological risk and childhood antisocial behavior among males: the moderating role of neonatal health risk. *Journal of Criminal Justice*, 47, 32–40. doi:10.1016/j.jcrimjus.2016.06.003.

Jackson, D. B., & Vaughn, M. G. (2018a). Maternal medical risks during pregnancy and childhood externalizing behavior. *Social Science & Medicine*, 207, 19–24. doi:10.1016/j.socscimed.2018.04.032.

Jackson, D. B., & Vaughn, M. G. (2018b). Promoting health equity to prevent crime. *Preventive Medicine*, 113, 91–94. doi:10.1016/j.ypmed.2018.05.009.

Jarjour, I. T. (2015). Neurodevelopmental outcome after extreme prematurity: a review of the literature. *Pediatric Neurology*, 52(2), 143–152. doi:10.1016/j.pediatrneurol.2014.10.027.

Jauniaux, E., & Burton, G. J. (2007). Morphological and biological effects of maternal exposure to tobacco smoke on the feto-placental unit. *Early Human Development*, 83(11), 699–706. doi:10.1016/j.earlhumdev.2007.07.016.

Kandel, E., & Mednick, S. A. (1991). Perinatal complications predict violent offending. *Criminology*, 29(3), 519–529. doi:10.1111/j.1745-9125.1991.tb01077.x.

Khandaker, G. M., Zimbron, J., Lewis, G., & Jones, P. B. (2013). Prenatal maternal infection, neurodevelopment and adult schizophrenia: a systematic review of population-based studies. *Psychological Medicine*, 43(2), 239–257. doi:10.1017/S0033291712000736.

Knopik, V. S., Maccani, M. A., Francazio, S., & McGeary, J. E. (2012). The epigenetics of maternal cigarette smoking during pregnancy and effects on child development. *Development and Psychopathology*, 24(4), 1377–1390. doi:10.1017/S0954579412000776.

LaGasse, L. L., Derauf, C., Smith, L. M., Newman, E., Shah, R., Neal, C., ... Lin, H. (2012). Prenatal methamphetamine exposure and childhood behavior problems at 3 and 5 years of age. *Pediatrics*, 129(4), 681–688.

Lambert, B. L., Bann, C. M., Bauer, C. R., Shankaran, S., Bada, H. S., Lester, B. M., ... Higgins, R. D. (2013). Risk-taking behavior among adolescents with prenatal drug exposure and extrauterine environmental adversity. *Journal of Developmental and Behavioral Pediatrics*, 34(9), 669–679. doi:10.1097/01.DBP.0000437726.16588.e2.

Lambert, B. L., & Bauer, C. R. (2012). Developmental and behavioral consequences of prenatal cocaine exposure: a review. *Journal of Perinatology: Official Journal of the California Perinatal Association*, 32(11), 819–828. doi:10.1038/jp.2012.90.

Lange, S., Probst, C., Rehm, J., & Popova, S. (2018). National, regional, and global prevalence of smoking during pregnancy in the general population: a systematic review and meta-analysis. *The Lancet Global Health*, 6(7), e769–e776. doi:10.1016/S2214-109X(18)30223-7.

Lee, P. A., Chernausek, S. D., Hokken-Koelega, A. C., & Czernichow, P. (2003). International Small for Gestational Age Advisory Board consensus development conference statement: management of short children born small for gestational age, April 24–October 1, 2001. *Pediatrics*, 111(6), 1253–1261. doi:10.1542/peds.111.6.1253.

Liew, Z., Ritz, B., Rebordosa, C., Lee, P., & Olsen, J. (2014). Acetaminophen use during pregnancy, behavioral problems, and hyperkinetic disorders. *JAMA Pediatrics*, 168(4), 313–320. doi:10.1001/jamapediatrics.2013.4914.

Liu, J. (2011). Early health risk factors for violence: conceptualization, evidence, and implications. *Aggression and Violent Behavior*, 16(1), 63–73. doi:10.1016/j.avb.2010.12.003.

Liu, J., Raine, A., Wuerker, A., Venables, P. H., & Mednick, S. (2009). The association of birth complications and externalizing behavior in early adolescents: direct and mediating effects. *Journal of Research on Adolescence*, 19(1), 93–111. doi:10.1111/j.1532-7795.2009.00583.x.

Liu, X., Agerbo, E., Ingstrup, K. G., Musliner, K., Meltzer-Brody, S., Bergink, V., & Munk-Olsen, T. (2017). Antidepressant use during pregnancy and psychiatric disorders in offspring: danish nationwide register based cohort study. *BMJ*, 358. doi:10.1136/bmj.j3668.

Lussier, P., Tzoumakis, S., Healey, J., Corrado, R. R., & Reebye, P. (2011). Pre/perinatal adversities and behavioural outcomes in early childhood: preliminary findings from the Vancouver longitudinal study. *International Journal of Child, Youth & Family Studies, 2*(1/2), 36.

MacKinnon, N., Kingsbury, M., Mahedy, L., Evans, J., & Colman, I. (2018). The association between prenatal stress and externalizing symptoms in childhood: evidence from the Avon Longitudinal Study of Parents and Children. *Biological Psychiatry, 83*(2), 100–108. doi:10.1016/j.biopsych.2017.07.010.

Mäki, P., Veijola, J., Räsänen, P., Joukamaa, M., Valonen, P., Jokelainen, J., & Isohanni, M. (2003). Criminality in the offspring of antenatally depressed mothers: a 33-year follow-up of the Northern Finland 1966 Birth Cohort. *Journal of Affective Disorders, 74*(3), 273–278. doi:10.1016/S0165-0327(02)00019-8.

Man, K. K. C., Chan, E. W., Ip, P., Coghill, D., Simonoff, E., Chan, P. K. L., ... Wong, I. C. K. (2017). Prenatal antidepressant use and risk of attention-deficit/hyperactivity disorder in offspring: population based cohort study. *BMJ, 357*, doi:10.1136/bmj.j2350.

Martin, R. P., Noyes, J., Wisenbaker, J., & Huttunen, M. O. (1999). Prediction of early childhood negative emotionality and inhibition from maternal distress during pregnancy. *Merrill-Palmer Quarterly, 45*(3), 370–391.

Mason, W. A., January, S.-A. A., Chmelka, M. B., Parra, G. R., Savolainen, J., Miettunen, J., ... Moilanen, I. (2016). Cumulative contextual risk at birth in relation to adolescent substance use, conduct problems, and risky sex: general and specific predictive associations in a Finnish birth cohort. *Addictive Behaviors, 58*, 161–166. doi:10.1016/j.addbeh.2016.02.031.

Mattson, S. N., Crocker, N., & Nguyen, T. T. (2011). Fetal alcohol spectrum disorders: neuropsychological and behavioral features. *Neuropsychology Review, 21*(2), 81–101. doi:10.1007/s11065-011-9167-9.

Maughan, B., Taylor, A., Caspi, A., & Moffitt, T. E. (2004). Prenatal smoking and early childhood conduct problems: testing genetic and environmental explanations of the association. *Archives of General Psychiatry, 61*(8), 836–843. doi:10.1001/archpsyc.61.8.836.

Mayes, L. C. (1999). Developing brain and in utero cocaine exposure: effects on neural ontogeny. *Development and Psychopathology, 11*(4), 685–714.

Mayes, L. C. (2002). A behavioral teratogenic model of the impact of prenatal cocaine exposure on arousal regulatory systems. *Neurotoxicology and Teratology, 24*(3), 385–395.

McGloin, J. M., Pratt, T. C., & Piquero, A. R. (2006). A life-course analysis of the criminogenic effects of maternal cigarette smoking during pregnancy a research note on the mediating impact of neuropsychological deficit. *Journal of Research in Crime and Delinquency, 43*(4), 412–426. doi:10.1177/0022427806292340.

Min, M. O., Minnes, S., Lang, A., Weishampel, P., Short, E. J., Yoon, S., & Singer, L. T. (2014). Externalizing behavior and substance use related problems at 15 years in prenatally cocaine exposed adolescents. *Journal of Adolescence, 37*(3), 269–279. doi:10.1016/j.adolescence.2014.01.004.

Moffitt, T. E. (1993). Adolescence-limited and life-course-persistent antisocial behavior: a developmental taxonomy. *Psychological Review, 100*(4), 674–701. doi:10.1037/0033-295X.100.4.674.

Mwaniki, M. K., Atieno, M., Lawn, J. E., & Newton, C. R. J. C. (2012). Long-term neurodevelopmental outcomes after intrauterine and neonatal insults: a systematic review. *The Lancet, 379*(9814), 445–452. doi:10.1016/S0140-6736(11)61577-8.

Ncube, C. N., Enquobahrie, D. A., Albert, S. M., Herrick, A. L., & Burke, J. G. (2016). Association of neighborhood context with offspring risk of preterm birth and low birthweight: a systematic review and meta-analysis of population-based studies. *Social Science & Medicine, 153*, 156–164. doi:10.1016/j.socscimed.2016.02.014.

O'Connor, M. J. (2014). Mental health outcomes associated with prenatal alcohol exposure: genetic and environmental factors. *Current Developmental Disorders Reports, 1*(3), 181–188. doi:10.1007/s40474-014-0021-7.

Obel, C., Linnet, K. M., Henriksen, T. B., Rodriguez, A., Järvelin, M. R., Kotimaa, A., ... Taanila, A. (2008). Smoking during pregnancy and hyperactivity-inattention in the offspring – comparing results from three Nordic cohorts. *International Journal of Epidemiology, 38*(3), 698–705. doi:10.1093/ije/dym290.

Parker, S. E., Lijewski, V. A., Janulewicz, P. A., Collett, B. R., Speltz, M. L., & Werler, M. M. (2016). Upper respiratory infection during pregnancy and neurodevelopmental outcomes among offspring. *Neurotoxicology and Teratology, 57*, 54–59. doi:10.1016/j.ntt.2016.06.007.

Passmore, E., McGuire, R., Correll, P., & Bentley, J. (2015). Demographic factors associated with smoking cessation during pregnancy in New South Wales, Australia, 2000–2011. *BMC Public Health, 15*(1), 398. doi:10.1186/s12889-015-1725-2.

Piquero, A. R., Gibson, C. L., Tibbetts, S. G., Turner, M. G., & Katz, S. H. (2002). Maternal cigarette smoking during pregnancy and life-course-persistent offending. *International Journal of Offender Therapy and Comparative Criminology, 46*(2), 231–248. doi:10.1177/0306624X02462008.

Popova, S., Lange, S., Probst, C., Gmel, G., & Rehm, J. (2017). Estimation of national, regional, and global prevalence of alcohol use during pregnancy and fetal alcohol syndrome: a systematic review and meta-analysis. *The Lancet Global Health*, *5*(3), e290–e299. doi:10.1016/S2214-109X(17)30021-9.

Pratt, T. C., McGloin, J. M., & Fearn, N. E. (2006). Maternal cigarette smoking during pregnancy and criminal/deviant behavior: a meta-analysis. *International Journal of Offender Therapy and Comparative Criminology*, *50*(6), 672–690. doi:10.1177/0306624x06286623.

Raine, A. (2013). *The anatomy of violence: the biological roots of crime*. New York, NY: Pantheon/Random House.

Raine, A., Brennan, P., & Mednick, S. A. (1997). Interaction between birth complications and early material rejection in predisposing individuals to adult violence: specificity to serious, early-onset violence. *The American Journal of Psychiatry*, *154*(9), 1265–1271. doi:10.1176/ajp.154.9.1265.

Richardson, G. A., Goldschmidt, L., Larkby, C., & Day, N. L. (2015). Effects of prenatal cocaine exposure on adolescent development. *Neurotoxicology and Teratology*, *49*, 41–48. doi:10.1016/j.ntt.2015.03.002.

Roza, S. J., Verhulst, F. C., Jaddoe, V. W., Steegers, E. A., Mackenbach, J. P., Hofman, A., & Tiemeier, H. (2008). Maternal smoking during pregnancy and child behaviour problems: the Generation R Study. *International Journal of Epidemiology*, *38*(3), 680–689. doi:10.1093/ije/dyn163.

Ruisch, I. H., Dietrich, A., Glennon, J. C., Buitelaar, J. K., & Hoekstra, P. J. (2018). Maternal substance use during pregnancy and offspring conduct problems: a meta-analysis. *Neuroscience & Biobehavioral Reviews*, *84*, 325–336. doi:10.1016/j.neubiorev.2017.08.014.

Salihu, H. M., & Wilson, R. E. (2007). Epidemiology of prenatal smoking and perinatal outcomes. *Early Human Development*, *83*(11), 713–720. doi:10.1016/j.earlhumdev.2007.08.002.

Sampson, R. J., & Winter, A. S. (2018). Poisoned development: assessing childhood lead exposure as a cause of crime in a birth cohort followed through adolescence. *Criminology*, *56*(2), 269–301. doi:10.1111/1745-9125.12171.

Samuelsson, M., Holsti, A., Adamsson, M., Serenius, F., Hägglöf, B., & Farooqi, A. (2017). Behavioral patterns in adolescents born at 23 to 25 weeks of gestation. *Pediatrics*, *140*(1), e20170199. doi:10.1542/peds.2017-0199.

Sayal, K., Heron, J., Golding, J., & Emond, A. (2007). Prenatal alcohol exposure and gender differences in childhood mental health problems: a longitudinal population-based study. *Pediatrics*, *119*(2), e426–e434. doi:10.1542/peds.2006-1840.

Schneider, S., Huy, C., Schuetz, J., & Diehl, K. (2010). Smoking cessation during pregnancy: a systematic literature review. *Drug and Alcohol Review*, *29*(1), 81–90. doi:10.1111/j.1465-3362.2009.00098.x.

Skoglund, C., Chen, Q., D'Onofrio, B. M., Lichtenstein, P., & Larsson, H. (2014). Familial confounding of the association between maternal smoking during pregnancy and ADHD in offspring. *Journal of Child Psychology and Psychiatry*, *55*(1), 61–68. doi:10.1111/jcpp.12124.

Smith, L. M., Diaz, S., LaGasse, L. L., Wouldes, T., Derauf, C., Newman, E., ... Strauss, A. (2015). Developmental and behavioral consequences of prenatal methamphetamine exposure: a review of the infant development, environment, and lifestyle (IDEAL) study. *Neurotoxicology and Teratology*, *51*, 35–44.

Sokol, R. J., Delaney-Black, V., & Nordstrom, B. (2003). Fetal alcohol spectrum disorder. *JAMA*, *290*(22), 2996–2999. doi:10.1001/jama.290.22.2996.

Stergiakouli, E., Thapar, A., & Davey Smith, G. (2016). Association of acetaminophen use during pregnancy with behavioral problems in childhood: evidence against confounding. *JAMA Pediatrics*, *170*(10), 964–970. doi:10.1001/jamapediatrics.2016.1775.

Streissguth, A. P., Bookstein, F. L., Barr, H. M., Sampson, P. D., O'Malley, K., & Young, J. K. (2004). Risk factors for adverse life outcomes in fetal alcohol syndrome and fetal alcohol effects. *Journal of Developmental and Behavioral Pediatrics*, *25*(4), 228–238. doi:10.1097/00004703-200408000-00002.

Substance Abuse and Mental Health Services Administration. (2011). *Results from the 2010 national survey on drug use and health: mental health findings*. Rockville, MD: Substance Abuse and Mental Health Services Administration.

Tibbetts, S. G. (2014). Prenatal and perinatal predictors of antisocial behavior: review of research and interventions. In M. DeLisi & K. M. Beaver (Eds.), *Criminological Theory: a Life-Course Approach* (2nd ed., Vol. 201, pp. 27–33). Sudbury, MA: Jones & Bartlett Publishers.

Tibbetts, S. G., & Piquero, A. R. (1999). The influence of gender, low birth weight, and disadvantaged environment in predicting early onset of offending: a test of Moffitt's interactional hypothesis. *Criminology*, *37*(4), 843–878. doi:10.1111/j.1745-9125.1999.tb00507.x.

Tibbetts, S. G., & Rivera, J. (2015). Prenatal and perinatal factors in the development of persistent criminality. In J. Morizot & L. Kazemian (Eds.), *The development of criminal and antisocial behavior: theory, research and practical applications* (pp. 167–180). Cham: Springer.

Tzoumakis, S., Carr, V. J., Dean, K., Laurens, K. R., Kariuki, M., Harris, F., & Green, M. J. (2018). Prenatal maternal smoking, maternal offending, and offspring behavioural and cognitive outcomes in early childhood. *Criminal Behaviour and Mental Health*. doi:10.1002/cbm.2089.

United Nations Children's Fund and World Health Organization. (2004). *Low birthweight: country, regional and global estimates*. New York: UNICEF.

Van den Bergh, B. R., van den Heuvel, M. I., Lahti, M., Braeken, M., de Rooij, S. R., Entringer, S., ... King, S. (2017). Prenatal developmental origins of behavior and mental health: the influence of maternal stress in pregnancy. *Neuroscience & Biobehavioral Reviews*. doi: 10.1016/j.neubiorev.2017.07.003.

Wakschlag, L. S., Pickett, K. E., Cook Jr., E., Benowitz, N. L., & Leventhal, B. L. (2002). Maternal smoking during pregnancy and severe antisocial behavior in offspring: a review. *American Journal of Public Health*, 92(6), 966–974. doi:10.2105/ajph.92.6.966.

Werenberg Dreier, J., Nybo Andersen, A.-M., Hvolby, A., Garne, E., Kragh Andersen, P., & Berg-Beckhoff, G. (2016). Fever and infections in pregnancy and risk of attention deficit/hyperactivity disorder in the offspring. *Journal of Child Psychology and Psychiatry*, 57(4), 540–548. doi:10.1111/jcp.12480.

Wilcox, A. J. (2001). On the importance – and the unimportance – of birthweight. *International Journal of Epidemiology*, 30(6), 1233–1241. doi:10.1093/ije/30.6.1233.

Williams, J. H. G., & Ross, L. (2007). Consequences of prenatal toxin exposure for mental health in children and adolescents. *European Child & Adolescent Psychiatry*, 16(4), 243–253. doi:10.1007/s00787-006-0596-6.

# 3
# RACIAL DISPARITIES IN HEALTH AND JUSTICE SYSTEM EXPOSURE
## Patterns and Explanations

*Graham C. Ousey and Tracy W.P. Sohoni*

## Introduction

The United States is remarkable for abundant wealth and technological sophistication. It is also remarkable for high levels of social inequality, particularly between racial groups. In this chapter, we explore patterns of racial/ethnic disparity within two institutional venues, health and criminal justice, for juveniles and adults. Prior scholarship on these issues has mostly developed in disconnected disciplinary silos (Jackson & Vaughn, 2018b; Ousey, 2017) with studies of health and disease the purview of physicians, nurses, epidemiologists, and medical sociologists and research on criminal justice processes the concern of criminologists and legal scholars. We peer through the silo walls, examining how racial/ethnic inequalities in these areas of social life are connected.

The remainder of the chapter is organized as follows. We begin with a background discussion of patterns of racial disparity in illness prevalence and mortality rates. It is followed by a description of observed disparities in incarceration between racial and ethnic groups. Next, we discuss theories that potentially explain: (1) why health and criminal justice outcomes are correlated; and (2) why racial disparities in illness prevalence and criminal justice system exposure are similar. We close with a brief discussion of how health, crime, and racial/ethnic inequality may be reduced.

### *Racial Disparities in Health in the United States*

Health and longevity statistics differ markedly for racial and ethnic subgroups in the U.S. population (Kawachi, Daniels, & Robinson, 2005; Wang & Beydoun, 2007). These discrepancies follow a familiar pattern, mimicking the contours of inequalities in employment (Hout, 2017), wealth (Shapiro, 2017), earnings (Peterson, Snipp, & Cheung, 2017), and education (Reardon & Fahle, 2017). Specifically, White Americans are advantaged relative to most non-white racial groups (Johnson, 2017; Williams & Sternthal, 2010) with African Americans experiencing the greatest health disadvantages and American Indians also faring poorly compared to Whites (Beydoun et al., 2016; National Center for Health Statistics, 2017). Of non-White racial groups, only Asian

Americans exhibit health outcomes that consistently compare favorably with Whites (National Center for Health Statistics, 2017; U.S. Department of Health and Human Services, 2018).

## *Disparities in Mortality*

Health inequities are well-illustrated by mortality data (Beydoun et al., 2016; Borrell, Dallo, & Nguyen, 2010; Richardus & Kunst, 2001). The all-cause death rate for 2016 was 18 percent higher for non-Hispanic African Americans than non-Hispanic Whites (U.S. Department of Health and Human Services (US DHHS), Centers for Disease Control and Prevention (CDC), National Center for Health Statistics (NCHS), 2018). Native Americans' all-cause mortality rates were roughly seven percent higher than for white non-Hispanics (U.S. Department of Health and Human Services (US DHHS), Centers for Disease Control and Prevention (CDC), National Center for Health Statistics (NCHS), 2018). Asian Americans had mortality rates 47 percent lower than non-Hispanic Whites (U.S. Department of Health and Human Services (US DHHS), Centers for Disease Control and Prevention (CDC), National Center for Health Statistics (NCHS), 2018). Interestingly, people of Hispanic/Latino origin (of any race) had nearly 30 percent lower mortality rates than non-Latinos (of any race). This difference reflects the so-called "Latino paradox," whereby Latinos do better than expected on various health outcomes despite relatively low socioeconomic status and poor access to healthcare (Borrell, Dallo, & Nguyen, 2010; Hummer et al., 2007; Markides & Coreil, 1986; Markides & Eschbach, 2005).

Although race disparities in mortality rates are present across the life span, the gap is most pronounced among juveniles and young adults. All-cause death rates for persons aged 65-plus were 7 percent higher for non-Hispanic Blacks than Whites (U.S. Department of Health and Human Services (US DHHS), Centers for Disease Control and Prevention (CDC), National Center for Health Statistics (NCHS), 2018). For young people aged 1 to 24, the disparity was substantially greater with all-cause death rates 60 percent higher for African Americans than Whites (U.S. Department of Health and Human Services (US DHHS), Centers for Disease Control and Prevention (CDC), National Center for Health Statistics (NCHS), 2018). Moreover, infant death rates (< 1 year of age) were 2.3 times greater for African Americans than Whites (U.S. Department of Health and Human Services (US DHHS), Centers for Disease Control and Prevention (CDC), National Center for Health Statistics (NCHS), 2018). Given the preceding data, it is easy to understand why African Americans live, on average, four years fewer than Whites (Kochanek, Murphy, & Xu, 2015).

## *Disparities in Physical Disease*

There are also marked racial disparities in the prevalence of many illnesses with Blacks again disadvantaged relative to Whites (Hayward & Heron, 1999; Johnson, 2017; Massoglia, 2008b). In general, this pattern holds for chronic non-infectious conditions such as diabetes, obesity, and heart disease (Centers for Disease Control, 2018; National Center for Health Statistics, 2017) and for serious infectious diseases including tuberculosis (Nahid et al., 2011), helicobacter pylori (McQuillan et al., 2004), HIV (Centers for Disease Control and Prevention, 2017a) and several STDs (Centers for Disease Control and Prevention, 2017b).

Racial/ethnic differences in disease prevalence occur for children and adolescents as well as adults. Asthma, one of the most common chronic conditions affecting U.S. youth, occurs at higher rates among Puerto Ricans and African Americans than among Whites or Mexican Americans (Price et al., 2013). Obesity is more prevalent for African American and Hispanic youth relative to White youth (Price et al., 2013; Singh, Siahpush, & Kogan, 2010). Prevalence of youth diabetes also differs by race, but the pattern depends on the disease type. Type 1 is most common among non-Hispanic White youths whereas Type II is most common for American Indian and African American youths (Centers for Disease Control and Prevention, 2018; Spanakis & Golden, 2013).

## *Disparities in Mental Illness*

Evidence of racial disparity in the prevalence of mental illnesses also exists, but the pattern is not simple. In general, non-White racial groups have a lower prevalence of (any) mental illness than Whites (Budhwhani, Hearld, & Chavez-Yenter, 2015). But nuances appear in the story. First, despite lower overall mental illness prevalence, evidence indicates that non-Hispanic Blacks who become ill are more likely to experience a persistent disorder than non-Hispanic Whites (Breslau et al., 2005). In addition, while some depressive disorders like major depression are less common among African Americans than Whites other depressive disorders, like dysthymia, are more common for African Americans (Riolo et al., 2005). Finally, some research suggests that non-Hispanic Blacks have higher lifetime prevalence of post-traumatic stress disorder (PTSD) or are more likely to be diagnosed with schizophrenia than non-Hispanic Whites (Blow et al., 2004; Coleman et al., 2017; Eack et al., 2012; Roberts et al., 2011).

Racial and ethnic differences in mental health conditions also occur for adolescents. Kilpatrick and colleagues (2003) examined racial/ethnic differences in PTSD, major depressive episodes and substance abuse/dependence among a national sample of adolescents aged 12 to 17. They found significant differences for both PTSD and substance use/dependence. For the former, both African American and Hispanic adolescents had higher odds (odds ratios of 2.5 and 4.1, respectively) than White adolescents. For the latter, African American adolescents reported 74 percent lower odds than Whites. No statistically significant racial/ethnic differences were observed for major depression episodes.

## *Disparities in the Healthy Life-Span*

Taken together, the preceding sections are strong evidence of racial differences in the prevalence of physical and mental illnesses. From this we can expect that racial groups differ in the share of their lives characterized by good health. One gauge of this difference is measured by "active life expectancy," which estimates the average number of years one can expect to live without activity limitations (Centers for Disease Control and Prevention, 2013a). Using data from 2008, the CDC estimated that, on average, White Americans were expected to live around 67 years without activity limitations due to chronic illness. In comparison, Black Americans were expected to live only 61 years without limitations (Centers for Disease Control and Prevention, 2013a). These disparities also show up in survey measures of self-rated health. For example, data from the Behavioral Risk Factor Surveillance System shows that in comparison to non-Hispanic Whites, a significantly higher percentage of non-Hispanic Blacks report their health as "fair or poor" (23.3 percent vs. 13.3 percent). Moreover, African Americans also report significantly more physically and mentally unhealthy days in the last month that do White respondents (Centers for Disease Control and Prevention, 2013b).

In sum, for adults and juveniles, health outcomes clearly vary by race and ethnicity. Exacerbating these disparities is the fact that, on average, there are differences in healthcare. Evidence suggests that African Americans have lower access to and utilization of medical services than Whites (Artiga et al., 2016). Moreover, while the Affordable Care Act has lowered the overall share of the population lacking health insurance and reduced disparities in coverage, key racial/ethnic differences in access and utilization persist (Artiga et al., 2016; Artiga, Foutz, & Damico, 2018).

## Racial Disparity in the Criminal Justice System

One of the dramatic developments in American society over the past 50 years has been the large and rapid expansion of the criminal justice system (Massoglia, 2008a; Pratt, 2009). This is evinced by incarceration trend data for the United States. In 1970, adult state and federal prisons held around 329,000 inmates, a rate near 160 prisoners per 100,000 population. By the mid-2010s, the total adult population in prisons and jails hovered around 2.2 million, a rate of nearly 870 per 100,000 (Kaeble & Cowhig, 2018). Although some decline has occurred in adult incarceration over the past several years, the current rate remains more than five times that observed in the early 1970s.

Juvenile incarceration also experienced dramatic changes during the past 50 years. However, there were two dramatically opposed periods of change, one before and one since the new millennium. In 1980, around 60,000 juveniles were confined in juvenile detention facilities (Cahalan & Parsons, 1986). By 2000, that figure nearly doubled to around 109,000 (National Juvenile Justice Network & Texas Policy Foundation, 2013). Since 2000, however, that growth has more than reversed. Indeed, by 2015, the number of juveniles in residential placement had dropped to less than half of the circa 2000 peak, sitting near 50,000 (National Juvenile Justice Network & Texas Public Policy Foundation, 2013). Thus, the past 50 years have been times of change in both adult and juvenile incarceration rates in the United States. Prior to 2000, that change involved increasing incarceration for both adults and juveniles. Immediately after 2000, juvenile rates fell. Adult rates continued to climb for several additional years before falling modestly during the 2010s. Notwithstanding the recent evidence of decline, overall incarceration rates remain historically high. Moreover, as we document below there are troubling racial disparities in incarceration in the United States.

Despite declining youth incarceration rates since 2000, racial disparities in confinement remain firm. In fact, in relative terms, the decline in the Black youth incarceration rate was smaller than the decline of the White youth incarceration rate (The Sentencing Project, 2017). Consequently, the Black/White youth incarceration rate ratio increased from 4.12 in 2001 to 5.03 in 2015 (The Sentencing Project, 2017). Youth incarceration rates for other racial and ethnic minority groups also exceed those of Whites. For American Indian juveniles, the rate of confinement to secure facilities is three times the rate of Whites; for Hispanics it is 1.65 times the rate for Whites (The Sentencing Project, 2017). The lone exception is for Asian American youth, whose incarceration rate is 73 percent lower than the rate for White American youth (The Sentencing Project, 2017). Minority youth are more likely to feel the impact of the "school to prison pipeline." African American students, for example, are only 16 percent of the student population but they make up 27 percent of students referred to law enforcement by schools (U.S. Department of Education for Civil Rights 2014). In sum, while the overall picture of youth incarceration portrays meaningful progress toward less criminal justice system confinement, a closer look shows a troubling persistence of substantial racial and ethnic inequity with African Americans bearing the largest burden. Research indicates that these disparities in incarceration reflect both racial differences in offending for some crimes, as well as differential treatment by the criminal justice system (Sampson & Lauritsen, 1997).

## Explaining the Association between Health and Criminal Justice Outcomes

The preceding pages illustrate the noteworthy racial disparities in both health and criminal justice outcomes in American society. They also underscore the fact that the pattern of racial/ethnic disparities in these outcomes are similar. This evidence begs important questions. Are health disparities and criminal justice disparities similar because each is caused by the same underlying social, political and economic forces? Are they similar because they causally affect one another?

Are there plausible explanations for the higher rates of illness, mortality, and criminal justice system exposure that exist for African Americans, and other racial/ethnic minorities? We address these questions in the paragraphs that follow.

## *Common Cause Theories*

Similarity in the racial patterning of health and criminal justice outcomes is potentially explained by theories of *common cause*. In general, these explanations assert that health and criminal justice system outcomes vary together because they respond to the same underlying causal forces. That which explains why Whites experience lower morbidity and mortality rates relative to people of color also explains why African Americans and Latinos are overexposed to incarceration. Specific mechanisms invoked by common cause theories vary but can broadly be distinguished based on whether they posit shared causes as features of the social structure or as characteristics or traits of individuals.

Social structure theories argue that broad features of the social organization of communities or places are what produce variations in health outcomes and determine differences in the risk of criminal justice system exposure. These theories emphasize that social, economic, political, and cultural conditions of communities create benefits or harms for resident populations. Deprivation theory is an example. It contends that the cause of many undesired outcomes, including poor health, high crime, and incarceration is socioeconomic deprivation. Populations in communities experiencing higher levels of poverty, unemployment, school dropout, family breakdown and civic disengagement (among others) are at greater risk for contracting diseases, more likely to experience diseases chronically, more likely to die early deaths from disease, more likely to engage in law-violating behavior, and more likely to be incarcerated for their criminal behavior. This is because these forms of economic, social, and political deprivation trigger greater exposure to risks factors (e.g., environmental toxins, infectious pathogens, inadequate childhood nutrition, stressful situations, criminal networks) and limit availability of protective factors (e.g., social supports, prosocial capital, health knowledge, medical care, legal resources), which proximally influence illness, crime, and related consequences (Barkan & Rocque, 2018; Cockerham, 2013; Link & Phelan, 1995). Supporting this argument, numerous studies report that resource deprivation measures are associated with the prevalence or rate of: physical and mental illness, health-risk behaviors, crime, arrests, and incarceration (Cohen et al., 2000; Ford & Browning, 2011, 2013; Kirk, 2008; Ousey, 2017; Ross, 2000; Sampson & Loeffler, 2010; Silver, Mulvey, & Swanson, 2002).

The deprivation theory also provides explanation of racial disparities in health and criminal justice system contact in the United States. According to the theory, rates of illness and criminal justice system contact should be greater for racial and ethnic groups experiencing higher rates of poverty and other forms of resource deprivation. Consistent with this argument, racial groups with the highest poverty rates (e.g., African Americans) have illness, mortality and incarceration rates substantially greater than groups with lower poverty rates (e.g., Whites, Asian Americans) (Carson, 2018; Macartney, Bishaw, & Fontenot, 2013; National Center for Health Statistics, 2016; Puzzanchera & Hockenberry, 2018; The Sentencing Project, 2017). Moreover, studies suggest that racial and ethnic disparities in crime, arrest, and health are associated with racial-ethnic differences in socioeconomic deprivation (Kirk, 2008; McNulty & Bellair, 2003; Williams & Sternthal, 2010).

A second common cause argument asserts that racial discrimination explains the disproportionate racial/ethnic concentration of disease, crime, arrests, and incarceration. It links historic and contemporary manifestations of systemic racism—slavery, Jim Crow, anti-miscegenation laws, school segregation, discriminatory bank-lending, gerrymandering, vote-suppression, white-flight, and residential segregation—to forms of racial inequality. Thus, it offers explanation for why the pattern of racial and ethnic disparities is similar for outcomes as diverse as health/illness and criminal justice system exposure (Phelan & Link, 2015; Barkan & Rocque, 2018; Burch, 2014; Ousey, 2017; Ousey & Lee, 2008; Williams & Collins, 2001; Kramer & Hogue, 2009). It also offers a theory of relative disadvantages faced by different racial and ethnic groups. In the United States, systemic racial discrimination has most severely impacted African Americans, accounting for why they tend to experience the greatest disadvantages in many social outcomes, including health and criminal justice. Finally, as was true for the resource deprivation perspective, this theory suggests that racial discrimination affects health and criminal justice outcomes through a host of intervening mechanisms, but clearly asserts systemic racism as the "fundamental" cause (Barkan & Rocque, 2018; Phelan & Link, 2015).

The theory of racial discrimination draws general empirical support from research which links a salient form of systemic racism, racial residential segregation, to various health and crime/criminal justice outcomes including: greater overall morbidity and mortality rates (Kramer & Hogue, 2009; Williams & Collins, 2001; Williams & Sternthal, 2010), higher rates of incarceration (Burch, 2014), elevated crime rates among African Americans (Feldmeyer, 2010; Krivo, Peterson, & Kuhl, 2009; Peterson & Krivo, 1993; Shihadeh & Flynn, 1996), greater between-race disparities in infant mortality and preterm births (Bird, 1995; LaVeist, 1989; Osypuk & Acevedo-Garcia, 2008; Polednak, 1991), more substantial racial disparity in homicide rates (Velez, Krivo, & Peterson, 2003), and greater black/white disparities in arrests for drug and weapons offenses (Ousey & Lee, 2008). Likewise, it is supported by scholarship showing that individuals with greater personal experiences and perceptions of racial discrimination are more likely to exhibit an array of mental and physical health problems (Williams & Mohammed, 2009), delinquency (Burt, Simons, & Gibbons, 2012), violence (Simons et al., 2006), problematic externalizing behaviors (Unnever, Cullen, & Barnes, 2016), and illegal drug use (Borrell et al., 2007; Gibbons et al., 2007).

Not all common cause explanations identify social-structural factors. An alternative suggests that specific individual-level characteristics produce greater risks of negative health outcomes and criminal justice system exposure. One example is Gottfredson and Hirschi's (1990) self-control theory. It assumes individuals are motivated by self-interest and seek to satisfy needs and wants quickly. Unhealthy eating, improper hygiene, promiscuity, lying, stealing, and aggression can help satisfy short-term needs, but at the cost of increased risk of illness, of legal consequences, and of shortening the life-span. The person with low self-control has difficulty seeing and properly weighing those costs. Since our society values health, law abidance and longevity, its task is teaching individuals to respect those values and exercise constraints needed for their attainment. Individuals must learn to correctly weigh future costs against their desires for immediate pleasure. According to Gottfredson and Hirschi's theory, self-control should emerge in kids between ages 5 and 10 as parents monitor their behavior and correct wrongdoing with appropriate sanctions. Proper parenting teaches that the pursuit of self-interest must be restrained in ways that limit risks of disease, jail and early death. However, because parenting is not always effective some individuals remain low in self-control and experience higher risks of criminal behavior, criminal justice exposure, and negative health consequences.

Empirical research supports the idea that self-control explains both crime involvement and poor health outcomes. Pratt & Cullen's (2000) meta-analysis concluded that self-control was one of the strongest individual-level crime correlates. Numerous subsequent studies bolster that conclusion. Low self-control has been found predictive of various types of criminal offending across diverse samples varying by age, national origin, and economic disadvantage or crime-risk level (for review, see Hay & Meldrum, 2016, pp. 58–61). Moreover, research shows an association between self-control and various health indicators including: body mass index (Crescioni et al., 2011; Schlam et al., 2013); exercise and good nutrition (Wills et al., 2007); depression, mental health, and psychiatric disorders (Boals, vanDellen, & Banks, 2011; Caspi et al., 1996; Miller, Barnes, & Beaver, 2011); an index of respiratory, periodontal, metabolic, inflammatory, and sexually transmitted infectious conditions (Moffitt et al., 2011); and early mortality (Kern & Friedman, 2008).

Gottfredson and Hirschi's (1990) theory attributes racial and ethnic differences in crime to group differences in self-control, which are the result of: "potentially large differences among racial groups ... in the elements of child-rearing" (153). And although their theory is not meant to explain health outcomes, its logic implies that White Americans experience lower disease prevalence and lower mortality rates because, on average, they have developed higher levels of self-control than African Americans and other people of color. Unfortunately, research addressing whether self-control theory explains racial disparities in crime or health outcomes is relatively scarce. Some basic support can be gleaned from studies that indicate Whites and non-Whites differ on measures of parenting practices or on self-control (Higgins & Ricketts, 2005; Pratt, Turner, & Piquero, 2004) and other studies which show that the experience of racism depletes self-control in racial minority groups (Gibbons et al., 2012). However, other research evidence runs counter to the idea that race-differences in self-control are responsible for race differences in crime and criminal justice system exposure. For example, some studies find that race remains a significant predictor of crime, even when race differences in self-control are controlled (Kirchner & Higgins, 2014; Longshore, 1998). And other work reports that self-control does not differ by race (Hay, 2001) or is not predictive of delinquency for Blacks (Higgins & Ricketts, 2005). Thus, at present, the research evidence is too shallow and findings too ambiguous to support strong conclusions about whether differences in self-control explain observed patterns of racial disparity in health and crime.

## Direct Causal Linkages between Health and Criminal Justice Outcomes

Another set of explanations focus on how health and criminal justice system exposure directly influence one another. One line of explanation proffers that health problems cause subsequent criminal justice system exposure by increasing criminal behavior. The second line suggests that causation works in the other direction, criminal justice system exposure causes subsequent illness or health problems. These perspectives are not unfriendly to the possibility that antecedent forces, such as resource deprivation, systemic racism, or individual traits may affect both prevalence of illness and criminal justice system exposure. But their core argument is that that net of antecedent effects, health problems and criminal justice system exposures have causal impact on one another. We briefly review research related to each of these causal pathways below.

### *Health Effects on Incarceration*

Do health conditions play a role in the genesis of crime and criminal justice exposure? And do racial disparities in health contribute to racial disparities in incarceration? Until recently, criminological scholarship neglected this connection. However, there is now growing scholarly interest in connections between health, crime and criminal justice (Jackson & Vaughn, 2018b).

Health conditions occurring in the earliest stages of life are one avenue linking health and criminal behavior. It is known that maternal prenatal health problems, including the experience of high levels of stress, negatively impact fetal health and development (Dunkel Schetter, 2011; Gourounti, Karpathiotaki, & Vaslamatzis, 2015; Weinstock, 2008). Moreover, maternal health risks also are associated with problematic externalizing behaviors in offspring. Jackson and Vaughn (2018a) report that male offspring exposed to a greater accumulation of maternal health factors (e.g., anemia, cardiac or lung disease, diabetes, preeclampsia, obesity) during the prenatal period have a significantly greater likelihood of developing persistent externalizing behavior problems (e.g., impulsivity, aggression, provocation, hyperactivity) during preschool and kindergarten ages. Reasons are not completely clear, but stress/anxiety processes, neuropsychological functions, and temperament are potentially salient intervening mechanisms for the observed effects (Jackson & Vaughn, 2018a).

Exposure to environmental toxins is another health risk that may affect criminal behavior. Research by Needleman and colleagues (Needleman, 2004; Needleman et al., 1979, 1996) showed that low levels of lead exposure creates health and behavioral consequences, especially for young children. Problems with neurological development, motor function, learning, cognition, and attention-deficits all appear at elevated rates in children with greater lead exposure (Needleman, 2004). Building on this work, a growing research literature suggests that lead exposure may help explain juvenile delinquency and violent crime (Dietrich et al., 2001; Martin & Wolfe, 2018; Needleman et al., 2002, 1996; Nevin, 2007; Reyes, 2007, 2015; Stretesky & Lynch, 2001, 2004; Wright et al., 2008).

Research also suggests that traumatic brain injuries (TBI) produce short- and long-term behavioral effects (LeÓn-CarriÓn & Ramos, 2003; Li & Liu, 2013). Prior brain injury is up to ten times more common among incarcerated than general populations (Schwartz, Connolly, & Valgardson, 2018). In addition, research from Sweden indicates that individuals who experienced TBI had more than three times the odds of violent behavior than individuals with no TBI (Fazel et al., 2011). Sibling comparisons revealed that the odds of violence were double for siblings with a TBI history relative to siblings without a TBI history (Fazel et al., 2011). However, some recent research suggests that while correlated, brain injury does not cause subsequent involvement in criminal behavior (Schwartz, Connolly, & Valgardson, 2018).

Adverse child experiences (ACE) include unhealthy social experiences such as physical, sexual and emotional abuse, physical or emotional neglect, and witnessing violence in the household or neighborhood context. They may contribute to an elevated prevalence of mental health problems and greater involvement with crime and the criminal justice system. Consistent with that argument, evidence indicates that individuals in the criminal justice system report higher levels of ACE (Reavis et al., 2013) and greater evidence of PTSD and other psychiatric disorders (Briere, Agee, & Dietrich, 2016) than general/non-incarcerated populations. Moreover, some research reports that ACE and related trauma exposures are associated with subsequent behavioral problems (Wolff & Shi, 2012), including violence (Duke et al., 2010). However, recent research suggests that the relationship between ACE and antisocial behavior may be non-causal (Connolly, 2018).

A major consequence of the behavioral effects linked to the negative health conditions noted above is racial disparity in the risk of incarceration, especially for African Americans. Race differences in exposure to lead, poor prenatal health, TBI and ACE are likely to produce group differences in the prevalence of negative behaviors, which subsequently yield racial disparities in criminal justice system exposure. Because of systemic racism, racial residential segregation has concentrated many African Americans in residential spaces with greater exposure to toxic environments. Indeed, research indicates communities with higher African American population shares have higher levels of exposure to lead (Sampson & Winter, 2016; Stretesky, 2003), concentrated poverty (DeNavas-Walt, Proctor, & Smith, 2014; Logan, 2014) and racial discrimination which are likely to negatively impact prenatal and early childhood health through increased exposure to stress, ACE or other traumatic events (Bruner, 2017; Nagahawatte & Goldenberg, 2008). Not surprisingly, Eitle and Turner (2003) found that African Americans had higher rates of lifetime stress, leading to race differences in offending (Eitle & Turner, 2003).

## *Incarceration Effects on Health*

Extant research indicates that risks of chronic physical disease are disproportionately elevated among correctional populations relative to the general population (Binswanger, Krueger, & Steiner, 2009; Cloud, 2014; National Commission on Correctional Health Care, 2002). Some of this disproportion may be the result of selection effects in which people with poor health are more likely to commit crime and face incarceration, but there is also reason to believe that incarceration negatively impacts health outcomes (Schnittker & John, 2007). Because incarceration rates are substantially greater for African Americans than Whites, it follows that racial disparities in health may be, in part, influenced by race differences in incarceration.

The impact of incarceration on health can play out in several ways. First, incarceration may increase exposure to infectious diseases (Cloud, 2014; Massoglia, 2008a, 2008b; National Commission on Correctional Health Care, 2002). Second, incarceration is a major life event and chronic stressor, both of which negatively impact health functioning (Massoglia, 2008a). Third, incarceration negatively impacts employment opportunities and disrupts family connections, which are associated with health (Massoglia, 2008b; Ross & Mirowsky, 1995; Ross, Mirowsky, & Goldsteen, 1990). Fourth, incarceration may negatively impact mental health conditions, such as mood disorders (Schnittker, Massoglia, & Uggen, 2012). Finally, incarceration effects on health may extend to the families and broader communities of incarcerated individuals. Several studies indicate that incarceration is associated with higher rates of infectious disease (Johnson & Raphael, 2009; Stuckler et al., 2008; Thomas & Torrone, 2008). Others show that parental incarceration is associated with elevated risks of behavioral problems and mental health issues among children (Turney, 2014; Wakefield & Wildeman, 2011). With over 2.7 million children experiencing the incarceration of a parent (Pew Charitable Trusts, 2010), it is a serious health concern.

The burden of incarceration is most heavily experienced by people of color (Massoglia, 2008b; Petit & Western, 2004). Moreover, evidence suggests that the health status of blacks has worsened relative to whites during the period of rising incarceration rates (Massoglia, 2008b). Consequently, race differences in exposure to incarceration may partly explain the persistent and growing health disparities between Blacks and Whites. Direct research evidence on this issue remains limited, but findings are suggestive. Massoglia (2008b) examines the effects of incarceration on race disparities in general health functioning. He reports that incarceration is associated with poorer general health functioning and that a substantial proportion of the racial disparity in general health functioning is explained by race differences in incarceration exposure. Additional evidence in Johnson and Raphael (2009) shows that higher black male incarceration rates explain much of the racial disparity in AIDS infection among women.

Beyond empirical evidence, there are logical reasons to expect that incarceration plays a role in racial disparities in health. Incarceration is selective; it disproportionally affects high-poverty, high minority communities (Burch, 2014). Moreover, incarceration destabilizes communities by escalating strains, reducing employment prospects and damaging the prosocial family relationships that are critical for economic viability and social organization (Clear, 2007; Rose & Clear, 1998). For example, high incarceration rates reduce the number of men, destabilizing marriage markets (Wolfers, Leonhardt, & Qualy, 2015) and depressing the prevalence of a key community-level protective factor. In addition, communities destabilized by incarceration likely result in feelings of stress and despair, particularly for juveniles. Consistent with this argument, research indicates that African American teenagers are less likely to believe their lives will extend to the age of 35 and beyond (Warner & Swisher, 2015). In sum, there are strong empirical and logical reasons behind the view that dramatic racial disparities in incarceration in the United States contribute to racial differences in disease prevalence and overall health.

## Conclusions and Future Directions

The link between incarceration and health has long been neglected. Thus, it is a positive development to see that an emerging body of social science research is now engaging questions related to the important intersection of these phenomena. In broad portrait, this literature highlights an essential fact, that health and incarceration are inequitably distributed by race and ethnicity with African Americans and other non-white groups bearing greater burdens. What explains these distributions of health and incarceration by race? Common cause theories provide one major perspective to account for racial and ethnic disparities in illnesses, crime and incarceration. They attribute the similar patterns of racial disparity in health and criminal justice outcomes to structural forces such as socioeconomic disadvantage and systemic racism, and possibly to individual traits that emerge from such structural forces (e.g., low self-control). Yet, in addition to common cause theories, social scientists have increasingly proffered arguments suggesting that health and criminal justice system contact are causally linked, perhaps reciprocally. These causal linkages sustain and exacerbate the racial disparities in health and criminal justice that emerge from common structural conditions. Racial differences in the prevalence of prenatal health factors, traumatic brain injuries, and exposure to environmental toxins and adverse childhood experiences are considered to be part of the reason why we so commonly find racial group differences in the prevalence of antisocial or aggressive behaviors and ultimately, incarceration. In subsequent turn, the resulting race differences in exposure to incarceration influence race differences in health conditions because they increase the likelihood of contracting infectious and stress-related illnesses during the period of incarceration or post-release. Moreover, the health impact of incarceration may radiate outward to extended families and communities through various mechanisms including infection transmission and the depletion of economic and social support mechanisms.

What can be done to address these connected problems of health and criminal justice exposure? We suggest that urgent efforts to ameliorate these problems are needed. Preventative and corrective programs should eschew the traditional idea that health and incarceration should be addressed separately, either through medical or criminal justice responses. In our minds, a superior strategy starts by viewing racial inequities in health and incarceration as two related indicators of unhealthy conditions in the socio-spatial environments inhabited by people of color in American society. In that sense, solutions should be directed at identifying and eradicating unhealthy conditions and fostering better physical, mental and behavioral health. Addressing prenatal health concerns and limiting exposures to stressors, toxins and traumatic injuries are essential and will likely pay large dividends in terms of not only fewer diseases and medical costs, but also in terms of less maladaptive behavior, crime, and incarceration. Likewise, we believe that reducing the overreliance on incarceration may impart significant benefits to vulnerable communities by stemming one key source of poor health. Perhaps the best way to reduce racial disparities in the negative health and criminal justice outcomes and improve overall population health is to tackle the common causes of poor health, crime and incarceration. Policies that better ensure that all citizens, regardless of race or ethnicity or income, have an economic safety net, access to affordable high-quality medical and mental health care, access to safe housing, and protection from environmental stressors and toxins will likely yield a cascade of long-term benefits for our society. These include overall improvements in physical and mental health, and reductions in accidents, injuries, antisocial behaviors and crimes. This strategy is a sustained commitment that likely involves a radical reshuffling of budgeting and cultural priorities. But if successful, it would substantially alter one of America's most prominent, but dubious, features, our high levels of racial and ethnic inequality across so many social institutions, health and criminal justice included.

# References

Artiga, S., Foutz, J., Cornachione, E., & Garfield, R. (2016). Key Facts on Health and Health Care by Race and Ethnicity. Kaiser Family Foundation. www.kff.org/disparities-policy/report/key-facts-on-health-and-health-care-by-race-and-ethnicity/.

Artiga, S., Foutz, J., & Damico, A. (2018). Health Coverage by Race and Ethnicity: Changes Under the ACA. Kaiser Family Foundation. www.kff.org/disparities-policy/issue-brief/health-coverage-by-race-and-ethnicity-changes-under-the-aca/.

Barkan, S.E., & Rocque, M. (2018). Socioeconomic Status and Racism as Fundamental Causes of Street Criminality. *Critical Criminology 26*(2), 211–231.

Beydoun, M.A., Beydoun, H.A., Mode, N., Dore, G.A., Canas, J.A., Eid, S.M., & Zonderman, A.B. (2016). Racial Disparities In Adult All-cause and Cause-specific Mortality Among Us Adults: Mediating and Moderating Factors. *BMC Public Health 16*(1), 1–13. 10.1186/s12889-016-3744-z.

Binswanger, I.A., Krueger, P.M., & Steiner, J.F. (2009). Prevalence of Chronic Medical Conditions Among Jail and Prison Inmates in the United States Compared With the General Population. *Journal of Epidemiology and Community Health 63*(11), 912–919.

Bird, S.T. (1995). Separate Black and White Infant Mortality Models: Differences in the Importance of Structural Variables. *Social Science and Medicine 41*(11), 1507–1512.

Blow, F.C., Zeber, J.E., McCarthy, J.F., Valenstein, M., Gillon, L., & Bingham, C.R. (2004). Ethnicity and Diagnostic Patterns in Veterans with Psychosis. *Social Psychiatry and Psychiatric Epidemiology 39*(10), 841–851.

Boals, A., vanDellen, M.R., & Banks, J.B. (2011). The Relationship between Self-control and Health: The Mediating Effect of Avoidant Coping. *Psychology & Health 26*(8), 1049–1062.

Borrell, L.N., Dallo, F.J., & Nguyen, N. (2010). Racial/Ethnic Disparities in All-cause Mortality in U.S. Adults: The Effect of Allostatic Load. *Public Health Reports 125*(November-December), 810–816.

Borrell, L.N., Jacobs, D.R.J., Williams, D.R., Pletcher, M.J., & Houston, T.K. (2007). Self- reported Racial Discrimination and Substance Use in the Coronary Artery Risk Development in Adults Study. *American Journal of Epidemiology 166*(9), 1068–1079.

Breslau, J., Kendler, K.S., Su, M., Gaxiola-Aguilar, S., & Kessler, R.C. (2005). Lifetime Risk and Persistence of Psychiatric Disorders Across Ethnic Groups in the United States. *Psychological Medicine 35*(3), 317–327.

Briere, J., Agee, E., & Dietrich, A. (2016). Cumulative Trauma and Current Posttraumatic Stress Disorder Status in General Population and Inmate Sample. *Psychological Trauma 8*(4), 439–446.

Bruner, C. (2017). ACE, Place, Race, and Poverty: Building Hope for Children. *Academic pediatrics 17*(7), S123–S129.

Budhwhani, H., Hearld, K.R., & Chavez-Yenter, D. (2015). Depression in Racial and Ethnic Minorities: The Impact of Nativity and Discrimination. *Journal of Racial and Ethnic Health Disparities 2*(1), 34–42.

Burch, T. (2014). The Old Jim Crow: Racial Residential Segregation and Neighborhood Imprisonment. *Law & Policy 36*(3), 223–255.

Burt, C.H., Simons, R.L., & Gibbons, F.X. (2012). Racial Discrimination, Ethnic–Racial Socialization, and Crime: A Micro-Sociological Model of Risk and Resilience. *American Sociological Review 77*(4), 648–677.

Cahalan, M.W., & Parsons, L.A. (1986). *Historical Corrections Statistics in the United States 1850–1984.* Washington, DC: U.S. Department of Justice, Bureau of Justice Statistics.

Carson, E.A. (2018). *Prisoners in 2016.* Washington, DC: U.S. Department of Justice, Office of Justice Programs, Bureau of Justice Statistics. www.bjs.gov/content/pub/pdf/p16.pdf. Accessed July 23, 2018.

Caspi, A., Moffitt, T.E., Newman, D.L., & Silva, P.A. (1996). Behavioral Observations at Age 3 Years Predict Adult Psychiatric Disorders. Longitudinal Evidence from A Birth Cohort. *Archives of General Psychiatry 53*(11), 1033–1039.

Centers for Disease Control and Prevention. (2013a). Expected Years of Life Free of Chronic Condition–Induced Activity Limitations—United States, 1999–2008. *MMWR 62*(Supplement 3), 87–92.

Centers for Disease Control and Prevention. (2013b). Health-Related Quality of Life—United States, 2006 and 2010. *MMWR 62*(Supplement 3), 105–111.

Centers for Disease Control and Prevention. (2017a). *HIV Surveillance Report, 2016, Volume 28.* www.cdc.gov/hiv/library/reports/hiv-surveillance.html. Published November 2017. Accessed July 13, 2018.

Centers for Disease Control and Prevention. (2017b). STDs in Racial and Ethnic Minorities, 2017. www.cdc.gov/std/stats16/minorities.htm. Accessed July 16, 2018.

Centers for Disease Control and Prevention. (2018). National Diabetes Statistics Report, 2017. www.cdc.gov/diabetes/pdfs/data/statistics/national-diabetes-statistics-report.pdf. Accessed July 13, 2018.

Clear, T.R. (2007). *Imprisoning Communities: How Mass Incarceration Makes Disadvantaged Neighborhoods Worse*. New York, NY: Oxford University Press.

Cloud, D. 2014. On Life Support: Public Health in the Age of Mass Incarceration. Vera Institute of Justice. www.vera.org/publications/on-life-support-public-health-in-the-age-of-mass-incarceration.

Cockerham, W.C. (2013). *Social Causes of Health and Disease*. Malden, MA: Polity Press.

Cohen, D., Spear, S., Scribner, R., Kissinger, P., Mason, K., & Wildgen, J. (2000). "Broken Windows" and the Risk of Gonorrhea. *American Journal of Public Health* 90(2), 230–236.

Coleman, K.J., Stewart, C., Waitzfelder, B.E., Zeber, J.E., Morales, L.S., Ahmed, A.T., & Simon, G.E. (2017). Racial/Ethnic Differences in Diagnoses and Treatment of Mental Health Conditions Across Healthcare Systems Participating in the Mental Health Research Network. *Psychiatric Services* 67(7), 749–757.

Connolly, E.J. (2018). Evaluating the Causal Effect of Adverse Childhood Experiences on Antisocial Behavior and Violent Victimization: A Longitudinal Sibling-Comparison Analysis. www.researchgate.net/publication/326017507_Evaluating_the_Causal_Effect_of_Adverse_Childhood_Experiences_on_Antisocial_Behavior_and_Violent_Victimization_A_Longitudinal_Sibling-Comparison_Analysis. DOI: 10.13140/RG.2.2.13330.76481.

Crescioni, A.W., Erlanger, J., Alquist, J.L., Conlon, K.E., Baumeister, R.F., Schatschneider, C., & Dutton, G.R. (2011). High Trait Self-control Predicts Positive Health Behaviors and Success in Weight Loss. *Journal of Health Psychology* 16(5), 750–759.

DeNavas-Walt, C., Proctor, B.D., & Smith, J.C. (2014). *Income and Poverty in the United States: 2013*. Washington, DC: United States Census Bureau.

Dietrich, K.N., Ris, M.D., Succop, P.A., Berger, O.G., & Bornschein, R.L. (2001). Early Exposure to Lead and Juvenile Delinquency. *Neurotoxicology & Teratology* 23(6), 511–518.

Duke, N.N., Pettingell, S.L., McMorris, B.J., & Borowsky, I.W. (2010). Adolescent Violence Perpetration: Associations with Multiple Types of Adverse Childhood Experiences. *Pediatrics* 125(4), e778-e786.

Dunkel Schetter, C. (2011). Psychological Science on Pregnancy: Stress Processes, Biopsychosocial Models, and Emerging Research Issues. *Annual Review of Psychology* 62, 531–558.

Eack, S.M., Bahorik, A.L., Newhill, C.E., Neighbors, H.W., & Davis, L.E. (2012). Interviewer-Perceived Honesty As A Mediator of Racial Disparities in the Diagnosis of Schizophrenia. *Psychiatric Services* 63(9), 875–880.

Eitle, D., & Turner, R.J. (2003). Stress Exposure, Race, and Young Adult Male Crime. *The Sociological Quarterly* 44(2), 243–269.

Fazel, S., Lichtenstein, P., Grann, M., & Långström, N. (2011). Risk of Violent Crime in Individuals with Epilepsy and Traumatic Brain Injury: A 35-Year Swedish Population Study. *PLoS Medicine* 8(12), e1001150. 10.1371/journal.pmed.1001150.

Feldmeyer, B. (2010). The Effects of Racial/Ethnic Segregation on Latino and Black Homicide. *The Sociological Quarterly* 51(4), 600–623.

Ford, J.L., & Browning, C.R. (2011). Neighborhood Social Disorganization and the Acquisition of Trichomoniasis Among Young Adults in the United States. *American Journal of Public Health* 101(9), 1696–1703.

Ford, J.L., & Browning, C.R. (2013). Neighborhoods and Infectious Disease Risk: Acquisition of Chlamydia During the Transition to Adulthood. *Journal of Urban Health: Bulletin of the New York Academy of Medicine* 91(1), 136–150.

Gibbons, F.X., O'Hara, R.E., Stock, M.L., Gerrard, M., Weng, C.Y., & Wills, T.A. (2012). The Erosive Effects of Racism: Reduced Self-control Mediates the Relation Between Perceived Racial Discrimination and Substance Use in African American Adolescents. *Journal of Personality and Social Psychology* 102(5), 1089–1104.

Gibbons, F.X., Yeh, H.C., Gerrard, M., Cleveland, M.J., Cutrona, C., Simons, R.L., & Brody, G.H. (2007). Early Experience With Racial Discrimination and Conduct Disorder as Predictors of Subsequent Drug Use: A Critical Period Hypothesis. *Drug and Alcohol Dependence* 88(Supplement 1), 27–37.

Gottfredson, M.R., & Hirschi, T. (1990). *A General Theory of Crime*. Stanford, CA: Stanford University Press.

Gourounti, C., Karpathiotaki, N., & Vaslamatzis, G. (2015). Psychosocial Stress in High Risk Pregnancy. *International Archives of Medicine* 8, 1–9.

Hay, C. (2001). Parenting, Self-control, and Delinquency: A Test of Self-Control Theory. *Criminology* 39(3), 707–736.

Hay, C., & Meldrum, R. (2016). *Self-Control and Crime Over the Life Course*. Thousand Oaks, CA: Sage.

Hayward, M.D., & Heron, M. (1999). Racial Inequality in Active Life Among Adult Americans. *Demography* 36(1), 77–91.

Higgins, G.E., & Ricketts, M.L. (2005). Self-Control Theory, Race, and Delinquency. *Journal of Ethnicity in Criminal Justice 3*(3), 5–22.

Hout, M. (2017). Employment. In Stanford Center on Poverty and Inequality (ed.), *State of the Union: The Poverty and Inequality Report, Pathways Magazine, Special Issue* (pp. 5–8).

Hummer, R.A., Powers, D.A., Pullum, S.G., Gossman, G.L., & Frisbie, W.P. (2007). Paradox Found (Again): Infant Mortality Among the Mexican-Origin Population in the United States. *Demography 44*(3), 441–457.

Jackson, D.B., & Vaughn, M.G. (2018a). Maternal Medical Risks during Pregnancy and Childhood Externalizing Behavior. *Social Science & Medicine 207*, 19–24. 10.1016/j.socscimed.2018.04.032.

Jackson, D.B., & Vaughn, M.G. (2018b). Promoting Health Equity to Prevent Crime. *Preventative Medicine 113*, 91–94. 10.1016/j.pmed.2018.05.009.

Johnson, R.C. (2017). Health. In Stanford Center on Poverty and Inequality (ed.), *State of the Union: The Poverty and Inequality Report, Pathways Magazine, Special Issue* (pp. 27–31).

Johnson, R.C., & Raphael, S. (2009). The Effects of Male Incarceration Dynamics on Acquired Immune Deficiency Syndrome Infection Rates Among African American Women and Men. *The Journal of Law and Economics 52*(2), 251–293.

Kaeble, D., & Cowhig, M. (2018). *Correctional Population in the United States, 2016*. U.S. Department of Justice, Office of Justice Programs, Bureau of Justice Statistics. NCJ251211. www.bjs.gov/content/pub/pdf/cpus16.pdf. Accessed July 19, 2018.

Kawachi, I., Daniels, N., & Robinson, D.E. (2005). Health Disparities by Race and Class: Why Both Matter. *Health Affairs 24*(2), 343–552.

Kern, M.L., & Friedman, H.S. (2008). Do Conscientious Individuals Live Longer? A Quantitative Review. *Health Psychology 27*(5), 505–512.

Kilpatrick, D.G., Ruggiero, K.J., Acierno, R., Saunders, B.E., Resnick, H.S., & Best, C.L. (2003). Violence and Risk of PTSD, Major Depression, Substance Abuse/Dependence, and Comorbidity: Results from the National Survey of Adolescents. *Journal of Consulting and Clinical Psychology 71*(4), 692–700.

Kirchner, E.E., & Higgins, G.E. (2014). Self-Control and Racial Disparities in Delinquency: A Structural Equation Modeling Approach. *American Journal of Criminal Justice 39*(3), 436–449.

Kirk, D. (2008). The Neighborhood Context of Racial and Ethnic Disparities in Arrest. *Demography 45*(1), 55–77.

Kochanek, K.D., Murphy, S.L., & Xu, J. (2015). Deaths: Final Data for 2011. *National vital Statistics Reports: From the Centers for Disease Control and Prevention, National Center for Health Statistics, National Vital STATISTICS SYSTEM 63*(3), 1–120.

Kramer, M.R., & Hogue, C.R. (2009). Is Segregation Bad for Your Health? *Epidemiology Reviews 31*(1), 178–194.

Krivo, L., Peterson, R.D., & Kuhl, D.C. (2009). Segregation, Racial Structure, and Neighborhood Violent Crime. *American Journal of Sociology 114*(6), 1765–1802.

LaVeist, T.A. (1989). Linking Residential Segregation and the Infant Mortality Race Disparity. *Sociology and Social Research 73*(2), 90–94.

LeÓn-CarriÓn, J., & Ramos, F.J.C. (2003). Blows to the Head During Development Can Predispose to Violent Criminal Behaviour: Rehabilitation of Consequences of Head Injury is a Measure for Crime Prevention. *Brain Injury 17*(3), 207–216.

Li, L., & Liu, J. (2013). The Effect of Pediatric Traumatic Brain Injury on Behavioral Health Outcomes: A Systematic Review. *Developmental Medicine & Child Neurology 55*(1), 37–45.

Link, B.G., & Phelan, J. (1995). Social Conditions as Fundamental Causes of Disease. *Journal of Health and Social Behavior, Extra Issue, Forty Years of Medical Sociology: The State of the Art and Directions for the Future* 80–94.

Logan, J.R. (2014). Separate and Unequal in Suburbia. *Census brief prepared for US2010. Brown University*, www.s4.brown.edu/us2010/Data/Report/report12012014.pdf.

Longshore, D. (1998). Self-Control and Criminal Opportunity: A Prospective Test of General Theory of Crime. *Social Problems 45*(1), 102–113.

Macartney, S., Bishaw, A., & Fontenot, K. (2013). Poverty Rates for Selected Detailed Race and Hispanic Groups by State and Place, 2007-2011. *American Community Survey Briefs*. Washington, DC: U.S. Bureau of Commerce, U.S. Census Bureau. www.census.gov/prod/2013pubs/acsbr11-17.pdf. Accessed July 24, 2018.

Markides, K.S., & Coreil, J. (1986). The Health of Hispanics in the Southwestern United States: An Epidemiologic Paradox. *Public Health Reports 101*(3), 253–265.

Markides, K.S., & Eschbach, K. (2005). Aging, Migration, and Mortality: Current Status of Research on the Hispanic Paradox. *The Journals of Gerontology Series B: Psychological Sciences and Social Sciences* 60(Special Issue 2), S68–S75.

Martin, T.E., & Wolfe, S. (2018). Lead Exposure, Concentrated Disadvantage, and Violent Crime Rates. *Justice Quarterly*. DOI: 10.1080/07418825.2018.1473462.

Massoglia, M. (2008a). Incarceration as Exposure: The Prison, Infectious Disease, and Other Stress-Related Illness. *Journal of Health and Social Behavior* 49(1), 56–71.

Massoglia, M. (2008b). Incarceration, Health and Racial Disparities in Health. *Law & Society Review* 42(2), 275–306.

McNulty, T.L., & Bellair, P.E. (2003). Explaining Racial and Ethnic Differences in Serious Adolescent Violent Behavior. *Criminology* 41(3), 709–746.

McQuillan, G.M., Kruszon-Moran, D., Kottiri, B.J., Curtin, L.R., Lucas, J.W., & Kington, R.S. (2004). Racial and Ethnic Differences in the Seroprevalence of 6 Infectious Diseases in the United States: Data from NHANES III, 1988–1994. *American Journal of Public Health* 94(11), 1952–1958.

Miller, H.V., Barnes, J.C., & Beaver, K.M. (2011). Self-Control and Health Outcomes in a Nationally-Representative Sample. *American Journal of Health Behavior* 35(1), 15–27.

Moffitt, T.E., Arseneault, L., Belsky, D., Dickson, N., Hancox, R.J., Harrington, H., & Caspi, A. (2011). A Gradient of Childhood Self-Control Predicts Health, Wealth and Public Safety. *PNAS* 108(7), 2693–2698.

Nagahawatte, N.T., & Goldenberg, R.L. (2008). Poverty, Maternal Health, and Adverse Pregnancy Outcomes. *Annals of the New York Academy of Sciences* 1136(1), 80–85.

Nahid, P., Horne, D.J., Jarlsberg, L.G., Reiner, A.P., Osmond, D., Hopewell, P.C., & Bibbins-Domingo, K. (2011). Racial Differences in Tuberculosis Infection in United States Communities: The Coronary Artery Risk Development in Young Adults Study. *Clinical Infectious Diseases* 53(3), 291–294.

National Center for Health Statistics. (2016). *Health, United States, 2015: With Special Feature on Racial and Ethnic Health Disparities*. Hyattsville, MD: National Center for Health Statistics.

National Center for Health Statistics. (2017). *Health, United States, 2016: With Chartbook on Long-term Trends in Health*. Hyattsville, MD: National Center for Health Statistics.

National Commission on Correctional Health Care. (2002). *The Health Status of Soon-To-Be-Released Inmates: A Report to Congress*. Chicago, IL: National Commission on Correctional Health Care.

National Juvenile Justice Network & Texas Public Policy Foundation. (2013). The Comeback States: Reducing Youth Incarceration in the United States. www.njjn.org/our-work/the-comeback-states-reducing-juvenile-incarceration-in-the-united-states.

Needleman, H.L. (2004). Lead Poisoning. *Annual Review of Medicine* 55, 209–222.

Needleman, H.L., Gunnoe, C., Leviton, A., Reed, R., Peresie, H., Maher, C., & Barret, P. (1979). Deficits in Psychological and Classroom Performance of Children with Elevated Dentine Lead Levels. *New England Journal of Medicine* 300(13), 689–695.

Needleman, H.L., McFarland, C., Ness, R.B., Fienberg, S.E., & Tobin, M.J. (2002). Bone Lead Levels in Adjudicated Delinquents: A Case Control Study. *Neurotoxicology and Teratology* 24(6), 711–717.

Needleman, H.L., Riess, J.A., Tobin, M.J., Biesecker, G.E., & Greenhouse, J.B. (1996). Bone Lead Levels and Delinquent Behavior. *JAMA* 275(5), 363–369.

Nevin, R. (2007). Understanding International Crime Trends: The Legacy of Preschool Lead Exposure. *Environmental Research* 104(3), 315–336.

Osypuk, T.L., & Acevedo-Garcia, D. (2008). Are racial Disparities in Preterm Birth Larger in Hypersegregated Areas? *American Journal of Epidemiology* 167(11), 1295–1304.

Ousey, G.C. (2017). Crime is Not the Only Problem: Examining Why Violence & Adverse Health Outcomes Co-vary Across Large U.S. Counties. *Journal of Criminal Justice* 50, 29–41.

Ousey, G.C., & Lee, M.R. (2008). Racial Disparity in Formal Social Control: An Investigation of Alternative Explanations of Arrest Rate Inequality. *Journal of Research in Crime and Delinquency* 45(3), 322–355.

Peterson, C.C., Snipp, M., & Cheung, S.Y. (2017). Earnings. In Stanford Center on Poverty and Inequality (ed.), *State of the Union: The Poverty and Inequality Report, Pathways Magazine, Special Issue* (pp. 32–35).

Peterson, R.D., & Krivo, L.J. (1993). Racial Segregation and Black Urban Homicide. *Social Forces* 71(4), 1001–1026.

Petit, B., & Western, B. (2004). Mass Imprisonment and The Life Course: Race and Class Inequality in U.S. Incarceration. *American Sociological Review* 69(2), 151–169.

Pew Charitable Trusts. (2010). *Collateral Costs: Incarceration's Effect on Economic Mobility*. Washington, DC: The Pew Charitable Trusts.

Phelan, J.C., & Link, B.G. (2015). Is Racism a Fundamental Cause of Health of Inequalities in Health? *Annual Review of Sociology 41*, 311–330.

Polednak, A.P. (1991). Black–White Differences in Infant Mortality in 38 Standard Metropolitan Statistical Areas. *American Journal of Public Health 81*(11), 1480–1482.

Pratt, T.C. (2009). *Addicted to Incarceration: Corrections Policy and the Politics of Misinformation in the United States*. Thousand Oaks, CA: Sage.

Pratt, T.C., & Cullen, F.T. (2000). The Empirical Status of Gottfredson & Hirschi's General Theory of cRime: A Meta-analysis. *Criminology 38*(3), 931–964.

Pratt, T.C., Turner, M.G., & Piquero, A. (2004). Parental Socialization and Community Context: A Longitudinal Analysis of the Structural Sources of Low Self-control. *Journal of Research in Crime and Delinquency 41*(3), 219–243.

Price, J.H., Khubchandani, J., McKinney, M., & Braun, R. (2013). Racial/Ethnic Disparities in Chronic Diseases of Youths and Access to Health Care in the United States. *BioMed Research International 2013*, 1–12. 10.1155/2013/787616.

Puzzanchera, C., & Hockenberry, S. (2018). National Disproportionate Minority Contact Databook. Developed by the National Center for Juvenile Justice for the Office of Juvenile Justice and Delinquency Prevention. www.ojjdp.gov/ojstatbb/dmcdb/. Accessed July 19, 2018.

Reardon, S.F., & Fahle, E.M. (2017). Education. In Stanford Center on Poverty and Inequality (ed.), *State of the Union: The Poverty and Inequality Report, Pathways Magazine, Special Issue* (pp. 20–23).

Reavis, J.A., Looman, J., Franco, K.A., & Rojas, B. (2013). Adverse Childhood Experiences and Adult Criminality: How Long Must We Live before We Possess Our Own Lives? *The Permanente Journal 17*(2), 44.

Reyes, J.W. (2007). Environmental Policy As Social Policy? The Impact of Childhood Lead Exposure on Crime. *The B.E. Journal of Economic Analysis & Policy 7*(1), 1935–1982.

Reyes, J.W. (2015). Lead Exposure and Behavior: Effects on Antisocial Risky Behavior Among Children and Adolescents. *Economic Inquiry 53*(3), 1580–1605.

Richardus, J.H., & Kunst, A.E. (2001). Black–White Differences in Infectious Disease Mortality in the United States. *American Journal of Public Health 91*(8), 1251–1253.

Riolo, S.A., Nguyen, T.A., Greden, J.F., & King, C.A. (2005). Prevalence of Depression by Race/Ethnicity: Findings from the National Health and Nutrition Examination Survey III. *American Journal of Public Health 95*(6), 998–1000.

Roberts, A.L., Gilman, S.E., Breslau, J., Breslau, N., & Koenen, K.C. (2011). Race/Ethnic Differences in Exposure to Traumatic Events, Development of Post-Traumatic Stress Disorder, and Treatment-Seeking for Post-Traumatic Stress Disorder in the United States. *Psychological Medicine 41*(1), 71–83.

Rose, D.R., & Clear, T.R. (1998). Incarceration, Social Capital, and Crime: Implications for Social Disorganization Theory. *Criminology 36*(3), 441–480.

Ross, C.E. (2000). Neighborhood Disadvantage and Adult Depression. *Journal of Health and Social Behavior 41*(2), 177–187.

Ross, C.E., & Mirowsky, J. (1995). Does Employment Affect Health? *Journal of Health and Social Behavior 36*(3), 230–243.

Ross, C.E., Mirowsky, J., & Goldsteen, K. (1990). The Impact of the Family on Health: The Decade in Review. *Journal of Marriage and the Family 52*(4), 1059–1078.

Sampson, R.J., & Lauritsen, J.L. (1997). Racial and Ethnic Disparities in Crime and Criminal Justice in the United States. *Crime and Justice 21*, 311–374.

Sampson, R.J., & Loeffler, C. (2010). Punishment's Place: The Local Concentration of Mass Incarceration. *Daedalus 139*(3), 20–31.

Sampson, R.J., & Winter, A.W. (2016). The Racial Ecology of Lead Poisoning: Toxic Inequality in Chicago Neighborhoods, 1995-2013. *DuBois Review 13*(2), 261–283.

Schlam, T.R., Wilson, N.L., Shoda, Y., Mischel, W., & Ayduk, O. (2013). Preschoolers' Delay of Gratification Predicts their Body Mass 30 Years Later. *Journal of Pediatrics 162*, 90–93.

Schnittker, J., & John, A. (2007). Enduring Stigma: The Long-Term Effects of Incarceration on Health. *Journal of Health and Social Behavior 48*(2), 115–130.

Schnittker, J., Massoglia, M., & Uggen, C. (2012). Out and Down: Incarceration and Psychiatric Disorders. *Journal of Health and Social Behavior 53*(4), 448–464.

Schwartz, J.A., Connolly, E.J., & Valgardson, B.A. (2018). An Evaluation of the Directional Relationship Between Head Injuries and Subsequent Changes in Impulse Control and Delinquency in a Sample of Previously Adjudicated Males. *Journal of Criminal Justice 56*, 70–80. https://doi.org/10.1016/j.jcrimjus.2017.08.004.

The Sentencing Project. (2017). Fact Sheet: Black Disparities in Youth Incarceration. www.sentencingproject.org/wp-content/uploads/2017/09/Black-Disparities-in-Youth-Incarceration.pdf.

Shapiro, T. (2017). Wealth. In Stanford Center on Poverty and Inequality (ed.), *State of the Union: The Poverty and Inequality Report, Pathways Magazine, Special Issue* (pp. 36–38).

Shihadeh, E.S., & Flynn, N. (1996). Segregation and Crime: The Effect of Black Social Isolation on the Rates of Black Urban Violence. *Social Forces* 74(4), 1325–1352.

Silver, E., Mulvey, E.P., & Swanson, J.W. (2002). Neighborhood Structural Characteristics and Mental Disorder: Faris and Dunham Revisited. *Social Science & Medicine* 55(8), 1457–1470.

Simons, R., Simons, L., Burt, C.H., Drummond, H., Stewart, E., Brody, G., & Cutrona, C. (2006). Supportive Parenting Moderates the Effect of Discrimination Upon Anger, Hostile View of Relationships, and Violence Among African American Boys. *Journal of Health and Social Behavior* 47(4), 374–389.

Singh, G.K., Siahpush, M., & Kogan, M.D. (2010). Rising Social Inequalities in U.S. Childhood Obesity, 2003-2007. *Annals of Epidemiology* 20(1), 40–52.

Spanakis, E.K., & Golden, S.H. (2013). Race/Ethnic Difference in Diabetes and Diabetic Complications. *Current Diabetes Reports* 13(6), 814–823. DOI: 10.1007/s11892-013-0421-9.

Stretesky, P., & Lynch, M.J. (2001). The Relationship Between Lead Exposure and Homicide. *Archives of Pediatric and Adolescent Medicine* 155(5), 579–582.

Stretesky, P., & Lynch, M.J. (2004). The Relationship Between Lead and Crime. *Journal of Health and Social Behavior* 45(2), 214–229.

Stretesky, P.B. (2003). The Distribution of Air Lead Levels Across U.S. Counties: Implications for the Production of Racial Inequality. *Sociological Spectrum* 23(1), 91–118.

Stuckler, D., Basu, S., McKee, M., & King, L. (2008). Mass Incarceration Can Explain Population Increases in TB and Multidrug-Resistant TB in European and Central Asian Countries. *Proceedings of the National Academy of Sciences* 105(36), 13280–13285.

Thomas, J.C., & Torrone, E. (2008). Incarceration as Forced Migration: Effects on Selected Community Health Outcomes. *American Journal of Public Health* 98(Supplement_1), S181-S184.

Turney, K. (2014). Stress Proliferation Across Generations? Examining the Relationship Between Parental Incarceration and Childhood Health. *Journal of Health and Social Behavior* 55(3), 302–319.

U.S. Department of Education Office for Civil Rights. (2014). Civil Rights Data Collection Data Snapshot: School Discipline. *Issue brief no. 1*. Washington, DC: U.S. Department of Education. https://ocrdata.ed.gov/downloads/crdc-school-discipline-snapshot.pdf.

U.S. Department of Health and Human Services (US DHHS), Centers for Disease Control and Prevention (CDC), National Center for Health Statistics (NCHS). Compressed Mortality File on CDC Wonder Online Database. http://wonder.cdc.gov. Accessed July 6, 2018.

Unnever, J.D., Cullen, F.T., & Barnes, J.C. (2016). Racial Discrimination, Weakened School Bonds, and Problematic Behaviors: Testing a Theory of African American Offending. *Journal of Research in Crime & Delinquency* 53(2), 139–164.

Velez, M.B., Krivo, L.J., & Peterson, R.D. (2003). Structural Inequality and Homicide: An Assessment of the Black-White Gap in Killings. *Criminology* 41(3), 645–672.

Wakefield, S., & Wildeman, C. (2011). Mass Imprisonment and Racial Disparities in Childhood Behavioral Problems. *Criminology & Public Policy* 10(3), 793–817.

Wang, Y., & Beydoun, M.A. (2007). The Obesity Epidemic in the United States–Gender, Age, Socioeconomic, Racial/ Ethnic,and Geographic Characteristics: A Systematic Review and Meta-Regression Analysis. *Epidemiologic Reviews* 29(1), 6–28.

Warner, T.D., & Swisher, R.R. (2015). Adolescent Survival Expectations: Variations by Race, Ethnicity, and Nativity. *Journal of Health and Social Behavior* 56(4), 478–494.

Weinstock, M. (2008). The Long-term Behavioural Consequences of Prenatal Stress. *Neuroscience and Biobehavioral Reviews* 32(6), 1073–1086.

Williams, D.R., & Collins, C. (2001). Racial Residential Segregation: A Fundamental Cause of Racial Disparities in Health. *Public Health Reports* 116(5), 404–416.

Williams, D.R., & Mohammed, S.A. (2009). Discrimination and Racial Disparities in Health: Evidence and Needed Research. *Journal of Behavioral Medicine* 32(1), 20–47.

Williams, D.R., & Sternthal, M. (2010). Understanding Racial/Ethnic Disparities in Health: Sociological Contributions. *Journal of Health and Social Behavior* 51(1 Supplement), S15-S27.

Wills, T.A., Isasi, C.R., Mendoza, D., & Ainette, M.G. (2007). Self-control Constructs Related to Measures of Dietary Intake and Physical Activity in Adolescents. *Journal of Adolescent Health* 41(6), 551–558.

Wolfers, J., Leonhardt, D., & Quealy, K. (2015). 1.5 Million Missing Black Men. *The New York Times* 20, A1.

Wolff, N., & Shi, J. (2012). Childhood and Adult Trauma Experiences of Incarcerated Persons and their Relationship to Adult Behavioral Health Problems and Treatment. *International journal of Environmental Research and Public Health 9*(5), 1908–1926.

Wright, J.P., Dietrich, K.N., Ris, M.D., Hornung, R.W., Wessel, S.D., Lanphear, B.P., ... Rae, M.N. (2008). Association of Prenatal and Childhood Blood Lead Concentrations with Criminal Arrests in Early Adulthood. *PLoS Medicine 5*(5), e101.

# 4
# INFLUENCES OF EARLY NUTRITION ON CHILD AND ADOLESCENT ANTISOCIAL BEHAVIOR

*Phoebe Um[1] and Jianghong Liu[1]*

[1]UNIVERSITY OF PENNSYLVANIA

## Introduction

The World Health Organization has declared aggression and violence significant public health issues with serious potential consequences to the individual and society at large. In addition to taking millions of lives per year, violence carries non-fatal consequences that follow individuals over a lifetime. Those who experience childhood maltreatment, intimate partner violence or sexual violence are at significantly increased risk for depression, sexually transmitted diseases, and likelihood of engaging in risky behaviors such as drug or alcohol abuse (World Health Organization, 2014). These behaviors in turn increase risk for developing chronic diseases later in life such as cancer, liver disease, cardiovascular disease, and diabetes (World Health Organization, 2014). Thus, violence and aggression are not purely social phenomena; rather, they are intricately related to other public health issues that create significant social and economic burdens on society. Identifying early risk factors of adult aggression and violence, such as aggression, delinquency, and violence that arise during childhood, is an important first step in preventing later criminal acts and antisocial tendencies later in life. Decades of research have identified several social and biological risk factors for antisocial and aggressive behavior in children and adults (Farrington, 2000; Iozzino, Ferrari, Large, Nielssen, & De Girolamo, 2015; Murray et al., 2018; Virkkunen, Goldman, Nielsen, & Linnoila, 1995; Webster-Stratton & Hammond, 1999), but fewer studies have focused specifically on vulnerabilities during very early childhood, including health factors such as nutrition. Indeed, among possible health risk factors, there is growing recognition that nutritional status may strongly contribute to the rise of such behaviors and therefore underscores the importance of identifying the ways in which early childhood health risk factors can be potentially modified to prevent future antisocial behaviors.

This chapter will explore such relationships by first introducing a novel biopsychosocial framework that conceptualizes the link between early health risk factors and developmental antisocial behaviors later in life. Further discussion of malnutrition will follow, including recent empirical findings to support the framework. Finally, implications and limitations of this new model will be briefly discussed.

# Framework for an Early Health Model for the Development of Antisocial Behavior

Although risk factors for violence and antisocial behaviors have been thoroughly discussed in the literature, early childhood factors, including early exposure to malnutrition and environment toxicants, have been comparably overlooked versus later childhood and adolescent issues. Yet these variables represent important and potentially modifiable conditions that, if supported by empirical findings, may help clarify causes of antisocial behavior and that can be suitable targets of intervention. The early health risk factor framework (Liu, 2011) presented here is built upon Liu's (2004) previous model of child externalizing behavior, which itself was derived from a biosocial model of violence (Raine, Brennan, & Farrington, 1997).

In the framework (Liu, 2011), biological factors by themselves are hypothesized to directly give rise to behavioral outcomes. Similarly, social risk factors can independently and directly lead to externalizing behaviors. Importantly, the framework emphasizes that the interaction between the biological and psychosocial risk factors, which are collectively defined as health risk factors, along with potential mediators, may account for the relationship between the predictors and the expected outcomes.

Preventable health risk factors for violence, such as low childhood and maternal weight, tobacco and alcohol use, iron deficiency, obesity, high cholesterol and blood pressure, and unsafe sexual practices, have considerable impact on longevity and quality of life, as worldwide estimates suggest they contribute to more than 29 million deaths annually (Ezzati, Lopez, Rodgers, & Murray, 2004). As such, these represented important targets of consideration in creating this new model.

## *Early Health Risk Factors*

Risk factors are defined as byproducts of biological and psychosocial processes during the pre-, peri-, and postnatal periods and are hypothesized to be predictors of adverse outcomes, including childhood externalizing behavior, juvenile delinquency, and adult violence. Of note, the early health risk factors outlined in this framework, which focus only on those occurring during the prenatal period and childhood, are known to impair brain functions, which would consequently be expected to influence behavior. As a result, not all early health risk factors can be exhaustively encompassed since some are still lacking empirical evidence demonstrating their relationship to neurological deficits and violent/aggressive behaviors. Further, an expansive discussion of all such factors is beyond the scope of this chapter. Rather, this chapter will describe the overall model, with further discussion concentrating specifically on malnutrition as an early health risk factor for aggression highly supported by the literature (Liu, 2011).

### *Biological Risk Factors*

During the pre-, peri-, and postnatal periods, pertinent biological risk factors include both genetic and maternal pathophysiological processes that can impede fetal growth and development (Liu & Wuerker, 2005; Peterson et al., 2015). It is unlikely that a single specific gene will be identified as a biologic cause for antisocial behavior. It is more likely that a confluence of genetic, neurotransmitter, temperamental, and pathophysiological processes are at play. While many early biological risk factors during the pre-and postnatal period may be linked to childhood externalizing behaviors, a few of the most important factors include maternal malnutrition; smoking, alcohol, and drug use during pregnancy; and birth complications (Liu, 2011).

## Psychosocial Risk Factors

Psychosocial risk factors have been hypothesized to be associated with an increased risk for negative behavioral outcomes, particularly child abuse and neglect, marital conflict, poor parenting, domestic and intimate partner violence, and unstable home life, including poverty, parental unemployment, family history of criminal behavior, and community violence. Other important considerations include high psychosocial stress, poor school attendance and performance, negative attitudes about pregnancy, pregnancy during adolescence, and psychiatric disorders, including substance abuse (Liu, 2011).

## Health Risk Factors: The Interaction between Biology and the Psychosocial Environment

As noted above, it is likely that the interaction between biology (e.g., genes) and environment offers the most plausible explanation for the development of antisocial behaviors above and beyond any effects of biology or environment in isolation. Therefore, consideration of biological and psychosocial environment offers understanding of two risk factors that are multiplicative. For example, birth complications, including delivery problems and early infancy, may predispose children to later violence (Liu, Raine, Wuerker, Venables, & Mednick, 2009; Tibbetts & Rivera, 2015) but can be due to both biological risk factors (e.g., poor nutrition) and psychosocial risk factors (e.g., antenatal stress) (Heaman et al., 2013; Staneva, Bogossian, Pritchard, & Wittkowski, 2015). The framework opines that the likelihood of early health factors leading to later externalizing behavior is maximized when biological risk factors interact with social risk factors. Adoption studies of the offspring of parents with antisocial or hostile behaviors have observed that such children are more likely to exhibit antisocial tendencies themselves. However, the likelihood of the child demonstrating antisocial tendencies is increased when these children are adopted into negative home environments (e.g., poverty, abusive parenting) (Liu, 2011).

Recently, epigenetics – the study of inherited alterations in gene expression brought about by mechanisms other than changes in the underlying DNA sequence – has gained increasing attention in health risk factor research as recognition of multiple influences on maternal-fetal pathways have emerged. Epigenetic factors appear important in predicting behavioral outcomes as they may impinge on the neurodevelopment of the fetus' growing brain. For example, exposure to environmental chemicals during the prenatal period may affect gene transcription, which may subsequently induce differential methylation of gene clusters involved with aggression or the regulation thereof (Provençal et al., 2014; Tremblay, Booij, Provençal, & Szyf, 2016). Given that biology and the social environment are intertwined and may even have synergistic effects as opposed to independent effects, they are collectively defined unitarily as "health risk factors" (Liu, 2011).

This framework also recognizes the reciprocal interaction between biological and psychosocial risk factors wherein biology may affect psychosocial risk factors (e.g., genetic predisposition to substance use) or, likewise, psychosocial experiences may affect biology (e.g., engaging in excessive substance use behaviors may "turn on" genes predisposing the individual toward addiction). For example, teenage pregnancy as one component of social adversity is generally viewed as a psychosocial risk factor, but it could be that genetic/biological traits (e.g., high hormone levels) may predispose some teenager to engage in sexual activities and become pregnant. Thus, this framework proposes that early health risk factors, which results from the interaction between biological and psychosocial risk factors, are critically important in predisposition of later aggression, hyperactivity, and delinquency.

## **Early Health Protective Factors (Prevention and Intervention)**

Protective factors should be introduced as early as possible before health risk factors arise, as they can potentially reduce the direct and interactive effects of biologic and socio-environmental contributors. The prenatal developmental period represents an important period in which the effects of protective factors may be maximized, given that the fetus is highly vulnerable to influences from the environment and from other health-related variables. Such factors increase resilience, enhance resistance to risk, and strengthen individual defenses against the development of negative outcomes. Thus, proper prenatal care, including regular physical examinations, proper nutrition, general healthy lifestyle, avoidance of toxic chemicals (e.g., tobacco and substance use), as well as strong parental bonding and family harmony, may offset the impact of risk factors and increase the likelihood of a positive outcome by encouraging normal fetal neurodevelopment and infant mental health. Finally, nutritional interventions during childhood or adulthood can serve as protective factors in reducing negative behavior (Liu, 2011).

### *The Mediating Factor of the Brain*

Mediating factors are those that help explain the mechanism of action when an outcome is observed, such as IQ. Low IQ mediates the relationship between prenatal biological factors and externalizing outcomes, including factors such as nutrition (Liu, 2004, 2011; Liu & Raine, 2017; Liu & Wuerker, 2005), maternal tobacco exposure (Daseking, Petermann, Tischler, & Waldmann, 2015), and maternal alcohol use (Wyper & Pei, 2016). Furthermore, longitudinal studies have suggested that neuropsychological deficits characterize child and adult violence and antisocial behavior (Raine, 2002), and early neurocognitive deficits precede the onset of these antisocial behaviors (Chamberlain, Derbyshire, Leppink, & Grant, 2016).

## Empirical Evidence of Prenatal and Early Childhood Health Risk Factors

Throughout the literature, there are several lines of empirical evidence supporting the components of this framework, including for the health risk factors of prenatal maternal smoking, malnutrition, lead exposure, birth complications, childhood head injury, maternal depression and stress, and child abuse. These health risk factors have been identified as being the most salient, are well-supported by the literature, and, to a large degree, are amenable to prevention and intervention strategies. This section will focus specifically on recent empirical findings in malnutrition research as a primary area of risk for childhood and adult externalizing/antisocial behavior, including highlights of possible brain mechanisms that may serve to explain their linkage (Liu & Raine, 2006) and in turn provide empirical support for the theoretical framework.

### *Malnutrition and Development of Antisocial Behaviors*

While the importance of nutrition in fetal brain development and throughout early childhood cannot be understated, it has been somewhat neglected by the literature. In post-industrialized nations, such as the United States, malnutrition is often overlooked and underestimated as a current problem. Moreover, while individuals may be able to meet caloric needs, adequate population-level intake of macronutrients, vitamins, minerals, amino acids, fatty acids, and micronutrients can lag, especially in low-income populations. Even in developed countries, impoverished populations often have diets that lack important vitamins and minerals due to the inability to access fresh fruits and produce. Using data from the National Health and Nutritional Examination Survey (NHANES) 2001–2008 (N=18,177), Agarwal, Reider, Brooks and Fulgoni (2015) found that over 40% of the US adult population had inadequate intakes of vitamin A, vitamin C, vitamin D, vitamin E, calcium, and magnesium (Agarwal, Reider, Brooks, & Fulgoni III, 2015). Nutrient-poor diets are especially impactful during periods of development (e.g. childhood and adolescence) and when occurring in women who are pregnant. Indeed, teenage mothers are especially susceptible to malnutrition, including low energy intake and iron deficiency that nears or meets definitions for anemia. Zinc, vitamin B, and protein have a significant impact on brain and central nervous system development, and their deficiencies have been strongly linked to cognitive difficulties and early antisocial behaviors. But the implications of malnutrition are not only at the level of brain growth but also manifest at the level of even earlier developmental processes, including neurogenesis, cell migration, and differentiation (Liu, Raine, Venables, & Mednick, 2006).

*Prenatal Malnutrition*

Epidemiology studies support the association between prenatal nutritional deficiencies and later neurodevelopmental and behavioral disorders. Neugebauer et al. (Neugebauer, Hoek, & Susser, 1999) conducted a large sample (N=100,543) retrospective cohort study in the 1960s to assess the relationship between prenatal nutritional deficiencies and the prevalence of offspring antisocial personality disorder among males in the Netherlands. During World War II, the Netherlands was subject to a period of nutritional deficiency and famine after the German army interfered with transport of food supplies into the country. Consequently, different regions of the Netherlands were subject to moderate (4200–6300 kJ/d) to severe (<4200 kJ/d) nutritional deficiency. The retrospective cohort study included men born during 1944–1946, the period of time during which regions of the Netherlands were experiencing differing levels of nutritional deficiencies. Participants were enrolled at the time of their military induction at age 18 years. Since nutritional deficiency was the predictor variable, participants were classified according to their expected exposure to prenatal nutritional deficiency based on the region in which they were born. The outcome measure of interest was whether these men had ASPD, which was diagnosed during medical examinations at the time of their military induction. Neugebauer et al. (Neugebauer, Hoek, & Susser, 1999) found that male offspring of mothers severely malnourished during the first and second trimesters of pregnancy had 2.5 times the normal rate of antisocial personality disorder in adulthood, suggesting a link between nutrition and antisocial behaviors.

More recently, in a study done on a Greek mother–child cohort, low maternal serum vitamin D levels during the first trimester were associated with children's behavioral difficulties, particularly ADHD symptoms, during preschool (Daraki et al., 2018). Research has emphasized the importance of key vitamins, such as Vitamin D, in biological functions central to fetal brain development, such as differentiation of brain cells, regulation of axonal growth and calcium signaling within the brain (Lambregts-Rommelse & Hebebrand, 2017). Fetuses are entirely dependent on maternal nutrient stores during this time, thus emphasizing the potential role of maternal nutritional health as a protective factor against children's behavior and conduct disorders.

*Malnutrition During Childhood*

Postnatal diet quality has also been associated with antisocial and externalizing behavior during childhood. In a prospective twin study that examined preschool diet and elementary school behavior reported that poor quality nutrition during preschool increased externalizing behavior during elementary behavior after controlling for genes and the shared environment (Jackson, 2016). While genes and the environment serve as important risk factors in the etiology of aggression and externalizing behavior, the results of this study suggest that eating behaviors play significant and independent roles in the development of antisocial behavior.

Studies have also reported robust relationships between micronutrient deficiencies during childhood and later neurobehavioral problems, aggression and delinquency. Children with protein, zinc, iron, and vitamin B deficiencies at age 3 years have been linked to greater antisocial, aggressive, and/or hyperactive behaviors at ages 8, 11, and 17 years and the effects are mediated by cognitive deficits (Liu, Raine, Venables, Dalais, & Mednick, 2003; Liu, Raine, Venables, & Mednick, 2004). Zinc deficiency has been specifically associated with greater violence and aggression (Liu, Raine, Venables, & Mednick, 2004; Watts, 1990), behavior problems (Liu et al., 2014) as well as hyperactivity (Brophy, 1986). A recent follow-up study of 1018 infants in Chile found that compared to iron sufficiency at 12 or 18 months of age, iron deficiency predicted greater adolescent behavior problems, such as oppositional defiance, rule-breaking problems and attention disorders (Doom et al., 2018). Low iron intake in children is also associated with aggression, conduct disorder, and juvenile delinquency (Rosen et al., 1985; Werbach, 1992). Furthermore, iron supplementation was shown improve cognitive and behavioral outcomes among non-iron deficient children with attention-deficit hyperactivity disorder (Sever, Ashkenazi, Tyano, & Weizman, 1997).

Interestingly, studies have shown that males are particularly sensitive to the effects of malnutrition on behavior. Early childhood household food insecurity and food insecurity persistence predicted adolescent behavioral misconduct in males, but not females (Jackson & Vaughn, 2017). Similarly, a study done in Colombian schoolchildren (N=1,042) reported that iron deficiency, anemia and low plasma vitamin B-12 during middle childhood were significantly associated with adolescent externalizing behavior in boys but not girls (Robinson et al., 2018). These observed sex differences may be a result of sexual dimorphisms in brain development. Males demonstrate a greater reduction in grey matter and a significantly higher rate of change in white matter volume than females during childhood and adolescence (Bava & Tapert, 2010; Lenroot et al., 2007). It is possible that these greater structural changes are more susceptible to changes promoted by external influences, such as malnutrition.

### *Malnutrition Effects on Antisocial Behavior across the Lifespan*

The effects of malnutrition are not static and may carry long-lasting implications. As noted above, malnutrition at age 3 years has been associated with higher scores for externalizing behavior problems at ages 8, 11, and 17 years (Liu, Raine, Venables, & Mednick, 2004). In this study, the participants were drawn from a birth cohort (N=1,795) in whom signs of malnutrition were assessed at age 3 years, cognitive measures were assessed at ages 3 and 11 years, and antisocial, aggressive, and hyperactive behavior was assessed at ages 8, 11, and 17 years. The authors found that, in relation to comparison subjects (N=1,206), the children with malnutrition signs at age 3 years (N=353) were more aggressive or hyperactive at age 8 years, had more externalizing problems at age 11, and had greater conduct disorder and excessive motor activity at age 17. The results were independent of psychosocial adversity and were not moderated by gender. There was a dose-response relationship between degree of malnutrition and degree of externalizing behavior at ages 8 and 17. Low IQ mediated the link between malnutrition and externalizing behavior at ages 8 and 11. These results indicate that malnutrition predisposes to neurocognitive deficits, which in turn predispose to persistent externalizing behavior problems throughout childhood and adolescence. The findings suggest that reducing early malnutrition may help reduce later antisocial and aggressive behavior

## Empirical Evidence of Prenatal and Early Childhood Health Protective Factors

### *The Impact of Omega-3 Interventions for Malnutrition*

As indicated in our early health risk framework, protective factors, including nutritional interventions, can serve to reduce biological vulnerability to aggressive behavior. In this section, we will use Omega-3 as an example of a dietary intervention that has shown to be effective in reducing antisocial behavior in several populations. Docosahexaenoic acid (DHA) and omega-3 long chain essential fatty acid deficiencies have been associated with higher aggression in humans (Stevens, Zentall, Abate, Kuczek, & Burgess, 1996; Stevens et al., 2003) and in animal models (DeMar et al., 2005), thus making it a potential target for dietary interventions aimed at reducing antisocial behavior.

Recent intervention research regarding the efficacy of omega-3 supplementation for aggression has shown promising results, particularly in children. In a randomized, placebo-controlled, parallel group trial, we found that omega-3 supplementation significantly reduced externalizing behavior problems in a community sample of 8–16 year old children, as reported by both caregivers and their children (Raine, Portnoy, Liu, Mahoomed, & Hibbeln, 2015). In this study, significant group x time interactions were found at 6 months (end of treatment) and 12 months (6 months post-treatment) for parents' reports of child externalizing and callous-unemotional traits. These results were replicated in several studies on both community (Raine et al., 2016) and clinical samples of children with externalizing behavior (Raine et al., 2018). Additionally, studies have shown that the benefits of child omega-3 supplementation are not only limited to the child; adult caregivers of children receiving omega-3 supplementation reported reductions in interpartner and child-directed physical assault as well as long-term reductions in psychological aggression that correlated with child externalizing behavior scores (Portnoy, Raine, Liu, & Hibbeln, 2018). These studies demonstrate the efficacy of omega-3 interventions on antisocial and aggressive behavior as well as its benefits that extend beyond the child to the family system as a whole.

The effect of nutritional supplement of Omega-3 fatty acid on antisocial behavior has also been shown in adolescent and adult populations. Gesch (2002) implemented a double-blind, randomized controlled intervention study among young adult prisoners givens either real food supplements (1260 mg linoleic acid, 160 mg gamma linolenic acid, 80 mg eicosapentaenoic acid and 44 mg docosahexaenoic acid) or placebo. Adolescents taking real nutritional supplements committed less offenses than those taking placebos. These findings were upheld by a replicated study by the Dutch Ministry of Justice, further strengthening the potential contributor and target of intervention for antisocial behavior (Gesch, 2014).

## Brain Dysfunction as a Possible Mechanism

The early health risk framework emphasizes *mediating* effects of brain dysfunction account for early health risk factor and antisocial behavior, which help explain the mechanism of action when an outcome is observed. The nature of how nutritional deficits contribute to aggressive and antisocial behavior is not well understood and has been relatively neglected from the research compared to other biological contributors to antisocial behavior (e.g., genetics, gender, neurotransmitter and hormonal abnormalities). However, evidence continues to grow underscoring malnutrition as a potential significant contributor to the alteration of brain dysfunction via three independent mechanisms (Liu, Raine, Venables, & Mednick, 2006): (1) decreased brain cell growth/development; (2) disruptions in neurochemistry; and (3) an increase in neurotoxic effects (Liu, Raine, Venables, & Mednick, 2006). The implication that malnutrition predisposes developing fetuses and children to brain dysfunction, which in turn predisposes to persistent externalizing behavior problems throughout childhood, is gaining support. Protein and micronutrients, such as zinc and iron, are necessary for development of healthy central nervous system structure and functioning (Gallagher, Newman, Green, & Hanson, 2005; Liu, Raine, Venables, & Mednick, 2006; Nakagawasai et al., 2006; Young & Leyton, 2002). Iron is associated with the dopamine pathway and is needed to metabolize serotonin and norepinephrine. Findings from animal models that indicate that iron deficiency may reduce dopamine transmission (Liu, Raine,

Venables, & Mednick, 2006), resulting in learning difficulties and impulsivity. Significant iron deficiencies have also been documented among incarcerated youth, as compared to non-incarcerated adolescents (Rosen et al., 1985).

Recently, increasing attention has been given to the role of the microbiome-gut-brain axis as the most likely mechanism underlying the observed relationship between malnutrition and neurobehavioral disorders. The microbiome-gut-brain axis posits a complex web of interactions between multiple systems, including the endocrine, neural, and immune pathways, that make up bidirectional communication between the gut and the brain. Animal studies have demonstrated a relationship between gut microbiota and the regulation of cognition, behavior and emotional regulation (Cryan & Dinan, 2012). Likewise, animals exposed to physical and psychosocial stress have shown alterations in gut microbiota and levels in inflammatory cytokines (Bailey et al., 2011; O'Mahony et al., 2009). Interestingly, evidence from human studies has suggested that the adult-like microbiota structure is established early in life, mirroring neurodevelopment (Lambregts-Rommelse & Hebebrand, 2017). These findings suggest that maintenance of a healthy microbiome-gut-brain axis, particularly during the first three years of life, plays an important role in the healthy cognitive, behavioral and emotional development of a child. However, the mechanisms underlying the effect of gut microbiota on central nervous system functioning have yet to be fully elucidated. Likewise, microbial-based interventions as a potential treatment for behavioral and cognitive disorders still require further investigation.

In sum, there is strong evidence to suggest a potential link between poor nutrition and development of antisocial behaviors, including aggression and other externalizing tendencies (Liu & Raine, 2006). This line of research will require further study to more clearly delineate possible causal effects of nutrition during the prenatal and postnatal periods on negative behavior. Malnutrition may represent a significant risk factor for antisocial behavior that is highly amenable to change through public health, school-based, and prenatal wellness programs. Given the wide-reaching effects of nutrition on brain development as a whole, greater attention to malnutrition could likely not only inform the treatment and prevention of conduct disorder in children, but cognitive outcomes and school performance as well.

## Implications of the Model: Prevention Strategies and Future Study

Our health risk factor model on better understanding the development of antisocial behavior may inform the creation of strategies to help prevent and reduce risk of antisocial behaviors at the public health level as well as by individuals. Malnutrition has ample empirical evidence of its linkage to aggression and externalizing tendencies, and it is amenable to change, thus making it an appropriate target for intervention. Nurses and other health professionals are especially well-positioned to contribute to primary prevention efforts given their frequent access to and close contact with parents and children (e.g., through health clinics, through schools, through community programs). Parental training and education, especially those targeted at pregnant women, can impart critical information about the importance of proper nutrition and diet, such as the use of folate during pregnancy. Secondary prevention should focus on high-risk populations, including young mothers and parents with a history of psychiatric illness (e.g., depression, substance use disorders). Behavior modification and cognitive techniques can help parents reduce aggression and externalizing behaviors in their offspring (Gagnon, Craig, Tremblay, Zhou, & Vitaro, 1995; Tremblay Richard, 2010) through both school- and home-based programs. Finally, future research should help elucidate factors accounting for individual differences and risk-stratification. Indeed, not every person undernourished as a young child will display antisocial behaviors later in life. A better understanding of exacerbating as well as ameliorating factors will help experts more clearly identify earlier which children are most at risk and potentially intervene before psychopathy is manifest.

## Acknowledgements

All phases of the author's research were supported by NIH grants from the National Institute of Environment Health Sciences (NIH/NIEHS, R01-ES018858; K02-ES019878-01), USA.

## References

Agarwal, S., Reider, C., Brooks, J. R., & Fulgoni III, V. L. (2015). Comparison of prevalence of inadequate nutrient intake based on body weight status of adults in the United States: An analysis of NHANES 2001–2008. *Journal of the American College of Nutrition*, 34(2), 126–134.

Bailey, M. T., Dowd, S. E., Galley, J. D., Hufnagle, A. R., Allen, R. G., & Lyte, M. (2011). Exposure to a social stressor alters the structure of the intestinal microbiota: Implications for stressor-induced immunomodulation. *Brain, Behavior, and Immunity*, 25(3), 397–407. doi: https://doi.org/10.1016/j.bbi.2010.10.023.

Bava, S., & Tapert, S. F. (2010). Adolescent brain development and the risk for alcohol and other drug problems. *Neuropsychology Review*, 20(4), 398–413. doi: 10.1007/s11065-010-9146-6.

Brophy, M. H. (1986). Zinc and childhood hyperactivity. *Biological Psychiatry*, 21(7), 704–705.

Chamberlain, S. R., Derbyshire, K. L., Leppink, E. W., & Grant, J. E. (2016). Neurocognitive deficits associated with antisocial personality disorder in non-treatment-seeking young adults. *Journal of the American Academy of Psychiatry and the Law Online*, 44(2), 218–225.

Cryan, J. F., & Dinan, T. G. (2012). Mind-altering microorganisms: The impact of the gut microbiota on brain and behaviour. *Nature Reviews Neuroscience*, 13, 701. doi: 10.1038/nrn3346

Daraki, V., Roumeliotaki, T., Koutra, K., Chalkiadaki, G., Katrinaki, M., Kyriklaki, A., ... Chatzi, L. (2018). High maternal vitamin D levels in early pregnancy may protect against behavioral difficulties at preschool age: The Rhea mother–Child cohort, Crete, Greece. *European Child & Adolescent Psychiatry*, 27(1), 79–88. doi: 10.1007/s00787-017-1023-x.

Daseking, M., Petermann, F., Tischler, T., & Waldmann, H.-C. (2015). Smoking during pregnancy is a risk factor for executive function deficits in preschool-aged children. *Geburtshilfe und Frauenheilkunde*, 75(1), 64.

DeMar, J. J., Ma, K., Bell, J., Igarashi, M., Greenstein, D., & Rapoport, S. (2005). One generation of n-3 polyunsaturated fatty acid deprivation increases depression and aggression test scores in rats. *The Journal of Lipid Research*, 47(1), 172–180.

Doom, J. R., Richards, B., Caballero, G., Delva, J., Gahagan, S., & Lozoff, B. (2018). Infant iron deficiency and iron supplementation predict adolescent internalizing, externalizing, and social problems. *The Journal of Pediatrics*, 195, 199–205.e192. doi: https://doi.org/10.1016/j.jpeds.2017.12.008

Ezzati, M., Lopez, A. D., Rodgers, A., & Murray, C. J. (2004). *Comparative Quantification of Health Risks: Global and Regional Burden of Disease Attributable to Selected Major Risk Factors*. Geneva: OMS.

Farrington, D. P. (2000). Psychosocial predictors of adult antisocial personality and adult convictions. *Behavioral Sciences & the Law*, 18(5), 605–622.

Gagnon, C., Craig, W. M., Tremblay, R. E., Zhou, R. M., & Vitaro, F. (1995). Kindergarten predictors of boys' stable behavior problems at the end of elementary school. *Journal of Abnormal Child Psychology*, 23(6), 751–766. doi: 10.1007/bf01447475.

Gallagher, E. A. L., Newman, J. P., Green, L. R., & Hanson, M. A. (2005). The effect of low protein diet in pregnancy on the development of brain metabolism in rat offspring. *The Journal of Physiology*, 568(2), 553–558. doi: 10.1113/jphysiol.2005.092825.

Gesch, B. (2014). Adolescence: Does good nutrition = good behaviour? *Nutr Health*, [Epub ahead of print].

Gesch, C. (2002). Influence of supplementary vitamins, minerals and essential fatty acids on the antisocial behaviour of young adult prisoners. Randomised, placebo-controlled trial. *British Journal of Psychiatry*, 181, 22–28.

Heaman, M., Kingston, D., Chalmers, B., Sauve, R., Lee, L., & Young, D. (2013). Risk factors for preterm birth and small-for-gestational-age births among Canadian women. *Paediatric and Perinatal Epidemiology*, 27(1), 54–61.

Iozzino, L., Ferrari, C., Large, M., Nielssen, O., & De Girolamo, G. (2015). Prevalence and risk factors of violence by psychiatric acute inpatients: A systematic review and meta-analysis. *PloS One*, 10(6), e0128536.

Jackson, D. B. (2016). The link between poor quality nutrition and childhood antisocial behavior: A genetically informative analysis. *Journal of Criminal Justice, 44*, 13–20. doi: https://doi.org/10.1016/j.jcrimjus.2015.11.007

Jackson, D. B., & Vaughn, M. G. (2017). Household food insecurity during childhood and adolescent misconduct. *Preventive Medicine, 96*, 113–117. doi: https://doi.org/10.1016/j.ypmed.2016.12.042

Lambregts-Rommelse, N., & Hebebrand, J. (2017). Editorial focused issue 'The role of nutrition in child and adolescent onset mental disorders'. *European Child & Adolescent Psychiatry, 26*(9), 1007–1010. doi: 10.1007/s00787-017-1041-8.

Lenroot, R. K., Gogtay, N., Greenstein, D. K., Wells, E. M., Wallace, G. L., Clasen, L. S., ... Giedd, J. N. (2007). Sexual dimorphism of brain developmental trajectories during childhood and adolescence. *NeuroImage, 36*(4), 1065–1073. doi: https://doi.org/10.1016/j.neuroimage.2007.03.053.

Liu, J. (2004). Childhood externalizing behavior: Theory and implications. *Journal of Child and Adolescent Psychiatric Nursing, 17*(3), 93–103.

Liu, J. (2011). Early health risk factors for violence: Conceptualization, evidence, and implications. *Aggression and Violent Behavior, 16*(1), 63–73.

Liu, J., Hanlon, A., Ma, C., Zhao, S., Cao, S., & Compher, C. (2014). Low blood zinc, iron, and other sociodemographic factors associated with behavior problems in preschoolers. *Nutrients, 6*(2), 530.

Liu, J., & Raine, A. (2006). The effect of childhood malnutrition on externalizing behavior. *Current Opinion in Pediatrics, 18*(5), 565–570.

Liu, J., & Raine, A. (2017). Nutritional status and social behavior in preschool children: The mediating effects of neurocognitive functioning. *Maternal & Child Nutrition, 13*(2). doi: 10.1111/mcn.12321.

Liu, J., Raine, A., Venables, P., & Mednick, S. (2006). Malnutrition, Brain Dysfunction, and Antisocial Criminal Behavior. In Adrian Raine (ed.), *Crime and Schizophrenia: Causes and Cures* (pp. 109–128). New York: Nova Science Publishers.

Liu, J., Raine, A., Venables, P. H., Dalais, C., & Mednick, S. A. (2003). Malnutrition at age 3 years and lower cognitive ability at age 11 years: Independence from psychosocial adversity. *Archives of Pediatrics & Adolescent Medicine, 157*(6), 593–600. doi: 10.1001/archpedi.157.6.593.

Liu, J., Raine, A., Venables, P. H., & Mednick, S. A. (2004). Malnutrition at age 3 years and externalizing behavior problems at ages 8, 11, and 17 years. *American Journal of Psychiatry, 161*(11), 2005–2013. doi: 10.1176/appi.ajp.161.11.2005.

Liu, J., Raine, A., Wuerker, A., Venables, P. H., & Mednick, S. (2009). The association of birth complications and externalizing behavior in early adolescents: Direct and mediating effects. *Journal of Research on Adolescence, 19*(1), 93–111.

Liu, J., & Wuerker, A. (2005). Biosocial bases of aggressive and violent behavior—Implications for nursing studies. *International Journal of Nursing Studies, 42*(2), 229–241.

Murray, J., Shenderovich, Y., Gardner, F., Mikton, C., Derzon, J. H., Liu, J., & Eisner, M. (2018). Risk factors for antisocial behavior in low-and middle-income countries: A systematic review of longitudinal studies. *Crime and Justice, 47*(1), 255–364.

Nakagawasai, O., Yamadera, F., Sato, S., Taniguchi, R., Hiraga, H., Arai, Y., ... Tadano, T. (2006). Alterations in cognitive function in prepubertal mice with protein malnutrition: Relationship to changes in choline acetyltransferase. *Behavioural Brain Research, 167*(1), 111–117. doi: https://doi.org/10.1016/j.bbr.2005.08.024.

Neugebauer, R., Hoek, H. W., & Susser, E. (1999). Prenatal exposure to wartime famine and development of antisocial personality disorder in early adulthood. *Jama, 282*(5), 455–462.

O'Mahony, S. M., Marchesi, J. R., Scully, P., Codling, C., Ceolho, A.-M., Quigley, E. M., ... Dinan, T. G. (2009). Early life stress alters behavior, immunity, and microbiota in rats: Implications for irritable bowel syndrome and psychiatric illnesses. *Biological Psychiatry, 65*(3), 263–267.

Peterson, B. S., Rauh, V. A., Bansal, R., Hao, X., Toth, Z., Nati, G., ... Semanek, D. (2015). Effects of prenatal exposure to air pollutants (polycyclic aromatic hydrocarbons) on the development of brain white matter, cognition, and behavior in later childhood. *JAMA Psychiatry, 72*(6), 531–540.

Portnoy, J., Raine, A., Liu, J., & Hibbeln, J. R. (2018). Reductions of intimate partner violence resulting from supplementing children with omega-3 fatty acids: A randomized, double-blind, placebo-controlled, stratified, parallel-group trial. *Aggressive Behavior*. doi: 10.1002/ab.21769.

Provençal, N., Suderman, M. J., Guillemin, C., Vitaro, F., Côté, S. M., Hallett, M., ... Szyf, M. (2014). Association of childhood chronic physical aggression with a DNA methylation signature in adult human T cells. *PloS One, 9*(4), e89839.

Raine, A. (2002). Annotation: The role of prefrontal deficits, low autonomic arousal, and early health factors in the development of antisocial and aggressive behavior in children. *Journal of Child Psychology and Psychiatry*, *43*(4), 417–434.

Raine, A., Ang, R. P., Choy, O., Hibbeln, J. R., Ho, R. M., Lim, C. G., … Ooi, Y. P. (2018). Omega-3 (ω-3) and social skills interventions for reactive aggression and childhood externalizing behavior problems: A randomized, stratified, double-blind, placebo-controlled, factorial trial. *Psychological Medicine*, *49*(2), 335–344.

Raine, A., Brennan, P., & Farrington, D. P. (1997). *Biosocial Bases of Violence* (pp. 1–20). New York: Springer.

Raine, A., Cheney, R. A., Ho, R., Portnoy, J., Liu, J., Soyfer, L., … Richmond, T. S. (2016). Nutritional supplementation to reduce child aggression: A randomized, stratified, single-blind, factorial trial. *Journal of Child Psychology and Psychiatry*, *57*(9), 1038–1046.

Raine, A., Portnoy, J., Liu, J., Mahoomed, T., & Hibbeln, J. R. (2015). Reduction in behavior problems with omega-3 supplementation in children aged 8–16 years: A randomized, double-blind, placebo-controlled, stratified, parallel-group trial. *Journal of Child Psychology and Psychiatry*, *56*(5), 509–520.

Robinson, S. L., Marín, C., Oliveros, H., Mora-Plazas, M., Richards, B. J., Lozoff, B., & Villamor, E. (2018). Iron deficiency, anemia, and low vitamin B-12 serostatus in middle childhood are associated with behavior problems in adolescent boys: Results from the Bogotá school children cohort. *The Journal of Nutrition*, *148*(5), 760–770. doi: 10.1093/jn/nxy029.

Rosen, G. M., Deinard, A. S., Schwartz, S., Smith, C., Stephenson, B., & Grabenstein, B. (1985). Iron deficiency among incarcerated juvenile delinquents. *Journal of Adolescent Health Care*, *6*(6), 419–423. doi: https://doi.org/10.1016/S0197-0070(85)80045-0.

Sever, Y., Ashkenazi, A., Tyano, S., & Weizman, A. (1997). Iron treatment in children with attention deficit hyperactivity disorder. *Neuropsychobiology*, *35*(4), 178–180.

Staneva, A., Bogossian, F., Pritchard, M., & Wittkowski, A. (2015). The effects of maternal depression, anxiety, and perceived stress during pregnancy on preterm birth: A systematic review. *Women and Birth*, *28*(3), 179–193.

Stevens, L., Zentall, S., Abate, M., Kuczek, T., & Burgess, J. (1996). Omega-3 fatty acids in boys with behavior, learning, and health problems. *Physiol Behav*, *59*(4–5), 915–920.

Stevens, L., Zhang, W., Peck, L., Kuczek, T., Grevstad, N., Mahon, A., … Burgess, J. (2003). Supplementation in children with inattention, hyperactivity, and other disruptive behaviors. *Lipids*, *38*(10), 1007–1021.

Tibbetts, S. G., & Rivera, J. (2015). Prenatal and perinatal factors in the development of persistent criminality. In Julien Morizot & Lila Kazemian (eds.), *The Development of Criminal and Antisocial Behavior* (pp. 167–180). Cham, Switzerland: Springer.

Tremblay, R. E., Booij, L., Provençal, N., & Szyf, M. (2016). The impact of environmental stressors on DNA methylation, neurobehavioral development, and chronic physical aggression: Prospects for early protective interventions. In Claude L. Hughes & Michael D. Waters (eds.), *Translational Toxicology: Defining a New Therapeutic Discipline* (pp. 295–319). Cham, Switzerland: Springer.

Tremblay Richard, E. (2010). Developmental origins of disruptive behaviour problems: The 'original sin' hypothesis, epigenetics and their consequences for prevention. *Journal of Child Psychology and Psychiatry*, *51*(4), 341–367. doi: 10.1111/j.1469-7610.2010.02211.x.

Virkkunen, M., Goldman, D., Nielsen, D. A., & Linnoila, M. (1995). Low brain serotonin turnover rate (low CSF 5-HIAA) and impulsive violence. *Journal of Psychiatry and Neuroscience*, *20*(4), 271.

Watts, D. L. (1990). Trace elements and neuropsychological problems as reflected in tissue mineral analysis (TMA) patterns. *Journal of Orthomolecular Medicine*, *5*(3), 159–166.

Webster-Stratton, C., & Hammond, M. (1999). Marital conflict management skills, parenting style, and early-onset conduct problems: Processes and pathways. *The Journal of Child Psychology and Psychiatry and Allied Disciplines*, *40*(6), 917–927.

Werbach, M. (1992). Nutritional influences on aggressive behavior. *Journal of Orthomolecular Medicine*, *7*(1), 45–51.

World Health Organization. (2014). Injuries and violence: The facts 2014. Retrieved from https://apps.who.int/iris/handle/10665/149798.

Wyper, K., & Pei, J. (2016). Neurocognitive difficulties underlying high risk and criminal behaviour in FASD: Clinical implications. In Monty Nelson & Marguerite Trussler (eds.), *Fetal Alcohol Spectrum Disorders in Adults: Ethical and Legal Perspectives* (pp. 101–120). Cham, Switzerland: Springer.

Young, S. N., & Leyton, M. (2002). The role of serotonin in human mood and social interaction: Insight from altered tryptophan levels. *Pharmacology Biochemistry and Behavior*, *71*(4), 857–865. doi: https://doi.org/10.1016/S0091-3057(01)00670-0.

# 5

# WHAT BECOMES OF THE PROBLEM CHILD?

## The Foundational Role of Temperament in Health and Juvenile Offending

*Matthew DeLisi*

### Introduction

Since antiquity, scholars have utilized temperament as an organizing construct to understand variance in emotional and behavioral regulation (Arikha, 2008; Kagan, 1998, 2010; Morizot, 2015) and have created typologies or archetypes of individuals that behave in relatively consistent ways across the life course. Temperament is the stable, largely innate tendency with which a person experiences the environment and regulates his or her responses to the environment. There is important variation in temperament such that some individuals by virtue of their relatively facile, easygoing, and compliant disposition enjoy behavioral advantages whereas other individuals by virtue of their peevish, dysregulated, and difficult disposition face behavioral disadvantages. With temperament, Mother Nature is surely no egalitarian. Due to its association to physiological processes and the autonomic nervous system, temperament is considered the biological foundation upon which personality rests. Unfortunately, despite its utility as a conceptual framework for understanding individual-level differences in conduct, for many years temperament was peripheral to the study of antisocial conduct from a criminological perspective. This changed with the prominent publication of DeLisi and Vaughn's (2014) temperament-based theory of antisocial behavior and criminal justice system involvement.

According to DeLisi and Vaughn (2014; also see, DeLisi & Vaughn, 2011, 2015, 2016), effortful control, negative emotionality, and the interaction between effortful control and negative emotionality explain conduct problems across childhood, adolescence, and adulthood. Specifically, those with low effortful control—the ability to inhibit a dominant response in favor of performing a subdominant response (Rothbart, 1989; Rueda, 2012)—are posited to have fundamental deficits in self-regulation that causes adjustment problems in the family, at school, and at work. Compared to their persons with adequate effortful control, those with low effortful control tend to display higher levels of externalizing and internalizing symptoms, have lower social competence, exhibit slower declines in conduct problems, display slower increases in social competence, and experience lower subjective well-being Those with lower effortful control are also prone to reduced health.

Those with high negative emotionality, particularly "red" negative emotions, such as anger and hostility as opposed to "blue" negative emotions, such as sadness, withdrawal, and depression, frequently experience traits and states with negative valences. These negative emotions in turn contribute to aversive, problematic interactions with others. Those with both low effortful control and high negative emotionality are theorized to be at significant risk for conduct problems, delinquency, and crime because of increased opportunities for inappropriate behavioral responses and conflict-laden exchanges with others. A unique feature of DeLisi and Vaughn's model is the explicit notion that these temperamental deficits not only increase variance in conduct problems, but also increase the likelihood of negative behavioral responses to the criminal justice system. In other words, these temperamental deficits also compromise compliance with court orders and the ability or willingness to conform to direction from law enforcement and correctional staff. In this regard, their theoretical model offers explanatory power in criminological and criminal justice contexts.

Although it is a newer criminological theory, there are already empirical tests that have proven to be supportive of DeLisi and Vaughn's general claims (Baglivio, Wolff, DeLisi, Vaughn, & Piquero, 2016; Baglivio, Wolff, Piquero, DeLisi, & Vaughn, 2017; DeLisi, Fox, Fully, & Vaughn, 2018; Garofalo & Velotti, 2017; Veeh, Renn, Vaughn, & DeLisi, 2018; Wolff, Baglivio, Piquero, Vaughn, & DeLisi, 2016), with all studies thus far confirming associations between effortful control, negative emotionality, and their interaction and various forms of antisocial behavior.[1] For example, drawing on data from nearly 30,000 youth selected from the Florida Department of Juvenile Justice, Wolff and colleagues (2016) found that those who had temperaments characterized by low effortful control and high negative emotionality along with community disadvantage were more likely to be recidivistic juvenile offenders despite a bevy of control variables that have been previously linked with delinquency and repeated antisocial conduct. In a related study using data from over 11,000 male juvenile offenders, Baglivio and colleagues (2017) found that youth who had parents with drug and alcohol problems and mental health symptoms were more likely to have difficult temperaments characterized by low effortful control and high negative emotionality. In turn, youth with these temperamental displays were more engaged in delinquent conduct and significantly more likely to recidivate after contact with the juvenile justice system.

Their study also provides insight into the early home environments of adolescents that have temperamental deficits and conduct problems. It is common for these youth to be reared by parents who themselves have significant behavior problems including substance use disorders, criminal offending and criminal justice system involvement, and other comorbid psychiatric conditions that engender all sorts of situations that pose health challenges. Serious delinquent youth often face food insecurity, unstable residency and transiency, and diverse forms of abuse and neglect (Ashiabi & O'Neal, 2008; Cicchetti & Toth, 1995; DeLisi, Trulson, Marquart, Drury, & Kosloski, 2011; Dunn et al., 2002; Hawkins, Catalano, & Miller, 1992; Trulson, Haerle, Caudill, & DeLisi, 2016). In this way, temperamental deficits are a powerful driver of chaotic, highly dysfunctional early-life home environments that engender children with similarly difficult temperamental displays and the accompanying negative behaviors.

## Current Focus

Temperament research illuminates the multitudinous ways that effortful/self-control and negative emotional displays contribute to serious behavioral problems and psychopathology. Although criminologists have provided support about temperamental associations with delinquency and related externalizing features, they have paid insufficient attention to the health behaviors and health consequences stemming from these temperamental deficits. The current chapter first briefly examines research on early-life temperamental problems that are consistent with DeLisi and Vaughn (2014) criminological model to understand the developmental sequencing of temperament-conduct problems, second examines the interrelations between adolescent temperamental deficits, delinquency, and adverse health behaviors, and third offers research suggestions to more fully integrate considerations of health and health behaviors within criminological-temperament research.

## Temperamental Underpinnings to Child Conduct Problems

Buttressed by scores of research studies, DeLisi and Vaughn's theory clearly presents temperament as a multifactorial construct and thus biosocial mechanisms contribute to temperamental deficits.[2] The more severe the temperamental disposition and the conduct problems are, the greater the heritability. In the Environmental Risk (E-Risk) Longitudinal Twin Study, for instance, there was evidence of a severe subgroup that had pervasive antisocial behavior according to assessments from mothers, teachers, interviewers, and the youth themselves. These pervasively antisocial youth were observed at age 5 and again at age 12 (Wertz et al., 2016). In males (who evince the most violent and serious conduct), the stability was $r = .74$ and 88% of the variance in the stability of pervasive antisocial conduct was attributable to genetic factors. Of course, genetic factors do not exist in isolation but interact with environmental contexts in sublime and multifaceted ways. Lorber, Del Vecchio, and Slep's (2015) study of the development of infant externalizing behavior is revealing of this. Drawing on a sample of 274 psychologically aggressive couples and whose infants were followed from birth to age 24 months, Lorber et al. reported evidence of a coherent externalizing repertoire characterized by physical aggression, defiance, distress to limitations (anger), and activity level. Distress to limitations or what DeLisi and Vaughn refer broadly as negative emotionality was the most stable temperamental features. Lorber and colleagues also found that externalizing features were significantly correlated with aversive and negative interactions occurring within the home including conflicts between parents, bonding problems between parents and infant, and harsh parenting—evidence of mutual exacerbation that is driven by the infant's temperamental deficits (Lorber & Egeland, 2011).[3]

In the first decade of life, effortful control has significant predictive validity years later during adolescence. For example, Caspi, Moffitt, Newman, and Silva (1996) reported that children in a New Zealand birth cohort described as undercontrolled at age three were threefold more likely than self-regulated children to be diagnosed with Antisocial Personality Disorder in early adulthood. Moreover, they were twice as likely to be repeat offenders and nearly five times more likely to be convicted of a violent crime. Compared to a control group, undercontrolled children were also more likely to attempt suicide and have alcohol problems. Stevenson and Goodman's (2001) examination of children selected from a large British birth cohort found that temper tantrums and effortful control deficits at age three were predictive of delinquency and violent criminal convictions during adulthood. In this sense, serious adult psychopathology was the distal outcome of effortful control problems observed as early as age three.

Similarly, Wang, Chassin, Eisenberg, and Spinrad (2015) found that deficits in effortful control during childhood were associated with pure forms of aggressive-antisocial behavior during adolescence. Pure forms of aggressive-antisocial behavior included guiltlessness, rule breaking, lying, cheating, use of profanity, cruelty to others, threats of others, fighting, firesetting, truancy, disobedience at home and at school, frequent screaming, stubbornness/sullenness, labile mood, and having a bad temper. Low effortful control coupled with impulsivity was also associated with pure depressive symptoms and comorbid depressive symptoms and aggressive-antisocial behavior. Drawing on data from 2,076 children from 13 birth cohorts drawn from Dutch birth registries, Althoff, Verhulst, Rettew, Hudziak, and Van der Ende

(2010) examined the adult outcomes of dysregulated temperament. Their sample contained children ages 4 to 18 and who were followed up 14 years later. They found evidence of a pathological subgroup of children whose temperament profile was characterized as "dysregulated profile." These youth displayed the greatest deficits in affective, behavior, and cognition as children, and about 1.5 decades later were significantly likely to meet diagnostic criteria for any anxiety disorder, any mood disorder, any disruptive behavior disorder, any drug abuse, and any major depression disorder.

Other studies reveal a similar pattern of results. Using data from the National Institute of Child Health and Human Development (NICHD) Study of Early Child Care and Youth Development, Runions and Keating (2010) found that children age six years with high levels of anger and low levels of inhibitory control, which is the behavioral modulation component of effortful control, were more aggressive according to mother reports. In another study using the NICHD data, Fanti and Henrich (2010) reported evidence for a small group of youth comprising about 8.4% of the sample who were characterized by chronic externalizing behaviors from age 2 years through age 12 years.[4] Children with difficult temperament were more than 50% likely to be in this chronic externalizing category. As these children developed into adolescence, their behavioral displays were dominated by inappropriate, risky behaviors. They were significantly likely to associate with similarly behaving peers and be excluded by conventionally behaved peers. In other words, temperamental deficits in childhood significantly impair relationships with parents, peers, and teachers and set the stage for similar maladjustment during adolescence.

## Temperamental Underpinnings to Adolescent Delinquency and Allied Health Problems

An array of studies has shown that adolescents that have difficult temperaments especially centering on self-regulation problems and/or high levels of negative emotionality are more likely to have behavior problems at home, school, and community, engage in substance use, and suffer from reduced mental and/or physical health (Caspi, Henry, McGee, Moffitt, & Silva, 1995b; Checa & Abundis-Gutierrez, 2017; Clark, Donnellan, Robins, & Conger, 2015; Crockett, Wasserman, Rudasill, Hoffman, & Kalutskaya, 2017; Odgers et al., 2007; Rodriguez, Tucker, & Palmer, 2016; Schwartz, Snidman, & Kagan, 1996; Windle, 1991). In longitudinal studies, it is often the case that difficult temperaments observed during various points in childhood not only remain largely stable, but also reveal associations with poor health behaviors during adolescence and even adulthood, such as drug abuse and dependence, risky sexual behaviors, risky driving behaviors, and risky criminal activity (Caspi et al., 1997, 1995a). A study of 631 participants from a community sample examined at age 13 and again at age 33 revealed that early adolescent temperamental irritability predicted Major Depressive Disorder, Generalized Anxiety Disorder, and Dysthymia (Stringaris, Cohen, Pine, & Leibenluft, 2009). Adolescents with lower effortful control have lower subjective wellbeing, experience more emotional distress, and are more likely to have family conflicts (Fosco, Caruthers, & Dishion, 2012). In addition, adolescents with reduced self-control are more likely to experience accidents and be involved in a host of delinquent activities (Tremblay, Boulerice, Arseneault, & Niscale, 1995). Some research produced findings that are closely consistent with DeLisi and Vaughn's temperament model. For instance, Yücel and colleagues (2015) studied a cohort of youth from age 12 to 19 and found that negative affectivity and effortful control were associated with significantly greater involvement in risk behaviors including substance use and gambling.

International data sources have produced a common refrain about linkages between temperamental deficits, health risk behaviors, and conduct problems. In the Tracking Adolescents' Individual Lives Survey (TRAILS), which is a prospective cohort study of Dutch adolescents, there is significant evidence that youth with lower self-control face a multitude of health risk behaviors. Compared to adolescents with adequate self-regulation, those with self-control deficits are less likely to regularly eat fruit and vegetables, more likely to skip breakfast, more likely to be physically inactive, more likely to be overweight or obese, more likely to smoke, more likely to use alcohol, and more likely to smoke marijuana (de Winter, Visser, Verhulst, Vollebergh, & Reijneveld, 2016). Drawing on data from the Dunedin Multidisciplinary Health and Development Study, Odgers et al. (2007) found associations between undercontrolled temperament and conduct problems throughout adolescence and into adulthood. What was particularly striking about their study was the medical and mental health burden that the most temperamentally uncontrolled group—life-course-persistent (LCP) offenders—carried. By age 32, LCP offenders suffered from a panoply of conditions including anxiety, major depressive disorder, multiple substance dependence disorders, PTSD, hospitalization, suicide attempt, homelessness, and multiple forms of violence perpetration. The prevalence of these health threats was dramatically higher than others, for instance, LCP offenders were nearly 26 times more likely than controls to attempt suicide, nearly 22 times more likely to be drug dependent, nearly 20 times more likely to be hospitalized for psychiatric impairment, and nearly 10 times more likely to be homeless.

Deficits in effortful control, negative emotionality, and their interaction of course are not limited to adolescence, but are enduring features of an individual's psychological and behavioral constitution (Tubman & Windle, 1995; Windle, 1992). This means that those who struggle to regulate their conduct and emotion will continue to suffer the behavioral and health consequences across adulthood. For example, White and Turner (2014) surveyed a university sample of students about the interrelations between angry rumination, the degree to which a person recurrently focuses on angry mood, effortful control, and various forms of aggression. Angry rumination was positively and effortful control was negatively correlated with both reactive aggression and proactive aggression. They also found that students who experienced greater angry rumination had lower effortful control and were prone to reactive forms of aggression. A study of 1,631 participants selected from the National Survey of Midlife Development in the United States II (MIDUS II) is revealing. Pease and Lewis (2015) examined the personality underpinnings of anger, a quintessential form of negative emotionality. Persons that were higher scoring on neuroticism and lower scoring on conscientiousness had significantly higher trait anger, outward expressions of anger, and aggression. All of these are consistent with externalizing and/or internalizing behaviors during adolescence (also see, Davis, Votruba-Drzal, & Silk, 2015).

Among a sample of university students ages 18 to 25, Burt, Boddy, and Bridgett (2015) reported significant associations between specific temperamental deficits and eating disorder symptoms. The findings were nearly identical to DeLisi and Vaughn's conceptual model. Burt, Boddy, and Bridgett (2015) found that emerging adults with lower effortful control were more likely to exhibit eating disorder symptoms. Negative emotionality was not significantly associated with eating disorders as a main effect; however, the interaction between high negative emotionality and low effortful control was the strongest predictor of eating disorder symptoms. Both temperamental features were also significantly correlated with childhood trauma.

Across developmental stages, effortful control is commonly referred to as self-control or self-regulation. In personality psychology, self-control is a facet of Conscientiousness along with industriousness, order, responsibility, traditionalism, and virtue. Youth with clinical deficits in effortful control will be low scoring on Conscientiousness because they are so low scoring on self-control and likely order and responsibility as well. This has important implications for conduct problems and health behaviors. For example, a study of late adolescents who were university students found that low Conscientiousness was correlated with greater depression, reduced physical activity/exercise, and less sleep in the health domain and worse grades, less school engagement, less favorable views of school, and relationship problems (Tackman, Srivastava, Pfeifer, & Dapretto, 2017).

In a large-scale meta-analysis, Bogg and Roberts (2004) found that Conscientiousness was significantly inversely associated with excessive alcohol use, drug use, unhealthy eating, risky driving, risky sexual behaviors, suicide, tobacco use, and violence including delinquency, criminal justice system involvement, interpersonal aggression, and sexual aggression. A novel feature of Bogg and Roberts' (2004) analysis was that they disaggregated the effects of Conscientiousness on health behaviors by age below or above 30 years. Generally, the effects of low Conscientiousness and by extension low effortful control were more damaging for excessive alcohol use, drug use, unhealthy eating, risky driving, and tobacco use among those persons that were age 30 and under.

Finally, in a landmark study, Moffitt and her colleagues (2011) recently evaluated the predictive validity of childhood self-control on a range of life outcomes during adulthood. The findings were startling. Persons who displayed low self-control during childhood reported a range of difficulties at age 32 years. These included worse physical health, greater depression, higher likelihood of drug dependence, lower socioeconomic status, lower income, greater likelihood of single-parenthood, worse financial planning, more financial struggles, and most importantly for a criminological audience, more criminal convictions. Indeed, 45% of participants with low self-control during childhood had criminal convictions at age 32, a level that is nearly fourfold higher than the prevalence of criminal convictions for persons who had higher childhood self-control.

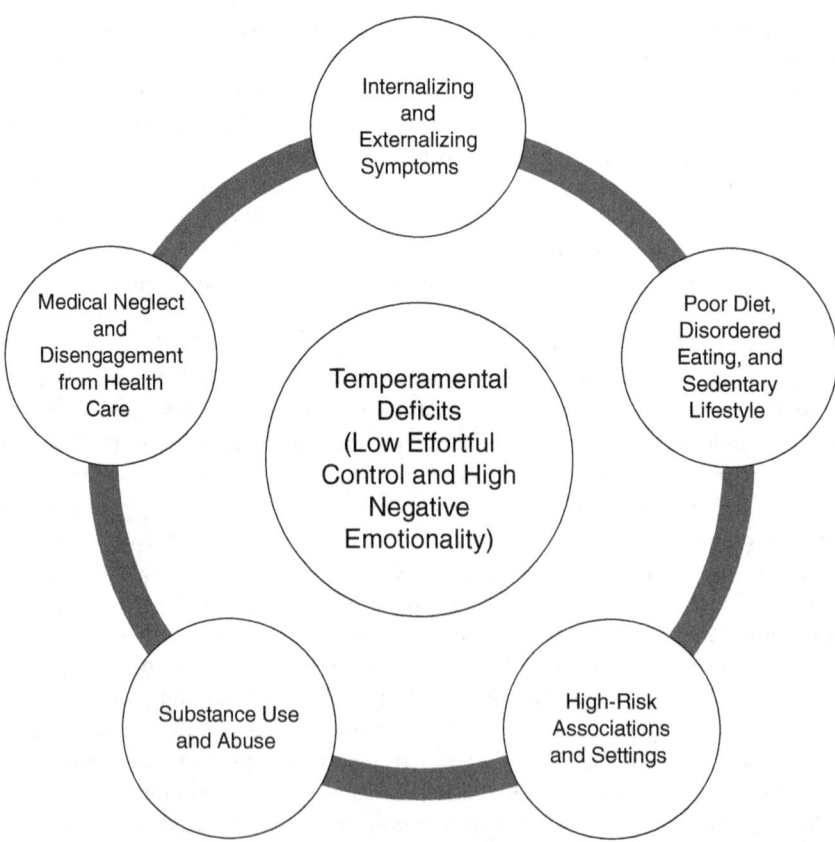

*Figure 5.1* Health consequences of temperamental deficits

A summary representation of the health problems associated with temperamental deficits is shown in Figure 5.1.

## Future Research Directions

In a variety of practitioner, researcher, and clinical roles, the current author has interviewed thousands of criminal offenders and read tens of thousands more criminal histories, delinquency histories, presentence reports, and related criminal justice system records. It is clear that powerful individual-level constructs relating to temperament and personality are consistent drivers of the myriad forms of antisocial conduct these offenders commit from childhood through adulthood. Adolescence is a critical life stage where various early-emerging behavioral tendencies and adverse childhood experiences manifest in serious delinquency and other imprudent behaviors that jeopardize the youth's likelihood of successful school completion and transition to adulthood. Many studies cited in the current chapter attest to this antisocial development. The following comments explore ways that health and health behaviors can be explored to more fully understand the temperament-delinquency nexus.

In juvenile justice settings, youth are often very eager to participate in data collection efforts. One reason why is that having researchers interact with youth in juvenile detention, or residential treatment centers, or confinement facilities breaks up the boredom and monotony of institutional life. But another reason is that seriously delinquent youth are often starving for a prosocial, conventionally-behaved, educated adult to show interest in them. Some offenders have reported to me that they can recall few experiences during their childhood and adolescence that were wholesome, supportive, or positive. Instead, these youth were relentlessly exposed to parental abuse, neglect, and apathy, substance use and other vice, and crime and violence.[5] Many reported parents that themselves had significant behavioral problems and who interacted with them in unpredictable ways (Dannerbeck, 2005). In other words, many serious offenders were effectively reared by low effortful control and negative emotionality, and the result was often similar temperamental and behavioral tendencies in their own life (Dodge, Greenberg, & Malone, 2008; Masten & Cicchetti, 2010; Masten et al., 2005). Such an upbringing produces a range of mental health problems spanning dysthymia, depression, PTSD, and chronic anger that—according to hundreds of offender self-reports—drives substance use and/or a nihilistic rage that drives their criminal offending.

A fruitful avenue for research is to explore the health of delinquent youth in a *holistic* sense. It is clear that temperamental deficits relating to effortful control and negative emotionality are correlated with conduct problems, but we do not understand the ways that temperament drives an offender's sense of personal health and mental health, and, more importantly, how that offender construes their health as a driver or determinant of their problem behaviors. For youth whose negative emotionality and general dysphoria is comprised mostly by sadness, depression, and hopelessness, behaviors such as disordered eating, self-harm, suicidal thoughts and behaviors, and drug experimentation are likely. For youth whose negative emotionality and general dysphoria is comprised mostly by anger, hostility, rage, contempt, and disgust, behaviors such as violent delinquency, violent victimization, and extreme risk taking are likely (see, Vaughn, Salas-Wright, DeLisi, & Larson, 2015). Temperament, particularly DeLisi and Vaughn's model, can help to articulate how specific emotional states and traits manifest in specific forms of adverse behaviors fraught with legal and health consequences.

Researchers should also explore temperament features of negative emotionality beyond anger and hostility. Rothbart (2007) has noted several forms of negative emotionality particularly in young children including frustration, the interruption of ongoing tasks or the blocking of goals, fear, the negative affect associated with the anticipation of distress, discomfort, the negative emotion relating to the sensory qualities of stimulation, light, sound, movement, and texture, sadness, the negative affect and lowered mood and energy related to exposure to object loss, disappointment, and suffering, and soothability, the rate of recovery from peak distress, excitement, or general arousal. Each form of negative affectivity can relate to specific moods that impact behavior, and of course, all of these negative emotions are seen in abundance during the tumultuous adolescent years. For instance, prior research has shown that anger and delinquent peer exposure mediate the linkages between childhood trauma and delinquency (Maschi, Bradley, & Morgen, 2008). Similar work should be done with frustration, fear, sadness, and others.

Health should be studied broadly to also encompass social and financial health. Serious delinquents often have their educational careers interrupted by stays in detention centers, suspensions, expulsions, and transfer to other juvenile justice settings. Whereas some youth complete their GED, many do not and their low educational attainment damages their vocational prospects and their broader development. For example, a study of nearly 20,000 emerging adults selected from the National Survey on Drug Use and Health found that high school dropout was significantly associated with smoking, drug use, diverse forms of crime, and suicide attempts (Maynard, Salas-Wright, & Vaughn, 2015). Indigence and a futile job future are thus intermingled with reduced mental health and health. Here, effortful control is a crucial variable. For instance, consider Moffitt et al.'s (2011, p. 2698, references omitted) concluding assessment,

> Modern history is seeing a marked increase in human longevity, requiring individuals to pay more strategic attention to their health and wealth to avoid disability and poverty in old age. Modern history has also seen marked increases in food availability, sedentary occupations, access to harmful addictive substances, ease of divorce, self-management of retirement savings, and imprisonment of law-breakers. These historical shifts are enhancing the value of individual self-control in modern life, not just for well-being but for survival.

Once one begins reading the literature on temperament and sees the long shadow it casts on behavior, it is difficult to overestimate its importance for understanding conduct problems and delinquency. Effortful control and negative emotionality are useful explanatory constructs for understanding a broad range of delinquent acts, including driving recklessly without wearing a seatbelt, carrying firearms and using them to rob, threaten, or shoot victims, compulsively using narcotics and staying awake for days or weeks before crashing, sleeping for several days only to begin the cycle again, and many others. Dozens of offenders have frankly admitted to the current author that they "should not be alive" given the assorted ways their behavior placed them in harm's way. Those health behaviors, health consequences, and health costs are yet another part of the long shadow of temperament.

## Notes

1 Several other criminological studies (Beaver, Hartman, & Belsky, 2015; Eme, 2018; Mathesius, Lussier, & Corrado, 2017; Waller et al., 2016; Walters, 2014, 2015) have produced research findings on temperament-externalizing behavior linkages that were compatible with but not specific tests of DeLisi and Vaughn's theory.
2 This is especially meaningful in understanding linkages between poor quality nutrition and childhood conduct problems. Using data from the Early Childhood Longitudinal Study, Birth Cohort, Jackson (2016) found that poor quality nutrition during the preschool period was robustly predictive of reduced self-regulation and conduct problems, and these associations were due overwhelmingly to genetic factors (approximately 80% of the variance) and shared environmental factors (also see, Jackson & Newsome, 2016). Similarly, analysis of data from the Fragile Families and Child Wellbeing Study found that both

transient and particularly pervasive household food insecurity were associated with lower self/effortful control and elevated delinquency among youth (Jackson, Newsome, Vaughn, & Johnson, 2018).

3  The associations between child temperament, parenting, and behavior problems are multi-directional. Several studies have shown for instance, that aversive child temperamental features such as negative emotionality, affectivity, or irritability is associated with inconsistent parental discipline, reduced parental acceptance of the child, and child conduct problems, all of which can exacerbate the child's underlying irritability (see, Lengua, 2002, 2006; Lengua & Kovacs, 2005; Moran et al., 2017; Stoltz, Beijers, Smeekens, & Deković, 2017). More generally, there are significant linkages between child temperament and parenting. A meta-analysis of 84 studies including 105 samples and 235 independent effect sizes found that children with more difficult temperaments of which reduced self-regulation and enhanced negative emotion are central are more vulnerable to negative parenting (Slagt, Dubas, Deković, & van Aken, 2016).

4  A repeated finding in criminology is the existence of a small subgroup of persons usually 5–10% of the population that accounts for the majority of antisocial acts and the overwhelming majority of severe violent acts in the population (DeLisi, 2005, 2016; Moffitt, 1993, 2018; Vaughn, DeLisi, Beaver, Perron, & Abdon, 2012; Vaughn, Salas-Wright, DeLisi, & Maynard, 2014; Vaughn et al., 2011; Wolfgang, Figlio, & Sellin, 1972). Although these studies did not focus on temperament per se, the current author suspects strong convergent validity between difficult/adverse temperamental style and serious, violent, and chronic delinquency.

5  The adverse childhood experiences and crime literature makes this developmental profile clear. For a recent overview of that literature, see Baglivio (2018).

## References

Althoff, R. R., Verhulst, F. C., Rettew, D. C., Hudziak, J. J., & Van der Ende, J. (2010). Adult outcomes of childhood dysregulation: A 14-year follow-up study. *Journal of the American Academy of Child & Adolescent Psychiatry*, *49*(11), 1105–1116.

Arikha, N. (2008). *Passions and tempers: A history of the humours.* New York: Harper Perennial.

Ashiabi, G. S., & O'Neal, K. K. (2008). A framework for understanding the association between food insecurity and children's developmental outcomes. *Child Development Perspectives*, *2*(2), 71–77.

Baglivio, M. T. (2018). On cumulative childhood traumatic exposure and violence/aggression: The implications of adverse childhood experiences (ACE). In A. T. Vazsonyi, D. J. Flannery, & M. DeLisi (Eds.), *The Cambridge handbook of violent behavior and aggression* (pp. 467–490). New York, NY: Cambridge University Press.

Baglivio, M. T., Wolff, K. T., DeLisi, M., Vaughn, M. G., & Piquero, A. R. (2016). Effortful control, negative emotionality, and juvenile recidivism: An empirical test of DeLisi and Vaughn's temperament-based theory of antisocial behavior. *The Journal of Forensic Psychiatry & Psychology*, *27*(3), 376–403.

Baglivio, M. T., Wolff, K. T., Piquero, A. R., DeLisi, M., & Vaughn, M. G. (2017). Multiple pathways to juvenile recidivism: Examining parental drug and mental health problems, and markers of neuropsychological deficits among serious juvenile offenders. *Criminal Justice and Behavior*, *44*(8), 1009–1029.

Beaver, K. M., Hartman, S., & Belsky, J. (2015). Differential susceptibility to parental sensitivity based on early-life temperament in the prediction of adolescent affective psychopathic personality traits. *Criminal Justice and Behavior*, *42*(5), 546–565.

Bogg, T., & Roberts, B. W. (2004). Conscientiousness and health-related behaviors: A meta-analysis of the leading behavioral contributors to mortality. *Psychological Bulletin*, *130*(6), 887–919.

Burt, N. M., Boddy, L. E., & Bridgett, D. J. (2015). Contribution of temperament to eating disorder symptoms in emerging adulthood: Additive and interactive effects. *Eating Behaviors*, *18*, 30–35.

Caspi, A., Begg, D., Dickson, N., Harrington, H., Langley, J., Moffitt, T. E., & Silva, P. A. (1997). Personality differences predict health-risk behaviors in young adulthood: Evidence from a longitudinal study. *Journal of Personality and Social Psychology*, *73*(5), 1052.

Caspi, A., Begg, D., Dickson, N., Langley, J., Moffitt, T. E., McGEE, R. O. B., & Silva, P. A. (1995a). Identification of personality types at risk for poor health and injury in late adolescence. *Criminal Behaviour and Mental Health*, *5*(4), 330–350.

Caspi, A., Henry, B., McGee, R. O., Moffitt, T. E., & Silva, P. A. (1995b). Temperamental origins of child and adolescent behavior problems: From age three to age fifteen. *Child Development*, *66*(1), 55–68.

Caspi, A., Moffitt, T. E., Newman, D. L., & Silva, P. A. (1996). Behavioral observations at age 3 years predict adult psychiatric disorders: Longitudinal evidence from a birth cohort. *Archives of General Psychiatry*, *53*, 1033–1039.

Checa, P., & Abundis-Gutierrez, A. (2017). Parenting and temperament influence on school success in 9–13 year olds. *Frontiers in Psychology, 8*, 543.

Cicchetti, D., & Toth, S. L. (1995). A developmental psychopathology perspective on child abuse and neglect. *Journal of the American Academy of Child & Adolescent Psychiatry, 34*(5), 541–565.

Clark, D. A., Donnellan, M. B., Robins, R. W., & Conger, R. D. (2015). Early adolescent temperament, parental monitoring, and substance use in Mexican-origin adolescents. *Journal of Adolescence, 41*, 121–130.

Crockett, L. J., Wasserman, A. M., Rudasill, K. M., Hoffman, L., & Kalutskaya, I. (2017). Temperamental anger and effortful control, teacher–child conflict, and externalizing behavior across the elementary school years. *Child Development*, in press.

Dannerbeck, A. M. (2005). Differences in parenting attributes, experiences, and behaviors of delinquent youth with and without a parental history of incarceration. *Youth Violence and Juvenile Justice, 3*(3), 199–213.

Davis, S., Votruba-Drzal, E., & Silk, J. S. (2015). Trajectories of internalizing symptoms from early childhood to adolescence: Associations with temperament and parenting. *Social Development, 24*(3), 501–520.

de Winter, A. F., Visser, L., Verhulst, F. C., Vollebergh, W. A., & Reijneveld, S. A. (2016). Longitudinal patterns and predictors of multiple health risk behaviors among adolescents: The TRAILS study. *Preventive Medicine, 84*, 76–82.

DeLisi, M. (2005). *Career criminals in society*. Thousand Oaks, CA: Sage.

DeLisi, M. (2016). Career criminals and the antisocial life course. *Child Development Perspectives, 10*(1), 53–58.

DeLisi, M., Fox, B. H., Fully, M., & Vaughn, M. G. (2018). The effects of temperament, psychopathy, and childhood trauma among delinquent youth: A test of DeLisi and Vaughn's temperament-based theory of crime. *International Journal of Law and Psychiatry, 57*, 53–60.

DeLisi, M., Trulson, C. R., Marquart, J. W., Drury, A. J., & Kosloski, A. E. (2011). Inside the prison black box: Toward a life course importation model of inmate behavior. *International Journal of Offender Therapy and Comparative Criminology, 55*(8), 1186–1207.

DeLisi, M., & Vaughn, M. G. (2011). The importance of neuropsychological deficits relating to self-control and temperament to the prevention of serious antisocial behavior. *International Journal of Child, Youth and Family Studies, 2*(1/2), 12–35.

DeLisi, M., & Vaughn, M. G. (2014). Foundation for a temperament-based theory of antisocial behavior and criminal justice system involvement. *Journal of Criminal Justice, 42*(1), 10–25.

DeLisi, M., & Vaughn, M. G. (2015). Ingredients for criminality require genes, temperament, and psychopathic personality. *Journal of Criminal Justice, 43*(4), 290–294.

DeLisi, M., & Vaughn, M. G. (2016). Presaging problem behavior: The mutuality of child temperament, parenting, and family environments from gestation to age three. In K. M. Beaver & A. Walsh (Eds.), *The ashgate research companion to biosocial theories of crime* (pp. 291–304). Burlington, VT: Ashgate Publishing Company.

Dodge, K. A., Greenberg, M. T., Malone, P. S., & Conduct Problems Prevention Research Group. (2008). Testing an idealized dynamic cascade model of the development of serious violence in adolescence. *Child Development, 79*(6), 1907–1927.

Dunn, M. G., Tarter, R. E., Mezzich, A. C., Vanyukov, M., Kirisci, L., & Kirillova, G. (2002). Origins and consequences of child neglect in substance abuse families. *Clinical Psychology Review, 22*(7), 1063–1090.

Eme, R. (2018). Sex differences in temperament: A partial explanation for the sex difference in the prevalence of serious antisocial behaviors. *Aggression and Violent Behavior*, in press.

Fanti, K. A., & Henrich, C. C. (2010). Trajectories of pure and co-occurring internalizing and externalizing problems from age 2 to age 12: Findings from the National Institute of Child Health and Human Development Study of Early Child Care. *Developmental Psychology, 46*(5), 1159–1175.

Fosco, G. M., Caruthers, A. S., & Dishion, T. J. (2012). A six-year predictive test of adolescent family relationship quality and effortful control pathways to emerging adult social and emotional health. *Journal of Family Psychology, 26*(4), 565–579.

Garofalo, C., & Velotti, P. (2017). Negative emotionality and aggression in violent offenders: The moderating role of emotion dysregulation. *Journal of Criminal Justice, 51*, 9–16.

Hawkins, J. D., Catalano, R. F., & Miller, J. Y. (1992). Risk and protective factors for alcohol and other drug problems in adolescence and early adulthood: Implications for substance abuse prevention. *Psychological Bulletin, 112*(1), 64–105.

Jackson, D. B. (2016). The link between poor quality nutrition and childhood antisocial behavior: A genetically informative analysis. *Journal of Criminal Justice, 44*, 13–20.

Jackson, D. B., & Newsome, J. (2016). The link between infant neuropsychological risk and childhood antisocial behavior among males: The moderating role of neonatal health risk. *Journal of Criminal Justice, 47*, 32–40.

Jackson, D. B., Newsome, J., Vaughn, M. G., & Johnson, K. R. (2018). Considering the role of food insecurity in low self-control and early delinquency. *Journal of Criminal Justice, 56*, 127–139.

Kagan, J. (1998). *Galen's prophecy: Temperament in human nature.* Boulder, CO: Westview.

Kagan, J. (2010). *The temperamental thread: How genes, culture, time, and luck make us who we are.* New York: Dana Press.

Lengua, L. J. (2002). The contribution of emotionality and self-regulation to the understanding of children's response to multiple risk. *Child Development, 73*(1), 144–161.

Lengua, L. J. (2006). Growth in temperament and parenting as predictors of adjustment during children's transition to adolescence. *Developmental Psychology, 42*(5), 819.

Lengua, L. J., & Kovacs, E. A. (2005). Bidirectional associations between temperament and parenting and the prediction of adjustment problems in middle childhood. *Journal of Applied Developmental Psychology, 26*(1), 21–38.

Lorber, M. F., Del Vecchio, T., & Slep, A. M. S. (2015). The emergence and evolution of infant externalizing behavior. *Development and Psychopathology, 27*(3), 663–680.

Lorber, M. F., & Egeland, B. (2011). Parenting and infant difficulty: Testing a mutual exacerbation hypothesis to predict early onset conduct problems. *Child Development, 82*(6), 2006–2020.

Maschi, T., Bradley, C. A., & Morgen, K. (2008). Unraveling the link between trauma and delinquency: The mediating role of negative affect and delinquent peer exposure. *Youth Violence and Juvenile Justice, 6*(2), 136–157.

Masten, A. S., & Cicchetti, D. (2010). Developmental cascades. *Development and Psychopathology, 22*(3), 491–495.

Masten, A. S., Roisman, G. I., Long, J. D., Burt, K. B., Obradović, J., Riley, J. R., ... & Tellegen, A. (2005). Developmental cascades: Linking academic achievement and externalizing and internalizing symptoms over 20 years. *Developmental Psychology, 41*(5), 733.

Mathesius, J., Lussier, P., & Corrado, R. (2017). Child and adolescent disposition model: An examination of the temperament factor structure within early childhood. *International Journal of Offender Therapy and Comparative Criminology, 61*(13), 1500–1526.

Maynard, B. R., Salas-Wright, C. P., & Vaughn, M. G. (2015). High school dropouts in emerging adulthood: Substance use, mental health problems, and crime. *Community Mental Health Journal, 51*(3), 289–299.

Moffitt, T. E. (1993). Adolescence-limited and life-course-persistent antisocial behavior: A developmental taxonomy. *Psychological Review, 100*(4), 674–701.

Moffitt, T. E. (2018). Male antisocial behaviour in adolescence and beyond. *Nature Human Behaviour, 1*, in press.

Moffitt, T. E., Arseneault, L., Belsky, D., Dickson, N., Hancox, R. J., Harrington, H., ... & Caspi, A. (2011). A gradient of childhood self-control predicts health, wealth, and public safety. *Proceedings of the National Academy of Sciences of the United States of America, 108*(7), 2693–2698.

Moran, L., Lengua, L. J., Zalewski, M., Ruberry, E., Klein, M., Thompson, S., & Kiff, C. (2017). Variable- and person-centered approaches to examining temperament vulnerability and resilience to the effects of contextual risk. *Journal of Research in Personality, 67*, 61–74.

Morizot, J. (2015). The contribution of temperament and personality traits to criminal and antisocial behavior development and desistance. In J. Morizot & L. Kazemian (Eds.), *The development of criminal and antisocial behavior* (pp. 137–165). New York, NY: Springer.

Odgers, C. L., Caspi, A., Broadbent, J. M., Dickson, N., Hancox, R. J., Harrington, H., ... & Moffitt, T. E. (2007). Prediction of differential adult health burden by conduct problem subtypes in males. *Archives of General Psychiatry, 64*(4), 476–484.

Pease, C. R., & Lewis, G. J. (2015). Personality links to anger: Evidence for trait interaction and differentiation across expression style. *Personality and Individual Differences, 74*, 159–164.

Rodriguez, C. M., Tucker, M. C., & Palmer, K. (2016). Emotion regulation in relation to emerging adults' mental health and delinquency: A multi-informant approach. *Journal of Child and Family Studies, 25*(6), 1916–1925.

Rothbart, M. K. (1989). Temperament and development. In G. A. Kohnstamm, J. E. Bates, & M. K. Rothbart (Eds.), *Temperament in childhood* (pp. 187–247). Chichester, England: John Wiley and Sons.

Rothbart, M. K. (2007). Temperament, development, and personality. *Current Directions in Psychological Science, 16*, 207–212.

Rueda, M. R. (2012). Effortful control. In M. Zentner & R. L. Shiner (Eds.), *Handbook of temperament* (pp. 145–167). New York: The Guilford Press.

Runions, K. C., & Keating, D. P. (2010). Anger and inhibitory control as moderators of children's hostile attributions and aggression. *Journal of Applied Developmental Psychology, 31*, 370–378.

Schwartz, C. E., Snidman, N., & Kagan, J. (1996). Early childhood temperament as a determinant of externalizing behavior in adolescence. *Development and Psychopathology, 8*(3), 527–537.

Slagt, M., Dubas, J. S., Deković, M., & van Aken, M. A. (2016). Differences in sensitivity to parenting depending on child temperament: A meta-analysis. *Psychological Bulletin, 142*(10), 1068–1110.

Stevenson, J., & Goodman, R. (2001). Association between behaviour at age 3 years and adult criminality. *The British Journal of Psychiatry, 179*(3), 197–202.

Stoltz, S., Beijers, R., Smeekens, S., & Deković, M. (2017). Diathesis stress or differential susceptibility? Testing longitudinal associations between parenting, temperament, and children's problem behavior. *Social Development, 26*(4), 783–796.

Stringaris, A., Cohen, P., Pine, D., & Leibenluft, E. (2009). Adult outcomes of youth irritability: A 20-year prospective community-based study. *American Journal of Psychiatry, 166*(9), 1048–1054.

Tackman, A. M., Srivastava, S., Pfeifer, J. H., & Dapretto, M. (2017). Development of conscientiousness in childhood and adolescence: Typical trajectories and associations with academic, health, and relationship changes. *Journal of Research in Personality, 67*, 85–96.

Tremblay, R. E., Boulerice, B., Arseneault, L., & Niscale, M. T. (1995). Does low self-control during childhood explain the association between delinquency and accidents in early adolescence? *Criminal Behaviour and Mental Health, 5*(4), 439–451.

Trulson, C. R., Haerle, D. R., Caudill, J. W., & DeLisi, M. (2016). *Lost causes: Blended sentencing, second chances, and the texas youth commission.* Austin, TX: University of Texas Press.

Tubman, J. G., & Windle, M. (1995). Continuity of difficult temperament in adolescence: Relations with depression, life events, family support, and substance use across a one-year period. *Journal of Youth and Adolescence, 24*(2), 133–153.

Vaughn, M. G., DeLisi, M., Beaver, K. M., Perron, B. E., & Abdon, A. (2012). Toward a criminal justice epidemiology: Behavioral and physical health of probationers and parolees in the United States. *Journal of Criminal Justice, 40*(3), 165–173.

Vaughn, M. G., DeLisi, M., Gunter, T., Fu, Q., Beaver, K. M., Perron, B. E., & Howard, M. O. (2011). The severe 5%: A latent class analysis of the externalizing behavior spectrum in the United States. *Journal of Criminal Justice, 39*(1), 75–80.

Vaughn, M. G., Salas-Wright, C. P., DeLisi, M., & Larson, M. (2015). Deliberate self-harm and the nexus of violence, victimization, and mental health problems in the United States. *Psychiatry Research, 225*(3), 588–595.

Vaughn, M. G., Salas-Wright, C. P., DeLisi, M., & Maynard, B. R. (2014). Violence and externalizing behavior among youth in the United States: Is there a severe 5%? *Youth Violence and Juvenile Justice, 12*(1), 3–21.

Veeh, C. A., Renn, T., Vaughn, M. G., & DeLisi, M. (2018). Traumatic brain injury, temperament, and violence in incarcerated youth: A mediation analysis based on DeLisi and Vaughn's theory of temperament and antisocial behavior. *Psychology, Crime & Law, 24*(10), 1016–1029.

Waller, R., Trentacosta, C. J., Shaw, D. S., Neiderhiser, J. M., Ganiban, J. M., Reiss, D., ... & Hyde, L. W. (2016). Heritable temperament pathways to early callous–unemotional behaviour. *The British Journal of Psychiatry, 209*(6), 475–482.

Walters, G. D. (2014). Pathways to early delinquency: Exploring the individual and collective contributions of difficult temperament, low maternal involvement, and externalizing behavior. *Journal of Criminal Justice, 42*(4), 321–326.

Walters, G. D. (2015). Early childhood temperament, maternal monitoring, reactive criminal thinking, and the origin (s) of low self-control. *Journal of Criminal Justice, 43*(5), 369–376.

Wang, F. L., Chassin, L., Eisenberg, N., & Spinrad, T. L. (2015). Effortful control predicts adolescent antisocial-aggressive behaviors and depressive symptoms: Co-occurrence and moderation by impulsivity. *Child Development, 86*(6), 1812–1829.

Wertz, J., Zavos, H., Matthews, T., Gray, R., Best-Lane, J., Pariante, C. M., Moffitt, T. E., & Arseneault, L. (2016). Etiology of pervasive versus situational antisocial behaviors: A multi-informant longitudinal cohort study. *Child Development, 87*(1), 312–325.

White, B. A., & Turner, K. A. (2014). Anger rumination and effortful control: Mediation effects on reactive but not proactive aggression. *Personality and Individual Differences, 56*, 186–189.

Windle, M. (1991). The difficult temperament in adolescence: Associations with substance use, family support, and problem behaviors. *Journal of Clinical Psychology, 47*(2), 310–315.

Windle, M. (1992). Temperament and social support in adolescence: Interrelations with depressive symptoms and delinquent behaviors. *Journal of Youth and Adolescence, 21*(1), 1–21.

Wolff, K. T., Baglivio, M. T., Piquero, A. R., Vaughn, M. G., & DeLisi, M. (2016). The triple crown of antisocial behavior: Effortful control, negative emotionality, and community disadvantage. *Youth Violence and Juvenile Justice, 14*(4), 350–366.

Wolfgang, M. E., Figlio, R. M., & Sellin, T. (1972). *Delinquency in a birth cohort*. Chicago, IL: University of Chicago Press.

Yücel, M., Whittle, S., Youssef, G. J., Kashyap, H., Simmons, J. G., Schwartz, O., ... & Allen, N. B. (2015). The influence of sex, temperament, risk-taking and mental health on the emergence of gambling: A longitudinal study of young people. *International Gambling Studies, 15*(1), 108–123.

# 6
# THE STRESS MECHANISMS OF ADOLESCENT PHYSICAL, MENTAL, AND BEHAVIORAL HEALTH

*Lisa A. Kort-Butler*

The experience of stress has implications for physical, mental, and behavioral health among adolescents. Research points to shared antecedents and common etiologies of these problems, as well as models that suggest one set of problems may precipitate the others (Hagan & Foster, 2003; Lee & Stone, 2012; Wade & Pevalin, 2005). Adolescence is often viewed as a period of storm-and-stress, but those experiences are a product of the cultural and social conditions in which adolescents live (Arnett, 1999). The stress paradigm posits a system of relationships among social structures, stressors, social and personal resources, and health outcomes (Aneshensel & Mitchell, 2014). The roots of and risks related to adolescents' physical, mental, and behavioral health needs are complex, but the stress paradigm offers a framework for understanding how life problems and the means to cope with them affect adolescents' ability to resist illnesses and to self-regulate behaviors.

This chapter reviews the theoretical underpinnings of the stress paradigm, drawing primarily on the stress process model, developed to understand the stress–health/mental health link (Pearlin, 1989), and general strain theory, developed to understand the stress–criminality link (Agnew, 1992). To begin, I highlight the biological forces and social realities surrounding the adolescent stress experience. Then, I describe the stress paradigm model dovetailing the stress process model and general strain theory. This is followed with a discussion of the nature of stressors and key domains of stress during adolescence, as well as the mechanisms by which stress impacts adolescents' health and well-being. Finally, I conclude the chapter with the implications of the stress paradigm for future research and policy.

## Biological Forces, Social Realities

Stress, at its most basic, is a physiological response. Stressors – also referred to as strains – are challenging events, demanding situations, or roadblocks to or absence of the means to pursue goals, which ignite a stress response (Aneshensel & Mitchell, 2014). Stressors activate processes along the hypothalamic-pituitary-adrenocortical (HPA) axis, designed to maintain increased energy and vigilance to deal with the threat posed by stressors (Lucas-Thompson et al., 2017). This promotes short-term adaptation – allostasis. If the situation is remedied or the person can cope, then readiness subsides. If not, however, then the physiological reaction may not subside, contributing to a dysregulation of allostasis. As stressors persist or accumulate, the person lives with an elevated allostatic load. This state compromises the body's neuroendocrine, immune, metabolic, and cardiovascular functioning, as well as stress resiliency, ultimately contributing to a range of negative health outcomes (Juster et al., 2010; McEwen & Gianaros, 2010).

Research confirms that the adolescent brain is still developing, with the limbic structures that drive the seeking of rewards, risks, and novel experiences outpacing the prefrontal control structures that regulate decision-making, emotional reactivity, and effective coping (Casey et al., 2011). Adolescents are capable of making rational decisions and understanding the risks associated with choices, but under stressful or emotionally charged situations the more developed limbic system takes control. These features of brain development shape how adolescents appraise and respond to stressors (McEwen & Gianaros, 2010). Moreover, stressful experiences influence the structure of the developing adolescent brain, adding to the complex mechanisms linking stress and well-being.

Yet adolescents are more than the sum of their biological responses. The experience of stress is deeply personal while embedded in social context, a consequence of social organization and an individual's location within it (Sigfusdottir et al., 2016). Importantly, stressful experiences are one way social structure is linked to well-being (Pearlin, 1999). Social conditions, structures of inequality, and socialization experiences shape the nature of stressors people confront, their assessment of those stressors, the resources they have available to cope with stressors, and their ability to deploy those resources in a way that successfully manages stress. Moreover, one's stage in the life course has particular importance in shaping the stressors one encounters and the range and effectiveness of coping responses.

Adolescence, while a period of biological and cognitive development, is also socially defined (Gore & Colten, 1991). It is a period in which young people begin to try out adult statuses, rehearse culturally appropriate role definitions, and solidify identities (Hagan & Foster, 2003). There are stressors unique to adolescence: adult expectations and family relationships, school pressures, peer relationships (e.g., dating, bullying), and higher risk for victimization. Differences in cognitive, emotional, and social development affect what adolescents see as stressful, the resources they can draw together to manage stress, and how they respond to perceived problems (Seiffge-Krenke et al., 2009). Learning to cope with stress effectively is among all the other developmental goals of adolescence.

## The Stress Paradigm

Both the stress process model (Pearlin, 1989, 1999) and general strain theory (Agnew, 1992, 2006) predict that the occurrence of stressful experiences can activate sequences that result in problems like poor health, poor mental health, and delinquency. The *stress process model* suggests that stressful experiences tax the individual's ability to adapt, putting pressure on the body or mind. The lack of personal and social resources detracts from healthy adaptation, and the inability to adapt threatens well-being. The connection between stress and adolescent physical and mental health has generally been supported (Compas et al., 2012; Low et al., 2012; Wickrama et al., 2015).

*General strain theory* explicates how negative emotional arousal generated by stressful experiences may be externalized into aggressive actions, substance use, or illicit behavior. Negative emotions – fear, depression, frustration, anger – create pressure for corrective action. People may use legal or illegal means to address these strains and alleviate the feelings they engender. Anger in particular is implicated in crime, while depression is implicated in substance use (Jang & Johnson, 2003). The likelihood that people turn to illegitimate actions is based on social psychological protective factors and criminal propensity. The connection between strain and delinquent outcomes has generally been supported (Moon et al., 2009; Sigfusdottir et al., 2012).

Both perspectives hinge on a variety of mechanisms connecting stressors and health-related outcomes, detailed below. The core process described by these theories is depicted in Figure 6.1 (see also Agnew, 2006; Aneshensel & Mitchell, 2014; Wheaton, 2010). Social conditions and structured inequalities shape the context in which the process unfolds, holding both distal and direct effects. When stressors occur, they are appraised. Subjective appraisal forms the basis of the individual's physiological and emotional arousal. Stressors can also have direct effects on physiological arousal and well-being, particularly in moments when appraisal or other elements of the process are overwhelmed (e.g., extreme or sudden trauma).

Personal and social resources, including coping style, self-esteem and mastery, and social support, influence stress appraisal and adaptation to stressors. Physiological and psychological responses to stressors, as well as behavioral responses (e.g., lashing out, self-medicating) may ultimately lead to disease, mental illness, and delinquency. Personal and social resources serve mediating functions, in which stressors activate or suppress coping responses, or even deplete resources, impacting well-being. They also act as moderating or buffering constructs, which may prevent, hinder, or advance healthy adaptations to stress. People with higher levels of these resources have a wider repertoire with which they can manage stress and are therefore more protected from its damaging effects.

Stressors act in an indeterminate manner, such that their impact is not limited to a single disease or disorder but may be manifested across a spectrum of physical and mental health outcomes (Aneshensel & Mitchell, 2014). General strain theory points to a variety of behavioral outcomes that can also be impacted by stressors: aggressive acts, instrumental acts (e.g., theft), and escapist acts (e.g., drug use, running away) (DeCoster & Kort-Butler, 2006). The harmful effects of exposure to stressors and vulnerability to stressful experiences are not inherent to a particular stressor or category of stressors; rather, problems result from an interaction with attributes and resources of the individual and their social circumstances. It is this continuum of outcomes that make the stress paradigm useful for understanding adolescent health and delinquency. To detect possible differences in the ways in which social groups manifest problems with well-being, and to observe the range and specificity of outcomes that strain might generate, it is necessary to bring together information about different outcomes.

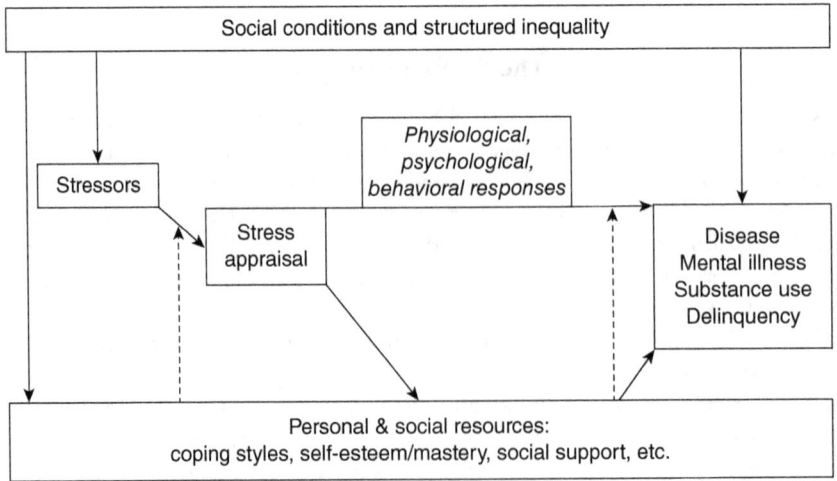

*Figure 6.1* Stress paradigm model
Note: Solid lines represent direct/mediating effects. Dashed lines represent moderating effects.

## Social Stressors

The universe of stressors can be placed along continuums of duration (discrete to chronic), severity, life course stage, and level of social context. Identifying separate types of stressors allows us to distinguish between the problems of identity threat and identity adjustment (e.g., life events) and the problems of continual vigilance and pressure (e.g., chronic stressors) (Wheaton et al., 2013, p. 304). Considering the level of context frames the range of stress exposure in a population, recognizing the several environments in which people are immediately embedded – families, schools, community groups – which themselves are bounded by neighborhoods or cities. Events happening at these mid-range levels may also be experienced as stressful, just as larger scale social stressors may have cascading effects on midrange situations and even interpersonal relationships. Taking context into account also clarifies the distinction not only among personally experienced stressors, but also witnessed, vicarious, and anticipated stressors (Agnew, 2002). The universe of stressors cannot be fully understood apart from social context, illustrating how stressful experiences overlap, intertwine, and proliferate in the lives of young people (Sigfusdottir et al., 2016).

### *Key Stress Domains for Adolescents*

For adolescents, family, school, and peer groups are key stress domains (DeCoster & Kort-Butler, 2006; Wade et al., 2014). *Families* may be the source of arguments and conflicts with parents or siblings, as well as a range of adverse experiences, such as economic hardship, abuse and neglect, domestic violence, divorce, parental incarceration, parental mental illness or substance use (Balistreri & Alvira-Hammond, 2016). Because *school* and school-related activities figure prominently in the lives of adolescents, problems at school, such as conflict with teachers, struggles with academic work, troubles with or exclusion from extracurricular activities, as well as a deleterious school environment, are unique sources of adolescent strain. *Peer relationships*, which adolescents are learning to navigate on their own, may be particularly meaningful, including peer pressures, arguments with friends, break-ups, social exclusion and rejection, dating violence, and bullying.

Normative changes and developmental tasks weave through these domains: concerns about body, identity, and fitting in; gaining independence; establishing and navigating romances; expectations and concerns about future educational and occupations goals (Knight et al., 2017; Seiffge-Krenke et al., 2009). Experiences of trauma and victimization, both experienced and witnessed, may be located within a specific domain but have cross-cutting and potentially long-lasting effects (Bouffard & Koeppel, 2014). Experiences of discrimination and stigma also have cross-cutting effects, especially as adolescents begin to confront these experiences on their own (DeCoster & Thompson, 2017). Neighborhoods themselves may be sources of strain (e.g., environmental hazards; social disadvantages) and frame the likelihood of encountering trauma and discrimination (Warner & Settersten, 2017). They also create de facto boundaries for families, schools, and peer relationships, shaping the strains experienced in those domains and the resources available to cope with strain.

### *Stress Proliferation*

Identifying different categories of stressors is helpful when thinking about the range of troubles adolescents might face, and how together they contribute to cumulative stress burden or accumulated strain (Thoits, 2010). Such distinctions are empirically and theoretically useful, but people's lived experiences are rarely so neatly categorized (Carr & Umberson, 2013). The concept of stress proliferation – the idea that stressors beget other stressors – recognizes that a stressful condition may disrupt or alter people's established roles and routines, and may also lead to stressors beyond the life domain in which it occurred (Pearlin et al., 2005). An acute problem – a sudden trauma, a negative life event – can have cascading consequences that become chronic in nature.

Proliferation may arise along two pathways. One, new stressors within a life domain may arise from an expansion of primary stressors (Pearlin et al., 2005). For example, parental separation may lead to an adolescent taking on new and stressful family responsibilities, such as caring for siblings and more household chores. Two, primary stressors in one domain may spillover, creating secondary stressors in another domain (DeCoster & Kort-Butler, 2006). For example, parental conflict may affect an adolescent's school performance.

Along both pathways, coping efforts must be directed at the original problem, trying to contain any spillover, and then dealing with the new stressors. These secondary stressors may become the more proximate causes of negative outcomes. As stressors accumulate and proliferate, or even become routine, newly arising conditions or events that are objectively minor may have greater potential to undermine health or promote risky behaviors (Botchkovar & Broidy, 2013). For example, Ferro and Boyle (2015) found in families of children with chronic illness, that stressor increased maternal and family stress, depleting the child's self-esteem, and increasing their risk for anxiety and depression. The proliferation process also clarifies how adverse early life circumstances are connected to stressors in adolescence and beyond, tying these early experiences to later well-being (Slocum, 2010).

## *Stress Appraisal*

Objective and subjective experiences of strain only partially overlap (Agnew, 2013). Objective stressors "set the stage" for the sorts of experiences that may be subjectively appraised as stressful. Experiences may be appraised as challenges when a person feels they have enough resources to cope with demands, or as threats when demands exceed resources (Yeager et al., 2016). Both activate physiological responses, although threat appraisals yield more prolonged reactions and allostasic dysregulation, potentially damaging long-term health and cognitive processes. Likewise, subjective perceptions of strain may prime delinquent outcomes (Froggio & Agnew, 2007). Strains perceived as unjust or of high magnitude or severity provoke emotional responses like anger. Strains of this nature may seem, from a subjective point of view, to overwhelm legitimate coping resources, reduce the perceived costs of illegitimate coping, and promote criminal or risky behaviors.

An adolescent's evaluation of their own skill set, capacities, and access to meaningful resources are fundamental to assessing an event (Seiffge-Krenke et al., 2009). A range of factors may influence the subjective evaluation of objective stressful experiences: individual factors (e.g., personality traits, personal goals and values, role-associated identities, self-esteem); social factors (e.g., social support; peer networks); life circumstances and environmental factors (e.g., family poverty, access to care); and prior attempts at coping with stressful experiences (Froggio & Agnew, 2007). McLeod (2012) emphasizes that people's interpretations of objective life experiences depend on their social location and broader, cultural ideologies. Meaning is negotiated in social context: families, friends, informal and formal groups, schools, communities. People's interpretation of stressors are likely evaluated by others, who help shape the appraisal process. Even in absence of direct interaction, people may compare their own evaluations against the imagined evaluations of others. The social context in which a stressful experience occurs and the appraisal of a stressful situation affect later responses.

## Mechanisms of the Stress Paradigm: Key Personal and Social Resources

Both the stress process model and general strain theory highlight the importance of social psychological and interpersonal resources in shaping the process by which stress affects well-being.

These resources include (but are not limited to) coping styles; self-esteem, mastery, and self-efficacy; and social support. As Figure 6.1 depicts, resources, like stressors, are tied to social structure and context, as well as socialization experiences. Thus, individuals vary in the extent to which they bring resources to bear on stressful situations. Because coping also varies developmentally, resources adolescents use to manage stress and their effectiveness may vary, with consequences for well-being.

Resources, although conceptually distinct, tend to be correlated. For example, adolescents with positive self-esteem are also likely to have higher levels of mastery and social support, just as social support buoys a strong sense of self (Cornwell, 2003; Kort-Butler, 2010). Consequently, people with higher combined levels of resources may be more resilient to the negative effects of stress. More is not always better, as not all resources have the same capacity to protect against strain (Sealock & Manasse, 2012). Resources may be more effective in they match-up to the strain domain, e.g., social support from teachers may be especially beneficial for school-related stressors (DeCoster & Kort-Butler, 2006). Effective coping may also require drawing on a combination of resources from different domains (Foster & Brooks-Gunn, 2009).

The mechanisms by which resources steer the stress process are multifaceted. They may influence how an individual appraises a stressor in the first place, how an individual experiences and responds to the stressor, and ultimately if/how the stressor undermines health and well-being. Stress researchers refer to processes of mediation and moderation (Aneshensel & Mitchell, 2014). The key is the availability of these resources to the individual to assist in interpreting and managing the experience of stress (i.e., appraisal and mediation, respectively), and/or their ability to buffer the deleterious effects of stressors on well-being (i.e., moderation). Over time, particularly in conditions of chronic stress, resources may become substantially weakened, as people repeatedly draw on them.

As *mediators*, resources provide an indirect link between stressful experiences and health outcomes. Resources may be involved in suppressing relationships, in which stressors lead people to "activate" resources, limiting the overall effect of stress on well-being (Wheaton et al., 2013). Resources may also operate in intervening relationships in which stressors deplete resources, resulting in a net negative effect on well-being. Mediating resources are tied to both the stressors that stimulate them and to health outcomes, explaining how stressors operate to undermine health. As *moderators*, resources may act as buffers between a stressful experience and deleterious outcomes, typically modeled as an interaction term. Those with low levels of resources are left more vulnerable to stress, whereas those with high levels of resources are shielded from the potentially damaging effects. Compared to mediators in the stress process model, moderators do not directly link stress and health per se; instead, they influence the impact of the stressor on the outcome (Pearlin & Bierman, 2013).

## *Coping Styles and Strategies*

Coping can broadly be defined as the efforts that people take on their own behalf in an attempt to avoid or lessen the impact of stress and its consequences (Pearlin, 1999). Coping styles are habitual preferences for dealing with problems, which are employed across different stressful situations (Thoits, 1995). Although adults may have habitual coping preferences, it is important to remember adolescents are still developing these preferences. There are several ways to categorize coping styles among adolescents; they share three broad themes (Compas et al., 2012; Seiffge-Krenke, 2000). An *active or approach-oriented coping style* entails actions to alter the stressor or being proactive in managing one's emotional reaction to stressor (e.g., seeking support, discussing the problem, acquiring information and material resources). An *internal or cognitive coping style* entails efforts to adapt to the stressor with cognitive reappraisal, or thinking over the problem and considering courses of action. An *avoidant coping style* entails attempts to physically or cognitively "get away" from a stressor or one's emotional response to it (e.g., withdrawal, distraction, denial).

Coping styles may influence stress appraisal and also act as moderating mechanisms that cushion (or amplify) the effect of the stressors on outcomes. Coping strategies, drawn from an individual's coping style, are behavioral and/or cognitive tactics to manage specific situational demands that are appraised as stressful (Carr & Umberson, 2013; Seiffge-Krenke et al., 2009). As mediators in the stress process, coping strategies may function to: change the situation from which stressors arise; manage the meaning of the situation in a way that reduces its threat; keep the symptoms of stress manageable; or inhibit the emergence of secondary stressors (Pearlin, 1999). Across adolescence there is typically an increase in the use of problem-solving strategies and a decline in avoidance strategies (Amirkhan & Auyeung, 2007). As adolescents try out different strategies, they may apply them inconsistently or inefficaciously (Zimmer-Gembeck & Skinner, 2011).

The relationship between coping styles and outcomes of the stress process is complex (Kort-Butler, 2009). An avoidant style may be beneficial in the short term, but inhibits problem-focused strategies, undermines a sense of control, thereby failing to buffer or even amplifying the impact of stress on physical and mental health. An active coping style facilitates problem-solving and a sense of control, buffering the negative effects of stress and promoting health. When it comes to behavioral health, however, an avoidant style may inhibit someone from acting out aggressively against the source of the stress; an attempt to ignore a situation may also promote a retreat to substance use. An active style may promote problem-solving, but conduct problems could ensue if such strategies are not tempered by restraint. Thus, active coping is generally most beneficial to well-being, but there may be conditions under which it is not and conditions under which avoidant coping is protective.

Matching strategy to stressor is also relevant. Active coping is associated with healthy functioning in the context of controllable stressors (i.e., the degree to which objective conditions of a stressor can be eliminated by resources or actions), but negatively associated with health when activated to manage uncontrollable stressors (Clarke, 2006). Internal/cognitive coping, in these circumstances, may be protective (Carr & Umberson, 2013). Under conditions of chronic stress, however, even effective situational strategies may dwindle over time, becoming less helpful. Maladaptive coping styles may arise as a way of "getting by" or surviving, but they may have long-term negative consequences for well-being.

## *Self-Esteem, Mastery, and Self-Efficacy*

Self-esteem is an evaluation that a person makes of themselves, expressing approval or disapproval regarding self-worth, rooted in self-comparison to others and reflected appraisals (Rosenberg, 1989). Low self-esteem among adolescents is tied to poorer mental health outcomes and delinquency (Keane & Loades, 2017; Mier & Ladny, 2018). Self-esteem is dynamic during adolescence, declining in early adolescence but rebounding in mid- to late-adolescence (Baldwin & Hoffman, 2002). Instability is linked to developmental experiences, including biological changes and shifts in roles, responsibilities, and personal identity. Self-esteem is also responsive to relationships with family and friends, life events, and school climate (Greene & Way, 2005).

A positive and resilient self-image is a crucial resource for combating the sometimes negative implications for the self that accompany personal changes and stressful experiences, as well as for buffering the emotional consequences of stress (Thoits, 1995). Self-esteem helps individuals resist the effects of stress, perhaps by making them less sensitive to its negative qualities, facilitating productive and legitimate coping efforts, and promoting healthy outcomes (Trzesniewski et al.,

2006). Self-esteem may mediate the effect of childhood and family stressors on emotional and behavior problems and substance use in adolescence (Arslan, 2016; Voisin et al., 2018).

Mastery is an individual's sense of their ability to control the forces that affect their life (Mirowsky & Ross, 2003). Self-efficacy, a similar construct, refers to the belief in one's capability to exercise control over events, to confront and handle problems, and to perform effectively by one's own efforts (Burger & Samuel, 2017). With this sense of personal control, a person may be more attentive to problems, and more active and successful in solving them. Like self-esteem, self-efficacy is dynamic during adolescence, fluctuating during times of transition, and is responsive to inputs from the social environment (Burger & Samuel, 2017).

A sense of mastery may directly reduce psychological distress and buffer the harmful effects of stress exposure on health (Mirowsky & Ross, 2003; Turner, 2010). People who have a high level of mastery may see stressors as less threatening and ominous and have a greater sense of self-confidence, which counteracts discouragement in the face of stress (Mirowsky & Ross, 2003). Although studies have tended to focus on life events or trauma, self-efficacy also has protective functions from adolescents' daily stress hassles and from the effects of neighborhood context (Dupéré et al., 2012; Schönfeld et al., 2016).

Mastery and self-efficacy facilitate legitimate coping efforts in the face of strain, as people with high levels of mastery are more likely to see their strain as manageable through nondelinquent means (Hoffmann & Cerbone, 1999). A sense of mastery may also make it less likely for individuals to externalize blame for stressful events, so they may seek personal solutions rather than acting out. However, Agnew (2006) also described a kind of criminal self-efficacy, the extent to which people feel they can solve problems illegitimately. Among some adolescents, particularly those exposed to chronic strains or precarious circumstances, self-efficacy may operate to facilitate delinquent outcomes (Tyler et al., 2014).

## *Social Support*

Just as family, teachers, and peers can be a source of stressors, they can also be important sources of support for adolescents (Yeung & Leadbeater, 2010). Social support is commonly conceptualized as the social resources on which one can rely in dealing with life problems and stressors, typically grounded in personal relationships but also tied to community-level resources (Cullen et al., 1999; Turner & Lloyd, 1999). Thoits (2011) theorizes that social support can be classified into active coping assistance and emotional sustenance. Active coping assistance involves another person taking instrumental action to address a stressor directly, providing information, giving advice, or offering encouragement or distractions. Emotional sustenance involves offering care, concern, or sympathy, validating feelings, or simply "being there" for a person.

Social support may thus provide adolescents a safe haven from negative experiences, offer a way to avoid or navigate stressors, foster resiliency, and facilitate legitimate coping responses in the face of stress (Capowich et al., 2001). Social support creates a context in which strong prosocial bonds form and in which parental and other social controls are most efficacious (Cullen, 1994). Parental support is an important source of stress buffering in adolescence, often operationalized as a subjective emotional bond that makes an adolescent feel supported and loved (Meadows et al., 2006). As adolescents mature into adulthood and begin to establish their own independent lives, support from others becomes more relevant. Social support – relevant sources, their meaning to the adolescent, and their effectiveness in buffering stress – ebb and flow during adolescence (Cornwell, 2003; Rueger et al., 2016). Evidence consistently demonstrates social support has both direct and buffering effects on well-being (Turner, 2010), including physical, mental, and behavioral health among adolescents (Chu et al., 2010; Wight et al., 2006).

Adolescents with consistent conventional social support are in a better position to handle stressors, although social context may shape how consequential that support is (Colvin et al., 2002; Wight et al., 2006). Additionally, it is important to recognize that social support involves a degree of social influence via role modeling and encouragement. Thoits (2011) focuses on the positive aspects of this support, but Colvin et al. (2002) contend the lack of positive support may lead people to seek out more illegitimate support sources. For example, Baron (2015) found adolescents who did not feel supported by parents were more likely to have peers supportive of illicit behavior. Support from such sources may influence stress responses along more problematic lines (Brezina & Azimi, 2018). Like other mechanisms in the stress process, the role of social support is nuanced, once source, type, consistency, and conventionality are considered.

## Additional Mechanisms

There are several concepts pertinent to adolescence for which there is some preliminary evidence of health-related effects. Mattering – the belief that others are dependent on us and we are important to others – is related to but conceptually distinct from self-esteem and social support, perhaps signaling a sense of social integration that protects from stressors (Lewis, 2017; Turner, 2010). A sense of optimism may be implicated in both stress appraisal and approach-oriented coping, buffering the impact of stressors on health and problem behavior (Knight et al., 2017). Finally, belief systems and values, including religiosity, frame meaning and stress appraisal, and may be tied to unique coping strategies and systems of support (Krok, 2015; Pearlin & Bierman, 2013).

In addition, general strain theory describes several other factors that connect strain and delinquency, focused around criminal propensity, such as the personality traits of negative emotionality and low constraint, beliefs that crime is justifiable or desirable, reduced social control (i.e., connections to others and conventional activities), and association with criminal others (Agnew, 2006). Delinquency and other risky behaviors are situational responses, so moderators are particularly relevant; people high in criminal propensity are more likely to make riskier decisions in a given situation. However, the inconsistent moderating effects of individual factors have led to research using composite moderators of propensity (Baron, 2018), with the idea that the overall standing on these factors may together affect the likelihood of responding to strain with crime (Agnew, 2013). This research is in its early stages, but the evidence also appears mixed (e.g., Craig et al., 2017; Moon & Morash, 2017). In part, the inconsistent moderating effects for criminal propensity may be due to the challenges of measuring situational responses in surveys, and the wide variation in how those concepts are operationalized.

## A Note on Status Differences

Adolescents' life experiences are shaped by status characteristics such as race-ethnicity (Brown et al., 2007), social class (Wade et al., 2014), gender (Sharp et al., 2005), and sexuality (Saewyc, 2011), which themselves intersect (Dowd et al., 2014; Goodman et al., 2005). Structured inequalities generate differences in the level and length of exposure to stressors, and produce stressors unique to social positions. Because structured inequalities are also linked to differences in resources, including those that buffer stress, adolescents in disadvantaged social positions may be more vulnerable to the effects of stress. Vulnerability does not necessarily mean resources operate differently. Rather, resources may less available, less impactful, or more easily depleted over time, weakening the ability to cope effectively with new or additional stressors. (Adkins et al., 2009).

## Further Considerations

Although the mechanisms are complex, stress is a risk factor for compromised physical, mental, and behavioral health in adolescence. These effects can be contemporaneous: the stressor is appraised, controllable, the adolescent has resources available, and successfully copes, with no deleterious effect on well-being. The adolescent may make mistakes in appraisal or in bringing the right resources to bear on a problem, resulting in a relatively temporary health problem or a deviant behavioral reaction until the situation can be resolved more effectively. In addition to contemporaneous effects, stressful experiences also create differential risk for precocious entry into and exit from social roles, which may contribute to maladjustment and health problems in young adulthood and beyond (Hagan & Foster, 2003). Research suggests that resources themselves likely shape which stressors people are either protected from or the extent to which they experience them. For some adolescents, stress proliferates, and poor health and harm accumulate as a result.

## *Poor Health as a Stressor*

The interrelationship among the co-occurring problems of youth remain undertheorized and understudied (Lee & Stone, 2012; McLeod et al., 2012). Adolescents who engage in delinquency tend to be less healthy than non-delinquents, and stress may partly account for this association (Junger et al., 2001). A criminal lifestyle during one's youth may lead to poor health later in life (Piquero et al., 2007), but among young people, health problems may themselves be a risk factor for mental health problems and delinquency. Chronic health conditions are associated with internalizing and externalizing disorders, as well as substance use and other health risk behaviors (Pinquart & Shen, 2011; Surís et al., 2008).

Following Agnew's (2006) conceptualization, poor health is a noxious stimuli that may interfere with the achievement of positively valued goals while removing positively valued stimuli from the ill person. Further, individuals may feel their illness is unfair and, depending on the nature of the illness, highly aversive. Poor physical health, as well as related strains such as not being able to access needed care or missing normative activities, may be experienced as stressful and are associated with repercussions that promote psychological distress, delinquency, and substance use (Ford, 2014; Stogner & Gibson, 2010).

Stress proliferation offers one explanation (Kort-Butler, 2017). For adolescents, health-related strains may lead to stressors in other life domains, such as difficulties with schoolwork, problems with teachers, and missing out on school and social activities, which become more proximate causes for illicit behaviors. If such behaviors persist, they may increase exposure to yet more stressors, which in turn may exacerbate health issues and problem behaviors (Slocum, 2010). Additionally, negative reactions from others to such behaviors may be sources of stress and stigma (McLeod et al., 2012), and signal a withdrawal of social supports that would otherwise have a protective function.

## *Directions for Research*

Research has identified a range of stressors that impact well-being, but the pursuit of understanding specific stressors is double-edged (Wheaton, 2010). On the one hand, by focusing on one type or domain of stressor, we may overlook how the burden associated with the accumulation of stressors undermines health. On the other hand, by relying only on general or count measures, we fail to detect how stressful experiences interact, spillover, and proliferate in the lives of young people. Additionally, the relative effects of objective versus subjective strains remains unsettled

(Moon & Morash, 2017). While subjective measures encapsulate the appraisal process, objective measures may capture the broader context of adolescents' lives. There is more to learn about how to quantify stressors and stress appraisal, how stress ebbs, flows, and/or accumulates in young people's lives, and whether the long-term effects can be averted or reversed (Sigfusdottir et al., 2016).

A particular challenge in studying stress mechanisms is that they can function statistically as both mediators and moderators (Aneshensel & Mitchell, 2014). Evidence demonstrates these factors are central to health and well-being under stressful circumstances, but understanding how, under what circumstances, for whom, and why mechanisms work remains a theoretical and empirical challenge. The appraisal of the stressor, the physical and emotional reaction to the stressor, the circumstances and context of the stressor, and the person's standing on a host of resources influence mediating and/or moderating effects of a particular mechanism. Research should consider the effects of these mechanisms within and across life domains (DeCoster & Kort-Butler, 2006; Foster & Brooks-Gunn, 2009). Proliferation may be contained if resources can be "matched" to life domains, just as coping resources may spillover to support coping in another domain. In addition, we need to explore beyond the individual and consider their social context, what Foster and Brooks-Gunn (2009) describe as multilevel mediators and moderators.

Increasingly sophisticated statistical capabilities have improved our ability to situate individuals in their social environments, as well as our ability to model mediating and moderating effects – alone and in combination. However, we remain restricted in our ability to "see" the process unfold; we need both quantitative and qualitative approaches (McLeod, 2012). Qualitative work can offer insight into how young people appraise stress and mobilize resources, and can be nuanced enough to attune to developmental periods. Interview- and focus group-based studies can explore stress perceptions (Spencer et al., 2018b), the meaning of stress (Rose et al., 2017), the intricacies of intervening mechanisms (Panuccio et al., 2012), and barriers to health care access (Ott et al., 2011).

Mixed methods that collect real-time data offer one approach that may be particularly useful for adolescent populations. For example, ecological momentary assessment using text messaging allows researchers to contact respondents with short survey questions throughout the day about stressful events and health risk behaviors (Tyler et al., 2018). Creative methodological approaches are needed to address remaining gaps in knowledge about the mechanisms through which stressors work to increase the likelihood of poor physical and mental health and harmful behaviors in adolescence.

## Conclusion

Adolescent well-being is dynamic, unfolding over time as young people try to negotiate the social world, a world in which they encounter stress and a world significantly structured by their social location and stage in the life course. Biosocial factors, brains mechanisms, and genetic interactions are important auxiliaries to the social psychological model of stress discussed in this chapter (Stogner, 2015). Structural, contextual, and developmental factors, and mechanisms such as stress appraisal, coping, self-esteem and mastery, and social support affect whether and how stress ultimately impacts health. Stress acts in an indeterminate manner, such that its impact is not limited to a single health outcome but may be manifested across a spectrum of physical, mental, and behavioral health. Policies designed to target exposure to stressors and promote equity in health care may help eliminate disparities in adolescent health and generally advance adolescent well-being (Jackson & Vaughn, 2018; Thoits, 2010; Turner, 2010).

We need more research, particularly cross-disciplinary research, to integrate fully across the stress process model and general strain theory. The stress paradigm has a tradition of openness and flexibility, in which new ideas and new evidence are used to specify, and to alter if necessary, the basic concepts and linkages among concepts (Wheaton, 2010, p. 250). Such theoretical and empirical advancements will help us to: better understand the unfolding of stress through childhood to young adulthood; identify the set of circumstances leading to one outcome versus another; and reveal the intertwining of physical, mental, and behavioral health issues (Grant et al., 2010). To craft effective interventions, it is crucial to understand intervening mechanisms and the relative impact of those mechanisms on health outcomes (Thoits, 2011, p. 156).

To that end, health and delinquency research typically emphasizes individual deficits and risky contexts. Yet, prevention and intervention strategies that focus on positive goals (e.g., enhancing strengths, building skills) are preferable to those focused on deficits (Hall et al., 2012, p. 54). Despite the complexities of the stress process, two recommendations emerge from the literature. The first is *bolstering conventional social support* (Agnew, 2006; Chu et al., 2010; Cullen et al., 1999). Social support fosters resiliency and legitimate coping in the face of strain, promoting healthy, prosocial adaptations. At the individual level, such efforts may focus on fostering supportive relationships with family members, teachers, and other adults in the community (DuBois et al., 2002; Johnson et al., 2011). Schools and communities can also be designed to foster supportive relationships through extracurricular or community groups (Eisman et al., 2018; National Research Council, 2002).

The second recommendation is *improving access to and providing comprehensive health care*, both in the public (Spencer et al., 2018a) and correctional settings (American Academy of Pediatrics, 2011). Access to quality care may help adolescents avoid health problems, help them recover more quickly, and/or help to monitor chronic conditions in order to reduce the risk of stress proliferation (Kort-Butler, 2017). Similarly, access to age-appropriate health care that is attuned to psychological and behavioral needs may help adolescents connect to intervention programs (Reijneveld et al., 2014). For instance, programs that assist adolescents in building a physically healthy lifestyle may benefit the way that young people feel about themselves, encourage valuation of conventional goals, and promote prosocial behavior (Semenza, 2018). Adequate, comprehensive care in juvenile residential facilities – where so many adolescents experience comorbidity, a history of accumulated stressors, and current stressful circumstances associated with offending and confinement – may also stem stress proliferation and concomitant harms.

# References

Adkins, D.E., Wang, V., Dupre, M.E., Van Den Oord, E.J., & Elder, G.H. Jr (2009). Structure and stress: Trajectories of depressive symptoms across adolescence and young adulthood. *Social Forces*, 88(1), 31–60.
Agnew, R. (1992). Foundation for a general strain theory of crime and delinquency. *Criminology*, 30(1), 47–87.
Agnew, R. (2002). Experienced, vicarious, and anticipated strain: An exploratory study on physical victimization and delinquency. *Justice Quarterly*, 19(4), 603–633.
Agnew, R. (2006). *Pressured into crime: An overview of general strain theory*. Los Angeles: Roxbury.
Agnew, R. (2013). When criminal coping is likely: An extension of general strain theory. *Deviant Behavior*, 34(8), 653–670.
American Academy of Pediatrics. (2011). Policy statement: Health care for youth in the juvenile justice system. *Pediatrics*, 128(6), 1219–1235.
Amirkhan, J., & Auyeung, B. (2007). Coping with stress across the lifespan: Absolute vs relative changes in strategy. *Journal of Applied Developmental Psychology*, 28(4), 298–317.
Aneshensel, C.S., & Mitchell, U.A. (2014). The stress process: Its origins, evolution, and future. In Johnson, R.J., Turner, R.J., & Link, B.G. (Eds.), *Sociology of mental health* (pp. 53–74). Cham: Springer.
Arnett, J.J. (1999). Adolescent storm and stress, reconsidered. *American Psychologist*, 54(5), 317.
Arslan, R. (2016). Psychological maltreatment, emotional and behavioral problems in adolescents: The mediating role of resilience and self-esteem. *Child Abuse & Neglect*, 52, 200–209.
Baldwin, S.A., & Hoffman, J.P. (2002). The dynamics of self-esteem: A growth-curve analysis. *Journal of Youth and Adolescence*, 31(2), 101–113.

Balistreri, K.S., & Alvira-Hammond, M. (2016). Adverse childhood experiences, family functioning and adolescent health and emotional well-being. *Public Health, 132*, 72–78.

Baron, S.W. (2015). Differential social support, differential coercion, and organized criminal activities. *Justice Quarterly, 32*(6), 1089–1117.

Baron, S.W. (2018). Strain, criminal propensity, and violence: Examining the role of the composite moderator in Agnew's extension to GST. *Crime & Delinquency*, doi.org/10.1177/0011128718787511.

Botchkovar, E., & Broidy, L. (2013). Accumulated strain, negative emotions, and crime: A test of general strain theory in Russia. *Crime and Delinquency, 59*(6), 837–860.

Bouffard, L.A., & Koeppel, M.D. (2014). Understanding the potential long-term physical and mental health consequences of early experiences of victimization. *Justice Quarterly, 31*(3), 568–587.

Brezina, T., & Azimi, A.M. (2018). Social support, loyalty to delinquent peers, and offending: an elaboration and test of the differential social support hypothesis. *Deviant Behavior, 39*(5), 648–663.

Brown, J.S., Meadows, S.O., & Elder, G.H. Jr (2007). Race-ethnic inequality and psychological distress: Depressive symptoms from adolescence to young adulthood. *Developmental Psychology, 43*(6), 1295.

Burger, K., & Samuel, R. (2017). The role of perceived stress and self-efficacy in young people's life satisfaction: A longitudinal study. *Journal of Youth and Adolescence, 46*(1), 78–90.

Capowich, G.E., Mazerolle, P., & Piquero, A. (2001). General strain theory, situational anger, and social networks: An assessment of conditioning influences. *Journal of Criminal Justice, 29*(5), 445–461.

Carr, D., & Umberson, D. (2013). The social psychology of stress, health, and coping. In DeLamater, J., & Ward, A. (Eds.), *Handbook of social psychology 2nd edn* (pp. 465–487). Dordrecht: Springer.

Casey, B.J., Jones, R.M., & Somerville, L.H. (2011). Braking and accelerating of the adolescent brain. *Journal of Research on Adolescence, 21*(1), 21–33.

Chu, P.S., Saucier, D.A., & Hafner, E. (2010). Meta-analysis of the relationships between social support and well-being in children and adolescents. *Journal of Social and Clinical Psychology, 29*(6), 624–645.

Clarke, A.T. (2006). Coping with interpersonal stress and psychosocial health among children and adolescents: A meta-analysis. *Journal of Youth and Adolescence, 35*(1), 10–23.

Colvin, M., Cullen, F.T., & Ven, T.V. (2002). Coercion, social support, and crime: An emerging theoretical consensus. *Criminology, 40*(1), 19–42.

Compas, B.E., Jaser, S.S., Dunn, M.J., & Rodriguez, E.M. (2012). Coping with chronic illness in childhood and adolescence. *Annual Review of Clinical Psychology, 8*, 455–480.

Cornwell, B. (2003). The dynamic properties of social support: Decay, growth, and staticity, and their effects on adolescent depression. *Social Forces, 81*(3), 953–978.

Craig, J.M., Cardwell, S.M., & Piquero, A.R. (2017). The effects of criminal propensity and strain on later offending. *Crime & Delinquency, 63*(13), 1655–1681.

Cullen, F.T. (1994). Social support as an organizing concept for criminology. *Justice Quarterly, 11*(4), 527–559.

Cullen, F.T., Wright, J.P., & Chamlin, M.B. (1999). Social support and social reform: A progressive crime control agenda. *Crime and Delinquency, 45*(2), 188–207.

DeCoster, S., & Kort-Butler, L.A. (2006). How general is general strain theory? Assessing determinacy and indeterminacy across life domains. *Journal of Research in Crime and Delinquency, 43*(4), 1–29.

DeCoster, S., & Thompson, M.S. (2017). Race and general strain theory: Microaggressions as mundane extreme environmental stresses. *Justice Quarterly, 34*(5), 903–930.

Dowd, J.B., Palermo, T., Chyu, L., Adam, E., & McDade, T.W. (2014). Race/ethnic and socioeconomic differences in stress and immune function in The National Longitudinal Study of Adolescent Health. *Social Science & Medicine, 115*, 49–55.

DuBois, D.L., Burk-Braxton, C., Swenson, L.P., Tevendale, H.D., Lockerd, E.M., & Moran, B.L. (2002). Getting by with a little help from self and others: Self-esteem and social support as resources during early adolescence. *Developmental Psychology, 38*(5), 822.

Dupéré, V., Leventhal, T., & Vitaro, F. (2012). Neighborhood processes, self-efficacy, and adolescent mental health. *Journal of Health and Social Behavior, 53*(2), 183–198.

Eisman, A.B., Lee, D.B., Hsieh, H.F., Stoddard, S.A., & Zimmerman, M.A. (2018). More than just keeping busy: The protective effects of organized activity participation on violence and substance use among urban youth. *Journal of Youth and Adolescence*, 10.1007/s10964-018-0868-8.

Ferro, M.A., & Boyle, M.H. (2015). The impact of chronic physical illness, maternal depressive symptoms, family functioning, and self-esteem on symptoms of anxiety and depression in children. *Journal of Abnormal Child Psychology, 43*(1), 177–187.

Ford, J.A. (2014). Poor health, strain, and substance use. *Deviant Behavior, 35*(8), 654–667.

Foster, H., & Brooks-Gunn, J. (2009). Toward a stress process model of children's exposure to physical family and community violence. *Clinical Child and Family Psychology Review, 12*(2), 71–94.

Froggio, G., & Agnew, R. (2007). The relationship between crime and "objective" versus "subjective" strains. *Journal of Criminal Justice, 35*(1), 81–87.

Goodman, E., McEwen, B.S., Dolan, L.M., Schafer-Kalkhoff, T., & Adler, N.E. (2005). Social disadvantage and adolescent stress. *Journal of Adolescent Health, 37*(6), 484–492.

Gore, S., & Colten, M.E. (1991). Introduction: Adolescent stress, social relationships, and mental health. In Colten, M.E., & Gore, S. (Eds.), *Adolescent stress: Causes and consequences* (pp. 1–14). New York: Aldine de Gruyter.

Grant, K.E., McMahon, S.D., Duffy, S.N., Taylor, J.J., & Compas, B.E. (2010). Stressors and mental health problems in childhood and adolescence. In Contrada, R., & Baum, A. (Eds.), *Handbook of stress science: Biology, psychology, and health* (pp. 359–372). New York: Springer.

Greene, M.L., & Way, N. (2005). Self-esteem trajectories among ethnic minority adolescents: A growth curve analysis of the patterns and predictors of change. *Journal of Research on Adolescence, 15*(2), 151–178.

Hagan, J., & Foster, H. (2003). S/He's a rebel: Toward a sequential stress theory of delinquency and gendered pathways to disadvantage in emerging adulthood. *Social Forces, 82*(1), 53–86.

Hall, J.E., Simon, T.R., Mercy, J.A., Loeber, R., Farrington, D.P., & Lee, R.D. (2012). Centers for Disease Control and Prevention's expert panel on protective factors for youth violence perpetration: Background and overview. *American Journal of Preventive Medicine, 43*(2), S1-S7.

Hoffmann, J.P., & Cerbone, F.G. (1999). Stressful life events and delinquency escalation in early adolescence. *Criminology, 37*(2), 343–374.

Jackson, D.B., & Vaughn, M.G. (2018). Promoting health equity to prevent crime. *Preventive Medicine, 113*, 91–94.

Jang, S.J., & Johnson, B.R. (2003). Strain, negative emotions, and deviant coping among African Americans: A test of general strain theory. *Journal of Quantitative Criminology, 19*(1), 80–105.

Johnson, M.K., Crosnoe, R., & Elder, G.H. (2011). Insights on adolescence from a life course perspective. *Journal of Research on Adolescence, 21*(1), 273–280.

Junger, M., Stroebe, W., & Van der Laan, A. (2001). Delinquency, health behavior, and health. *British Journal of Health Psychology, 6*(2), 103–120.

Juster, R.P., McEwen, B.S., & Lupien, S.J. (2010). Allostatic load biomarkers of chronic stress and impact on health and cognition. *Neuroscience & Biobehavioral Reviews, 35*(1), 2–16.

Keane, L., & Loades, M. (2017). Low self-esteem and internalizing disorders in young people – a systematic review. *Child and Adolescent Mental Health, 22*(1), 4–15.

Knight, K.E., Ellis, C., Roark, J., Henry, K.L., & Huizinga, D. (2017). Testing the role of aspirations, future expectations, and strain on the development of problem behaviors across young and middle adulthood. *Deviant Behavior, 38*(12), 1456–1473.

Kort-Butler, L.A. (2009). Coping styles and sex differences in depressive symptoms and delinquent behavior. *Journal of Youth and Adolescence, 38*(1), 122–136.

Kort-Butler, L.A. (2010). Experienced and vicarious victimization: Do social support and self-esteem prevent delinquent responses? *Journal of Criminal Justice, 38*(4), 496–505.

Kort-Butler, L.A. (2017). Health-related strains and subsequent delinquency and marijuana use. *Youth & Society, 49*(8), 1077–1103.

Krok, D. (2015). Religiousness, spirituality, and coping with stress among late adolescents: A meaning-making perspective. *Journal of Adolescence, 45*, 196–203.

Lee, E.J., & Stone, S.I. (2012). Co-occurring internalizing and externalizing behavioral problems: the mediating effect of negative self-concept. *Journal of Youth and Adolescence, 41*(6), 717–731.

Lewis, D.M. (2017). A matter for concern: young offenders and the importance of mattering. *Deviant Behavior, 38*(11), 1318–1331.

Low, N.C., Dugas, E., O'Loughlin, E., Rodriguez, D., Contreras, G., Chaiton, M., & O'Loughlin, J. (2012). Common stressful life events and difficulties are associated with mental health symptoms and substance use in young adolescents. *BMC Psychiatry, 12*(1), 10.1186/1471-244X-12-116.

Lucas-Thompson, R.G., Lunkenheimer, E.S., & Dumitrache, A. (2017). Associations between marital conflict and adolescent conflict appraisals, stress physiology, and mental health. *Journal of Clinical Child & Adolescent Psychology, 46*(3), 379–393.

McEwen, B.S., & Gianaros, P.J. (2010). Central role of the brain in stress and adaptation: Links to socioeconomic status, health, and disease. *Annals of the New York Academy of Sciences, 1186*(1), 190–222.

McLeod, J.D. (2012). The meanings of stress: Expanding the stress process model. *Society and Mental Health, 2*(3), 172–186.

McLeod, J.D., Uemura, R., & Rohrman, S. (2012). Adolescent mental health, behavior problems, and academic achievement. *Journal of Health and Social Behavior, 53*(4), 482–497.

Meadows, S.O., Brown, J.S., & Elder, G.H. (2006). Depressive symptoms, stress, and support: Gendered trajectories from adolescence to young adulthood. *Journal of Youth and Adolescence*, 35(1), 89–99.

Mier, C., & Ladny, R.T. (2018). Does self-esteem negatively impact crime and delinquency? A meta-analytic Review of 25 Years of evidence. *Deviant Behavior*, 39(8), 1006–1022.

Mirowsky, J., & Ross, C.E. (2003). *Social causes of psychological distress, 2nd edn*. New York: Routledge.

Moon, B., & Morash, M. (2017). A test of general strain theory in South Korea: A focus on objective/subjective strains, negative emotions, and composite conditioning factors. *Crime & Delinquency*, 63(6), 731–756.

Moon, B., Morash, M., McClusky, C.P., & Hwang, H. (2009). A comprehensive test of general strain theory: Key strains, situational- and trait-based negative emotions, conditioning factors, and delinquency. *Journal of Research in Crime and Delinquency*, 46, 182–212.

National Research Council. (2002). *Community programs to promote youth development*. Washington, DC: National Academies Press.

Ott, M.A., Rosenberger, J.G., McBride, K.R., & Woodcox, S.G. (2011). How do adolescents view health? Implications for state health policy. *Journal of Adolescent Health*, 48(4), 398–403.

Panuccio, E.A., Christian, J., Martinez, D.J., & Sullivan, M.L. (2012). Social support, motivation, and the process of juvenile reentry: An exploratory analysis of desistance. *Journal of Offender Rehabilitation*, 51(3), 135–160.

Pearlin, L.I. (1989). The sociological study of stress. *Journal of Health and Social Behavior*, 30(3), 241–256.

Pearlin, L.I. (1999). The stress concept revisited. in Aneshensel, C.S., & Phelan, J.C. (Eds.), *Handbook of the sociology of mental health* (pp. 395–415). New York: Kluwer Academic/Plenum Publishers.

Pearlin, L.I., & Bierman, A. (2013). Current issues and future directions in research into the stress process. In Aneshensel, C.S., Phelan, J.C., & Bierman, A. (Eds.), *Handbook of the sociology of mental health* (pp. 325–340). Dordrecht: Springer.

Pearlin, L.I., Schieman, S., Fazio, E.M., & Meersman, S.C. (2005). Stress, health, and the life course: Some conceptual perspectives. *Journal of Health and Social Behavior*, 46(2), 205–219.

Pinquart, M., & Shen, Y. (2011). Behavior problems in children and adolescents with chronic physical illness: A meta-analysis. *Journal of Pediatric Psychology*, 36(9), 1003–1016.

Piquero, A.R., Daigle, L.E., Gibson, C., Piquero, N.L., & Tibbetts, S.G. (2007). Are life-course-persistent offenders at risk for adverse health outcomes? *Journal of Research in Crime & Delinquency*, 44(2), 185–207.

Reijneveld, S.A., Wiegersma, P.A., Ormel, J., Verhulst, F.C., Vollebergh, W.A., & Jansen, D.E. (2014). Adolescents' use of care for behavioral and emotional problems: types, trends, and determinants. *PLoS One*, 9(4), e93526. 10.1371/journal.pone.0093526.

Rose, T., Sharpe, T.L., Shdaimah, C., & deTablan, D. (2017). Exploring coping among urban youth through photovoice. *Qualitative Social Work*, 10.1177/1473325017693684.

Rosenberg, M. (1989). *Society and the adolescent self-image, revised edition* Middletown, CT: Wesleyan University Press.

Rueger, S.Y., Malecki, C.K., Pyun, Y., Aycock, C., & Coyle, S. (2016). A meta-analytic review of the association between perceived social support and depression in childhood and adolescence. *Psychological Bulletin*, 142(10), 107–1067.

Saewyc, E.M. (2011). Research on adolescent sexual orientation: Development, health disparities, stigma, and resilience. *Journal of Research on Adolescence*, 21(1), 256–272.

Schönfeld, P., Brailovskaia, J., Bieda, A., Zhang, X.C., & Margraf, J. (2016). The effects of daily stress on positive and negative mental health: Mediation through self-efficacy. *International Journal of Clinical and Health Psychology*, 16(1), 1–10.

Sealock, M.D., & Manasse, M. (2012). An uneven playing field: The impact of strain and coping skills on treatment outcomes for juvenile offenders. *Journal of Criminal Justice*, 40(3), 238–248.

Seiffge-Krenke, I. (2000). Causal links between stressful events, coping style, and adolescent symptomatology. *Journal of Adolescence*, 23(6), 675–691.

Seiffge-Krenke, I., Aunola, K., & Nurmi, J.E. (2009). Changes in stress perception and coping during adolescence: The role of situational and personal factors. *Child Development*, 80(1), 259–279.

Semenza, D.C. (2018). Health behaviors and juvenile delinquency. *Crime & Delinquency*, 64, 1394–1416.

Sharp, S.F., Brewster, D., & Love, S.R. (2005). Disentangling strain, personal attributes, affective response and deviance: A gendered analysis. *Deviant Behavior*, 26(2), 133–157.

Sigfusdottir, I.D., Kristjansson, A.L., & Agnew, R. (2012). A comparative analysis of general strain theory. *Journal of Criminal Justice*, 40, 117–127.

Sigfusdottir, I.D., Kristjansson, A.L., Thorlindsson, T., & Allegrante, J.P. (2016). Stress and adolescent well-being: the need for an interdisciplinary framework. *Health Promotion International*, 32(6), 1081–1090.

Slocum, L.E. (2010). General strain theory and the development of stressors and substance use over time: An empirical examination. *Journal of Criminal Justice*, 38(6), 1100–1112.

Spencer, D.L., McManus, M., Call, K.T., Turner, J., Harwood, C., White, P., & Alarcon, G. (2018a). Health care coverage and access among children, adolescents, and young adults, 2010–2016: Implications for future health reforms. *Journal of Adolescent Health, 62*(6), 667–673.

Spencer, R., Walsh, J., Liang, B., Mousseau, A.M.D., & Lund, T.J. (2018b). Having it all? A qualitative examination of affluent adolescent girls' perceptions of stress and their quests for success. *Journal of Adolescent Research, 33*(1), 3–33.

Stogner, J., & Gibson, C.L. (2010). Healthy, wealthy, and wise: Incorporating health issues as a source of strain in Agnew's general strain theory. *Journal of Criminal Justice, 38*(6), 1150–1159.

Stogner, J.M. (2015). DAT1 and alcohol use: differential responses to life stress during adolescence. *Criminal Justice Studies, 28*(1), 18–38.

Surís, J.C., Michaud, P.A., Akre, C., & Sawyer, S.M. (2008). Health risk behaviors in adolescents with chronic conditions. *Pediatrics, 122*(5), e1113-e1118. 10.1542/peds.2008-1479.

Thoits, P.A. (1995). Stress, coping, and social support processes: Where are we? What next?. *Journal of Health and Social Behavior*, Extra Issue, 53–79.

Thoits, P.A. (2010). Stress and health: Major findings and policy implications. *Journal of Health and Social Behavior, 51*, S41-S53.

Thoits, P.A. (2011). Mechanisms linking social ties and support to physical and mental health. *Journal of Health and Social Behavior, 52*, 145–161.

Trzesniewski, K.H., Donnellan, M.B., Moffitt, T.E., Robins, R.W., Poulton, R., & Caspi, A. (2006). Low self-esteem during adolescence predicts poor health, criminal behavior, and limited economic prospects during adulthood. *Developmental Psychology, 42*(2), 381.

Turner, R.J. (2010). Understanding health disparities: The promise of the stress process model. In Avison, W.R., Aneshensel, C.S., Schieman, S., & Wheaton, B. (Eds.), *Advances in the conceptualization of the stress process* (pp. 3–21). New York: Springer.

Turner, R.J., & Lloyd, D.A. (1999). The stress process and the social distribution of depression. *Journal of Health and Social Behavior, 40*, 374–404.

Tyler, K.A., Kort-Butler, L., & Swendener, A. (2014). The effect of victimization, mental health, and protective factors on crime and illicit drug use among homeless young adults. *Violence & Victims, 29*(2), 348–362.

Tyler, K.A., Olson, K., & Ray, C.M. (2018). Understanding the link between victimization and alcohol use among homeless youth using ecological momentary assessment. *Socius, 4*, 10.1177/2378023118779832.

Voisin, D.R., Kim, D.H., Bassett, S.M., & Marotta, P.L. (2018). Pathways linking family stress to youth delinquency and substance use: exploring the mediating roles of self-efficacy and future orientation. *Journal of Health Psychology*, 10.1177/1359105318763992.

Wade, R., Shea, J.A., Rubin, D., & Wood, J. (2014). Adverse childhood experiences of low-income urban youth. *Pediatrics, 134*(1), e13–e20. http://pediatrics.aappublications.org/content/134/1/e13.

Wade, T.J., & Pevalin, D.J. (2005). Adolescent delinquency and health. *Canadian Journal of Criminology and Criminal Justice, 47*(4), 619–654.

Warner, T.D., & Settersten, R.A. (2017). Why neighborhoods (and how we study them) matter for adolescent development. *Advances in Child Development and Behavior, 52*, 105–152.

Wheaton, B. (2010). The stress process as a successful paradigm. In Avison, W.R., Aneshensel, C.S., Schieman, S., & Wheaton, B. (Eds.), *Advances in the conceptualization of the stress process* (pp. 231–252). New York: Springer.

Wheaton, B., Young, M., Montazer, S., & Stuart-Lahman, K. (2013). Social stress in the twenty-first century. In Aneshensel, C.S., Phelan, J.C., & Bierman, A. (Eds.), *Handbook of the sociology of mental health* (pp. 299–323). Dordrecht: Springer.

Wickrama, K.A., Lee, T.K., & O'Neal, C.W. (2015). Stressful life experiences in adolescence and cardiometabolic risk factors in young adulthood. *Journal of Adolescent Health, 56*(4), 456–463.

Wight, R.G., Botticello, A.L., & Aneshensel, C.S. (2006). Socioeconomic context, social support, and adolescent mental health: A multilevel investigation. *Journal of Youth and Adolescence, 35*, 109–120.

Yeager, D.S., Lee, H.Y., & Jamieson, J.P. (2016). How to improve adolescent stress responses: Insights from integrating implicit theories of personality and biopsychosocial models. *Psychological Science, 27*(8), 1078–1091.

Yeung, R., & Leadbeater, B. (2010). Adults make a difference: The protective effects of parent and teacher emotional support on emotional and behavioral problems of peer-victimized adolescents. *Journal of Community Psychology, 38*(1), 80–98.

Zimmer-Gembeck, M.J., & Skinner, E.A. (2011). The development of coping across childhood and adolescence: An integrative review and critique of research. *International Journal of Behavioral Development, 35*(1), 1–17.

# 7
# ADVERSE CHILDHOOD EXPERIENCES, DELINQUENCY, AND HEALTH
## Implications for Juvenile Justice Systems

*Michael Baglivio*

One could argue life is analogous to a base runner in a baseball game. The goal is to reach home plate and score a run. "Scoring a run" assuredly differs across individuals; whereas one may wish for a loving family, another good health, yet another a successful job, to mention just a few. To be sure, we all have desired outcomes we're striving to achieve. The reality is, some people start at the beginning and have to navigate to first base, second, third, and finally to reach home plate. Others, metaphorically start on third base and only have 90 feet to go. In this chapter the case is made, using empirical support across samples, methodologies, and outcomes, that exposure to adverse childhood experiences (ACE), including abuses, neglect, and household dysfunctions, position exposed individuals on the most difficult path with respect to the baseball analogy. Focus is given throughout the chapter to the effects of cumulative traumatic exposure during the first 18 years of life on the intersections of delinquency and health, and ultimately exploring implications of ACE for juvenile justice systems.

### Adverse Childhood Experiences: Conceptualization of the ACE Score

Adverse childhood experiences (ACE) refer to exposure to childhood maltreatment usually considered prior to the age of 18. The conceptualization of ACE in this chapter predominately includes types of abuse (physical, sexual, and emotional), neglect (physical and emotional), and household dysfunction (parental mental health problems, parental separation/divorce, parental substance abuse, parental jail/prison history, and violent treatment towards mother/domestic violence). These ten distinct ACE exposures are those espoused by the US Centers for Disease Control and Prevention (CDC, 2017). The CDC and the San Diego Department of Preventive Medicine at Kaiser Permanente (an integrated managed care consortium) collaborated on two waves of data collection from 1995 to 1997 during which 17,421 well-educated, middle-class patients completed a retrospective questionnaire detailing ACE exposure. The survey, the Adverse Childhood Experiences Questionnaire, sought to examine the relationship between the cumulative traumatic exposure and adult health (see Felitti et al., 1998).

The Felitti et al. (1998) ACE Study, as it has become known, first introduced the notion of the composite ACE score, being a person's cumulative number of the reported ten ACE exposures. Each ACE is captured as a binary (yes–no) indicator, such that an affirmative response to a history of any given ACE receives 1 point, irrespective of the intensity, frequency, or duration of exposure. For example, a positive response for physical abuse receives 1 point whether there were 1 or 100 incidents of such abuse, and regardless of the duration or severity of the abuse. The ACE score ranges from 0 (not having been exposed to any of the traumas/abuse types) to 10 (having been exposed to all 10). While there have been critiques of the ACE score with respect to the need for additional items beyond the 10 ACEs (such as witnessing violence in the community and low socioeconomic status; see Cronholm et al., 2015; Finkelohor, Shattuck, Turner, & Hamby, 2013, 2015), whether self-reported abuse/neglect and child welfare system substantiated abuse are equivalent (Chiu, Ryan, & Herz, 2011; but see Baglivio et al., 2016; Drake, Jonson-Reid, Way, & Chung, 2003), as well as findings regarding the importance of frequency, duration, and severity of abuse and neglect (see for example, Smith & Thornberry, 1995), higher ACE scores have been linked to a plethora of negative health and behavioral consequences (Anda, Butchart, Felitti, & Brown, 2010; Anda et al., 2006; Felitti et al., 1998). Children who have experienced four or more ACEs have up to 12 times the odds of experiencing heart disease, cancer, chronic lung disease, skeletal fractures, and liver disease in adulthood (Felitti et al., 1998).

Additional relationships between higher ACE scores and detrimental outcomes include immediate chromosome damage (Shalev et al., 2013), as well as functional changes to the developing brain (Anda et al., 2010; Cicchetti, 2013; Danese & McEwen, 2012; Painter & Scannapieco, 2013; Teicher et al., 2003), which have implications for the ability to self-regulate behavior and emotional responses, increase antisocial behavior, violence, substance abuse, and suicidal behavior (Evans-Chase, 2014). Furthermore, greater ACE exposure has demonstrated links to risky sexual behaviors, including 50 or more sexual partners, intercourse before age 15 (Hillis, Anda, Felitti, & Marchbanks, 2001), and becoming pregnant as a teenager (Hillis et al., 2004). A retrospective cross sectional study of 1,500 UK residents demonstrated higher cumulative ACE scores increased the odds of smoking, heavy drinking, morbid obesity, poor educational and employment outcomes, recent involvement in violence, and almost nine times the odds of incarceration (Bellis, Lowey, Leckenby, Hughes, & Harrison, 2013).

Central to our understanding of the effect of ACEs is the notion that they be considered as a composite score capturing multiple exposure types. Studies demonstrate ACEs are common, highly interrelated, and exert a powerful cumulative effect on human development (Anda et al., 2010). Baglivio and Epps (2016) demonstrated that of youth experiencing one ACE exposure, 67.5% reported four or more additional exposures among 64,329 juvenile offenders. The co-occurrence and cumulative effect of these experiences, termed a "cumulative stressor approach", necessitates their examination as a collective composite, as a single abuse type analysis misses the broader context in which they occur. The ACE score as a measure of the cumulative traumatic stress exposure during childhood is consistent with our understanding of the effects of traumatic stress on neurodevelopment (Anda et al., 2006, 2010).

## ACE Exposure among Juvenile Offenders

As the current focus is the intersection of ACEs, delinquency, and health, it is critical to explore the prevalence of ACE exposure among adolescent offenders in relation to that found in general population studies. ACE exposure was surprisingly common in the original ACE Study sample, but has been demonstrated even more pervasive in poor, minority, marginalized, and oppressed populations (Baglivio, Wolff, Epps, & Nelson, 2017; Eckenrode, Smith, McCarthy, & Dineen,

2014; Larkin, Felitti, & Anda, 2014). The first published work on ACE exposure of an all-juvenile offender sample showed dramatic prevalence differences from the largely white, upper middle class adult sample used in the original ACE Study. Specifically, the 64,329 juvenile offenders were 13 times less likely to report no ACE exposures (2.8% compared to 36% for the ACE Study adults) and four times more likely to report four or more ACEs (50% compared to 13%; Baglivio et al., 2014).

Perhaps more stunning are findings that ACE exposure increases the deeper adolescent offenders penetrating the juvenile justice system. A study of New Mexico juvenile offenders who were committed for incarceration (the most restrictive juvenile justice placement) showed not only do these youth have higher ACE scores on average than the original ACE Study, and a random sample of New Mexico adults, but they evidenced an 86% prevalence rate of four or more ACEs, in comparison to the 50% for the Florida study examining all juvenile offenders (Cannon, Davis, Hsi, & Bochte, 2016). Additionally, subsets of juvenile offending groups have higher ACE scores, on average, than others, such as juveniles who sexually offend (Levenson et al., 2017), with considerable nuances across racial and ethnic groups and across offense types (DeLisi et al., 2017).

Notably, these studies differed in methodology with respect to the instruments used to assess the ACE score, which limits the generalizability of the results. However, for this chapter Florida data was re-examined to provide ACE prevalence rates for youth with no, one, and two or more residential commitment placements prior to aging out of the juvenile system (prior to age 18). Of note, 67% of the juvenile offenders were never placed in a residential facility by age 18, 26% had one placement, and 7% of the 64,329 juvenile offenders had two of more stays in a long-term residential facility (typically 6–9 months). Those without residential placement had an average ACE score of 3.34, those with one placement 4.21 and those with two or more placements evidenced an average ACE score of 4.65; all differences were significant across groups, with a moderate effect size (F = 2086.07, $p < .001$, $d = .52$).

The supplemental analysis of the Baglivio et al. (2014) data verify the relationship between deeper penetration into the juvenile justice system and a higher average ACE score. This is evidenced by youth with no residential placements being 13 times more likely to have no ACE exposures than youth with two or more placements (3.9% compared to .03%), and almost ¾ of the two or more residential placement youth having exposure to four or more ACE types, compared to only 43% of youth with no residential placement histories (see Figure 7.1). Again, it is essential that all of the 64,329 juvenile offenders have "aged out", meaning the entirety of both their juvenile offending "career" and their ACE exposure prior to age 18 was considered.

## ACE Exposure: Relationship to Delinquency, Juvenile Offending, and Violence

Higher ACE scores have been linked to crime, violence, and incarceration in adulthood (see, for example, Bellis et al., 2013). However, much of that work involved retrospective recall of ACE exposure. As such, there may be selection effects whereby individuals finding themselves in precarious situations tend to externalize blame and may be more likely to attribute such ill-fated circumstances to past wrongs, such as ACE exposure (Bremner, 1999; Della Femina, Yeager, & Lewis, 1990; Dube, Williamson, Thompson, Felitti, & Anda, 2004; Williams, 1995). However, prospective studies have confirmed the "Cycle of Violence" (Widom, 1989) relationship between childhood maltreatment indicators and crime and delinquency (Barrett, Katsiyannis, Zhang, & Zhang, 2014; English, Widom, & Brandford, 2002; Maxfield & Widom, 1996; Smith & Thornberry, 1995; Stouthamer-Loeber, Loeber, Homish, & Wei, 2001; Widom, 1989; Zingraff, Leiter, Myers, & Johnsen, 1993). Additionally, exposure to violence predicts violent juvenile offending,

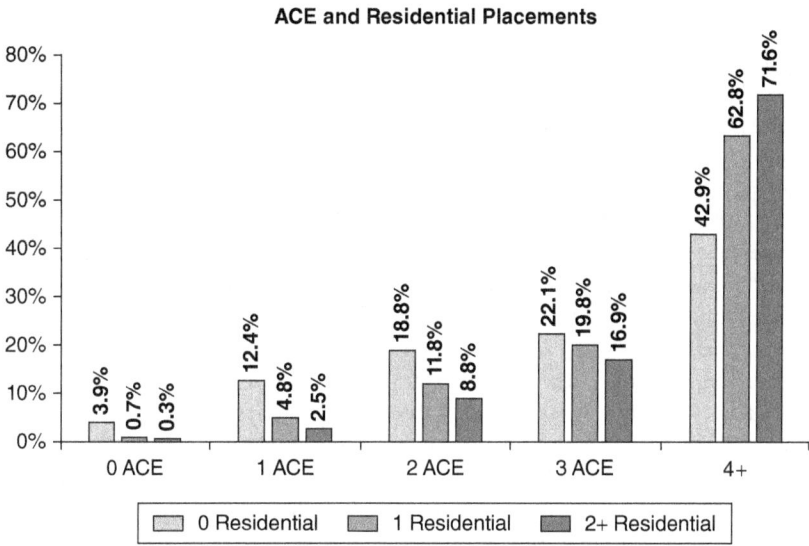

*Figure 7.1* ACE prevalence by long-term juvenile justice residential placements

the rate of exposure matters (Nofziger & Kurtz, 2005), and maltreatment is associated with an earlier onset of offending and increased frequency of offending (Wiig, Widom, & Tuell, 2003).

Extensive prospective work specifically using the ACE score as a measure of cumulative traumatic stress has led to similar findings with respect to juvenile delinquency. Wolff and colleagues employed a sample of 27,867 juvenile offenders to examine whether higher ACE scores predicted subsequent recidivism, as well as a shorter time to re-offense, net of demographic and common risk factor controls (Wolff, Baglivio, & Piquero, 2017). Findings demonstrated greater cumulative traumatic exposure (higher ACE scores) was associated with a shorter time to failure (higher ACE score youth recidivate faster); a finding that held for both male and female youthful offenders, yet was more nuanced when further disaggregated in gender and race/ethnicity subsamples.

Examining over 64,000 Florida juvenile offenders, Baglivio and colleagues demonstrated that higher ACE scores distinguishes an early onset and a persistent level of offending through late adolescence from other patterns of offending, net of extensive controls across demographic, individual risk, familial risk, and personal history domains (Baglivio, Wolff, Piquero, & Epps, 2015). This early onset, chronic offending group (7% of the sample) averaged approximately 18 arrests through late adolescence. These results supplement additional work which demonstrated that *each* additional ACE exposure increased the odds of becoming a serious, violent, and chronic (SVC) offender by age 18 by 35 times (Fox, Perez, Cass, Baglivio, & Epps, 2015), work illustrating ACEs exert both a direct effect and an indirect effect through adolescent problem behaviors and maladaptive personality traits on SVC offending (Perez, Jennings, & Baglivio, 2018), and that ACE exert a direct effect on recidivism, and an indirect effect through negative emotionality (Wolff & Baglivio, 2017). The implications of ACE on life-course offending was further illustrated among the Cambridge Study in Delinquent Development sample (Craig, Piquero, Farrington, & Ttofi, 2017). That ACE scores can predict both a shorter time to recidivism for juvenile offenders, as well as identify early-onset and chronic offending trajectories through age 18, even with substantial control for other prominent risk factors, demonstrates the status of early life traumatic events as a prolific risk for juvenile offending.

Only one study to date has examined the role of ACE in placement into juvenile justice residential programs. Analyzing a sample of 4,733 juvenile offenders first arrested at age 12 demonstrated each additional ACE exposure increased the likelihood the 12-year-old would eventually be placed into a long-term juvenile justice residential facility by 20% (Zettler, Wolff, Baglivio, Craig, & Epps, 2017). With respect to race/ethnicity and gender, ACEs increased the odds of future residential placement for Black and Hispanic males, as well as Black females, but not for White males, White females, or Hispanic females. Specifically examining these deepest end juvenile justice placements, youthful offenders held in long-term residential facilities, Baglivio and colleagues studied the timing of childhood maltreatment on juvenile recidivism (Baglivio et al., 2016). Additionally, that study examined the direct effects of childhood traumatic events (ACE scores) on delinquency, as well as their indirect effects through official/substantiated child welfare involvement. Findings demonstrated the effect of ACE on recidivism was indirect, in that it increased the odds of official child welfare system placement, and that child welfare placement increased recidivism likelihood. Furthermore, across all racial subgroups, higher ACE scores had a significant effect on the likelihood of child welfare placement, yet child welfare placement exerted a significant effect on recidivism for White and Hispanic youth, but not for Black youth. Integral to the question of timing, findings indicated that earlier child welfare involvement (prior to juvenile justice system involvement) is more detrimental than concurrent juvenile justice and child welfare system involvement when it does matter. This finding is highly relevant to policy as it indicates earlier exposure to childhood maltreatment may be more crucial than adolescent exposure, with respect to juvenile offending (but see Ryan, Williams, & Courtney, 2013; Smith, Thornberry, & Ireland, 2004).

## ACE and Adolescent Health

ACE exposure has been linked to a host of health problems in adulthood, as noted above, often in a dose-response fashion (see Felitti et al., 1998). Less work has been conducted on adolescent health, and even less using prospective methodologies to allow examining causality rather than association. Importantly, however, the line of inquiring is growing.

### *Mental Health*

A prospective two-wave study design using a large, diverse sample of 1,093 high school seniors examined ACE exposure and mental health outcomes two years later (Schilling, Aseltine, & Gore, 2007). ACE exposure was related to depressive symptoms, frequency of substance abuse, and frequency of externalizing behaviors. With the exception of sexual abuse, no gender differences were found in the effects of individual ACE types on depression or drug use. In terms of race/ethnicity differences, where they did exist, the study found stronger effects of ACE on mental health outcomes among White youth (Schilling et al., 2007). An additional prospective study of over 3,000 children from the Fragile Families and Child Wellbeing Study found higher ACE exposure by age five predicted externalizing and internalizing behaviors warranting professional attention, as well as the odds of an ADHD diagnosis by age nine (Hunt, Slack, & Berger, 2017). Additionally, ACEs were more strongly related to externalizing behaviors and ADHD diagnosis for Black children, while White children evidenced a stronger ACE-internalizing behavior relationship.

Using the ACE Study data, while retrospective, indicated a strong graded relationship between higher ACE scores and initiating alcohol use in early adolescence, which held for all four birth cohorts examined among the 8,417 adults (Dube et al., 2006). A study specific to juvenile offenders examined 64,329 youth regarding the direct and indirect effects of ACE on suicide attempts using generalized structural equation modeling (Perez, Jennings, Piquero, & Baglivio, 2016). They found close to 0% of those youth without any ACE exposure had a suicide attempt by age 18, while 24% of those with an ACE score of 9 had engaged in suicidal behavior (and a 1.49 increase in odds for each additional ACE exposure). Furthermore, higher ACE scores increased the youth's aggression levels, their level of impulsivity, school difficulties, and problems with substance abuse, while controlling for demographic measures (Perez et al., 2016). The mediation analysis indicated, while ACE still exert a significant direct effect on suicidal behavior, there was evidence of partial mediation by aggression and impulsivity, which in turn significantly increased suicidal behavior, but no effects for substance abuse and school difficulties actually decreased the odds of suicide attempts. These analyses indicate that some of the effects of ACE on suicidal behavior can be explained by the effect of ACE on increasing aggression and impulsivity, but that ACE exposure still exerts a significant direct effect by increasing the likelihood a juvenile offender exhibits suicidal behavior.

## *Physical Health*

Similar to mental health outcomes, the examination of physical health relationships to ACE exposure among adolescents is ever-growing. In the prospective Consortium for Longitudinal Studies of Child Abuse and Neglect (LONGSCAN) study, exposure to 5 or more ACEs from ages 6 to 12 was associated with a 224% increased odds of any health complaint, 369% increased odds of an illness requiring a doctor, and a 337% increased odds of caregiver's reports of child's somatic complaints among 805 12-year-old children (Flaherty et al., 2009). These results were supported by additional work showing recent ACE exposure (within the last two years) of 14-year-olds was more strongly related to health problems than older exposures (Flaherty et al., 2013). Finally, cumulative exposure to ACEs from 4 to 16 years of age increased self-report health concerns and needing medical care for a serious or ongoing health problem at age 18 among 802 LONGSCAN participants (Thompson et al., 2015). While cross sectional methodologically, a recent study found higher family functioning moderated the negative effects of ACE on adolescent health (Balistreri & Alvira-Hammond, 2016). Family functioning included items related to frequent family meals, higher coping with parenting demands by caregivers, parental involvement, and stress on the family, which may be useful for policy makers and practitioners to consider to mitigate the implications of ACE exposure on those already exposed. In a recent analysis of children involved in the child welfare system, for each additional ACE exposure before age 5, there was a 32% greater likelihood of mental health problems, and also a 21% increased odds of having a chronic medical condition (Kerker et al., 2015). Over 98% of all the children in the sample were exposed to at least one ACE, with a mean of 3.6 exposures, demonstrating this special population (youth involved in the child welfare system) also at increased risk of ACE exposure compared to non-involved youth (Kerker et al., 2015).

## *Teenage Pregnancy and Fetal Death*

From the original ACE Study data, 16% of women with zero ACE exposure reported teen pregnancy, compared to 53% of those with ACE scores of 7 or higher (Hillis et al., 2004). This equated to the odds of a women with 7 or more ACE exposures having been pregnant in adolescence were 5.6 times that of a women with no ACE exposures, even after adjusting for race, education, and age at interview. Furthermore, having experienced fetal death was associated with higher ACE exposure such that those with ACE scores of 5 or more were 1.8 times as likely to experience fetal death (after adjusting for age, race, and education). Perhaps as stunning as these results, when the teenage pregnancy increased the likelihood of high stress, uncontrollable anger, and serious problems with families, employment, and finances only among women with higher ACE exposures, not among those with no ACE exposure during childhood (Hillis et al., 2004).

## Human Trafficking

Intuitive links between childhood trauma and adversity and eventual human trafficking can certainly be made. To empirically test these hypotheses, the prevalence of ACEs among human trafficking victims, and the predictive ability of ACEs with respect to human trafficking was examined among 913 juvenile justice-involved youth with officially reported human trafficking victimization and a matched comparison group of 913 juvenile offenders without such reports (Reid, Baglivio, Piquero, Greenwald, & Epps, 2017). The mean ACE score was significantly higher among the offenders with human trafficking reports, by about 1 exposure type. Additionally, the odds of being a victim of human trafficking was 2.52 times higher for girls who experienced sexual abuse, and an astonishing 8.21 times higher for boys experiencing sexual abuse (Reid et al., 2017). Equally importantly, a few of the specific ACE types predictive of human trafficking did differ by gender. Physical and emotional abuse were not predictive of human trafficking for girls (all other ACE types were), but only among girls who were not also sexually abused. Among boys, only emotional abuse and sexual abuse were predictive of human trafficking.

## Residential Mobility, ACEs and Health

One characteristic not often considered in conjunction with cumulative traumatic stress is residential mobility. A retrospective study of 8,116 adults completing surveys regarding childhood residential mobility, ACEs and health problems indicated the risk for high residential mobility during childhood (experiencing at least eight moves) had a dose-response relationship with ACE exposure (Dong et al., 2005). Additionally, compared with those who never moved, those with eight or more childhood moves had 1.3 times the odds of smoking as an adult, and 2.5 times the odds of suicide. Interestingly, including the number of ACEs in predictive models reduced the effect of mobility on health problems, indicating the apparent relationship between mobility and health risks is largely explained by ACE exposure (Dong et al., 2005).

## Implications for Juvenile Justice Systems

The body of work reviewed and presented above illustrates childhood maltreatment and traumatic exposure (1) is common, (2) is more prevalent among at-risk and special populations such as juvenile offenders, (3) and exerts a deleterious effect on a host of negative proximal and long-term outcomes ranging from rather immediate changes to the developing brain to physical health, mental health, and behavioral indicators, including delinquency and crime. This knowledge has rather stark implications for practitioners and policy makers encompassing juvenile justice systems. A potential four-tier strategy is outlined below.

### Tier 1: ACE Prevention

Clearly, the most obvious of implications, and the first tier of a proposed strategy is the need for prevention. ACEs are entirely preventable, and the studies outlined above all demonstrate those without exposure to adverse childhood trauma demonstrate significantly and substantive greater success across outcomes than those with such ACE exposures, often in a dose-response, graded fashion. As ACE exposure is a direct predictor of these maladaptive outcomes, the prevention of such adverse experiences may play a pivotal role in affecting the path toward them. Enhanced prenatal care and assistance, parent and family training interventions, and home visitation programs have all shown potential in reducing adverse experiences and improving child development (Cohen, Piquero, & Jennings, 2010; Zigler & Hall, 1989), while also consistently affecting subsequent delinquent and criminal behavior (see Olds et al., 1997, 1998; Piquero, Farrington, Welsh, Tremblay, & Jennings, 2009; Piquero et al., 2016). Targeted prevention efforts may avert youth from experiencing childhood adversity in the first place, with hopes of steering youth from negative health repercussions and maladaptive behavior.

### Tier 2: ACE Screening, Staff Training, and Service Referrals

A second tier effort should arguably be the implementation of universal ACE screening across juvenile justice system programs and partners. Understanding and recognition of ACE exposure and its implications for children and adolescents is critical. Staff training in both of these facets (understanding ACEs and their effects and identification of exposures among clients/youth) is undoubtable a large component to the second tier of universal screening. Similar recommendations have been levied toward primary care physician practices to include implementation of screening programs or tools, training clinicians to recognize and discuss psychosocial issues with youth and their families, and providing professionals with community resource lists including referrals to parenting programs (Flynn et al., 2015). Similarly, those in juvenile justice systems need not only the understanding of ACE and the implications of maltreatment, as well as training and tools to conduct screening, but also protocols for referral for further assessment and linkages to community-based providers in order to refer youth and families for potentially needed services. As we have stated in the past, the simplicity of the ACE score reinforces the policy implications as the costs to implement a ten-item additive yes/no binary screening tool are limited (Wolff, Baglivio, & Piquero, 2017). The effectiveness of the process lies in the understanding and buy-in that cumulative traumatic exposure and childhood maltreatment are drivers of antisocial behavior and negative health outcomes, which may be assuredly difficult for some juvenile justice practitioners, and the need for referral to services.

### Tier 3: Targeted Mental Health and Trauma-Informed Intervention Service Provision

The third tier to enhancing juvenile justice response to childhood traumatic exposure is intervention. As shown above, adolescents enter the juvenile justice system with ACE exposure far exceeding that of the general population. Intervention efforts should ensure that the screening results of each youth's ACE exposure are used in matching youth with appropriate treatment, if juvenile delinquency is to be redirected from persistence and transition into early adulthood, and if we are to mitigate the suffering of deleterious health repercussions evidenced among ACE exposed individuals. We know that intervention at the earliest age possible is the most advantageous to thwart the long-term effects of toxic stress (Welsh & Loeber, 2013). One intervention specifically designed to address traumatic exposure which has some demonstrated success is Trauma-Focused CBT (TF-CBT; Cohen, Mannarino, & Deblinger, 2017). TF-CBT has demonstrated effectiveness in addressing internalizing and externalizing problem behaviors of children and adolescents with cumulative traumatic exposure (Cohen, Deblinger, Mannarino, & Steer, 2004; Cohen, Mannarino, & Deblinger, 2010; Mannarino, Cohen, & Deblinger, 2014). Of note, further research should be conducted to examine the efficacy of TF-CBT with justice-involved youth.

We have seen that ACE exposure itself influences a host of risk factors across individual, familial, and personal characteristics, including anger-irritability, aggression, substance abuse, parental supervision, and school misbehavior. As we have opined previously, a

> wide range of evidence-based prevention and intervention strategies exists for lessening the influence of these risk factors including early-family/child training programs (Piquero et al., 2009), self-regulation modification (Evans-Chase, 2014; Evans-Chase, Kim, & Zhou, 2013) and self-control modification (Piquero, Jennings, & Farrington, 2010) programs, as well as substance abuse treatment strategies (Vaughn & Howard, 2004). All of these programs should be made available to youth presenting such risk upon entry into the juvenile justice system.
>
> (Baglivio et al., 2015, p. 239)

Additionally, as ACEs have been implicated with negative emotionality and aggression in juvenile recidivism (Wolff & Baglivio, 2017), interventions addressing anger management are warranted (Goldstein et al., 1986; Holmqvist, Hill, & Lang, 2009; Reddy & Goldstein, 2001), as are more holistic interventions which include the families and often community connections as well, such as Multi-systemic Therapy, Nurse-Family Partnerships, and Functional Family Therapy (Olds, 2007; Sawyer & Borduin, 2011; Sexton & Turner, 2010).

As ACE exposure has demonstrated strong linkages to subsequent offending and negative health outcomes across samples, including a broad scope of research examining Florida's juvenile offenders, a research agenda must be set to examine potential moderating and mediating mechanisms in an attempt to mitigate those effects. For example, Craig and colleagues demonstrated that higher ACE exposure increases the likelihood of recidivism among youth who engaged in moderate-to-high substance use, yet this effect was not evidenced among juvenile offenders with little-to-no substance use (Craig, Intravia, Wolff, & Baglivio, 2017). Useful to practitioners and justice system policy, these effects were largely consistent across race/ethnicity and sex. Interestingly, using the same sample of approximately 28,000 Florida juvenile offenders, stronger social bonds (positive, prosocial ties to family, peers and community) did not reduce the deleterious effects of greater ACE exposure on recidivism (Craig, Baglivio, Wolff, Piquero, & Epps, 2017). These results, contrary to expectations, indicate how essential it is to empirically test hypotheses prior to juvenile justice agencies or practitioners rushing to implement policies or practices. Recommendations of interventions are warranted, but even more so are evaluations as to whether those properly implemented services actually mitigate the undesirable outcomes.

## Tier 4: Systems Alignment

A juvenile justice strategy to address the implications of adverse childhood exposure types would seem remiss without consideration that a percentage of justice-involved youth are dually involved in the child welfare system, and of course have had involvement with the school system. Youth with dual involvement have more extensive ACE exposure, on average, than single-system youth (see Baglivio et al., 2016). These systems must commit to "fundamentally changing the manner in which the child welfare, juvenile justice, education and behavioral health systems align their case practices in relation to dually-involved and dually-adjudicated youth" (Baglivio et al., 2016, p. 649). Best practices call for identification of dually involved youth as early as possible, sharing of data and information, potentially a court liaison position, as well as a team approach to ensure a single, comprehensive strategy in addressing the youth's case, rather than a silo, fragmented care approach. Additionally, a one judge/one family approach is optimal, rather than youth and families navigating separate courts at any given time. Systems alignment and information sharing will be instrumental to ensuring youth and families do not "slip through the cracks" as agencies and systems pass youth from one to the next. A coordinated, aligned approach, such as that espoused by the Crossover Youth Practice Model (CYPM; Stewart, Lutz, & Herz, 2010) is optimal.

## Conclusion

A rich body of research now exists detailing the damaging effects of childhood maltreatment, through abuse, neglect, and household dysfunction, on the most basic facets of human life: behavior and health. The effects are consistent, transcend samples and methodologies, and cross multiple outcomes. The effects are usually indicated to be graded, such that each additional ACE exposure increases the likelihood of poor outcome. While there have certainly been critiques of the ACE score levied, the simplicity of a short screener of binary exposures may have led to its proliferation and ease of use, which is not to be minimized. Juvenile justice system-involved youth are especially vulnerable due to their increased exposure and the nature of the circumstances many of those youth are faced with on a daily basis. A need exists for further research, especially related to gender and race/ethnicity differences in ACE prevalence, as well as efficacy of various interventions to mitigate ACE effects on health and behavior. The implications of ACE exposure in increasing racial/ethnic inequality are greatly understudied. As example, one in four Black 23-year-olds have had a father incarcerated (an ACE exposure) at some point, compared to one in 30 for Whites (Wakefield & Wildeman, 2014). In addition to continuing to build and enhance the research agenda, there are steps juvenile justice systems can take now. Prevention, screening, staff training, targeted intervention, and systems alignment with child welfare are readily identified best practices. The literal future of these children hangs in the balance.

## References

Anda, R. F., Butchart, A., Felitti, V. J., & Brown, D. W. (2010). Building a framework for global surveillance of the public health implications of adverse childhood experiences. *American Journal of Preventive Medicine*, *39*, 93–98.

Anda, R. F., Felitti, V. J., Bremner, J. D., Walker, J. D., Whitfield, C., Perry, B. D., Dube, S. R., & Giles, W. H. (2006). The enduring effects of abuse and related adverse experiences in childhood: A convergence of evidence from neurobiology and epidemiology. *European Archives of Psychiatry and Clinical Neuroscience*, *256*, 174–186.

Baglivio, M. T., & Epps, N. (2016). The interrelatedness of Adverse Childhood Experiences among high-risk juvenile offenders. *Youth Violence and Juvenile Justice*, *14(3)*, 179–198.

Baglivio, M. T., Epps, N., Swartz, K., Huq, M. S., Sheer, A., & Hardt, N. S. (2014). The prevalence of Adverse Childhood Experiences (ACE) in the lives of juvenile offenders. *Journal of Juvenile Justice*, *3(2)*, 1–23.

Baglivio, M. T., Wolff, K. T., Epps, N., & Nelson, R. (2017). Predicting Adverse Childhood Experiences: The importance of neighborhood context in youth trauma among delinquent youth. *Crime & Delinquency*, *63(2)*, 166–188.

Baglivio, M. T., Wolff, K. T., Piquero, A. R., Bilchik, S., Jackowski, K., Greenwald, M. A., & Epps, N. (2016). Maltreatment, child welfare, and recidivism in a sample of deep-end crossover youth. *Journal of Youth and Adolescence*, *45(4)*, 625–654.

Baglivio, M. T., Wolff, K. T., Piquero, A. R., & Epps, N. (2015). The relationship between Adverse Childhood Experiences (ACE) and juvenile offending trajectories in a juvenile offender sample. *Journal of Criminal Justice*, *43*, 229–241.

Balistreri, K. S., & Alvira-Hammond, M. (2016). Adverse Childhood Experiences, family functioning and adolescent health and emotional well-being. *Public Health*, *132*, 72–78.

Barrett, D. E., Katsiyannis, A., Zhang, D., & Zhang, D. (2014). Delinquency and recidivism: A multicohort, matched-control study of the role of early adverse experiences, mental health problems, and disabilities. *Journal of Emotional and Behavioral Disorders*, *22(1)*, 3–15.

Bellis, M. A., Lowey, H., Leckenby, N., Hughes, K., & Harrison, D. (2013). Adverse childhood experiences: Retrospective study to determine their impact on adult health behaviors and health outcomes in a UK population. *Journal of Public Health, 36*(1), 81–91.

Bremner, J. D. (1999). Does stress damage the brain? *Biological Psychiatry, 45*, 797–805.

Cannon, Y., Davis, G., Hsi, A., & Bochte, A. (2016). *Adverse childhood experiences in the New Mexico juvenile justice population*. New Mexico: New Mexico Sentencing Commission.

Centers for Disease Control and Prevention. (2017). Injury prevention and control: Adverse Childhood Experiences (ACE) study. Available online: www.cdc.gov/violenceprevention/acestudy/. Accessed 20 February 2018.

Chiu, Y., Ryan, J. P., & Herz, D. C. (2011). Allegations of maltreatment and delinquency: Does risk of juvenile arrest vary substantiation status? *Children and Youth Services Review, 33*, 855–860.

Cicchetti, D. (2013). Annual research review: Resilient functioning in maltreated children – past, present, and future perspectives. *Journal of Child Psychology and Psychiatry, 54*, 402–422.

Cohen, J. A., Deblinger, E., Mannarino, A. P., & Steer, R. A. (2004). A multisite, randomized controlled trial for sexually abused children with PTSD problems. *Journal of the American Academy of Children and Adolescent Psychiatry, 43*, 393–402.

Cohen, J. A., Mannarino, A. P., & Deblinger, E. (2010). Trauma-focused cognitive-behavioral therapy for traumatized children. *Evidence-based Psychotherapies for Children and Adolescents, 2*, 295–311.

Cohen, J. A., Mannarino, A. P., & Deblinger, E. (2017). *Treating trauma and traumatic grief in children and adolescents*, 2nd ed. New York, NY: Guilford Press.

Cohen, M. A., Piquero, A. R., & Jennings, W. G. (2010). Estimating the costs of bad outcomes for at-risk youth and the benefits of early childhood interventions to reduce them. *Criminal Justice Policy Review, 21*, 391–434.

Craig, J. M., Baglivio, M. T., Wolff, K. T., Piquero, A. R., & Epps, N. (2017). Do social bonds buffer the impact of Adverse Childhood Experiences on reoffending? *Youth Violence and Juvenile Justice, 15*(1), 3–20.

Craig, J. M., Intravia, J., Wolff, K. T., & Baglivio, M. T. (2017). What can help? Examining levels of substance (non)use as a protective factor in the effect of ACEs on crime. *Youth Violence and Juvenile Justice*, advance online publication, 10.1177/1541204017728998.

Craig, J. M., Piquero, A. R., Farrington, D. P., & Ttofi, M. M. (2017). A little risk goes a long way: Adverse childhood experiences and life-course offending in the Cambridge study. *Journal of Criminal Justice, 53*, 34–45.

Cronholm, P. F., Forke, C. M., Wade, R., Bair-Merritt, M. H., Davis, M., Harkins-Schwarz, M., Pachter, L. M., & Fein, J. A. (2015). Adverse childhood experiences: Expanding the concept of adversity. *American Journal of Preventive Medicine, 49*(3), 354–361.

Danese, A., & McEwen, B. S. (2012). Adverse childhood experiences, allostasis, allostatic load, and age-related disease. *Physiology and Behavior, 106*, 29–39.

DeLisi, M., Alcala, J., Kusow, A., Hochstetler, A., Heirigs, M. H., Caudill, J. W., Trulson, C. R., & Baglivio, M. T. (2017). Adverse Childhood Experiences, commitment offense, and race/ethnicity: Are the effects crime-, race-, and ethnicity-specific? *International Journal of Environmental Research and Public Health, 14*, 331–343.

Della Femina, D., Yeager, C. A., & Lewis, D. O. (1990). Child abuse: Adolescent records vs. adult recall. *Child Abuse and Neglect, 14*, 227–231.

Dong, M., Anda, R. F., Felitti, V. J., Williamson, D. F., Dube, S. R., Brown, D. W., & Giles, W. H. (2005). Childhood residential mobility and multiple health risks during adolescence and adulthood: The hidden role of Adverse Childhood Experiences. *Archives of Pediatrics Adolescent Medicine, 159*, 1104–1110.

Drake, B., Jonson-Reid, M., Way, I., & Chung, S. (2003). Substantiation and recidivism. *Children Maltreatment, 8*, 248–260.

Dube, S. R., Miller, J. W., Brown, D. W., Giles, W. H., Felitti, V. J., Dong, M., & Anda, R. F. (2006). Adverse childhood experiences and the association with ever using alcohol and initiating alcohol use during adolescence. *Journal of Adolescent Health, 38*, 444.e1–444.e10.

Dube, S. R., Williamson, D. F., Thompson, T., Felitti, V. J., & Anda, R. F. (2004). Assessing the reliability of retrospective reports of adverse childhood experiences among adult HMO members attending a primary care clinic. *Child Abuse and Neglect, 28*, 729–737.

Eckenrode, J., Smith, E. G., McCarthy, M. E., & Dineen, M. (2014). Income inequality and child maltreatment in the United States. *Pediatrics, 133*(3), 454–461.

English, D. J., Widom, C. S., & Brandford, C. (2002). *Childhood victimization and delinquency, adult criminality, and violent criminal behavior: A replication and extension*. Final Report to National Institute of Justice.

Evans-Chase, M. (2014). Addressing trauma and psychosocial development in juvenile justice-involved youth: A synthesis of the developmental neuroscience, juvenile justice and trauma literature. *Laws, 3*, 744–758.

Evans-Chase, M., Kim, M., & Zhou, H. (2013). Risk-taking and self-regulation: A systematic review of the analysis of delinquency outcomes in the juvenile justice intervention literature 1996–2009. *Criminal Justice and Behavior, 40*, 608–628.

Felitti, V. J., Anda, R. F., Nordenberg, D., Williamson, D. F., Spitz, A. M., Edwards, V., Koss, M. P., & Marks, J. S. (1998). Relationship of childhood abuse and household dysfunction to many of the leading causes of death in adults: The Adverse Childhood Experiences Study. *American Journal of Preventive Medicine, 14*(4), 245–258.

Finkelohor, D., Shattuck, A., Turner, H., & Hamby, S. (2013). Improving the Adverse Childhood Experiences Study scale. *Pediatrics, 167*(1), 70–75.

Finkelohor, D., Shattuck, A., Turner, H., & Hamby, S. (2015). A revised inventory of Adverse Childhood Experiences. *Child Abuse & Neglect, 48*, 13–21.

Flaherty, E. G., Thompson, R., Dubowitz, H., Harvey, E. M., English, D. J., Proctor, L. J., & Runyan, D. K. (2013). Adverse Childhood Experiences and child health in early adolescence. *Pediatrics, 167*(7), 622–629.

Flaherty, E. G., Thompson, R., Litrownik, A. J., Zolotor, A. J., Dubowitz, H., Runyan, D. K., English, D. J., & Everson, M. D. (2009). Adverse childhood exposures and reported health at age 12. *Academic Pediatrics, 9*, 150–156.

Flynn, A. B., Fothergill, K. E., Wilcox, H. C., Coleclough, E., Horwitz, R., Ruble, A., Burkey, M. D., & Wissow, L. S. (2015). Primary care interventions to prevent or treat traumatic stress in childhood: A systematic review. *Academic Pediatrics, 15*, 480–492.

Fox, B. H., Perez, N., Cass, E., Baglivio, M. T., & Epps, N. (2015). Trauma changes everything: Examining the relationship between Adverse Childhood Experiences and serious, violent and chronic juvenile offenders. *Child Abuse & Neglect, 46*, 153–163.

Goldstein, A. P., Glick, B., Reiner, S., Zimmerman, D., Coultry, T. M., & Gold, D. (1986). Aggression replacement training: A comprehensive intervention for the acting out delinquent. *Journal of Correctional Education, 37*, 120–126.

Hillis, S. D., Anda, R. F., Dube, S. R., Felitti, V. J., Marchbanks, P. A., & Marks, J. S. (2004). The association between Adverse Childhood Experiences and adolescent pregnancy, long-term psychosocial consequences, and fetal death. *Pediatrics, 2*, 320–327.

Hillis, S. D., Anda, R. F., Felitti, V. J., & Marchbanks, P. A. (2001). Adverse Childhood Experiences and sexual risk behaviors in women: A retrospective cohort study. *Family Planning Perspective, 5*, 206–211.

Holmqvist, R., Hill, T., & Lang, A. (2009). Effects of aggression replacement training in young offender institutions. *International Journal of Offender Therapy and Comparative Criminology, 53*, 74–92.

Hunt, T. K. A., Slack, K. S., & Berger, L. M. (2017). Adverse Childhood Experiences and behavioral problems in middle childhood. *Child Abuse & Neglect, 67*, 391–402.

Kerker, B. D., Zhang, J., Nadeem, E., Stein, R. E. K., Hurlburt, M. S., Heneghan, A., Landsverk, J., & Horwitz, S. M. (2015). Adverse Childhood Experiences and mental health, chronic medical conditions, and development in young children. *Academic Pediatrics, 15*, 510–517.

Larkin, H., Felitti, V. J., & Anda, R. F. (2014). Social work and Adverse Childhood Experiences research: Implications for practice and health policy. *Social Work in Public Health, 29*, 1–16.

Levenson, J. S., Baglivio, M. T., Wolff, K. T., Epps, N., Royall, W., Gomez, K., & Kaplan, D. (2017). You learn what you live: Prevalence of childhood adversity in the lives of juveniles arrested for sexual offenses. *Advances in Social Work, 18*(1), 313–334.

Mannarino, A. P., Cohen, J. A., & Deblinger, E. (2014). Trauma-focused cognitive behavioral therapy. In Timmer, S., & Urquiza, A. (Eds.), *Evidence-based approaches for the treatment of maltreated children* (pp. 165–185). Rotterdam, The Netherlands: Springer.

Maxfield, M. G., & Widom, C. S. (1996). The cycle of violence: Revisited 6 years later. *Archives of Pediatric Adolescence, 150*(4), 390–395.

Nofziger, S., & Kurtz, D. (2005). Violent lives: A lifestyle model linking exposure to violence to juvenile violent offending. *Journal of Research in Crime and Delinquency, 42*(1), 3–26.

Olds, D. L. (2007). Preventing crime with prenatal and infancy support of parents: The nurse-family partnership. *Victims & Offenders, 2*, 205–225.

Olds, D. L., Eckenrode, J., Henderson, C. R., Kitzman, H., Powers, J., Cole, R., & Luckey, D. (1997). Long-term effects of home visitation on maternal life course and child abuse and neglect: Fifteen-year follow-up of a randomized trial. *Journal of the American Medical Association, 278*, 637–643.

Olds, D. L., Henderson, C. R., Cole, R., Eckenrode, J., Kitzman, H., Luckey, D., & Powers, J. (1998). Long-term effects of nurse home visitation on children's criminal and antisocial behavior: 15-year follow-up of a randomized controlled trial. *Journal of the American Medical Association, 280*, 1238–1244.

Painter, K., & Scannapieco, M. (2013). Child maltreatment: The neurobiological aspects of posttraumatic stress disorder. *Journal of Evidence-Based Social Work, 10*, 276–284.

Perez, N. M., Jennings, W. G., & Baglivio, M. T. (2018). The path to serious, violent, chronic delinquency: The harmful aftermath of Adverse Childhood Experiences. *Crime & Delinquency, 64(1)*, 3–25.

Perez, N. M., Jennings, W. G., Piquero, A. R., & Baglivio, M. T. (2016). Adverse Childhood Experiences and suicide attempts: The mediating influence of personality development and problem behaviors. *Journal of Youth and Adolescence, 45(8)*, 1527–1545.

Piquero, A. R., Farrington, D. P., Welsh, B. C., Tremblay, R., & Jennings, W. G. (2009). Effects of early family/parent training programs on antisocial behavior and delinquency. *Journal of Experimental Criminology, 5*, 83–120.

Piquero, A. R., Jennings, W., & Farrington, D. P. (2010). On the malleability of self-control: Theoretical and policy implications regarding a General Theory of Crime. *Justice Quarterly, 27*, 803–834.

Piquero, A. R., Jennings, W. G., Diamond, B., Farrington, D. P., Tremblay, R. E., Welsh, B., & Reingle Gonzalez, J. M. (2016). A meta-analysis update on the effects of early family/parent training programs on antisocial behavior and delinquency. *Journal of Experimental Criminology, 12*, 229–248.

Reddy, L. A., & Goldstein, A. P. (2001). Aggression replacement training: A multimodal intervention for aggressive adolescents. *Residential Treatment for Children & Youth, 18*, 47–62.

Reid, J. A., Baglivio, M. T., Piquero, A. R., Greenwald, M. A., & Epps, N. (2017). Human trafficking of minors and childhood adversity in Florida. *American Journal of Public Health, 107(2)*, 306–311.

Ryan, J. P., Williams, A. B., & Courtney, M. E. (2013). Adolescent neglect, juvenile delinquency and the risk of recidivism. *Journal of Youth and Adolescence, 42*, 454–465.

Sawyer, A. M., & Borduin, C. M. (2011). Effects of multisystemic therapy through midlife: A 21.9 year follow-up to a randomized clinical trial with serious and violent juvenile offenders. *Journal of Consulting and Clinical Psychology, 79*, 643–652.

Schilling, E. A., Aseltine, R. H., & Gore, S. (2007). Adverse Childhood Experiences and mental health in youth adults: A longitudinal survey. *BMC Public Health, 7*, 30–40.

Sexton, T. L., & Turner, C. W. (2010). The effectiveness of functional family therapy for youth with behavioral problems in a community practice setting. *Journal of Family Psychology, 3*, 339–348.

Shalev, I., Moffitt, T., Sugden, K., Williams, B., Houts, R. M., Danese, A., Mill, J., Arseneault, L., & Caspi, A. (2013). Exposure to violence during childhood is associated with telomere erosion from 5 to 10 years of age: A longitudinal study. *Molecular Psychiatry, 18*, 576–581.

Smith, C., & Thornberry, T. P. (1995). The relationship between childhood maltreatment and adolescent involvement in delinquency. *Criminology, 33*, 451–481.

Smith, C., Thornberry, T. P., & Ireland, T. O. (2004). Adolescent maltreatment and its impact: Timing matters. *The Prevention Researcher, 11*, 7–11.

Stewart, M., Lutz, L., & Herz, D. H. (2010). *Crossover youth practice model*. Washington, DC: Center for Juvenile Justice Reform, Georgetown University McCourt School of Public Policy.

Stouthamer-Loeber, M., Loeber, R., Homish, D. L., & Wei, E. (2001). Maltreatment of boys and the development of disruptive and delinquent behavior. *Developmental Psychopathology, 13(4)*, 941–955.

Teicher, M. H., Andersen, S. L., Polcari, A., Anderson, C. M., Navalta, C. P., & Kim, D. M. (2003). The neurobiological consequences of early stress and childhood maltreatment. *Neuroscience & Biobehavioral Reviews, 27(1–2)*, 33–34.

Thompson, R., Flaherty, E. G., English, D. J., Litrownik, A. J., Dubowitz, H., Kotch, J. B., & Runyan, D. K. (2015). Trajectories of Adverse Childhood Experiences and self-reported health at age 18. *Academic Pediatrics, 15*, 503–509.

Vaughn, M. G., & Howard, M. O. (2004). Adolescent substance abuse treatment: A synthesis of controlled evaluations. *Research on Social Work Practice, 14*, 323–335.

Wakefield, S., & Wildeman, C. (2014). *Children of the prison boom: Mass incarceration and the future of American inequality*. New York, NY: Oxford University Press.

Welsh, B. C., & Loeber, R. (2013). Taking stock of criminology and a criminologist for the ages: Reflections on milestones and the future of criminology and on one of its scholars – David Farrington. *Criminal Behaviour and Mental Health, 23*, 77–85.

Widom, C. S. (1989). The cycle of violence. *Science, 244*, 160–166.

Wiig, J., Widom, C. S., & Tuell, J. A. (2003). *Understanding child maltreatment and juvenile delinquency: Foundations for effective responses: From research to effective program, practice, and systemic solutions*. Washington, DC: Child Welfare League of America, Inc.

Williams, L. M. (1995). Recovered memories of abuse in women with documented child sexual victimization histories. *Journal of Trauma and Stress, 8*, 649–673.

Wolff, K. T., & Baglivio, M. T. (2017). Adverse Childhood Experiences, negative emotionality, and pathways to juvenile recidivism. *Crime & Delinquency, 63*(12), 1495–1521.

Wolff, K. T., Baglivio, M. T., & Piquero, A. R. (2017). The relationship between Adverse Childhood Experiences and recidivism in a sample of juvenile offenders in community-based treatment. *International Journal of Offender Therapy and Comparative Criminology, 61*(11), 1210–1242.

Zettler, H., Wolff, K. T., Baglivio, M. T., Craig, J. M., & Epps, N. (2017). The racial and gender differences in the impact of Adverse Childhood Experiences on juvenile residential placement. *Youth Violence and Juvenile Justice*, advance online publication, 10.1177/1541204017698213.

Zigler, E., & Hall, N. W. (1989). Physical child abuse in America: Past, present, and future. In Cicchetti, D., & Carlson, V. (Eds.), *Child maltreatment: Theory and research on the causes and consequences of child abuse and neglect* (pp. 38–75). New York, NY: Cambridge University Press.

Zingraff, M. T., Leiter, J., Myers, K. A., & Johnsen, M. C. (1993). Child maltreatment and youthful problem behavior. *Criminology, 31*(2), 173–202.

# 8
# THE HEALTH CONSEQUENCES OF INCARCERATION FOR FAMILIES

*Kristin Turney and Martha Morales Hernandez*

### Introduction

The number of incarcerated individuals in the United States has risen dramatically in the last half century. In 2016, 6.6 million individuals were incarcerated in a local jail, a state prison, or a federal prison in the United States (Kaeble & Cowhig, 2018). This high number has captured the attention of researchers across a variety of disciplines, practitioners, and policymakers in efforts to understand the consequences of incarceration for those who both directly and indirectly experience it. Research highlights that incarceration has deleterious consequences for currently and formerly incarcerated individuals and that incarceration has broader consequences for families and communities (Travis, Western, & Redburn, 2014).

Currently and formerly incarcerated individuals are not solitary individuals. Instead, currently and formerly incarcerated individuals have many familial connections, identifying with roles such as romantic partner, parent, and child (Chung & Hepburn, 2018). It is therefore unsurprising that incarceration is a stressor that is consequential for aspects of family life, altering the structure and function of families who experience the stressor (Arditti, 2012; Comfort, 2008; Turanovic, Rodriguez, & Pratt, 2012; Wildeman & Muller, 2012). Incarceration is associated with an increased likelihood of union dissolution (Massoglia, Remster, & King, 2011; Turney, 2015a), impaired relationship quality (Turney, 2015b), challenges in the co-parental relationship (Geller, 2013; Turney & Wildeman, 2013), and reduced contact with parents (Turney, 2014a). Incarceration is a stressor that reverberates throughout families.

The stress process perspective, which highlights how stressors are both concentrated among disadvantaged groups and create health disadvantages (Pearlin, 1989), suggests that incarceration may have deleterious health consequences for family members. Accordingly, a burgeoning literature investigates the physical and mental health consequences of family member incarceration. In this chapter, we review both theoretical and empirical literature linking incarceration to family member health. First, we provide an overview of the stress process perspective. Following previous research (Pearlin, 1989; Turney, 2014b; Turney, Wildeman, & Schnittker, 2012), we conceptualize incarceration as a stressor for the incarcerated individual and those connected to the incarcerated individual via family ties (including romantic partners, children, and other family members). Next, we review empirical findings linking incarceration to the physical and mental health of incarcerated individuals and their family members, focusing mostly on the proliferation to family members.

## Incarceration in the Stress Process Perspective

The stress process perspective provides a useful theoretical lens for understanding the familial health consequences of incarceration. Four aspects of the stress process perspective are especially useful for understanding this relationship: (1) social groups are unequally exposed to stressors; (2) stressors have deleterious consequences for physical and mental health; (3) stressors can proliferate in two ways, first by proliferating to create additional stressors and second by proliferating to those connected to the individual experiencing the stressor; and (4) social support and coping resources can buffer the deleterious health consequences of stressors. We describe each of these aspects below, highlighting the role of incarceration as a stressor.

### *Unequal Exposure to Stressors*

First, the stress process perspective suggests that groups from disadvantaged social contexts are more likely to experience stress than their counterparts from more advantaged social contexts (Pearlin, 1989). Indeed, incarceration is a stressor that is unequally distributed across the population. For example, Blacks and Hispanics are more likely than Whites to experience forms of criminal justice contact such as incarceration (Sugie & Turney, 2017; Western & Pettit, 2010). Disparities in exposure to incarceration also persist according to socioeconomic status, with economically disadvantaged individuals more likely to experience incarceration than economically advantaged individuals and those with lower educational attainment more likely to experience incarceration than their counterparts (Wakefield & Uggen, 2010).

Accordingly, experiencing family member incarceration is unequally distributed across the population. Consider the risk of exposure to parental incarceration. Notably, children of color are most at risk for experiencing parental incarceration (Turney & Haskins, Forthcoming). Demographic estimates show that about 25% of Black children and 10% of Latino children, compared to 4% of White children, are expected to experience parental incarceration (Sykes & Pettit, 2014). The risk of parental incarceration is also structured by indicators of socioeconomic status. Children who live in poverty are three times more likely than other children to experience parental incarceration (Murphey & Cooper, 2015). Children with parents who did not graduate high school are more likely than other children to experience parental incarceration. For example, 15% of White children and 62% of Black children born to parents without a high school degree, compared to 2% and 10%, respectively, of children born to parents with some college, can expect to experience parental incarceration by age 17 (Sykes & Pettit, 2014).

### *Consequences of Stressors for Physical and Mental Health*

Second, the stress process perspective suggest that stressors have consequences for physical and mental health (Pearlin, 1989; Thoits, 2010). Stressors such as job loss, death of a family member, and divorce have deleterious consequences for mental health outcomes including depressive symptoms, major depressive disorder, substance abuse, and alcohol dependence (Turner, 2003; Turner & Avison, 2003; Turner & Lloyd, 1999; Turner, Wheaton, & Lloyd, 1995). In fact, the consequences of chronic strains on the mental health of individuals are more powerful than the negative events or traumas that precipitated the chronic strain (Turner, Wheaton, & Lloyd, 1995).

Scholars have theorized incarceration as a stressor (Foster, 2012; Massoglia, 2008a; Turney, 2014b; Turney, Wildeman, & Schnittker, 2012). During incarceration, individuals are limited in their time outside of their cell, have an enforced routine, and face uncertainty about their lives upon release, all of which may be consequential for physical and mental health. By extension, experiencing the incarceration of a family member is a consequential stressor for physical and mental health (Pearlin, 1989; Pearlin, Aneshensel, & LeBlanc, 1997).

## *Stress Proliferation within and across Individuals*

Third, the stress process perspective suggests that stressors can proliferate in two ways, with stressors accumulating within individuals and with stressors proliferating from one individual to others connected to that individual.

The first dimension of stress proliferation, the within-individual stress proliferation, involves the emergence of multiple stressors resulting from one stressor. In other words, initial stressors (often called primary stressors) can accumulate and give rise to additional stressors (often called secondary stressors). These primary and secondary stressors pile on the lives of individuals, facilitating an entanglement of stressors that may be different from what they started with (Pearlin, Aneshensel, & LeBlanc, 1997). Thus, being exposed to a new stressor leads to another event or triggers more strains (Pearlin, 1989).

The second dimension of stress proliferation is the transferring of stress from one person to another, sometimes called stress contagion (Barr et al., 2018; Wethington, 2000). In this type of stress proliferation, stressors in one person's life can lead to stressors in another person's life. Pearlin et al. (2005) discuss how an individual linked by a shared membership in a specific role may be subject to experiencing the initial stressors encountered by only one member. Thoits (2010) further elaborates this process in one of the most important relationships—that between children and parents—and suggests that stressors parents experience could have consequences for the stressors that their children encounter. This transfer of stressors is important to highlight because it demonstrates that there could be reproduction of social disadvantages from one generation onto another.

In particular, the stressor of incarceration can proliferate within individuals. The confinement associated with incarceration is a stressful experience (Sykes, 2007). Given the primary stressors that are associated with incarceration (such as confinement, regimentation, and isolation), incarcerated or formerly incarcerated individuals experience multiple stressors simultaneously (Pearlin, 1989; Turner & Avison, 2003; Wheaton, 1994). For example, the primary stressor of incarceration could develop into additional, or secondary, stressors such as difficultly finding employment upon release or strained relationships with family members. Both these primary and secondary stressors can affect the health of the incarcerated individual and his or her family members.

Additionally, the stressor of incarceration can transfer from an individual to his/her family members, both directly and indirectly influencing their health. The effects might be direct, as experiencing family member incarceration may facilitate depression or anxiety. But the effects might also be indirect. For example, one of the most prominent stressors that is heightened through family member incarceration is financial insecurity. This is particularly true when incarcerated individuals were primary or important sources of income for their families (Comfort, 2008; Schwartz-Soicher, Geller, & Garfinkel, 2011; Western, 2006), and this financial insecurity likely has deleterious health consequences (Burgard & Kalousova, 2015). Similarly, it is challenging for incarcerated individuals to maintain strong relationships with family members, which may facilitate health problems among those family members (Lopoo & Western, 2005; Massoglia, Remster, & King, 2011). Furthermore, stigma can be experienced by the person who is incarcerated and it can spread to people who associated with the incarcerated individual (Braman, 2004). In summary, stress proliferating from incarceration can affect physical and mental health of family members.

## Coping and Social Support as Buffers

Finally, the stress process perspective suggests that coping and social support buffers the relationship between stressors and health. Coping is an action—either cognitive or behavioral—made by an individual to reduce, master, or manage life strains and stress (Lazarus & Folkman, 1984; Pearlin & Schooler, 1978). Individuals have coping resources that can buffer the deleterious consequences of a stressor, reducing the accompanying adverse mental and physical health risks of stress (Taylor & Stanton, 2007). Specifically, extensive research has focused around the usage of coping resources and availability of them to individuals. In having different pockets of support and resources, individuals are better able to cope with the stressors in their life and, by extension, the deleterious effects of stress are reduced (Billings & Moos, 1981; Kessler & Essex, 1982; Pearlin & Schooler, 1978).

Indeed, coping can moderate the effects of stress on the incarcerated and their family members. Incarceration presents a unique and straining set of challenges that prompts those affected by it to find ways to cope. Research has shown how imprisoned mothers, in efforts to cope with not being fully present, have conversations with their children and loved ones about their actions and scheduling frequent visitations (Celinska & Siegel, 2010; Enos, 2001). Maintaining this source of social or familial support results in families managing the stressor of incarceration that may moderate the relationship between incarceration and health. Another result of incarceration is that family members are left to cope with stigma associated with incarceration, thus building networks and shielding themselves or their children from understanding the issue of their incarcerated family member (Nurse, 2002). Avoidance of the stressor could be understood as a successful coping strategy because it may help the children get past the stressor during its duration.

## Research Linking Incarceration and Health

The stress process perspective suggests that incarceration is a stressor that can have spillover consequences on the health of family members. In this section, we review research linking incarceration and health, some of which is explicitly grounded in the stress process perspective. We first briefly summarize the relatively large literature that examines how incarceration is associated with one's own physical and mental health. We then more comprehensively summarize the smaller literature that examines the health consequences of incarceration for family members of the incarcerated. Currently and formerly incarcerated individuals are embedded within families and their incarceration can have proliferating consequences for their romantic partners, children, and other family members (i.e., parents and siblings).

## Consequences of Incarceration for Individual Physical and Mental Health

A relatively large literature examines the physical and mental health consequences of incarceration for currently and formerly incarcerated individuals (for reviews, see Massoglia & Pridemore, 2015; Wildeman & Muller, 2012; Wildeman & Wang, 2017). Overall, this research suggests three key findings.

First, current incarceration can be protective for some aspects of individual health. Specifically, incarcerated individuals have lower mortality rates than comparable individuals who are not incarcerated (Patterson, 2010). This research suggests incarceration can provide a respite from substance abuse and violence and that incarceration can provide an opportunity for health care that might be inaccessible on the outside, both of which may shield against mortality (Binswanger et al., 2007; though see Baćak & Wildeman, 2015). Other research, though, finds the protective function of incarceration does not extend to mental health (Turney, Wildeman, & Schnittker, 2012).

Second, any beneficial consequences of incarceration dissipate upon release, whereas formerly incarcerated individuals are more likely than their not formerly incarcerated counterparts to have physical and mental health impairments. An incarceration history is associated with a greater likelihood of mortality (Binswanger et al., 2007); severe health limitations (Schnittker & John, 2007); infectious diseases (Hammett, 2006; Massoglia, 2008a); chronic diseases (Binswanger, Krueger, & Steiner, 2009); health limitations (Turney & Wildeman, 2015a); fair or poor health (Curtis, 2011; see also Massoglia, 2008b); mental health conditions including major depressive disorder, bipolar disorder, and dysthymia (Esposito et al., 2017; Massoglia, 2008b; Porter & Novisky, 2017; Schnittker, Massoglia, & Uggen, 2012; Sugie & Turney, 2017; Turney & Wildeman, 2015a; Turney, Wildeman, & Schnittker, 2012); substance use including heavy drinking and illicit drug use (Turney & Wildeman, 2015a; Yi, Turney, & Wildeman, 2017); health behaviors including fast food consumption and smoking (Porter, 2014); and sleep problems including short sleep duration and insomnia (Testa & Porter, 2017).

Third, research highlights that stress proliferation processes may link incarceration to physical and mental health outcomes. For example, one study suggests that incarceration is a primary stressor that leads to secondary stressors related to reintegration (including reductions in socioeconomic status and impairments in family functioning), and the accumulation of both primary and secondary stressors is associated with depression (Turney, Wildeman, & Schnittker, 2012).

## *Health Consequences of Incarceration for Romantic Partners*

The consequences of incarceration for physical and mental health do not end with the consequences for the incarcerated individual. Instead, the consequences of incarceration proliferate to family members of the incarcerated. One strain of research documents deleterious health consequences for romantic partners connected to incarcerated individuals. For example, Megan Comfort, drawing on years of ethnographic field work and in-depth interviews with women visiting men in a California prison, finds that women in romantic relationships with incarcerated men—even though they themselves are not incarcerated—undergo secondary prisonization, a form of socialization to correctional norms. Women describe this experience of secondary prisonization, which can include the loss of liberty experienced while visiting, as both traumatic and anxiety-producing (Comfort, 2008).

Quantitative research examining the health consequences of incarceration generally finds that romantic partner incarceration can have deleterious and lasting health consequences for women connected to incarcerated men. Much of this research uses data from the Fragile Families and Child Wellbeing Study, a longitudinal survey of mostly unmarried parents in urban areas who had a child together around the turn of the century. One study using these data finds that women who share children with recently incarcerated fathers, compared to those who share children with not recently incarcerated fathers, are more likely to have major depressive disorder and life dissatisfaction (Wildeman, Schnittker, & Turney, 2012; see also Wildeman, Lee, & Comfort, 2013). This study uses a series of rigorous modeling strategies to account for the fact that these two groups of women—those connected to recently incarcerated fathers and those connected to not recently incarcerated fathers—differ across a number of dimensions even before their exposure to their partner's incarceration, and the association between romantic partner incarceration and mental health persists across these modeling strategies. Further, this study considers three sets of mechanisms that might explain the association between romantic partner incarceration and mental health—economic wellbeing and hardship, relationship status and quality, and parenting quality and stress—and find that these mechanisms (and, in particular, parenting quality and stress) explain this association (Wildeman, Schnittker, & Turney, 2012).

Other quantitative research, also using Fragile Families data, suggests additional negative consequences for the health and wellbeing of women who share children with incarcerated men. For example, one study finds that women who share children with recently incarcerated men are more likely than their counterparts to engage in substance use, including heavy drinking, illicit drug use, and smoking. This study also finds that the association between partner incarceration and substance sue is partially explained by changes in mothers' economic wellbeing and mothers' depression and that the association between partner incarceration and drug use, in particular, is concentrated among non-Hispanic Black women (Bruns & Lee, 2018).

Additionally, another study documents that romantic partner incarceration is associated with perceptions of social support, an important dimension of health and wellbeing that may buffer the negative consequences of incarceration on physical and mental health (Thoits, 2010; Turney, Schnittker, & Wildeman, 2012). This study finds that women who share children with a currently or recently incarcerated father, compared to other women, report less in-kind support (measured by the availability of a loan for $200, place to live, and emergency childcare) and less large financial support (measured by the availability of a loan for $1,000, co-signer for $1,000, and co-signer for $5,000). Therefore, incarceration may produce a double disadvantage for romantic partners, by simultaneously increasing the need for support and decreasing the availability of support (Turney, Schnittker, & Wildeman, 2012).

## *Health Consequences of Incarceration for Children*

Additionally, research documents that the health consequences of incarceration extend to the children of the currently and formerly incarcerated (for reviews, see Foster & Hagan, 2015; Haskins & Turney, 2017; Murray, Farrington, & Sekol, 2012; Turney & Goodsell, 2018; Wildeman, Goldman, & Turney, 2018). Parental incarceration, on average, has deleterious consequences for physical and mental health from infancy through adulthood.

First, parental incarceration can be consequential for mental health. For example, research using the 2011–2012 National Survey of Children's Health (NSCH), a nationally representative survey of children in the United States, shows that the incarceration of a residential parent is independently associated with a greater likelihood of learning disabilities, attention deficit disorder and attention deficit hyperactivity disorder (ADD/ADHD), behavioral or conduct problems, developmental delays, and speech or language problems. These associations persist even after adjusting for demographic, socioeconomic, and familial characteristics (Turney, 2014b).

Other research, using data from the Fragile Families study, suggests that the health consequences of parental incarceration (at least the consequences for young children's behaviors) may be limited to paternal incarceration (and not maternal incarceration). Research shows that paternal incarceration is associated with aggressive behaviors among three-year-old children (Geller et al., 2009); aggressive behaviors and attention problems among five-year-old children (Geller et al., 2012; Wildeman, 2010); and internalizing, externalizing, and delinquency among nine-year-old children (Haskins, 2014, 2015; Turney, 2017a; see also Jackson & Vaughn, 2017). Research also shows that maternal incarceration is not independently associated with behaviors among five- and nine-year-old children; instead, observed differences in behaviors between children who do and do not experience maternal incarceration result from characteristics associated with selection into experiencing maternal incarceration such as poverty and family instability (Wildeman & Turney, 2014; see also Turney & Wildeman, 2015b). Other research shows that children of incarcerated parents are more likely than their counterparts to experience unmet mental health care needs, suggesting that the children most in need of mental health care are the least likely to receive it (Turney, 2017b).

Studies focusing on adolescent and young adult outcomes finds that both paternal and maternal incarceration has deleterious consequences for health. For example, research using the National Longitudinal Study of Adolescent to Adult Health (Add Health), a longitudinal and nationally representative sample of adolescents in seventh through 12th grade in 1994–1995, finds that paternal incarceration is positively associated with substance role problems and that maternal incarceration is positively associated with depressive symptoms (Foster & Hagan, 2015; see also Lee, Fang, & Luo, 2013; Roettger et al., 2011).

Second, parental incarceration can be consequential for physical health. Most research addressing the link between parental incarceration and physical health uses Add Health data (though see Turney, 2014b). For example, one study finds that adolescents girls who experience parental incarceration, compared to those who do not, have a higher body mass index. This study also finds that these associations persist after adjusting for an array of characteristics associated with both incarceration and BMI and that these associations persist into adulthood. This study also finds no association between parental incarceration and BMI among boys or men, suggesting that parental incarceration may be a stressful experience that facilitates gendered responses (Roettger & Boardman, 2012). Other research finds that parental incarceration, net of characteristics associated with experiencing parental incarceration, is positively associated with cholesterol, asthma, migraines, HIV/AIDS, and fair/poor health in adulthood (Lee, Fang, & Luo, 2013). Parental incarceration is also positively associated with low-grade inflammation via C-reactive protein (CRP) levels among adult women (Boch & Ford, 2015).

## *Health Consequences of Incarceration for Other Family Members*

Though most research on the spillover health consequences of incarceration focuses on romantic partners and children connected to the incarcerated, there is a small (and burgeoning) literature that considers the health of other family members such as parents and siblings (see Chung & Hepburn, 2018). One study of African-American mothers in Chicago finds that mothers who experience the incarceration of a son, compared to those who do not, experience greater psychological distress. This study also finds that the association between son's incarceration and psychological distress is strongest for recent incarcerations and that this association can be explained by financial difficulties and greater caregiving burdens (Green et al., 2006).

Other research uses data from the National Survey of American Life (NSAL), a nationally representative sample of Blacks and non-Hispanic Whites in the United States, to investigate the association between family member incarceration and psychological distress among men. This study finds that, after adjusting for characteristics associated with incarceration (including chronic strains such as criminal victimization), there is no average association between family member incarceration and psychological distress. However, this study also finds heterogeneity in the consequences of family member incarceration, with formerly incarcerated individuals who experience family member incarceration having lower psychological distress than their not formerly incarcerated counterparts who experience family member incarceration (Brown, Bell, & Patterson, 2016). Other research documents that the re-entry period may be a stressful time that poses unique mental health burdens on the family members of the reentering individual (Braman, 2004; Grieb et al., 2014; Western, 2018).

Finally, research using data from the NSAL shows that the health consequences of family member incarceration may extend to physical health outcomes. One study shows that family member incarceration is associated with an increased likelihood of obesity, having a heart attack or stroke, and being in fair or poor health among women. This study also shows no association between family member incarceration and health among men, suggesting women are especially vulnerable to physical health consequences (Lee et al., 2014; see also Lee & Wildeman, 2013).

## Conclusion

As detailed above, the stress process perspective is a useful theoretical framework for understanding the deleterious consequences of incarceration for the health of family members connected to the incarcerated. A burgeoning literature shows that incarceration has deleterious health consequences for both the incarcerated and those connected to them. The incarceration of parents, romantic partners, and children is a stressor that proliferates across the family unit to compromise physical and mental health. And, further, given the concentration of this stressor among already vulnerable groups, this suggests that family member incarceration can both create and exacerbate health inequalities.

The stress process perspective also provides several opportunities to extend our existing knowledge about the health consequences of family member incarceration. Consider two possibilities for future research. First, the stress process perspective suggests that stressors will be more consequential among groups who are most commonly exposed to the stressor (Pearlin, 1989). Accordingly, this perspective posits that family member incarceration will be more deleterious for physical and mental health of people of color, the poor, and those residing in disadvantaged neighborhoods. Second, the stress process perspective suggests that coping and social support will buffer the deleterious consequences of stressors (Pearlin, 1989). Accordingly, this perspective suggests that having available emotional or instrumental support will reduce the deleterious consequences of the stressor of family member incarceration. However, despite theoretical reasons to expect heterogeneity in the relationship between family member incarceration and health (with the former suggesting heterogeneity by demographic groups and the latter suggesting heterogeneity by coping and social support), little research considers these contingencies. Understanding these contingencies could further advance our understanding of incarceration in the stress process perspective. It could also advance our understanding of how and under what conditions incarceration creates and exacerbates health inequalities, a critical endeavor given the concentration of incarceration among those most at risk for health problems.

## Acknowledgment

This project was funded by the Foundation for Child Development and the William T. Grant Foundation.

## References

Arditti, J. A. (2012). *Parental incarceration and the family: Psychological and social effects of imprisonment on children, parents, and caregivers.* New York: NYU Press.

Baćak, V., & Wildeman, C. (2015). An empirical assessment of the "healthy prisoner hypothesis". *Social Science & Medicine, 138*(8), 187–191.

Barr, A. B., Simons, L. G., Simons, R. L., Beach, S. R., & Philibert, R. A. (2018). Sharing the burden of the transition to adulthood: African American young adults' transition challenges and their mothers' health risk. *American Sociological Review, 83*(1), 143–172.

Billings, A. G., & Moos, R. H. (1981). The role of coping responses and social resources in attenuating the stress of life events. *Journal of Behavioral Medicine, 4*(2), 139–157.

Binswanger, I. A., Krueger, P. M., & Steiner, J. F. (2009). Prevalence of chronic medical conditions among jail and prison inmates in the U.S.A. compared with the general population. *Journal of Epidemiology and Community Health, 63*(11), 912–919.

Binswanger, I. A., Stern, M. F., Deyo, R. A., Heagerty, P. J., Cheadle, A., Elmore, J. G., & Koepsell, T. D. (2007). Release from prison—A high risk of death for former inmates. *New England Journal of Medicine, 356*(2), 157–165.

Boch, S. J., & Ford, J. L. (2015). C-reactive protein levels among US adults exposed to parental incarceration. *Biological Research for Nursing, 17*(5), 574–584.

Braman, D. (2004). *Doing time on the outside: Incarceration and family life in urban America*. Ann Arbor, MI: University of Michigan Press.

Brown, T. N., Bell, M. L., & Patterson, E. J. (2016). Imprisoned by empathy: Familial incarceration and psychological distress among African American men in the National Survey of American Life. *Journal of Health and Social Behavior, 57*(2), 240–256.

Bruns, A., & Lee, H. (2018). Partner incarceration and women's substance use. Presented at the Annual Meeting of the Population Association of America.

Burgard, S. A., & Kalousova, L. (2015). Effects of the great recession: Health and well-being. *Annual Review of Sociology, 41*, 181–201.

Celinska, K., & Siegel, J. A. (2010). Mothers in trouble: Coping with actual or pending separation from children due to incarceration. *The Prison Journal, 90*(4), 447–474.

Chung, P. H., & Hepburn, P. (2018). Mass imprisonment and the extended family. *Sociological Science, 5*, 335–360.

Comfort, M. (2008). *Doing time together: Love and family in the shadow of the prison*. Chicago: University of Chicago Press.

Curtis, M. A. (2011). The effect of incarceration on urban fathers' health. *American Journal of Men's Health, 5*(4), 341–350.

Enos, S. (2001). *Mothering from the inside: Parenting in a women's prison*. New York: SUNY Press.

Esposito, M. H., Lee, H., Hicken, M. T., Porter, L. C., & Herting, J. R. (2017). The consequences of contact with the criminal justice system for health in the transition to adulthood. *Longitudinal and Life Course Studies, 8*(1), 57–74.

Foster, H. (2012). The strains of maternal imprisonment: Importation and deprivation stressors for women and children. *Journal of Criminal Justice, 40*(3), 221–229.

Foster, H., & Hagan, J. (2015). Punishment regimes and the multilevel effects of parental incarceration: Intergenerational, intersectional, and interinstitutional models of social inequality and systemic exclusion. *Annual Review of Sociology, 41*, 135–158.

Geller, A. (2013). Paternal incarceration and father–child contact in Fragile Families. *Journal of Marriage and Family, 75*(5), 1288–1303.

Geller, A., Cooper, C. E., Garfinkel, I., Schwartz-Soicher, O., & Mincy, R. B. (2012). Beyond absenteeism: Father incarceration and child development. *Demography, 49*(1), 49–76.

Geller, A., Garfinkel, I., Cooper, C. E., & Mincy, R. B. (2009). Parental incarceration and child well-being: Implications for urban families. *Social Science Quarterly, 90*(5), 1186–1202.

Green, K. M., Ensminger, M. E., Robertson, J. A., & Juon, H. S. (2006). Impact of adult sons' incarceration on African American mothers' psychological distress. *Journal of Marriage and Family, 68*(2), 430–441.

Grieb, S. M. D., Crawford, A., Fields, J., Smith, H., Harris, R., & Matson, P. (2014). "The stress will kill you": Prisoner reentry as experienced by family members and the urgent need for support services. *Journal of Health Care for the Poor and Underserved, 25*(3), 1183–1200.

Hammett, T. M. (2006). HIV/AIDS and other infectious diseases among correctional inmates: Transmission, burden, and an appropriate response. *American Journal of Public Health, 96*(6), 974–978.

Haskins, A., & Turney, K. (2017). The demographic landscape and sociological implications of parental incarceration for childhood inequality. In Wildeman, C., Haskins, A., & Poehlmann-Tynan, J. (Eds.), *When parents are incarcerated: Interdisciplinary research and interventions to support children* (pp. 9–28). Washington, DC: American Psychological Association Press.

Haskins, A. R. (2014). Unintended consequences: Effects of paternal incarceration on child school readiness and later special education placement. *Sociological Science, 1*, 141–157.

Haskins, A. R. (2015). Paternal incarceration and child-reported behavioral functioning at age 9. *Social Science Research, 52*(7), 18–33.

Jackson, D. B., & Vaughn, M. G. (2017). Parental incarceration and child sleep and eating behaviors. *The Journal of Pediatrics, 185*, 211–217.

Kaeble, D., & Cowhig, M. (2018). *Correctional populations in the United States, 2016*. Washington, DC: U.S. Department of Justice, Office of Justice Programs, Bureau of Justice Statistics. https://www.bjs.gov/content/pub/pdf/cpus16.pdf. Accessed June 2, 2019.

Kessler, R. C., & Essex, M. (1982). Marital status and depression: The importance of coping resources. *Social Forces, 61*(2), 484–507.

Lazarus, R. S., & Folkman, S. (1984). The coping process: An alternative to traditional formulations. In *Stress, appraisal, and coping*. New York: Springer.

Lee, H., & Wildeman, C. (2013). Things fall apart: Health consequences of mass imprisonment for African American women. *The Review of Black Political Economy, 40*(1), 39–52.

Lee, H., Wildeman, C., Wang, E. A., Matusko, N., & Jackson, J. S. (2014). A heavy burden: The cardiovascular health consequences of having a family member incarcerated. *American Journal of Public Health, 104*(3), 421–427.

Lee, R. D., Fang, X., & Luo, F. (2013). The impact of parental incarceration on the physical and mental health of young adults. *Pediatrics, 131*(4), e1188–e1195.

Lopoo, L. M., & Western, B. (2005). Incarceration and the formation and stability of marital unions. *Journal of Marriage and Family, 67*(3), 721–734.

Massoglia, M. (2008a). Incarceration as exposure: The prison, infectious disease, and other stress-related illnesses. *Journal of Health and Social Behavior, 49*(1), 56–71.

Massoglia, M. (2008b). Incarceration, health, and racial disparities in health. *Law & Society Review, 42*(2), 275–306.

Massoglia, M., & Pridemore, W. A. (2015). Incarceration and health. *Annual Review of Sociology, 41*, 291–310.

Massoglia, M., Remster, B., & King, R. D. (2011). Stigma or separation? Understanding the incarceration-divorce relationship. *Social Forces, 90*(1), 133–155.

Murphey, D., & Cooper, P. M. (2015). *Parents behind bars: What happens to their children.* Washington, DC: Child Trends.

Murray, J., Farrington, D. P., & Sekol, I. (2012). Children's antisocial behavior, mental health, drug use, and educational performance after parental incarceration: A systematic review and meta-analysis. *Psychological Bulletin, 138*(2), 175–210.

Nurse, A. (2002). *Fatherhood arrested: Parenting from within the juvenile justice system.* Nashville, TN: Vanderbilt University Press.

Patterson, E. J. (2010). Incarcerating death: Mortality in US state correctional facilities, 1985–1998. *Demography, 47*(3), 587–607.

Pearlin, L. I. (1989). The sociological study of stress. *Journal of Health and Social Behavior, 30*(3), 241–256.

Pearlin, L. I., Aneshensel, C. S., & LeBlanc, A. J. (1997). The forms and mechanisms of stress proliferation: The case of AIDS caregivers. *Journal of Health and Social Behavior, 38*(3), 223–236.

Pearlin, L. I., Schieman, S., Fazio, E. M., & Meersman, S. C. (2005). Stress, health, and the life course: Some conceptual perspectives. *Journal of Health and Social Behavior, 46*(2), 205–219.

Pearlin, L. I., & Schooler, C. (1978). The structure of coping. *Journal of Health and Social Behavior, 19*(1), 2–21.

Porter, L. C. (2014). Incarceration and post-release health behavior. *Journal of Health and Social Behavior, 55*(2), 234–249.

Porter, L. C., & Novisky, M. A. (2017). Pathways to depressive symptoms among former inmates. *Justice Quarterly, 34*(5), 847–872.

Roettger, M. E., & Boardman, J. D. (2012). Parental incarceration and gender-based risks for increased body mass index: Evidence from the National Longitudinal Study of Adolescent Health in the United States. *American Journal of Epidemiology, 175*(7), 636–644.

Roettger, M. E., Swisher, R. R., Kuhl, D. C., & Chavez, J. (2011). Paternal incarceration and trajectories of marijuana and other illegal drug use from adolescence into young adulthood: Evidence from longitudinal panels of males and females in the United States. *Addiction, 106*(1), 121–132.

Schnittker, J., & John, A. (2007). Enduring stigma: The long-term effects of incarceration on health. *Journal of Health and Social Behavior, 48*(2), 115–130.

Schnittker, J., Massoglia, M., & Uggen, C. (2012). Out and down: Incarceration and psychiatric disorders. *Journal of Health and Social Behavior, 53*(4), 448–464.

Schwartz-Soicher, O., Geller, A., & Garfinkel, I. (2011). The effect of paternal incarceration on material hardship. *Social Service Review, 85*(3), 447–473.

Sugie, N. F., & Turney, K. (2017). Beyond incarceration: Criminal justice contact and mental health. *American Sociological Review, 82*(4), 719–743.

Sykes, B. L., & Pettit, B. (2014). Mass incarceration, family complexity, and the reproduction of childhood disadvantage. *The Annals of the American Academy of Political and Social Science, 654*(1), 127–149.

Sykes, G. M. (2007). *The society of captives: A study of a maximum security prison.* Princeton, NJ: Princeton University Press.

Taylor, S. E., & Stanton, A. L. (2007). Coping resources, coping processes, and mental health. *Annual Review of Clinical Psychology, 3*, 377–401.

Testa, A., & Porter, L. C. (2017). No rest for the wicked? The consequences of incarceration for sleep problems. *Society and Mental Health, 7*(3), 196–208.

Thoits, P. A. (2010). Stress and health: Major findings and policy implications. *Journal of Health and Social Behavior, 51*(S), S41–S53.

Travis, J., Western, B., & Redburn, S. (2014). *The growth of incarceration in the United States: Exploring causes and consequences*. Washington, DC: The National Academies Press.

Turanovic, J. J., Rodriguez, N., & Pratt, T. C. (2012). The collateral consequences of incarceration revisited: A qualitative analysis of the effects on caregivers of children of incarcerated parents. *Criminology, 50*(4), 913–959.

Turner, R. J. (2003). The pursuit of socially modifiable contingencies in mental health. *Journal of Health and Social Behavior, 44*(1), 1–17.

Turner, R. J., & Avison, W. R. (2003). Status variations in stress exposure: Implications for the interpretation of research on race, socioeconomic status, and gender. *Journal of Health and Social Behavior, 44*(4), 488–505.

Turner, R. J., & Lloyd, D. A. (1999). The stress process and the social distribution of depression. *Journal of Health and Social Behavior, 40*(4), 374–404.

Turner, R. J., Wheaton, B., & Lloyd, D. A. (1995). The epidemiology of social stress. *American Sociological Review, 60*(1), 104–125.

Turney, K. (2014a). The intergenerational consequences of mass incarceration: Implications for children's co-residence and contact with grandparents. *Social Forces, 93*(1), 299–327.

Turney, K. (2014b). Stress proliferation across generations? Examining the relationship between parental incarceration and childhood health. *Journal of Health and Social Behavior, 55*(3), 302–319.

Turney, K. (2015a). Liminal men: Incarceration and relationship dissolution. *Social Problems, 62*(4), 499–528.

Turney, K. (2015b). Hopelessly devoted? Relationship quality during and after incarceration. *Journal of Marriage and Family, 77*(2), 480–495.

Turney, K. (2017a). The unequal consequences of mass incarceration for children. *Demography, 54*(1), 361–389.

Turney, K. (2017b). Unmet health care needs among children exposed to parental incarceration. *Maternal and Child Health Journal, 21*(5), 1194–1202.

Turney, K., & Goodsell, R. (2018). Parental incarceration and children's wellbeing. *Future of Children, 28*(1), 147–164.

Turney, K., & Haskins, A. (Forthcoming). Parental incarceration and children's wellbeing: Findings from the Fragile Families and Child Wellbeing Study. In Eddy, J. M. & Poehlmann-Tynan, J. (Eds.), *Children of incarcerated parents: A handbook for researchers and practitioners (Second Edition)*. New York: Springer.

Turney, K., Schnittker, J., & Wildeman, C. (2012). Those they leave behind: Paternal incarceration and maternal instrumental support. *Journal of Marriage and Family, 74*(5), 1149–1165.

Turney, K., & Wildeman, C. (2013). Redefining relationships: Explaining the countervailing consequences of paternal incarceration for parenting. *American Sociological Review, 78*(6), 949–979.

Turney, K., & Wildeman, C. (2015a). Self-reported health among recently incarcerated mothers. *American Journal of Public Health, 105*(10), 2014–2020.

Turney, K., & Wildeman, C. (2015b). Detrimental for some? Heterogeneous effects of maternal incarceration on child wellbeing. *Criminology & Public Policy, 14*(1), 125–156.

Turney, K., Wildeman, C., & Schnittker, J. (2012). As fathers and felons: Explaining the effects of current and recent incarceration on major depression. *Journal of Health and Social Behavior, 53*(4), 465–481.

Wakefield, S., & Uggen, C. (2010). Incarceration and stratification. *Annual Review of Sociology, 36*, 387–406.

West, H. C., & Sabol, W. J. (2009). *Prison inmates at midyear 2008: Statistical tables*. Washington, DC: Bureau of Justice Statistics.

Western, B. (2006). *Punishment and inequality in America*. New York: Russell Sage Foundation.

Western, B. (2018). *Homeward: Life in the year after prison*. New York: Russell Sage Foundation.

Western, B., Braga, A. A., Davis, J., & Sirois, C. (2015). Stress and hardship after prison. *American Journal of Sociology, 120*(5), 1512–1547.

Western, B., & Pettit, B. (2010). Incarceration & social inequality. *Daedalus, 139*(3), 8–19. doi: 10.1162/DAED_a_00019.

Wethington, E. (2000). Contagion of stress. In Thye, S. R., Lawler, E. (Eds.), *Advances in group processes* (Vol. 17, pp. 229–253). Bingley, UK: Emerald Group Publishing Limited.

Wheaton, B. (1994). Sampling the stress universe. In Avison, W. R. & Gotlib, I. H. (Eds.), *Stress and mental health: Contemporary issues and prospects for the future* (pp. 77–114). New York: Springer.

Wildeman, C. (2010). Paternal incarceration and children's physically aggressive behaviors: Evidence from the Fragile Families and Child Wellbeing Study. *Social Forces, 89*(1), 285–309.

Wildeman, C., Goldman, A. W., & Turney, K. (2018). Parental incarceration and child health in the United States. *Epidemiologic Reviews, 40*(1), 146–156.

Wildeman, C., Lee, H., & Comfort, M. (2013). A new vulnerable population? The health of female partners of men recently released from prison. *Women's Health Issues, 23*(6), e335–e340.

Wildeman, C., & Muller, C. (2012). Mass imprisonment and inequality in health and family life. *Annual Review of Law and Social Science, 8,* 11–30.

Wildeman, C., Schnittker, J., & Turney, K. (2012). Despair by association? The mental health of mothers with children by recently incarcerated fathers. *American Sociological Review, 77*(2), 216–243.

Wildeman, C., & Turney, K. (2014). Positive, negative, or null? The effects of maternal incarceration on children's behavioral problems. *Demography, 51*(3), 1041–1068.

Wildeman, C., & Wang, E. A. (2017). Mass incarceration, public health, and widening inequality in the USA. *The Lancet, 389*(10077), 1464–1474.

Yi, Y., Turney, K., & Wildeman, C. (2017). Mental health among jail and prison inmates. *American Journal of Men's Health, 11*(4), 900–909.

# PART II

# Behavioral, Mental, and Physical Health Conditions

# 9
# TRAUMATIC BRAIN INJURY AND JUSTICE-INVOLVED YOUTH
## Assessment and Intervention

*Christopher A. Veeh and Tanya Renn*

In 2005, the United States Supreme Court decided in *Roper v. Simmons* (543 U.S. 551) that the execution of youth 17 years of age and younger violated the Eighth Amendment to the U.S. Constitution that prohibits cruel and unusual punishment. The basis for this groundbreaking decision was findings from developmental neuroscience that showed the prefrontal cortex, an area vital to the regulation of behavior, did not fully mature until the early twenties (Gogtay et al., 2004). Following *Roper v. Simmons*, the Supreme Court continued to rely on developmental neuroscience in a series of decisions that rolled back the tough-on-crime measures instituted in the 1990s, such as life sentences without the possibility for parole (Cohen & Casey, 2014).

This revolution in the understanding of the development and function of the adolescent brain fundamentally changed how youth are managed in the criminal justice system. No longer are youth with early offenses viewed as irredeemable, the so called "super predators." Rather, youth are increasingly viewed, as expressed in the Supreme Court decisions, to be in-development and not yet equipped with the necessary cognitive abilities to regulate their behaviors like adults, particularly in emotionally charged situations (Cohen-Gilbert & Thomas, 2013; Grose-Fifer, Rodrigues, Hoover, & Zottoli, 2013) and in the presence of peers (Chein, Albert, O'Brien, Uckert, & Steinberg, 2011).

Parallel to this path breaking work on the development of the adolescent brain, a separate line of investigation was beginning to explore traumatic brain injury (TBI) – or a head injury that disrupts the normal function of the brain (Centers for Disease Control and Prevention [CDC], 2017) – among youth involved in the criminal justice system. Hux and colleagues (1998), in an influential article, described the similarity in behavioral profiles between youth with TBI and youth in criminal justice system; specifically, in terms of impulsivity and challenges with selective attention and behavior control. Over the last two decades, research into TBI within youth in the juvenile justice system has shown the rate of TBI to be disproportionately higher than nondelinquent youth (Farrer, Frost, & Hedges, 2013). These findings are particularly concerning given the numerous deleterious consequences that a history of TBI can have on the developing brain of a youth and their long-term success as adults.

Therefore, the current chapter details the research into the prevalence of TBI in youth in the criminal justice system and what that means for their success in the community following engagement in the criminal justice system. Next, the need for widespread adoption of standardized and validated assessment tools for TBI is discussed. Finally, the chapter concludes with a look at stress and coping theory and how that can inform the development of innovative interventions targeted for youth with TBI in the criminal justice system.

## Traumatic Brain Injury

TBI is primarily caused by either a bump, blow, or jolt to the head or a penetrating head injury that causes the normal function of the brain to be disrupted (Faul & Coronado, 2015). Teenagers between the age of 15 to 19 years of age as well as children under the age of 4 are at high risk of suffering a TBI (Langlois, Rutland-Brown, & Thomas, 2006). The rate of injury is substantial within youth and adolescents, leading to more than 640,000 TBI-related emergency department visits for children 14 years or younger during a single year in 2013 (Taylor, Bell, Breiding, & Xu, 2017). This is an increase since 2007, which may be the product of increased awareness of TBI as opposed to a substantive increase in the rate of injury. Regardless, these rates of TBI and the resulting consequences make TBI the leading cause of death for children and adolescents in high income countries (Maas et al., 2017).

There is a range of TBI events that can be experienced, ranging from severe to mild. The most commonly used ways to measure the severity of a TBI is either through an assessment tool, such as the Glasgow Coma Scale (GCS) or the Abbreviated Injury Severity Scale (AIS; Corrigan, Selassie, & Orman, 2010), or the length of unconsciousness experienced by an individual following a TBI. In severe injuries the consequences of a TBI can be quite pronounced, including loss of consciousness (LOC) for longer than 24 hours to even coma or death. On the other end of spectrum, mild traumatic brain injury (mTBI) can result in fairly minor immediate consequences such as a LOC of less than 30 minutes and bouts of dizziness, disorientation, and headaches (Corrigan et al., 2010). Moderate levels of TBI fall directly between severe and mild with experiences of a LOC ranging between 30 minutes and 24 hours.

The issue of TBI has gained increased salience within society because of high-profile events surrounding professional football players or United States military personnel attacked with improvised explosive devices in Iraq and Afghanistan. Consequently, the type of injury often associated with TBI is a violent sports collusion or a bomb explosion. However, this is not representative of most TBI events. Approximately 80% of TBIs are, in fact, mild injuries from a fall or blow to the head that result in brief symptoms and never lead to a hospital visit (Corrigan et al., 2010). While any one of these mTBIs in isolation can have fairly limited effects on an individual, the accumulation of multiple TBI events, regardless of severity, can have deleterious consequences for a youth. For example, Dams-O'Connor and colleagues (2013) found that multiple TBIs in a community sample of youth 16 years of age or younger increased reported symptomatology and negatively impact a youth's cognitive processing speed and verbal learning ability. Beyond even these sequela, more recent research has also shown that repeated events of mTBI can change the structure of the brain by reducing the cortical thickness in the prefrontal cortex, which was associated with slower cognitive processing (Urban et al., 2017).

## TBI within Justice-Involved Youth

Research into the epidemiology of TBI has found the occurrence of injury not to be randomly disrupted throughout the population, rather TBI is disproportionately experienced by children with certain characteristics. TBI is most pronounced in young males of color – specifically African Americans and Native Americans – who grow up in poverty, misuse alcohol and/or drugs, and assessed to have deficiencies in impulse control (Hughes et al., 2015). These are similar characteristics of youth that also experience disproportionately involvement in the criminal justice system. Therefore, like many issues in TBI research, it has been an open question whether TBI leads to antisocial behavior or, on the flip side, youth at-risk for antisocial behavior engage in the types of impulsive acts that make the occurrence of a TBI more likely.

Systematic reviews of the current literature on prevalence rates of TBI among justice-involved youth by both Farrer et al. (2013) and Hughes et al. (2015) have substantiated the hypothesis that youth in the criminal justice system report significantly higher rates of TBI then their counterparts without a criminal justice history. Overall, the prevalence rate of TBI within justice involved youth as ranged between 30% and 71.2% (Farrer et al., 2013; Hughes et al., 2015). The research conducted by Farrer et al. (2013) is particularly instructive because they were able to identify a set of five studies that compared the prevalence of TBI in justice-involved youth to a matched control group with no justice involvement. Across these five studies, the likelihood of TBI was found to be 3.37 times higher in the justice-involved youth.

## Negative Outcomes Associated with TBI

### *Violence*

The disproportionately higher rate of TBI within justice-involved youth and adolescents is an important public health issue because of the multitude of negative effects it can have on a youth in both the short and long term as he or she transitions into adulthood. Perhaps most significantly, a history of TBI has shown to have a robust relationship with future violent behavior. In two separate longitudinal birth cohorts, one in Sweden and a second in New Zealand, the report of a TBI in childhood significantly increased the likelihood for an individual to commit a violent crime as an adult (Fazel, Lichtenstein, Grann, & Langstrom, 2011; McKinlay, Corrigan, Horwood, & Fergusson, 2014). Parallel results were also found in a community sample of youth and young adults living in an urban area of the United States, with more recent events of TBI showing the strongest relationship to violent behavior (Stoddard & Zimmerman, 2011). Even when looking within a sample of only justice-involved youth in the United Kingdom, Williams and colleagues (2010) found that those youth with the most complex TBI histories (i.e., self-reports of three or more TBI events) were significantly more likely to be violent compared to their justice-involved peers with fewer or no history of TBI.

### *Anxiety, Depression, and Suicidality*

Beyond the increased likelihood for violent behavior, a history of TBI can also have a detrimental impact on a youth's level of anxiety, depression, and suicidality. Important epidemiological research examining these various factors was recently published by Gabriela Ilie and colleagues looking at a representative sample of youth in Ontario, Canada. A history of TBI was shown to increase the use of medications for depression and anxiety by 2.45 times as well as substantially elevate rates of reporting both suicidal ideation and well as suicide attempts (Ilie et al., 2014). These findings have been replicated within samples of justice-involved youth. For example, youth in the justice system that report TBI have shown to have higher levels of psychological distress, including symptoms of both anxiety and depression (Moore, Indig, & Haysom, 2014; Perron & Howard, 2008; Vaughn, Salas-Wright, DeLisi, & Perron, 2014; Williams et al., 2010). In terms of suicidality, the research is fairly preliminary among samples of justice-involved youth. Chitsabesan and colleagues (2015) found elevated rates of both deliberate self-harm and suicide risk factors in those youth who reported TBI relative to their justice-involved counterparts without TBI.

## *Alcohol and Drug Use*

The relationship between the occurrence of TBI youth and the increased use of alcohol and drugs has been replicated in multiple studies, including in large-scale epidemiological studies in both Canada (Ilie et al., 2015) and New Zealand (McKinlay et al., 2014). For example, McKinlay and colleagues (2014) followed an entire cohort of individuals in Christchurch, New Zealand, from birth to adulthood and found that a TBI episode in childhood increased the risk for alcohol and drug dependence in young adulthood. Looking specifically at justice-involved youth, the increased use and misuse of substances has also been found to be associated with TBI in multiple studies (Davies, Williams, Hinder, Burgess, & Mounce, 2012; Moore et al., 2014; Perron & Howard, 2008; Williams et al., 2010). However, not all results point in the same direction; Vaughn et al. (2014) failed to find a significant association between TBI and substance use when controlling for important confounds (i.e., impulsivity and psychological distress).

These mixed results highlight the argument that research has yet to disentangle whether TBI is a cause of increased substance use, or whether the use of alcohol and drugs is a part of a behavioral repertoire that makes an individual more likely to use alcohol and drugs as well as participate in activities that increase the likelihood of TBI. Kort-Butler (2017) recently conducted a study with 894 college students in the U.S. to investigate this issue and found a history of TBI to be weakly related to prescription drug use. Any relationship between TBI and the use of marijuana or binge drinking was accounted for by prior delinquency and risk-taking behaviors. While the findings of Kort-Butler are important to consider, the longitudinal birth-cohort study by McKinlay and colleagues (2014) provides particularly compelling evidence that, on average, TBI in childhood and adolescence does lead to increased alcohol and drug use.

## *Cognitive Deficits*

Cognitive deficits that are related to a history of TBI are another important factor to consider for youth with head injuries in the criminal justice system. The most vulnerable area of injury among youth with TBI has shown to be the prefrontal cortex (Wilde et al., 2005) – the same area that is still developing into the early twenties. The prefrontal cortex is particularly vulnerable in a TBI because of the anatomical structure of the human skull, where the orbital bones create a bony structure that the prefrontal cortex is pushed into when external force is applied to the head.

### *Executive Functioning*

Trauma to the prefrontal cortex is strongly associated with deficiencies in executive functioning (Stuss, 2011). Executive functioning is a group of cognitive processes and behavioral abilities "to facilitate the initiation, planning, regulation, sequencing, and achievement of complex goal-oriented behavior and thought" (Ogilvie, Stewart, Chan, & Shum, 2011, p. 1065). A recent meta-analysis looking across a range of measure of executive functioning found that poor executive functioning is strongly associated with antisocial behavior, including criminality and externalizing behavior disorder (Ogilvie et al., 2011). This strong relationship between deficient executive functioning and antisocial behavior is particularly important for youth both at-risk for involvement with the criminal justice system or making an attempt to become disentangled from its bureaucracy.

One of the most important aspects of executive functioning is its role in self-regulation across several domains including emotion, cognitive, and behavior (Beaver, Wright, & DeLisi, 2007; Ganesalingam,

Sanson, Anderson, & Yeates, 2006). History of TBI has shown a robust association to decreased ability to regulate both emotions and behaviors following the injury (Ganesalingam et al., 2006; McDonald, Rushby, Kelly, & de Sousa, 2014). Studies with justice-involved youth have also found that a history of TBI is associated with both increased levels of impulsivity and decreased self-regulation (Schwartz, Connolly, & Brauer, 2017; Schwartz, Connolly, & Valgardson, 2018; Vaughn et al., 2014). Moreover, the recent study by Schwartz and colleagues (2018) used data from the Pathways to Desistance study to investigate the temporal relationship between head injury and a youth's level of self-control. The pattern of results aligned with the casual explanation that head injuries caused significant decreases in self-control among the adjudicated youth (Schwartz et al., 2018).

## Working Memory

Damage to the prefrontal cortex from a history of TBI in childhood has also been shown to have a negative impact on individuals' working memory, in terms of both verbal and visual-spatial memory (Gorman, Barnes, Swank, & Ewing-Cobbs, 2017; Gorman, Barnes, Swank, Prasad & Ewing-Cobbs, 2012). Working memory is defined as the "mental workspace in which task-relevant information is monitored, processed, and maintained in order to respond to immediate environmental demands" (Gorman et al., 2017, p. 127). Specifically, when thinking about the consequences for youth in the criminal justice system, working memory is vital for long-term success because it is strongly associated with proficiency in completing multi-step instructions (Christopher et al., 2012). Almost every action a youth is required to undertake to move off criminal justice supervision, whether that be participation in treatment or finishing their education, requires the ability to successfully identify goals and then follow a multi-step process to complete the goal over an extended period of weeks or even months.

## Personality

A history of TBI is also related to a disorder called personality change due to TBI (Max et al., 2006). The *Diagnostic Manual and Statistical Manual for Mental Disorders* has identified five types of personality change that result from a TBI: affective liability, aggression, disinhibited, apathetic, and paranoid (Max et al., 2015). Overall, the impact of personality change due to TBI has been most pronounced within individuals that have experienced a severe TBI event, with little or no personality change after a mild or moderate TBI (Max et al., 2000).

For youth in the criminal justice system, the effects of TBI on personality, specifically in terms of aggression and disinhibition, can have potentially long-term detrimental effects on their ability to not become involved in situations that may result in contact with law enforcement. One instructive way to think of this is through the lens of Vaughn and Delisi's temperament theory of antisocial behavior (2014a, 2014b, 2015). According to temperament theory, the dynamic interplay between the personality characteristics of poor effortful control (i.e., disinhibition) and high negative emotionality (i.e., aggression) make the likelihood of future antisocial or criminal behavior very likely. Therefore, the very aspects of personality most likely to be negatively impacted by a history of TBI are those aspects of personality robustly demonstrated to increase antisocial behavior (Baglivio, Wolff, DeLisi, Vaughn, & Piquero, 2016; Wolff, Baglivio, Piquero, Vaughn, & DeLisi, 2016). In fact, in a recent cross-sectional study looking at over 200 youth incarcerated in a residential long-term facility, a youth's temperament mediated 54% of the total effect between TBI and the self-report of violent behavior (Veeh, Renn, Vaughn, & DeLisi, 2018a). The negative impact of TBI on a youth's temperament can have important consequences as the individual makes attempt to navigate both their time under the supervision of criminal justice authorities as well as the day-to-day stress in the community.

## Assessment of TBI

Studies into TBI with youth in the criminal justice system have consistently called for the adoption of standardized screening tools that can assist in making systematic assessment of a youth's history of TBI. A fundamental issue facing the assessment of TBI is that the youth are being asked to remember events over his or her entire lifetime that resulted in a loss consciousness. Events that by their very outcome, the loss of consciousness, makes them difficult to remember. Therefore, one of the most important issues facing both research and practice with justice-involved youth is the adoption of assessment tools that have been tested for their ability to accurately capture an individual's TBI history.

Existing research into TBI within criminal justice samples is still fairly limited, with a total of 17 studies identified in a recent systematic review of the literature, and of those 17, only seven looked at juvenile offending (Allely, 2016). Despite the small number of studies, comparisons between them have proven difficult because of the wide variation in methods that were used to assess for a history of TBI. This is one of the most important limitations to the still ambiguous picture (i.e., prevalence rates range between 30% and 71.2%; Farrer et al., 2013; Hughes et al., 2015) that exists surrounding TBI among youth in the criminal justice system.

Many studies have relied on a single question that asks an individual if he or she has experienced a head injury that resulted in a loss of consciousness (LOC) for a specified time frame. The most common cutoff is 30 minutes in order to follow the guidelines for differentiating between mTBI and a moderate or severe injury. The decision to exclude all injuries considered mTBI results in a truncated view of the prevalence of TBI within the criminal justice population. Moreover, it provides the respondent to the question no structured way to think over a decade or more of their life history whether a TBI event may have occurred. Simply conducting a free recall of all TBI events within one's life without any prompted guidance would be difficult for anyone. Fortunately, there exist a number of standardized assessment tools, such as, the Traumatic Brain Injury Questionnaire (TBIQ; Diamond, Harzke, Magaletta, Cummins, & Frankowski, 2007) and the Brain Injury Screening Index (BISI; The Disabilities Trust, 2018). However, for the purposes of this chapter, we would like to focus on the most widely used and researched assessment tool for TBI, the Ohio State University TBI Identification Method (OSU-TBI-ID; Bogner & Corrigan, 2009; Corrigan & Bogner, 2007).

The OSU-TBI-ID is a brief instrument tool that assesses for a history of TBI with five brief questions (e.g., In your lifetime, have you ever been hospitalized or treated in an emergency room following an injury to your head or neck?). If the respondent indicates an affirmative response to any of the five questions, the OSU-TBI-ID provides tables where a researcher or practitioner can then delve into each instance of TBI by documenting the occurrence of LOC, the length of LOC, and the age of the event. Finally, the OSU-TBI-ID prompts a question about repeated events of TBI and for how long each of those episodes lasted. The brief structure of the tool makes it easily scalable to situations that require the assessment of a large number of individuals; for example, when youth first enter into the juvenile court system or are sentenced to a residential facility. Thus, the OSU-TBI-ID can serve as an effective first line of defense in making sure that TBI is systematically assessed within youth in the criminal justice system, where they can then be triaged into more in-depth neuropsychological assessments.

The OSU-TBI-ID is the only TBI assessment tool to be specifically validated within a sample of adult prisoners. Bogner and Corrigan (2009) examined the reliability and validity of the OSU-TBI-ID among 210 men and women incarcerated in a state prison facility. The study showed strong results in the assessment's test/retest reliability and its predictive validity of common cognitive and behavioral deficits caused by TBI. However, a definite limitation of the OSU-TBI-ID is that there has yet to be any published work looking into whether the effectiveness of the assessment also extends into juveniles in the criminal justice system. Therefore, the OSU-TBI-ID should be used with caution when assessing juveniles until there is evidence that empirically supports the assessment's usage with the population.

## Interventions for TBI

The systematic assessment of youth involved in the criminal justice system is an important first step to developing a complete picture of TBI within the population. However, once a youth is assessed to have a history of TBI, the next question is what should be done to help the youth be successful once he or she leaves the justice system. Currently, most rehabilitation programs fail to consider cognitive deficits that may be present in participants. This is problematic since the basic premise underlying many rehabilitation programs is for the youth to uptake the treatment information and then apply that knowledge to navigate their lives in the community. For youth with a history of trauma to the prefrontal cortex caused by multiple TBI events, his or her ability to execute identified goals that require the completion of multi-step instructions will be difficult at best. Thus, it is imperative that once a youth is assessed to have a TBI history, interventions are available that can help address possible cognitive deficits.

One of the most promising targets for interventions with justice-involved youth with TBI is the coping strategies used to manage difficult and/or stressful situations in day-to-day life. For over 20 years, experts in the field of neuropsychological rehabilitation have identified coping strategies to be one of the most important factors in determining an individual's outcome following TBI (Kendall & Terry, 1996; Krpan, Anderson, & Stuss, 2013; Moore & Stambrook, 1995). According to stress and coping theory, a coping strategy is a "person's cognitive and behavioral efforts to manage (reduce, minimize, master, or tolerate) the internal and external demands of the person-environment transaction that is appraised as taking or exceeding the person's resources" (Folkman, Lazarus, Gruen, & DeLongis, 1986, p. 572). Coping strategies are commonly grouped into two types: (1) active strategies that attempt to directly manage a taxing situation by changing it or developing skills to change it, and (2) avoidance strategies that aim to distract oneself from a taxing situation or the emotional reaction to the situation (Lazarus, 1993).

TBI has shown to have a detrimental impact on an individual's ability to use active coping strategies, thus leading to greater reliance on avoidant styles of coping (Krpan, Levine, Stuss, & Dawson, 2007). For example, in research with adults in the community, the incidence of moderate to severe TBI was both related to lower use of active coping strategies as well as a more frequent use of avoidant strategies (Finset & Andersson, 2000; Tomberg, Toomela, Pulver, & Tikk, 2005). Unfortunately, the frequent use of avoidant coping strategies is related to a variety of negative outcomes among individuals with a moderate to severe TBI history, including: anxiety, depression, and a self-reported low quality-of-life (Anson & Ponsford, 2006a; Gould, Ponsford, Johnston, & Schönberger, 2011; Wolters, Stapert, Brands, & van Heugten, 2010, 2011; Wolters Gregorio, Gould, Spitz, van Heugten, & Ponsford, 2014). Similar results regarding the increased use of avoidance coping strategies have also been found among individuals that report a history of mild TBIs (Scheenen, van der Horn, de Koning, van der Naalt, & Spikman, 2017; van der Naalt et al., 2017); nevertheless, the most pronounced effects on an individual's use of coping strategy have been associated with a history that includes moderate and/or severe TBIs (Rakers et al., 2018).

Research into the relationship between TBI and coping strategy within justice-involved individuals, whether juvenile or adults, has been limited. The only research that has examined the effect of TBI on coping strategy within a justice-involved population is a recent investigation with 227 male and female incarcerated youth. This cross-sectional study found that youth who reported a TBI with loss of consciousness for 20 minutes or great reported higher use of avoidant coping strategies (i.e., internalization, acting-out, and partying) but no difference was reported in the use of active strategies (i.e., prosocial and expressing; Veeh, Vaughn, & Renn, 2018b). Most importantly for the purposes of intervention science, mediation analysis was used to examine whether the use of avoidant coping strategies explained the relationship between TBI and higher rates of both anxiety/depression and substance use. Results found that using avoidant coping strategies explained between 40 to 50% of the effect TBI had on rates of depression/anxiety and substance use (Veeh et al., 2018b).

Therefore, as suggested by the preliminary findings from Veeh et al. (2018b), interventions that effectively target an individual's coping by promoting active strategies to deal with stressful situations may be able to ameliorate, on average, the impact TBI has on increased anxiety/depression and substance use. Initial work has been conducted with community-based adults with TBI on the designing and testing of an intervention based on principles of cognitive-behavioral therapy (CBT) that targets coping (see Anson & Ponsford, 2006b). Interventions that target coping and are based on high-quality CBT implemented with fidelity provide particular promise given that CBT is shown to be one of the most effective modalities of treatment with justice-involved youth (Lipsey, 2012). However, while the intervention designed by Anson and Ponsford (2006b) is a promising direction for working with justice-involved youth with TBI, there is still much work to be completed before it can be considered an evidence-based intervention. A comprehensive agenda of intervention research – including pilot, efficacy, and effectiveness trials – must be undertaken to ensure a coping intervention based on CBT principles is appropriate for justice-involved youth with TBI.

In addition to interventions focused on coping strategies, there also exist a range of evidence-based practices developed by the field of cognitive rehabilitation that may be useful for justice-involved youth with TBI (see Cicerone et al., 2011). For example, as described previously, TBI most acutely impacts the prefrontal cortex, which is likely to result in deficits to an individual's executive functioning. The practice standard within cognitive rehabilitation is to utilize metacognitive strategies (i.e., strategies to think about one's thinking) for individuals with TBI that are assessed to have deficits in their executive functioning (Cicerone et al., 2011).

A specific, evidence-based intervention that utilizes metacognitive strategies to focus on goal planning and execution is called Goal Management Training (GMT; Krasny-Pacini, Chevignard, & Evans, 2014). GMT is structured around five steps that correspond to important aspects of goal directed behavior (Levine et al., 2000). Step one directs the participant to develop a catchphrase that can help orient him or her towards a goal that needs to be accomplished. Step two is identifying a specific goal, which is followed by step three where the goal is broken down into subgoals. Step four is studying the subgoals and thinking through action steps to complete the subgoal. Step five focuses on executing the action steps and monitoring progress to ensure the goal is achieved. Overall, metacognitive strategies, such as GMT, have shown preliminary effectiveness in improving adaptive behavior within children and adolescents but mixed findings regarding executive functions (Resch, Rosema, Hurks, de Kloet, & van Heugten, 2018).

Cognitive rehabilitation interventions hold great promise in providing evidence-based strategies to work with justice-involved youth with TBI. However, there exists a lack of research looking into the effectiveness of cognitive rehabilitation interventions with children and adolescents outside of clinical settings (Ross, Dorris, & McMillan, 2011). Translation of cognitive rehabilitation interventions into either a residential treatment facility or a community-based correctional program must be undertaken, which then need to be followed by pilot testing of those interventions to identify possible adaptations appropriate for justice-involved youth. Moreover, current correctional rehabilitation programs should be reviewed for possible opportunities where approaches, such as metacognitive strategies, can be implemented in tandem with programming that already exists for justice-involved youth.

## Conclusion

The disproportionate rate of TBI among youth in the criminal justice system is a vitally important public health issue, both for the youth as well as the larger community. A similar revolution to that which took place following the *Roper v. Simmons* decision at the Supreme Court also needs to occur for youth with histories of trauma to their brain. Correctional agencies across the United States need to adopt the types of evidence-based approaches to both assessment and intervention detailed in this chapter to ensure youth with TBI are being properly managed.

Robert Sapolsky (2017), a neuroendocrinologist and scholar on human behavior, has written about how the behaviors we often criminally punish individuals for as acts of their own free will are the product of biology that we have yet to completely understand. Therefore, the criminal justice system and the public officials that design it would be served well by developing a sense of humility to not "act irrevocably" (Sapolsky, 2017, p. 608). Rather, we should continue to recalibrate our approach to youth in the criminal justice system in line with sentiments expressed by the Supreme Court in *Roper v. Simmons* by acting thoughtfully and considering comprehensively the entire range of cognitive disabilities and deficits, including TBI, that make youth more likely to enter the criminal justice system.

## References

Alley, C. S. (2016). Prevalence and assessment of traumatic brain injury in prison inmates: A systematic PRISMA review. *Brain Injury*, *30*, 1161–1180. https://doi.org/10.1080/02699052.2016.1191674

Anson, K., & Ponsford, J. (2006a). Coping and emotional adjustment following traumatic brain injury. *Journal of Head Trauma Rehabilitation*, *21*, 248–259. https://doi.org/10.1097/00001199-200605000-00005

Anson, K., & Ponsford, J. (2006b). Evaluation of a coping skills group following traumatic brain injury. *Brain Injury*, *20*, 167–178. https://doi.org/10.1080/02699050500442956

Baglivio, M. T., Wolff, K. T., DeLisi, M., Vaughn, M. G., & Piquero, A. R. (2016). Effortful control, negative emotionality, and juvenile recidivism: An empirical test of DeLisi and Vaughn's temperament-based theory of antisocial behavior. *The Journal of Forensic Psychiatry & Psychology*, *27*, 376–403. https://doi.org/10.1080/14789949.2016.1145720

Beaver, K. M., Wright, J. P., & DeLisi, M. (2007). Self-control as an executive function: Reformulating Gottfredson and Hirschi's parental socialization thesis. *Criminal Justice and Behavior*, *34*, 1345–1361. https://doi.org/10.1177/0093854807302049

Bogner, J., & Corrigan, J. D. (2009). Reliability and predictive validity of the Ohio State University TBI identification method with prisoners. *The Journal of Head Trauma Rehabilitation*, *24*, 279–291. https://doi.org/10.1097/HTR.0b013e3181a66356

Centers for Disease Control and Prevention [CDC]. (2017). *Traumatic brain injury & concussion*. Retrieved from www.cdc.gov/traumaticbraininjury

Chein, J., Albert, D., O'Brien, L., Uckert, K., & Steinberg, L. (2011). Peers increase adolescent risk taking by enhancing activity in the brain's reward circuitry. *Developmental Science*, *14*, F1-F10. https://doi.org/10.1111/j.1467-7687.2010.01035.x

Chitsabesan, P., Lennox, C., Williams, H., Tariq, O., & Shaw, J. (2015). Traumatic brain injury in juvenile offenders: Findings from the comprehensive health assessment tool study and the development of a specialist linkworker service. *Journal of Head Trauma Rehabilitation*, *30*, 106–115. https://doi.org/10.1097/HTR.0000000000000129

Christopher, M. E., Miyake, A., Keenan, J. M., Pennington, B., DeFries, J. C., Wadsworth, S. J., & Olson, R. K. (2012). Predicting word reading and comprehension with executive function and speed measures across development: A latent variable analysis. *Journal of Experimental Psychology*, *141*, 470–488. https://doi.org/10.1037/a0027375

Cicerone, K. D., Langenbahn, D. M., Braden, C., Malec, J. F., Kalmar, K., Fraas, M., … Azulay, J. (2011). Evidence-based cognitive rehabilitation: Updated review of the literature from 2003 through 2008. *Archives of Physical Medicine and Rehabilitation*, *92*, 519–530. https://doi.org/10.1016/j.apmr.2010.11.015

Cohen, A. O., & Casey, B. J. (2014). Rewiring juvenile justice: The intersection of developmental neuroscience and legal policy. *Trends in Cognitive Sciences*, *18*, 63–65. https://doi.org/10.1016/j.tics.2013.11.002

Cohen-Gilbert, J. E., & Thomas, K. M. (2013). Inhibitory control during emotional distraction across adolescence and early adulthood. *Child Development, 84*, 1954–1966. https://doi.org/10.1111/cdev.12085

Corrigan, J. D., & Bogner, J. (2007). Initial reliability and validity of the Ohio State University TBI identification method. *The Journal of Head Trauma Rehabilitation, 22*, 318–329. https://doi.org/10.1097/01.HTR.0000300227.67748.77

Corrigan, J. D., Selassie, A. W., & Orman, J. A. L. (2010). The epidemiology of traumatic brain injury. *The Journal of Head Trauma Rehabilitation, 25*, 72–80. https://doi.org/10.1097/HTR.0b013e3181ccc8b4

Dams-O'Connor, K., Spielman, L., Singh, A., Gordon, W. A., Lingsma, H. F., Maas, A. I., ... Schnyer, D. M. (2013). The impact of previous traumatic brain injury on health and functioning: A TRACK-TBI study. *Journal of Neurotrauma, 30*, 2014–2020. https://doi.org/10.1089/neu.2013.3049

Davies, R. C., Williams, W. H., Hinder, D., Burgess, C. N., & Mounce, L. T. (2012). Self-reported traumatic brain injury and postconcussion symptoms in incarcerated youth. *The Journal of Head Trauma Rehabilitation, 27*(3), E21-E27. https://doi.org/10.1097/HTR.0b013e31825360da

DeLisi, M., & Vaughn, M. G. (2014a). Foundation for a temperament-based theory of antisocial behavior and criminal justice system involvement. *Journal of Criminal Justice, 42*, 10–25. https://doi.org/10.1016/j.jcrimjus.2013.11.001

DeLisi, M., & Vaughn, M. G. (2014b). Temperament as a biosocial construct for understanding antisocial behavior. In M. DeLisi & M. G. Vaughn (Eds.), *The Routledge international handbook of biosocial criminology* (pp. 331–335). New York, NY: Routledge.

DeLisi, M., & Vaughn, M. G. (2015). Ingredients for criminality require genes, temperament, and psychopathic personality. *Journal of Criminal Justice, 43*, 290–294. https://doi.org/10.1016/j.jcrimjus.2015.05.005

Diamond, P. M., Harzke, A. J., Magaletta, P. R., Cummins, A. G., & Frankowski, R. (2007). Screening for traumatic brain injury in an offender sample: A first look at the reliability and validity of the traumatic brain injury questionnaire. *The Journal of Head Trauma Rehabilitation, 22*, 330–338. https://doi.org/10.1097/01.HTR.0000300228.05867.5c

Farrer, T. J., Frost, R. B., & Hedges, D. W. (2013). Prevalence of traumatic brain injury in juvenile offenders: A meta-analysis. *Child Neuropsychology, 19*, 225–234. https://doi.org/10.1080/09297049.2011.647901

Faul, M., & Coronado, V. (2015). Epidemiology of traumatic brain injury. *Handbook of Clinical Neurology, 127*, 3–13. https://doi.org/10.1016/B978-0-444-52892-6.00001-5

Fazel, S., Lichtenstein, P., Grann, M., & Langstrom, N. (2011). Risk of violent crime in individuals with epilepsy and traumatic brain injury: A 35-year Swedish population study. *PLoS Medicine, 8*. https://doi.org/10.1371/journal.pmed.1001150

Finset, A., & Andersson, S. (2000). Coping strategies in patients with acquired brain injury: Relationships between coping, apathy, depression and lesion location. *Brain Injury, 14*, 887–905. https://doi.org/10.1080/026990500445718

Folkman, S., Lazarus, R., Gruen, R., & DeLongis, A. (1986). Appraisal, coping, health status, and psychological symptoms. *Journal of Personality and Social Psychology, 50*, 571–579. https://doi.org/10.1037/0022-3514.50.3.571

Ganesalingam, K., Sanson, A., Anderson, V., & Yeates, K. O. (2006). Self-regulation and social and behavioral functioning following childhood traumatic brain injury. *Journal of the International Neuropsychological Society, 12*, 609–621. https://doi.org/10.1017OS1355617706060796

Gogtay, N., Giedd, J. N., Lusk, L., Hayashi, K. M., Greenstein, D., Vaituzis, A. C., ... Rapoport, J. L. (2004). Dynamic mapping of human cortical development during childhood through early adulthood. *Proceedings of the National Academy of Sciences, 101*, 8174–8179. https://doi.org/10.1073/pnas.0402680101

Gorman, S., Barnes, M. A., Swank, P. R., & Ewing-Cobbs, L. (2017). Recovery of working memory following pediatric traumatic brain injury: A longitudinal analysis. *Developmental Neuropsychology, 42*, 127–145. https://doi.org/10.1080/87565641.2017.1315581

Gorman, S., Barnes, M. A., Swank, P. R., Prasad, M., & Ewing-Cobbs, L. (2012). The effects of pediatric traumatic brain injury on verbal and visual-spatial working memory. *Journal of the International Neuropsychological Society, 18*, 29–38. https://doi.org/10.1017/S1355617711001251

Gould, K., Ponsford, J., Johnston, L., & Schönberger, M. (2011). Predictive and associated factors of psychiatric disorders after traumatic brain injury: A prospective study. *Journal of Neurotrauma, 28*, 1155–1163. https://doi.org/10.1089/neu.2010.1528

Grose-Fifer, J., Rodrigues, A., Hoover, S., & Zottoli, T. (2013). Attentional capture by emotional faces in adolescence. *Advances in Cognitive Psychology, 9*, 81–91. https://doi.org/10.5709/acp-0134-9

Hughes, N., Williams, W. H., Chitsabesan, P., Walesby, R. C., Mounce, L. T., & Clasby, B. (2015). The prevalence of traumatic brain injury among young offenders in custody: A systematic review. *Journal of Head Trauma Rehabilitation, 30*, 94–105. https://doi.org/10.1097/HTR.0000000000000124

Hux, K., Bond, V., Skinner, S., Belau, D., & Sanger, D. (1998). Parental report of occurrences and consequences of traumatic brain injury among delinquent and non-delinquent youth. *Brain Injury, 12*, 667–681. https://doi.org/10.1080/026990598122232

Ilie, G., Mann, R. E., Boak, A., Adlaf, E. M., Hamilton, H., Asbridge, M., ... Cusimano, M. D. (2014). Suicidality, bullying and other conduct and mental health correlates of traumatic brain injury in adolescents. *PloS One, 9*(4), e94936. https://doi.org/10.1371/journal.pone.0094936

Ilie, G., Mann, R. E., Hamilton, H., Adlaf, E. M., Boak, A., Asbridge, M., ... Cusimano, M. D. (2015). Substance use and related harms among adolescents with and without traumatic brain injury. *The Journal of Head Trauma Rehabilitation, 30*(5), 293–301. https://doi.org/10.1097/HTR.0000000000000101

Kendall, E., & Terry, D. (1996). Psychosocial adjustment following closed head injury: A model for understanding individual differences and predicting outcome. *Neuropsychological Rehabilitation, 6*, 101–132. https://doi.org/10.1080/713755502

Kort-Butler, L. A. (2017). Head injury and substance use in young adults. *Substance Use & Misuse, 52*, 1019–1026. https://doi.org/10.1080/10826084.2016.1268632

Krasny-Pacini, A., Chevignard, M., & Evans, J. (2014). Goal management training for rehabilitation of executive functions: A systematic review of effectiveness in patients with acquired brain injury. *Disability and Rehabilitation, 36*, 105–116. https://doi.org/10.3109/09638288.2013.777807

Krpan, K., Anderson, N., & Stuss, D. (2013). Obstacles to remediating coping following traumatic brain injury. *NeuroRehabilitation, 32*, 721–728. https://doi.org/10.3233/NRE-130897

Krpan, K., Levine, B., Stuss, D., & Dawson, D. (2007). Executive function and coping at one-year post traumatic brain injury. *Journal of Clinical and Experimental Neuropsychology, 29*, 36–46. https://doi.org/10.1080/13803390500376816

Langlois, J., Rutland-Brown, W., & Thomas, K. (2006). *Traumatic brain injury in the United States: Emergency department visits, hospitalizations, and deaths*. Atlanta, GA: Centers for Disease Control and Prevention, National Center for Injury Prevention.

Lazarus, R. (1993). Coping theory and research: Past, present, and future. *Psychosomatic Medicine, 55*, 234–247. https://doi.org/10.1097/00006842-199305000-00002

Levine, B., Robertson, I. H., Clare, L., Carter, G., Hong, J., Wilson, B. A., ... Stuss, D. T. (2000). Rehabilitation of executive functioning: An experimental–clinical validation of Goal Management Training. *Journal of the International Neuropsychological Society, 6*, 299–312. https://doi.org/10.1017/S1355617700633052

Lipsey M. (2012). Effective interventions for juvenile offenders. In T. Bliesener & A. Beelmann (Eds.), *Antisocial behavior & crime: Contributions of developmental and evaluation research to prevention and intervention* (pp. 181–198). Boston, MA: Hogrefe Publishing.

Maas, A. I., Menon, D. K., Adelson, P. D., Andelic, N., Bell, M. J., Belli, A., ... Citerio, G. (2017). Traumatic brain injury: Integrated approaches to improve prevention, clinical care, and research. *The Lancet Neurology, 16*, 987–1048. https://doi.org/10.1016/S1474-4422(17)30371-X

Max, J. E., Koele, S. L., Castillo, C. C., Lindgren, S. D., Arndt, S., Bokura, H., ... Sato, Y. (2000). Personality change disorder in children and adolescents following traumatic brain injury. *Journal of the International Neuropsychological Society, 6*(3), 279–289. https://doi.org/10.1017/S1355617700633039

Max, J. E., Levin, H. S., Schachar, R. J., Landis, J., Saunders, A. E., Ewing-Cobbs, L., ... Dennis, M. (2006). Predictors of personality change due to traumatic brain injury in children and adolescents six to twenty-four months after injury. *The Journal of Neuropsychiatry and Clinical Neurosciences, 18*(1), 21–32. https://doi.org/10.1176/jnp.18.1.21

Max, J. E., Wilde, E. A., Bigler, E. D., Hanten, G., Dennis, M., Schachar, R. J., ... Yang, T. T. (2015). Personality change due to traumatic brain injury in children and adolescents: Neurocognitive correlates. *The Journal of Neuropsychiatry and Clinical Neurosciences, 27*(4), 272–279. https://doi.org/10.1176/appi.neuropsych.15030073

McDonald, S., Rushby, J., Kelly, M., & de Sousa, A. (2014). Disorders of emotion and social cognition following traumatic brain injury. In H. S. Levin, D. K. Shum, & R. K. Chan (Eds.), *Understanding traumatic brain injury: Current research and future directions* (pp. 133–162). New York: Oxford University Press.

McKinlay, A., Corrigan, J., Horwood, L. J., & Fergusson, D. M. (2014). Substance abuse and criminal activities following traumatic brain injury in childhood, adolescence, and early adulthood. *The Journal of Head Trauma Rehabilitation, 29*, 498–506. https://doi.org/10.1097/HTR.0000000000000001

Moore, A., & Stambrook, M. (1995). Cognitive moderators of outcome following traumatic brain injury: A conceptual model and implications for rehabilitation. *Brain Injury, 9*, 109–130. https://doi.org/10.3109/02699059509008185

Moore, E., Indig, D., & Haysom, L. (2014). Traumatic brain injury, mental health, substance use, and offending among incarcerated young people. *The Journal of Head Trauma Rehabilitation, 29*, 239–247. https://doi.org/10.1097/HTR.0b013e31828f9876

Ogilvie, J. M., Stewart, A. L., Chan, R. C., & Shum, D. H. (2011). Neuropsychological measures of executive function and antisocial behavior: A meta-analysis. *Criminology, 49*, 1063–1107. https://doi.org/10.1111/j.1745-9125.2011.00252.x

Perron, B. E., & Howard, M. O. (2008). Prevalence and correlates of traumatic brain injury among delinquent youths. *Criminal Behaviour and Mental Health, 18*, 243–255. https://doi.org/10.1002/cbm.702

Rakers, S. E., Scheenen, M. E., Westerhof-Evers, H. J., de Koning, M. E., van der Horn, H. J., van der Naalt, J., & Spikman, J. M. (2018). Executive functioning in relation to coping in mild versus moderate-severe traumatic brain injury. *Neuropsychology, 32*, 213–219. https://doi.org/10.1037/neu0000399

Resch, C., Rosema, S., Hurks, P., de Kloet, A., & van Heugten, C. (2018). Searching for effective components of cognitive rehabilitation for children and adolescents with acquired brain injury: A systematic review. *Brain Injury, 32*, 679–692. https://doi.org/10.1080/02699052.2018.1458335

Roper v. Simmons, 543 U.S. 551. (2005)

Ross, K. A., Dorris, L., & McMillan, T. O. M. (2011). A systematic review of psychological interventions to alleviate cognitive and psychosocial problems in children with acquired brain injury. *Developmental Medicine & Child Neurology, 53*, 692–701. https://doi.org/10.1111/j.1469-8749.2011.03976.x

Sapolsky, R. M. (2017). *Behave: The biology of humans at our best and worst.* New York: Penguin Press.

Scheenen. M., van der Horn, H., de Koning, M., van der Naalt, J., & Spikman, J. (2017). Stability of coping and the role of self-efficacy in the first year following mild traumatic brain injury. *Social Science & Medicine, 181*, 184–190. https://doi.org/10.1016/j.socscimed.2017.03.025

Schwartz, J. A., Connolly, E. J., & Brauer, J. R. (2017). Head injuries and changes in delinquency from adolescence to emerging adulthood: The importance of self-control as a mediating influence. *Journal of Research in Crime and Delinquency.* https://doi.org/10.1177/0022427817710287

Schwartz, J. A., Connolly, E. J., & Valgardson, B. A. (2018). An evaluation of the directional relationship between head injuries and subsequent changes in impulse control and delinquency in a sample of previously adjudicated males. *Journal of Criminal Justice, 56*, 70–80. https://doi.org/10.1016/j.jcrimjus.2017.08.004

Stoddard, S. A., & Zimmerman, M. A. (2011). Association of interpersonal violence with self-reported history of head injury. *Pediatrics, 127*, 1074–1079. https://doi.org/10.1542/peds.2010-2453

Stuss, D. T. (2011). Traumatic brain injury: Relation to executive dysfunction and the frontal lobes. *Current Opinion in Neurology, 24*, 584–589. https://doi.org/10.1097/WCO.0b013e32834c7eb9

Taylor, C. A., Bell, J. M., Breiding, M. J., & Xu, L. (2017). Traumatic brain injury-related emergency department visits, hospitalizations, and deaths – United States, 2007 and 2013. *Morbidity and Mortality Weekly Report – Surveillance Summaries, 66*(9), 1–16. https://doi.org/10.15585/mmwr.ss6609a1

The Disabilities Trust Foundation. (2018). *Brain injury screening index.* Retrieved from www.thedtgroup.org/foundation/brain-injury-screening-index

Tomberg, T., Toomela, A., Pulver, A., & Tikk, A. (2005). Coping strategies, social support, life orientation and health-related quality of life following traumatic brain injury. *Brain Injury, 19*, 1181–1190. https://doi.org/10.1080/02699050500150153

Urban, K. J., Riggs, L., Wells, G. D., Keightley, M., Chen, J. K., Ptito, A., ... Sinopoli, K. J. (2017). Cortical thickness changes and their relationship to dual-task performance following mild traumatic brain injury in youth. *Journal of Neurotrauma, 34*, 816–823. https://doi.org/10.1089/neu.2016.4502

van der Naalt, J., Timmerman, M., de Koning, M., van der Horn, H., Scheenen, M., Jacobs, B., Hageman, G., Yilmaz, T., Roks, G., & Spikman, J. (2017). Early predictors of outcome after mild traumatic brain injury (UPFRONT): An observational cohort study. *The Lancet Neurology, 16*, 532–540. https://doi.org/10.1016/S1474-4422(17)30117-5

Vaughn, M. G., Salas-Wright, C. P., DeLisi, M., & Perron, B. (2014). Correlates of traumatic brain injury among juvenile offenders: A multi-site study. *Criminal Behaviour and Mental Health, 24*, 188–203. https://doi.org/10.1002/cbm.1900

Veeh, C. A., Renn, T., Vaughn, M. G., & DeLisi, M. (2018a). Traumatic brain injury, temperament, and violence in incarcerated youth: A mediation analysis based on Delisi and Vaughn's theory of temperament and antisocial behavior. *Psychology, Crime & Law, 24*, 1016–1029. https://doi.org/10.1080/1068316X.2018.1497632

Veeh, C. A., Vaughn, M. G., & Renn, T. (2018b). *Coping strategies and traumatic brain injury in incarcerated youth: A mediation analysis.* Manuscript submitted for publication.

Wilde, E. A., Hunter, J. V., Newsome, M. R., Scheibel, R. S., Bigler, E. D., Johnson, J. L., ... Levin, H. S. (2005). Frontal and temporal morphometric findings on MRI in children after moderate to severe traumatic brain injury. *Journal of Neurotrauma, 22*, 333–344. https://doi.org/10.1089/neu.2005.22.333

Williams, W. H., Cordan, G., Mewse, A. J., Tonks, J., & Burgess, C. N. (2010). Self-reported traumatic brain injury in male young offenders: A risk factor for re-offending, poor mental health and violence? *Neuropsychological Rehabilitation, 20*, 801–812. https://doi.org/10.1080/09602011.2010.519613

Wolff, K. T., Baglivio, M. T., Piquero, A. R., Vaughn, M. G., & DeLisi, M. (2016). The triple crown of antisocial behavior: Effortful control, negative emotionality, and community disadvantage. *Youth Violence and Juvenile Justice, 14*, 350–366. https://doi.org/10.1177/1541204015599042

Wolters, G., Stapert, S., Brands, I., & van Heugten, C. (2010). Coping styles in relation to cognitive rehabilitation and quality of life after brain injury. *Neuropsychological Rehabilitation, 20*, 587–600. https://doi.org/10.1080/09602011003683836

Wolters, G., Stapert, S., Brands, I., & van Heugten, C. (2011). Coping following acquired brain injury. *Journal of Head Trauma Rehabilitation, 26*, 150–157. https://doi.org/10.1097/HTR.0b013e3181e421dc

Wolters Gregório, G., Gould, K., Spitz, G., van Heugten, C., & Ponsford, J. (2014). Changes in self-reported pre- to postinjury coping styles in the first 3 years after traumatic brain injury and the effects on psychosocial and emotional functioning and quality of life. *Journal of Head Trauma Rehabilitation, 29*, E43–E53. https://doi.org/10.1097/HTR.0b013e318292fb00

# 10
# SLEEP AND DELINQUENCY
## An Emerging Area of Research

*Samantha S. Clinkinbeard and Pete Simi*

Sleep is a widely discussed topic, commonly included in news media stories regarding the most effective ways to achieve optimal sleep quality and quantity. Media headlines even go so far as to describe insufficient sleep as "catastrophic" and "killing" us (Bradberry, 2016; Johnston, 2017). Sleep issues have been recognized as an important public health problem in the US and across the globe (Becker, Langberg, & Byars, 2015; Institute of Medicine, 2006; Owens, 2014). According to the National Sleep Foundation Sleep Health Index, approximately one third of Americans report their sleep quality as fair or poor and the majority of adults get less than the recommended amount of sleep each night (Knutson et al., 2017). Children and teens are especially vulnerable to sleep deficits and problems due to the developmental changes, school schedules, and "screen" time (WBA Market Research, 2006). Research during the last several decades have linked sleep problems and debt to a variety of psychological and physical aspects of health and to performance in work and school environments (Hamilton, Nelson, Stevens, & Kitzman, 2007; Roberts, Roberts, & Duong, 2009; Wells & Vaughn, 2012). Among adolescents, sleep issues have been associated with impaired driving skills (Garner et al., 2015), mood and emotion regulation (Baum et al., 2013), inattention during the daytime (Beebe, 2011), suicidality (McGlinchey & Harvey, 2015; McKnight-Eily et al., 2011), and academic performance (Dewald, Meijer, Oort, Kerkhof, & Bögels, 2010), just to name a few. In the last decade, one negative effect that has received growing attention is delinquency and risky behavior. Though there is growing evidence that sleep is linked to delinquent behavior, the research in this area is still nascent and there are a number of questions yet to be answered. In this chapter we will review the empirical literature that currently exists with regard to sleep and delinquency and outline needs for future research.

### Sleep in the Adolescent Life Course

In 2010, the American Medical Association adopted a resolution sponsored by the American Academy of Sleep Medicine, stating: "RESOLVED, That our American Medical Association identify adolescent insufficient sleep and sleepiness as a public health issue ..." (American Academy of Sleep Medicine, 2010). The 2006 *Sleep in America Poll* found that most adolescents in the United States do not get the optimal 9 hours of sleep recommended for that age group. Further, the proportion of teens getting optimal sleep (35% among 6th to 8th graders) decreases significantly at they get older (9% among 9th to 12th graders) (WBA Market Research, 2006). Studies from several other countries around the world have reported similar findings (Huang, Wang, & Guilleminault, 2010; Loessl et al., 2008; Owens, 2014; Yang, Kim, Patel, & Lee,

2005). Further, many teens attempt to "catch up" on the weekends reporting wild swings in bedtimes, waketimes, and sleep duration between weekdays and weekends (Owens, 2014; WBA Market Research, 2006).

The recognized need for sleep is driven by two processes, the sleep-wake component and the circadian rhythm component (Borbely, 1982). Simply put, the intrinsic sleep–wake component compels us to seek out sleep by creating a pressure or need to sleep that grows the longer we stay awake. This pressure also reduces as we get sleep. The circadian rhythm component is associated with hormones and a sort of "internal clock" that guides our sleep and wake time preferences. Ideally these two processes work in concert with one another to help us reach our goal of optimal sleep; however, this balance can be easily disturbed by developmental changes or social and environmental influences (Becker, Langberg, & Byars, 2015; Carskadon, 2011; Crowley, Wolfson, Tarokh, & Carskadon, 2018). Both of these cycles experience shifts in adolescence, starting at puberty. The building of internal sleep pressure based on time since last slept is slowed and the "internal clock" for many pubertal adolescents is shifted towards wanting to stay awake later at night and sleeping later in the morning (Becker, Langberg, & Byars, 2015; Carskadon, 2011; Hagenauer, Perryman, Lee, & Carskadon, 2009).

This period of time from late childhood to early adulthood in which youth are receiving progressively less sleep and in which their sleep architecture is changing, is also a time of important biological, social, and psychological development. Among other tasks, adolescents must reconcile the cognitive transition from concrete to abstract thinking, increased complexity in moral understanding, changes in physical shape and sexual interests, movement away from primary reliance on parents and the growing importance of peers in their self-concepts (Christie & Viner, 2005; Dahl, 2004; Nottelmann et al., 1987; Steinberg & Morris, 2001). One hallmark of adolescence is the difficulty often experienced in the regulation of emotion and behavior. Thanks to hormonal and neurological changes, adolescents experience intense emotions coupled with an increasing desire to experience intense thrills and excitement (Dahl, 2004). While the increase in sensation-seeking is often activated with the onset of puberty, the prefrontal cortex, which is known for executive functioning (e.g., cognitive control and self-regulation), continues to develop long past this point, indicating a critical mismatch in the emotions, desires, and skills of adolescents (Blakemore & Choudhury, 2006; Dahl, 2004). Increased cognitive skills allows adolescents to predict consequences and improve decision-making under low arousal conditions, yet they struggle to make those same responsible decisions under emotional arousal (Dahl, 2004). Again, all of this happens during a time in which the majority of adolescents receive borderline or insufficient sleep and sleep deficits increase with each passing year (Owens, 2014; WBA Market Research, 2006).

Thus far, we know that adolescents are sleep-deprived and simultaneously dealing with asynchronous development of emotions, desires, and executive functioning. Coincidentally (or not) this is also the same period in the life course during which delinquent behavior is most prevalent. Typical onset ranges from late childhood to early adolescence with delinquent behavior peaking around 15–19 and then declining in the early 20s (Hirschi & Gottfredson, 1983; Pratt, 2015; Sampson & Laub, 2005, 2006).

## *Sleep and Delinquency, Does It Matter?*

Research over the last decade has begun to explore the possible relationship between sleep and delinquency, and the general conclusion, is "Yes, but ..." To some extent, it is difficult to talk about the sleep and delinquency literature as a unified whole. The literature consists of studies that explore a variety of definitions of both concepts. When it comes to sleep, some studies look at sleep problems or sleep quality, while others look at sleep duration, and few include indicators of both. The ways in which sleep problems and sleep duration are operationalized are rarely the same from one study to the next, making comparisons of findings difficult. Regarding the conceptualization of delinquency, the variation in definition and measurement is even more pronounced. To some extent the literature in this area has taken a broad view and looked at risky behavior, which can refer to anything from failing to use a safety belt to alcohol or drug use to participating in various forms of delinquency.

For the purposes of this chapter, we focus primarily on studies that conceptualized delinquency as the outcome variable of investigation, which itself is often defined in a number of ways. It should be noted that there is also a subset of literature that explores the relationship between sleep and alcohol and drug use. Although these are not typically characterized in scales of delinquency, they do represent status offenses or delinquent acts. Though it is beyond the scope of this chapter, future work should look at integrating the findings on sleep and drug and alcohol use and delinquent behavior. In the sections below, we first review the empirical literature on the outcomes of sleep duration and sleep quality before turning to the discussion of methodological issues and recommendations for future work.

## Sleep Duration

Short and Weber (2018) addressed the question of sleep duration and risk-taking in a recent meta-analysis of 26 studies looking at adolescents between the ages of 10 and 19. The authors concluded that there was a meaningful relationship between sleep duration and risk-taking and noted that effect sizes were similar across several different types of risk-taking. Overall, insufficient sleep across different operationalizations was associated with 1.43 times greater odds of risk-taking among adolescents (Short & Weber, 2018). Risk domains included measures of drug use, alcohol use, smoking, road safety, sexual risk-taking, violent/delinquent behavior and trait sensation-seeking. Though there was enough information to conclude modest effects with regard to violence/delinquency and trait risk-taking there was insufficient data to allow confident comparisons between these and the other categories of risk (Short & Weber, 2018). Thus, we still need more sleep research specific to delinquency and violence.

If we focus specifically on measures of delinquency, the results are somewhat mixed. A handful of studies have utilized nationally representative data from the National Longitudinal Study of Adolescent to Adult Health (Add Health). In our 2011 study, we found that youth who reported sleeping five, six, or seven hours a night also reported significantly higher levels of involvement in property delinquency (e.g., deliberately damaging property, taking something from a store without paying) than the reference group that slept eight to ten hours. Higher reports of violent delinquency (e.g., get into a physical fight, hurt someone badly enough to need bandages) occurred only for those reporting five or fewer hours of sleep (Clinkinbeard, Simi, Evans, & Anderson, 2011). Using the same wave of data but a smaller twin sample, and different control variables, Barnes and Meldrum (2015) found evidence of a modest relationship between sleep duration and non-violent delinquency and drug use but not violent delinquency. All of these relationships were rendered non-significant once the shared genetic and environmental variance of twin pairs was considered (Barnes & Meldrum, 2015).

While both we (Clinkinbeard, Simi, Evans, & Anderson, 2011) and Barnes and Meldrum (2015) focused on the first wave of the Add Health (mean age ≈ 15), Peach and Gaultney (2013) extended that work into later waves. They found significant direct effects of sleep duration and delayed bedtime on delinquency at Wave II (mean age ≈ 16) but not Wave III (mean age ≈ 22) or Wave IV (mean age ≈ 28). Further, they found evidence of indirect effects through sensation-seeking and impulse control at all waves (Peach & Gaultney, 2013). McGlinchey and Harvey (2015) did not look specifically at duration, but instead focused on the relationship between late bedtimes and risky behavior. They found cross-sectional relationships between late bedtimes and several risky behaviors (all coded as dichotomous, present/absent variables), including criminal[1] and violent activities, and drug and alcohol use at Waves II and III. Late bedtimes at Wave II also predicted criminal activity, alcohol abuse, and drug use, but not violence longitudinally at Wave III. Taken together these findings from the Add Health could indicate that sleep is more important for delinquent or criminal behavior in adolescence compared to early adulthood and that timing of sleep/wake may be important in addition to actual duration.

Utilizing data from the Fragile Families and Child Well-being Study, Jackson and Vaughn (2017) found that each additional hour of sleep (as reported by the youth's parents) was associated with an 18% decrease in delinquency, a result that was unchanged when accounting for ADHD symptoms. Backman and colleagues (2015) found that sleeping less than seven hours was associated with both property and violent delinquency. In their study, the effects of sleep were stronger for violent than property delinquency (Backman et al., 2015). A study in Taiwan found that sleep duration of less than six hours had a direct effect on adolescent conduct problems, after controlling for prior behavior (Lin & Yi, 2015), while another study in the Netherlands found a significant longitudinal relationship between time in bed and delinquent and aggressive behaviors (Meijer, Reitz, Deković, van Den Wittenboer, & Stoel, 2010). Finally, Meldrum and Restivo (2014) found that sleep duration was associated with a variety of risky behaviors, including fighting, but this finding was consistent at only the most extreme levels of sleep deprivation. Though moderate sleep deprivation did not predict all of the risky behaviors, all levels of sleep deprivation were associated with common adolescent behavior such as drinking alcohol and texting while driving (Meldrum & Restivo, 2014).

As noted above, the relationship between sleep duration and delinquent behavior is mixed in the literature. Several studies, including one meta-analysis (Short & Weber, 2018), have found evidence of a relationship between sleep deprivation and delinquent behavior (Backman et al., 2015; Clinkinbeard, Simi, Evans, & Anderson, 2011; Hildenbrand, Daly, Nicholls, Brooks-Holliday, & Kloss, 2013; Holley, Hill, & Stevenson, 2011; Jackson & Vaughn, 2017; Lin & Yi, 2015; Peach & Gaultney, 2013), however, other studies did not find significant effects of delinquent or violent behavior (Barnes & Meldrum, 2015; O'Brien & Mindell, 2005). That said, there is support for a relationship between sleep duration and the broad umbrella of risky behaviors (Catrett & Gaultney, 2009; McGlinchey & Harvey, 2015; McKnight-Eily et al., 2011; Meldrum & Restivo, 2014; O'Brien & Mindell, 2005; Short & Weber, 2018). Status offenses such as underage alcohol use or illicit drug use are regularly found to be associated with sleep deprivation (e.g., McKnight-Eily et al., 2011; Sosnowski, Kliewer, & Lepore, 2016; Vazsonyi et al., 2015; Wong, Roberson, & Dyson, 2015). Within the sleep duration literature, it seems that the effects may be stronger during early to mid-adolescence (Peach & Gaultney, 2013) and at deprivation extremes (e.g., less than five or six hours; Clinkinbeard, Simi, Evans, & Anderson, 2011; Meldrum & Restivo, 2014).

## Sleep Problems or Sleep Quality

In addition to sleep duration or deprivation, a number of studies have focused on sleep quality or problems. Similar to duration, the specific measurement of sleep quality/problems varies across studies. A common approach to measurement of sleep problems is to generate a sleep problems scale score from items such as trouble sleeping, tired during the day, trouble getting back to sleep after waking in the middle of the night, trouble getting to sleep, desire for more sleep, etc. Other sleep problems include reports of insomnia, weekend-delay or weekend-oversleep (i.e., differences between sleep duration during the week on weekends).

Several studies report evidence of a cross-sectional relationship between sleep issues and different types of delinquency (Backman et al., 2015; Catrett & Gaultney, 2009; Chang et al., 2017; Hambrick, Rubens, Brawner, & Taussig, 2018; Lin & Yi, 2015; Vail-Smith, Felts, & Becker, 2009). For example, in one of the earliest studies of sleep and delinquency, O'Brien and Mindell (2005) found that higher scores on daytime sleepiness and a sleep-wake problems scale were associated with more reports of violent behavior and other risky behaviors. Backman and colleagues (2015) also discovered evidence of a relationship with violent behavior, finding that teenagers in Finland who reported frequent (i.e., three to five times a week) and persistent (i.e., for more than a year) sleep problems reported higher rates of property and violent delinquency. One study utilizing actigraphic and self-report measures with a sample of at-risk 13-year-olds found that those who reported poorer sleep quality and who had more daytime sleep (i.e., naps) reported more delinquency (Stone, Cuellar, Miller-Loncar, LaGasse, & Lester, 2015).

Catrett and Gaultney (2009) found within wave effects of insomnia on delinquency though the results were not significant when predicting delinquency from insomnia at an earlier wave. Other research, however, has shown evidence of a longitudinal relationship between sleep quality and delinquent behavior. In an early longitudinal investigation, Meijer and colleagues (2010) found a linear relationship between sleep problems and delinquency and aggressive behaviors. In a study of Taiwanese adolescents, Chang and colleagues (2017) found a significant relationship between sleep problems and reports of delinquency a year later. In another study, utilizing data from the Taiwan Youth Project, sleep problems had a significant effect on conduct problems in both cross-sectional and longitudinal analyses (Lin & Yi, 2015). In some of these studies, direct effects of sleep problems that were initially significant are either partially or fully mediated by the introduction of other variables such as ADHD symptoms (Jackson & Vaughn, 2017) or self-control measures (Meldrum, Barnes, & Hay, 2015).

## Sleep Quality Vs. Sleep Quantity

As mentioned earlier, it is difficult to succinctly summarize the findings in the literature on sleep and delinquency due to a variety of conceptualizations and operationalizations. Many studies of sleep and risky behavior focus *either* on sleep duration *or* on some indicator of sleep problems or sleep quality. Because there is evidence that time spent in bed in not necessarily correlated with reports of sleep problems, Meijer and colleagues (2010) argue that there is a qualitative conceptual difference between sleep duration and sleep problems. Thus, we have to be cautious about direct comparisons between studies that include indicators of duration and those that include indicators of quality. Even within each of the concepts, summary statements remain difficult. Although there is a meta-analysis of sleep duration and risky behavior (Short & Weber, 2018), it is limited in the information specific to delinquency, and a similar meta-analysis of sleep problems and risky or delinquent behavior does not yet exist.

Although it is relatively rare, there is occasional within-study overlap of sleep duration and quality. Lin and colleagues (2015) reported direct and indirect longitudinal effects of both sleep problems and sleep duration (i.e., short sleep) on conduct problems. Similarly, Meijer and colleagues (2010) found longitudinal relationships between time in bed and sleep problems and delinquent and aggressive behavior. Both sleep duration and problems were significantly related to delinquency in a study conducted by Jackson and Vaughn (2017), but only the effects of sleep duration remained significant after accounting for ADHD symptoms. Backman and colleagues (2015) found both problems and duration to significantly predict delinquency, though the effects of duration were stronger. O'Brien and Mindell (2005), on the other hand, found significant relationships between problems and violence but not duration. To better understand the relationship between sleep and delinquency, it is important to expand upon the research which directly compares the effects of sleep problems and duration.

## Methodological Issues

### *Overreliance on Self-Reports*

The bulk of the research looking at sleep issues and related consequences, including risky or delinquent behavior, rely heavily on self-reports of sleep duration or problematic sleep. While at least one study reported relative consistency between self-reports of average sleep times (hours and minutes), daily time diaries and actigraphy tools (Wolfson et al., 2003), a more recent study suggests that people commonly overestimate the amount of actual sleep they receive (Arora, Broglia, Pushpakumar, Lodhi, & Taheri, 2013). Further, in many cases, self-report questions on surveys are rounded to closest hour (e.g., Barnes & Meldrum, 2015; Clinkinbeard, Simi, Evans, & Anderson, 2011) which combines a number of people together that maybe shouldn't be (e.g., those who sleep 6 hours and 10 minutes and those that sleep 6 hours and 45 minutes). Even if self-reports of bedtimes and wake times are relatively accurate, that may not be precise enough. At least one study investigating the relationship between sleep and a variety of issues, found that of multiple sleep indicators, *actual sleep minutes* (measured via actigraphy) was the most effective predictor, accounting for 18% of the variance in conduct problems (Holley, Hill & Stevenson, 2011). That is, it was not the length of time from head hitting the pillow until rising in the morning, but the *actual minutes* of sleep (i.e., subtracting out periods of wakefulness, of which most of us are unaware). Finally, self-report studies, particularly those utilizing sleep duration measures, typically rely on only one or two survey items. Even some of the most elaborate designs (e.g., twin studies; Barnes & Meldrum, 2015) rely on single item indicators of sleep.

Considering the overreliance on self-report measures, future research should prioritize more precise indicators of sleep duration and problems. For example, time diaries rely on participants self-reports but they are more precise than single item-indicators that ask participants to estimate *average* or *typical* daily sleep. Though time diaries can be burdensome for participants, cell-phone technology can be used to ease the burden and capture relationships between multiple variables over time (Anderson, Clinkinbeard, Barnum, & Augustyn, 2016). In addition, wearable devices utilizing actigraphy are commonly utilized in sleep labs or medical research but are rarely used by social scientists exploring sleep and delinquency (see for exception, Holley, Hill, & Stevenson, 2011; Stone, Cuellar, Miller-Loncar, LaGasse, & Lester, 2015). These devices are more precise than time diaries and self-reports of averages. Further, they can provide additional information about wakefulness, time spent in different sleep stages, and other indicators that could be of interest. Criminologists would be well-advised to partner with researchers already doing clinical sleep research, as it would be relatively easy to add measures of delinquency to studies already utilizing state-of-the art technology for tracking sleep. Further, as sleep tracking technology continues to improve and the popularity of wearable fitness trackers continues to increase, researchers may be able to utilize technology that participants already own, reducing the expense of research designs with more precise indicators.

### **Need for Longitudinal and Experimental Research**

Most of the research investigating the relationship between sleep and delinquency has relied on cross-sectional designs, and, thus, one of the most common limitations noted is the lack of clarity regarding the direction of effects. In fact, while most studies assume that the relationship flows from sleep to delinquency, at least a couple studies have explored the opposite (Ireland & Culpin, 2006; Meijer, Reitz, Deković, van Den Wittenboer, & Stoel, 2010). Even studies that control for genetic variation, cannot confidently comment on the direction of the effects (Barnes & Meldrum, 2015). A few studies have controlled for prior behavior or explored longer-term effects by looking at sleep in one wave and examining the extent to which it might predict delinquency at a later wave. Thus far, however, research has been silent on the long-term accumulation of sleep problems or deprivation as it might relate to delinquency. In other words, are there differences between people who experience modest, short-lived problems and those that experience problems or deprivation over weeks, months, or years? Related to this, designs are necessary that allow for the exploration of both short and long-term effects and examination of the co-development and/or potentially reciprocal nature of sleep and delinquency.

Experimental or randomized control designs are often considered the "gold standard" of rigor in research, and it is not uncommon for clinical or medical researchers to utilize these types of designs when investigating the effects of sleep. Experimental designs are missing, however, from the literature on sleep and delinquency. One approach is the "one night of sleep deprivation" model in which some participants are assigned to stay up overnight or get shortened sleep while a control group gets regular sleep (see for example, Ballesio, Cerolini, Ferlazzo, Cellini, & Lombardo, 2018; McKenna, Dickinson, Orff, & Drummond, 2007). Group performance on various tasks are then compared between the two groups. With a little creativity, this type of model could be applied to minor deviant or risk-taking outcomes in the form of provoked aggression and/or willingness to violate minor rules (see for examples of behavioral outcomes in experiments; Cohen, Nisbett, Bowdle, & Schwarz, 1996; Fischer, Aydin, Kastenmüller, Frey, & Fischer, 2012). Further, varying sleep duration protocols or bedtimes could be assigned to groups over longer periods of times (e.g., several days or a few weeks) and compared to outcomes reporting. Where ethical concerns exist, alternative quasi-experimental and propensity-score designs could be utilized. Such designs could also focus on potential intervening mechanisms such as self-control and decision-making.

## Future Research in the Area of Sleep and Delinquency

The previous section highlighted a number of methodological priorities for future research (e.g., longitudinal designs, use of multiple indicators, utilizing technological advances in sleep tracking, and experimental research). We also have a few substantive suggestions for future research.

### *Mediators and Moderators*

A focus on mediators and moderators related to the sleep and delinquency relationship is an important area of future work. Although the strength of the relationship varies somewhat across operationalizations of sleep and delinquency, there is enough evidence to confirm that a relationship does indeed exist. More work is needed to better understand the mechanisms or intervening processes that are affected by sleep and ultimately contribute to risk-taking or delinquent behavior. A better understanding of the intervening mechanisms might also bring some consistency to the literature. That is, because researchers control for a variety of factors but do so inconsistently across studies, differential findings could, to some extent, be a product of full or partial mediation by control variables. Though there are only a couple studies thus far that look specifically at mediators of sleep and delinquency, a few variables that have gained support include emotional well-being, defiant attitudes, academic performance, and self-control (Lin & Yi, 2015; Meldrum, Barnes, & Hay, 2015).

Self-control, in particular, should be central to future research on the relationship between sleep and delinquency. Though in the criminological literature self-control was once assumed to be static after late childhood (Gottfredson & Hirschi, 1990), the long-term stability of self-control is no longer taken for granted (Burt, Simons, & Simons, 2006; Burt, Sweeten, & Simons, 2014; Clinkinbeard, Barnum, & Rhodes, 2018; Hay & Forrest, 2006; Meldrum, Young, & Weerman, 2012; Na & Paternoster, 2012). Informed by the strength model of self-control (Baumeister & Heatherton, 1996; Baumeister, Vohs, & Tice, 2007), which posits that self-control is a finite resource that can be depleted through effort and strengthened through rest and practice, Meldrum and colleagues (2015) explored the relationships between sleep, self-control, and delinquency. Specifically, they utilized data from the Study of Early Child Care and Youth Development and found that self-control fully mediated the relationship between self-reported sleep problems and delinquency (Meldrum, Barnes, & Hay, 2015). The authors acknowledge that the study was not designed to fully "unpack the black box" regarding the specific neurological or psychological processes that bridge self-control and delinquency (Meldrum, Barnes, & Hay, 2015), but this is certainly a promising development in the area of sleep and delinquency. As noted earlier, several studies have reported that even minor sleep deprivation can have important implications for executive functioning processes, and poor sleep quality may be associated with deficits in decision-making and decreased motivation to engage in cognitive control (Becker, Langberg, & Byars, 2015). Thus, we agree with Meldrum and colleagues (2015) that this line of research should be prioritized and that it should be explored using additional indicators of sleep and the preferred methodologies mentioned in the previous section.

In addition to exploring variables that mediate the relationship between sleep and delinquency, a number of studies have suggested that sleep may serve as an important link between other risk factors and delinquency. For example, there is evidence that the relationship between different types of trauma, adverse childhood experiences, and victimization may be at least partially mediated by sleep problems (Chang et al., 2017; Hambrick, Rubens, Brawner, & Taussig, 2018; Sosnowski, Kliewer, & Lepore, 2016). Future research might also consider whether sleep could mediate or moderate the effects of other predictors of delinquency (e.g., parental monitoring, peer influence). For example, one could imagine how quality sleep could provide a buffer between antisocial peers and delinquent behavior by allowing for more quality decision-making. Further, it is important to determine the extent to which sleep could act differently between various at-risk populations. Various studies with at-risk populations (e.g., victims, children with prenatal drug exposure, clinical samples) have reported a significant relationship between sleep and various forms of deviant or antisocial behavior (Hambrick, Rubens, Brawner, & Taussig, 2018; Jackson & Vaughn, 2017; Stephens et al., 2013; Stone, Cuellar, Miller-Loncar, LaGasse, & Lester, 2015). A thus far unexplored question is whether sleep deficits might be more important for at-risk populations. In other words, whereas low-risk populations might be able to easily weather the effects of moderate sleep deficits, the consequences of poor sleep could be more detrimental to at-risk adolescents.

## *Individual Variation*

Another area that is ripe for exploration is the way in which demographic characteristics intersect with sleep and delinquency. To date, gender has not been extensively studied; however, a few interesting findings have surfaced. Peach and Gaultney (2013) found that males were more sensitive than females to the effects of sleep duration and bedtime delay on delinquency. In a study by Meijer and colleagues (2010), boys with below average time in bed and low sleep quality were more aggressive than girls but when time in bed exceeded the mean with poor sleep quality, girls' aggression scores were higher. The findings from these studies warrant further investigation of gender in the sleep and delinquency relationship. Socioeconomic status and race also deserve attention. Although they have yet to be explored directly in the sleep and delinquency context, there is evidence that both race and SES matter with regard to sleep. For example, African Americans report less sleep and more sleep problems than Whites (WBA Market Research, 2010). Further, adults and children from low SES backgrounds have been found to have more sleep issues than those who are higher on the SES continuum (Grandner et al., 2010; Mezick et al., 2008; Owens, 2014).

Genetic contributions to the sleep and delinquency relationship also deserve more attention. Sleep is a complex process and much of the specifics remain unclear to scientists. That said, there is some evidence that genetic mutations may play a role in the timing, duration, and other features of sleep (Shi, Wu, Ptáček, & Fu, 2017). Barnes and Meldrum (2015) argue that a significant limitation of the sleep and delinquency literature is the inability to exclude possible spuriousness resulting from unaccounted genetic influences. Barnes and Meldrum (2015) explored the relationship between sleep duration and bedtime and several outcomes, including violent and non-violent delinquency. Once shared environmental and genetic contributions were accounted for, the only outcomes that remained significant were depression and self-control (Barnes & Meldrum, 2015). Though the study had limitations (e.g., no measure of sleep quality and single-item indicator of sleep duration), the findings highlight the importance of accounting for genetic contributions.

## *Institutional Environments*

In 2014 the American Academy of Pediatrics released a statement recommending that middle and high schools should not start until at least 8:30 in the morning (American Academy of Pediatrics, 2014). This statement was released in response to evidence that adolescents in the United States tend to be sleep-deprived and that such sleep deprivation can have negative consequences. Though many schools still start earlier than recommended, some schools and districts across the country have made shifts to their school start times. Research has shown that delayed start times do, in fact, lead to more sleep by adolescents (Owens, Belon, & Moss, 2010; Wahlstrom, Berger, & Widome, 2017). Typically, youth do not go to bed earlier, but instead, sleep in a bit later in the morning, leading to additional sleep. As school start times continue to change, delinquency researchers should examine school conduct reports and related indicators before and after such changes or compare across districts with different start times. Later start times could also have the unintentional consequence of shortening the time in which adolescents are unsupervised in the afternoon hours, when the majority of delinquent behavior occurs (Office of Juvenile Justice and Delinquency Prevention, 2014).

## Conclusion

Although a growing number of studies have examined sleep and delinquency during the last decade, a variety of questions remain unanswered. The relationship between sleep and delinquency depends to some extent on how sleep is measured, how delinquency is defined, the age of the study population, and which variables are included as controls. Several likely mediators of sleep and delinquency have been identified in the research and more effort should be directed towards understanding these intervening mechanisms and how sleep relates to typical risk and protective factors for delinquency (e.g., parental attachment, adverse childhood experiences, anti-social peers). Further, sleep itself may sometimes be the mediator, especially for various types of victimization as they relate to delinquent or antisocial behavior. Also, as pointed out by Barnes and Meldrum (2015), because genetics can play a role in sleep, more research needs to investigate the genetic contributions to the sleep and delinquency relationship. Finally, future research should prioritize longitudinal and experimental designs. Though sleep is certainly not a "silver bullet," education and screening related to sleep should be commonly integrated into prevention/intervention initiatives. Sleep may be a behavior that is relatively easy to impact and is something that parents can monitor more directly than other potential influences (e.g., peers) because it takes place within the home. Even when/if sleep does not always have a direct effect on violent or delinquent behaviors it is likely to impact intervening variables (e.g., self-control) and is a vital part of general well-being and health such that optimal sleep quality and quantity is always a priority.

## Note

1 The items used by McGlinchey and Harvey to measure "criminal activity" were similar to the property and non-violent delinquency variables used by others (Barnes & Meldrum, 2015; Clinkinbeard, Simi, Evans, & Anderson, 2011).

## References

American Academy of Pediatrics. (2014). Let them sleep: AAP recommends delaying start times of middle and high schools to combat teen sleep deprivation [Press release]. Retrieved from www.aap.org/en-us/about-the-aap/aap-press-room/Pages/Let-Them-Sleep-AAP-Recommends-Delaying-Start-Times-of-Middle-and-High-Schools-to-Combat-Teen-Sleep-Deprivation.aspx

American Academy of Sleep Medicine. (2010). AMA resolution acknowledges the problem of insufficient sleep in adolescents. Retrieved from https://aasm.org/ama-resolution-acknowledges-the-problem-of-insufficient-sleep-in-adolescents/

Anderson, A., Clinkinbeard, S., Barnum, T., & Augustyn, R. (2016). Examining behaviors using respondents' cell phones and a burst design: Drinking and activities across the first year of college among transitioning freshmen. *Journal of Developmental and Life Course Criminology*, 2(1), 64–84.

Arora, T., Broglia, E., Pushpakumar, D., Lodhi, T., & Taheri, S. (2013). An investigation into the strength of the association and agreement levels between subjective and objective sleep duration in adolescents. *PLoS ONE*, 8(8), 1–1. doi:10.1371/journal.pone.0072406.

Backman, H., Laajasalo, T., Saukkonen, S., Salmi, V., Kivivuori, J., & Aronen, E. T. (2015). Are qualitative and quantitative sleep problems associated with delinquency when controlling for psychopathic features and parental supervision? *Journal of Sleep Research*, 24(5), 543–548. doi:10.1111/jsr.12296.

Ballesio, A., Cerolini, S., Ferlazzo, F., Cellini, N., & Lombardo, C. (2018). The effects of one night of partial sleep deprivation on executive functions in individuals reporting chronic insomnia and good sleepers. *Journal of Behavior Therapy and Experimental Psychiatry*, 60, 42–45. doi:10.1016/j.jbtep.2018.02.002.

Barnes, J. C., & Meldrum, R. C. (2015). The impact of sleep duration on adolescent development: A genetically informed analysis of identical twin pairs. *Journal of Youth and Adolescence*, 44(2), 489–506. doi:10.1007/s10964-014-0137-4.

Baum, K. T., Desai, A., Field, J., Miller, L. E., Rausch, J., & Beebe, D. W. (2013). Sleep restriction worsens mood and emotion regulation in adolescents. *Journal of Child Psychology and Psychiatry*, 55(2), 180–190. doi:10.1111/jcp.12125.

Baumeister, R. F., & Heatherton, T. F. (1996). Self-regulation failure: An overview. *Psychological Inquiry*, 7(1), 1.

Baumeister, R. F., Vohs, K. D., & Tice, D. M. (2007). The strength model of self-control. *Current Directions in Psychological Science*, 16(6), 351–355. doi:10.1111/j.1467-8721.2007.00534.x.

Becker, S., Langberg, J., & Byars, K. (2015). Advancing a biopsychosocial and contextual model of sleep in adolescence: A review and introduction to the special issue. *Journal of Youth and Adolescence*, 44(2), 239–270. doi:10.1007/s10964-014-0248-y.

Beebe, D. W. (2011). Cognitive, behavioral, and functional consequences of inadequate sleep in children and adolescents. *Pediatric Clinics of North America*, 58(3), 649–665. doi:10.1016/j.pcl.2011.03.002.

Blakemore, S.-J., & Choudhury, S. (2006). Development of the adolescent brain: Implications for executive function and social cognition. *Journal of Child Psychology and Psychiatry*, 47(3–4), 296–312. doi:10.1111/j.1469-7610.2006.01611.x.

Borbely, A. A. (1982). A two process model of sleep regulation. *Human Neurobiology*, 1, 195–204.

Bradberry, T. (2016). Sleep deprivation is killing you and your career. *Huffington Post*. Retrieved from www.huffingtonpost.com/dr-travis-bradberry/sleep-deprivation-is-kill_b_12051550.html

Burt, C. H., Simons, R. L., & Simons, L. G. (2006). A longitudinal test of the effects of parenting and the stability of self-control: Negative evidence for the general theory of crime. *Criminology*, *44*(2), 353–396. doi:10.1111/j.1745-9125.2006.00052.x.

Burt, C. H., Sweeten, G., & Simons, R. L. (2014). Self-control through emerging adulthood: Instability, multidimensionality, and criminological significance. *Criminology*, *52*(3), 450–487. doi:10.1111/1745-9125.12045.

Carskadon, M. A. (2011). Sleep in adolescents: The perfect storm. *Pediatric Clinics of North America*, *58*(3), 637–647. doi:10.1016/j.pcl.2011.03.003.

Catrett, C. D., & Gaultney, J. F. (2009). Possible insomnia predicts some risky behaviors among adolescents when controlling for depressive symptoms. *Journal of Genetic Psychology*, *170*(4), 287–309.

Chang, L.-Y., Wu, W.-C., Wu, C.-C., Lin, L. N., Yen, L.-L., & Chang, H.-Y. (2017). The role of sleep problems in the relationship between peer victimization and antisocial behavior: A five-year longitudinal study. *Social Science & Medicine*, *173*, 126–133. doi:10.1016/j.socscimed.2016.11.025.

Christie, D., & Viner, R. (2005). Adolescent development. *BMJ: British Medical Journal (International Edition)*, *330*(7486), 301–304.

Clinkinbeard, S. S., Barnum, T. C., & Rhodes, T. N. (2018). The other side of the coin: Exploring the effects of adolescent delinquency on young adult self-control. *Journal of Criminal Justice*, *56*, 86–97. doi:10.1016/j.jcrimjus.2017.08.001.

Clinkinbeard, S. S., Simi, P., Evans, M. K., & Anderson, A. L. (2011). Sleep and delinquency: Does the amount of sleep matter? *Journal of Youth and Adolescence*, *40*(7), 916–930. doi:10.1007/s10964-010-9594-6.

Cohen, D., Nisbett, R. E., Bowdle, B. F., & Schwarz, N. (1996). Insult, aggression, and the southern culture of honor: An 'experimental ethnography'. *Journal of Personality and Social Psychology*, *70*(5), 945–960. doi:10.1037/0022-3514.70.5.945.

Crowley, S. J., Wolfson, A. R., Tarokh, L., & Carskadon, M. A. (2018). An update on adolescent sleep: New evidence informing the perfect storm model. *Journal of Adolescence*, *67*, 55–65. doi:10.1016/j.adolescence.2018.06.001.

Dahl, R. E. (2004). Adolescent brain development: A period of vulnerabilities and opportunities. Keynote address. *Annals of the New York Academy of Sciences*, *1021*(1), 1–22. doi:10.1196/annals.1308.001.

Dewald, J. F., Meijer, A. M., Oort, F. J., Kerkhof, G. A., & Bögels, S. M. (2010). The influence of sleep quality, sleep duration and sleepiness on school performance in children and adolescents: A meta-analytic review. *Sleep Medicine Reviews*, *14*(3), 179–189. doi:10.1016/j.smrv.2009.10.004.

Fischer, J., Aydin, N., Kastenmüller, A., Frey, D., & Fischer, P. (2012). The delinquent media effect: Delinquency-reinforcing video games increase players attitudinal and behavioral inclination toward delinquent behavior. *Psychology of Popular Media Culture*, *1*(3), 201–205. doi:10.1037/a0028114.

Garner, A. A., Miller, M. M., Field, J., Noe, O., Smith, Z., & Beebe, D. W. (2015). Impact of experimentally manipulated sleep on adolescent simulated driving. *Sleep Medicine*, *16*(6), 796–799. doi:10.1016/j.sleep.2015.03.003.

Gottfredson, M. R., & Hirschi, T. (1990). *A general theory of crime*. Stanford, CA: Stanford University Press.

Grandner, M. A., Patel, N. P., Gehrman, P. R., Xie, D., Sha, D., Weaver, T., & Gooneratne, N. (2010). Who gets the best sleep? Ethnic and socioeconomic factors related to sleep complaints. *Sleep Medicine*, *11*(5), 470–478. doi:10.1016/j.sleep.2009.10.006.

Hagenauer, M. H., Perryman, J. I., Lee, T. M., & Carskadon, M. A. (2009). Adolescent changes in the homeostatic and circadian regulation of sleep. *Developmental Neuroscience*, *31*(4), 276–284. doi:10.1159/000216538.

Hambrick, E. P., Rubens, S. L., Brawner, T. W., & Taussig, H. N. (2018). Do sleep problems mediate the link between adverse childhood experiences and delinquency in preadolescent children in foster care? *Journal of Child Psychology and Psychiatry*, *59*(2), 140–149. doi:10.1111/jcpp.12802.

Hamilton, N. A., Nelson, C. A., Stevens, N., & Kitzman, H. (2007). Sleep and psychological well-being. *Social Indicators Research*, *82*(1), 147–163. doi:10.1007/s11205-006-9030-1.

Hay, C., & Forrest, W. (2006). The development of self-control: Examining self-control theory's stability thesis. *Criminology*, *44*(4), 739–774.

Hildenbrand, A. K., Daly, B. P., Nicholls, E., Brooks-Holliday, S., & Kloss, J. D. (2013). Increased risk for school violence-related behaviors among adolescents with insufficient sleep. *Journal of School Health*, *83*(6), 408–414. doi:10.1111/josh.12044.

Hirschi, T., & Gottfredson, M. (1983). Age and the explanation of crime. *American Journal of Sociology*, *89*(3), 552–584.

Holley, S., Hill, C. M., & Stevenson, J. (2011). An hour less sleep is a risk factor for childhood conduct problems. *Child: Care, Health and Development, 37*(4), 563–570. doi:10.1111/j.1365-2214.2010.01203.x.

Huang, Y.-S., Wang, C.-H., & Guilleminault, C. (2010). An epidemiologic study of sleep problems among adolescents in north taiwan. *Sleep Medicine, 11*(10), 1035–1042. doi:10.1016/j.sleep.2010.04.009.

Institute of Medicine. (2006). *Sleep disorders and sleep deprivation: An unmet public health problem.* Washington, DC: National Academies Press.

Ireland, J. L., & Culpin, V. (2006). The relationship between sleeping problems and aggression, anger, and impulsivity in a population of juvenile and young offenders. *Journal of Adolescent Health, 38*(6), 649–655. doi:10.1016/j.jadohealth.2005.05.027.

Jackson, D. B., & Vaughn, M. G. (2017). Sleep and preteen delinquency: Is the association robust to ADHD symptomatology and ADHD diagnosis? *Journal of Psychopathology and Behavioral Assessment, 39*(4), 585–595. doi:10.1007/s10862-017-9610-1.

Johnston, I. (2017). 'Catastrophic' lack of sleep in modern society is killing us, warns leading sleep scientist. *Independent.* Retrieved from www.independent.co.uk/news/sleep-deprivation-epidemic-health-effects-tired-heart-disease-stroke-dementia-cancer-a7964156.html

Knutson, K. L., Phelan, J., Paskow, M. J., Roach, A., Whiton, K., Langer, G., ... Hirshkowitz, M. (2017). The national sleep foundation's sleep health index. *Sleep Health: Journal of the National Sleep Foundation, 3*(4), 234–240. doi:10.1016/j.sleh.2017.05.011.

Lin, W.-H., & Yi, C.-C. (2015). Unhealthy sleep practices, conduct problems, and daytime functioning during adolescence. *Journal of Youth and Adolescence, 44*(2), 431–446. doi:10.1007/s10964-014-0169-9.

Loessl, B., Valerius, G., Kopasz, M., Hornyak, M., Riemann, D., & Voderholzer, U. (2008). Are adolescents chronically sleep-deprived? An investigation of sleep habits of adolescents in the southwest of Germany. *Child: Care, Health and Development, 34*(5), 549–556. doi:10.1111/j.1365-2214.2008.00845.x.

McGlinchey, E. L., & Harvey, A. G. (2015). Risk behaviors and negative health outcomes for adolescents with late bedtimes. *Journal of Youth and Adolescence, 44*(2), 478–488. doi:10.1007/s10964-014-0110-2.

McKenna, B. S., Dickinson, D. L., Orff, H. J., & Drummond, S. P. A. (2007). The effects of one night of sleep deprivation on known-risk and ambiguous-risk decisions. *Journal of Sleep Research, 16*(3), 245–252. doi:10.1111/j.1365-2869.2007.00591.x.

McKnight-Eily, L. R., Eaton, D. K., Lowry, R., Croft, J. B., Presley-Cantrell, L., & Perry, G. S. (2011). Relationships between hours of sleep and health-risk behaviors in us adolescent students. *Preventive Medicine, 53*(4/5), 271–273. doi:10.1016/j.ypmed.2011.06.020.

Meijer, A. M., Reitz, E., Deković, M., van Den Wittenboer, G. L. H., & Stoel, R. D. (2010). Longitudinal relations between sleep quality, time in bed and adolescent problem behaviour. *Journal of Child Psychology and Psychiatry, 51*(11), 1278–1286. doi:10.1111/j.1469-7610.2010.02261.x.

Meldrum, R. C., Barnes, J. C., & Hay, C. (2015). Sleep deprivation, low self-control, and delinquency: A test of the strength model of self-control. *Journal of Youth and Adolescence, 44*(2), 465–477. doi:10.1007/s10964-013-0024-4.

Meldrum, R. C., & Restivo, E. (2014). The behavioral and health consequences of sleep deprivation among us high school students: Relative deprivation matters. *Preventive Medicine: An International Journal Devoted to Practice and Theory, 63,* 24–28. doi:10.1016/j.ypmed.2014.03.006.

Meldrum, R. C., Young, J. T. N., & Weerman, F. M. (2012). Changes in self-control during adolescence: Investigating the influence of the adolescent peer network. *Journal of Criminal Justice, 40*(6), 452–462. doi:10.1016/j.jcrimjus.2012.07.002.

Mezick, E. J., Matthews, K. A., Hall, M., Strollo, P. J., Buysse, D. J., Kamarck, T. W., ... Reis, S. E. (2008). Influence of race and socioeconomic status on sleep: Pittsburgh sleep score project. *Psychosomatic Medicine, 70*(4), 410–416. doi:10.1097/PSY.0b013e31816fdf21.

Na, C., & Paternoster, R. (2012). Can self-control change substantially over time? Rethinking the relationship between self- and social control. *Criminology, 50*(2), 427–462. doi:10.1111/j.1745-9125.2011.00269.x.

Nottelmann, E. D., Susman, E. J., Dorn, L. D., Inoff-Germain, G., Loriaux, D. L., Cutler, G. B., & Chrousos, G. P. (1987). Developmental processes in early adolescence: Relations among chronologic age, pubertal stage, height, weight, and serum levels of gonadotropins, sex steroids, and adrenal androgens. *Journal of Adolescent Health Care, 8*(3), 246–260. doi:10.1016/0197-0070(87)90428-1.

O'Brien, E. M., & Mindell, J. A. (2005). Sleep and risk-taking behavior in adolescents. *Behavioral Sleep Medicine, 3*(3), 113–133. doi:10.1207/s15402010bsm0303_1.

Office of Juvenile Justice and Delinquency Prevention. (2014). OJJDP statistical briefing book. Retrieved from www.ojjdp.gov/ojstatbb/offenders/qa03301.asp?qaDate=2010

Owens, J. (2014). Insufficient sleep in adolescents and young adults: An update on causes and consequences. *Pediatrics, 134*(3), e921–e932. doi:10.1542/peds.2014-1696.

Owens, J., Belon, K., & Moss, P. (2010). Impact of delaying school start time on adolescent sleep, mood, and behavior. *Archives of Pediatrics & Adolescent Medicine, 164*(7), 608–614. doi:10.1001/archpediatrics.2010.96.

Peach, H. D., & Gaultney, J. F. (2013). Sleep, impulse control, and sensation-seeking predict delinquent behavior in adolescents, emerging adults, and adults. *Journal of Adolescent Health, 53*(2), 293–299. doi:10.1016/j.jadohealth.2013.03.012.

Pratt, T. C. (2015). A self-control/life-course theory of criminal behavior. *European Journal of Criminology, 13*(1), 129–146. doi:10.1177/1477370815587771.

Roberts, R. E., Roberts, C. R., & Duong, H. T. (2009). Sleepless in adolescence: Prospective data on sleep deprivation, health and functioning. *Journal of Adolescence, 32*(5), 1045–1057. doi:10.1016/j.adolescence.2009.03.007.

Sampson, R. J., & Laub, J. H. (2005). A life-course view of the development of crime. *The ANNALS of the American Academy of Political and Social Science, 602*(1), 12–45. doi:10.1177/0002716205280075.

Sampson, R. J., & Laub, J. H. (2006). Life-course desisters? Trajectories of crime among delinquent boys followed to age 70. *Criminology, 41*(3), 555–592. doi:10.1111/j.1745-9125.2003.tb00997.x.

Shi, G., Wu, D., Ptáček, L. J., & Fu, Y.-H. (2017). Human genetics and sleep behavior. *Current Opinion in Neurobiology, 44*, 43–49. doi:10.1016/j.conb.2017.02.015.

Short, M. A., & Weber, N. (2018). Sleep duration and risk-taking in adolescents: A systematic review and meta-analysis. *Sleep Medicine Reviews, 41*, 185–196. doi:10.1016/j.smrv.2018.03.006.

Sosnowski, D. W., Kliewer, W., & Lepore, S. J. (2016). The role of sleep in the relationship between victimization and externalizing problems in adolescents. *Journal of Youth and Adolescence, 45*(9), 1744–1754. doi:10.1007/s10964-016-0506-2.

Steinberg, L., & Morris, A. S. (2001). Adolescent development. *Annual Review of Psychology, 52*(1), 83.

Stephens, R. J., Chung, S. A., Jovanovic, D., Guerra, R., Stephens, B., Sandor, P., & Shapiro, C. M. (2013). Relationship between polysomnographic sleep architecture and behavior in medication-free children with ts, adhd, ts and adhd, and controls. *Journal of Developmental and Behavioral Pediatrics, 34*(9), 688–696. doi:10.1097/DBP.0000000000000012.

Stone, K. C., Cuellar, C. R., Miller-Loncar, C. L., LaGasse, L. L., & Lester, B. M. (2015). Poor actigraphic and self-reported sleep patterns predict delinquency and daytime impairment among at-risk adolescents. *Sleep Health, 1*(3), 177–183.

Vail-Smith, K., Felts, W. M., & Becker, C. (2009). Relationship between sleep quality and health risk behaviors in undergraduate college students. *College Student Journal, 43*(3), 924–930.

Vazsonyi, A. T., Harris, C., Terveer, A. M., Pagava, K., Phagava, H., & Michaud, P.-A. (2015). Parallel mediation effects by sleep on the parental warmth-problem behavior links: Evidence from national probability samples of georgian and swiss adolescents. *Journal of Youth and Adolescence, 44*(2), 331–345. doi:10.1007/s10964-014-0167-y.

Wahlstrom, K. L., Berger, A. T., & Widome, R. (2017). Relationships between school start time, sleep duration, and adolescent behaviors. *Sleep Health, 3*(3), 216–221. doi:10.1016/j.sleh.2017.03.002.

WBA Market Research. (2006). *2006 sleep in America poll: Summary of findings*. National Sleep Foundation. Retrieved from http://sleepfoundation.org/sites/default/files/2006_summary_of_findings.pdf.

WBA Market Research. (2010). *2010 sleep in America poll*. National Sleep Foundation. Retrieved from http://sleepfoundation.org/sites/default/files/nsaw/NSF%20Sleep%20in%20%20America%20Poll%20-%20Summary%20of%20Findings%20.pdf.

Wells, M. E., & Vaughn, B. V. (2012). Poor sleep challenging the health of a nation. *Neurodiagnostic Journal, 52*(3), 233–249.

Wolfson, A. R., Carskadon, M. A., Acebo, C., Seifer, R., Fallone, G., Labyak, S. E., & Martin, J. L. (2003). Evidence for the validity of a sleep habits survey for adolescents. *Sleep: Journal of Sleep and Sleep Disorders Research, 26*(2), 213–216. doi:10.1093/sleep/26.2.213.

Wong, M. M., Roberson, G., & Dyson, R. (2015). Prospective relationship between poor sleep and substance-related problems in a national sample of adolescents. *Alcoholism, Clinical and Experimental Research, 39*(2), 355–362. doi:10.1111/acer.12618.

Yang, C.-K., Kim, J. K., Patel, S. R., & Lee, J.-H. (2005). Age-related changes in sleep/wake patterns among korean teenagers. *Pediatrics, 115*(Supplement 1), 250.

# 11
# THE IMPACT OF YOUTH WITH PSYCHOPATHIC TRAITS ON HEALTH
## A Social-Ecological Perspective

*Dennis E. Reidy, Katherine W. Bogen, and Scott O. Lilienfeld*

### Psychopathy and Psychopathic Traits

Psychopathic personality (psychopathy) comprises a loosely correlated set of interpersonal, affective, and behavioral features that includes superficial charm, social poise, dishonesty, grandiosity, guiltlessness, callousness, promiscuous sexual behavior, and poor impulse control (Cleckley, 1941; Hare, 1996; Lykken, 1995). Many theorists hypothesize that deficient emotional processing, a process pivotal during early development, is a core deficit of psychopathy – if not *the* core deficit – that disrupts healthy socialization (Reidy et al., 2015; Reidy, Lilienfeld, Berke, Gentile, & Zeichner, 2016). Psychopaths are hybrid beings in that they frequently create a positive first impression on others, rendering them adept at deception, manipulation, romantic seduction, and on occasions, outright physical aggression. Not surprisingly, this condition is commonly found in clinical and forensic settings, especially the latter. However, growing data indicate that psychopathy manifests along a dimension – rather than a dichotomy – of severity (e.g., Edens, Marcus, Lilienfeld, & Poythress, 2006; Edens, Marcus, & Vaughn, 2011; Guay, Ruscio, Knight, & Hare, 2007; Murrie, Marcus, Douglas, Lee, Salekin, & Vincent, 2007), suggesting the presence of these traits in the general population.

A large body of evidence points to the presence of psychopathic traits (PT) in children and adolescents that manifest similarly to those of adults (Blair, 2013; Frick & White, 2008; Lynam & Gudonis, 2005; Viding & McCrory, 2012). In children and adolescents, callous-unemotional (CU) traits, which largely mirror the core affective-interpersonal features of psychopathy seen in adults, appear in particular to designate a largely distinctive subset of youth at risk to begin offending early and persist significantly longer than their peers (Frick, Ray, Thornton, & Kahn, 2014; Reidy et al., 2015, 2017). Such traits encompass a relative absence of guilt and empathy, weak social attachments to parents and other children, paucity of deep emotions, and lack of caring regarding one's behavior or its impact on other people. These traits, operationalized as the newly introduced "limited prosocial emotions" (LPE) specifier for conduct disorder in the fifth edition of the *Diagnostic and Statistical Manual of Mental Disorders* (DSM-5; American Psychiatric Association, 2013), can be reliably and validly assessed early in life, perhaps even as young as three years of age (Cardinale & Marsh, 2017; Hyde, Shaw, & Hariri, 2013; Kimonis et al., 2016;

Willoughby et al., 2011, 2014). Moreover, these early emerging traits have demonstrated predictive ability similar to that seen in adults (Kimonis et al., 2016; Longman, Hawes, & Kohlhoff, 2016; Willoughby et al., 2014).

Admittedly, there continue to be number of unresolved debates regarding the construct validity of psychopathic traits in youth (Berg et al., 2013; Lahey, 2014; Latzman, Lilienfeld, Latzman, & Clark, 2013); but, these important ongoing debates aside, psychopathic traits are at least moderately predictive of antisocial and violent behavior, which are frequent correlates of adult psychopathy as well (Leistico, Salekin, DeCoster, & Rogers, 2008; Reidy et al., 2015, 2017). Nevertheless, for scientific, ethical, and legal reasons, there is considerable hesitation to apply the term "psychopath" to children and adolescents (Edens, Skeem, Cruise, & Cauffman, 2001; Seagrave & Grisso, 2002). On the scientific front, pronounced levels of certain psychopathic traits (e.g., impulsivity, irresponsibility, sensation-seeking) may reflect normative transient behaviors in developing youth. Although personality is relatively stable in adults, especially older adults, it is still be evolving in children and adolescents (Buss, 1995; Roberts & DelVechio, 2000). Indeed, a nontrivial proportion of youth exhibiting psychopathic traits demonstrate a pronounced decline in these traits over time, whereas others (admittedly a small proportion) manifest stable high psychopathic traits but never engage in violent and delinquent behavior (Fontaine, McCrory, Boivin, Moffitt, & Viding, 2011). As such, applying a label of psychopath may imply unwarranted stability of such features and pathologize largely normative behavior (e.g., Edens, Skeem, Cruise, & Cauffman, 2001).

In addition, such labels risk potentially stigmatizing youth and adversely influencing the manner in which adults and peers may interact with them. This, in turn, may decrease the likelihood that youth with high levels of psychopathic traits receive appropriate intervention that may motivate them to abstain or desist from delinquency. In addition, such labels may bias jurors against children with marked psychopathic traits as more dangerous, malicious and psychopathic than other children (Edens, Mowle, Clark, & Magyar, 2017), raising the possibility that this specifier is tied to stigma in courtroom settings. From here out, we refer to youth with these characteristics as PT youth or youth with psychopathic traits.

## The Public Health Model

In ascertaining the impact of psychopathy on juvenile delinquency and the juvenile justice system, one must consider how the health of the individual, the community, and society at large contribute the development and function of these systems. In doing so, one inevitably highlights the public health significance of psychopathy. Public health, defined as the science of protecting and improving the health of individuals and their communities (Centers for Disease Control and Prevention, 2018), combines research, healthcare practice, community readiness, prevention, education, promotion of healthy lifestyles, and institutional responses to health crises to improve and maximize the health of a given population. For example, individuals working in public health are responsible for education, dissemination, collection, and monitoring of data on vaccinations. This public health emphasis allows institutions to *predict* infectious outbreaks such as influenza, *communicate* the severity of the outbreak to the wider community, *manage* the outbreak through public education campaigns, *mitigate* the impact and extent through the facilitation of low cost, accessible treatments, and *prevent* future outbreaks through the study of such infectious disease outbreaks (Aledort, Lurie, Wasserman, & Bozzette, 2007). In aggregate, public health is wide-reaching and includes such activities as the planning and execution of responses to the national opioid crisis (Kolodny et al., 2015), HIV and AIDS (World Health Organization, 2016), hurricanes and other natural disasters (Eisenman, Cordasco, Asch, Golden, & Glik, 2007), gun violence (Hemenway & Miller, 2013), obesity (Nestle & Jacobson, 2000), intimate partner violence (Garcia-Moreno &

Watts, 2011), and disparities in health status across groups (Braveman, 2003; Tulchinsky & Varavikova, 2010), to name just a few. Public health as a field and a practice has broad implications for the growth and success of communities and the individuals within them.

Understanding how health, including mental and behavioral health, manifests as a function of the larger population requires an understanding of the social determinants of health. These determinants are the forces that drive and shape the health of individuals within a population. Health is influenced not only by genetic factors, but by the wider contexts into which people are born and develop. The latter encompass the social and physical makeup of their environment, including access to care, quality of education, workplace safety, ability to maintain income, availability of affordable housing, and quality of interpersonal relationships. These determinants of health allow researchers to explore and explain why certain populations are able to achieve and sustain greater health than others. Likewise, these determinants may explain why certain populations are equally at risk for adverse health and criminal adjudication. For example, we know that poverty, crime, and chronic health ailments tend to all congregate in certain populations (e.g., Haan, Kaplan, & Camacho, 1987; Nikulina, Widom, & Czaja, 2011; Piquero, Daigle, Gibson, Piquero, & Tibbetts, 2007). Further, examination of the social determinants of health allows researchers, practitioners, policy-makers, and community stakeholders to take effective action to alleviate health inequities by intervening to address the pertinent health determinants.

The social ecological model (Bronfenbrenner, 1977) has often been applied to trace the influence of the social determinants of health, and their compounding effects on various populations. This model addresses the relationship between a person and his or changing environment, including not only immediate social settings, but larger social networks through which human beings learn, grow, and function. Bronfenbrenner's evaluation of social ecology allows public health researchers and practitioners to trace the determinants of health across social "levels," including *individual, relational, organizational, community,* and *societal*. In this chapter, we argue for the importance of viewing and treating psychopathy (especially among youth) through a public health lens and facilitating the development of appropriate goals for its treatment and management. In doing so, we adopt the social ecological framework to consider if, and how PT youth might affect individual, interpersonal, organizational, community, and population health.

This chapter is not intended to be an exhaustive discussion of the multitude of ways that psychopathy might impact the health of individuals and their communities. Rather, we intend it to facilitate a broader discussion among researchers and health practitioners in the service of stimulating the adoption of a public health approach to psychopathy, crime, and eventually health. Ultimately, such an approach holds out the promise of improving the health potential of society. Further, we hope that this chapter will begin to illuminate ways in which psychopathy may have multiplicative, compounding effects at various levels of the social ecology, and how effective intervention at one level may have cascading effects across various spheres of public health.

## The Individual and Relational Impact of Psychopathy

In examining the public health risk of youth with psychopathic traits, we must first address the immediate risk to individuals with whom they interact. Elsewhere, we have argued, as have others, that psychopathy and PT youth are pressing public health concerns given their links to violence (Coid & Yang, 2011; Reidy et al., 2015, 2017). The association between psychopathy and violence is well established and has been documented across diverse populations of age, gender, ethnicity, forensic, and sampling strategy (Reidy, Kearns, & DeGue, 2013; Reidy et al., 2015, 2017; Reidy, Shelley-Tremblay, & Lilienfeld, 2011). Although youth and adults with psychopathic traits comprise an infinitesimal proportion of the population, they are responsible for a disproportionate amount of violence (Coid & Yang, 2011; Reidy et al., 2015; Vaughn, Salas-Wright, Delisi, & Maynard, 2014) and are therefore responsible for a disproportionate amount of the adverse health of the population. Violence is globally recognized as a public health problem because of the mental and physical health implications of victimization (Krug, Dahlberg, Mercy, Zwi, & Lozano, 2002; Reidy et al., 2015; U.S. Department of Health, Education, and Welfare, 1979). Not surprisingly, victims of violence often experience numerous physical injuries that necessitate medical attention and potentially hospitalization. However, the consequences extend far beyond the initial sustained injuries. Victims of violence experience a myriad of sequelae that include chronic physical ailments (e.g., including sexually transmitted infections, heart disease, gastrointestinal disorders, and pelvic inflammatory disease); mental health difficulties (e.g., post-traumatic stress, anxiety, depression, and suicidal ideation); and behavioral health problems (e.g., substance abuse and risky sexual behavior) (Basile et al., 2016; David-Ferdon et al., 2016; Niolon et al., 2017).

A true grasp of the potential health impact of psychopathy across the life-course is not possible without considering the early stage at which this impact may begin. Compared with other children, youth with marked psychopathic traits are more likely to perpetuate school violence and bullying through social dominance and physical aggression (Barry et al., 2007; Chabrol, Leeuwen, Rodgers, Séjourné, 2009; Fanti & Kimonis, 2012; Ragatz, Anderson, Fremouw, & Schwartz, 2011; Verona & Patrick, 2015). Such victimization is associated with numerous negative health sequela and potential consequences for young victims, including anxiety and depression, suicidal thoughts and attempts, and in some cases, perhaps even psychotic symptoms (Takizawa, Maughan, & Arseneault, 2014; Wolke, Copeland, Angold, & Costello, 2013). The potential outcomes of bullying also include lower academic performance and educational achievement in adolescence, which, in turn, is connected to lower earning potential and a greater number of adverse health outcomes in adulthood (Brown & Taylor, 2008; Fonagy, Twemlow, Vernberg, Sacco, & Little, 2005; Wolke, Copeland, Angold, & Costello, 2013). In fact, PT youth may potentially unfavorably impact educational attainment for a multitude of youth by creating a hostile environment with norms that condone bullying and aggression (Neuman et al., 2011; Vanderbilt & Augustyn, 2010). Thus, PT youth could potentially precipitate lasting effects on both adolescent and adult health outcomes through their aggressive and derisive treatment of peers.

Yet, it is not through violence alone that PT youth confer risk on their peers. Psychopathic traits are particularly salient in the context of adolescent risk behaviors. Notably, adolescents are already more likely to make risky decisions (e.g., driving recklessly, fighting, engaging in unprotected sex) than adults, especially in the presence of their peers (Gardner & Steinberg, 2005; Steinberg, 2005), and pronounced psychopathic traits appear to exacerbate these risky choices. Frick and White (2008) observed that PT youth experience less distress regarding action-consequences and frequently display thrill-seeking and novelty-seeking behaviors. There is a close relationship between thrill/novelty seeking and substance use (Bardo, Donohew, & Harrington, 1996), suggesting that PT youth may be particularly prone to alcohol and drug use (Baskin-Sommers, Waller, Fish, & Hyde, 2015; Taylor & Lang, 2006; Walsh, Allen, & Kosson, 2007). Notably, substance use among adolescence may contribute to a larger social norm within a school or community environment that such use is normal, acceptable, or "cool." Some have also raised the possibility that substance use can infiltrate adolescent social networks in a manner that resembles social contagion (e.g., Ali, Amialchuk, & Dwyer, 2011; Dishion & Tipsord, 2011; Rende, Slomkowski, Lloyd-Richardson, & Niaura, 2005: but see Shalizi & Thomas, 2011 for a discussion of the problems with parsing social contagion from homophily). For example, Fujimoto and Valente (2012) demonstrated that the effect of peer influence on alcohol use existed across four levels of indirectly connected peers (i.e., friends of friends of friends of friends). Cohen and Prinstein (2006) similarly found that adolescent males were likely to publicly and privately subscribe to attitudes of their peers about engaging in aggression, substance use, and health risk behavior.

In a related vein, some theorists have speculated that adolescent sexual behavior and pregnancy spreads through a social contagion phenomenon similar to substance use (Rodgers & Rowe, 1993; Rodgers, Rowe, & Buster, 1998; Rowe & Rodgers, 1994). Evidence does indicate that associating with deviant peers, such as ones involved with substance use and delinquency, is connected to engaging in sexual risk behavior (Dishion & Tipsord, 2011; Kotchick, Shaffer, Miller, & Forehand, 2001; Miller, Forehand, & Kotchick, 2000) Thus, PT youth may indirectly exert an impact on sexual risk behaviors (e.g., early sexual debut, unprotected sex, sex under the influence of drugs and alcohol, sex with multiple partners) of their peers (Anderson, Zheng, & McMahon, 2017; Fulton, Marcus, & Zeigler-Hill, 2014; Kastner & Sellbom, 2012; Thornton et al., 2017). In addition to these more developmentally common risk behaviors, PT adolescents also appear prone to engage in sexual coercion and violence (DeGue & DiLillo, 2004; Gretton, McBride, Hare, O'Shaughnessy, & Kumka, 2001; Reidy, Kearns, & DeGue, 2013; Reidy et al., 2017). All of these sexual risk behaviors place youth with PT traits not only at risk for contracting sexually transmitted infections, but to transmit infections to multiple peers, who in turn may transmit these infections to others (Decker, Silverman, & Raj, 2005; Goesling, Colman, Trenholm, Terzian, & Moore, 2014; Kaestle, Halpern, Miller, & Ford, 2005; Sandfort, Orr, Hirsch, & Santelli, 2008).

Taken together, it is possible that the presence of peers with psychopathic traits have a meaningful impact on adolescents, particularly in regards to exacerbating and reinforcing the "normality" of aggressive and risk-taking behaviors. Youth with psychopathic traits are therefore potentially change-making agents at the individual and relational levels of the social ecology, with their individual behavior having possible far-reaching implications for the health and safety of other adolescents. Such effects may be particularly apparent in schools, and thus health promotion strategies may be strengthened by considering the ripple-effects of PT youth within school settings.

## The Community and Societal Impact of Psychopathy

On April 20, 1999, 18-year-old Eric Harris and 17-year-old Dylan Klebold entered their high school in Columbine, Colorado, and began shooting students and staff indiscriminately. Over the course of 45 minutes they shot and killed 13 people, and injured another 21. But there were far more than 34 victims that day, as a community and a country mourned the event. Single egregious acts of violence, such as this one, have the potential to provoke numerous sequelae at multiple levels of the social ecology (e.g., Hoffman & Kruczek, 2011).

There is no compelling research evidence that PT youth are more likely than other youth to commit school shooting or acts of mass violence. Nevertheless, some experts have suggested that psychopathic persons make up a substantial proportion of mass violence perpetrators. For example, in his review of more than 150 mass murderers, Stone (2015) reported that approximately 16% were psychopathic or manifested significant degree of psychopathic traits. This finding is in line with Langman (2013), who reported that approximately 20% of the 35 school shooters he reviewed fell into the psychopathic category of his typology, including Eric Harris. Nevertheless, the judgments are made on an *ex post facto* basis without the benefit of a formal validated assessment of psychopathy. Still, many of these perpetrators appear to possess some of the core psychopathic traits of emotional callousness and lack of empathy, even if they do not all manifest diagnostic levels of psychopathy. Thus, implementing strategies to prevent the development of these characteristics in youth may spare a number of individuals from violent victimization. Even more so, it may prevent the large-scale effects of one single act of violence on society at large.

The physical and psychological consequences for the survivors of these events and their families are obvious. Yet, the impact of the seemingly growing number of rampage attacks has the potential to affect the surrounding communities, too. Much like the victims, first-responders and medical staff are at risk of developing posttraumatic stress disorder, depression, and substance use disorders after responding to mass casualty events (Geronazzo-Alman et al., 2017; Grieger, Fullerton, Ursano, & Reeves, 2003; North et al., 2002; Ursano, Fullerton, Vance, & Kao, 1999; Walker, McKune, Ferguson, Pyne, & Rattray, 2016). Further, even some of those in the community not directly exposed to such violent events are at risk of adverse health outcomes (Galea & Resnick, 2005; Marshall et al., 2007). Following a mass murder in Oslo, Norway, by Anders Breivik in 2011, there was a spike in distress among the broader general population of Norway (Thoresen, Flood Aakvaag, Wentzel-Larsen, Dyb, & Kristian Hjemdal, 2012). Similarly, the terrorist attacks on New York City on September 11, 2001 caused clinically significant, albeit temporary, PTSD symptoms in the general U.S. population of people not directly affected (Galea & Resnick, 2005; Marshall et al., 2007; Shuster et al., 2001; Silver, Holman, MCIntosh, Poulin, & Gil-Rivas, 2002). Of course, as personal/social and physical proximity to the attacks increased, so too did the severity and chronicity of the subsequent psychopathology and distress.

Moreover, the consequences of these acts can reach beyond the immediate community to afflict society as a whole by exacerbating the cycle of violence. Violence, much like infectious disease, may in many cases be contagious (Huesmann, 2012; Loftin, 1986; Slutkin, 2012). Green, Horel, and Papachristos (2017) investigated gun violence in Chicago, Illinois, over an eight-year period to test the probabilistic spread of violence through a contagion model. These authors reported that among 138,000+ individuals involved in 11,000+ gun violence episodes, social contagion accounted for a substantial proportion of all events (Green, Horel, & Papachristos, 2017). Towers and colleagues (2015) reported that mass killings involving firearms were catalyzed by similar attacks in the immediately preceding days. They further found that the contagion pattern resembled what would be expected from a contagion driven by widespread media attention and did not resemble a geo-spatial proximity contagion pattern. This result is not unexpected given the widespread national media coverage that frequently follows one of these traumatic attacks and the general trend of media to prioritize violence in their coverage (Scharrer, 2008). Further, beyond directly inciting similar violent attacks, we know that frequent exposure to violence in vivo contributes to desensitization and beliefs that violence is common and acceptable, which precipitates future violence (Dishion & Tipsord, 2011; Guerra, Huesmann, & Spindler, 2003; Huesmann et al., 2017; Karlsson, Temple, Weston, & Le, 2016; Kennedy & Ceballo, 2016; Mrug, Madan, & Windle, 2016; Shukla & Wiesner, 2016; Tarabah, Badr, Usta, & Doyle, 2016). However, exposure to the reporting of violence via print and television news may in some cases also engender desensitization and promote norms that condone violence (Haq, 2017; Scharrer, 2008; Van der Molen, 2004). For example, Scharrer (2008) found that as individuals read more print news and watched more television news they reported less emotional distress to violence, judged acts of violence to be less violent, and rated violence as more commonplace. This cultivation of norms that condone violence is a critical problem for communities given that such norms have repeatedly been linked to perpetration of violence (e.g., Archer, 2000; Capaldi, Knoble, Shortt, & Kim, 2012; Foshee et al., 2005; Foshee, Linder, MacDougall, & Bangdiwala, 2001; Simon et al., 2001; Smith-Darden, Kernsmith, Reidy, & Cortina, 2017; Vagi et al., 2013). Thus, acts of mass violence may have the potential to precipitate similar such acts, but also to insidiously change the norms of an entire society via news media coverage, although more research is needed to corroborate this possibility.

Of note, Towers and colleagues found no association between mass shootings and prevalence rates of mental illness. Unfortunately, mental illness is frequently the scapegoat in these events and one consequence is that media stories about mass shootings increase the public's negative perceptions of persons with mental illness (McGinty, Webster, & Barry, 2013; McGinty, Webster, Jarlenski, & Barry, 2014). This outcome is unfortunate for many reasons, not the least of which is the fact that the overwhelming majority of people with mental illness are not dangerous (Gold, 2013); but especially because it may prevent persons with genuine mental health problems from seeking help (Clement et al., 2015; Gold, 2013). Failure to seek treatment would likely prolong suffering of those individuals and could impair functioning in other domains of life (e.g., social, educational, employment).

Admittedly, far more investigation is necessary to confirm whether psychopathic traits predispose youth to mass acts of violence. Moreover, it is unlikely that psychopathy explains the majority of mass violence events. Nevertheless, given that a single act can provoke distress in communities and nations; incite a chain of future acts of extreme violence; potentially desensitize communities to violence and propagate norms that condone it; and increase public attitudes that stigmatize and exacerbate the functioning of persons with mental health afflictions, stopping even a small fraction of these events may have exponential health effects. Thus undertaking activities aimed at preventing delinquent behavioral outcomes of psychopathy (e.g., Caldwell, McCormick, Wolfe, & Umstead, 2012; Kolko et al., 2009; McDonald, Dodson, Rosenfield, & Jouriles, 2011) may reduce psychological distress, adverse health, and violence in communities and society.

## Implications

Despite scientific controversies surrounding psychopathic traits (e.g., Lahey, 2014), the relevance of these traits to the health system seems undeniable considering the severity and chronicity with which PT youth tend to commit violence (Reidy et al., 2017). Elsewhere, we have contended that altering the phenotypic expression of psychopathic traits could substantially reduce collective levels of violence, thereby boosting the overall health and social functioning of a considerable proportion of the population (Coid & Yang, 2011; Reidy et al., 2015, 2017). However, we herein argue that adverse health effects of PT youths' behavior (1) may not be conferred through violence alone, and (2) may diffuse across the social ecology affecting those not directly victimized. As such, PT youth probably exert a compounding effects on the health of their peers, their communities, and potentially even society.

We argue that this pervasive effect is, in large part, due to their impact on the social determinants of health. For example, PT youths' sexual violence and sexual risk behavior may translate into an increased rate of unintended adolescent pregnancies (Miller et al., 2010). Teen mothers (and their babies) are at risk for a multitude of health complications, including preterm delivery, low birth weight, and neonatal mortality (Basch, 2011; Jutte et al., 2010). They are also more likely to report suicidal thoughts, perform worse academically, and are less likely to graduate high-school and attend college (Basch, 2011; Jutte et al., 2010; Lammers, Ireland, Resnick, & Blum, 2000). Subsequently, teen mothers' potential earnings and consequent access to proper nutrition, preventive medical care, and education (i.e., social determinants of health) for themselves and their babies is diminished. And unfortunately, daughters of adolescent mothers are more likely to become teen mothers themselves contributing to a cycle of health deprivation (Jutte et al., 2010; Meade, Kershaw, & Ickovics, 2008).

Additionally, the influence of PT youth may precipitate the early initiation of substance use among peers. Onset of substance use at this early age is associated with the development of addiction, psychopathology, and social and occupational deficits (Brooks, Harris, Thrall, & Woods, 2002; Friedman, Terras, & Zhu, 2004; Kandel & Kandel, 2015; Schleider & Weisz, 2016; Wagner & Anthony, 2002; Wu et al., 2004). The introduction of psychoactive substances into the body hinders brain maturation processes and may result in structural and functional abnormalities and cause neurocognitive deficits (Mills, Goddings, Clasen, Giedd, & Blakemore, 2014;

Squeglia, Jacobus, & Tapert, 2009; Squeglia et al., 2015). Consequently, substance-using youth perform worse academically, are less likely to graduate high-school (Kelly et al., 2015; Townsend, Flisher, & King, 2007), and ultimately have an estimated life expectancy of almost 10 years shorter (Gasper, 2011). Among adolescents, the individual effects of substance use, dropping out of school, and poor mental health are dangerous, but in combination they may be lethal, as substance use among adolescents is associated with a risk of suicide (Woods et al., 1997; Wu et al., 2004).

Youth with psychopathic traits may also influence the educational attainment of entire social groups by fostering hostile environments and norms that promote aggressive victimization. This outcome can impede academic performance, and perhaps long-term educational and financial achievement of students in these settings. Notably, education and income are critical determinants of health associated with chronic health problems and mortality (Chetty et al., 2016; Herd, Goesling, & House, 2007). In particular, higher educational attainment is associated with delayed disease onset, while income level influences the disease progression after onset (Herd, Goesling, & House, 2007). Thus, even for those who manage to overcome educational deficits to secure stable financial resources and access to health care, they are still more likely to experience disease, even if it may be better managed.

Likewise, chronic perpetration of extreme acts of violence may propagate desensitization to violence and cultivate norms that condone violence within communities, forcing people in those communities to live in chronic fear of victimization. Living under such circumstances is connected the development of psychiatric disorders in adolescence that often persist into adulthood (Aneshensel & Sucoff, 1996; Fowler, Tompsett, Braciszewski, Jacques-Tiura, & Baltes, 2009; Zinzow et al., 2009). This is pertinent because mental health diagnoses are associated with the more missed days at work, decreased social functioning and close relationships, cardiovascular disease, and chronic disease (Keyes, 2007). They may also increase the risk of youth becoming involved with the juvenile justice system (Abram et al., 2004; Copeland, Miller-Johnson, Keeler, Angold, & Costello, 2007). In a related vein, PT youth may corrupt their peers by cultivating norms that encourage risk-taking behavior, which likewise increases the potential for juvenile adjudication. Thus, efforts to alter the behavioral manifestations associated with psychopathic traits in youth may minimize juvenile justice involvement not only for PT youth, but for their peers.

Moreover, the diffused impact of psychopathy may not be restricted to PT youth in the community. It is likely that the corruptive effect of PT youth in forensic setting adversely impacts the health of other adjudicated youth. Whether by creating a dangerous and hostile environment via violence and intimidation, encouraging the disruptive behaviors of others, or disrupting treatment services, PT youth may impede the ability of their adjudicated peers to benefit from services intended to address behavioral and mental health and to prepare them for positive re-entry into their community. Thus, health promotion is served by prevention of deviant manifestations of psychopathy before it can lead to the adjudication of youth, but also by addressing it within incarcerated populations.

In past writings (e.g., Reidy, Kearns, & DeGue, 2013; Reidy et al., 2015, 2017), we have highlighted the efficacy of the Mendota Juvenile Treatment Center (MJTC) in reducing both the violence and the psychopathic traits of affected youth (Caldwell, 2011; Caldwell, McCormick, Wolfe, & Umstead, 2012; Caldwell, Skeem, Salekin, & Van Rybroek, 2006). This program appears particularly suited for youth psychopathic traits due to its alignment with their propensity toward reward-dominant neurobehavioral conditioning (Reidy et al., 2017). In fact, several early intervention programs employing similar principles have been effective in reducing levels of psychopathic traits in young children (Kolko et al., 2009; McDonald, Dodson, Rosenfield, & Jouriles, 2011). It is likely that core principles of these programs (i.e., decreased focus on punishment and increased focus on positively reinforcing prosocial behavior) would benefit most youth, regardless of the presence of psychopathic traits. Thus, programs of this nature might be gainfully implemented with youth at earlier developmental stages to prevent the potential leaching effects of psychopathic traits across the social ecology.

Rarely has psychopathy been considered a public health issue. This oversight is regrettable. Most frequently, this phenomenon has been researched and addressed clinically by the forensic system in relation to problem behavior that has already appeared. Notably, in both the public health and forensic systems, we often adopt a myopic focus in attempting to reduce or prevent a targeted behavior or health outcome. However, we believe that by altering the phenotypic expression of psychopathy to prevent the socially deviant behavioral manifestations, we may be addressing a cross-cutting risk factor for both adjudication and adverse health of the individual and the community. Admittedly, psychopathy is only one of countless factors that influence population health and its impact is merely a fraction of those factors. Nevertheless, this is true of all health factors and that fraction represents a substantial degree of affliction for a substantial number of individuals. As such, preventing psychopathy, or at least minimizing its destructive behavioral manifestations, is both a risk reduction and health promotion imperative.

## References

Abram, K. M., Teplin, L. A., Charles, D. R., Longworth, S. L., McClelland, G. M., & Dulcan, M. K. (2004). Posttraumatic stress disorder and trauma in youth in juvenile detention. *Archives of General Psychiatry*, *61*(4), 403–410.

Aledort, J. E., Lurie, N., Wasserman, J., & Bozzette, S. A. (2007). Non-pharmaceutical public health interventions for pandemic influenza: An evaluation of the evidence base. *BMC Public Health*, 7, 208.

Ali, M. M., Amialchuk, A., & Dwyer, D. S. (2011). The social contagion effect of marijuana use among adolescents. *PloS One*, *6*(1), e16183.

American Psychiatric Association. (2013). *Diagnostic and statistical manual of mental disorders, fifth edition* (DSM-5). Washington, DC: Author.

Anderson, S. L., Zheng, Y., & McMahon, R. J. (2017). Predicting risky sexual behavior: The unique and interactive roles of childhood conduct disorder symptoms and callous-unemotional traits. *Journal of Abnormal Child Psychology*, *45*(6), 1147–1156.

Aneshensel, C. S., & Sucoff, C. A. (1996). The neighborhood context of adolescent mental health. *Journal of Health and Social Behavior*, *37*(4), 293–310.

Archer, J. (2000). Sex differences in aggression between heterosexual partners: A meta-analytic review. *Psychological Bulletin*, *126*, 650–681.

Bardo, M. T., Donohew, R. L., & Harrington, N. G. (1996). Psychobiology of novelty seeking and drug seeking behavior. *Behavioural Brain Research*, *77*(1–2), 23–43.

Barry, T. D., Thompson, A., Barry, C. T., Lochman, J. E., Adler, K., & Hill, K. (2007). The importance of narcissism in predicting proactive and reactive aggression in moderately to highly aggressive children. *Aggressive Behavior*, *33*, 185–197.

Basch, C. E. (2011). Teen pregnancy and the achievement gap among urban minority youth. *Journal of School Health*, *81*, 614–618.

Basile, K. C., DeGue, S., Jones, K., Freire, K., Dills, J., Smith, S. G., & Raiford, J. L. (2016). *STOP SV: A technical package to prevent sexual violence*. Atlanta, GA: National Center for Injury Prevention and Control, Centers for Disease Control and Prevention.

Baskin-Sommers, A. R., Waller, R., Fish, A. M., & Hyde, L. W. (2015). Callous-unemotional traits trajectories interact with earlier conduct problems and executive control to predict violence and substance use among high risk male adolescents. *Journal of Abnormal Child Psychology*, *43*(8), 1529–1541.

Berg, J. M., Lilienfeld, S. O., Reddy, S. D., Latzman, R. D., Roose, A., Craighead, L. W., Pace, T. W., & Raison, C. L. (2013). The inventory of callous and unemotional traits: A construct-validation analysis in an at-risk sample. *Assessment*, *20*, 532–544.

Blair, R. J. R. (2013). The neurobiology of psychopathic traits in youths. *Nature Reviews Neuroscience*, *14*, 786–799.

Braveman, P. A. (2003). Monitoring equity in health and healthcare: A conceptual framework. *Journal of Health, Population and Nutrition*, *21*, 181–192.

Bronfenbrenner, U. (1977). Toward an experimental ecology of human development. *American Psychologist*, *32*, 513.

Brooks, T. L., Harris, S. K., Thrall, J. S., & Woods, E. R. (2002). Association of adolescent risk behaviors with mental health symptoms in high school students. *Journal of Adolescent Health*, *31*(3), 240–246.

Brown, S., & Taylor, K. (2008). Bullying, education and earnings: Evidence from the National Child Development Study. *Economics of Education Review*, *27*(4), 387–401.

Buss, A. H. (1995). *Personality: Temperament, social behavior, and the self*. Boston, MA: Allyn & Bacon.

Caldwell, M., Skeem, J., Salekin, R., & Van Rybroek, G. (2006). Treatment response of adolescent offenders with psychopathy features: A 2-year follow-up. *Criminal Justice and Behavior*, *33*(5), 571–596.

Caldwell, M. F. (2011). Treatment-related changes in behavioral outcomes of psychopathy facets in adolescent offenders. *Law and Human Behavior*, *35*(4), 275–287.

Caldwell, M. F., McCormick, D., Wolfe, J., & Umstead, D. (2012). Treatment-related changes in psychopathy features and behavior in adolescent offenders. *Criminal Justice and Behavior*, *39*(2), 144–155.

Capaldi, D. M., Knoble, N. B., Shortt, J. W., & Kim, H. K. (2012). A systematic review of risk factors for Intimate Partner Violence. *Partner Abuse*, *3*, 231–280.

Cardinale, E. M., & Marsh, A. A. (2017). The reliability and validity of the Inventory of Callous Unemotional Traits: A meta-analytic review. *Assessment*. DOI:1073191117747392.

Centers for Disease Control and Prevention. (2018). Introduction to public health. www.cdc.gov/publichealth101/public-health.html. Accessed June 4, 2019.

Chabrol, H., Van Leeuwen, N., Rodgers, R., & Séjourné, N. (2009). Contributions of psychopathic, narcissistic, Machiavellian, and sadistic personality traits to juvenile delinquency. *Personality and Individual Differences*, *47*(7), 734–739.

Chetty, R., Stepner, M., Abraham, S., et al. (2016). The association between income and life expectancy in the United States, 2001–2014. *JAMA*, *315*(16), 1750–1766.

Cleckley, H. (1941). *The mask of sanity: An attempt to reinterpret the so-called psychopath*. St. Louis, MO: The C.V. Mosby Company.

Clement, S., Schauman, O., Graham, T., et al. (2015). What is the impact of mental health-related stigma on help-seeking? A systematic review of quantitative and qualitative studies. *Psychological Medicine*, *45*, 11–27.

Cohen, G. L., & Prinstein, M. J. (2006). Peer contagion of aggression and health risk behavior among adolescent males: An experimental investigation of effects on public conduct and private attitudes. *Child Development*, *77*(4), 967–983.

Coid, J., & Yang, M. (2011). The impact of psychopathy on violence among the household population of Great Britian. *Social Psychiatry & Psychiatric Epidemiology*, *46*, 473–480.

Copeland, W. E., Miller-Johnson, S., Keeler, G., Angold, A., & Costello, E. J. (2007). Childhood psychiatric disorders and young adult crime: A prospective, population-based study. *American Journal of psychiatry*, *164*(11), 1668–1675.

David-Ferdon, C., Vivolo-Kantor, A. M., Dahlberg, L. L., Marshall, K. J., Rainford, N., & Hall, J. E. (2016). *A comprehensive technical package for the prevention of youth violence and associated risk behaviors*. Atlanta, GA: National Center for Injury Prevention and Control, Centers for Disease Control and Prevention.

Decker, M. R., Silverman, J. G., & Raj, A. (2005). Dating violence and sexually transmitted disease/HIV testing and diagnosis among adolescent females. *Pediatrics*, *116*(2), e272-e276.

DeGue, S., & DiLillo, D. (2004). Understanding perpetrators of nonphysical sexual coercion: Characteristics of those who cross the line. *Faculty Publications, Department of Psychology*, 126. University of Nebraska-Lincoln Digital Commons.

Dishion, T. J., & Tipsord, J. M. (2011). Peer contagion in child and adolescent social and emotional development. *Annual Review of Psychology*, *62*, 189–214.

Edens, J. F., Marcus, D. K., Lilienfeld, S. O., & Poythress, N. G., Jr. (2006). Psychopathic, not psychopath: Taxometric evidence for the dimensional structure of psychopathy. *Journal of Abnormal Psychology*, *115*, 131–144.

Edens, J. F., Marcus, D. K., & Vaughn, M. G. (2011). Exploring the taxometric status of psychopathy among youthful offenders: Is there a juvenile psychopath taxon? *Law and Human Behavior*, *35*(1), 13–24.

Edens, J. F., Mowle, E. N., Clark, J. W., & Magyar, M. S. (2017). A psychopath by any other name?: Juror perceptions of the DSM-5 "limited prosocial emotions" specifier. *Journal of Personality Disorders*, *31*, 90–109.

Edens, J. F., Skeem, J. L., Cruise, K. R., & Cauffman, E. (2001). Assessment of "juvenile psychopathy" and its association with violence: A critical review. *Behavioral Sciences and the Law*, *19*, 53–80.

Eisenman, D. P., Cordasco, K. M., Asch, S., Golden, J. F., & Glik, D. (2007). Disaster planning and risk communication with vulnerable communities: Lessons from Hurricane Katrina. *American Journal of Public Health*, *97*(Supplement_1), S109-S115.

Fanti, K. A., & Kimonis, E. R. (2012). Bullying and victimization: The role of conduct problems and psychopathic traits. *Journal of Research on Adolescence, 22*(4), 617–631.

Fonagy, P., Twemlow, S. W., Vernberg, E., Sacco, F. C., & Little, T. D. (2005). Creating a peaceful school learning environment: The impact of an antibullying program on educational attainment in elementary schools. *Medical Science Monitor, 11*(7), CR317-CR325.

Fontaine, N. M. G., McCrory, E. J. P., Boivin, M., Moffitt, T. E., & Viding, E. (2011). Predictors and outcomes of joint trajectories of callous-unemotional traits and conduct problems in childhood. *Journal of Abnormal Psychology, 120*, 730–742.

Foshee, V., Linder, F., MacDougall, J., & Bangdiwala, S. (2001). Gender differences in the longitudinal predictors of adolescent dating violence. *Preventive Medicine, 32*, 128–141.

Foshee, V. A., Bauman, K. E., Ennett, S. T., Suchindran, C., Benefield, T., & Linder, G. (2005). Assessing the effects of the dating violence prevention program "Safe Dates" using random coefficient regression modeling. *Prevention Science, 6*, 245–258.

Fowler, P. J., Tompsett, C. J., Braciszewski, J. M., Jacques-Tiura, A. J., & Baltes, B. B. (2009). Community violence: A meta-analysis on the effect of exposure and mental health outcomes of children and adolescents. *Development and Psychopathology, 21*(1), 227–259.

Frick, P. J., Ray, J. V., Thornton, L. C., & Kahn, R. E. (2014). Can callous-unemotional traits enhance the understanding, diagnosis, and treatment of serious conduct problems in children and adolescents? A comprehensive review. *Psychological Bulletin, 140*, 1–57.

Frick, P. J., & White, S. F. (2008). Research review: The importance of callous-unemotional traits for developmental models of aggressive and antisocial behavior. *Journal of Child Psychology & Psychiatry, 49*, 359–375.

Friedman, A. S., Terras, A., & Zhu, W. (2004). Early adolescence substance use/abuse as predictor to employment in adulthood: Gender differences. *Journal of Child Adolescent Substance Abuse, 13*, 49–60.

Fujimoto, K., & Valente, T. W. (2012). Social network influences on adolescent substance use: Disentangling structural equivalence from cohesion. *Social Science & Medicine, 74*(12), 1952–1960.

Fulton, J. J., Marcus, D. K., & Zeigler-Hill, V. (2014). Psychopathic personality traits, risky sexual behavior, and psychological adjustment among college-age women. *Journal of Social and Clinical Psychology, 33*(2), 143–168.

Galea, S., & Resnick, H. (2005). Posttraumatic stress disorder in the general population after mass terrorist incidents: Considerations about the nature of exposure. *CNS Spectrums, 10*(2), 107–115.

Garcia-Moreno, C., & Watts, C. (2011). Violence against women: An urgent public health priority. *Bulletin of the World Health Organization, 89*, 2.

Gardner, M., & Steinberg, L. (2005). Peer influence on risk taking, risk preference, and risky decision making in adolescence and adulthood: An experimental study. *Developmental Psychology, 41*(4), 625.

Gasper, J. (2011). Revisiting the relationship between adolescent drug use and high school dropout. *Journal of Drug Issues, 41*(4), 587–618.

Geronazzo-Alman, L., Eisenberg, R., Shen, S., et al. (2017). Cumulative exposure to work-related traumatic events and current post-traumatic stress disorder in New York City's first responders. *Comprehensive Psychiatry, 74*, 134–143.

Goesling, B., Colman, S., Trenholm, C., Terzian, M., & Moore, K. (2014). Programs to reduce teen pregnancy, sexually transmitted infections, and associated sexual risk behaviors: A systematic review. *Journal of Adolescent Health, 54*(5), 499–507.

Gold, L. H. (2013). Gun violence: Psychiatry, risk assessment, and social policy. *Journal of the American Academy of Psychiatry and the Law, 41*(3), 337–343.

Green, B., Horel, T., & Papachristos, A. V. (2017). Modeling contagion through social networks to explain and predict gunshot violence in Chicago, 2006 to 2014. *JAMA Internal Medicine, 177*(3), 326–333.

Gretton, H. M., McBride, M., Hare, R. D., O'Shaughnessy, R., & Kumka, G. (2001). Psychopathy and recidivism in adolescent sexual offenders. *Criminal Justice & Behavior, 28*, 427–449.

Grieger, T. A., Fullerton, C. S., Ursano, R. J., & Reeves, J. J. (2003). Acute stress disorder, alcohol use, and perception of safety among hospital staff after the sniper attacks. *Psychiatric Services, 54*, 1383–1387.

Guay, J. P., Ruscio, J., Knight, R. A., & Hare, R. D. (2007). A taxometric analysis of the latent structure of psychopathy: Evidence for dimensionality. *Journal of Abnormal Psychology, 116*(4), 701.

Guerra, N. G., Huesmann, R. L., & Spindler, A. (2003). Community violence exposure, social cognition, and aggression among urban elementary school children. *Child Development, 74*(5), 1561–1576.

Haan, M., Kaplan, G. A., & Camacho, T. (1987). Poverty and health prospective evidence from the alameda county study. *American Journal of Epidemiology, 125*(6), 989–998.

Haq, A. (2017). News violence and desensitization of news viewers in Pakistan (Doctoral dissertation). Retrieved from https://repository.hkbu.edu.hk/etd_oa/397/

Hare, R. D. (1996). Psychopathy: A clinical construct whose time has come. *Criminal Justice & Behavior, 23,* 25–54.

Hemenway, D., & Miller, M. (2013). Public health approach to the prevention of gun violence. *New England Journal of Medicine, 368*(21), 2033–2035.

Herd, P., Goesling, B., & House, J. S. (2007). Socioeconomic position and health: The differential effects of education versus income on the onset versus progression of health problems. *Journal of Health & Social Behavior, 48*(3), 223–238.

Hoffman, M. A., & Kruczek, T. (2011). A bioecological model of mass trauma: Individual, community, and societal effects. *The Counseling Psychologist, 39*(8), 1087–1127.

Huesmann, L. R. (2012, February). The contagion of violence: The extent, the processes, and the outcomes. In D. M. Patel, R. M. Taylor (Eds.) & Institute of Medicine, National Research Council of the National Academies, *Social and economic costs of violence: Workshop summary* (pp. 63–69). Washington, DC, US: National Academies Press.

Huesmann, R. L., Dubow, E. F., Boxer, P., Landau, S. F., Gvirsman, S. D., & Shikaki, K. (2017). Children's exposure to violent political conflict stimulates aggression at peers by increasing emotional distress, aggressive script rehearsal, and normative beliefs favoring aggression. *Development and Psychopathology, 29*(1), 39–50.

Hyde, L. W., Shaw, D. S., & Hariri, A. R. (2013). Understanding youth antisocial behavior using neuroscience through a developmental psychopathology lens: Review, integration, and directions for research. *Developmental Review, 33*(3), 168–223.

Jutte, D. P., Roos, N. P., Brownell, M. D., Briggs, G., MacWilliam, L., & Roos, L. L. (2010). The ripples of adolescent motherhood: Social, educational, and medical outcomes for children of teen and prior teen mothers. *Academic Pediatrics, 10*(5), 293–301.

Kaestle, C. E., Halpern, C. T., Miller, W. C., & Ford, C. A. (2005). Young age at first sexual intercourse and sexually transmitted infections in adolescents and young adults. *American Journal of Epidemiology, 161*(8), 774–780.

Kandel, D., & Kandel, E. (2015). The Gateway Hypothesis of substance abuse: Developmental, biological and societal perspectives. *Acta Paediatrica, 104*(2), 130–137.

Karlsson, M. E., Temple, J. R., Weston, R., & Le, V. D. (2016). Witnessing interparental violence and acceptance of dating violence as predictors for teen dating violence victimization. *Violence against Women, 22*(5), 625–646.

Kastner, R. M., & Sellbom, M. (2012). Hypersexuality in college students: The role of psychopathy. *Personality and Individual Differences, 53*(5), 644–649.

Kelly, A. B., Evans-Whipp, T. J., Smith, R., Chan, G. C., Toumbourou, J. W., Patton, G. C., & Catalano, R. F. (2015). A longitudinal study of the association of adolescent polydrug use, alcohol use and high school non-completion. *Addiction, 110*(4), 627–635.

Kennedy, T. M., & Ceballo, R. (2016). Emotionally numb: Desensitization to community violence exposure among urban youth. *Developmental Psychology, 52*(5), 778–789.

Keyes, C. L. (2007). Promoting and protecting mental health as flourishing: A complementary strategy for improving national mental health. *American Psychologist, 62*(2), 95.

Kimonis, E. R., Fanti, K. A., Anastassiou-Hadjicharalambous, X., Mertan, B., Goulter, N., & Katsimicha, E. (2016). Can callous-unemotional traits be reliably measured in preschoolers? *Journal of Abnormal Child Psychology, 44*(4), 625–638.

Kolko, D. J., Dorn, L. D., Bukstein, O. G., Pardini, D., Holden, E. A., & Hart, J. (2009). Community vs. clinic-based modular treatment of children with early-onset ODD or CD: A clinical trial with a 3-year follow-up. *Journal of Abnormal Child Psychology, 37,* 591–609.

Kolodny, A., Courtwright, D. T., Hwang, C. S., Kreiner, P., Eadie, J. L., Clark, T. W., & Alexander, G. C. (2015). The prescription opioid and heroin crisis: A public health approach to an epidemic of addiction. *Annual Review of Public Health, 36,* 559–574.

Kotchick, B. A., Shaffer, A., Miller, K. S., & Forehand, R. (2001). Adolescent sexual risk behavior: A multi-system perspective. *Clinical Psychology Review, 21*(4), 493–519.

Krug, E. G., Dahlberg, L. L., Mercy, J. A., Zwi, A. B., & Lozano, R. (Eds.). (2002). *World report on violence and health.* Geneva: World Health Organization.

Lahey, B. B. (2014). What we need to know about callous-unemotional traits: Comment on Frick, Ray, Thornton, and Kahn (2014). *Psychological Bulletin, 140*(1), 58–63.

Lammers, C., Ireland, M., Resnick, M., & Blum, R. (2000). Influences on adolescents' decision to postpone onset of sexual intercourse: A survival analysis of virginity among youths aged 13 to 18 years. *Journal of Adolescent Health, 26,* 42–48.

Langman, P. (2013). Thirty-five rampage school shooters: Trends, patterns, and typology. In N. Bockler, T. Seager, P. Sitzer, & W. Heitmeyer (Eds.), *School shootings: International research, case studies, and concepts for prevention* (pp. 131–156). New York, NY: Springer.

Latzman, R. D., Lilienfeld, S. O., Latzman, N. E., & Clark, L. A. (2013). Exploring callous and unemotional traits in youth via general personality traits: An eye toward DSM-5. *Personality Disorders: Theory, Research, and Treatment, 4*, 191–202.

Leistico, A. M. R., Salekin, R. T., DeCoster, J., & Rogers, R. (2008). A large-scale meta-analysis relating the Hare measures of psychopathy to antisocial conduct. *Law and Human Behavior, 32*(1), 28–45.

Loftin, C. (1986). Assaultive violence as a contagious social process. *Bulletin of the New York Academy of Medicine, 62*(5), 550.

Longman, T., Hawes, D. J., & Kohlhoff, J. (2016). Callous–unemotional traits as markers for conduct problem severity in early childhood: A meta-analysis. *Child Psychiatry & Human Development, 47*(2), 326–334.

Lykken, D. T. (1995). *The antisocial personalities*. Hillsdale, NJ: Erlbaum.

Lynam, D. R., & Gudonis, L. (2005). The development of psychopathy. *Annual Review of Clinical Psychology, 1*, 381–407.

Marshall, R. D., Bryant, R. A., Amsel, L., Suh, E. J., Cook, J. M., & Neria, Y. (2007). The psychology of ongoing threat: Relative risk appraisal, the September 11 attacks, and terrorism-related fears. *American Psychologist, 62*(4), 304.

McDonald, R. M., Dodson, C., Rosenfield, D., & Jouriles, E. N. (2011). Effects of a parenting intervention on features of psychopathy in children. *Journal of Abnormal Child Psychology, 39*, 1013–1023.

McGinty, E. E., Webster, D. W., & Barry, C. L. (2013). Effects of news media messages about mass shootings on attitudes toward persons with serious mental illness and public support for gun control policies. *American Journal of Psychiatry, 170*(5), 494–501.

McGinty, E. E., Webster, D. W., Jarlenski, M., & Barry, C. L. (2014). News media framing of serious mental illness and gun violence in the United States, 1997–2012. *American Journal of Public Health, 104*(3), 406–413.

Meade, C. S., Kershaw, T. S., & Ickovics, J. R. (2008). The intergenerational cycle of teenage motherhood: An ecological approach. *Health Psychology, 27*(4), 419.

Miller, E., Decker, M. R., McCauley, H. L., et al. (2010). Pregnancy coercion, intimate partner violence and unintended pregnancy. *Contraception, 81*(4), 316–322.

Miller, K. S., Forehand, R., & Kotchick, B. A. (2000). Adolescent sexual behavior in two ethnic minority samples: A multi-system perspective. *Adolescence, 35*, 313–333.

Mills, K. L., Goddings, A. L., Clasen, L. S., Giedd, J. N., & Blakemore, S. J. (2014). The developmental mismatch in structural brain maturation during adolescence. *Developmental Neuroscience, 36*, 147–160.

Mrug, S., Madan, A., & Windle, M. (2016). Emotional desensitization to violence contributes to adolescents' violent behavior. *Journal of Abnormal Child Psychology, 44*(1), 75–86.

Murrie, D. C., Marcus, D. K., Douglas, K. S., Lee, Z., Salekin, R. T., & Vincent, G. (2007). Youth with psychopathy features are not a discrete class: A taxometric analysis. *Journal of Child Psychology and Psychiatry, 48*(7), 714–723.

Nestle, M., & Jacobson, M. F. (2000). Halting the obesity epidemic: A public health policy approach. *Public Health Reports, 115*, 12.

Neuman, J. H., Baron, R. A., Einarsen, S., Hoel, H., Zapf, D., & Cooper, C. (2011). Social antecedents of bullying: A social interactionist perspective. In S. Einarsen, H. Hoel, D. Zapf & C. Cooper (Eds.), *Bullying and harassment in the workplace: Developments in theory, research, and practice* (pp. 201–225). Boca Raton, FL: CRC Press.

Nikulina, V., Widom, C. S., & Czaja, S. (2011). The role of childhood neglect and childhood poverty in predicting mental health, academic achievement and crime in adulthood. *American Journal of Community Psychology, 48*(3–4), 309–321.

Niolon, P. H., Kearns, M., Dills, J., Rambo, K., Irving, S., Armstead, T., & Gilbert, L. (2017). *Preventing intimate partner violence across the lifespan: A technical package of programs, policies, and practices*. Atlanta, GA: National Center for Injury Prevention and Control, Centers for Disease Control and Prevention.

North, C. S., Tivis, L., McMillen, J. C., Pfefferbaum, B., Cox, J., Spitznagel, E. L., … Smith, E. M. (2002). Coping, functioning, and adjustment of rescue workers after the Oklahoma City bombing. *Journal of Traumatic Stress, 15*, 171–175.

Piquero, A. R., Daigle, L. E., Gibson, C., Piquero, N. L., & Tibbetts, S. G. (2007). Research note: Are life-course-persistent offenders at risk for adverse health outcomes? *Journal of Research in Crime and Delinquency, 44*(2), 185–207.

Ragatz, L. L., Anderson, R. J., Fremouw, W., & Schwartz, R. (2011). Criminal thinking patterns, aggression styles, and the psychopathic traits of late high school bullies and bully-victims. *Aggressive Behavior, 37*(2), 145–160.

Reidy, D. E., Kearns, M. C., & DeGue, S. (2013). Reducing psychopathic violence: A review of the treatment literature. *Aggression & Violent Behavior, 18*, 527–538.

Reidy, D. E., Kearns, M. C., DeGue, S., Lilienfeld, S. O., Massetti, G., & Kiehl, K. A. (2015). Why psychopathy matters: Implications for public health and violence prevention. *Aggression & Violent Behavior, 24*, 214–225.

Reidy, D. E., Krusemark, E., Kosson, D. S., Kearns, M. C., Smith-Darden, J. P., & Kiehl, K. A. (2017). The development of severe and chronic violence among youth: The role of psychopathic traits and reward processing. *Child Psychiatry & Human Development, 48*, 967–982.

Reidy, D. E., Lilienfeld, S. O., Berke, D. S., Gentile, B., & Zeichner, A. (2016). Psychopathy traits and violent assault among men with and without history of arrest. *Journal of Interpersonal Violence*. DOI: 0886260516660972.

Reidy, D. E., Shelley-Tremblay, J. F., & Lilienfeld, S. O. (2011). Psychopathy, reactive aggression, and precarious proclamations: A review of behavioral, cognitive, & biological research. *Aggression & Violent Behavior, 16*, 512–524.

Rende, R., Slomkowski, C., Lloyd-Richardson, E., & Niaura, R. (2005). Sibling effects on substance use in adolescence: Social contagion and genetic relatedness. *Journal of Family Psychology, 19*(4), 611.

Roberts, B. W., & DelVechio, W. F. (2000). The rank-order consistency of personality traits from childhood to old age: A quantitative review of longitudinal studies. *Psychological Bulletin, 26*, 3–25.

Rodgers, J. L., & Rowe, D. C. (1993). Social contagion and adolescent sexual behavior: A developmental EMOSA model. *Psychological Review, 100*(3), 479.

Rodgers, J. L., Rowe, D. C., & Buster, M. (1998). Social contagion, adolescent sexual behavior, and pregnancy: A nonlinear dynamic EMOSA model. *Developmental Psychology, 34*(5), 1096.

Rowe, D. C., & Rodgers, J. L. (1994). A social contagion model of adolescent sexual behavior: Explaining race differences. *Social Biology, 41*(1–2), 1–18.

Sandfort, T. G., Orr, M., Hirsch, J. S., & Santelli, J. (2008). Long-term health correlates of timing of sexual debut: Results from a national US study. *American Journal of Public Health, 98*(1), 155–161.

Scharrer, E. (2008). Media exposure and sensitivity to violence in news reports: Evidence of desensitization? *Journalism & Mass Communication Quarterly, 85*(2), 291–310.

Schleider, J. L., & Weisz, J. R. (2016). Mental health and implicit theories of thoughts, feelings, and behavior in early adolescents: Are girls at greater risk? *Journal of Social and Clinical Psychology, 35*(2), 130.

Seagrave, D., & Grisso, T. (2002). Adolescent development and measurement of juvenile psychopathy. *Law & Human Behavior, 26*, 219–239.

Shalizi, C. R., & Thomas, A. C. (2011). Homophily and contagion are generically confounded in observational social network studies. *Sociological Methods & Research, 40*(2), 211–239.

Shukla, K., & Wiesner, M. (2016). Relations of delinquency to direct and indirect violence exposure among economically disadvantaged, ethnic-minority mid-adolescents. *Crime & Delinquency, 62*(4), 423–445.

Shuster, M. A., Stein, B. D., Jaycox, L. H., et al. (2001). A national survey of stress reactions after the September 11, 2001, terrorist attack. *New England Journal of Medicine, 345*, 1507–1512.

Silver, R. C., Holman, E. A., McIntosh, D. N., Poulin, M., & Gil-Rivas, V. (2002). Nationwide longitudinal study of psychological responses to September 11. *JAMA, 288*, 1235–1244.

Simon, T. R., Anderson, M., Thompson, M. P., Crosby, A. E., Shelley, G., & Sacks, J. J. (2001). Attitudinal acceptance of intimate partner violence among U.S. adults. *Violence and Victims, 16*, 115–126.

Slutkin, G. (2012). Violence is a contagious disease. In *Contagion of violence: Workshop summary* (pp. 94–111). Washington, DC: National Academy Press. Available at http://cureviolence.org/wp-content/uploads/2015/05/Violence-is-a-Contagious-Disease.pdf.

Smith-Darden, J. P., Kernsmith, P. D., Reidy, D. E., & Cortina, K. S. (2017). In search of modifiable risk and protective factors for teen dating violence. *Journal of Research on Adolescence, 27*(2), 423–435.

Squeglia, L. M., Jacobus, J., & Tapert, S. F. (2009). The influence of substance use on adolescent brain development. *Clinical EEG and Neuroscience, 40*(1), 31–38.

Squeglia, L. M., Tapert, S. F., Sullivan, E. V., Jacobus, J., Meloy, M., Rohlfing, T., & Pfefferbaum, A. (2015). Brain development in heavy-drinking adolescents. *American Journal of Psychiatry, 172*(6), 531–542.

Steinberg, L. (2005). Cognitive and affective development in adolescence. *Trends in Cognitive Sciences, 9*(2), 69–74.

Stone, M. H. (2015). Mass murder, mental illness, and men. *Violence and Gender, 2*(1), 51–86.

Takizawa, R., Maughan, B., & Arseneault, L. (2014). Adult health outcomes of childhood bullying victimization: Evidence from a five-decade longitudinal British birth cohort. *American Journal of Psychiatry, 171*, 777–784.

Tarabah, A., Badr, L. K., Usta, J., & Doyle, J. (2016). Exposure to violence and children's desensitization attitudes in Lebanon. *Journal of Interpersonal Violence, 31*(18), 3017–3038.

Taylor, J., & Lang, A. R. (2006). Psychopathy and substance use disorders. In C. J. Patrick (Ed.), *Handbook of psychopathy* (pp. 495–511). New York, NY: Guilford Press.

Thoresen, S., Flood Aakvaag, H., Wentzel-Larsen, T., Dyb, G., & Kristian Hjemdal, O. (2012). The day Norway cried: Proximity and distress in Norwegian citizens following the 22nd July 2011 terrorist attacks in Oslo and on Utøya Island. *European Journal of Psychotraumatology, 3*, 19709.

Thornton, L. C., Frick, P. J., Ray, J. V., Wall Myers, T. D., Steinberg, L., & Cauffman, E. (2017). Risky sex, drugs, sensation seeking, and callous unemotional traits in justice-involved male adolescents. *Journal of Clinical Child & Adolescent Psychology, 48*(1), 68–79.

Towers, S., Gomez-Lievano, A., Khan, M., Mubayi, A., & Castillo-Chavez, C. (2015). Contagion in mass killings and school shootings. *PLoS One, 10*(7), e0117259.

Townsend, L., Flisher, A. J., & King, G. (2007). A systematic review of the relationship between high school dropout and substance use. *Clinical Child and Family Psychology Review, 10*(4), 295–317.

Tulchinsky, T. H., & Varavikova, E. A. (2010). The new public health. *Public Health Reviews, 32*(1), 25–53.

Ursano, R. J., Fullerton, C. S., Vance, K., & Kao, T. C. (1999). Posttraumatic stress disorder and identification in disaster workers. *American Journal of Psychiatry, 156*(3), 353–359.

U.S. Department of Health, Education, and Welfare. (1979). *Healthy people: The Surgeon General's report on health promotion and disease prevention.* (Publication 79-55071). Washington, DC: Public Health Service, Office of Assistant Secretary for Health and Surgeon General.

Vagi, K. J., Rothman, E. F., Latzman, N. E., Tharp, A. T., Hall, D. M., & Breiding, M. J. (2013). Beyond correlates: A review of risk and protective factors for adolescent dating violence. *Journal of Youth and Adolescence, 42*(4), 633–649.

Van der Molen, J. H. W. (2004). Violence and suffering in television news: Toward a broader conception of harmful television content for children. *Pediatrics, 113*(6), 1771–1775.

Vanderbilt, D., & Augustyn, M. (2010). The effects of bullying. *Paediatrics and Child Health, 20*(7), 315–320.

Vaughn, M. G., Salas-Wright, C. P., Delisi, M., & Maynard, B. R. (2014). Violence and externalizing behavior among youth in the United States: Is there a severe 5%? *Youth Violence & Juvenile Justice, 12*, 3–21.

Verona, E., & Patrick, C. J. (2015). Psychobiological aspects of antisocial personality disorder, psychopathy, and violence. *Psychiatric Times, 32*(3), 49.

Viding, E., & McCrory, E. J. (2012). Genetic and neurocognitive contributions to the development of psychopathy. *Development and Psychopathology, 24*, 969–983.

Wagner, F. A., & Anthony, J. C. (2002). From first drug use to drug dependence: Developmental periods of risk for dependence upon marijuana, cocaine, and alcohol. *Neuropsychopharmacology, 26*, 479–488.

Walker, A., McKune, A., Ferguson, S., Pyne, D. B., & Rattray, B. (2016). Chronic occupational exposures can influence the rate of PTSD and depressive disorders in first responders and military personnel. *Extreme Physiology & Medicine, 5*(1), 8.

Walsh, Z., Allen, L. C., & Kosson, D. S. (2007). Beyond social deviance: Substance use disorders and the dimensions of psychopathy. *Journal of Personality Disorders, 21*(3), 273–288.

Willoughby, M. T., Waschbusch, D. A., Moore, G. A., & Propper, C. B. (2011). Using the ASEBA to screen for callous unemotional traits in early childhood: Factor structure, temporal stability, and utility. *Journal of Psychopathology and Behavioral Assessment, 33*(1), 19–30.

Willoughby, M. T., Mills-Koonce, W. R., Gottfredson, N. C., & Wagner, N. J. (2014). Measuring callous unemotional behaviors in early childhood: Factor structure and the prediction of stable aggression in middle childhood. *Journal of Psychopathology and Behavioral Assessment, 36*(1), 30–42.

Wolke, D., Copeland, W. E., Angold, A., & Costello, E. J. (2013). Impact of bullying in childhood on adult health, wealth, crime, and social outcomes. *Psychological Science, 24*(10), 1958–1970.

Woods, E. R., Lin, Y. G., Middleman, A., Beckford, P., Chase, L., & DuRant, R. H. (1997). The associations of suicide attempts in adolescents. *Pediatrics, 99*(6), 791–796.

World Health Organization. (2016). *Consolidated guidelines on the use of antiretroviral drugs for treating and preventing HIV infection: Recommendations for a public health approach.* Geneva, Switzerland: World Health Organization.

Wu, P., Hoven, C. W., Liu, X., Cohen, P., Fuller, C. J., & Shaffer, D. (2004). Substance use, suicidal ideation and attempts in children and adolescents. *Suicide and Life-Threatening Behavior, 34*(4), 408–420.

Zinzow, H. M., Ruggiero, K. J., Resnick, H., Hanson, R., Smith, D., Saunders, B., & Kilpatrick, D. (2009). Prevalence and mental health correlates of witnessed parental and community violence in a national sample of adolescents. *Journal of Child Psychology and Psychiatry, 50*(4), 441–450.

# 12
# ALCOHOL AND DRUG MISUSE, DELINQUENCY, AND HEALTH

*Christopher P. Salas-Wright*

## Introduction

The present chapter is an exploration of three critically important and profoundly interrelated constructs: adolescent alcohol and other drug (AOD) misuse, juvenile delinquency, and health. Often empirical studies—my own work included—examine the ways in which AOD misuse is intertwined with delinquency and crime, and a vast body of research has documented the profound implications of AOD misuse for risk of acute and chronic health conditions. Moreover, multiple chapters in this *Routledge Handbook* provide insight into how youth involvement in violence and crime relates to risk of health problems. But far less attention has been dedicated to considering these three constructs simultaneously. The objective of the present chapter is to present core principles related to *AOD misuse, delinquency*, and *health*, and to highlight the ways in which drinking, drug use, violence, crime, criminal justice system involvement, health risk behavior, health conditions, and health promotion touch upon one another.

This brief chapter is organized around five main points intended to build upon one another in a stepwise fashion. We will begin by examining [1] the substantial body of literature showing that AOD misuse and delinquency are tightly linked with a particular emphasis on considering *how* (i.e., the influence of one behavior on the other) and *why* (i.e., shared biological and environmental sources of risk) this is the case. Next, our attention will shift to [2] the ways in which we know drinking and illicit drug use are related to risk for acute and chronic health conditions before [3] considering how together AOD misuse and delinquency are independent, overlapping, and synergistic behaviors that serve to increase risk of adverse health consequences. Subsequently, we will consider how [4] a biosocial life course perspective that considers both genetic and neurological factors as well as social and contextual influences can be used to understand the complex interplay between AOD misuse, delinquency, and health over years, decades, and even generations. Finally, we will conclude by discussing [5] what all of this may mean for prevention and intervention researchers seeking to foster the healthy development of youth and to short-circuit behavioral and health problems that emerge early on in life.

## Point One

### *AOD Misuse and Delinquency are Tightly Linked*

There is little doubt that a strong association exists between adolescent drinking and drug use and involvement in delinquent behaviors. A number of my own recent studies using data from the National Survey on Drug Use and Health (NSDUH) can be used to illustrate this rather straightforward point. For example, my colleagues and I found that teenagers reporting recent binge drinking were roughly two times more likely than non-binge drinkers to report having attacked someone with the intent to seriously injure them during the previous year (Salas-Wright, Reingle Gonzalez, Vaughn, Schwartz, & Jetelina, 2016a). In this same study, we found that the prevalence of violent attacks among 13-year-olds reporting no alcohol use was roughly 7% as compared to a rate of 31% among those reporting having 5 or more drinks on a single occasion during the previous month.

Of course, these findings are not limited to alcohol use. DeLisi and colleagues (2015) found that, compared to youth with low levels of substance use morbidity, young people exhibiting polydrug abuse/dependence were more than four times more likely to be arrested for robbery, ten times more likely to be arrested for larceny or theft, and more than 17 times more likely to be arrested for possession or sale of illicit drugs. In our work, we have also found that the relationship works the other way around. For instance, we recently found that the prevalence of past year substance use disorder was 6% among youth reporting no involvement in violence, but was 22% among those reporting episodic involvement and 36% among repeatedly violent youth (Salas-Wright, Vaughn, Reingle Gonzalez, Fu, & Clark Goings, 2016c). Vaughn and colleagues (2015) also found—using data from the National Epidemiologic Survey on Alcohol and Related Conditions (NESARC)—that 29% of adults who spent time in juvenile detention facilities met criteria for a substance use disorder as compared to 10% of those who reported no juvenile justice system contact as teens. These are but several studies among literally hundreds of scientific papers that make crystal clear that there is a strong connection between AOD misuse and delinquency.

Scholars have highlighted a number of compelling explanations for the observed relationship between AOD misuse and delinquency (Salas-Wright & Todic, 2014; Vaughn, Maynard, Salas-Wright, & DeLisi, 2018; Vaughn, Salas-Wright, & Reingle Gonzalez, 2016, 2018). One particularly salient conceptualization is that of the externalizing spectrum. This framework argues that an array of risky adolescent behaviors—ranging from minor property crimes and trying tobacco or alcohol to more severe behaviors such as habitual illicit drug use, violent attacks, or weapon carrying—should be understood as not categorically distinct but rather points along a theoretical severity gradient or externalizing spectrum (Beauchaine & Hinshaw, 2015; Vaughn, Salas-Wright, DeLisi, & Maynard, 2014). From this vantage point, it should not be considered surprising that AOD misuse and delinquency are correlated; rather, these phenomena are best understood as distinct but conceptually related markers of underlying externalizing risk. This underlying risk typically is understood as being influenced by both biological and social risk and protective factors (Salas-Wright, Vaughn, & Reingle Gonzalez, 2016). For instance, we know that certain biological factors such as risk propensity or sensation seeking, both of which have a strong genetic component and are heritable (Bezdjian, Baker, & Tuvblad, 2011; Hur & Bouchard, 1997), are related to risk of AOD misuse and delinquency among young people (Harden, Quinn, & Tucker-Drob, 2012; Sargent, Tanski, Stoolmiller, & Hanewinkel, 2010). Similarly, it is well-established that social and contextual factors, such as childhood adversity and parental monitoring, relate not just to risk of AOD misuse or delinquency, but have well documented links to both outcomes (Barnes, Hoffman, Welte, Farrell, & Dintcheff, 2006; O'Brien, Salas-Wright, Vaughn, & LeCloux, 2015; Vaughn et al., 2017). To be sure, this research is in keeping with the central tenets of problem behavior theory which suggests that externalizing behaviors are interconnected via underlying linkages in the social ecology of youth and the desire to express independence from parental and social control (Jessor, 1987).

We have strong evidence that there is a cross-sectional association between AOD misuse and delinquency during adolescence, and we know that externalizing behavior during childhood is an important predictor of later AOD misuse during adolescence (Englund, Egeland, Oliva, & Collins, 2008; Moffitt, Caspi, Harrington, & Milne, 2002). However, empirical evidence on the direct causal links between AOD misuse and delinquency is a bit tenuous as it is sometimes difficult to establish causality or to discern directionality and timing (Salas-Wright et al., 2016b). There are certainly compelling theoretical reasons to think about how AOD misuse—via direct intoxication and the impaired judgment that accompanies it or the of the effect of chronic use on neurological executive functioning systems—would place youth at greater risk of illegal behavior. And scholars have made coherent arguments about how involvement in delinquency can place youth in peer networks and social ecologies in which substance use risk is elevated (Jessor, 1987). And yet, our understanding of the precise ways in which AOD misuse and the delinquency influence one another remains incomplete. Whatever the thorny causal issues, we stand on steady ground in thinking about these two phenomena as deeply interrelated.

## Point Two

### *We Often Talk about the Health Implications of AOD Misuse (But Not Delinquency)*

One of the core assertions of this *Routledge Handbook* is that many of us often do not think—at least not in a systematic fashion—about the relationship between delinquency and health. Some may dispute that point, but few would deny that we are a lot more accustomed to talking about the health implications of AOD misuse then we are about the links between delinquency and health. For example, scholars, practitioners, and the public understand that alcohol intoxication is a major factor in many automobile accidents and other traumatic events such as falls or drownings (Havard, Shakeshaft, & Sanson-Fisher, 2008). And most, if not all of us, are familiar with the central message of organizations like Mothers against Drunk Driving (Fell & Voas, 2006) and the idea that excessive drinking can make us profoundly sick.

There is also general consensus that use of drugs like marijuana, during the adolescent years in particular, is a source of risk for healthy neurological and physical development (Volkow, Baler, Compton, & Weiss, 2014). Unfortunately, many of us also are reminded daily, by our local newspapers and community groups, that the use of opioids and other legal and illicit substances can and does lead to overdose and death (Rudd, Aleshire, Zibbell, & Gladden, 2016). And, of course, we know that the long-term consequences of risky drinking, drug use, and substance use disorders can contribute to risk for myriad chronic health conditions such as heart disease, lung disease, liver and kidney disease, and cancer (Rehm *et al.*, 2009; Whiteford *et al.*, 2013).

Simply, we find it easy to talk about alcohol, drugs, and health in our contemporary lexicon. (*Of course drinking too much is bad for your health! Of course consuming fentanyl can kill you!*) As we will discuss below, failing to include delinquency as part of this conversation misses a hugely important component of understanding how AOD misuse and health are connected. And thinking simultaneously—and intentionally—about drinking, drug use, health, *and delinquency* together opens up many new insights and possibilities.

## Point Three

### *Drinking and Drug Use are Related to Delinquent Behaviors that We Know are Linked to Risk of Serious Health Consequences*

If we were to draw a line from AOD misuse to health outcomes among adolescents, more often than not our line would pass directly through juvenile delinquency. In the case of underage drinking, we see compelling evidence that the overwhelming majority of the social costs associated with adolescent drinking are due to violent delinquency and car accidents (Miller, Levy, Spicer, & Taylor, 2006; Pacific Institute for Research and Evaluation, n.d.). Experimental data makes clear that alcohol intoxication can impair judgment and lead to diminished inhibitory control and impulsive and poor decision-making (Dick et al., 2010; George, Rogers, & Duka, 2005). To put it bluntly, bad and impulsive decisions can include things like lashing out or punching someone in the face (and, in turn, getting punched in the face or worse) or driving drunk or getting into a car being driven by someone whose reactions and judgments are impaired by alcohol or other drugs. If self-control is the *Tyrannosaurs rex* of criminology (DeLisi, 2011), substances that impair our decision making and inhibitory control should be viewed as dangerous conspirators.

Beyond acute intoxication, sustained AOD misuse can also create serious problems related to victimization and health risk. For instance, in our recent work using national data, my colleagues and I found that risk of traumatic brain injury was more than two times greater among those with illicit drug use disorders as compared to those who did not meet diagnostic criteria (Vaughn et al., 2018). Moreover, in our earlier work, using data from a sample of adolescents convicted for serious criminal offenses in Arizona and Pennsylvania, we found that substance use morbidity significantly predicted risk of traumatic brain injury and that youth reporting serious head trauma were more likely to report subsequent drug offenses after conviction (Perron et al., 2014; Vaughn, Salas-Wright, Delisi, & Perron, 2014). It seems quite clear from these and other studies that young people who are consistently involved in illicit drug use are substantially more likely to receive a seriously traumatic blow to the head. And this makes perfect sense given that we know that drug seeking behaviors can often require youth to pass through contexts of elevated risk for victimization (Koo, Chitwood, & Sánchez, 2008) and that drug use can also lead to becoming parts of peer groups involved in other high-risk behaviors that can lead to injury (Dishion, Capaldi, Spracklen, & Li, 1995; Salas-Wright, Olate, & Vaughn, 2013, 2015). Beyond head injury, it is also clear that adolescent AOD use substantially increases the likelihood that youth will become involved in the criminal justice system and, in turn, be exposed to the myriad health risks that this entails (see Chapters 3, 8, 9 and others in this *Handbook*). Moreover, our research has also shown that criminal justice system involved individuals are more likely to experience medical problems, such as sexually-transmitted infections and hepatitis, that are closely related to AOD misuse and risk-taking (Vaughn, Salas-Wright, DeLisi, & Piquero, 2014).

There are many ways that AOD misuse relates to health problems, but—particularly among adolescents—perhaps the most important pathway linking drinking and illicit drug use with health is by means of involvement in delinquent and antisocial behavior. Adolescents who misuse AOD are far more likely to be involved in risky behaviors and spend time in social groups or environments where victimization is far more likely. And young people who drink and use illicit drugs unquestionably place themselves at greater risk for criminal justice system involvement and health-related sequelae related to juvenile detention and/or incarceration. In a word, it is challenging to attempt to understand how AOD misuse influences adolescent health without taking very seriously the role of delinquency and the criminal justice system.

## Point Four

### *A Biosocial Life Course Perspective Helps to Pull All of This Together*

Previously, my colleagues and I have highlighted the insights afforded by a biosocial life course perspective for understanding AOD misuse and delinquency (see Salas-Wright et al., 2016b). This perspective considers behavioral health risk as influenced by biological factors, such as our brains and genetics, that interact with social and environmental conditions, such as parenting, school, and peer influences. Moreover, in keeping with the work of Glen Elder and others, it considers how factors such as when events take place in our lives shape our life course trajectories, including those related to AOD use, crime, and health (Elder, 1998; Elder & Rockwell, 1979; Hser, Longshore, & Anglin, 2007; Piquero, Jennings, & Barnes, 2012).

For the purposes of this chapter, a biosocial life course perspective can also be applied to thinking about the complex interplay between our biology, life experiences, and social contexts and how this relates to drinking and drug use, delinquency and externalizing behavior, and short-term and long-term health outcomes. The life course perspective highlights the ways in which disruptive behaviors early on in life can be viewed as important markers—that call out for prevention and early intervention efforts, as discussed below—for later risk of AOD misuse, problem behavior, and the health implications that accompany these outcomes (Vaughn, Salas-Wright, & Reingle Gonzalez, 2016). In the same way, it helps us to consider how early AOD use initiation can lead to very serious health risk outcomes such as violent victimization, trauma, and chronic health conditions over the course of years and even decades (Hser, Longshore, & Anglin, 2007). To be sure, a life course framework also helps us to see how childhood disruptive behavior, early AOD use initiation, and delinquency relate to risk of criminal justice system contact, which we are understanding more and more to be profoundly bad for your health (Massoglia & Pridemore, 2015; Vaughn et al., 2014).

The central insight here is that adolescent drinking and drug use and juvenile delinquency together contribute to risk for immediate health problems related to victimization and trauma, but they also placed young people on life course trajectories that—via risky developmental pathways and/or criminal justice system contact—are profoundly related to longer-term and chronic health conditions as well as mortality (Rehm *et al.*, 2009; Whiteford *et al.*, 2013). A biosocial life course perspective helps to pull all of this together as it allows us to see the complex unfolding of AOD misuse, delinquency, and health over time.

## Point Five

### *When It Comes to Prevention and Intervention, a Multicomponent Approach Makes Sense*

In this final section, we do well to keep things simple. As discussed above, we know that [a] AOD misuse and delinquency are profoundly connected and that [b] together and independently these externalizing behaviors relate to both short-term and long-term health outcomes across the life course. As such, it seems straightforward that we should [c] be thoughtful about this interplay in efforts to prevent or address adolescent drinking and drug use, delinquency, and adverse health outcomes. In fact, in a world where funding for programs to address the challenges and problems experienced by youth is always limited, it would be profoundly shortsighted to overlook opportunities that allow for synergistic impact. To this end, scholars focused on HIV prevention have discussed the importance of "bundling" or multicomponent interventions designed to target multiple risk behaviors in a single prevention or intervention program (Ickovics, 2008).

In my own work, with support from the National Institute on Alcohol Abuse and Alcoholism, I am in the early stages of adapting an evidence-based AOD use prevention program to include an emphasis on aggressive and violent behavior during the middle school years. It is well-established that the program I am adapting—*keepin' it* REAL or *ki*R (Hecht *et al.*, 2003)—yields positive outcomes for youth alcohol, marijuana, and overall substance use (Kulis *et al.*, 2005). And there is some evidence that, despite no explicit references to violence or delinquency, that *ki*R participation may lead to lower rates of theft and weapon use among youth (Nieri, Apkarian, Kulis, & Marsiglia, 2015). Given the interrelatedness of AOD misuse and delinquency, this makes intuitive sense—and it also makes practical sense to try to address both outcomes together. Moreover, it seems likely that discussing how both AOD misuse and delinquency are related to risk of victimization, trauma, serious injury, and longer-term health problems will be an important way of pulling the different elements of the multicomponent program together. As part of our evaluation, we will examine not only AOD misuse and violence/delinquency, but also outcomes related to serious health risk (e.g., riding in a car with an intoxicated driver, head trauma). It would not surprise me at all to see that teaching youth to make good decisions about alcohol, drugs, and crime will have a direct impact on their health.

## Conclusion

In sum, we have covered five main points. *First*, we know that adolescent drinking and drug use are tightly linked with risk of involvement in delinquent behavior and criminal justice system involvement. While the direct causal links between these factors are not always easy to identify, it is certainly fair to say that where we see one of these behaviors we are far more likely to see the other as well. *Second*, despite the profound interrelatedness of AOD misuse and delinquency, we are much more comfortable talking about how drinking and drug misuse relates to health than we are in thinking about how behaviors like fighting, theft, and drug selling relate to our health. Certainly this makes some sense as AOD misuse literally involves ingesting substances that change our biology and have the potential to make a sick or even end our lives prematurely. That being said, the *third* point is that we know that the relationship between AOD misuse and both short- and long-term health problems often is mediated by involvement in delinquency. For instance, the lion's share of serious health outcomes resulting from underage drinking is due not to alcohol poisoning, but to interpersonal violence and car crashes (both of which relate as much to delinquency as they do to AOD misuse).

*Fourth*, we make the case that a biosocial life course approach—one that takes seriously the influence of biology and social context, and the ways that early life experiences unfold over time—helps to pull the first three points together. Problem behavior during adolescence increases risk of victimization and trauma-related health outcomes, but it also relates to risk of later acute and chronic health problems across the several decades that comprise the life course. *Fifth* and finally, given the interrelatedness of AOD misuse, delinquency, and health, it makes good sense to think about how our efforts to address youth well-being and development might touch on AOD misuse, delinquency, and health in order to achieve synergistic gain. In a world of limited funding and time, it would seem to be foolish to make all the effort to prevent adolescent drinking or drug use and to not consider how delinquency and health might also be part of the conversation. Similarly, if we hope to impact the health of individuals across the life course, there is no doubt that adolescent drinking, drug use, and the delinquency are all essential parts of the puzzle.

**Author Note:** Research reported in this publication was supported by the National Institute on Alcohol Abuse and Alcoholism of the National Institutes of Health under Award Number K01AA026645. The content is solely the responsibility of the authors and does not necessarily represent the official views of the National Institutes of Health.

# References

Barnes, G. M., Hoffman, J. H., Welte, J. W., Farrell, M. P., & Dintcheff, B. A. (2006). Effects of parental monitoring and peer deviance on substance use and delinquency. *Journal of Marriage and Family, 68*(4), 1084–1104.

Beauchaine, T. P., & Hinshaw, S. P. (2015). *The Oxford Handbook of Externalizing Spectrum Disorders.* New York, NY: Oxford University Press.

Bezdjian, S., Baker, L. A., & Tuvblad, C. (2011). Genetic and environmental influences on impulsivity: A meta-analysis of twin, family and adoption studies. *Clinical Psychology Review, 31*(7), 1209–1223.

DeLisi, M. (2011). Self-control theory: The Tyrannosaurus rex of criminology is poised to devour criminal justice. *Journal of Criminal Justice, 2*(39), 103–105.

DeLisi, M., Vaughn, M. G., Salas-Wright, C. P., & Jennings, W. G. (2015). Drugged and dangerous: Prevalence and variants of substance use comorbidity among seriously violent offenders in the United States. *Journal of Drug Issues, 45*(3), 232–248.

Dick, D. M., Smith, G., Olausson, P., Mitchell, S. H., Leeman, R. F., O'Malley, S. S., & Sher, K. (2010). Understanding the construct of impulsivity and its relationship to alcohol use disorders. *Addiction Biology, 15*(2), 217–226.

Dishion, T. J., Capaldi, D., Spracklen, K. M., & Li, F. (1995). Peer ecology of male adolescent drug use. *Development and Psychopathology, 7*(4), 803–824.

Elder Jr, G. H. (1998). The life course as developmental theory. *Child Development, 69*(1), 1–12.

Elder Jr, G. H., & Rockwell, R. C. (1979). The life-course and human development: An ecological perspective. *International Journal of Behavioral Development, 2*(1), 1–21.

Englund, M. M., Egeland, B., Oliva, E. M., & Collins, W. A. (2008). Childhood and adolescent predictors of heavy drinking and alcohol use disorders in early adulthood: A longitudinal developmental analysis. *Addiction, 103*(s1), 23–35.

Fell, J. C., & Voas, R. B. (2006). Mothers against drunk driving (MADD): The first 25 years. *Traffic Injury Prevention, 7*(3), 195–212.

George, S., Rogers, R. D., & Duka, T. (2005). The acute effect of alcohol on decision making in social drinkers. *Psychopharmacology, 182*(1), 160–169.

Harden, K. P., Quinn, P. D., & Tucker-Drob, E. M. (2012). Genetically influenced change in sensation seeking drives the rise of delinquent behavior during adolescence. *Developmental Science, 15*(1), 150–163.

Havard, A., Shakeshaft, A., & Sanson-Fisher, R. (2008). Systematic review and meta-analyses of strategies targeting alcohol problems in emergency departments: interventions reduce alcohol-related injuries. *Addiction, 103*(3), 368–376.

Hecht, M. L., Marsiglia, F. F., Elek, E., Wagstaff, D. A., Kulis, S., Dustman, P., & Miller-Day, M. (2003). Culturally grounded substance use prevention: an evaluation of the keepin'it REAL curriculum. *Prevention Science, 4*(4), 233–248.

Hser, Y. I., Longshore, D., & Anglin, M. D. (2007). The life course perspective on drug use: A conceptual framework for understanding drug use trajectories. *Evaluation Review, 31*(6), 515–547.

Hur, Y. M., & Bouchard, T. J. (1997). The genetic correlation between impulsivity and sensation seeking traits. *Behavior Genetics, 27*(5), 455–463.

Ickovics, J. R. (2008). "Bundling" HIV prevention: Integrating services to promote synergistic gain. *Preventive Medicine, 46*(3), 222–225.

Jessor, R. (1987). Problem-behavior theory, psychosocial development, and adolescent problem drinking. *British Journal of Addiction, 82*(4), 331–342.

Koo, D. J., Chitwood, D. D., & Sánchez, J. (2008). Violent victimization and the routine activities/lifestyle of active drug users. *Journal of Drug Issues, 38*(4), 1105–1137.

Kulis, S., Marsiglia, F. F., Elek, E., Dustman, P., Wagstaff, D. A., & Hecht, M. L. (2005). Mexican/Mexican American adolescents and keepin'it REAL: An evidence-based substance use prevention program. *Children & Schools, 27*(3), 133–145.

Massoglia, M., & Pridemore, W. A. (2015). Incarceration and health. *Annual Review of Sociology, 41*, 291–310.

Miller, T. R., Levy, D. T., Spicer, R. S., & Taylor, D. M. (2006). Societal costs of underage drinking. *Journal of Studies on Alcohol and Drugs, 67*(4), 519–528.

Moffitt, T. E., Caspi, A., Harrington, H., & Milne, B. J. (2002). Males on the life-course-persistent and adolescence-limited antisocial pathways: Followup at age 26 years. *Development and Psychopathology, 14*(1), 179–207.

Nieri, T., Apkarian, J., Kulis, S., & Marsiglia, F. F. (2015). Effects of a youth substance use prevention program on stealing, fighting, and weapon use. *Journal of Primary Prevention, 36*(1), 41–49.

O'Brien, K., Salas-Wright, C. P., Vaughn, M. G., & LeCloux, M. (2015). Childhood exposure to a parental suicide attempt and risk for substance use disorders. *Addictive Behaviors, 46*, 70–76.

Pacific Institute of Research and Evaluation. (n.d.). *Underage Drinking Costs*. Calverton, MD: Author.

Perron, B. E., Vaughn, M. G., Ryan, J., Salas-Wright, C. P., Ruffolo, M., & Guerrero, E. (2014). Self-reported head injuries among delinquent youth. In M. DeLisi & M. G. Vaughn (Eds.), *Routledge International Handbook of Biosocial Criminology* (pp. 300–314). New York: Routledge.

Piquero, A. R., Jennings, W. G., & Barnes, J. C. (2012). Violence in criminal careers: A review of the literature from a developmental life-course perspective. *Aggression and Violent Behavior, 17*(3), 171–179.

Rehm, J., Mathers, C., Popova, S., Thavorncharoensap, M., Teerawattananon, Y., & Patra, J. (2009). Global burden of disease and injury and economic cost attributable to alcohol use and alcohol-use disorders. *The Lancet, 373*(9682), 2223–2233.

Rudd, R. A., Aleshire, N., Zibbell, J. E., & Gladden, R. M. (2016). Increases in drug and opioid overdose deaths—United States, 2000–2014. *American Journal of Transplantation, 16*(4), 1323–1327.

Salas-Wright, C. P., Olate, R., & Vaughn, M. G. (2013). Religious coping, spirituality, and substance use and abuse among youth in high-risk communities in San Salvador, El Salvador. *Substance Use and Misuse, 48*(9), 769–783.

Salas-Wright, C. P., Olate, R., & Vaughn, M. G. (2015). Substance use, violence, and HIV risk behavior in El Salvador and the United States: cross-national profiles of the SAVA syndemic. *Victims & Offenders, 10*(1), 95–116.

Salas-Wright, C. P., Reingle Gonzalez, J. M., Vaughn, M. G., Schwartz, S. J., Jetelina, K. K. (2016a). Age-related changes in the relationship between alcohol use and violence from early adolescence to young adulthood. *Addictive Behavior Reports, 4*, 13–17.

Salas-Wright, C. P. & Todic, J. (2014). Alcohol and drug misuse as a biosocial source of crime. In M. DeLisi & M. G. Vaughn (Eds.), *Routledge International Handbook of Biosocial Criminology* (pp. 558–570). New York: Routledge.

Salas-Wright, C. P., Vaughn, M. G., & Reingle Gonzalez, J. M. (2016b). *Drug Abuse and Antisocial Behavior: A Biosocial Life-Course Approach*. New York, NY: Palgrave Macmillan.

Salas-Wright, C. P., Vaughn, M. G., Reingle Gonzalez, J. M., Fu, Q. J., & Clark Goings, T. T. (2016c). Attacks intended to seriously harm and co-occurring drug use among youth in the United States. *Substance Use and Misuse, 51*(13), 1681–1692.

Sargent, J. D., Tanski, S., Stoolmiller, M., & Hanewinkel, R. (2010). Using sensation seeking to target adolescents for substance use interventions. *Addiction, 105*(3), 506–514.

Vaughn, M. G., Maynard, B. R., Salas-Wright, C. P., & DeLisi, M. (2018). The severe 5% and psychopathy. In M. DeLisi (Ed.), *Routledge International Handbook of Psychopathy and Crime* (pp. 526–543). New York, NY: Routledge.

Vaughn, M. G., Salas-Wright, C. P., DeLisi, M., & Maynard, B. R. (2014). Violence and externalizing behavior among youth in the United States: Is there a severe 5%? *Youth Violence and Juvenile Justice, 12*(1), 3–21.

Vaughn, M. G., Salas-Wright, C. P., DeLisi, M., Maynard, B. R., & Boutwell, B. (2015). Prevalence and correlates of psychiatric disorders among former juvenile detainees in the United States. *Comprehensive Psychiatry, 59*, 107–116.

Vaughn, M. G., Salas-Wright, C. P., Delisi, M., & Perron, B. E. (2014). Correlates of traumatic brain injury among juvenile offenders: A multi-site study. *Criminal Behaviour and Mental Health, 24*(3), 188–203.

Vaughn, M. G., Salas-Wright, C. P., DeLisi, M., & Piquero, A. R. (2014). Health associations of drug-involved and criminal-justice-involved adults in the United States. *Criminal Justice and Behavior, 41*(3), 318–336.

Vaughn, M. G., Salas-Wright, C. P., Huang, J., Qian, Z., Terzis, L., & Helton, J. (2017). Adverse childhood experiences among immigrants to the United States. *Journal of Interpersonal Violence, 32*(10), 1543–1564.

Vaughn, M. G., Salas-Wright, C. P., John, R., Holzer, K. J., Qian, Z., & Veeh, C. (2018). Traumatic brain injury and psychiatric co-morbidity in the United States. *Psychiatric Quarterly*. Advance online publication. doi:10.1007/s11126-018-9617-0.

Vaughn, M. G., Salas-Wright, C. P., & Reingle Gonzalez, J. M. (2016). Addiction and crime: The importance of asymmetry in offending and the life-course. *Journal of Addictive Diseases, 35*(4), 213–217.

Vaughn, M. G., Salas-Wright, C. P., & Reingle Gonzalez, J. M. (2018). Biosocial foundations of addiction and violent delinquency. In A. T. Vazsonyi, D. J. Flannery, M. DeLisi (Eds.), *The Cambridge Handbook of Violent Behavior and Aggression* (2nd, pp. 206–220). New York, NY: Cambridge University Press.

Volkow, N. D., Baler, R. D., Compton, W. M., & Weiss, S. R. (2014). Adverse health effects of marijuana use. *New England Journal of Medicine, 370*(23), 2219–2227.

Whiteford, H. A., Degenhardt, L., Rehm, J., Baxter, A. J., Ferrari, A. J., Erskine, H. E., ... & Burstein, R. (2013). Global burden of disease attributable to mental and substance use disorders: findings from the Global Burden of Disease Study 2010. *The Lancet, 382*(9904), 1575–1586.

# 13

# KEY HEALTH BEHAVIORS ACROSS THE LIFE COURSE

## The Salience of Comorbid Substance Use and Depression

*Abby K. Johnson and Megan Bears Augustyn*

The Centers for Disease Control and Prevention identifies "health risk behaviors" as those risk behaviors that are the primary contributors to morbidity and mortality (see also Millstein et al., 1992). These behaviors include depressive symptomology, substance use, unhealthy dietary behaviors, and criminal offending, among others. Health risk behaviors tend to be common among youth, increase with age through adolescence, and can persist into adulthood for some individuals (D'Amico, Ellickson, Collins, Martino, & Klein, 2005; Eaton et al., 2010). Moreover, these behaviors often do not occur in isolation (De La Haye, D'Amico, Miles, Ewing, & Tucker, 2014; Lytle, Kelder, Perry, & Klepp, 1995), often resulting in a cumulative, detrimental effect on individual functioning (e.g., MacArthur et al., 2012).

We focus on the development of depression and problem substance use, as these two, often co-occurring, key health risk behaviors have particularly deleterious consequences for development and are disproportionately high among individuals that encounter the juvenile and criminal justice systems. Moreover, depression and substance use are two of the largest public health threats, particularly among adolescents (Substance Abuse and Mental Health Services Administration [SAMHSA], 2016). Their co-morbidity is particularly problematic with deleterious consequences for cognitive, social and emotional development, which ensure health and well-being later in life (Steinberg, 2015).

The goals of this chapter are as follows. First, we review the prevalence and incidence of substance use and depressive disorders, respectively, over the life course, highlighting, in particular, the prevalence of each disorder among individuals intertwined in the juvenile and criminal justice systems. Second, we discuss the co-morbidity of these two disorders and review potential causes for co-morbidity. Finally, we conclude with a discussion of the challenges faced by the juvenile and criminal justice systems as each incurs a non-trivial proportion of individuals with co-occurring disorders, yet, by in large, lack the resources to identify and treat the causes of the manifest behaviors (i.e., offending), which often further entrenches an individual into the juvenile, and/or criminal justice system.

## Substance Use Disorders

A substance use disorder is distinguished by the excessive or unhealthy consumption of one of the following substances: alcohol, marijuana, cocaine, heroin, hallucinogens, inhalants, and the nonmedical use of prescription-type psychotherapeutic drugs (Diagnostic and Statistical Manual of Mental Disorders—Fifth Edition [DSM-V]).[1] It encompasses both abuse and dependence. Substance abuse is characterized by maladaptive use and dependence is more severe in nature, marked by compulsive drug seeking behavior, tolerance, and withdrawal symptomology (American Psychiatric Association [APA], 2000). Substance abuse is of concern given that it can significantly impair functioning across individual, social, work, family, and physical health domains. Moreover, consequences of substance abuse can worsen with time, as the individual becomes more dependent/tolerant of the substance(s).

Although a majority of individuals in the United States (90%) use alcohol or drugs (mostly alcohol) at some point, only a portion develop a substance use disorder. Demographically, males are nearly three times more likely to develop a substance use disorder compared to females, and males are more likely to initiate substance use altogether (Van Etten & Anthony, 2001). Finally, the relationship between socioeconomic status and substance use disorders is less clear, as some studies suggest that those of higher income status are more likely to abuse alcohol, while those of lower income status more likely to abuse drugs (SAMHSA, 2011). In a similar vein, prevalence rates for alcohol use disorders (AUD) and drug use disorders (DUD) are often reported separately as use tends to vary as a function of race/ethnicity and type of substance (Huang et al., 2006). Native Americans have the highest rates of alcohol use disorders (12.1%), followed by non-Hispanic Whites (8.9%), Hispanic Americans (7.9%), non-Hispanic Blacks (6.9%), and Asian Americans (4.5%). Native Americans also have the highest rates of drug use disorders (4.9%; more than twice as high as any other race), followed by non-Hispanic Blacks (2.4%), non-Hispanic Whites (1.9%), Hispanic Americans (1.7%) and Asian Americans (1.7%; Huang et al., 2006). In total, approximately 8% (i.e., 21.5 million) of the United States population has a substance use disorder.

### *Substance Use Disorders across the Life Course*

Most people begin using substances in adolescence or early adulthood (Schulte & Hser, 2014). Although the peak age of use varies across substances, substance use, in general, begins to increase in prevalence at age 12, and the highest rates of use occur between the ages of 19 and 21. Specifically, alcohol use and tobacco use peak at age 21, marijuana use peaks at age 19, and other illicit drug use peaks at age 20; on average, use tends to taper thereafter (Schulte & Hser, 2014). Unfortunately, an experimental or adolescent/early adulthood limited trajectory of use is not the case for all individuals; substance use can begin earlier in the life course and/or escalate from moderated use to problematic use and a disorder in a matter of months (Jordan & Andersen, 2017). Most substance use disorders develop during late adolescence and early adulthood; 20 is the average age of onset for all substance use disorders (Kessler et al., 2005).

### *Substance Use Disorders in Adolescence*

Substance use tends to follow a sequence from tobacco and alcohol use, to cannabis use, and then more dangerous and illicit substance use, including opioids, heroin or cocaine use Rutter, 1996). Estimates suggest anywhere from three to nine percent of adolescents (ages 12–17) in the United States meet the diagnostic criteria for a substance use disorder. This is likely an underestimation since substance use disorders in adolescence are usually in the early stages and diagnostic criteria are less standardized for adolescents given the developmental, psychological and social differences between adolescents and adults for whom many diagnostic criteria (e.g., DSM-V) were developed (Hawkins, Van Horn, & Arthur, 2004; Mericle et al., 2015; Peiper, Ridenour, Hochwalt, & Coyne-Beasley, 2016). Relatedly, the specific prevalence rate of substance use disorders increases with age due to increased abused and diagnostic relevance (Peiper, Ridenour, Hochwalt, & Coyne-Beasley, 2016).

### *Substance Use Disorders in Adulthood*

Roughly 9% of adults in the U.S. have a substance use disorder. In 2014, approximately 20.2 million adults (age 18 and over) had a substance use disorder in the past year. Of those, 16.3 million had an alcohol use disorder and 6.2 million had an illicit drug use disorder. Of these individuals, a little over 2 million had both an alcohol and illicit drug use disorder (Lipari & Van Horn, 2017). Notably, individuals ages 18 to 25 (i.e., "emerging adults") are the most at risk for substance use disorders. After emerging adulthood, rates tend to decrease with age as individuals "mature out" of substance use, thereby decreasing the risk for developing a disorder (Schulte & Hser, 2014). High mortality rates associated with substance use disorders also contribute to the declining prevalence of a substance use disorder in later adulthood (Hser, Hoffman, Grella, & Anglin, 2001).

### *Substance Use Disorders in the Juvenile and Criminal Justice Systems*

Considering that substance use is illegal for adolescence (i.e. alcohol use prior to the age of 21 and illicit drugs are uniformly prohibited by law with the exception of cannabis use in some states) substance use disorders are particularly pertinent within the context of the juvenile and criminal justice systems (Bureau of Justice Statistics, 2018). Approximately 10% of juvenile arrests and 13% of adult arrests are for drug possession. Estimates suggest that nearly 50% of youth in the juvenile justice system have a substance use disorder (SAMHSA, 2017b; Teplin, Abram, McClelland, Dulcan, & Mericle, 2002) and many more youth who are arrested self-report regular substance use (McClelland, Teplin & Abram, 2004).

Approximately 25% of adult arrests are for drug offenses (i.e., possession or sale). Additionally, nearly a quarter of drug and property offenders reported committing crime in order to get money for drugs (Bureau of Justice Statistics, 2018). Overall, it is estimated that approximately 50% of prisoners are struggling with substance use disorder (NIDA, 2018), with the most commonly abused substances being alcohol, marijuana, and methamphetamines (SAMHSA, 2017b).

Though the juvenile and criminal justice systems are some of the largest sources of referrals for substance abuse treatment programs, questions remain regarding whether offenders who are willing to participate in treatment actually receive treatment and whether the quality of the treatment that they receive will reduce substance abuse (Byron, 2014). For instance, only a fraction of inmates with a substance use disorder receive any type of treatment (NIDA, 2018). This is unfortunate as treatment outcomes for prisoners with substance use disorders are extremely promising in terms of recidivism reduction, the overall health and prosperity of the individual, and societal economic burden (NIDA, 2018). Effective and accessible treatment for inmates is especially important for younger offenders, as substance abuse treatment for juveniles is likely to curtail the risk of future offending (particularly if it can simultaneously target criminogenic attitudes that support substance use and offending) and relapse in later years (Chassin, 2008; Loeber, Farrington, & Petechuk, 2003).

## Depression

The National Institute of Mental Health (NIMH, 2017) defines a Major Depressive Disorder (MDD) as "a common but serious mood disorder [which] causes severe symptoms that affect how [one] feels, thinks, and handles daily activities, such as sleeping, eating or working." Symptomatology of depression varies, but often includes a combination of cognitive, emotional, and physical symptoms (Centers for Disease Control [CDC], 2014).[2] To meet the criteria for a major depressive disorder, an individual must experience at least five of the following symptoms for at least two weeks: anhedonia (markedly diminished interest or pleasure in daily activities), depressed/irritable mood, impaired decision-making, excessive self-reproach or guilt, thoughts of death, changes in appetite and/or weight, sleep/energy disruptions (sleeping excessively and never feeling rested, or being unable to fall or stay asleep), psychomotor problems, or fatigue. At least one of the five symptoms must be anhedonia or depressed/irritable mood.

Clinicians often categorize depression as "mild," "moderate," or "severe." Further, a depression diagnosis may be classified as "with" or "without" psychotic symptoms, "chronic" (lasting two or more years), and "in or out of remission" (APA, 2013).

Major or clinical levels of depression, otherwise called depressive disorders, affect roughly 20 million individuals in the United States each year (NIMH, 2017; World Health Organization [WHO], 2018). Moreover, a depressive disorder will affect 15% of people in the U.S.—roughly 50 million individuals—at some point in their lifetime.

Some people are at a greater risk for developing a depressive disorder compared to others. Depressive disorders are twice as common in females than in males (Albert, 2015; CDC, 2018), though interestingly, the female to male ratio tends to become more equivocal with age. Across race/ethnicity, non-Hispanic Black and Hispanics-Americans generally have the highest rates of depressive disorders (9.2% and 8.2%), followed closely by non-Hispanic Whites (7.9%)[3] and non-Hispanic Asian-Americans (7.9%; CDC, 2018). In regard to socioeconomic status, there is negative relationship between income and depressive disorders. For example, 3.5% of individuals who are over 400% higher than the Federal Poverty Line (FPL) have a (or history of a) depressive disorder compared to 15.8% of individuals who fall below the FPL (CDC, 2018).

## *Depression across the Life Course*

Individuals between the ages of 18 and 25 have the highest rates of depressive disorders (NIMH, 2017), and the median age of onset is 32.5 years old (in contrast, the median age of onset for anxiety disorders is 11 and substance use disorders is 20; Kessler et al., 2005). This is highly indicative that depressive disorders occur at nearly all stages of the life course.

## *Depression in Adolescence*

Epidemiological data suggests that an estimated 5% of adolescents (age 10–19) are diagnosed with a depressive disorder each year (Thapar, Collishaw, Pine, & Thapar, 2012), though rates are as high as 20% in later adolescence (Lewinsohn, Rohde, Klein, & Seeley, 1999). Neurocognitive research posits that psychological changes during this time put adolescents at greater risk for sensation seeking, risk taking, impulsivity, mood fluctuations, psychological distress, and a heightened stress response (Angold & Costello, 2006; Kessler et al., 2005). According to the Substance Abuse and Mental Health Services Administration (SAMHSA, 2017a) these traits, in conjunction with biology (i.e., biological predisposition, family history of major depressive disorder) and the environmental stressors of adolescent development, may increase adolescents' vulnerability for psychological health consequences such as a depressive disorder.

Other characteristics may put some adolescents at an even greater risk for developing a depressive disorder. Adolescent females are at greater risk when they experience early pubertal development, while the opposite is true for adolescent males (though generally, depressive disorders are more prevalent in adolescent females; Thapar, Collishaw, Pine, & Thapar, 2012). Additional individual risk factors include psychosocial adversity, a disrupted family environment, and adverse childhood experiences (e.g., abuse, parental divorce, or trauma; see Thapar, Collishaw, Pine, & Thapar, 2012).

### *Depression in Adulthood*

Developmental experts often separate adulthood into sub-developmental stages, namely, emerging-, mid-, and older- adulthood. Because substages of adulthood often look quite different in terms of responsibility, subjective norms, and, physiological development, the manifestation of depressive disorders differs between each stage.

Between 5 and 10% of adults are diagnosed with a depressive disorder each year (CDC, 2018). As is the case with most behavioral disorders, depressive disorders often manifest in adulthood as a result of psychosocial stressors interacting with a genetic predisposition (Lohoff, 2010). In emerging adulthood in particular, environmental stressors involve transitions to major developmental milestones such as moving away from home, entering the job market, settling down with a romantic partner, and/or becoming a parent (see Thapar, Collishaw, Pine, & Thapar, 2012 for a review). In contrast, acute or chronic disease, economic strain, unemployment, minority status, general physical health, and being overworked are believed to be the biggest environmental contributors to depression in mid- and older adulthood (Köhler et al., 2018).

### *Depression in the Juvenile Justice and Criminal System.*

The rates of depressive disorders among offenders within the juvenile and criminal justice systems are concerning, as mental disorders tend to be vastly overrepresented in these populations (e.g., Grande, Hallman, Caldwell, & Underwood, 2011; Otto, Greenstein, Johnson, & Friedman, 1992). Approximately 50–75% of the two million youth that interact with the juvenile justice system meet the criteria for a mental health disorder and 40–80% of detained youth meet the criteria for a mental health disorder (Goldstein, Olubadewo, Redding, & Lexcen, 2005; Grisso, 2004, 2008; Teplin, Abram, McClelland, Dulcan, & Mericle, 2002). Notably, 20% of these youth have a mental disorder that is classified as "severe" (Grisso, 2008). Estimates suggest that approximately 15 to 30% of youth involved with the juvenile justice system have a depressive disorder (Weiss & Garber, 2003), which is three times higher than the adolescent population (Grisso, 1999).

Estimates suggest that over two million individuals with some form of mental health disorder, most often a depressive disorder (of in addition to other mental health disorders), go to jail each year (National Alliance on Mental Illness [NAMI], 2018). Fazel and Seewald (2012) found that the prevalence of depressive disorders ranged from 10–26% within prison systems, though that estimate is likely on the low end as many inmates (an estimated additional 8–12%) reported "mental health problems," and many other individuals were likely undiagnosed (Fazel & Seewald, 2012).

Despite such high prevalence rates, clinical efforts in the juvenile and criminal justice systems are focused more on externalizing behaviors (i.e., aggression) as opposed to internalizing symptomatology (SAMHSA, 2017b). This may be related to the fact that at most, only 5% of all violent crimes are committed by those with a serious mental health disorder such as major depression (SAMHSA, 2017b). Depressive disorders tend to not be a direct "cause" of offending. Instead, individuals with depressive disorders are more likely to experience some form of criminal justice contact given that they are more likely to experience financial strain (either themselves or their family of origin), substance abuse, victimization, and homelessness, all of which may indirectly or directly increase the risk for offending (for a review see Fazel & Seewald, 2012). Individuals with a history of depressive disorders are more likely to engage in illegal behavior (e.g., the making or selling of drugs) to make ends meet (National Healthcare for the Homeless Council, 2012). Alternatively, someone suffering from depressive disorder may self-medicate with illicit substances, bringing one into the purview of the juvenile or criminal justice system as a drug offender (Bureau of Justice Statistics, 2018).

Unfortunately, most offenders with a depressive disorder do not receive mental health care despite mandated efforts by the juvenile and criminal justice systems (Adams & Ferrandino, 2008). Current estimates from the National Institute of Health ([NIH]; Byron, 2014) suggest that over 350,000 offenders with mental health strain leave the criminal justice system untreated each year. In addition, one-third of diagnosed mental health disorders among incarcerated/detained individuals require ongoing care upon release (Goldstein, Olubadewo, Redding, & Lexcen, 2005; Grisso, 2008). Appropriate and continued treatment, if needed, may reduce the risk for recidivism (NIDA, 2018), which would be beneficial given that recidivism rates are nearly 230% higher for those with mental health disorders (via subsequent homelessness, worsened psychiatric states, worse psychiatric care, and financial strain; Baillargeon, Binswanger, Penn, Williams, & Murray, 2009).

## Co-Morbidity of Depression and Substance Use

Co-occurring or co-morbid disorders refer to a person who meets the DSM-IV criteria for at least one mental health disorder (i.e., a depressive disorder) and one substance use disorder (i.e., alcohol disorder or illicit drug use disorder). The disorders must be independent of one another as symptoms cannot simply be a cluster stemming from a single disorder (Flynn & Brown, 2008). According to the National Epidemiologic Survey on Alcohol and Related Conditions (Conway, Compton, Stinson, & Grant, 2006) the prevalence of substance abuse and dependence is twice as high among those with a depressive disorder than that of the general population. Moreover, an estimated 40% of individuals with a substance use disorder also have a co-occurring mental health disorder (SAMHSA, 2017a).

In order to meet criteria for co-occurring disorders, SAMHSA (2017a) requires that the disorders occur simultaneously or within one year of each other. More than eight million adults in the United States have co-occurring mental health and substance use disorders (SAMHSA, 2017a). Put another way, an estimated 3.1% of adult women and 4.1% of adult men have co-occurring disorders. Alcohol-dependent individuals are almost four times more likely to experience a depressive disorder (Hasin, Stinson, Ogburn, & Grant, 2007). Moreover, roughly a third of individuals who have abused marijuana in their lifetime also meet criteria for lifetime history of a depressive disorder (Conway, Compton, Stinson, & Grant, 2006).

Regrettably, co-occurring disorders add complexities to the nature and treatment of both disorders, particularly among populations in which treatment may be more limited (Hasin & Kilcoyne, 2012). For instance, substance abuse can interfere with adherence to treatment for depressive disorders and vice versa, and such interferences can result in more costly and less effective treatment overall (Burns, Teesson, & O'Neill, 2005). Indeed, Greenfield and colleagues (1998) found that alcohol-dependent individuals relapsed or consumed alcohol more quickly after treatment compared to those who did not experience a co-occurring depressive disorder.

Unfortunately, due to the relatively limited knowledge on the treatment of co-occurring disorders, many affected individuals receive care for only one of the two disorders (Horsfall, Cleary, Hunt, & Walter, 2009). Less than 7% of all individuals with co-occurring disorders receive treatment for both (SAMHSA, 2017a). This is especially concerning considering the relationship between depression, substance abuse and suicide (American Association of Suicidology, 2014). Suicide attempts are six times higher among individuals who struggle with mental health disorders and drug abuse/addiction (Dragisic, Dickov, Dickov, & Mijatovic, 2015).

## *Co-Occurring Disorders across the Life Course*

While depressive disorders and substance use both steadily increase through adolescence and generally peak in early adulthood, research suggests that trajectories for co-occurring disorders, more generally, do not follow suit. Extant research suggests that the association between substance use disorders and depressive disorders may be strongest in early adolescence (Schuler, Vasilenko, & Lanza, 2015). In other words, adolescents at risk for more problematic substance use are also those who are more likely to develop a depressive disorder (Schuler, Vasilenko, & Lanza, 2015). More than 340,000 adolescents have a co-occurring depression and substance use disorder. Specifically, adolescents who had experienced a depressive episode in the past year were twice as likely to be heavy alcohol drinkers (SAMHSA, 2017a), and Patton and colleagues (2002) found that adolescents who used marijuana weekly or more were twice as likely to develop a depressive disorder. In general, youth who abuse substances are nearly four times more likely to have a co-occurring depressive disorder (Costello, Armstrong, & Erkanli, 2000).

In contrast to co-occurring disorders in adolescence, much less attention has been given to the prevalence of co-occurring disorders in adulthood. Nonetheless, estimates suggest that approximately eight million adults in the U.S. have co-occurring mental health and substance use disorders.

## Theoretical Foundations for Co-Morbidity

Evidence clearly suggests that substance use disorders and mental health disorders, including depressive disorders, often co-occur. Mueser and colleagues (1998) identify four models for the development of co-occurring disorders: (1) the common risk factor model, which identified shared risk factors for both mental health disorders and substance abuse; (2) the secondary substance abuse disorder model, which suggests that mental health issues increase the risk for developing a substance use disorder; (3) the secondary mental health disorder model, which suggests that substance abuse occurs prior to a mental health disorder among individuals who likely would not develop a mental health disorder independently; and (4) the bi-directional model, which argues that the presence of either disorder increases the vulnerability for developing the other disorder. In their review of the literature, Mueser, Bond, Drake, and Resnick (1998) found the most support for the common risk factor- and the secondary substance abuse disorder model.

The common risk factor model suggests that shared risk factors, either biological or environmental, predispose an individual to both a substance use disorder and a depressive disorder/mental health disorder. In all likelihood, it is the interaction of one's genetics and environment that sets the stage for co-occurring disorders.

## *Biological Risk*

The biological underpinnings of co-occurring disorders are best understood in terms of neuropsychology and brain functioning. Within the brain, chemicals are relayed by neurons via electric and chemical messages during the process of neurotransmission. These electrical and chemical messages facilitate the release of molecules called neurotransmitters; distinct receptors receive the neurotransmitters and generate an electrical impulse (Larimore, 2017). Neurotransmitters, namely serotonin and dopamine (among others), play critical roles in the function of emotion regulation and mood (Hartwell, Tolliver, & Brady, 2009). Certain genes are responsible for disruptions or deficiencies of neurotransmitters in the brain, which, in turn may increase the likelihood of the development of a depressive disorder (NIH, 2007) and/or substance use disorder. For example, serotonin and dopamine deficiencies are closely linked to depressive disorders (Nautiyal & Hen, 2017), and play a major role in the facilitation of intermittent drug use to addiction (Müller & Homberg, 2015). Likewise, those with serotonin and dopamine deficiencies are also more sensitive to the boost of both brain chemicals that accompany drug use, increasing the likelihood of substance abuse and addiction among individuals who are already at risk for mental health disorders such as clinical depression (Müller & Homberg, 2015).

Genetics also predispose individuals to maladaptive brain structures, which disrupt the processes by which neurotransmitters are released and received. Neuropsychological research generally supports the notion that genetics could contribute to comorbidity, as patients suffering from mental health disorders and substance use disorders often experience overlapping abnormalities in the brain, specifically in the basal ganglia, the amygdala, and the prefrontal cortex (NIDA, 2010; SAMHSA, 2016). As such, it may be that an individual with such abnormalities is at a greater risk for developing co-occurring disorders.

## *Environmental Risk*

While there is compelling evidence that genetic factors can account for the risk for co-occurring disorders, factors external to the individual may play a larger role in comorbidity (see Cerdá, Sagdeo, Johnson, & Galea, 2010 for a review). For instance, stress, trauma, and adverse childhood experiences significantly impact psychological processing and regulation, which could put an individual at a greater risk for developing co-occurring disorders (NIDA, 2018). Research supports the influence of adverse childhood experiences—defined as "stressful or traumatic events including abuse or neglect"—on adverse health outcomes (Dube, Anda, Felitti, Edwards, & Croft, 2002; Felitti et al., 1998; Nurius, Green, Logan-Greene, & Borja, 2015). The effects of adverse childhood experiences are a graded dose-response, such that the intensity and frequency of the experience are related to the degree of stress, which often manifests in internalizing (depressive disorder) and externalizing (substance use disorder) symptomatology. As such, children and adults with a history of adverse childhood experiences are at an increased risk for substance use disorders, major depressive disorders, and the co-occurrence of the two (Cicchetti & Toth, 2005), irrespective of genetic predisposition.

Both the secondary substance abuse disorder model and the secondary mental disorder models are behavioral based, suggesting that it is a combination of both biological and environmental influences that leads to comorbidity. More specifically, an individual may develop one disorder due to genetic or environmental causes (or both). The manifestation of one disorder, then, increases the risk for developing the other. For instance, a substance use disorder may lead to the development of a mental health disorder because substance use negatively impacts the motivational and reward centers of the brain (Nestler, 2014). Specifically, substance abuse can facilitate molecular, functional and structural changes in the brain, and these changes may interfere with the ways in which the brain regulates serotonin and dopamine. In turn, deregulated brain chemistry increases the risk for the development of a co-occurring mental health disorder such as a depressive disorder (Robinson & Kolb, 2004).

The self-medication hypothesis, which is within the purview of the secondary substance abuse disorder model, is perhaps the most supported of all theories regarding co-occurring disorders. It poses that individuals cope with untreated mental or physical ailments through substance use, and, in turn, develop an addiction to the substance (Khantzian, 1997). Indeed, among hospitalized drug abusers, most individuals reported using drugs to alleviate symptoms of depression (Weiss, Griffin, & Mirin, 1992). Additional research indicates that many people who use psychodelic drugs do not use them for the euphoric effect; rather, these drugs are used to manage behavioral symptoms (Müller & Schumann, 2011). Bolton, Robinson, and Sareen (2009) found that roughly a quarter of individuals with mood disorders such as depressive disorders self-medicated with alcohol and/or drugs. Thus, the reinforcement and relief that substance use provides for individuals with mental health issues spawns the development of co-occurring substance use disorders. Unfortunately, self-medication is more likely in populations who have little or no access to adequate health care (Steele, Dewa, & Lee, 2007).

## A Special Consideration: Comorbidity and the Juvenile and Criminal Justice Systems

Peters, Wexler, and Lurigio (2015) argued that comorbid disorders are the rule rather than the exception among justice-involved individuals. In fact, comorbid disorders are more common among justice-involved persons than the general population and consume a significant amount of public health, justice system, and community resources (Council of State Governments, 2002; Peters, Wexler, & Lurigio, 2015). Elevated rates of co-occurring substance use and mental health disorders are higher among justice-involved populations in comparison to the general population due to the fact that those with comorbid or co-occurring disorders have more dynamic criminogenic risk factors (such as homelessness, criminal attitudes and peers, and employment problems; Morgan, Fisher, Duan, Mandracchia, & Murray, 2010; Osher, 2013; Skeem & Bibeau, 2008) and those arrested for drug crimes (i.e., possession and sale) have higher rates of co-occurring disorders (Lurigio & Swartz, 2000; Osher, 2013).

Adding further complexity to comorbidity among justice-involved populations is the fact that the combinations of disorders as well as the severity and course vary significantly among justice-involved individuals (Kessler et al., 2005; Flynn & Brown, 2008; Peters, Wexler, & Lurigio, 2015). Unfortunately, precise estimates of comorbid disorders (in terms of specific combinations and the severity of each disorder) are lacking due to barriers discussed subsequently. While rates of mental health disorders are three to six times higher in detained/incarcerated populations (Prins, 2014; Steadman et al, 2009), one estimate suggested that among juvenile detainees with a mental health disorder, nearly three-fifths of females and nearly 75% of males also have at least one substance use disorder (Abram et al., 2003). Among jail and prison inmates with mental health disorders, rates of substance use disorders are higher than those without mental health problems (60% vs. 40% for jail inmates and 74% vs. 56% for prison inmates, Mumola & Karberg, 2006). As such, it is estimated that 10% of male jail inmates and 20% of female jail inmates have co-occurring mental health and substance use disorders. Notably, co-occurring disorders are higher among incarcerated populations in comparison to those who are in community-based corrections.

### *Implications for the Justice System*

In their summary of research of comorbid disorders among justice-involved individuals, Peters and colleagues (2015) noted that while those with co-occurring disorders are more likely to be arrested, these individuals pose additional challenges for either the juvenile or criminal justice system personnel. For instance, those with co-occurring mental health disorders (i.e., mood disorders and not antisocial personality features) are more likely to violate conditions of community supervision (including drug and alcohol restrictions), if incarcerated, these individuals are more difficult to manage in custodial settings. Moreover, those with co-occurring mental health and substance use disorders are more likely to recidivate and be incarcerated (or re-incarcerated) in the year following discharge. Given the relationship between co-occurring mental health disorders and substance use disorders and recidivism, there has been a surge in interest in addressing these co-occurring disorders while one is part of either the juvenile or criminal justice system in order to rehabilitate the offender and attempt to stop the revolving door of justice system participation.

## *Implications for Treatment*

Effective treatment, which ultimately reduces the symptomology associated with either a substance use disorder and depressive disorder as well as reduces the likelihood of recidivism, is often impeded by numerous barriers. First, and foremost, is resource availability. If a correctional system does not have the resources to treat or manage either disorder, the discussion about treatment is moot. If resources for treatment are available, identification and assessment of disorders is met with its own challenges. Personnel at each stage of the juvenile and criminal justice system must have access to relevant instruments (by age and disorder) in order to identify those in need of services. Some instruments may require clinician administration (e.g., Drug Use Screening Inventory-Revised) whereas others can be administered by those without clinical experience anyone via paper and pencil (e.g., Children's Depression Inventory; Brief Jail Mental Health Screen; Mental Health Screening Form-III; Simple Screening Instrument, Texas Christian University Drug Screen-II). Moreover, screening and treatment assignment is often done according to a triage model, where those who need immediate attention and intervention receive services first (Grisso & Underwood, 2004) leaving many with comorbid disorders to go untreated if a disorder is classified as mild or intermittent.

Among those for whom co-occurring disorders are identified, next is the debate over which disorder should be "treated" first. For instance, mental health providers may be unwilling to provide services unless the substance abuse has stopped or substance abuse treatment providers may be unwilling to provide care unless mental health symptoms are under control. In times of great distress, the disorder that results in the most self-harm to the individual should be addressed first. However, for most individuals, simultaneous treatment will likely be most advantageous (given the shared etiology and reciprocity of symptomology).

The delivery of services, if any, to those who are under the purview of either the juvenile or criminal justice system can also undermine the effectiveness for the treatment of one or both disorders. For instance, many jails and prisons do not provide medication assisted treatment for substance use disorders (Ludwig & Peters, 2014) or have limited medication supplies that do not allow an offender to continue with current medication (Daniel, 2007). Moreover, treatment delivery that does not account for the co-morbidity of the disorders as well as other dynamic criminogenic risk factors (e.g., antisocial attitudes or antisocial associates) will fail to result in effective treatment (Andrews & Bonta, 2014; Osher, 2008). There is a low degree of individuals who are licensed or have acquired the training to treat both mental health and substance use disorders. As a result, many treatment agencies that operate in either the juvenile or criminal justice systems are largely unprepared to deal with co-occurring disorders.

Effective treatment more often than not requires care that extends past one's charge with either the juvenile or criminal justice system. Routine and on-going maintenance of the disorder should be a part of everyday life (Kazdin, 1994) and individuals need to be taught relapse prevention skills with continued reinforcement. For many justice-involved individuals, though, economic resources to obtain continued care for either one's depressive disorder and/or substance use disorder(s) are limited. Therefore, continued care is unlikely unless mandated and paid for by the state through the juvenile or criminal justice system (or Medicaid in the case of a mental health disorder such as a depressive disorder).

Other barriers to effective treatment for co-occurring disorders, which exist among the general population as well as justice-involved individuals, include the assessment of both disorders with age-appropriate instruments, treatment readiness by the individual, poor therapeutic alliance of treatment models (and how these models may stand in contrast to juvenile and criminal justice treatment models; Garcia & Weisz, 2002), and therapist-client racial/ethnic match (Garcia & Weisz, 2002).

## *Effective Care*

Given the barriers for treatment of those with co-occurring disorders, particularly those that are involved in either the juvenile or criminal justice systems, Drake and colleagues (2001) identified several components of effective treatment for those with co-occurring disorders. These include services that provide motivational and social support, a comprehensive, multisystem approach, multiple therapeutic modalities, culturally sensitivity and competence among practitioners, and a long-term perspective that includes transition and aftercare services and support. Drake and colleagues (2001) also argued that family involvement is critical in the effectiveness of interventions for adolescents (and likely adults as well).

A growing body of research-based evidence has demonstrated that community based treatment for co-occurring disorders hold promise for effectiveness among justice-involved populations. These include Illness Management and Recovery, integrated group treatment, cognitive-behavioral therapy, therapeutic communities, assertive community treatment, social skills training, and the use of medications to treatment both mental health and substance use issues (NIDA, 2010; Peters, Wexler, & Lurigio, 2015). These treatments are most effective if they treat both the mental health disorder and the substance use disorder(s) as primary conditions, acknowledge the reciprocity between the etiology and symptoms, and have strong therapeutic alliance (Peters, Wexler, & Lurigio, 2015). In fact, Sacks and colleagues (2004, 2012) found that recidivism and reincarceration rates among Therapeutic Community participants in both prison settings and community-based corrections were significantly lower than recidivism and reincarceration rates among those who received traditional mental health services from the criminal justice system. Moreover, Hawkins (2009) notes that while very few adolescent-based programs have been evaluated for co-occurring disorders, motivational enhancement/cognitive behavioral therapy (Dennis et al., 2004) and Multisystemic Therapy (Henggeler, Melton, & Smith, 1992) are promising as evaluations of effectiveness did not exclude youth with co-occurring disorders or a history of juvenile justice involvement. Nonetheless, programs that effectively address any disorder as well as comorbid disorders are not offered universally; most treatment programs that attend to a single disorder or comorbid disorders occur among juvenile or criminal justice (correctional) systems that have strong organizational support and funding for evidence-based practices (Taxman et al., 2008).

We echo the claims of Peters and colleagues (2015) that reforms that invest resources to address co-occurring disorders, whether by diverting non-violent offenders with co-occurring disorders to community-based treatments or providing effective treatment programs within the confines of detention/incarceration of the juvenile and criminal justice system and providing a continuity of care for those discharged from confinement is a wise decision. It will not only benefit the individual offender with co-occurring disorders but it will benefit society as well as it may have the potential to increase public safety and stop the revolving door of justice system involvement (and cost for taxpayers) for at least some.

## Notes

1 Notably, the DSM-5 no longer uses the terms, "substance abuse" and "substance dependence." Rather, the preferred terminology is "substance use disorders."

2 According to the Diagnostic and Statistical Manual of Mental Disorders, Fifth Edition (American Psychiatric Association, 2013) in order to meet criteria for Major Depressive Disorder, an individual must experience five of the nine depressive symptoms characteristic of MDD for at least two weeks. Additionally, one of the five symptoms must be "depressed mood" or "anhedonia."

3 Among American Indian and Alaskan Natives, no national-level data exists on the prevalence of major depression (Garrett, Baldridge, Benson, Crowder, & Aldrich, 2015).

## References

Abram, K. M., Teplin, L. A., McClelland, G. M., & Dulcan, M. K. (2003). Comorbid psychiatric disorders in youth in juvenile detention. *Archives of General Psychiatry*, *60*(11), 1097–1108.

Adams K., & Ferrandino J. (2008). Managing mentally ill inmates in prisons. *Criminal Justice Behavior*, *35*(8), 913–927.

Albert, P. R. (2015). Why is depression more prevalent in women? *Journal of Psychiatry & Neuroscience: JPN*, *40*(4), 219–221. doi:10.1503/jpn.150205.

American Association of Suicidology. (2014). Depression and suicide risk. Retrieved from www.suicidology.org/portals/14/docs/resources/factsheets/2011/depressionsuicide2014.pdf

American Psychiatric Association. (2000). American Psychiatric Association task force on DSM-IV. *Diagnostic and statistical manual of mental disorders: DSM-IV-TR*. 4th ed. Washington, DC: American Psychiatric Association, 513–517.

American Psychiatric Association. (2013). *Diagnostic and statistical manual of mental disorders (DSM-5®)*. Arlington, VA: American Psychiatric Pub.

Andrews, D. A., & Bonta, J. (2014). *The psychology of criminal conduct*. New York: Routledge.

Angold, A., & Costello, E. J. (2006). Puberty and depression. *Child and Adolescent Psychiatric Clinics*, *15*(4), 919–937.

Baillargeon, J., Binswanger, I. A., Penn, J. V., Williams, B. A., & Murray, O. J. (2009). Psychiatric disorders and repeat incarcerations: The revolving prison door. *American Journal of Psychiatry*, *166*(1), 103–109.

Bolton, J. M., Robinson, J., & Sareen, J. (2009). Self-medication of mood disorders with alcohol and drugs in the National Epidemiologic Survey on Alcohol and Related Conditions. *Journal of Affective Disorders*, *115*(3), 367–375. doi:10.1016/j.jad.2008.10.003.

Bureau of Justice Statistics. (2018). *Drug and crime facts: Drug use and crime*. Retrieved from www.bjs.gov/content/dcf/duc.cfm

Burns, L., Teesson, M., & O'Neill, K. (2005). The impact of comorbid anxiety and depression on alcohol treatment outcomes. *Addiction*, *100*(6), 787–796. doi:10.1111/j.1360-0443.2005.001069.x.

Byron, R. (2014). Criminals need mental health care: Psychiatric treatment is far better than imprisonment for reducing recidivism. *Scientific American*. Retrieved from www.scientificamerican.com/article/criminals-need-mental-health-care/

Centers for Disease Control. (2014). *Depression in the U.S. household population, 2009–2012*. Retrieved from www.cdc.gov/nchs/data/databriefs/db172.htm

Centers for Disease Control. (2018). *Prevalence of depression among adults aged 20 and over: Untied States, 2013–2016*. Retrieved from www.cdc.gov/nchs/products/databriefs/db303.htm

Cerdá, M., Sagdeo, A., Johnson, J., & Galea, S. (2010). Genetic and environmental influences on psychiatric comorbidity: A systematic review. *Journal of Affective Disorders*, *126*(1–2). doi:10.1016/j.jad.2009.11.006.

Chassin, L. (2008). Juvenile justice and substance use. *The Future of Children*, *18*(2), 165–183.

Cicchetti, D., & Toth, S. L. (2005). Child maltreatment. *Annual Review of Clinical Psychology*, *1*, 409–438.

Conway, K. P., Compton, W., Stinson, F. S., & Grant, B. F. (2006). Lifetime comorbidity of DSM-IV mood and anxiety disorders and specific drug use disorders: Results from the national epidemiologic survey on alcohol and related conditions. *The Journal of Clinical Psychiatry*, *67*(2), 247–257.

Costello, E. J., Armstrong, T. D., & Erkanli, A. (2000). Report on the developmental epidemiology of comorbid psychiatric and substance use disorders. Presented to the National Institute on Drug Abuse. Durham, NC: Duke University Medical Center.

Council of State Governments. (2002). Criminal justice/mental health consensus project. Retrieved from www.ncjrs.gov/pdffiles1/nij/grants/197103.pdf

D'Amico, E. J., Ellickson, P. L., Collins, R. L., Martino, S., & Klein, D. J. (2005). Processes linking adolescent problems to substance-use problems in late young adulthood. *Journal of Studies on Alcohol*, *66*(6), 766–775.

Daniel, A. E. (2007). Care of the mentally ill in prisons: Challenges and solutions. *Journal of the American Academy of Psychiatry and the Law*, *35*, 406–410.

De La Haye, K., D'Amico, E. J., Miles, J. N., Ewing, B., & Tucker, J. S. (2014). Covariance among multiple health risk behaviors in adolescents. *PloS one, 9*(5), e98141.

Dennis, M., Godley, S. H., Diamond, G., Tims, F. M., Babor, T., Donaldson, J., Liddle, H., Titus, J. C., Kaminer, Y., Webb, C., Hamilton, N., & Funk, R. (2004). The Cannabis Youth Treatment (CYT) study: Main findings from two randomized trials. *Journal of Substance Abuse Treatment, 27*(3), 197–213.

Dragisic, T., Dickov, A., Dickov, V., & Mijatovic, V. (2015). Drug addiction as risk for suicide attempts. *Materia Socio-Medica, 27*(3), 188–191. doi:10.5455/msm.2015.27.188-191.

Drake, R. E., Goldman, H. H., Leff, H. S., Lehman, A. F., Dixon, L., Mueser, K. T., & Torrey, W. C. (2001). Implementing evidence-based practices in routine mental health service settings. *Psychiatric Services, 52*(2), 179–182.

Dube, S., Anda, R., Felitti, V., Edwards, V., & Croft, J. (2002). Adverse childhood experiences and personal alcohol abuse as an adult. *Addictive Behaviors, 27*, 713–725.

Eaton, D. K., Kann, L., Kinchen, S., Shanklin, S., Ross, J., Hawkins, J., ... & Lim, C. (2010). Youth risk behavior surveillance-United States, 2009. *MMWR Surveillence Summary, 59*(5), 1–142.

Fazel, S., & Seewald, K. (2012). Severe mental illness in 33 588 prisoners worldwide: Systematic review and meta-regression analysis. *The British Journal of Psychiatry, 200*(5), 364–373.

Felitti, V. J., Anda, R. F., Nordenberg, D., Williamson, D. F., Spitz, A. M., Edwards, V., & Marks, J. S. (1998). Relationship of childhood abuse and household dysfunction to many of the leading causes of death in adults: The Adverse Childhood Experiences (ACE) study. *American Journal of Preventive Medicine, 14*(4), 245–258.

Flynn, P. M., & Brown, B. S. (2008). Co-occurring disorders in substance abuse treatment: Issues and prospects. *Journal of Substance Abuse Treatment, 34*(1), 36–47.

Garcia, J. A., & Weisz, J. R. (2002). When youth mental health care stops: Therapeutic relationship problems and other reasons for ending youth outpatient treatment. *Journal of Consulting and Clinical Psychology, 70*(2), 439.

Garrett, M., Baldridge, D., Benson, W., Crowder, J., & Aldrich, N. (2015). Mental health disorders among an invisible minority: Depression and dementia among American Indian and Alaska native elders. *The Gerontologist, 55*(2), 227–236. doi:10.1093/geront/gnu181.

Goldstein, N., Olubadewo, O., Redding, R., & Lexcen, F. (2005). Mental health disorders: The neglected risk factor in juvenile delinquency.

Grande, T., Hallman, J., Caldwell, K., & Underwood, L. (2011). Using the BASC-2 to assess mental health needs of incarcerated juveniles: Implications for treatment and release. *Corrections Today, 73*(5), 100–102.

Greenfield, S., Weiss, R., Muenz, L., Vagge, L., Kelly, J., Bello, L., & Michael J. (1998). The effect of depression on return to drinking: A prospective study. *Archives of General Psychiatry, 55*(3), 259–265.

Grisso, T. (1999). Juvenile offenders and mental illness. *Psychiatry, Psychology and Law, 6*(2), 143–151.

Grisso, T. (2004). *Double jeopardy: Adolescent offenders with mental disorders.* Chicago, IL: University of Chicago Press.

Grisso, T. (2008). Adolescent offenders with mental disorders. *The Future of Children, 18*(2), 143–164.

Grisso, T., & Underwood, L. A. (2004). Screening and Assessing mental health and substance use disorders among youth in the juvenile justice system. A resource guide for practitioners. *US Department of Justice.*

Hartwell, K. J., Tolliver, B. K., & Brady, K. T. (2009). Biologic commonalities between mental illness and addiction. *Primary Psychiatry, 16*(8), 33.

Hasin, D., & Kilcoyne, B. (2012). Comorbidity of psychiatric and substance use disorders in the United States: Current issues and findings from the NESARC. *Current Opinion in Psychiatry, 25*(3), 165–171. doi:10.1097/YCO.0b013e3283523dcc.

Hasin, D. S., Stinson, F. S., Ogburn, E., & Grant, B. F. (2007). Prevalence, correlates, disability, and comorbidity of DSM-IV alcohol abuse and dependence in the United States: Results from the National Epidemiologic Survey on Alcohol and Related Conditions. *Archives of General Psychiatry, 64*(7), 830–842.

Hawkins, E. H. (2009). A tale of two systems: Co-occurring mental health and substance abuse disorders treatment for adolescents. *Annual Review of Psychology, 60*, 197–227.

Hawkins, J. D., Van Horn, M. L., & Arthur, M. W. (2004). Community variation in risk and protective factors and substance use outcomes. *Prevention Science, 5*(4), 213–220.

Henggeler, S. W., Melton, G. B., & Smith, L. A. (1992). Family preservation using multisystemic therapy: An effective alternative to incarcerating serious juvenile offenders. *Journal of Consulting and Clinical Psychology, 60*(6), 953–961.

Horsfall, J., Cleary, M., Hunt, G. E., & Walter, G. (2009). Psychosocial treatments for people with co-occurring severe mental illnesses and substance use disorders (dual diagnosis): A review of empirical evidence. *Harvard Review of Psychiatry, 17*(1), 24–34. doi:10.1080/10673220902724599.

Hser, Y. I., Hoffman, V., Grella, C. E., & Anglin, M. D. (2001). A 33-year follow-up of narcotics addicts. *Archives of General Psychiatry, 58*(5), 503–508.

Huang, B., Grant, B. F., Dawson, D. A., Stinson, F. S., Chou, S. P., Saha, T. D., ... & Pickering, R. P. (2006). Race-ethnicity and the prevalence and co-occurrence of diagnostic and statistical manual of mental disorders, alcohol and drug use disorders and Axis I and II disorders: United States, 2001 to 2002. *Comprehensive Psychiatry, 47*(4), 252–257.

Jordan, C. J., & Andersen, S. L. (2017). Sensitive periods of substance abuse: Early risk for the transition to dependence. *Developmental Cognitive Neuroscience, 25*, 29–44.

Kazdin, A. E. (1994). Methodology, design, and evaluation in psychotherapy research. In A. E. Bergin & S. L. Garfield (Eds.), *Handbook of psychotherapy and behavior change* (pp. 19–71). Oxford, UK: John Wiley & Sons.

Kessler, R. C., Berglund, P., Demler, O., Jin, R., Merikangas, K. R., & Walters, E. E. (2005). Lifetime prevalence and age-of-onset distributions of DSM-IV disorders in the national comorbidity survey replication. *Archives of General Psychiatry, 62*(6), 593–602.

Khantzian, E. J. (1997). The self-medication hypothesis of substance use disorders: A reconsideration and recent applications. *Harvard Review of Psychiatry, 4*(5), 231–244. doi:10.3109/10673229709030550.

Köhler, C. A., Evangelou, E., Stubbs, B., Solmi, M., Veronese, N., Belbasis, L., Bortolato, B., Melo, M. C. A., Coelho, C. A., Fernandes, B. S., Olfson, M., Ioannidis, J. P. A., & Carvalho, A. F. (2018). Mapping risk factors for depression across the lifespan: an umbrella review of evidence from meta-analyses and Mendelian randomization studies. *Journal of Psychiatric Research, 103*, 189–207.

Larimore, J. (2017). *Neuroscience basics: A guide to the brain's involvement in everyday activities.* Cambridge, MA: Academic Press.

Lewinsohn, P. M., Rohde, P., Klein, D. N., & Seeley, J. R. (1999). Natural course of adolescent major depressive disorder: I. Continuity into young adulthood. *Journal of the American Academy of Child & Adolescent Psychiatry, 38*(1), 56–63.

Lipari, R. N. & Van Horn, S. L. (2017). *Trends in substance use disorders among adults aged 18 or older.* The CBHSQ Report: June 29, 2017. Rockville, MD: Center for Behavioral Health Statistics and Quality, Substance Abuse and Mental Health Services Administration.

Loeber, R., Farrington, D. P., & Petechuk, D. (2003). *Child delinquency: Early intervention and prevention.* Washington, DC: US Department of Justice, Office of Justice Programs, Office of Juvenile Justice and Delinquency Prevention.

Lohoff, F. W. (2010). Overview of the genetics of major depressive disorder. *Current Psychiatry Reports, 12*(6), 539–546. doi:10.1007/s11920-010-0150-6.

Ludwig, A. S., & Peters, R. H. (2014). Medication-assisted treatment for opioid use disorders in correctional settings: An ethics review. *International Journal of Drug Policy, 25*(6), 1041–1046.

Lurigio, A. J., & Swartz, J. A. (2000). Changing the contours of the criminal justice system to meet the needs of persons with serious mental illness. *Criminal Justice, 3*, 45–108.

Lytle, L. A., Kelder, S. H., Perry, C. L., & Klepp, K. I. (1995). Covariance of adolescent health behaviors: The Class of 1989 study. *Health Education Research, 10*(2), 133–146.

MacArthur, G. J., Smith, M. C., Melotti, R., Heron, J., Macleod, J., Hickman, M., ... & Lewis, G. (2012). Patterns of alcohol use and multiple risk behaviour by gender during early and late adolescence: The ALSPAC cohort. *Journal of Public Health, 34*(suppl_1), i20–i30.

McClelland, G. M., Teplin, L. A., & Abram, K. M. (2004). *Detection and prevalence of substance use among juvenile detainees.* Washington, DC: US Department of Justice, Office of Justice Programs, Office of Juvenile Justice and Delinquency Prevention.

Mericle, A. A., Arria, A. M., Meyers, K., Cacciola, J., Winters, K. C., & Kirby, K. (2015). National trends in adolescent substance use disorders and treatment availability: 2003–2010. *Journal of Child & Adolescent Substance Abuse, 24*(5), 255–263.

Millstein, S. G., Irwin, C. E., Adler, N. E., Cohn, L. D., Kegeles, S. M., & Dolcini, M. M. (1992). Health-risk behaviors and health concerns among young adolescents. *Pediatrics, 89*(3), 422–428.

Morgan, R. D., Fisher, W. H., Duan, N., Mandracchia, J. T., & Murray, D. (2010). Prevalence of criminal thinking among state prison inmates with serious mental illness. *Law and Human Behavior, 34*(4), 324–336.

Mueser, K. T., Bond, G. R., Drake, R. E., & Resnick, S. G. (1998). Models of community care for severe mental illness: A review of research on case management. *Schizophrenia Bulletin, 24*(1), 37–74.

Müller, C. P., & Homberg, J. R. (2015). The role of serotonin in drug use and addiction. *Behavioural Brain Research, 277*, 146–192.

Müller, C. P., & Schumann, G. (2011). Drugs as instruments: A new framework for non-addictive psychoactive drug use. *Behavioral and Brain Sciences, 34*(6), 293–310.

Mumola, C. J., & Karberg, J. C. (2006). *Drug use and dependence, state and federal prisoners, 2004*. Retrieved from www.bjs.gov/content/pub/pdf/dudsfp04.pdf

National Alliance on Mental Illness. (2018). *Jailing people with mental illness*. Retrieved from www.nami.org/Learn-More/Public-Policy/Jailing-People-with-Mental-Illness

National Health Care for the Homeless Council. (2012). *Criminal justice, homelessness, & health*. Nashville, TN. Retrieved from www.nhchc.org/wp-content/uploads/2011/09/Criminal-Justice-2012.pdf

National Institute of Mental Health. (2017). *Depression*. Retrieved from www.nimh.nih.gov/health/topics/depression/index.shtml

National Institute on Drug Abuse. (2010). *Comorbidity: Addiction and other mental illnesses*. Retrieved from www.drugabuse.gov/sites/default/files/rrcomorbidity.pdf

National Institute on Drug Abuse. (2018). *Common physical and mental health comorbidities with substance use disorders*. Retrieved from https://d14rmgtrwzf5a.cloudfront.net/sites/default/files/1155-common-physical-and-mental-health-comorbidities-with-substance-use-disorders.pdf

National Institutes of Health. (2007). *NIH Curriculum supplement series: Information about mental illness and the brain*. Bethesda, MD. Retrieved from www.ncbi.nlm.nih.gov/books/NBK20369/

Nautiyal, K. M., & Hen, R. (2017). Serotonin receptors in depression: From A to B. *F1000Research, 6*, 123. doi:10.12688/f1000research.9736.1.

Nestler, E. J. (2014). Epigenetic mechanisms of drug addiction. *Neuropharmacology, 76*, 259–268.

Nurius, P. S., Green, S., Logan-Greene, P., & Borja, S. (2015). Life course pathways of adverse childhood experiences toward adult psychological well-being: A stress process analysis. *Child Abuse & Neglect, 45*, 143–153.

Osher, F. C. (2008). Integrated mental health/substance abuse responses to justice involved persons with co-occurring disorders. *Journal of Dual Diagnosis, 4*(1), 3–33.

Osher, F. C. (2013). Integrating mental health and substance abuse services for justice-involved persons with co-occurring disorders. Retrieved from http://gainscenter.samhsa.gov

Otto, R. K., Greenstein, J., Johnson, M. K., & Friedman, R. (1992). Prevalence of mental disorders in the juvenile justice system. In Cocozza, J. (ed.), *Responding to the mental health needs of youth in the juvenile justice system*. Seattle, WA: The National Coalition for the Mentally Ill in the Criminal Justice System.

Patton, G. C., Coffey, C., Carlin, J. B., Degenhardt, L., Lynskey, M., & Hall, W. (2002). Cannabis use and mental health in young people: Cohort study. *British Medical Journal, 325*(7374), 1195–1198.

Peiper, N. C., Ridenour, T. A., Hochwalt, B., & Coyne-Beasley, T. (2016). Overview on prevalence and recent trends in adolescent substance use and abuse. *Child and Adolescent Psychiatric Clinics, 25*(3), 349–365.

Peters, R. H., Wexler, H. K., & Lurigio, A. J. (2015). Co-occurring substance use and mental disorders in the criminal justice system: A new frontier of clinical practice and research. *American Psychological Association, 38*(1), 1–6.

Prins, S. J. (2014). Prevalence of mental illnesses in US state prisons: A systematic review. *Psychiatric Services, 65*(7), 862–872.

Robinson, T. E., & Kolb, B. (2004). Structural plasticity associated with exposure to drugs of abuse. *Neuropharmacology, 47*, 33–46.

Rutter, M. (1996). Transitions and turning points in developmental psychopathology: As applied to the age span between childhood and mid-adulthood. *International Journal of Behavioral Development, 19*, 603–626.

Sacks, S., Sacks, J. Y., McKendrick, K., Banks, S., & Stommel, J. (2004). Modified TC for MICA offenders: Crime outcomes. *Behavioral Sciences & the Law, 22*(4), 477–501.

Sacks, S., Chaple, M., Sacks, J. Y., McKendrick, K., & Cleland, C. M. (2012). Randomized trial of a reentry modified therapeutic community for offenders with co-occurring disorders: Crime outcomes. *Journal of Substance Abuse Treatment, 42*(3), 247–259.

SAMHSA. (2011). *Results from the 2010 National survey on drug use and health: Summary of national findings, NSDUH Series H-41, HHS Publication No. (SMA) 11-4658*. Rockville, MD: Substance Abuse and Mental Health Services Administration.

SAMHSA. (2016). *Chapter 2: The neurobiology of substance use, misuse, and addiction*. Washington, DC: U.S. Department of Health and Human Services.

SAMHSA. (2017a). *Key substance use and mental health indicators in the United States: Results from the 2016 national survey on drug use and health (HHS Publication No. SMA 17-5044, NSDUH Series H-52)*. Rockville, MD. Retrieved from www.samhsa.gov/data/

SAMHSA. (2017b). *Criminal and juvenile justice*. Rockville, MD. Retrieved from www.samhsa.gov/criminal-juvenile-justice

Schuler, M. S., Vasilenko, S. A., & Lanza, S. T. (2015). Age-varying associations between substance use behaviors and depressive symptoms during adolescence and young adulthood. *Drug and Alcohol Dependence, 157*, 75–82.

Schulte, M. T., & Hser, Y. I. (2014). Substance use and associated health conditions throughout the lifespan. *Public Health Reviews, 35*(2). doi: 10.1007/BF03391702.

Skeem, J., & Bibeau, L. (2008). How does violence potential relate to crisis intervention team responses to emergencies? *Psychiatric Services, 59*(2), 201–204.

Steadman, H. J., Osher, F. C., Robbins, P. C., Case, B., & Samuels, S. (2009). Prevalence of serious mental illness among jail inmates. *Psychiatric Services, 60*(6), 761–765.

Steele, L., Dewa, C., & Lee, K. (2007). Socioeconomic status and self-reported barriers to mental health service use. *The Canadian Journal of Psychiatry, 52*(3), 201–206.

Steinberg, L. (2015). *Age of opportunity: Lessons from the new science of adolescence.* New York: Houghton Mifflin Harcourt Publishing Company.

Taxman, F. S., Cropsey, K. L., Melnick, G., & Perdoni, M. L. (2008). COD services in community correctional settings: An examination of organizational factors that affect service delivery. *Behavioral Sciences & the Law, 26*(4), 435–455.

Teplin, L. A., Abram, K. M., McClelland, G. M., Dulcan, M. K., & Mericle, A. A. (2002). Psychiatric disorders in youth in juvenile detention. *Archives of General Psychiatry, 59*(12), 1133–1143.

Thapar, A., Collishaw, S., Pine, D. S., & Thapar, A. K. (2012). Depression in adolescence. *The Lancet, 379*(9820), 1056–1067.

Van Etten, M. L., & Anthony, J. C. (2001). Male–female differences in transitions from first drug opportunity to first use: Searching for subgroup variation by age, race, region, and urban status. *Journal of Women's Health & Gender-Based Medicine, 10*(8), 797–804.

Weiss, B., & Garber, J. (2003). Developmental differences in the phenomenology of depression. *Development and Psychopathology, 15*(2), 403–430.

Weiss, R. D., Griffin, M. L., & Mirin, S. M. (1992). Drug abuse as self-medication for depression: An empirical study. *The American Journal of Drug and Alcohol Abuse, 18*(2), 121–129. doi:10.3109/00952999208992825.

World Health Organization. (2018). *Depression.* Retrieved from www.who.int/news-room/fact-sheets/detail/depression

# 14
# THE HEALTH CONSEQUENCES OF VICTIMIZATION

*Chad Posick and Kalynn Gruenfelder*

## Introduction

Violence is a serious public health concern that has received considerable attention from academics and practitioners. This attention is for good reason. Exposure to violence is prevalent in society and this exposure comes at great expense to those directly affected as well as their communities as a whole. For instance, the 2011 National Survey of Children's Exposure to Violence II (NatSCEV) study concluded that almost 60% of children (57.7%) were exposed to physical, sexual, property, maltreatment, or witnessing violence in their lifetime. Almost half of all children (48.4%) were exposed to more than one of the previously mentioned forms of violence (Finkelhor et al., 2015).

The National Child Abuse and Neglect Data System (NCANDS) reported that over three million reports were made to child service agencies in 2014 which included over six-and-a-half million children (DHHS, 2014). Youth and young adults ages 12–24 are victimized at some of the highest rates around 41 per every 100,000 individuals (Morgan & Kena, 2017). Obviously, abuse is not isolated to children and adolescents. Over 10 million individuals report physical domestic violence a year – about 1 in 3 women and 1 in 4 men (Black et al., 2011). In all, victimization touches individuals across the US of every race, sex, and age.

The consequences of victimization are significant. A host of negative social and biological outcomes are the result of exposure to violence impacting individuals across their lifecourse. Of course, the most serious negative health outcome of violence is death. Almost 18,000 people died as the result of homicide in 2015 (5.5 per 100,000 people in the US overall and 11 per 100,000 people for those between the ages 25–34) (Murphy et al., 2017). For those who survive their exposure to violence, other health maladies are inflicted. A short list of these maladies include: fear of becoming a repeat victim, negative emotionality, post-traumatic stress disorder, physical injury, and contracting sexually transmitted diseases (Black et al., 2011; Posick, 2014). These outcomes will be discussed in detail throughout this chapter.

Given the prevalence of exposure to victimization and the potentially severe health consequences, in-depth considerations of this topic are warranted. Luckily, a rather large literature base exists on the role of victimization on negative health outcomes that can be synthesized and discussed in order to establish promising approaches to reduce poor health outcomes in individuals. In this chapter, we will review the direct impacts of victimization on health, discuss the mediators and moderators of the victimization → health link, and review promising approaches to reduce the negative health consequences of victimization.

## Direct Effects of Violence on Health

Perhaps one of the most prevalent consequence of victimization is on **mental health**. Victims of violence (and property crime) often have some level of emotional distress and many have severe reactions related to anxiety, depression, and anger (Norman et al., 2012; Springer et al., 2007). In their study of abused children, Banyard, Williams, and Siegel (2001) found that both childhood sexual abuse and childhood abuse was related to various mental health conditions in adulthood including anxious arousal, depression, disassociation, avoidant behavior, and sexual dysfunction. Individuals who experienced sexual and physical abuse were also more likely to experience other forms of trauma leading to "cumulative effects" and lifelong feelings of powerlessness and betrayal. Other studies have similarly found that those who are exposed to trauma, abuse, and neglect also experience other stressful life events that accumulate negative effects across childhood and adolescence into adulthood (see Cecil et al., 2017; Horwitz et al., 2001). As the frequency of abuse increases, so does the severity of mental health symptoms (Horwitz et al., 2001).

Children who are sexually abused are also more likely to have had psychiatric treatment than their non-abused counterparts. In one study, both males and females who were sexually abused received counseling at greater rates than non-abused children for disorders including anxiety disorders, personality disorders, and major affective disorders. Interestingly, they found that males were more than twice as likely as females to seek treatment (22.8% vs. 10.2%) (Spataro et al., 2004). Along with sexual abuse, emotional abuse has been found as a main factor behind psychiatric treatment for males and females (Cecil et al., 2017).

The behavioral consequences of experiencing the emotional distress following abuse and neglect can be very serious. Children who have experienced physical and sexual abuse are several times more likely to have attempted suicide than non-abused children. These children are also more likely to exhibit risky sexual behavior (Norman et al., 2012). A longitudinal study carried out by Herrenkohl and colleagues (2013) followed study participants for over 30 years and found that participants who were abused in childhood were over twice as likely to experience moderate to severe depression and anxiety in adulthood compared to those who were not abused. Exposure to violence often leads to hopelessness which, in turn, leads to various problems related to emotional health. This is particularly so for females (Umlauf et al., 2015).

Along with mental health, **physical health** also suffers after experiencing victimization. As previously mentioned, death can be a physical consequence of victimization but it is relatively rare. Minor forms of negative physical health outcomes are more common than death. In a study conducted by Springer and colleagues (2007), abuse was linked with a host of negative physical health problems such as high blood pressure, liver problems, heart trouble, ulcers, circulation problems, and even allergies. The impact of abuse on these physical problems were generally weaker than for mental health but still significant. The impact of intimate partner violence increases a host of chronic physical health conditions and persistent injury among both men and women (Coker et al., 2002).

The abuse → physical health link was expanded upon in subsequent studies. Afifi and her co-authors (2016) revealed that abuse was related to high blood pressure, arthritis, fatigue, stroke, and cancer. Robust relationships were found between abuse and back problems, migraine headaches, and bowel disease. Victimization by peers increased negative somatic symptoms and sleep disturbance in a study conducted by Herge, La Greca, and Chan (2015). Individuals exposed to victimization by their peers reported headaches, nausea, and "feeling sick" as well as trouble falling asleep and staying asleep in the weeks after their victimization.

Exposure to trauma increases inflammation, which itself is linked to several disorders. Inflammation is a regular, and necessary, process where white blood cells ready themselves to protect the body against infection. This process often results in redness or swollenness around the areas carrying out the defense. Exposure to traumatic experiences can increase inflammation in the body even when it is not totally necessary. Cumulative stress in childhood can result in chronic inflammation in adulthood (Rasmussen et al., 2018). Inflammation also leads to a reduction of regulatory T-cells which has been associated with several physical health problems. Individuals with reduced t-cell production suffer from inflammatory bowel disorder and rheumatoid arthritis to a greater extent than those with normal levels of t-cells (Hemmings et al., 2017).

The most severe and **chronic offenders** are also those who have experienced high levels of trauma in their life. As individuals experience a greater number of traumatic events, their chances of becoming a violent, chronic offender also increases (Fox et al., 2015). Indeed, exposure to victimization increases a wide variety of offenses including property crime, violent crime, and drug use (Posick, 2013; Zimmerman & Posick, 2016). In fact, exposure to victimization increases the risk of offending across the life-course; however, the impact attenuates over time (Farrell & Zimmerman, 2018). The knowledge base on the victim-offender overlap is clear that aggressive and antisocial behavior is a common behavioral consequence of exposure to victimization.

One of the more consequential impacts of victimization is on **brain health**. The hippocampus is an important brain region involved with learning and memory. Additionally, the hippocampus regulated the functioning of the hypothalamic pituitary adrenal axis which influences the response to environmental stress. Individuals who have experienced victimization show reduced hippocampal volume compared to controls (including non-victimized twins). The impact of victimization on hippocampal volume is greatest in middle childhood and less so in early childhood and adolescence (Karl et al., 2006; Teicher & Samson, 2016).

Not only is the hippocampus a target of victimization but so are other brain regions, particularly those in the pre-frontal cortex. The anterior cingulate cortex, dorsolateral prefrontal cortex, and orbitofrontal cortex are all modified by victimization experiences. Changes in these brain regions often disrupt neurotransmitters and neurohormones both of which are related to regulating stress and other emotions. These modifications may be adaptive responses to increase the chance of survival and reproduction (Teicher & Samson, 2016).

A robust finding in the victimization literature is that exposure to victimization can lead to several **negative lifestyle and health-related outcomes**. Being bullied and victimized by peers can have significant impact on individual health including sleeping behaviors. A meta-analysis conducted on 21 studies of over 360,000 youth found that peer victimization is associated with loss of sleep and other sleep-related problems. The effect was pronounced for younger children than older adolescence (van Geel, Goemans, & Vedder, 2016).

Along with sleep, physical activity often diminishes after being exposed to a traumatic experience. In a study of adolescent males and females, peer victimization was correlated with a reduction in physical activity. The link from victimization to diminished physical activity was depression and loneliness. Victimization increased feelings of depression and loneliness which then led to a reduction in physical activity (Storch et al., 2006).

A host of eating disorders are also related to victimization. Binge eating (Brewerton, Cotton, & Kilpatrick, 2018), purging (Brewerton et al., 2015), and other eating-disordered behavior like "driving for thinness" (Kimber et al., 2017) have resulted from exposure to victimization. These disorders not only have direct effects on the body but also exacerbate existing conditions. Broader unhealthy eating patterns are common among victims of violence as well. For example, consumption of energy drinks, one unhealthy eating behavior, was found to increase as exposure to violence increased (Jackson et al., 2018). The victimization-energy drink consumption link was found for property and violent crime and was especially pronounced for females.

When considering the direct effects of exposure to victimization on mental, physical, and behavioral health, it is not surprising that violence is a significant public health issue. To gain a better understanding of *how* exposure to victimization leads to negative health outcomes, it is necessary to dig further into the mechanisms that mediate, or link, victimization experiences to those health outcomes. One important mediator is the brain. In the next section, we discuss how exposure to victimization negatively impacts the brain which then leads to myriad mental, physical, and behavioral health issues.

## The Mediators of the Victimization to Poor Health Link

When linking victimization to socio-behavioral health, it is necessary to explore how the environmental exposure to violence impact **brain structure and function**. The effects of childhood victimization (i.e., neglect, physical abuse, sexual abuse, and emotional abuse) have appreciable impact on the brain and stretch across the lifespan. Teicher and Samson (2016) found childhood trauma accounts for nearly half of the risk for future psychiatric disorders. Neuroimaging studies identified links between changes in brain structure and function and adverse events in childhood. Researchers focused on areas involved in the limbic system, specifically the hippocampus, amygdala, and the cerebral cortex, finding decreased brain volume in adults with histories of abuse.

The theories that explain neurobiological changes caused from childhood adversity do so primarily from the perspective of "limbic irritability," which explains the damage the limbic system endures from stress. The limbic system is the oldest part of the brain which regulates basic emotions (e.g., fear) and forms memories (Carlson, 2013); therefore, chronic stress can negatively impact basic emotions and memory function. Teicher et al. (2003) posited areas of the brain that are vulnerable to early stress have "a protracted postnatal development, a high density of glucocorticoid receptors, and some degree of postnatal neurogenesis" (p. 34). For example, stressful events trigger the release of stress hormones and neurotransmitters that affect vulnerable brain regions and alters the way the stress systems work. Specifically, stressful events trigger multiple stress-response systems, including the glucocorticoid, noradrenergic, and vasopressin-oxytocin systems, resulting in the release of neurotransmitters, which, in turn, affect basic brain processes, such as neurogenesis, synaptic overproduction, pruning, and myelination during sensitive periods of development. Researchers believe that the introduction of stress causes the brain to not function as it is supposed to function (Teicher et al., 2003; Teicher & Samson, 2016).

Researchers interested in the neurobiological effects of victimization often focus on the hippocampus because of its involvement in the limbic system (i.e., forms and retrieves memories; Nadel, Campbell, & Ryan, 2007) and its dense population of glucocorticoid receptors, making it vulnerable to the release of excessive glucocorticoids (e.g., cortisol), which are involved in the stress response (Sapolsky, Krey, & McEwen, 1985). Continued exposure to cortisol results in cell loss and no glucocorticoid receptor recovery in the hippocampus in rats, potentially accounting for quicker functional deterioration (Sapolsky, Krey, & McEwen, 1985).

Prior research uncovered similar patterns between early-life stress and the volume of the hippocampus in humans. Meta-analyses found adult survivors of childhood victimization appear to have smaller hippocampi when compared to adults without a history of abuse, such that the more severe the abuse, the smaller the hippocampi (Karl et al., 2006; Teicher & Samson, 2016). In addition, research suggests that female hippocampi are less vulnerable to the effects of stress. Karl et al. (2006) found that adult men with prior exposure to adversity showed the greatest decrease in hippocampal volume compared to adult women with prior exposure. Genetic variation also appears to play a role between changes in hippocampal structure, childhood victimization, and gender. Males carrying the short allele of the serotonin transporter-linked polymorphic genotype exposed to severe childhood adversity showed decreased volume while the same effect was not seen in females, indicating an interaction between gender, genetic variation, and severity of childhood adversity (Everaerd et al., 2012). The attenuation of glucocorticoid receptors in the hippocampus results in decreased regulation of the stress response, leading to a stronger stress response (Teicher et al., 2002).

Interestingly, the correlation between hippocampal volume and early adversity is not as strong in juveniles suggesting this effect only becomes evident in adulthood (Karl et al., 2006; Teicher & Samson, 2016). Of the 16 studies analyzed by Teicher and Samson (2016), nine showed no significant attenuation. Only two studies found an increase in volume (Tupler & De Bellis, 2006; Whittle et al., 2013); however, one of those two studies found a significant decrease in hippocampal growth in participants over the next four years (Whittle et al., 2013). Furthermore, Teicher and Samson (2016) found an older mean age of participants in studies that showed attenuation compared to those that did not find not. They proposed the existence of a silent period between the exposure of a traumatic event and the measurable neurological changes because attenuation emerges sometime between puberty and adulthood, explaining the mixed results.

The amygdala is another region of interest to researchers examining the effects of victimization. It is a region in the limbic system that is considered the "emotional hub" of the brain containing a high density of glucocorticoid receptors and grows rapidly postnatally, making it vulnerable to the excessive levels of cortisol experienced during periods of stress (Uematsu et al., 2012). The amygdala also plays an important role in the limbic system, identifying emotional cues and potential threats. The effects of trauma on the amygdala appear complex. People with early exposure to maltreatment showed an increase in amygdala volume (Lupien et al., 2011; Mehta et al., 2009; Tottenham et al., 2010); however, early trauma exposure followed by future stress (e.g., combat stress in adulthood, multiple trauma exposures in childhood, psychopathology) leads to decreased amygdala volume (Kuo, Kaloupek, & Woodward, 2012; Malykhin et al., 2012; Whittle et al., 2013). Furthermore, those without early trauma exposure and later combat stress in adulthood, showed no decrease in amygdala volume (Kuo, Kaloupek, & Woodward, 2012). Decreased amygdala volume results in an increased fear and anxiety response to events because of the region's decreased ability to inhibit the stress response (Teicher et al., 2002).

Due to its high density of glucocorticoid receptors, the cerebral cortex is another brain region particularly vulnerable to stress (Sinclair et al., 2011). When broken down into smaller parts, researchers uncovered specific effects of victimization depending on the specific region of the cerebral cortex. The limbic cortex is more sensitive to stress between infancy and early childhood, when the density of glucocorticoid receptors on the glial cells are greatest (Sarrieau et al., 1986). Studies consistently found diminished development (i.e., decreased volume, decreased thickness, indicating cell loss or dysfunction) in the anterior cingulate cortex in the right and left sides of the region (Teicher & Samson, 2016).

Another region of the cerebral cortex, the prefrontal cortex (the decision-making center of the brain), is most vulnerable to stress during late-adolescence to early adulthood, when the density of glucocorticoid receptors on the pyramidal cells are greatest (Sarrieau et al., 1986). Childhood trauma is consistently associated with weakened development in prefrontal cortex regions, particularly the dorsolateral prefrontal cortex and the orbitofrontal cortex (Teicher & Samson, 2016). Debilitated development in these cerebral cortical regions (i.e., anterior cingulate cortex, dorsolateral prefrontal cortex, and orbitofrontal cortex) affect decision-making, emotion regulation and neuro-plastic functioning, influencing inhibition control (Koob & Volkow, 2010) suggesting altered executive functioning skills.

Researchers have not only found that victimization affects the structure of the brain, but also that victimization affects the functioning (i.e., processes) of the brain. Consistently, functional imaging studies found increased amygdala reactivity in those with a history of trauma compared to those without a history (Teicher & Samson, 2016). van Den Bulk et al. (2016) found adolescents with Post-Traumatic Stress Disorder (PTSD) and a history of childhood sexual abuse showed significantly greater amygdala activation, or hyper-vigilance, when viewing emotional faces compared to a control group and a group of adolescents with an internalizing disorder, then a fast habituation effect comparable to all groups. These results may explain greater threat-detection behaviors in those with PTSD.

One of the ways in which victimization can penetrate the body biologically is through epigenetic changes. Epigenetics refers to changes that occur to DNA without modifying the underlying genetic code. Epigenetic processes occur naturally in the body and are often influenced by genes themselves. However, emerging evidence is providing strong support for the environment as one mechanism of epigenetic changes in the body. In particular, stressful life events, including victimization, may influence epigenetic process such as DNA methylation. Methylation of DNA reduces gene expression and may influence subsequent socio-behavioral health.

Evidence for the role of victimization on DNA methylation and subsequent behavior is illustrated in bullying studies using twins. Monozygotic twins (who share 100% of their DNA) can be used to account for genetic, environmental, and epigenetic changes that occur due to external factors. Ouellet-Morin and collaborators (2013) examined why two monozygotic twins might differ (i.e., be discordant) in their response to stress in childhood despite their identical genetic make-up and family environment. They found that there were DNA methylation patterns in the bullied twin that were not present in the non-bullied twin. Specifically, the bullied twin had more methylation of the SERT gene which controls for the transportation of serotonin. This resulted in a reduction in cortisol response to stress. This, in turn, is often related to depression and anxiety-related disorders (e.g., PTSD). While a new area of research, epigenetics may provide an integral research path toward greater understanding of how victimization experiences can influence biological processes.

Exposure to victimization or threat of victimization is one of the most severe environmental threats and can substantially impact the HPA axis by disrupting homeostasis. When stress creates added demand on the body, the hypothalamus kicks into gear secreting corticotrophin-releasing hormone (CRH). In turn, this hormone adrenocorticotropic hormone (ACTH) in the pituitary. ACTH activates the production of cortisol (a glucocorticoid) in the adrenal cortex. Thus, the name hypothalamic pituitary adrenal axis. Normal HPA axis functioning is key to returning the body back to homeostasis or equilibrium. Problems with HPA axis functioning can leads to several negative mental and physical health issues (Kudielka & Kirschbaum, 2005).

Methylation and other biological changes that occur as the result of victimization often impact what is known as the hypothalamic pituitary adrenal axis or HPA Axis. Environmental stimuli that signal threat to health and well-being activate a series of actions in the body. Specifically, coordinated responses occur within the brain and among neuroendocrine pathways. This coordination involved the parasympathetic and sympathetic nervous systems along with the HPA (Ellis, Del Giudice, & Shirtcliff, 2013).

The mediating factors that link victimization to health outcomes are essential to understanding the complete picture of the negative results of exposure to violence. These factors are also integral to prevention and intervention efforts which we get to in the final section. Before discussing what can be done to reduce rates of violence and the negative outcomes of victimization, the factors that worsen or assuage the results of victimization are discussed.

## The Moderating and Conditioning Factors in the Victimization to Poor Health Link

Research has also uncovered factors that either insulate against the harmful effects of victimization or exacerbated these effects. In other words, there are environmental factors that moderate of condition the relationship between victimization and poor health outcomes. Living in **poverty** is one of the mainstays in theories about crime causation. Crime, especially violent crime, is a problem of inner-city neighborhoods and it is the impoverished who are the most effected. From a purely sociological perspective, poverty causes crime. Yet, poverty does not *do* anything. It must cause a change in the individual who then acts antisocially. Research has now identified that living in poverty has profound impacts on human biological functioning and, of course, on the brain.

Communities marked by poverty face multiple problems ranging from lack of access to nutritious food to lack of jobs to exposure to violence. Each of these problems places substantial stress on the brain. Chronic exposure to these stressors leads to an abundance of messages being sent from the limbic system that overwhelms the prefrontal cortex. When the prefrontal cortex becomes inundated by these messages it becomes extremely difficult to make long-term plans, exhibit self-control, and complete tasks (Babcock, 2014; Bernheim, Ray, & Yeltekin, 2015).

There are also notable **sex differences** in HPA functioning (although many studies have also found few sex differences in HPA response to stress – see Kudielka & Kirschbaum, 2005). Regardless of age, HPA activation is quicker in females and females produce more cortisol after exposure to stress (Goel et al., 2011). However, many HPA sex differences become pronounced after puberty and are related to gonadal hormone changes that occur in males but not females. During puberty, the gonads in males increase their production of testosterone (mainly through a reduction in maximum cortisol levels). The increase in testosterone blunts the HPA axis reducing the stress response in males. At least one study suggests that stress from victimization during adolescence is a greater predictor of subsequent depression in females than in males (Heim et al., 2009). Sex differences in the response to stress are integral to the development of effective mental health interventions which are discussed at the end of this chapter.

Victim recovery might also vary be biological sex. In a study on the impact of traumatic violent exposure on sleep patterns, researchers found that the impact of trauma on sleep disturbance was great for females than males. Further, while the sleep patterns of males and females both improved over time, the improvement was quicker and more pronounced among males (Umlauf et al., 2015).

## Violence Prevention and Intervention through Public Health-Focused Practice and Policy

Despite the prevalence of violence and the negative health consequences that almost always follow, research has enabled a close consideration of what might prevent victimization and what might also alleviate the negative outcomes of victimization. While some of these approaches might be controversial – such as using genetic information to guide interventions – most are straightforward and offer much promise to improving health and behavior. These cautionary notes and promising strategies will be discussed in the final section.

Prior research shows youth are exposed to less violence in the **community** if there is a variety of youth organizations available (Gardner & Brooks-Gunn, 2009). The presence of youth organizations deters violent crime at the neighborhood level. This in turn, limits youths' potential exposure to violence within the community. Relatedly, youth service organizations have the potential to instill and develop self-control, which not only reduces violent behavior in the individual but can also assist those who have deficiencies or damage to brain areas such as the prefrontal cortex due to exposure to violence (Zimmerman, Welsh, & Posick, 2015).

The Life Skills Training (LST) is a prevention program directed toward children in a **school** setting. The aim of the program is to address different factors, such as cognitive, attitudinal, social, and psychological factors related to problematic behaviors like substance use and violence. LST is shown to be effective in reducing substance use and violence (e.g., verbal aggression, fighting, delinquency; Botvin, Griffin, & Nichols, 2006). Overall, this can lead to a reduction in exposure to school violence.

Efforts on college campuses have also been proven effective in reducing exposure to violence. One effort in particular, the Green Dot intervention, is shown to reduce violent victimization rates on campuses with the intervention compared to campuses without the intervention. The Green Dot effort is intended to inform bystanders of how to intervene to prevent violence as well as establish a community that is intolerant of violence (Coker et al., 2015).

Given the negative health effects of violence and victimization, **family intervention** programs have been developed and tested in the hopes of decreasing abuse, neglect, and behavioral problems while increasing the welfare of families to mitigate potential health disparities. The Nurse-Family Partnership, developed by David Olds, was created to improve the lives of vulnerable mothers, their children, and their families by teaching mothers positive health-related behaviors, emphasizing proper care for their children, and improving the life course of mothers ("Mission," 2018; Olds et al., 1998b).

Study results from follow-up studies indicate improved mother life course (i.e., fewer children, less time using public assistance), less substantiated child maltreatment reports among families with low to moderate domestic violence exposure (Eckenrode et al., 2017), and decreased criminal behaviors by the child (Olds et al., 1998b). Olds et al. (1998a) found that within the first two years of life, 4% of unmarried teen mothers who received home visits by nurses abused or neglected their children compared to 19% of the comparison group. Furthermore, Eckenrode et al. (2017) found improved mother life course (i.e., fewer children, less time using public assistance) accounted for almost half the total effect the program had on decreasing child maltreatment. The decreases in violent behavior in families in this program reduces the chances of adults and children facing early-life, adversity-related, negative outcomes.

Another evidence-based, family based intervention is Multisystemic Therapy (MST). MST is designed to address the risk factors associated with antisocial behavior in youth, from an individual, family, peer, school, and neighborhood level. Outcome results showed a decrease in violence, substance use, child maltreatment, and psychopathological symptoms. Furthermore, family relations improved (Henggeler & Schaeffer, 2016). Similarly, family counseling programs that follow domestic abuse are shown to be effective. When mothers and children are counseled in joint sessions, research indicates that internalized and externalized symptomology can be alleviated (Hackett, McWhirter, & Lesher, 2016).

The treatment effects of **behavioral interventions** vary widely depending on the target behavior and population being served. For example, cognitive behavioral therapy appears to be effective in treating anger problems and behavioral interventions seem to be effective for younger offenders of serious violent or sexual offenses (McGuire, 2008); however, Barnett and Howard (2018) found insufficient evidence for the use of cognitive behavioral therapy in treating individuals with sexual offenses. Furthermore, cognitive behavioral therapy appears to be ineffective for people with antisocial personality disorder (Barnett & Howard, 2018). More work is needed in this area to determine best practices.

## References

Afifi, T. O., MacMillan, H. L., Boyle, M., Cheung, K., Taillieu, T., Turner, S., & Sareen, J. (2016). Child abuse and physical health in adulthood. *Health Reports, 27*(3), 10–18.

Babcock, E. D. (2014). *Using brain science to design new pathways out of poverty.* Boston, MA: Crittenton Women's Union.

Banyard, V. L., Williams, L. M., & Siegel, J. A. (2001). The long-term mental health consequences of child sexual abuse: An exploratory study of the impact of multiple traumas in a sample of women. *Journal of Traumatic Stress, 14*(4), 697–715.

Barnett, G. D., & Howard, F. F. (2018). What doesn't work to reduce reoffending? *European Psychologist, 23*(2), 111–129.

Bernheim, B. D., Ray, D., & Yeltekin, Ş. (2015). Poverty and self-control. *Econometrica, 83*(5), 1877–1911.

Black, M. C., Basile, K. C., Breiding, M. J., Smith, S. G., Walters, M. L., Merrick, M. T., & Stevens, M. R. (2011). *The national intimate partner and sexual violence survey: 2010 summary report.* Atlanta, GA: National Center for Injury Prevention and Control, Centers for Disease Control and Prevention, *19*, 39–40.

Botvin, G. J., Griffin, K. W., & Nichols, T. D. (2006). Preventing youth violence and delinquency through a universal school-based prevention approach. *Prevention Science, 7*, 403–408.

Brewerton, T. D., Cotton, B. D., & Kilpatrick, D. G. (2018). Sensation seeking, binge-type eating disorders, victimization, and PTSD in the National Women's Study. *Eating Behaviors.* Online First. *30*, 120–124.

Brewerton, T. D., Dansky, B. S., O'Neil, P. M., & Kilpatrick, D. G. (2015). The number of divergent purging behaviors is associated with histories of trauma, PTSD, and comorbidity in a national sample of women. *Eating disorders, 23*(5), 422–429.

Carlson, N. R. (2013). *Physiology of behavior*, 11th edition. Boston, MA: Pearson.

Cecil, C. A., Viding, E., Fearon, P., Glaser, D., & McCrory, E. J. (2017). Disentangling the mental health impact of childhood abuse and neglect. *Child Abuse & Neglect, 63*, 106–119.

Coker, A. L., Davis, K. E., Arias, I., Desai, S., Sanderson, M., Brandt, H. M., & Smith, P. H. (2002). Physical and mental health effects of intimate partner violence for men and women. *American Journal of Preventive Medicine, 23*(4), 260–268.

Coker, A. L., Fisher, B. S., Bush, H. M., Swan, S. C., Williams, C. M., Clear, E. R., & DeGue, S. (2015). Evaluation of the Green Dot bystander intervention to reduce interpersonal violence among college students across three campuses. *Violence against Women, 21*(12), 1507–1527.

DHHS (2014). U.S. Department of Health & Human Services, Administration for Children and Families, Administration on Children, Youth and Families, Children's Bureau. (2016). *Child maltreatment 2014.* Available from: www.acf.hhs.gov/programs/cb/research-data-technology/statistics-research/child-maltreatment.

Eckenrode, J., Campa, M. I., Morris, P. A., Henderson Jr., C. R., Bolger, K. E., Kitzman, H., & Olds, D. L. (2017). The prevention of child maltreatment through the nurse family partnership program: Mediating effects in a long-term follow-up study. *Child Maltreatment, 22*(2), 92–99. doi:10.1177/1077559516685185.

Ellis, B. J., Del Giudice, M., & Shirtcliff, E. A. (2013). Beyond allostatic load: The stress response system as a mechanism of conditional adaptation. *Child and Adolescent Psychopathology, 2*, 251–284.

Everaerd, D., Gerritsen, L., Rijpkema, M., Frodl, T., van Oostrom, I., Franke, B., Fernandez, G., & Tendolkar, I. (2012). Sex modulates the interactive effect of the serotonin transporter gene polymorphism and childhood adversity on hippocampal volume. *Neuropsychopharmacology, 37*(8), 1848–1855. doi:10.1038/nnpp.2012.32.

Farrell, C., & Zimmerman, G. M. (2018). Is exposure to violence a persistent risk factor for offending across the life course? Examining the contemporaneous, acute, enduring, and long-term consequences of exposure to violence on property crime, violent offending, and substance use. *Journal of Research in Crime and Delinquency, 55*(6), 728–765. doi: 0022427818785207.

Finkelhor, D., Turner, H., Shattuck, A., Hamby, S., & Kracke, K. (2015). *Children's exposure to violence, crime, and abuse: An update.* Washington, DC: US Department of Justice, Office of Justice Programs, Office of Juvenile Justice and Delinquency Prevention.

Fox, B. H., Perez, N., Cass, E., Baglivio, M. T., & Epps, N. (2015). Trauma changes everything: Examining the relationship between adverse childhood experiences and serious, violent and chronic juvenile offenders. *Child Abuse & Neglect, 46*, 163–173.

Gardner, M., & Brooks-Gunn, J. (2009). Adolescents' exposure to community violence: Are neighborhood youth organizations protective? *Journal of Community Psychology, 37*(4), 505–525.

Goel, N., Workman, J. L., Lee, T. T., Innala, L., & Viau, V. (2011). Sex differences in the HPA axis. *Comprehensive Physiology*, *4*(3), 1121–1155.

Hackett, S., McWhirter, P. T., & Lesher, S. (2016). The therapeutic efficacy of domestic violence victim interventions. *Trauma, Violence, & Abuse*, *17*(2), 123–132.

Heim, C., Bradley, B., Mletzko, T., Deveau, T. C., Musselmann, D. L., Nemeroff, C. B., ... & Binder, E. B. (2009). Effect of childhood trauma on adult depression and neuroendocrine function: sex-specific moderation by CRH receptor 1 gene. *Frontiers in Behavioral Neuroscience*, *3*(41), 1–10.

Hemmings, S. M., Malan-Müller, S., van Den Heuvel, L. L., Demmitt, B. A., Stanislawski, M. A., Smith, D. G., ... & Marotz, C. A. (2017). The microbiome in posttraumatic stress disorder and trauma-exposed controls: An exploratory study. *Psychosomatic Medicine*, *79*(8), 936–946.

Henggeler, S. W., & Schaeffer, C. M. (2016). Multisystemic therapy: Clinical overview, outcomes, and implementation research. *Family Process*, *55*(3), 514–528.

Herge, W. M., La Greca, A. M., & Chan, S. F. (2015). Adolescent peer victimization and physical health problems. *Journal of Pediatric Psychology*, *41*(1), 15–27.

Herrenkohl, T. I., Hong, S., Klika, J. B., Herrenkohl, R. C., & Russo, M. J. (2013). Developmental impacts of child abuse and neglect related to adult mental health, substance use, and physical health. *Journal of Family Violence*, *28*(2), 191–199.

Horwitz, A. V., Widom, C. S., McLaughlin, J., & White, H. R. (2001). The impact of childhood abuse and neglect on adult mental health: A prospective study. *Journal of Health and Social Behavior*, *42*(2), 184–201.

Jackson, D. B., Leal, W. E., Posick, C., Vaughn, M. G., & Olivan, M. (2018). The role of adolescent victimization in energy drink consumption: Monitoring the future, 2010–2016. *Journal of Community Health*. Online First. *43*(6), 1137–1144.

Karl, A., Schaefer, M., Malta, L. S., Dorfel, D., Rohleder, N., & Werner, A. (2006). A meta-analysis of structural brain abnormalities in PTSD. *Neuroscience & Biobehavioral Reviews*, *30*(7), 1004–1031. doi:10.1016/j.neubiorev.2006.03.004.

Kimber, M., McTavish, J. R., Couturier, J., Boven, A., Gill, S., Dimitropoulos, G., & MacMillan, H. L. (2017). Consequences of child emotional abuse, emotional neglect and exposure to intimate partner violence for eating disorders: A systematic critical review. *BMC Psychology*, *5*(1), 33.

Koob, G. F. & Volkow, N. D. (2010). Neurocircuitry of addiction. *Neuropsychopharmacology*, *35*(4), 217–238. doi:10.1038/npp.2009.

Kudielka, B. M., & Kirschbaum, C. (2005). Sex differences in HPA axis responses to stress: A review. *Biological Psychology*, *69*(1), 113–132.

Kuo, J. R., Kaloupek, D. G., & Woodward, S. H. (2012). Amygdala volume in combat-exposed veterans with and without posttraumatic stress disorder: A cross-sectional study. *Archives of General Psychiatry*, *69*(10), 1080–1086.

Lupien, S. J., Parent, S., Evans, A. C., Tremblay, R. E., Zelazo, P. D., Corbo, V., ... & Seguin, J. R. (2011). Larger amygdala but no change in hippocampal volume in 10-year-old children exposed to maternal depressive symptomatology since birth. *Proceedings of the National Academy of Sciences of the United States of America*, *108*(34), 14324–14329. http://dx.doi.org.libez.lib.georgiasouthern.edu/10.1073/pnas.1105371108.

Malykhin, N. V., Carter, R., Hegadoren, K. M., Seres, P., & Coupland, N. J. (2012). Fronto-limbic volumetric changes in major depressive disorder. *Journal of Affective Disorders*, *136*(3), 1104–1113. doi:10.1016/j.jad.2011.10.038.

McGuire, J. (2008). A review of effective interventions for reducing aggression and violence. *Philosophical Transactions of the Royal Society*, *363*, 2577–2597.

Mehta, M. A., Golembo, N. I., Nosarti, C., Colvert, E., Mota, A., Williams, S. C., ... & Sonuga- Barke, E. J. (2009). Amygdala, hippocampal and corpus callosum size following severe early institutional deprivation: The English and Romanian adoptees study pilot. *Journal of Child Psychology and Psychiatry*, *50*(8), 943–951. doi:10.1111/j.1469-7610.2009.02084.x.

Mission, vision, and values. (2018). Retrieved from www.nursefamilypartnership.org/about/mission-vision-values/

Morgan, R. E., & Kena, G. (2017). *Criminal victimization, 2016*. Department of Justice. Office of Justice Programs. Bureau of Justice Statistics.

Murphy, S. L., Xu, J., Kochanek, K. D., Curtin, S. C., & Arias, E. (2017). Deaths: Final data for 2015. *National Vital Statistics Report*, *66*(6), 1–73. Centers for Disease Control and Prevention.

Nadel, L., Campbell, J., & Ryan, L. (2007). Autobiographical memory retrieval and hippocampal activation as a function of repetition and the passage of time. *Neural Plasticity*, *2007*, 90472. doi:10.1155/2007/90472.

Norman, R. E., Byambaa, M., De, R., Butchart, A., Scott, J., & Vos, T. (2012). The long-term health consequences of child physical abuse, emotional abuse, and neglect: A systematic review and meta-analysis. *PLoS Medicine*, *9*(11), e1001349.

Olds, D., Henderson Jr., C., Kitzman, H., Eckenrode, J., Cole, R., & Tarelbaum, R. (1998a). The promise of home visitation: Results of two randomized trials. *Journal of Community Psychology*, *26*(1), 5–21.

Olds, D., Henderson Jr., C. R., Cole, R., Eckenrode, J., Kitzman, H., Luckey, D., ... Powers, J. (1998b). Long-term effects of nurse home visitation on children's criminal and antisocial behavior. *The Journal of the American Medical Association*, *280*(14), 1238–1244.

Ouellet-Morin, I., Wong, C. C. Y., Danese, A., Pariante, C. M., Papadopoulos, A. S., Mill, J., & Arseneault, L. (2013). Increased serotonin transporter gene (SERT) DNA methylation is associated with bullying victimization and blunted cortisol response to stress in childhood: A longitudinal study of discordant monozygotic twins. *Psychological Medicine*, *43*(9), 1813–1823.

Posick, C. (2013). The overlap between offending and victimization among adolescents: Results from the second international self-report delinquency study. *Journal of Contemporary Criminal Justice*, *29*(1), 106–124.

Posick, C. (2014). Victimization and reporting to the police: The role of negative emotionality. *Psychology of Violence*, *4*(2), 210–223.

Rasmussen, L. J. H., Moffitt, T. E., Eugen-Olsen, J., Belsky, D. W., Danese, A., Harrington, H., ... & Caspi, A. (2018). Cumulative childhood risk is associated with a new measure of chronic inflammation in adulthood. *Journal of Child Psychology and Psychiatry*. Online First. *60*(2), 199–208.

Sapolsky, R. M., Krey, L. C., & McEwen, B. S. (1985). Prolonged glucocorticoid exposure reduces hippocampal neuron number: Implications for aging. *The Journal of Neuroscience*, *5*(5), 1222–1227.

Sarrieau, A., Dussaillant, M., Agid, F., Philibert, D., Agid, Y., & Rostene, W. (1986). Autoradiographic localization of glucocorticosteroid and progesterone binding sites in the human post-mortem brain. *Journal of Steroid Biochemistry*, *25*(5B), 717–721. doi:10.1016/0022-4731(86)90300-6.

Sinclair, D., Webster, M. J., Wong, J., & Weickert, C. S. (2011). Dynamic molecular and anatomical changes in the glucocorticoid receptor in human cortical development. *Molecular Psychiatry*, *16*(5), 504–515. doi:10.1038/mp.2010.28.

Spataro, J., Mullen, P. E., Burgess, P. M., Wells, D. L., & Moss, S. A. (2004). Impact of child sexual abuse on mental health: Prospective study in males and females. *The British Journal of Psychiatry*, *184*(5), 416–421.

Springer, K. W., Sheridan, J., Kuo, D., & Carnes, M. (2007). Long-term physical and mental health consequences of childhood physical abuse: Results from a large population-based sample of men and women. *Child Abuse & Neglect*, *31*(5), 517–530.

Storch, E. A., Milsom, V. A., DeBraganza, N., Lewin, A. B., Geffken, G. R., & Silverstein, J. H. (2006). Peer victimization, psychosocial adjustment, and physical activity in overweight and at-risk-for-overweight youth. *Journal of Pediatric Psychology*, *32*(1), 80–89.

Teicher, M. H., Andersen, S. L., Polcari, A., Anderson, C. M., & Navalta, C. P. (2002). Developmental neurobiology of childhood stress and trauma. *Psychiatric Clinics of North America*, *32*(2), 397–426.

Teicher, M. H., Andersen, S. L., Polcari, A., Anderson, C. M., Navalta, C. P., & Kim, D. M. (2003). The neurobiological consequences of early stress and childhood maltreatment. *Neuroscience & Biobehavioral Reviews*, *27*(1–2), 33–44. doi:10.1016/s0149-7634(03)00007-1.

Teicher, M. H., & Samson, J. A. (2016). Annual research review: enduring neurobiological effects of childhood abuse and neglect. *Journal of Child Psychology and Psychiatry*, *57*(3), 241–266.

Tottenham, N., Hare, T. A., Quinn, B. T., McCarry, T. W., Nurse, M., Gilhooly, T., ... & Casey, B. J. (2010). Prolonged institutional rearing is associated with atypically large amygdala volume and difficulties in emotion regulation. *Developmental Science*, *13*(1), 46–61.

Tupler, L. A. & De Bellis, M. D. (2006). Segmented hippocampal volume in children and adolescents with posttraumatic stress disorder. *Biological Psychiatry*, *59*(6), 523–529.

Uematsu, A., Matsui, M., Tanaka, C., Takahashi, T., Noguchi, K., Suzuki, M., & Nishijo, H. (2012). Development trajectories of amygdala and hippocampus from infancy to early adulthood in healthy individuals. *PLoS ONE*, *7*(10), e46970. doi: 10.1371/journal.pone.0046970.

Umlauf, M. G., Bolland, A. C., Bolland, K. A., Tomek, S., & Bolland, J. M. (2015). The effects of age, gender, hopelessness, and exposure to violence on sleep disorder symptoms and daytime sleepiness among adolescents in impoverished neighborhoods. *Journal of Youth and Adolescence*, *44*(2), 518–542.

van Den Bulk, B. G., Somerville, L. H., van Hoof, M. J., van Lang, N. D. J., van der Wee, N. J. A., Crone, E. A., & Vermeiren, R. R. J. M. (2016). Amygdala habituation to emotional faces in adolescents with internalizing disorders, adolescents with childhood sexual abuse, related PTSD and healthy adolescents. *Developmental Cognitive Neuroscience*, *21*, 15–25. doi:10.1016/j.dcn.2016.08.002.

van Geel, M., Goemans, A., & Vedder, P. H. (2016). The relation between peer victimization and sleeping problems: A meta-analysis. *Sleep Medicine Reviews, 27*, 89–95.

Whittle, S., Dennison, M., Vijayakumar, N., Simmons, J. G., Yucel, M., Lubman, D. I., ... & Allen, N. B. (2013). Childhood maltreatment and psychopathology affect brain development during adolescence. *Journal of the American Academy of Child and Adolescent Psychiatry, 52*(9), 940–952. doi:10.1037/t03988-000.

Zimmerman, G. M., & Posick, C. (2016). Risk factors for and behavioral consequences of direct versus indirect exposure to violence. *American Journal of Public Health, 106*(1), 178–188.

Zimmerman, G. M., Welsh, B. C., & Posick, C. (2015). Investigating the role of neighborhood youth organizations in preventing adolescent violent offending: Evidence from Chicago. *Journal of Quantitative Criminology, 31*(4), 565–593.

# 15
# THE PREVALENCE AND DYNAMICS OF TEEN DATING VIOLENCE

*Vithya Murugan, Annah K. Bender, Elise Trombetta, and Caroline Dilts*

### Introduction and Overview

The purpose of this chapter will be to define teen dating violence (TDV) and describe its prevalence, its consequences for health and mental health, risk and protective factors, and promising areas for future research. A key point to note is that TDV has received comparatively greater research, policy, and practice attention in the United States than other parts of the world. Therefore, much of what is known regarding TDV risk factors, correlates, and outcomes, as well as the policies and programs that have been implemented to address TDV, will be presented from a U.S. perspective. However, rates of interpersonal violence (some of which meets the definition of TDV) from abroad, as well as recommendations for changing social norms around gender-based violence from the World Health Organization (WHO), do exist and we have endeavored to include such information, where relevant, as areas where the field remains wide open to scholarly inquiry, theory and policy development, and prevention/intervention work.

A secondary aim of this chapter is to provide an overview of current research on effective means of preventing teen dating violence and intervening with teen victims and perpetrators. We will summarize the relatively small, yet quickly growing, body of research conducted primarily with the support of the National Institute of Justice (NIJ) and the Centers for Disease Control and Prevention (CDC). Again, because most of the published studies evaluating or testing prevention and intervention programs have taken place in the U.S., our focus will be primarily on what has been proven effective among American youth. We first begin with a description of teen dating violence, what it is and what it is not, and what factors distinguish it from intimate partner violence (IPV) in adult relationships.

### *Teen Dating Violence is Often Reciprocal*

Most studies of TDV, when taken together, indicate that girls and boys involved in an abusive dating relationship often identify as both victim and perpetrator (Mulford & Giordano, 2008; Reppucci et al., 2013). Among couples involved in abusive relationships, half reported rates of mutual aggression in a study of 1,300 Ohio seventh, ninth, and eleventh graders (Giordano, 2007); a similar study found that two-thirds of 1,200 youth in Long Island reported mutual violence (e.g. slapping, hitting, verbal abuse). In couples where there is a sole aggressor, girls may be more likely to identify as the aggressors in physically and emotionally abusive relationships and boys in sexually abusive relationships (Goncy, Sullivan, Farrell, Mehari, & Garthe, 2017). One explanation for the higher rates of female aggression and mutual violence among teens is that large power imbalances between girls and boys are uncommon compared to adults (Mulford & Giordano, 2008). In many heterosexual relationships where IPV occurs, for example, males wield greater physical and social control over their partners, whereas a teen girl is not likely to be dependent on her boyfriend for housing or child support. In fact, the study of Ohio teens found that youth perceived they had "equal say" in their relationships, and if there was a power imbalance, boys were more likely to perceive that girls had the upper hand (Giordano, 2007). Despite greater reciprocity of violence in teen dating relationships, however, certain similarities to adult IPV remain—among them sex differences in motivations for violence. One study found that girls cited "self-defense" more often than do boys as a reason for using violence against a dating partner, whereas boys more commonly cited the need to "exert control" when using physical violence against a date (O'Keefe, 1997). Another study found that boys were also more likely to respond with laughter when a date was physically aggressive with them (Molidor & Tolman, 1998). Furthermore, the consequences of violent victimization are most keenly felt by girls, who are more likely to suffer immediate and long-term negative consequences such as depression and suicidal ideation (Ackard, Eisenberg, & Neumark-Sztainer, 2007; Olshen, McVeigh, Wunsch-Hitzig, & Rickert, 2007). Although research on TDV has primarily been conducted among heterosexual couples, same-sex victims of TDV are more likely to experience depression and violent delinquency than opposite-sex victims (Gehring & Vaske, 2017), suggesting that sexual minority status is another important factor in understanding the short- and long-term consequences of TDV, among which a general lack of helpful information or services tailored to same-sex adolescent couples is paramount. The trajectory of TDV also represents an important shift between the sexes as adolescents move through their teen years into emerging adulthood. TDV tends to increase in prevalence and severity between early to late adolescence, with older teens (aged 14–18) reporting more victimization and aggression than younger teens (Goncy et al., 2017). However, there were important sex differences in this trajectory, with boys less likely to perpetrate violence than girls and demonstrating a decrease in both victimization and perpetration over time compared with girls, who showed an increase in both (Ibid.).

## *Teens Think about Dating and Dating Violence Differently than Adults*

The teen brain is a very different organ than an adult one. The brain structures responsible for executive function, social cognition, and integrative processing are still developing well into young adulthood. The emerging field of adolescent neuroscience has implications for TDV especially in relation to connectivity, impulsivity, and the damaging effects of stress, anxiety, and depression that often result from experiencing dating violence. Beyond the biological differences between teens and adults are the developmental stages and the tasks associated with each in adolescence. In a report to the NIJ, a team of researchers identified numerous discrepancies between adolescents' understanding of TDV and that of adult caregivers (Concept Systems, 2014). Findings from group sessions and concept mapping with youth and adults indicate that youth conceptualize teen dating relationships as progressing through stages, and note difficulties in maintaining self-awareness while in a romantic relationship (Ibid.). Because teens also have less life and dating experience than do adults, communicating and relating to partner may be immature or unrealistic, which could lead to maladaptive coping strategies such as physical or emotional abuse. Focus groups with middle school students revealed that physical aggression was frequently the manifestation of an inability to communicate effectively with a partner and the resultant feelings of frustration (Fredland Ricardo, Campbell, Sharps, Kub, & Yonas, 2005). Many teens also hold somewhat idealistic views of intimacy and relationships, and may become disillusioned to the point of violence when conflict emerges with a partner (Montgomery, 2005).

## *The Role of Peers in Teen Dating Relationships and TDV*

Peers play an important role in TDV as both risk and protective factors (Oudekerk, Blachman-Denmer, & Mulford, 2014). Peers are a vital component of an adolescent's social network that can affect everything from attitudes and health behaviors (such as sexual debut and contraception use) to relationship quality. One of the first articles to review theory and prevention initiatives in the then-emergent field of TDV was published in 1999 and conceptualized TDV within a framework of adolescent development (Wekerle & Wolfe, 1999). From early adolescence until the initiation of dating relationships—usually around ages 15 and 16—teens look to their peer networks to meet their needs for emotional intimacy, companionship, and nurturance. Therefore, the quality of these friendships may exert a significant impact on teens' perceptions of dating, including their attitudes toward dating in general, sex, and the acceptability of violence within relationships. Another critical consideration that emphasizes the importance of peers in TDV is the very public nature of most teen relationships. Teens frequently interact with each other in settings where there is little privacy—school or after-school activities, or other public spaces such as movie theaters, shopping centers, and even within the home where adults and siblings are likely to be present. Even when teens are not together physically, they are often interacting with each other virtually, by phone, text messages, social media, video games, and other digital spheres. Projecting an image of the relationship is therefore of great importance to most teens, and if that relationship becomes violent or unhealthy, they may feel embarrassed or isolated from their friends or larger peer network. In one study, for example, a focus group of boys told researchers that if a girl hit them in front of their friends, they would hit her back to save face (Fredland et al., 2005). Risky social environment—including peer delinquency and attitudes toward dating violence—was the strongest correlate of physical and psychological perpetration and victimization when examined in a model that also included neighborhood quality and family background (Oudekerk, Blachman-Denmer, & Mulford, 2014). However, peers can also be exceptional protective factors or help-seekers in the aftermath of TDV, as they are frequently the "first responders" (p. 4) to dating violence and can also encourage victims to seek help from a trusted adult or formal source. Overall, far less is known or understood about TDV than adult IPV, and this chapter's overview of TDV will reflect that gap and will attempt, where possible, to identify areas for cross-cutting themes and research.

## Definitions

Also called adolescent dating violence or intimate partner violence among adolescents, teen TDV refers to several types of abuse occurring among persons age 12 to 18 who are involved (or were formerly involved together) in a romantic and consensual relationship (National Institute of Justice [NIJ], 2018). The Centers for Disease Control & Prevention (CDC) further defines as a type of intimate partner violence occurring between two young people in a close relationship and delineates the subtypes of abuse as follows: *physical violence* (hurting or trying to hurt another person by use of physical force); *sexual violence* (forcing or attempting to force a partner into a sex act, sexual touching, or a non-physical sexual event such as sexting when the other person does not consent); *stalking*; and *psychological aggression* (a form of verbal or non-verbal communication with the intent to harm another person mentally or emotionally, or to exert control over another person). Teten and colleagues (2009) expand the definition of psychological aggression in TDV to include the following: "Psychological abuse may also include isolating a partner from her or his friends and family, controlling or jealous behavior, and acts of dominance such as assertion of power over decision making, put-downs, and name calling" (p. 923).

Varying terminology used interchangeably (e.g. "dating violence", "relationship aggression", "intimate partner violence"), and other phrases has posed several problems for researchers because the fluidity of the definitions and thus, measurement, from one study to another may not be inclusive of all types of violence (physical, sexual, stalking, and psychological). For instance, some studies do not include psychological aggression in their definition of TDV (i.e. Banyard & Cross, 2008; Clayton, Lowry, Basile, Demissie, & Bohm, 2017; Cohen, Shorey, Menon, & Temple, 2018). Furthermore, there is evidence suggesting that the subtypes of dating violence may emanate from distinct risk factors (although many share common ones, such as exposure to violence in the family of origin) (Teten, Ball, Valle, Noonan, & Rosenbluth, 2009). The authors cite the example of sexually aggressive boys, who report significantly more non-sexual aggression as well as prior sexual abuse than do non-sexually aggressive boys (Teten et al., 2009). Thus, specificity of terminology is essential for understanding the prevalence, causes, consequences, and patterns of TDV.

As with IPV and other forms of abusive or bullying behavior, TDV can take place in person or electronically, such as repeated texting or posting sexual pictures of a partner online without consent. Cyber dating violence, defined as the use of technology to harass, control, or abuse a dating partner, appears to be fairly common among teens. In a study of over 5,000 youth teens spread across three states, approximately one in ten youth, all of whom had dated in the past year, reported they had perpetrated some form of cyber dating violence (Zweig, Dank, Yahner, & Lachman, 2013). As with other forms of electronic abuse, such as cyber bullying, research suggests that LGBTQ+ youth are more likely to be victimized by cyber dating violence than their heterosexual peers (Dank, Lachman, Zweig, & Yahner, 2014).

Another implication for the precise measurement of TDV is carefully defining and separating characteristics common in many teen relationships from abusive (or potentially abusive) forms of interaction. Teasing and name-calling are frequently normalized by teens as part of a dating relationship, but these behaviors can develop into abuse and/or serious forms of violence. Personal interviews with 956 adolescents revealed that respondents who self-report violence are more likely to report other negative relationship behaviors, such as jealousy, verbal conflict, and cheating (Giordano, Soto, Manning, & Longmore, 2010). Additionally, in the fluid and unstable pattern characteristic of many teen relationships—abusive or not—relationship "churning", or the cycling in and out of a dating relationship with the same person, may be an additional risk factor for relationship problems, unhealthy conflict, and/or violence. Researchers from Ohio identified associations between so-called relationship churning and physical violence (adolescents involved in on/off relationships were twice as likely as those who were either stably broken up or stably together to report physical violence in their relationships) and verbal abuse (churners were half again as likely to report verbal abuse as non-churners) (Halpern-Meekin, Manning, Giordano, & Longmore, 2013).

## Prevalence, Risks, and Consequences of TDV

### Prevalence

There is great variation in prevalence rates gleaned across studies that may be attributed to differences in methodology, definitions of TDV used, and/or populations studied. Nevertheless, TDV remains a serious public health problem. According to the National Intimate Partner and Sexual Violence Survey (NISVS), nearly 23% of females and 14% of males first experienced some form of TDV prior to the age of 18.

According to the 2017 Youth Risk Behavior Surveillance System (YRBSS), 8% of students in grades 9 to 12 report that they have experienced physical TDV in the past 12 months (e.g., being hit, slammed into something, or injured with an object or weapon). The prevalence of having experienced physical TDV was higher among female (9.1%) than male (6.5%) students; higher among black female (13.1%) and Hispanic female (9.2%) than black male (7.1%) and Hispanic male (5.9%) students, respectively. The prevalence of having experienced physical dating violence was higher among gay, lesbian, and bisexual (17.2%) and not sure (14.1%) than heterosexual (6.4%) students. Among female students, the prevalence was higher among lesbian and bisexual (16.9%) than heterosexual (7.1%) students. Among male students, the prevalence was higher among gay and bisexual (16.8%) and not sure (14.1%) than heterosexual (5.8%) students.

Additionally, according to the 2017 YRBSS, 6.9% of students in grade 9 to 12 report having been forced to do "sexual things" (e.g., kissing, touching, or being physically forced to have sexual intercourse) they did not want to do one or more times during the 12 months before the survey by someone they were dating or going out with (i.e. TDV). The prevalence of having experienced sexual dating violence was higher among female (10.7%) than male (2.8%) students; higher among white female (11.1%), black female (6.8%), and Hispanic female (11.4%) than white male (2.6%), black male (2.7%), and Hispanic male (2.5%) students, respectively. The prevalence of having experienced sexual dating violence was higher among gay, lesbian, and bisexual (15.8%) and not sure (14.1%) than heterosexual (5.5%) students. Among female students, the prevalence was higher among lesbian and bisexual (16.3%) than heterosexual (9.3%) students. Among male students, the prevalence was higher among gay and bisexual (13.5%) than heterosexual (2.1%) students. The prevalence also was higher among heterosexual female (9.3%) than heterosexual male (2.1%) students.

Prevalence rates for emotional and psychological abuse are higher than both physical and sexual TDV, perhaps due to the pervasiveness of electronics and technology. According to the National Longitudinal Survey of Adolescent Health, between 20 and 30% of teens in grades 7 to 12 report being verbally or psychologically abused in the previous year. Approximately 16% of youth age 12 to 21 have been insulted; 23% have been sworn at, and 4% have been threatened by a partner.

The National Survey of Teen Relationships and Intimate Violence (STRiV), an NIJ-funded study, is the first to provide a comprehensive national portrait of teen dating violence with detailed measurements of both victims and perpetrators of TDV (NIJ, 2018). This study found that approximately two-thirds of youths (ages 12–18) who were in a relationship or had been in one in the past year reported that they had been victimized (69%) or perpetrated violence (63%). Furthermore, this study found that psychological abuse was the most common type of abuse victimization reported (over 60%), followed by physical and sexual TDV both 18%. Fewer adolescents reported perpetrating acts of physical TDV (12%) and sexual TDV (12%). This study also corroborated findings from other studies that found a significant overlap between victimization and perpetration; 84% of victims also perpetrated abuse. This finding highlights the importance of prevention and intervention programming focused on the "fluidity of these roles" among youth in dating relationships (NIJ, 2018).

## *Risk Factors*

Extant studies have focused on a multitude of individual, familial, peer, and community level risk factors for TDV victimization and perpetration. However, a lack of longitudinal data limits the causal connections that can be made between risk factors and TDV. Despite this limitation, correlational research suggests that risk factors for TDV victimization and perpetration include: increase in age; low self-esteem, anger, or depressed mood; experience with and exposure to stressful life events (e.g., past history of sexual abuse, prior victimization, family violence); participation in risky behaviors (e.g., substance abuse, alcohol use, violence); lack of parental supervision and support; acceptance of rape myths and the justification of violence against women; having a friend involved in dating violence; living in poverty; and exposure to neighborhood and community violence (Foshee et al., 2011; Offenhauer & Buchalter, 2011). Additionally, there are certain risk factors of TDV that are developmentally appropriate in youth, including limited relationship experience, vulnerability to peer pressure, and unsophisticated communication skills (Mulford & Giordano, 2008).

## Consequences

TDV has negative short- and long-term consequences on adolescent health and well-being. Youth who have experienced TDV are more likely to perform poorly in school; develop eating disorders; engage in unhealthy behaviors (e.g., drinking, smoking, taking drugs); become pregnant or have an STD; attempt suicide and report symptoms of depression and anxiety; and exhibit anti-social behaviors (Banyard & Cross, 2008; Wincentak, Connolly, & Card, 2017). Additionally, due to the critical period of adolescence, victims of TDV also experience difficulty establishing and maintaining healthy relationships, intimacy with a partner, and a positive adult identity.

## Theoretical Explanations for TDV

TDV is a relatively nascent area of inquiry. Over the past couple of decades, as TDV has garnered more scholarly attention, there has been an increase in the amount of public and private funds that have been allocated for research, education, and prevention programs. As a result, numerous theories have been offered to address social structures, cultural norms, and personal behaviors that perpetuate and sustain TDV. A glaring critique of existing theoretical frameworks are their relevance to individuals of racial and ethnic minority groups and those exposed to other forms of oppression, such as heterosexism and classism. Though there is no single theory that can fully explain the phenomenon of TDV, the following section provides an overview and critique of some of the most widely used theories and frameworks to understand TDV.

## Attachment Theory

Attachment theory posits that children form mental representations of relationships based on their history with significant caregivers (Bowlby, 1980). As such, these mental representations function as both a "prototype and template for forging future relationships" including romantic relationships (Wekerle & Wolfe, 1999; p. 442). Healthy partnerships are grounded in secure attachment models that are derived from consistent and responsive childrearing, while dysfunctional relationships are grounded in insecure working models, derived from inconsistent or unresponsive caregiving (Wekerle & Wolfe, 1999). Insecure attachment styles that result from experiences of child maltreatment (physical, sexual, and emotional trauma) serve as a risk factor for perpetration and victimization of TDV because they expose children to clear and delineated power differentials in the context of significant relationships. "Aggression and a sense of personal entitlement overlap with the victimizer role, and passivity and a sense of personal deprivation overlap with the victim role" (Wekerle & Wolfe, 1999, p. 443). As such, when adolescents are choosing dating partners, their attachment models inform their understanding of relationships and their expectations of themselves and their partners.

## Social Learning Theory

Psychologist, Albert Bandura (1977), to explain aggression exhibited by young children, developed social learning theory. Social learning theory is an integration of cognitive learning theory (which suggests that learning is influenced by psychological factors) and behavioral learning theory (which suggests that learning is influenced by the observation of external stimuli). One way that social learning theory pertains to dating violence is that children learn abusive behaviors when they are young by observing and imitating behaviors that adults model for them. As children transition to adolescence and later, adulthood, these behaviors are reinforced by society (Kelly et al., 2012; Lawson, 2012). For example, male children are more likely to grow up to assault female intimates if their parents abused them or if they observed their fathers assaulting their spouses (Hines & Malley-Morrison, 2005). Additionally, social learning theory has also been studied in peer group contexts, particularly among college males. The argument is that peer groups reinforce particular attitudes and behaviors that are socially desirable and appropriate according the group, irrespective of legality (Akers, 1973; Pratt et al., 2010; Sutherland, 1947). According to Schwartz and DeKeseredy (1997) men in college may associate with peer groups that foster, legitimize and endorse violence, thus causing men to engage in violence against women.

## *Ecological Framework*

The ecological framework emerged from the work of American developmental psychologist Urie Bronfenbrenner. Bronfenbrenner (1977) originally posited that in order to understand human development, the entire ecological context in which growth occurs must be accounted for. As it pertains to violence against women, the ecological framework views violence as the result of the interaction of factors at four major levels: the individual, relationship, community and societal levels. According to the World Health Organization, the individual level encompasses an individual's personal history and biological factors that influence how they behave and how susceptible they are to becoming victims or perpetrators of violence. Examples of factors at the individual level include: being the victim of child maltreatment, having psychological and/or personality disorders and having a substance abuse history. At the relationship level, the individual's relationships with family, friends, intimate partners and peers influence their risks of becoming a victim or perpetrator of violence. For example, having a parent who exerts violence over the other parent may increase the likelihood of becoming a victim or perpetrator of violence. The community level encompasses the contexts in which social relations occur, such as the neighborhood the individual resides or the school that they attend. Risk factors in neighborhoods that may affect the likelihood of becoming a victim or perpetrator of violence include unemployment and population density. Lastly, the societal level encompasses factors that dictate whether or not violence is tolerated; this includes: patriarchal values, socio-economic inequality, and enforcement of the law.

## Measurement

The ways in which TDV is defined dictates how it is measured, assessed, and ultimately, addressed. Below is a review and critique of standardized measures that have been used to assess TDV in both nationally representative and community-based studies.

### *Measurements*

#### *Conflict Tactics Scale-2 (CTS-2)*

The CTS-2 is the most widely used and cited quantitative measure of conflict between partners in a dating, cohabitating, or marital relationship (Yun, 2011). While it has primarily been used to assess IPV in adult relationships, it is increasingly being modified and used to assess TDV (Exner-Cortens, Gill, & Eckenrode, 2016). The CTS2 is a 78-item measure that ascertains negotiation, psychological aggression, physical assault, injury, and sexual coercion within an intimate context. Although the measurement tool has respectable psychometric properties including Cronbach's alpha ranging from .79 to .95 and evidence of convergent, discriminant, and factorial validity (Thompson, Basile, Hertz, & Sitterle, 2006), there are several limitations to this measurement.

Violence is situated in the context of settling disputes which implicitly discourages respondents from sharing their experiences with abuse that is control-based or that arises from an unknown cause. Additionally, the CTS-2 does not capture the context in which the abuse occurred or the motivation behind the abuse (e.g., self-defense, control).

### Conflict in Adolescent Dating Relationships Inventory (CADRI).

The CADRI was developed by Wolfe et al. (2001) to assess both victimization and perpetration of physical, psychological, and sexual dating violence. The items included in the CADRI were developed using several adult measures such as the CTS-2, the Psychological Maltreatment of Women Inventory, literature reviews, expert panels, and a pilot study (Exner-Cortens, Gill, & Eckenrode, 2016).

The CADRI is a 76-item self-report survey of students' use of a variety of strategies to resolve conflict within their most recent dating relationship. The instrument includes six scales (physical violence, sexual abuse, relational aggression, threatening behaviors, emotional abuse, and adaptive resolution) and a total value of dating violence. Each of the items within the scales are calculated relative to the respondent's own behavior (i.e., perpetration) and their partner's behavior (i.e., victimization) on a four point scale (0 = never, 1 = seldom, 2 = sometimes, 3 = often). Results from previous studies of the measure demonstrated acceptable psychometric properties (Wolfe et al., 2001). Wolfe and colleagues reported Cronbach alpha values ranging from .83 to .87 during the initial development and validation of the CADRI.

The CADRI, similar to the CTS-2, is also subject to limitations. Inherent in self-reported measurement is the interpretation of the individual regarding what is being asked of them. According to Wolfe et al. (2001), gender-based differences may exist in terms of how individuals interpret a particular item. Additionally, similar to the CTS-2, the CADRI does not account of the context in which violence was perpetrated or the subjective meaning made of the experience.

### The Sexual Experiences Survey (SES)

The SES was developed in the late 1970s to assess a thorough range of sexual victimization achieved through verbal coercion to physical force. The original measure consists of 12 yes/no items assessing whether or not participants have experienced sexual victimization. According to Koss et al. (2007), the scale's primary innovations included the use of non-judgmental specific language and avoidance of legal terms to facilitate the respondents' abilities to identify and recall experiences that encapsulate the forms of unwanted sexual experiences. As recent as 2007, Koss and colleagues revised the original SES to address some of its prior limitations. This new measure (SES-SFV) was the product of a three-year collaboration with nine researchers who have all used the original SES in their own work. The SES-SFV contains ten items, seven of which assess specific unwanted sexual experiences with five response choices that ask how many times this happened in the past year and since the participant was 14 years of age. The eighth question asks for the age of the participant. The ninth questions assess multiple victimizations and gender of the person who engaged in the unwanted contact with the participant. Finally, the last question ascertains if the participant has ever been raped, allowing the participant to utilize her own definition of rape. The SES-SFV is a marked improvement from the original in that it now uses a Likert scale, as opposed to the yes/no format. In addition, the new version not only allows participants to recall events of unwanted sexual contact in the past 12-months, like traditional scales assessing violence, it also allows the participants to recall events since age 14 (a longer period of time). In addition, the SES-SFV is one of few existing scales that measure sexual violence in a non-intimate partner context. Yet, similarly to other measurement tools of violence against women, the SES-SFV does not capture the victim's subjective experience with violence.

## TDV Policies, Programs, and Services

### Policies

Though there is a growing recognition of the consequences and pervasiveness of TDV, there are few policies that are directly related to TDV prevention and intervention. Relatively few teens and adolescents pursues legal remedies (e.g., legal case, protection order) to address TDV (Offenhauer & Buchalter, 2011). A barrier for teens seeking legal recourse is parental consent requirement for protection orders, transitional living services, and mental health services; this is an especially striking barrier for teens who are emancipated and/or do have difficulty confiding in their parents/guardians. Another barrier is that some TDV policies are couched under the auspices of adult IPV. As such, there are provisions that define IPV as between intimate partners who are married, cohabitating, or have children. As such, teenagers who live with their parents, as most do, are precluded from such policies.

Across the nation, many schools require policies related to TDV, including providing age-appropriate education about the prevalence and dynamics of TDV, mandated reporting, and victim service referrals. Specific laws, such as the Lindsey Burke Act, require that education policies incorporate TDV more directly to the curriculum.

### Programs

Most programs pertaining to TDV are school or community-based and focus on primary prevention (e.g., Safe Dates, Avery-Leaf, Positive Adolescent Training Choices). As such, these programs focus on raising awareness regarding TDV, combatting pro-violence beliefs and gender stereotypes, and increasing communication strategies (Offenhauer & Buchalter, 2011). There is much variability type and length of programming, participant characteristics, and outcome measurement and therefore, it is difficulty to meaningfully assess the effectiveness of these programs at preventing TDV (Offenhauer & Buchalter, 2011).

Additionally, there is an overwhelming lack on intervention studies specifically for victims of TDV. However, there have been efforts from the National Resource Center on Domestic Violencethat offers resources to victims primarily in the form of online support for victims. The NRCDV also sponsors several events throughout the year to help bring awareness to the issue of TDV, such as It's Time to Talk days, Break the Cycle, and Love is Not Abuse which provide useful information for victims and bystanders, offering evidence-based advice on how to remove oneself from an abusive relationship. However, the effectiveness of such programming has not been studied.

### Services

Shelter services (Sullivan & Bybee, 1999); advocacy (Sullivan & Bybee, 1999); supportive counseling (Golding, 1999); and screening in healthcare settings (Ghandour, Campbell, & Lloyd, 2015) have been empirically documented to be effective at mitigating the harmful effects of IPV in adult populations. However, there is limited documentation of the adaptation of such services for TDV victims and the effectiveness of these services for victims of TDV.

## Conclusion

The purpose of this chapter was to summarize the body of evidence on TDV. As demonstrated by this review, TDV is a relatively new area of inquiry. As such, there are opportunities wide open to scholarship, theory and practice development, and prevention/intervention work. Below, is a brief list of implications derived from this review:

- National surveillances of TDV been instrumental in elucidating the scope and magnitude of TDV. Yet there are methodological limitations to such studies. For example, most extant studies are conducted within the school context. As such these studies precluding teens who are drops out or those were otherwise absent during data collection, for participation in the study. Additionally, many extant studies use self-reported and non-comprehensive (e.g., ignoring the context, not accounting for subjective meaning of violence act) measures. Lastly, almost all surveillances of TDV are cross-sectional. Therefore, causation cannot be established between risk factors and consequences of TDV.
- Teens and adolescents conceptualize, identify, and eventually address TDV differently than adults due to developmental, generational, and legal (i.e. age and what constitutes as a minor) factors. For example, unlike IPV among adults, there is a significant overlap between victimization and perpetration. As such, prevention and interventions efforts must be specifically tailored and targeted to the unique needs of teens and adolescents.

## References

Ackard, D. M., Eisenberg, M. E., & Neumark-Sztainer, D. (2007). Long-term impact of adolescent dating violence on the behavioral and psychological health of male and female youth. *The Journal of Pediatrics, 151*(5), 476–481.

Akers, R. L. (1973). *Deviant behavior: A social learning approach*. Belmont, CA: Wadsworth Pub. Co.

Bandura, A. (1977). Self-efficacy: Toward a unifying theory of behavioral change. *Psychological Review, 84*(2), 191.

Banyard, V. L., & Cross, C. (2008). Consequences of teen dating violence: Understanding intervening variables in ecological context. *Violence Against Women, 14*(9), 998–1013.

Bowlby, J. (1980). *Attachment and loss: Loss, sadness and depression, vol. 3*. New York, NY: Basic Books.

Bronfenbrenner, U. (1977). Toward an experimental ecology of human development. *American Psychologist, 32*(7), 513.

Clayton, H. B., Lowry, R., Basile, K. C., Demissie, Z., & Bohm, M. K. (2017). Physical and sexual dating violence and nonmedical use of prescription drugs. *Pediatrics, 140*(6), e20172289.

Cohen, J. R., Shorey, R. C., Menon, S. V., & Temple, J. R. (2018). Predicting teen dating violence perpetration. *Pediatrics, 141*(4), e20172790.

Concept Systems. (2014). Teen dating relationships: Understanding and comparing youth and adult conceptualizations, final report. www.ncjrs.gov/pdffiles1/nij/grants/248464.pdf. Accessed June 6, 2019.

Dank, M., Lachman, P., Zweig, J. M., & Yahner, J. (2014). Dating violence experiences of lesbian, gay, bisexual, and transgender youth. *Journal of Youth and Adolescence, 43*(5), 846–857.

Exner-Cortens, D., Gill, L., & Eckenrode, J. (2016). Measurement of adolescent dating violence: A comprehensive review (Part 1, behaviors). *Aggression and Violent Behavior, 27*, 64–78.

Foshee, V. A., Reyes, H. L. M., Ennett, S. T., Suchindran, C., Mathias, J. P., Karriker-Jaffe, K. J., ... & Benefield, T. S. (2011). Risk and protective factors distinguishing profiles of adolescent peer and dating violence perpetration. *Journal of Adolescent Health, 48*(4), 344–350.

Fredland, N. M., Ricardo, I. B., Campbell, J. C., Sharps, P. W., Kub, J. K., & Yonas, M. (2005). The meaning of dating violence in the lives of middle school adolescents: A report of a focus group study. *Journal of School Violence, 4*(2), 95–114.

Gehring, K. S., & Vaske, J. C. (2017). Out in the open: The consequences of intimate partner violence for victims in same-sex and opposite-sex relationships. *Journal of Interpersonal Violence, 32*(23), 3669–3692.

Ghandour, R. M., Campbell, J. C., & Lloyd, J. (2015). Screening and counseling for intimate partner violence: A vision for the future. *Journal of Women's Health, 24*(1), 57–61.

Giordano, P. (2007, December). Recent research on gender and adolescent relationships: implications for teen dating violence research/prevention. In *Presentation at the US Departments of Health and Human Services and Justice Workshop on Teen Dating Violence: Developing a Research Agenda to Meet Practice Needs*, Crystal City, VA.

Giordano, P., Soto, D. A., Manning, W. D., & Longmore, M. A. (2010). The characteristics of romantic relationships associated with teen dating violence. *Social Science Research, 39*(6), 863–874.

Golding, J. M. (1999). Intimate partner violence as a risk factor for mental disorders: A meta-analysis. *Journal of Family Violence, 14*(2), 99–132.

Goncy, E. A., Sullivan, T. N., Farrell, A. D., Mehari, K. R., & Garthe, R. C. (2017). Identification of patterns of dating aggression and victimization among urban early adolescents and their relations to mental health symptoms. *Psychology of Violence, 7*(1), 58.

Halpern-Meekin, S., Manning, W. D., Giordano, P. C., & Longmore, M. A. (2013). Relationship churning, physical violence, and verbal abuse in young adult relationships. *Journal of Marriage and Family, 75*(1), 2–12.

Hines, D., & Malley-Morrison, K. (2005). *Family violence in the United States: Defining, understanding, and combating abuse*. Thousand Oaks, CA: Sage Publications, Inc.

Kelly, A. B., Chan, G. C., Toumbourou, J. W., O'Flaherty, M., Homel, R., Patton, G. C., & Williams, J. (2012). Very young adolescents and alcohol: Evidence of a unique susceptibility to peer alcohol use. *Addictive Behaviors, 37*(4), 414–419.

Koss, M. P., Abbey, A., Campbell, R., Cook, S., Norris, J., Testa, M., … & White, J. (2007). Revising the SES: A collaborative process to improve assessment of sexual aggression and victimization. *Psychology of Women Quarterly, 31*(4), 357–370.

Lawson, E. (2012). Single mothers, absentee fathers, and gun violence in Toronto: A contextual interpretation. *Women's Studies, 41*(7), 805–828.

Molidor, C., & Tolman, R. M. (1998). Gender and contextual factors in adolescent dating violence. *Violence Against Women, 4*(2), 180–194.

Montgomery, M. J. (2005). Psychosocial intimacy and identity: From early adolescence to emerging adulthood. *Journal of Adolescent Research, 20*(3), 346–374.

Mulford, C., & Giordano, P. C. (2008). Teen dating violence: A closer look at adolescent romantic relationships. *National Institute of Justice Journal, 261*(1), 31–40.

National Institute for Justice. (2018, February 8). Teen dating violence. www.nij.gov/topics/crime/intimate-partner-violence/teen-dating-violence/pages/welcome.aspx

O'Keefe, M. (1997). Predictors of dating violence among high school students. *Journal of Interpersonal Violence, 12*(4), 546–568.

Offenhauer, P., & Buchalter, A. (2011, June). Teen dating violence: A literature review and annotated bibliography. In *A report prepared by the Federal Research Division, Library of Congress under an interagency agreement with the Violence and Victimization Research Division, National Institute of Justice*. www.ncjrs.gov/pdffiles1/nij/grants/235368.pdf. Accessed 6 June, 2019.

Olshen, E., McVeigh, K. H., Wunsch-Hitzig, R. A., & Rickert, V. I. (2007). Dating violence, sexual assault, and suicide attempts among urban teenagers. *Archives of Pediatrics & Adolescent Medicine, 161*(6), 539–545.

Oudekerk, B., Blachman-Denmer, D., & Mulford, C. (2014). *Teen dating violence: How peers can affect risk & protective factors*. Washington, DC: U.S. Department of Justice, Office of Justice Programs. www.ncjrs.gov/pdffiles1/nij/248337.pdf

Pratt, T. C., Cullen, F. T., Sellers, C. S., Winfree, Jr, L. T.,, Madensen, T. D., Daigle, L. E., … & Gau, J. M. (2010). The empirical status of social learning theory: A meta-analysis. *Justice Quarterly, 27*(6), 765–802.

Reppucci, N. D., Oudekerk, B. A., Guarnera, L., Nagel, A., Reitz-Krueger, C., Walker, T., & Warner, T. (2013). A review of the findings from Project DATE: Risky relationships and teen dating violence among at-risk adolescents. *Final report for National Institute of Justice, grant*, (2009-IJ).

Schwartz, M. D., & DeKeseredy, W. (1997). *Sexual assault on the college campus: The role of male peer support*. Thousand Oaks, CA: Sage Publications.

Sullivan, C. M., & Bybee, D. I. (1999). Reducing violence using community-based advocacy for women with abusive partners. *Journal of Consulting and Clinical Psychology, 67*(1), 43.

Sutherland, E. H. (1947). *Principles of criminology* (4th). Philadelphia, PA: J. B. Lippincott.

Teten, A. L., Ball, B., Valle, L. A., Noonan, R., & Rosenbluth, B. (2009). Considerations for the definition, measurement, consequences, and prevention of dating violence victimization among adolescent girls. *Journal of Women's Health, 18*(7), 923–927.

Thompson, M. P., Basile, K. C., Hertz, M. F., & Sitterle, D. (2006). *Measuring intimate partner violence victimization and perpetration: A compendium of assessment tools*. Atlanta, GA: Centers for Disease Control and Prevention, National Center for Injury Prevention and Control.

Wekerle, C., & Wolfe, D. A. (1999). Dating violence in mid-adolescence: Theory, significance, and emerging prevention initiatives. *Clinical Psychology Review*, *19*(4), 435–456.

Wincentak, K., Connolly, J., & Card, N. (2017). Teen dating violence: A meta-analytic review of prevalence rates. *Psychology of Violence*, 7(2), 224.

Wolfe, D. A., Scott, K., Reitzel-Jaffe, D., Wekerle, C., Grasley, C., & Straatman, A. L. (2001). Development and validation of the conflict in adolescent dating relationships inventory. *Psychological Assessment*, *13*(2), 277.

Yun, S. H. (2011). Factor structure and reliability of the revised Conflict Tactics Scales' (CTS2) 10-factor model in a community-based female sample. *Journal of Interpersonal Violence*, *26*(4), 719–744.

Zweig, J. M., Dank, M., Yahner, J., & Lachman, P. (2013). The rate of cyber dating abuse among teens and how it relates to other forms of teen dating violence. *Journal of Youth and Adolescence*. *42*(7), 1063–1077.

# 16
# HEALTH FOCUSED CRIMINOLOGY
## Lead, Crime, and the Use of Quantitative Genetics to Examine Causality

*Brian B. Boutwell and Stephen J. Watts*

### Introduction

Recent years have started to witness an efflorescence of research approaching the study of criminal and antisocial behavior via the lens of public health (e.g. Beckley et al., 2018; Jackson & Vaughn, 2017; Jackson et al., 2017; Muller et al., 2018). The growth of this scholarship is not necessarily surprising given that, while predisposition toward criminogenic behaviors is partly heritable (Barnes et al., 2011; Chabris et al., 2014; Polderman et al., 2015; Turkheimer, 2000), *non-genetic* factors also (and virtually always) explain significant portions of the variance for criminogenic behaviors, and these non-genetic factors likely evince some of their influence via health related channels (Gottfredson & Hirschi, 1990; Muller et al., 2018; Wright et al., 2008). While we discuss one of these potent health risk factors momentarily it is important to pause first and return to the issue of partial heritability for human behavioral outcomes, as it underscores an important reality about environmental effects and the search for causal influences on behavior (Turkheimer, 2000).

In particular, it suggests that when experimental control of independent variables is largely not possible—as is the case with most health criminological and personality psychology research—some specific research designs are more helpful than others with trying to discern whether putative environmental risk factors exert a causal influence on crime (Rothman & Greenland, 2005; Wilson & Wilson, 2016; Wright et al., 2015). The distinguishing factor of these designs involves utilizing variations of the classical twin design in order to hold constant both genetic and familial variables that might otherwise confound the association between environmental risk and some behavioral outcome like crime (Barnes et al., 2014; Plomin et al., 2013; Turkheimer, 2000; Turkheimer & Harden, 2014).

These designs might be thought of as examining research questions from a pseudo-counterfactual point of view, such as: "what behaviors might emerge if one twin is more impulsive than their cotwin?" or "how might developmental outcomes differ for one twin who has more exposure to delinquent peers than their co-twin (Turkheimer & Harden, 2014)?" By approaching research questions in this manner—examining the differences between twins for exposure to some risk factor, or differences in personality traits—researchers are essentially posing a type of counterfactual question of "what would've happened in the life of this individual, had one personality trait/temperamental factor/social risk factor differed, and everything else (home environment and genome) remained the same?" (see Lee, 2012; Pearl & Mackenzie, 2018).

Compared to classical twin designs, and the sheer number of them that exist, studies of the type mentioned above remained comparatively more limited (discordant twin designs). Nonetheless, these types of research designs are beginning to penetrate into the study of crime, and the field of criminology more broadly (see, Lewis et al., 2019). Yet, over a century of sociological and criminological insights have unveiled a host of social and environmental factors that correlate with violence—some more consistently than others—and so much work remains in examining traditional crime correlates within the framework of quasi-experimental types of twin designs (Barnes et al., 2014).

Along these lines, there is one environmental and health relevant risk factor that is particularly poised to benefit from this type of design, as it seems on the precipice of fairly strong causal inference. Exposure to the heavy metal toxin lead between the ages of 0 and roughly 70 months in human beings has been linked consistently to a number of clinically and behaviorally deleterious outcomes. Disruption in brain development and functioning has been observed in humans (using associational data), and in non-human subjects (using experimental designs). What is striking is that the regions of the brain impacted by lead exposure are those also linked with behavioral inhibition, gratification delay, executive functioning, and aspects of general intelligence (Bellinger et al., 1992; Cecil et al., 2008; Fergusson et al., 1988; Needleman & Leviton, 1979; Needleman et al., 1990), thus seeming to draw a line between exposure, biological influence, and behavior. Indeed, longitudinal studies spanning decades of development have suggested that individuals exposed to lead prenatally are considerably more likely to be convicted of a violent crime in adulthood (Wright et al., 2008).

Below, we very briefly review this rapidly growing body of research, and then conclude by discussing how causal inference could be improved on this topic with the use of genetically sensitive research designs. To be sure, prior scholars have discussed the topic of lead exposure, and the difficulties surrounding causal inference and confounding (see Beckley et al., 2018; Ernhart, 1995; Wilson & Wilson, 2016). Yet, the issue remains unresolved and worthy of further consideration. Moreover, we seek to expand the discussion by exploring the advantages of quantitative genetics and what these designs have to offer the field of health criminology as a whole. To the extent that the long-term correlations of lead with behavioral outcomes are indeed causal (in a counterfactual sense), it could offer a powerful mechanism for prevention and intervention efforts in the public policy and public health arenas.

## Early Life Lead Exposure, Behavior, and Psychopathology

The research to date on lead exposure seems relatively clear that it is correlated with negative outcomes during childhood, and on through adulthood. The literature on lead exposure and neuropsychological deficits in particular is quite developed. Lead exposure in this literature has been tied to lower cognitive functioning (Bellinger et al., 1992; Fergusson et al., 1988; Needleman & Gatsonis, 1990; Nevin, 2000; Pocock et al., 1994; Reuben et al., 2017), decreased brain volume (Cecil et al., 2008), lower school achievement (Bellinger et al., 1992; Fergusson et al., 1988), and attentional problems/impulsivity (Cho et al., 2010; Minder et al., 1994).

Arguably the largest literature concerning the neuropsychological consequences of lead exposure concerns intelligence, as measured by IQ or other standardized test scores (see generally the recent review by Muller et al., 2018). Children exposed to lead score comparatively lower than their peers on standardized IQ tests (see Jusko et al., 2007; Lanphear et al., 2005). And these early differences can persist into adulthood, with a study by Reuben and colleagues (2017) finding that those who had high blood levels as children had lower IQ test scores when they were retested at 38 years old. This correlation between lead exposure and IQ scores is paralleled in research that has shown that lead exposure also correlates with poorer performance on school tests, as well. A study by Zhang and colleagues (2013) found that elevated blood lead levels correlate with lower test scores in math, science, and reading tests, while Reyes (2015) reported in a sample of Massachusetts school children that a reduction in the percentage of children with elevated blood lead levels correlated with a reduction in the share of children who performed below satisfactory levels on school tests.

Another growing literature concerns lead exposure and its correlation with attentional difficulties and impulsivity. Studies in both clinical and nationally representative samples have shown a relationship between lead exposure and hyperactivity (Braun et al., 2006; Mendelsohn et al., 1998; Nigg et al., 2010). While these studies are cross-sectional, some more recent research has provided more compelling causal evidence. Winter and Sampson (2017), utilizing data from the Project on Human Development in Chicago Neighborhoods, reported that children with comparatively high levels of blood lead were more impulsive in adolescence. This finding held while controlling for an extensive set of individual and neighborhood-level covariates.

## Lead Exposure and Crime

In short, a vast literature exists that connects lead exposure to neuropsychological deficits. At the same time, there also exists a fairly robust literature on the connection between lead exposure and crime, including violent crime. Moreover, this literature has suggested lead exposure has a relationship with crime at both the individual (Needleman et al., 2002; Nevin, 2000; Wasserman et al., 1998) and macro levels (Barrett, 2017; Boutwell et al., 2016; Nevin, 2007; Reyes, 2007; Stretesky & Lynch, 2001, 2004; Taylor et al., 2016). At the individual level, in one of the earliest studies on lead exposure, Byers and Lord (1943) noted that children with lead poisoning were often at risk for being violent. In a prospective longitudinal study of 195 urban, inner city youths, Dietrich and colleagues (2001) found that prenatal and postnatal exposure to lead associated with delinquent and antisocial behaviors in adolescence, including marijuana use. Using this same sample, Wright and colleagues (2008) found that prenatal and postnatal blood lead concentrations associated with higher rates of total arrest, and arrests for offenses specifically involving violence. Similarly, Needleman and colleagues (2002) found in a case-control study of 194 youths adjudicated delinquent in Pennsylvania that delinquent juveniles had much higher bone lead concentrations than non-delinquent juveniles.

While some of these studies are cross-sectional, several studies have used data drawn from longitudinal samples to show a correlation between lead exposure and crime (Amato et al., 2013; Dietrich et al., 2001; Wright et al., 2008). A very recent study, analyzing a birth cohort from New Zealand, reported that elevated blood levels, measured at age 11, correlated to some extent with offending outcomes, though it should be noted (as the authors do in the paper) that the associations were inconsistent and often failed to survive statistical correction for being male (Beckley et al., 2018). A similar literature has shown that lead concentrations in the environment relate to crime at the macro level. Stretesky and Lynch (2004) looked at county level data in the United States and found that air-lead levels correlated with both property and violent crime rates. These scholars found a similar association between air-lead levels and homicide specifically at the county level in the United States (Stretesky & Lynch, 2001). Also on the topic of homicide, Feigenbaum and Muller (2016) found that the use of lead water pipes in the early twentieth century in the United States correlated with higher homicide rates at the city-level. Finally, Boutwell and colleagues (2016) found that greater lead exposure at the census-tract level was associated with increased violent, non-violent, and total crime in St. Louis, MO. This macro-level correlation between lead and crime rates observed in the literature is so consistent, in fact, that some scholars have argued that reduced air-lead levels in the latter part of the twentieth century in the United States were one of the factors influencing the crime decline of the 1990s (see

Aizer & Currie, 2017; Nevin, 2007; Reyes, 2007). Overall, the research is clear that increased lead exposure, whether at the individual or aggregate level, correlates with higher crime rates, and specifically higher violent crime rates.

## Lead Exposure and Crime: ADHD and a Possible Causal Chain

The prior sections have identified an association in the research literature between lead exposure and neuropsychological deficits and lead exposure and crime. However, a question remains as to whether lead exposure has an association with crime that is more direct, or whether this association is mediated by one, or several, of the neuropsychological deficits associated with lead exposure. As an example of how this might work, we will briefly review the literature on attention deficit/hyperactivity disorder (ADHD), which has been linked to both lead exposure and crime.

Among children and adolescents, attention deficit/hyperactivity disorder is one of the more commonly diagnosed disorders. Research has made clear that ADHD is an important contributor to antisocial behavior during childhood and into later adolescence (Pratt et al., 2002; Schilling et al., 2011; Watts, 2018). ADHD has been tied to minor delinquency and substance use, but also more serious violent and property crime (Ellis & Walsh, 2000). And this line of research is clear that ADHD is a significant risk factor for crime even when accounting for the presence of other, correlated disorders, such as oppositional defiant disorder (ODD) and conduct disorder (CD) (Loeber et al., 1995; Moffitt, 1990; Van Lier et al., 2007). Also, individuals with ADHD have more frequent contact with the criminal justice system, and the correctional population includes a disproportionate number of offenders who can or have been diagnosed with ADHD (Gudjonsson et al., 2009; Mannuzza et al., 2008; Rösler et al., 2004; Savolainen et al., 2012; Young et al., 2009).

But what are the causes of ADHD? While a detailed etiology is not yet precisely known, numerous studies have shown that much of the variance in the disorder are accounted for by genetic factors that vary in the population, with heritability estimates of ADHD found to be at about 80 percent on average, regardless of whether it's measured as a dimensional spectrum or a categorical trait (Bobb et al., 2006; Schilling et al., 2011). Importantly, this still leaves roughly 20 percent of ADHD variability to the environment, and numerous studies to date have established an association between lead exposure and ADHD symptomatology.

Research has suggested that exposure to lead in either the prenatal or postnatal period can increase risks for ADHD (Nicolescu et al., 2010), even at levels of lead exposure that not are not substantially above average (Boucher et al., 2012). This second finding suggests that much like with ADHD, the risks or resilience associated with lead exposure may be heritable (Schilling et al., 2011). And depending on the type of measurement of symptomatology, lead exposure can relate to the predominantly inattentive, predominantly hyperactive-impulsive, or the combined type of ADHD (Nigg et al., 2010).

The literature is clear that lead exposure relates to crime, lead exposure relates to ADHD, and ADHD relates to crime, but an unresolved issue is whether these variables connect in a causal chain. Does lead exposure partly influence crime because of its relationship to ADHD and comorbid disorders? Is there a mediating relationship at play? Also, does lead exposure also influence crime through its effects on ADHD and the known effects of ADHD on problems in school (Frazier et al., 2007; Watts, 2018)? These are questions concerning causal relationships that still need to be explored, yet remain an area primed for researchers in the field of health criminology.

## Lingering Questions about Causality

Rothman and Greenland (2005) pointed out several particularly vexing aspects of causal inference in epidemiological research in general, yet one worth spending some time with is the concern of strong selection bias and non-random exposures to various exogenous risk factors (like lead). Regional geography, occupational status (i.e., blue collar versus white collar), educational attainment, socio-economic status, along with a range of other factors can often either elevate or diminish the likelihood of an individual coming into contact with heavy metal pollutants like lead. Philosophically, and more recently mathematically, causal inference is rooted in the notion of a counterfactual, which involves considering what would have transpired, had some exposure to treatment *never* happened at all (see Lee, 2012; Pearl & Mackenzie, 2018; Rothman & Greenland, 2005), an idea which ultimately hinges on the ability to *control* the exposure (i.e., rule out spurious predictors).

For the current discussion, this would mean directly exposing an individual to lead, observing the outcome, and then rewinding the clock of time, withholding lead exposure, and then observing once again the outcome of their life. A true counterfactual of this type, observing the same individual both receive and not receive some treatment, is impossible. Instead we often seek to approximate it by constructing statistically equivalent groups using random assignment and exposing one group to the key independent variable (i.e., an experiment) (Lee, 2012). Yet, ethical constraints rightly preclude endangering subjects in the manner in which randomized lead exposure would—at a minimum—jeopardize the health of expectant mothers, young infants, or both.

This, of course, is not a new challenge for medical and epidemiological research, as a similar difficulty emerged when trying to disentangle selection bias from causation for nicotine smoking and cancer decades ago (see Pearl & Mackenzie, 2018). At the time, the statistician Francis Galton argued fiercely that any association between the two variables—smoking and lung cancer—was confounded by then unmeasured genetic influences that predicted both propensity to smoke as well as vulnerability to cancer (Lee, 2012; Pearl & Mackenzie, 2018). Without the ability to conduct randomized trials in humans, researchers were left trying to approach experimental control using statistical correction (Pearl & Mackenzie, 2018). Certainly, randomized trials in animals painted a compelling picture for causal effects between smoking and cancer, yet associations in humans were correlational, and no matter how strong, or robust an association, causal inference is limited unless key criteria are met. While we lack the space to outline those criteria herein, suffice it to say that one *can* make reasonable causal inference using non-experimental research tools such as instrumental variables, and most relevant for the current discussion, twin and family designs (Lee, 2012). And it warrants mentioning, of course, that scientists ultimately converged on the idea that smoking did indeed exert a causal effect on cancer.

Identical twins represent genetic clones of one another, sharing virtually all of their distinguishing DNA. Fraternal twins share as much genetic material as full siblings (50 percent), yet share a prenatal environment, while full siblings (50 percent), half siblings (25 percent), and adopted siblings (0 percent) share varying degrees of genetic material, as well as a rearing environment (Barnes et al., 2014; Plomin et al., 2013). By utilizing knowledge about genetic overlap, quantitative geneticists are able to tease apart the variance for a given outcome that is attributable to genetic factors from that which is due to environmental factors (Polderman et al., 2015). More importantly, this type of data can be utilized as a form of naturally occurring experiment in which genetic material is randomly shuffled between twins and siblings at conception.

To provide a specific example, identical twins can be used as genetic controls of one another, which allows researchers to examine the effect of "treatment" (any key independent variable) on some outcomes. Perhaps one twin smokes and the other does not, one twin consumes more dietary fat while the other is vegetarian, one twin associates with deviant peers and other does not, or one twin practices a particular religion with zeal while the other does not (Turkheimer & Harden, 2014). To the extent that these differences correspond to differences in the outcome of interest—perhaps the twin who smokes develops cancer and their cotwin does not—it provides a powerful mechanism for causal inference as it systematically controls for all genetic and familial confounds without the need to actually measure (or even have knowledge of) all of the relevant confounds (Lee, 2012).

An example from the literature on schizophrenia also helps to provide a more concrete example of how such designs are useful in observational data. Sariaslan and colleagues (2014) were interested in further examining the link that had emerged between risk for schizophrenia and residence in dense, urban settings. Prior scholarship on the topic revealed a correlation between residence in urban areas and schizophrenia, yet the obvious problem—which mirrors that of lead exposure—involved lingering concerns about causality versus selection bias. Using data from a national registry of Swedish citizens, Sariaslan and his team (2014) examined over 2 million subjects, analyzing data from over 1 million cousins and 1 million full siblings in particular (thus, a variant on the classical twin design). Once the researchers corrected for unobserved familial confounds, the urbanicity-schizophrenia association disappeared. What this means is that the correlation between the epidemiological risk factor (urbanicity) and the outcome was primarily attributable to risk factors already concentrated in the families (partly genetic and partly environmental in origin). Put differently, the findings strongly challenged the presumption of a causal effect emanating from the environment.

While designs of the this nature have been used to examine a variety of independent and dependent variables—from psychopathy and crime, to religiosity and delinquency (Lewis et al., 2019; Turkheimer & Harden, 2014)—to our knowledge no one has yet undertaken such an analysis around lead exposure and ADHD, or lead exposure and violence. In reality, such a study is not difficult to envision, it would simply involve collection of blood lead exposure information from children early in the life-course, in addition to the typical developmental and behavioral data typically collected in twin and family studies in the social sciences. One difficulty with including twins at all, of course, is the fact that they share a prenatal environment and thus any lead exposure is likely going to expose both fetuses and perhaps at levels so similar as to not provide enough variation for meaningful analyses.

Nonetheless, it is plausible to consider that even in scenarios where twins are both exposed to lead exposure, one twin may nonetheless bear a heavier burden of blood lead than their cotwin, so it would still be informative to analyze data from twins—if only to examine questions of absorption differences in siblings, and the factors that might increase the vulnerability of one twin versus the other. Are male twins in a mixed sex pair of fraternal twins more likely to uptake lead compared to their sibling, for example? Yet, no matter if it does prove implausible to analyze twins for this research question, divergent sibling designs can still be utilized with full and half siblings, and while these designs do not control for all genetic confounds, they do offer useful insight into potential causal effects, and they obfuscate the need to measure and control for possible family confounders in the manner of traditional social science designs (i.e., OLS regression) (see Boutwell et al., 2017a; Sariaslan et al., 2014).

For the question of lead exposure, then, and possible causal pathways from exposure to violence, there are two largely open questions that need resolving. First, if we suspect lead exposure is indeed exerting some causal effect on violence and crime later in life then we need to investigate that question using the causal inference tools afforded from twin and family designs. To the extent that those studies align with prior evidence—that they reveal an effect of lead on violence—it will lead us to the second unresolved issue, which is what phenotypes lie along the way from lead exposure to violence. As we've mentioned, ADHD seems to represent a reasonably plausible candidate, but similar types of studies will need to be conducted examining lead exposure and ADHD using twin designs. More broadly, we contend that the burgeoning field of health criminology—which seems poised to make key contributions to our understanding of criminal and antisocial behavior—will nonetheless reap a large benefit from a reliance on twin and family designs.

## References

Aizer, A., & Currie, J. (2017). *Lead and juvenile delinquency: New evidence from linked birth, school and juvenile detention records* (No. w23392). Cambridge, MA: National Bureau of Economic Research. www.nber.org/papers/w23392

Amato, M. S., Magzamen, S., Imm, P., Havlena, J. A., Anderson, H. A., Kanarek, M. S., & Moore, C. F. (2013). Early lead exposure (< 3 years old) prospectively predicts fourth grade school suspension in Milwaukee, Wisconsin (USA). *Environmental Research, 126*, 60–65.

Barnes, J. C., Beaver, K. M., & Boutwell, B. B. (2011). Examining the genetic underpinnings to Moffitt's developmental taxonomy: A behavioral genetic analysis. *Criminology, 49*(4), 923–954.

Barnes, J. C., Wright, J. P., Boutwell, B. B., Schwartz, J. A., Connolly, E. J., Nedelec, J. L., & Beaver, K. M. (2014). Demonstrating the validity of twin research in criminology. *Criminology, 52*(4), 588–626.

Barrett, K. L. (2017). Exploring community levels of lead (Pb) and youth violence. *Sociological Spectrum, 37*(4), 205–222.

Beckley, A. L., Caspi, A., Broadbent, J., Harrington, H., Houts, R. M., Poulton, R., ... Moffitt, T. E. (2018). Association of childhood blood lead levels with criminal offending. *JAMA Pediatrics, 172*(2), 166–173.

Bellinger, D. C., Stiles, K. M., & Needleman, H. L. (1992). Low-level lead exposure, intelligence and academic achievement: A long-term follow-up study. *Pediatrics, 90*(6), 855–861.

Bobb, A. J., Castellanos, F. X., Addington, A. M., & Rapoport, J. L. (2006). Molecular genetic studies of ADHD: 1991 to 2004. *American Journal of Medical Genetics Part B: Neuropsychiatric Genetics, 141*(6), 551–565.

Boucher, O., Jacobson, S. W., Plusquellec, P., Dewailly, É., Ayotte, P., Forget-Dubois, N., ... Muckle, G. (2012). Prenatal methylmercury, postnatal lead exposure, and evidence of attention deficit/hyperactivity disorder among Inuit children in Arctic Quebec. *Environmental Health Perspectives, 120*(10), 1456–1461.

Boutwell, B. B., Connolly, E. J., Barbaro, N., Shackelford, T. K., Petkovsek, M., & Beaver, K. M. (2017). On the genetic and environmental reasons why intelligence correlates with criminal victimization. *Intelligence, 62*, 155–166.

Boutwell, B. B., Nelson, E. J., Emo, B., Vaughn, M. G., Schootman, M., Rosenfeld, R., & Lewis, R. (2016). The intersection of aggregate-level lead exposure and crime. *Environmental Research, 148*, 79–85.

Boutwell, B. B., Nelson, E. J., Qian, Z., Vaughn, M. G., Wright, J. P., Beaver, K. M., ... Rosenfeld, R. (2017b). Aggregate-level lead exposure, gun violence, homicide, and rape. *PLoS One, 12*(11), e0187953.

Braun, J. M., Kahn, R. S., Froehlich, T., Auinger, P., & Lanphear, B. P. (2006). Exposures to environmental toxicants and attention deficit hyperactivity disorder in US children. *Environmental Health Perspectives, 114*(12), 1904–1909.

Byers, R. K., & Lord, E. E. (1943). Late effects of lead poisoning on mental development. *American Journal of Diseases of Children, 66*(5), 471–494.

Cecil, K. M., Brubaker, C. J., Adler, C. M., Dietrich, K. N., Altaye, M., Egelhoff, J. C., ... Lanphear, B. P. (2008). Decreased brain volume in adults with childhood lead exposure. *PLoS Medicine, 5*(5), e112.

Chabris, C. F., Lee, J. J., & Benjamin, D. J. (2014). Erratum: Why it is hard to find genes associated with social science traits: Theoretical and empirical considerations (American Journal of Public Health (2013) 103 (S152-S166)). *American Journal of Public Health, 104*(1), 1–5.

Cho, S. C., Kim, B. N., Hong, Y. C., Shin, M. S., Yoo, H. J., Kim, J. W., ... Kim, H. W. (2010). Effect of environmental exposure to lead and tobacco smoke on inattentive and hyperactive symptoms and neurocognitive performance in children. *Journal of Child Psychology and Psychiatry, 51*(9), 1050–1057.

Dietrich, K. N., Douglas, R. M., Succop, P. A., Berger, O. G., & Bornschein, R. L. (2001). Early exposure to lead and juvenile delinquency. *Neurotoxicology and Teratology, 23*(6), 511–518.

Ellis, L. & Walsh, A. (2000). *Criminology: A Global Perspective*. Boston, MA: Allyn & Bacon.

Ernhart, C. B. (1995). Inconsistencies in the lead-effects literature exist and cannot be explained by "effect modification". *Neurotoxicology and Teratology, 17*(3), 227–233.

Feigenbaum, J. J., & Muller, C. (2016). Lead exposure and violent crime in the early twentieth century. *Explorations in Economic History, 62*, 51–86.

Fergusson, D. M., Fergusson, J. E., Horwood, L. J., & Kinzett, N. G. (1988). A longitudinal study of dentine lead levels, intelligence, school performance and behaviour: Part II. Dentine lead and cognitive ability. *Journal of Child Psychology and Psychiatry, 29*(6), 793–809.

Frazier, T. W., Youngstrom, E. A., Glutting, J. J., & Watkins, M. W. (2007). ADHD and achievement: Meta-analysis of the child, adolescent, and adult literatures and a concomitant study with college students. *Journal of Learning Disabilities, 40*(1), 49–65.

Gottfredson, M. R., & Hirschi, T. (1990). *A General Theory of Crime*. Palo Alto, CA: Stanford University Press.

Gudjonsson, G. H., Sigurdsson, J. F., Young, S., Newton, A. K., & Peersen, M. (2009). Attention Deficit Hyperactivity Disorder (ADHD). How do ADHD symptoms relate to personality among prisoners? *Personality and Individual Differences*, 47(1), 64–68.

Jackson, D. B., & Vaughn, M. G. (2017). Household food insecurity during childhood and adolescent misconduct. *Preventive Medicine*, 96, 113–117.

Jackson, D. B., Vaughn, M. G., & Salas-Wright, C. P. (2017). Poor nutrition and bullying behaviors: A comparison of deviant and non-deviant youth. *Journal of Adolescence*, 57, 69–73.

Jusko, T. A., Henderson Jr., C. R., Lanphear, B. P., Cory-Slechta, D. A., Parsons, P. J., & Canfield, R. L. (2007). Blood lead concentrations< 10 μg/dL and child intelligence at 6 years of age. *Environmental Health Perspectives*, 116(2), 243–248.

Lanphear, B. P., Hornung, R., Khoury, J., Yolton, K., Baghurst, P., Bellinger, D. C., ... Rothenberg, S. J. (2005). Low-level environmental lead exposure and children's intellectual function: An international pooled analysis. *Environmental health perspectives*, 113(7), 894–899.

Lee, J. J. (2012). Correlation and causation in the study of personality. *European Journal of Personality*, 26(4), 372–390.

Lewis, R. H., Connolly, E. J., Boisvert, D. L., & Boutwell, B. B. (2019). A behavioral genetic analysis of the cooccurrence between psychopathic personality traits and criminal behavior. *Journal of Contemporary Criminal Justice*, 35(1), 52–68.

Loeber, R., Green, S. M., Keenan, K., & Lahey, B. B. (1995). Which boys will fare worse? Early predictors of the onset of conduct disorder in a six-year longitudinal study. *Journal of the American Academy of Child & Adolescent Psychiatry*, 34(4), 499–509.

Mannuzza, S., Klein, R. G., & Moulton III, J. L. (2008). Lifetime criminality among boys with ADHD: A prospective follow-up study into adulthood using official arrest records. *Psychiatry Research*, 160(3), 237–246.

Mendelsohn, A. L., Dreyer, B. P., Fierman, A. H., Rosen, C. M., Legano, L. A., Kruger, H. A., ... Courtlandt, C. D. (1998). Low-level lead exposure and behavior in early childhood. *Pediatrics*, 101(3), e10–e10.

Minder, B., Das-Smaal, E. A., JM Brand, E. F., & Orlebeke, J. F. (1994). Exposure to lead and specific attentional problems in schoolchildren. *Journal of Learning Disabilities*, 27(6), 393–399.

Moffitt, T. E. (1990). Juvenile delinquency and attention deficit disorder: Boys' developmental trajectories from age 3 to age 15. *Child Development*, 61(3), 893–910.

Muller, C., Sampson, R. J., & Winter, A. S. (2018). Environmental inequality: The social causes and consequences of lead exposure. *Annual Review of Sociology*, 44, 263–282.

Needleman, H. L., & Gatsonis, C. A. (1990). Low-level lead exposure and the IQ of children. *JAMA*, 263(5), 673–678.

Needleman, H. L., & Leviton, A. (1979). Neurologic effects of exposure to lead. *The Journal of Pediatrics*, 94(3), 505–506.

Needleman, H. L., McFarland, C., Ness, R. B., Fienberg, S. E., & Tobin, M. J. (2002). Bone lead levels in adjudicated delinquents: A case control study. *Neurotoxicology and Teratology*, 24(6), 711–717.

Needleman, H. L., Schell, A., Bellinger, D., Leviton, A., & Allred, E. N. (1990). The long-term effects of exposure to low doses of lead in childhood: An 11-year follow-up report. *New England Journal of Medicine*, 322(2), 83–88.

Nevin, R. (2000). How lead exposure relates to temporal changes in IQ, violent crime, and unwed pregnancy. *Environmental Research*, 83(1), 1–22.

Nevin, R. (2007). Understanding international crime trends: The legacy of preschool lead exposure. *Environmental Research*, 104(3), 315–336.

Nicolescu, R., Petcu, C., Cordeanu, A., Fabritius, K., Schlumpf, M., Krebs, R., ... Winneke, G. (2010). Environmental exposure to lead, but not other neurotoxic metals, relates to core elements of ADHD in Romanian children: Performance and questionnaire data. *Environmental Research*, 110(5), 476–483.

Nigg, J. T., Nikolas, M., Mark Knottnerus, G., Cavanagh, K., & Friderici, K. (2010). Confirmation and extension of association of blood lead with attention-deficit/hyperactivity disorder (ADHD) and ADHD symptom domains at population-typical exposure levels. *Journal of Child Psychology and Psychiatry*, 51(1), 58–65.

Pearl, J., & Mackenzie, D. (2018). *The book of why: The new science of cause and effect*. New York, NY: Basic Books.

Plomin, R., DeFries, J. C., Knopik, V. S., & Neiderhiser, J. M. (2013). *Behavioral genetics*. New York, NY: Worth Publishers.

Pocock, S. J., Smith, M., & Baghurst, P. (1994). Environmental lead and children's intelligence: A systematic review of the epidemiological evidence. *BMJ*, 309(6963), 1189–1197.

Polderman, T. J., Benyamin, B., De Leeuw, C. A., Sullivan, P. F., Van Bochoven, A., Visscher, P. M., & Posthuma, D. (2015). Meta-analysis of the heritability of human traits based on fifty years of twin studies. *Nature Genetics*, 47(7), 702–709.

Pratt, T. C., Cullen, F. T., Blevins, K. R., Daigle, L., & Unnever, J. D. (2002). The relationship of attention deficit hyperactivity disorder to crime and delinquency: A meta-analysis. *International Journal of Police Science & Management*, *4*(4), 344–360.

Reuben, A., Caspi, A., Belsky, D. W., Broadbent, J., Harrington, H., Sugden, K., ... Moffitt, T. E. (2017). Association of childhood blood lead levels with cognitive function and socioeconomic status at age 38 years and with IQ change and socioeconomic mobility between childhood and adulthood. *JAMA*, *317*(12), 1244–1251.

Reyes, J. W. (2007). Environmental policy as social policy? The impact of childhood lead exposure on crime. *The BE Journal of Economic Analysis & Policy*, *7*(1). doi: 10.2202/1935-1682.1796.

Reyes, J. W. (2015). Lead policy and academic performance: Insights from Massachusetts. *Harvard Educational Review*, *85*(1), 75–107.

Rösler, M., Retz, W., Retz-Junginger, P., Hengesch, G., Schneider, M., Supprian, T., ... Thome, J. (2004). Prevalence of Attention Deficit–Hyperactivity Disorder (ADHD) and comorbid disorders in young male prison inmates. *European Archives of Psychiatry and Clinical Neuroscience*, *254*(6), 365–371.

Rothman, K. J., & Greenland, S. (2005). Causation and causal inference in epidemiology. *American Journal of Public Health*, *95*(S1), S144–S150.

Sariaslan, A., Larsson, H., D'onofrio, B., Långström, N., Fazel, S., & Lichtenstein, P. (2014). Does population density and neighborhood deprivation predict schizophrenia? A nationwide Swedish family-based study of 2.4 million individuals. *Schizophrenia Bulletin*, *41*(2), 494–502.

Savolainen, J., Hughes, L. A., Mason, W. A., Hurtig, T. M., Ebeling, H., Moilanen, I. K., ... Taanila, A. M. (2012). Antisocial propensity, adolescent school outcomes, and the risk of criminal conviction. *Journal of Research on Adolescence*, *22*(1), 54–64.

Schilling, C. M., Walsh, A., & Yun, I. (2011). ADHD and criminality: A primer on the genetic, neurobiological, evolutionary, and treatment literature for criminologists. *Journal of Criminal Justice*, *39*(1), 3–11.

Stretesky, P. B., & Lynch, M. J. (2001). The relationship between lead exposure and homicide. *Archives of Pediatrics & Adolescent Medicine*, *155*(5), 579–582.

Stretesky, P. B., & Lynch, M. J. (2004). The relationship between lead and crime. *Journal of Health and Social Behavior*, *45*(2), 214–229.

Taylor, M. P., Forbes, M. K., Opeskin, B., Parr, N., & Lanphear, B. P. (2016). The relationship between atmospheric lead emissions and aggressive crime: An ecological study. *Environmental Health*, *15*(1), 23.

Turkheimer, E. (2000). Three laws of behavior genetics and what they mean. *Current Directions in Psychological Science*, *9*(5), 160–164.

Turkheimer, E., & Harden, K. P. (2014). Behavior genetic research methods: Testing quasi-causal hypotheses using multivariate twin data. In H. T. Reis & C. M. Judd (Eds.), *Handbook of research methods in social and personality psychology* (pp. 159–187). New York, NY: Cambridge University Press.

Van Lier, P. A., Der Ende, J. V., Koot, H. M., & Verhulst, F. C. (2007). Which better predicts conduct problems? The relationship of trajectories of conduct problems with ODD and ADHD symptoms from childhood into adolescence. *Journal of Child Psychology and Psychiatry*, *48*(6), 601–608.

Wasserman, G. A., Staghezza-Jaramillo, B., Shrout, P., Popovac, D., & Graziano, J. (1998). The effect of lead exposure on behavior problems in preschool children. *American Journal of Public Health*, *88*(3), 481–486.

Watts, S. J. (2018). ADHD symptomatology and criminal behavior during adolescence: Exploring the mediating role of school factors. *International Journal of Offender Therapy and Comparative Criminology*, *62*(1), 3–23.

Wilson, I. H., & Wilson, S. B. (2016). Confounding and causation in the epidemiology of lead. *International Journal of Environmental Health Research*, *26*(5–6), 467–482.

Winter, A. S., & Sampson, R. J. (2017). From lead exposure in early childhood to adolescent health: A Chicago birth cohort. *American Journal of Public Health*, *107*(9), 1496–1501.

Wright, J. P., Barnes, J. C., Boutwell, B. B., Schwartz, J. A., Connolly, E. J., Nedelec, J. L., & Beaver, K. M. (2015). Mathematical proof is not minutiae and irreducible complexity is not a theory: A final response to Burt and Simons and a call to criminologists. *Criminology*, *53*(1), 113–120.

Wright, J. P., Dietrich, K. N., Ris, M. D., Hornung, R. W., Wessel, S. D., Lanphear, B. P., ... Rae, M. N. (2008). Association of prenatal and childhood blood lead concentrations with criminal arrests in early adulthood. *PLoS Medicine*, *5*(5), e101.

Young, S., Gudjonsson, G. H., Wells, J., Asherson, P., Theobald, D., Oliver, B., ... Mooney, A. (2009). Attention deficit hyperactivity disorder and critical incidents in a Scottish prison population. *Personality and Individual Differences*, *46*(3), 265–269.

Zhang, N., Baker, H. W., Tufts, M., Raymond, R. E., Salihu, H., & Elliott, M. R. (2013). Early childhood lead exposure and academic achievement: Evidence from Detroit public schools, 2008–2010. *American Journal of Public Health*, *103*(3), e72–e77.

# PART III

# Prevention, Policy, and Health Promotion Systems

# 17
# EARLY CHILDHOOD RISK FACTORS, PREVENTION AND INTERVENTION

*Ruth Paris, Jessica Dym Bartlett, and Corinne Beaugard*

## Introduction

There is no period of life more foundational to individual health and development over the lifespan than early childhood. A strong start in life is one of the most potent predictors of positive outcomes in adolescence and adulthood. Conversely, the first few years of life are a sensitive period of brain development during which young children are most vulnerable to harmful effects of trauma and adversity (National Scientific Council on the Developing Child, 2007). Over one million new neural connections form per second during this rapid stage of brain development, setting the stage for a child's acquisition and integration of increasingly complex skills across multiple developmental domains. While innate characteristics (e.g., genetics) shape a young child's developing capacities, his or her experiences in the world (e.g., relationships, environments) also have a powerful influence on the developing brain, and in turn on the child's immediate and long-term functioning (Center on the Developing Child, 2010).

Thus, early childhood is the most opportune time for implementing interventions to prevent untoward outcomes later in life, as well as the most cost efficient. For example, for every dollar spent on high-quality, comprehensive early childhood education programs for children from vulnerable backgrounds, there is an estimated 7% annual return on investment when offered to preschoolers, and a 13% annual return on investment per year when delivered to children birth to five (García, Heckman, Leaf, & Prados, 2016). Thus, efforts to create supportive childrearing environments beginning as early in life as possible is the most efficacious way to set the stage for positive youth development. This chapter explores the complexity of early development in the presence of multiple, interacting risk and protective factors, as well as the prevention and intervention programs that have been found to address common developmental disruptions and promote resilience.

## Risk Factors that Influence Early Childhood Development

### Individual-Level Risk Factors

Psychopathology can emerge as early as the first few years of life (Lyons-Ruth et al., 2017; Zeanah & Zeanah, 2019). In fact, contemporary research shows a number of psychiatric disorders can be observed in young children. Evidence suggests that approximately 16% of children between the ages of two and five years old have diagnosable psychiatric disorders (Egger & Angold, 2006), and the continuity of their symptoms from early to middle childhood is similar to the persistence of symptoms in adolescents and adults (Briggs-Gowan, Carter, Bosson-Heenan, Guyer, & Horwitz, 2006; Bufferd, Dougherty, Carlson, Rose, & Klein, 2012). In part, early psychopathology and its persistence over time stem from characteristics of children that are present before, during, or after birth that place a child at increased risk for poor developmental outcomes (National Research Council & Institute of Medicine [NRC & IOM], 2009a).

Commonly studied risk factors at the individual level include genetic predisposition and expression, alterations to typical brain structure and functioning, exposure to teratogens in utero, complications during pregnancy and birth, poor physical health, disability, low intelligence, and temperament (Krieger & Stringaris, 2015; Samuelsson et al., 2017). Early life stress—even in utero—may be transmitted to the infant through gene methylation (Monk et al., 2016), epigenetic changes, and alterations to the stress response system that result in altered gene expression and changes to the brain which in turn lead to heightened vulnerability to subsequent psychiatric disorders (Monk, Spicer, & Champagne, 2012). Preterm birth and low birthweight also are associated with impairments later in life, such as attention, behavior, and emotional problems in middle childhood and adolescence (Bhutta, Cleves, Casey, Cradock, & Anand, 2002; Fevang, Hysing, Markestad, & Sommerfelt, 2016; Johnson et al., 2010; Samuelsson et al., 2017). In addition, there is a large body of research identifying a "difficult" infant temperament as a risk factor for later psychopathology (Krieger & Stringaris, 2015; Rothbart, Posner, & Hershey, 1995). However, for the purposes of informing interventions to prevent or ameliorate risk in children's lives, maintaining a focus on risk factors that are malleable is most useful (Fraser, Richman, Galinsky, & Day, 2009).

One note of caution is that individual factors do not predestine children to follow specific developmental pathways. Predicting psychopathology in adolescence and adulthood from individual characteristics identified very early in life is an imprecise science at best, and a harmful, stigmatizing prophecy at worst. Many traits of young children are not stable over time, and short-term fluctuations in psychological well-being are normative (Bornstein et al., 2015). For example, most toddlers who regularly engage in disruptive behaviors cease these behaviors before reaching their third birthday (Baillardgeon et al., 2007). Here the concepts of *multifinality* and *equifinality* are useful. Specifically, two children with the same set of risk factors may have different life outcomes (*mulifinality*); moreover, two children with different risk factors may develop similar problems (*equifinality*) (Cicchetti & Rogosch, 1996). Perhaps most important, development is multiply determined, and the emergence of psychopathology cannot be solely attributed to individual characteristics. Rather, it is best understood as a product of interactions between a child and the social and environmental contexts in which he or she lives (Bronfenbrenner & Morris, 2006).

## *Parent – and Family – Level Risk Factors*

Family context in early childhood contributes to the development of psychopathology in adolescence and later life. More specifically, relationships with primary caregivers play a dominant role. Over the last 40 years, a central framework used by scholars to understand these relationships is attachment theory. Originally described by Bowlby (1982), the theory emphasizes that infants are biologically driven to form attachment relationships with caregivers in order to support their early dependent states. With time, the young child is able to use the caregiver as a secure base, allowing him/her to explore the environment, and return to the caregiver for protection and comfort (Sroufe, 2005).

Myriad studies have utilized the theory and the laboratory process developed to assess differences in attachment behaviors called the Strange Situation Procedure (SSP; Ainsworth, Blehar,

Waters, & Wall, 2015). Ainsworth and colleagues described three organizational patterns showing how toddlers and parents negotiate attachment behavior: secure, anxious–avoidant, and anxious–ambivalent. Main and Solomon (1986) later added the disorganized pattern to describe attachment behaviors seen in many seriously maltreated children. Toddlers demonstrating *secure* attachment patterns show an ability to display emotions and rely on their parents to help regulate their distress. In contrast, toddlers with *anxious–avoidant* attachment patterns show their distress but seemingly do not look to their parents for comfort. *Anxious–ambivalent* pattern toddlers look to their parents for comfort, but seem unable to be soothed by them. Toddlers with *disorganized* attachment patterns appear to lack a coherent strategy for connecting with a parent when in distress and display bizarre or uncoordinated behaviors. Each of these patterns involve a parenting style that may include attunement, sensitivity, support, disengagement, intrusiveness, hostility, and/or abuse among others (Rosenblum, Dayton, & Muzik, 2019).

Foundationally, attachment theory purports that parents' sensitive caregiving primarily determines children's attachment security, not unique individual characteristics of the child. Over time, the child internalizes the experiences he/she has with a caregiver in order to develop their own internal working models, including views of the self, others and the nature of relationships. As the growing child interacts with the environment, these working models influence development (Groh, Fearon, van IJzendoorn, Bakermans-Kranenburg, & Roisman, 2017).

Generally, studies have found evidence that attachment relationships can predict child developmental adaptations or maladaptations (Groh et al., 2017; Sroufe, 2005). Secure attachment relationships are thought to buffer life stressors and should be seen as a protective but not necessarily predictive of life course development. Longitudinal studies since the 1970s have enabled researchers to demonstrate modest connections between attachment security in early childhood and later development in psychological, cognitive, interpersonal and other domains (Thompson, 2016). Given our understanding of early attachments, we see that childhood disorders such as Reactive Attachment Disorder (RAD) and Disinhibited Social Engagement Disorder (DSED) can arise from conditions of severe social and interpersonal neglect, although even in those conditions most children do not develop these disorders (Zeanah & Gleason, 2015). Overall, we understand that the relationship between early attachments and later outcomes is not linear but complex and transactional. A child with an anxious–avoidant or disorganized attachment style early in life may have an increased likelihood of behavioral, interpersonal or emotional challenges, but as with individual level risk factors, there is no assurance of specific outcomes (Sroufe, 2005).

In addition to the parent–child relationship, larger family systems play an important role in early and later child development (Cowan & Cowan, 2003). From a systems perspective, functioning among family members within structures, communication patterns and roles influence child behavior and development (Minuchin, 1985). Challenges in the family system such as intimate partner violence or parental substance misuse, can contribute to problems in family functioning, such as absent caregivers or role diffusion, and ultimately lead to untoward outcomes for young children (Levendosky, Bogat, Bernard, & Garcia, 2018; Salo & Flykt, 2013). Families that are well organized, have established routines and offer good supervision to young children promote adaptive behavioral development (Labella & Masten, 2018). Importantly, young children that are exposed to family violence, including child maltreatment, are more likely to become aggressive themselves (Cicchetti & Toth, 2015; Van Horn & Lieberman, 2012). More broadly, family risk factors such as low socioeconomic status, poverty or other chronic stress can result in the emergence of violent behavior in children and adolescents (Labella & Masten, 2018).

## Environmental – Level Risk Factors

At the environmental level (Bronfenbrenner & Morris, 2006) various risk factors can influence early child development. Those considered here as exemplars include, broad socioeconomic status (SES), food and housing insecurity and exposure to community violence. Economic hardship during childhood is a known predictor of problematic developmental outcomes. Research on SES indicates broadly that poverty during early childhood within a household or within a neighborhood is predictive of lower IQ scores, lower cognitive and verbal skills, poorer working memory, and inhibitory control dysfunction (Duncan, Brooks-Gunn, & Klebanov, 1994; Hackman & Farah, 2009; McLoyd, 1998; NICHD, 2005). Low SES interferes with children's opportunity in early educational settings (McLoyd, 1998) and those who experience chronic poverty-related stress are at risk for increased allostatic load, a risk factor for internalizing disorders and memory impairment in adolescence (Blair, Raver, Granger, Mills-Koonce, & Hibel, 2011; Evans, Schamberg, & McEwen, 2009).

Households with children are at a greater risk to be food insecure (Slopen, Fitzmaurice, Williams, & Gilman, 2010) and insecurity during early childhood increases developmental risks by two thirds, is correlated with poor/fair child health, and increases incidence of children's hospitalizations (Rose-Jacobs et al., 2008; Cook et al., 2013). Children raised in food insecure homes are more likely to experience internalizing and externalizing problems, obesity and type II diabetes (Shonkoff, Boyce, & McEwen, 2009; Slopen et al., 2010) and hyperactivity and inattention during childhood (Melchior et al., 2012).

Additionally, housing insecurity during early childhood predicts greater involvement with child welfare, as lack of housing is viewed as potential child maltreatment. Households with children are more likely to report a housing problem including frequent moves, inability to pay rent, overcrowding, and suboptimal living conditions (Cutts et al., 2011; Pascoe, Wood, Duffee, & Kuo, 2016). Furthermore, children are more likely to suffer negative health consequences of poor living conditions compared to adults and the problematic correlates include poorer academic performance, less medical care, teen pregnancy, and substance misuse (Weitzman et al., 2013).

Exposure to community violence, another environmental risk factor, can trigger irregular arousal states and post-traumatic stress disorder (Lynch, 2003). Witnessing violence is linked to the onset of externalizing and internalizing symptoms, as well as decreased self-esteem, negative perceptions of care givers, and problematic social relationships (Cooley-Strickland et al., 2009; Lynch, 2003; Schwartz & Hopmeyer Gorman, 2003). Community violence correlates with lower academic achievement for middle and high school students and lower IQ and reading scores in middle school students (Bowen & Bowen, 1999; Templin et al., 2003).

## Examples of Disruptions to Early Childhood Development

### Overview

In the following section, we identify and examine three major contributors that are known to disrupt optimal processes in early childhood and often lead to negative outcomes for older children and adolescents. They include parental mental health disorders, parental substance misuse and child abuse and neglect.

### Parental Mental Health Disorders

As described above, early childhood development depends in large part upon the consistent presence of an emotionally available adult capable of providing sensitive and responsive care (Bakermans-Kranenburg & van Ijzendoorn, 2007; Easterbrooks, Bartlett, Beeghly, & Thompson,

2012). When a parent's mental health is compromised, the quality of parent–child interactions may be as well. Maternal depression has been linked to insensitive, intrusiveness, unrealistic, or negative perceptions of the child, few positive interactions, limited physical affection, infrequent verbal interactions, and risk for abuse and neglect (Field, 1995; Spatz Widom, DuMont, & Czaja, 2007). Similarly, high levels of parental stress and anxiety is associated with insensitive, neglectful, and harsh parenting (Crnic, Gaze, & Hoffman, 2005; Deater-Deckard & Scarr, 1996).

Parental depression is the most common mental health disorder in families—approximately 15.6 million children have parents with severe or major depression (NRC & IOM, 2009b). Further, it often co-occurs with other mental health or substance use disorders (75% of depressed adults have at least one other mental health diagnosis), which may further impede parenting quality (Carter, Garrity-Rokous, Chazan Cohen, Little, & Briggs-Gowan, 2001). Mothers are at especially high risk for depression during the childbearing years (Wilhelm, 2006); an estimated 40–60% report depressive symptoms (Knitzer, Theberge, & Johnson, 2008) and between 10% and 15% suffer from major depressive disorder (Ertel, Rich-Edwards, & Koenen, 2011). Rates of maternal depression are especially high during the perinatal period (Ertel et al., 2011). Studies on paternal depression are less common, but research suggests rates are only slightly lower than mothers (Kane & Garber, 2004)—11% versus 14% during the postpartum period (Paulson, Dauber, & Leiferman, 2006).

Parental mental health disorders appears to be most harmful to children during the first few years of life, a sensitive period of development during which a child is reliant on adults for healthy brain and interpersonal development (Center on the Developing Child at Harvard University, 2009; Easterbrooks et al., 2012). But the deleterious effects of parental depression on children may persist into adolescence and adulthood (Ertel et al., 2011). Children of depressed mothers are more likely than are children of non-depressed mothers to experience disruptions to their stress response system (Dawson et al., 2001; Field et al., 2004), difficulties with self-regulation (Tronick & Gianino, 1986), problems with attachments (Martins & Gaffan, 2000), and internalizing problems (Ashman, Dawson, Panagiotides, Yamada, & Wilkinson, 2002). And when both parents are affected by mental health problems, poor child outcomes are especially likely. An estimated 25% of children with two depressed parents develop serious psychological or behavioral problems, compared to 6% when neither parent has a mental health disorder (Weitzman, Rosenthal, & Liu, 2011).

Negative impacts of parental depression on children are most likely when a parent's depression begins early in the child's life and is severe and chronic (Ashman, Dawson, & Panagiotides, 2008; Campbell, Morgan-Lopez, Cox, McLoyd, NICHD ECCRN, 2009). In addition, the presence or absence of environmental risk and protective factors (Chen & Kovacs, 2013) influence a child's adaptation to a parent's depression. Social isolation, financial instability, and family violence may compound depression's harmful effects, whereas social support, financial resources, and mental health treatment can help buffer a child from its negative effects (NRC & IOM, 2009a). Finally, characteristics of young children (i.e., genetic predispositions, temperament) shape their vulnerability or resilience to parental mental illness (Downey & Coyne, 1990; Lovejoy, Graczyk, O'Hare, & Neuman, 2000).

## *Parental Substance Misuse*

Similar to mental health disorders, parents with substance use disorders (SUDs) often experience challenges in their parenting capacities and practices. They may have family histories of substance misuse, complex trauma, and co-occurring mental health disorders, including posttraumatic stress disorder (PTSD). These conditions are highly correlated with suboptimal parenting, including less sensitivity and structuring, and greater intrusiveness (Back, Sonne, Killeen, Dansky, & Brady,

2003; Kaltenbach, 2013; Salo et al., 2010). Given the importance of the attachment relationship for an infant's overall development, the lack of attunement and consistency often seen in parents with SUDs can compromise an infant's "secure base" (Salo & Flykt, 2013). Substance-related disruptions in the brain's oxytocin and dopamine levels and receptors, which play a significant role in reward processing, diminish the maternal pleasure that usually accompany parenting a young child (Light et al., 2004; Rutherford, Potenza, & Mayes, 2013). Studies have found postpartum mothers who misused substances to have reduced neurobiological activity in response to infant cries and faces (Landi et al., 2011). Many opioid and substance-exposed newborns can have difficulties regulating states of sleep and hunger, thus they may need more parental help. However, parents with SUDs may be less able to read and respond to babies' cues, demonstrating intrusive behaviors which over ride infant-led interactions (Hans, Bernstein, & Henson, 1999; Pajulo et al., 2012). Given the centrality of the attachment relationship in young children's development, a mother's decreased responsiveness to her infant, intrusiveness, and the dysregulation of the mother-infant dyad are particularly detrimental (Salo & Flykt, 2013).

In utero exposure to substances can manifest in deleterious outcomes for infants (SAMHSA, 2019), including Neonatal Abstinence Syndrome (NAS) for those exposed to opioids. NAS contributes to problematic infant neurobehavior and long-term behavior challenges such as hyperactivity, short attention span, and memory problems, all of which can lead to longer-term developmental and behavioral difficulties (Behnke, Smith, Committee on Substance Abuse, & Committee on Fetus and Newborn, 2013). In utero exposure may not be the most significant risk factor for children. Exposure to parental substance misuse and concomitant environmental stressors such as inadequate housing, insufficient income, and domestic violence along with suboptimal parent–child relationships can have developmental and environmental consequences for these children, including in the physical, intellectual, social and emotional realms (Salo & Flykt, 2013). Children with a parent who has an SUD versus those who do not are more likely to have lower socioeconomic status, increased difficulties in academic and social settings and family functioning, and to be involved with the child welfare system (Peleg-Oren & Teichman, 2006). Estimates run as high as 61% of infants and 41% of older children in out-of-home care are from families with active substance misuse (Wulczyn, Ernst, & Fisher, 2011).

## *Child Abuse and Neglect*

Child abuse and neglect can lead to serious disruptions in development beginning early in a child's life. Very young children are more likely than any other age group to experience abuse and neglect, and most vulnerable to suffer negative consequences (U.S. Department of Health and Human Services [USDHHS], 2018). In 2016, referrals in the United States alleged the maltreatment of 7.4 million children; approximately one-quarter (28.5%) of confirmed victims were younger than 3 years old and the victimization rate was highest for children under one year.

The experience of abuse and neglect is especially detrimental to young children because it is typically perpetrated by the very adults who are responsible for their social, emotional, and physical well-being—over 91% of child victims are maltreated by one or both of their parents (USDHHS, 2018). Not surprisingly, then, social-emotional disturbances have been commonly observed in young maltreated children, including difficulty forming healthy attachments, deficits in understanding, recognizing, processing, expressing, and regulating emotions (Curtis & Cicchetti, 2013; Messman-Moore, Walsh, & DiLillo, 2010; Pollak & Sinha, 2002; Shipman & Zeman, 1999; Young & Widom, 2014), and limited engagement in prosocial behavior (Koenig, Cicchetti, & Rogosch, 2004). In addition, child abuse and neglect can lead to impairments in brain structure and functioning associated with long-term negative consequences for children's cognitive and language development (Tarullo, 2012), physical health conditions (Felitti & Anda,

2009), juvenile delinquency (Gold, Wolan, Sullivan, & Lewis, 2011), intimate partner violence (Fang & Corso, 2007), and child abuse and neglect in the next generation (Bartlett & Easterbrooks, 2012; Bartlett, Kotake, Fauth, & Easterbrooks, 2017; Berzenski, Yates, & Egeland, 2014; Sidebotham & Heron, 2006). There is also scientific consensus that abuse and neglect in childhood is related to depression in adulthood, and beginning linkages between childhood maltreatment and other major mental health disorders.

Child maltreatment also tends to co-occur with other childhood adversities, which can exacerbate its harmful effects. For example, numerous studies have found a strong association between poverty and child neglect (Drake & Pandey, 1996; Sedlak et al., 2010; Slack, Holl, McDaniel Yoo, & Bolger, 2004). In addition, intimate partner violence (IPV) is common among families involved with the child welfare system, with estimates ranging from 30% to 60% (Appel & Holden, 1998; Edleson, 1999; Herrenkohl, Sousa, Tajima, Herrenkohl, & Moylan, 2008). There is mounting evidence to suggest young children suffer more negative outcomes in the presence of more than one type of family violence (De la Vega, de la Osa, Ezpeleta, Granero, & Domenech, 2011; Kaslow, 2008), and that an accumulation of adversities including child abuse and neglect can lead to some of the most common diseases and leading causes of deaths many decades later (Felitti et al., 1998; Shonkoff et al., 2009).

## Impact of Early Childhood Disruptions on Later Childhood and Adolescence

Early adverse childhood experiences (ACEs) are implicated in not so distant negative outcomes during adolescence. Studies analyzing the relationship between childhood traumas and consequences during adolescence assess frequencies for out of home placement, juvenile delinquency, emotional and psychological distress, and physical health. The focus of this chapter is implications of challenges in early childhood, however most research on adolescent outcomes does not tend to focus on the specific age when adverse experiences occur. Rather, the frequency, severity, and type of experience receive the abundance of analytical consideration. The age of onset of childhood adverse experiences is negatively correlated with frequency and chronicity of problematic events, suggesting that more severe challenges may be connected to the earliest phases of development (Bolger, Patterson, & Kupersmidt, 1998).

Research on ACEs considers a variety of physically and emotionally stressful experiences. The ten commonly considered ACEs are emotional abuse, physical abuse, sexual abuse, emotional neglect, physical neglect, family violence, household substance misuse, household mental illness, parental separation or divorce, and household member incarceration (Baglivio et al., 2014). Other ACE studies include measures of extreme financial hardship, neighborhood violence, and conflict due to race or ethnicity (Bethell, Newacheck, Hawes, & Halfon, 2014). Negative outcomes in adolescence are assessed via their correlation to a selection of ACEs, with particular attention to physical abuse and neglect. The following discussion analyzes the likelihood for the most common and detrimental outcomes of the varieties of traumas encompassed under ACEs during adolescence.

### *Physical Health*

Increased attention to the social determinants of health for adolescents is critical given the potential for lifelong chronic health conditions to develop during this period (Bethell, Newacheck, Hawes, & Halfon, 2014). Adolescents with ACEs were more likely to have chronic health concerns, require special healthcare needs, have illnesses requiring physician treatment, and have somatic concerns (Bethell, Newacheck, Hawes, & Halfon, 2014; Flaherty et al., 2013).

There is a dose-response effect in that adolescents with higher ACE scores are more susceptible to negative health outcomes and behaviors, including smoking (Baglivio et al., 2014; Bethell, Newacheck, Hawes, & Halfon, 2014; Dong et al., 2005). Adolescents in the foster care system warrant special consideration for their complex vulnerabilities and are at increased risk for physical health concerns, including sexually transmitted infections (Courtney, Terao, & Bost, 2004; Simms, Dubowitz, & Szilagyi, 2000).

Child maltreatment and ACEs are statistically correlated with higher rates of sexual activity prior to age 14 and adolescent pregnancy (Dong et al., 2005; Hillis et al., 2004). Early childhood physical abuse predicts higher rates of teen pregnancy, pregnancy outside of marriage, and teen parenthood (Lansford et al., 2007). Compared to adolescents raised by their birth parents, foster youth are significantly more likely to become pregnant and to have live births (Courtney, Terao, & Bost, 2004).

## *School and Social Experiences*

School performance and relationships with peers are significant features of adolescent functioning and both are moderated by ACEs. Decreased school engagement, poorer attendance, and grade repetition are correlated with cumulative ACEs (Bethell, Newacheck, Hawes, & Halfon, 2014). Childhood neglect and abuse, specifically, are implicated in adolescents' poor academic achievement, increased incidences of school-based discipline and poor self-esteem and peer attachment (Eckenrode, Laird, & Doris, 1993; Lim & Lee, 2017). Youth who experienced various types of maltreatment struggle with popularity amongst their peers, higher rates of conflict with peers, and fewer reciprocal friendships. Sexual abuse and earlier onset of maltreatment are associated with lower self-esteem (Bolger, Patterson, & Kupersmidt, 1998). The importance of peer relationships during this stage of development and the pressure to have successful social experiences, which operate as protective factors, make social support for this group of teens especially critical for positive development.

## *Psychological Features*

A particular concern is the development of psychosocial distress and disorder during adolescence, which can occur as a fully manifested diagnosable condition or as a maladaptive pattern of behaviors and cognitions. Adolescents with a history of childhood stressors are less able to regulate experiences of emotional distress and are more prone to engage in maladaptive strategies, including rumination (McLaughlin, 2016). Furthermore, they are more likely to assess others' behaviors as hostile or aggressive and not appraise hostile or aggressive actions as morally wrong (Lansford et al., 2007).

ACEs, particularly emotional and physical abuse and neglect, are correlated with increased rates of affective distress, a range of mental health disorders as well as substance misuse in adolescents (Arseneault et al., 2011; Collin-Vézina, Coleman, Milne, Sell, & Daigneault, 2011; Dong et al., 2005; Dube et al., 2006; Greeson et al., 2011; McLaughlin, 2016; Schilling, Aseltine, Robert, & Gore, 2007). In some cases, the cumulative effect of multiple ACEs increase statistical significance for negative outcomes, like exposure to domestic violence and early childhood maltreatment and the likelihood of antisocial behaviors during adolescence (Sousa et al., 2011). The manifestation of internalizing behaviors, like anxiety, depression, and self-mutilation, is greater amongst women with histories of ACEs, while men are more likely to manifest externalizing and antisocial behaviors (Baglivio et al., 2014; Mendle, Leve, Van Ryzin, & Natsuaki, 2014; Schilling et al., 2007). Of significant concern is the correlation between childhood maltreatment and the increased rate of suicide attempts prior to age 18 (Dong et al., 2005; Jonson-Reid, M., Kohl & Drake, 2012).

## *Juvenile Delinquency*

Although instances of child maltreatment are not directly predictive of future incarceration, as demonstrated through the concept of multi-finality, they are correlated with markers of juvenile delinquency. Childhood traumatic experiences are detected at statistically significant levels in the juvenile detained population, especially amongst those with emotional dysregulation and externalized antisocial behaviors. In this population, childhood maltreatment is correlated with maladaptive emotional and behavioral outcomes and these youth have more likely experienced parental incarceration, witnessed violence, or out of home placement (Krischer & Sevecke, 2008; Evans-Chase, 2014). Additionally, emotional neglect is significantly correlated with antisocial psychopathy in girls, while physical and emotional abuse in males is associated with poor anger control and serious criminal behavior. Children who had experienced physical abuse prior to age five were more likely to have been arrested as a juvenile for violent and nonviolent offenses, to perpetrate acts of relationship violence, and to exhibit aggressive externalizing behaviors (Lansford et al., 2007).

## Protective Factors

Protective factors—the characteristics and conditions that ameliorate risk for disruptions in development and psychopathology—operate by reducing risk factors, buffering children from adversity, and supporting competence (Garmezy, Masten, & Tellegen, 1984; Zeanah & Zeanah, 2019). The study of protective factors that support resilience, a dynamic process of positive adaptation in the face of significant adversity (Luthar, Cicchetti, & Becker, 2000), dates back to the 1970s, when researchers began to notice that some children with severely mentally ill parents or living in low SES families were faring unexpectedly well compared to their peers (Garmezy, 1970; Werner & Smith, 1977). These early studies primarily highlighted personal qualities of children that protected them from the potentially deleterious effects of adverse experiences (Masten & Garmezy, 1985); subsequently, research has highlighted the importance of environmental factors and the interactions among individual and contextual influences on development (Cicchetti, 2010; Luthar et al., 2000). Below, we briefly summarize the research on protective factors at the level of the individual, family, and community, beginning in early childhood.

### *Individual-Level Protective Factors*

Extant research on individual-level protective factors (e.g., biological makeup, knowledge, and skills associated with resilience) suggests that certain personal attributes of young children at high risk for negative outcomes increase the odds of healthy development over the life course (Hawkins, 2006; Jenson, 2010; Werner, 2000). Individual-level protective factors observed in early childhood include average or above intelligence, an "easy" temperament, and strong executive function and self-regulation skills (National Scientific Council on the Developing Child, 2015; Werner, 2000).

Many of the early skills that serve as protective factors (e.g., impulse control, problem-solving and managing strong emotions), often disrupted by exposure to severe stress and trauma, can be taught through coaching and practice (Babcock, 2014; Murray, Rosanbalm, Christopoulos, & Hamoudi, 2015). However, individual-level factors alone are not likely sufficient to produce positive life outcomes for children at high risk for problems later in life. The development of foundational skills to cope with adversity is dependent upon the presence of nurturing adults and environments that provide a safe place for children to learn (National Scientific Council on the

Developing Child, 2015; Rosanbalm & Murray, 2017). Thus, it is essential to consider the influence of the multiple contexts in which young children are embedded (e.g., families, neighborhoods, schools) on their developmental trajectories (Bronfenbrenner & Morris, 2006; Luthar et al., 2000).

## *Family and Community Protective Factors*

Protective factors within the family and community offset the potential for negative physical and emotional health outcomes. Communication among family members during difficult transitions supports the health of the child and family unit. When parents and service providers are able to have developmentally appropriate conversations with children about the challenges faced by the household, children are more likely to have continued positive relationships with parents even after dramatic stressors such as incarceration or deportation (Brabeck & Xu, 2010; Murray, Farrington, & Sekol, 2012). The family dynamic generally is a critical piece of children's resilience, as strong and bonded units offer children protection from hazards such as witnessing violence (Weitzman et al., 2013). More broadly, the concept of family resilience, referencing an entire family's ability to withstand and rebound from adversity (Walsh, 1996), serves as a protective factor for all of its members, but most especially the children.

At the community level, high quality educational environments, including those that address toxic stress (NSCDC, 2014), are shown to diminish negative consequences for children somewhat by mediating the correlation between low SES and poor cognitive outcomes (Melhuish et al., 2008). Similarly, support for health and nutrition during the perinatal period along with standard developmental screening can serve to protect and support positive child outcomes (Center on the Developing Child at Harvard University, 2016; National Scientific Council on the Developing Child [NSCDC], 2014). Additionally, when community services are coordinated, such as early intervention and child welfare, the positive outcomes for children are bolstered.

## **Early Childhood Prevention and Intervention**

Preventive interventions in early childhood are programs and initiatives designed to reduce risk factors and increase protective factors during the first years of life, a sensitive period of development during which experiences shape brain development and influence the likelihood of subsequent developmental disruptions and psychopathology (Zeanah & Zeanah, 2019). The National Research Council and Institute of Medicine (NRC & IOM, 2009a) reviewed the evidence from the prevention science literature and concluded that preventive interventions are most likely to be successful when they are interdisciplinary, implemented through a coordinated, community-level system of care, modify young children's environment and experiences to promote healthy brain development, and address the developmental nature of mental, emotional, and behavioral disorders. However, specific approaches vary, and there is strong evidence of effectiveness across a wide range of strategies, including parenting programs (e.g., The Incredible Years; Triple P), home visiting (e.g., Healthy Families; Nurse Family Partnership), and high-quality, comprehensive early care and education (e.g., Carolina Abcedarian Project, Perry Preschool Program). Examples of positive program impacts cited in the literature on preventive interventions include increases in school readiness and academic achievement, and reductions in child abuse and neglect, family violence, problem behaviors, conduct disorder, depression, anxiety, and substance misuse during childhood and adolescence (Belfield, Nores, Barnett, & Schweinhart, 2006; DuMont et al., 2008; Englund, White, Reynolds, Schweinhart, & Campbell, 2014; Olds et al., 1997; Ramey & Campbell, 1984; Sanders, Markie-Dadds, Tully, & Bor, 2000; Webster-Stratton, 1998).

Preventive interventions can be implemented in a range of settings—home, school, community, or broader culture—and may be *universal* (targeted to an entire population or the general public; e.g., high-quality child care), *selective* (targeted to subgroups of a population who are at higher than average risk for developing disorders due to biological, psychological, or social risk factors; e.g., home visiting), or *indicated* (targeted to individuals already exhibiting signs of disorders but who have not yet met the clinical criteria; e.g., interventions to address early behavior problems) (NRC & IOM, 2009b, p. 66). However, interventions that address the needs of both parents and children simultaneously are among the most promising.

## *Two-Generation Programs*

A large body of evidence suggests that two-generational programs are particularly effective in achieving a wide range of positive outcomes for young children and their families under high-risk conditions, including poverty, adolescent parenthood, and child abuse and neglect (Green et al., 2014; Michalopoulos, Faucetta, Warren, & Mitchell, 2017; U.S. Department of Health and Human Services [USDHHS], 2010; Vogel, Brooks-Gunn, Martin, & Klute, 2013). Rather than serving only children or parents alone, two-generation approaches target both young children and their parents, as well as parent–child relationships. Some of the most widely disseminated two-generation approaches include Head Start, Early Head Start, and home visiting.

### *Head Start and Early Head Start*

Head Start (HS) is a large-scale federal program established in 1965 as a comprehensive, center-based program for preschoolers (ages three and four) and their families with incomes below the poverty line. Early Head Start (EHS) began 30 years later, offering comprehensive services (center-based, home-based, or both) to pregnant women, parents, and children (under age three) living in poverty. Both programs focus on school readiness, health, mental health, and family well-being, and follow strict federal quality standards; together they have served over 34 million children (National Head Start Association [NHSA], 2018).

Rigorous evaluations have shown considerable benefits that were especially strong for Hispanic and African-American children, dual language learners, children who are homeless or in foster care, and children whose mothers did not graduate high school (USDHHS, 2010; Love et al., 2005). EHS has been found to reduce spanking and emergency room visits, increase positive parent–child interactions and support for learning and development in the home, and improve maternal employment and education outcomes. Impacts remained for children's social-emotional skills, parenting quality and parental well-being two years after children left the program (USDHHS, 2010). HS has shown lasting positive impacts on children's cognitive, language, and social-emotional development, problem behaviors, and health status, and parenting quality (USDHHS, 2010). While some effects appear to dissipate over time, the Brookings Institute's recent economic analysis concluded "Head Start not only enhances eventual educational attainment, but also has a lasting positive impact on behavioral outcomes ... Furthermore, it improves parenting practices—potentially providing additional benefits to the next generation" (Schanzenbach & Bauer, 2016, p. 8). Neither program is fully funded; HS serves 31% of eligible children and EHS serves 7% of eligible children (NHSA, 2018).

## Home Visiting

Home visiting is a method of service delivery in which pregnant mothers, parents, and their children, birth to five, receive services and supports for both generations from trained professionals or paraprofessionals who meet with families in their home. States support home visiting programs through federal, state, and foundation funds (Supplee, 2016). This approach to prevention has become an increasingly common since 2010, when Congress authorized the Maternal, Infant, and Early Childhood Home Visiting (MIECHV) program, and major expansion of evidence-based home visiting services. States and tribal communities that use MIECHV funding must use models that have met strict criteria for evidence of effectiveness. MIECHV programs primarily serve economically disadvantaged families, focus on improving parenting and child development, and tailor services to each family's needs. The most frequently selected models of home visiting are Early Head Start (Home Based Program Option), Healthy Families America, Nurse-Family Partnership, and Parents as Teachers (Duggan et al., 2018).

Numerous studies, including randomized controlled trials (RCTs), have been conducted on home visiting programs (e.g., Jacobs et al., 2015; Olds et al., 1997), but the most comprehensive study to date is the federally mandated evaluation of MIECHV, the Mother and Infant Home Visiting Program Evaluation (MIHOPE; Michalopoulos et al., 2017). MIHOPE included the four aforementioned home visiting models and randomly assigned approximately 4,200 families to receive either MIECHV services or information on community services. The results revealed positive, statistically significant effects (with little variation among families with different characteristics), including but not limited to: the quality of the home environment, the frequency of psychological aggression toward the child, the number of Medicaid-paid child emergency department visits, and child behavior problems, women's general health, health insurance coverage, and reductions in depressive symptoms. Evidence-based home visiting has been implemented in all 50 states, the District of Columbia, 5 territories, and 25 tribal communities, with approximately 300,000 families served in 2017. However, an estimated 18.1 million pregnant women and families with children under six years old could benefit from home visiting services, suggesting many families are not being reached (National Home Visiting Resource Center, 2018).

## *Therapeutic Interventions*

Therapeutic interventions in early childhood can be placed under the prevention framework as they promote a young child's return to a typical developmental trajectory, even when addressing behavioral symptoms that may be present, and prevent further delays or symptoms. Under the National Research Council and Institute of Medicine spectrum (NRC & IOM, 2009b) interventions may be considered prevention when they are *indicated* for minor behavioral symptoms, or *treatment* when a young child has an identifiable disorder. In either situation, the intervention may target the infant, the parent's mental health and behavior and/or the parent–child relationship. Widely disseminated interventions focused on young children and their parents considered evidence-based or a promising practice are Child–Parent Psychotherapy, Attachment and Biobehavioral Catch-up and the Circle of Security Program.

### Child–Parent Psychotherapy (CPP)

Child–Parent Psychotherapy is a relationship-based, dyadic treatment for young children who have been exposed to family and community violence or other traumatic events. The central foundation of CPP is based on theory and research indicating that young children's responses to danger are both organized by and can be changed through their attachment relationships (Lieberman & Van Horn, 2005). As a two-generation approach, CPP involves both the young child and caregiver(s) and addresses the impact of traumatic exposure on the child, the parent and the parent–child relationship. The parent's unresolved experiences and attachment styles are considered in relation to their perceptions of and interactions with their child (Berlin, Zeanah, & Lieberman, 2016). Typically offered for one year in weekly sessions comprised of play and unstructured interactions, CPP addresses the child's mental health symptoms, parental perceptions and behaviors and promotes attachment security. By working to enhance a parent's reflective functioning (RF; Slade, 2005), the ability for the parent to attune to and accurately interpret their child's mental states, the clinician promotes the relationship between parent and child, which can serve to ameliorate symptoms and promote a child's development.

In five randomized trials, CPP has shown efficacy in reducing child behavior problems and trauma symptoms in both children and mothers, improving representations of self and caregivers in maltreated preschoolers, and shifting attachment categories towards greater security in maltreated preschoolers (Cicchetti, Rogosch, & Toth, 2006; Lieberman, Van Horn, & Ghosh Ippen, 2005; Lieberman, Weston, & Pawl, 1991; Toth, Rogosch, Manly, & Cicchetti, 2006). It has been disseminated world-wide and specifically through learning communities within the National Child Traumatic Stress Network in the U.S.

### *Attachment and Biobehavioral Catch-Up (ABC)*

Attachment and Biobehavioral Catch-up is a short-term, ten-session parenting intervention delivered in parents' homes. It was developed with attachment theory in mind along with research findings regarding best practices for maltreated children or those who had many disruptions in care. Children are typically anywhere from 6 months to 36 months old. Primary foci of the intervention include: nurturing the distressed child, following the child's lead with delight and avoiding harsh or scary behavior. ABC is manualized and offers parent coaches specific material to review for each of the ten sessions. Video clips of other parents and of the sessions themselves are used as examples and to reinforce optimal parenting behaviors. Central to ABC are the frequent comments (one per minute) made by the parent coaches to draw attention to target behaviors. This type of regular feedback is seen as helpful in order for participants to implement the new style of parenting (Dozier & Bernard, 2019).

ABC is supported by two randomized trials, one with infants in foster care and the other with infants or toddlers being cared for by their biological mothers who were receiving services through child welfare agencies (Bernard et al., 2012; Bick & Dozier, 2013; Dozier et al., 2009). The intervention demonstrated positive effects on child secure attachment, caregivers' sensitive behaviors, cognitive flexibility and hormonal cortisol regulation. Given the promising evidence base, the short-term nature and its manualization, ABC is being widely disseminated in family service and child welfare programs working for the betterment of vulnerable parents and young children (Berlin, Zeanah, & Lieberman, 2016).

### *Circle of Security (COS)*

The Circle of Security program is an attachment-based intervention typically offered in a group setting to parents (either in a 20-week intensive or a shorter 10-week version), but can also be offered individually. The young child is held in mind and discussed by the trained intervener and parent, but is not present in the session. COS teaches parents about attachment and encourages them to reflect on their own histories and parenting behaviors. Central in the COS work is a graphic that depicts key aspects of attachment such as a child's need for autonomy and connection and a parent's behavior that can support these needs. The concept of "shark music" is explained to parents to help them think about why certain child behaviors might feel threatening to the parent and subsequently prompt a negative response, even though the behavior might not actually be dangerous. Parents are encouraged to reflect on their own histories and why their "shark music" might get activated (Coyne, Powell, Hoffman, & Cooper, 2019).

Although COS in its various forms has been widely disseminated, the evidence base is weaker than for CPP and ABC (Mercer, 2015). It is viewed as a promising practice given the two studies that have demonstrated positive effects of the intervention, even though they examine different versions. The first evaluation of the 20-week parenting group using a pre-posttreatment design found decreases among children in insecure and disorganized attachment classifications (Hoffman, Marvin, Cooper, & Powell, 2006). The second study used a randomized trial to evaluate a four-session home-based version of COS for low income mothers and their irritable infants. No main effects were found for the intervention, however highly irritable infants in the COS group were more likely to be securely attached and children of mothers with self-reported secure attachment styles were more likely to be securely attached in the COS group (Berlin, Zeanah & Lieberman, 2016).

## Summary and Conclusion

This chapter seeks to elevate the focus on early development in an effort to explain its vital importance for our understanding of adolescent health and delinquency. Its basic premises are to appreciate the importance of the first years of life, the risk and protective factors that contribute to challenges during that period and their long-term implications, and the absolute necessity of intervening early in order to avoid negative outcomes and promote resilience. A developmental perspective for understanding adolescents necessitates thinking about early prevention, because making differences in young children's lives are the best ways to promote positive youth outcomes. As the concepts of multifinality and equifinality espouse, there are few definitively causal relationships among the risk factors we reviewed and poor health and delinquency in adolescence. Yet, countless studies point to the increased probability of problematic outcomes with early, frequent and ongoing adverse experiences.

Early childhood is full of complexity and possibility, and the best time of life to affect change. Regardless of varied risks, the likelihood of inevitable growth and development is great. As we have discussed in this chapter, promotion of multilevel protective factors when children are young has been shown to decrease the likelihood of substantial difficulties later in life. Prevention and intervention programs offered at multiple levels in the early years have consistently demonstrated their ability to achieve positive outcomes for individuals, families and communities thereby avoiding significant short- and long-term financial, interpersonal and other costs (CDCHU, 2010). Those interested in the health and well-being of adolescents would be well-served to look closely at the possibilities in the early years of life.

## References

Ainsworth, M. D. S., Blehar, M., Waters, E., & Wall, S. N. (2015). *Patterns of attachment: A psychological study of the strange situation* (Classic ed.). New York: Routledge.

Appel, A. E., & Holden, G. W. (1998). The co-occurrence of spouse and physical child abuse: A review and appraisal. *Journal of Family Psychology*, 12(4), 578–599.

Arseneault, L., Cannon, M., Fisher, H. L., Polanczyk, G., Moffitt, T. E., & Caspi, A. (2011). Childhood trauma and children's emerging psychotic symptoms: A genetically sensitive longitudinal cohort study. *American Journal of Psychiatry*, 168(1), 65–72. doi:10.1176/appi.ajp.2010.10040567

Ashman, S. B., Dawson, G., Panagiotides, H., Yamada, E., & Wilkinson, C. W. (2002). Stress hormone levels of children of depressed mothers. *Development & Psychopathology*, 14(2), 333–349.

Ashman, S. B., Dawson, G., & Panagiotides, H. (2008). Trajectories of maternal depression over 7 years: Relations with child psychophysiology and behavior and role of contextual risks. *Development and Psychopathology*, 20(1), 55–77.

Babcock, E. (2014). *Using brain science to design new pathways out of poverty.* Crittenton Women's Union. Retrieved January 12, 2019 from www.liveworkthrive.org/

Back, S. E., Sonne, S. C., Killeen, T., Dansky, B. S., & Brady, K. T. (2003). Comparative profiles of women with PTSD and comorbid cocaine or alcohol dependence. *The American Journal of Drug and Alcohol Abuse*, 29(1), 169–189.

Baglivio, M. T., Epps, N., Swartz, K., Huq, M. S., Sheer, A., & Hardt, N. S. (2014). The prevalence of adverse childhood experiences (ACE) in the lives of juvenile offenders. *Journal of Juvenile Justice*, 3(2), 1.

Baillardgeon, R. H., Normand, C. L., Seguin, J. R., Zoccolillo, M., Japel, C., Perusses, D., ... Tremblay, R. E. (2007). The evolution of problem and social competence behaviors during toddlerhood: A prospective population-based cohort survey. *Infant Mental Health Journal*, 28(1), 12–38.

Bakermans-Kranenburg, M. J., & van Ijzendoorn, M. H. (2007). Research review: Genetic vulnerability or differential susceptibility in child development: The case of attachment. *Journal of Child Psychology and Psychiatry*, 48(12), 1160–1173.

Bartlett, J. D., & Easterbrooks, M. A. (2012). Links between physical abuse in childhood and child neglect among adolescent mothers. *Children and Youth Services Review*, 34, 2164–2169.

Bartlett, J. D., Kotake, C., Fauth, R., & Easterbrooks, M. A. (2017). Intergenerational transmission of child abuse and neglect: Do maltreatment type, perpetrator, and substantiation status matter? *Child Abuse & Neglect*, 63, 84–94.

Behnke, M., Smith, V. C., & Committee on Substance Abuse, & Committee on Fetus and Newborn. (2013). Prenatal substance abuse: Short-and long-term effects on the exposed fetus. *Pediatrics*, 131(3), e1009–e1024.

Belfield, C. R., Nores, M., Barnett, S., & Schweinhart, L. (2006). The high/scope Perry preschool program: Cost-benefit analysis using data from the age-40 follow up. *Journal of Human Resources*, 41(1), 162–190.

Berlin, L., Zeanah, C. & Lieberman, A. (2016). Prevention and intervention programs to support early attachment security. In J. Cassidy & P. Shaver (Eds.), *Handbook of attachment: Theory, research and clinical applications* (pp. 739–758). New York: Guilford Press.

Bernard, K., Dozier, M., Bick, J., Lewis-Morrarty, E., Lindhiem, O., & Carlson, E. (2012). Enhancing attachment organization among maltreated children: Results of a randomized clinical trial. *Child Development*, 83(2), 623–636.

Berzenski, S. R., Yates, T. M., & Egeland, B. (2014). A multidimensional view of continuity in intergenerational transmission of child maltreatment. In J. E. Korbin & R. D. Krugman (Eds.), *Handbook of child maltreatment* (pp. 115–129). New York: Springer Science and Business Media.

Bethell, C. D., Newacheck, P., Hawes, E., & Halfon, N. (2014). Adverse childhood experiences: Assessing the impact on health and school engagement and the mitigating role of resilience. *Health Affairs (Project Hope)*, 33(12), 2106–2115. doi:10.1377/hlthaff.2014.0914

Bhutta, A. T., Cleves, M. A., Casey, P. H., Cradock, M. M., & Anand, K. J. S. (2002). Cognitive and behavioral outcomes of school aged children who were born preterm. *Journal of the American Medical Association*, 288(6), 728–737.

Bick, J., & Dozier, M. (2013). The effectiveness of an attachment-based intervention in promoting foster mothers' sensitivity toward foster infants. *Infant Mental Health Journal*, 34(2), 95–103.

Blair, C., Raver, C. C., Granger, D., Mills-Koonce, R., Hibel, L., & Family Life Project Key Investigators, & The Family Life Project Key Investigators. (2011). Allostasis and allostatic load in the context of poverty in early childhood. *Development and Psychopathology*, 23(3), 845–857. doi:10.1017/S0954579411000344

Bolger, K. E., Patterson, C. J., & Kupersmidt, J. B. (1998). Peer relationships and self-esteem among children who have been maltreated. *Child Development*, 69(4), 1171–1197. doi:10.1111/j.1467-8624.1998.tb06166.x

Bornstein, M. H., Putnick, D. L., Gartstein, M. A., Hahn, C., Auestad, N., & O'Connor, D. L. (2015). Infant temperament: Stability by age, gender, birth order, term status, and SES. *Child Development*, 86(3), 844–863.

Bowen, N. K., & Bowen, G. L. (1999). Effects of crime and violence in neighborhoods and schools on the school behavior and performance of adolescents. *Journal of Adolescent Research*, 14(3), 319–342. doi:10.1177/0743558499143003

Bowlby, J. (1982). *Attachment: Attachment and loss: Volume 1. Attachment* (2nd ed.). New York: Basic Books. (Original work published in 1969).
Brabeck, K., & Xu, Q. (2010). The impact of detention and deportation on Latino immigrant children and families: A quantitative exploration. *Hispanic Journal of Behavioral Sciences*, 32(3), 341–361. doi:10.1177/0739986310374053
Briggs-Gowan, M. J., Carter, A. S., Bosson-Heenan, J., Guyer, A. E., & Horwitz, S. M. (2006). Are infant–toddler social-emotional and behavioral problems transient? *Journal of the American Academy of Child and Adolescent Psychiatry*, 45, 849–858.
Bronfenbrenner, U., & Morris, P. A. (2006). The bioecological model of human development. In R. M. Lerner & W. Damon (Eds.), *Handbook of child psychology: Theoretical models of human development* (pp. 793–828). Hoboken, NJ: John Wiley & Sons Inc.
Bufferd, S. J., Dougherty, L. R., Carlson, G. A., Rose, S., & Klein, D. N. (2012). Psychiatric disorders in preschoolers: Continuity from ages 3 to 6. *American Journal of Psychiatry*, 169, 1157–1164.
Campbell, S., Morgan-Lopez, A. A., Cox, M., McLoyd, V., & NICHD ECCRN. (2009). A latent class analysis of maternal depressive symptoms over 12 years and offspring adjustment in adolescence. *Journal of Abnormal Psychology*, 3, 479–493.
Carter, A. S., Garrity-Rokous, F. E., Chazan-Cohen, R., Little, C., & Briggs-Gowan, M. J. (2001). Maternal depression and comorbidity: Predicting early parenting, attachment security, and toddler social-emotional problems and competencies. *Journal of the American Academy of Child and Adolescent Psychiatry*, 40(1), 18–26.
Center on the Developing Child at Harvard University. (2009). *Maternal depression can undermine the development of young children: Working paper no. 8*. Retrieved December 16, 2018 from http://developingchild.harvard.edu/wp-content/uploads/2009/05/Maternal-Depression-Can-Undermine-Development.pdf
Center on the Developing Child at Harvard University. (2010). *The Foundations of lifelong health are built in early childhood*. Retrieved January 30, 2019 from https://developingchild.harvard.edu/resources/the-foundations-of-lifelong-health-are-built-in-early-childhood/
Center on the Developing Child at Harvard University. (2016). *From best practices to breakthrough impacts: A science-based approach to building a more promising future for young children and families*. Retrieved from www.developingchild.harvard.edu.
Chen, H., & Kovacs, P. (2013). Working with families in which a parent has depression: A resilience perspective. *Families in Society*, 94(2), 114–120.
Cicchetti, D. (2010). Resilience under conditions of extreme stress: A multilevel perspective. *World Psychiatry*, 9(3), 145–154.
Cicchetti, D., & Rogosch, F. A. (1996). Equifinality and multifinality in developmental psychopathology. *Development and Psychopathology*, 8, 597–600.
Cicchetti, D., Rogosch, F. A., & Toth, S. L. (2006). Fostering secure attachment in infants in maltreating families through preventive interventions. *Development and Psychopathology*, 18(3), 623–649.
Cicchetti, D., & Toth, S. L. (2015). Multilevel developmental perspectives on child maltreatment. *Development and Psychopathology*, 27(4 Pt 2), 1385–1386. doi:10.1017/S0954579415000814
Collin-Vézina, D., Coleman, K., Milne, L., Sell, J., & Daigneault, I. (2011). Trauma experiences, maltreatment-related impairments, and resilience among child welfare youth in residential care. *International Journal of Mental Health and Addiction*, 9(5), 577–589. doi:10.1007/s11469-011-9323-8
Cook, J. T., Black, M., Chilton, M., Cutts, D., Ettinger de Cuba, S., Heeren, T. C., Rose-Jacobs, R., Sandel, M., Casey, P. H., Coleman, S., Weiss, I., & Frank, D. A. (2013). Are food insecurity's health impacts underestimated in the US population? Marginal food security also predicts adverse health outcomes in young US children and mothers. *Advances in Nutrition*, 4(1), 51–61.
Cooley-Strickland, M., Quille, T. J., Griffin, R. S., Stuart, E. A., Bradshaw, C. P., & Furr-Holden, D. (2009). Community violence and youth: Affect, behavior, substance use, and academics. *Clinical Child and Family Psychology Review*, 12(2), 127–156. doi:10.1007/s10567-009-0051-6
Courtney, M. E., Terao, S, & Bost, N. (2004, February 22). *Midwest evaluation of the adult functioning of former foster youth: Conditions of youth preparing to leave state care*. Chicago, IL: Chapin Hall Center for Children at the University of Chicago.
Cowan, P. A., & Cowan, C. P. (2003). Normative family transitions, normal family processes, and healthy child development. In F. Walsh (Ed.), *Normal family processes: Growing diversity and complexity* (pp. 424–459). New York: Guilford Press.
Coyne, J., Powell, B., Hoffman, K., & Cooper, G. (2019). The circle of security. In C. H. Zeanah (Ed.), *Handbook of infant mental health, 4th edition* (pp. 500–513). New York: Guilford Press.

Crnic, K., Gaze, C., & Hoffman, C. (2005). Cumulative parenting stress across the preschool period: Relations to maternal parenting and child behaviour at age 5. *Infant and Child Development*, 14(2), 117–132. doi: https://doi.org/10.1002/icd.384

Curtis, W. J., & Cicchetti, D. (2013). Affective facial expression processing in 15-month-old infants who have experienced maltreatment: An event-related potential study. *Child Maltreatment*, 18, 140–154.

Cutts, D. B., Meyers, A. F., Black, M. M., Casey, P. H., Chilton, M., Cook, J. T., ... Frank, D. A. (2011). US housing insecurity and the health of very young children. *American Journal of Public Health*, 101(8), 1508–1514. doi:10.2105/AJPH.2011.300139

Dawson, G., Ashman, S. B., Hessl, D., Spieker, S., Frey, K., Panagiotides, H., & Embry, L. (2001). Autonomic and brain electrical activity in securely- and insecurely-attached infants of depressed mothers. *Infant Behavior and Development*, 2, 135–149.

De la Vega, A., de la Osa, N., Ezpeleta, L., Granero, R., & Domenech, J. M. (2011). Differential effects of psychological maltreatment on children of mothers exposed to intimate partner violence. *Child Abuse & Neglect*, 35(7), 524–531.

Deater-Deckard K, & Scarr S. (1996). Parenting stress among dual-earner mothers and fathers: Are there gender differences? *Journal of Family Psychology*, 10, 45–59.

Dong, M., Anda, R. F., Felitti, V. J., Williamson, D. F., Dube, S. R., Brown, D. W., & Giles, W. H. (2005). Childhood residential mobility and multiple health risks during adolescence and adulthood: The hidden role of adverse childhood experiences. *Archives of Pediatrics & Adolescent Medicine*, 159(12), 1104–1110. doi:10.1001/archpedi.159.12.1104

Downey, G., & Coyne, J. C. (1990). Children of depressed parents: An integrative review. *Psychological Bulletin*, 108(1), 50–76. doi:10.1037/0033-2909.108.1.50

Dozier, M., & Bernard, K. (2019). Attachment and biobehavioral catch-up. In C. H. Zeanah (Ed.), *Handbook of infant mental health, 4th Edition* (pp. 514–526). New York: Guilford Press.

Dozier, M., Lindhiem, O., Lewis, E., Bick, J., Bernard, K., & Peloso, E. (2009). Effects of a foster parent training program on young children's attachment behaviors: Preliminary evidence from a randomized clinical trial. *Child and Adolescent Social Work Journal*, 26(4), 321–332.

Drake, B., & Pandey, S. (1996). Understanding the relationship between neighborhood poverty and specific types of child maltreatment. *Child Abuse & Neglect*, 20(11), 1003–1018. doi:10.1016/0145-2134(96)00091-9

Dube, S. R., Miller, J. W., Brown, D. W., Giles, W. H., Felitti, V. J., Dong, M., & Anda, R. F. (2006). Adverse childhood experiences and the association with ever using alcohol and initiating alcohol use during adolescence. *Journal of Adolescent Health*, 38(4), 444.e1–444.e10. doi:10.1016/j.jadohealth.2005.06.006

Duggan, A., Portilla, X. A., Filene, J. H., Crowne, S. S., Hill, C. J., Lee, H., & Knox, V. (2018). *Implementation of evidence-based early childhood home visiting: Results from the mother and infant home visiting program evaluation*. OPRE Report 2018-76A. Washington, DC: Office of Planning, Research, and Evaluation, Administration for Children and Families, U.S. Department of Health and Human Services.

DuMont, K., Mitchell-Herzfeld, S., Greene, R., Lee, E., Lowenfels, A., Rodriguez, M., & Dorabawila, V. (2008). Healthy families New York (HFNY) randomized trial: Effects on early child abuse and neglect. *Child Abuse and Neglect*, 32(3), 295–315.

Duncan, G. J., Brooks-Gunn, J., & Klebanov, P. K. (1994). Economic deprivation and early childhood development. *Child Development*, 65(2), 296–318. doi:10.1111/j.1467-8624.1994.tb00752.x

Easterbrooks, M. A., Bartlett, J. D., Beeghly, M., & Thompson, R. A. (2012). Social and emotional development in infancy. In R. M. Lerner, M. A. Easterbrooks, & J. Mistry (Eds.), *Handbook of psychology: Vol. 6. Developmental psychology* (2nd ed., pp. 91–120). Editor-in-Chief: I. B. Weiner: Hoboken, NJ: Wiley.

Eckenrode, J., Laird, M., & Doris, J. (1993). School performance and disciplinary problems among abused and neglected children. *Developmental Psychology*, 29(1), 53–62.

Edleson, J. L. (1999). The overlap between child maltreatment and woman battering. *Violence against Women*, 5(2), 134–154.

Egger, H. L., & Angold, A. (2006). Common emotional and behavioral disorders in preschool children: Presentation, nosology, and epidemiology. *Journal of Child Psychology and Psychiatry*, 47(3–4), 313–337.

Englund, M., White, B., Reynolds, A. J., Schweinhart, L., & Campbell, F. A. (2014). Health outcomes of the abecedarian, child-parent center and high-scope perry preschool programs. In A. J., Reynolds, A. J. Rolnick, & J. A. Temple (Eds.), *Health and education in early childhood: Predictors, interventions and policies* (pp. 257–285). New York: Cambridge University Press.

Ertel, K. A., Rich-Edwards, J. W., & Koenen, K. C. (2011). Maternal depression in the United States: Nationally representative rates and risks. *Journal of Women's Healthy*, 20(11), 1609–1617.

Evans, G. W., Schamberg, M. A., & McEwen, B. S. (2009). Childhood poverty, chronic stress, and adult working memory. *Proceedings of the National Academy of Sciences of the United States of America*, 106(16), 6545–6549. doi:10.1073/pnas.0811910106

Evans-Chase, M. (2014). Addressing trauma and psychosocial development in juvenile justice-involved youth: A synthesis of the developmental neuroscience, juvenile justice and trauma literature. *Laws*, 3(4), 744–758.

Fang, X., & Corso, P. S. (2007). Child maltreatment, youth violence, and intimate partner violence: Developmental relationships. *American Journal of Preventive Medicine*, 33(4), 281.

Felitti, V. J., & Anda, R. (2009). The relationship of adverse childhood experiences to adult medical disease, psychiatric disorders and sexual behavior: Implications for healthcare. In R. A. Lanius, E. Vermetten, & C. Pain (Eds.), *The impact of early life trauma on health and disease: The hidden epidemic* (pp. 77–87). New York: Cambridge University Press.

Felitti, V. J., Anda, R. F., Nordenberg, D., Williamson, D. F., Spitz, A. M., Edwards, V., ... Marks, J. S. (1998). Relationship of childhood abuse and household dysfunction to many of the leading causes of death in adults: The adverse childhood experiences (ACE) study. *American Journal of Preventive Medicine*, 14(4), 245–258. doi:10.1016/S0749-3797(98)00017-8

Fevang, S. K., Hysing, M., Markestad, T., & Sommerfelt, K. (2016). Mental health in children born extremely preterm without severe neurodevelopmental disabilities. *Pediatrics*, 137(4), e20153002.

Field, T. (1995). Infants of depressed mothers. *Infant Behavior & Development*, 18(1), 1–13.

Field, T., Diego, M., Dieter, J., Hernandez-Reif, M., Schanberg, S., Kuhn, C., Yando, R., & Bendell, D. (2004). Prenatal depression effects on the fetus and the newborn. *Infant Behavior and Development*, 27, 216–229.

Flaherty, E. G., Thompson, R., Dubowitz, H., Harvey, E. M., English, D. J., Proctor, L. J., & Runyan, D. K. (2013). Adverse childhood experiences and child health in early adolescence. *JAMA Pediatrics*, 167(7), 622–629. doi:10.1001/jamapediatrics.2013.22

Fraser, M., Richman, J. M., Galinsky, M. J., & Day, S. H. (2009). *Intervention research: Developing social programs*. New York: Oxford University Press.

García, J. L., Heckman, J. J., Leaf, D. E., & Prados, M. J. (2016). *The life-cycle benefits of an influential early childhood program*. Retrieved January 30, 2019 from heckmanequation.org/www/assets/2017/01/F_Heckman_CBAOnePager_120516.pdf

Garmezy, N. (1970). Process and reactive schizophrenia: Some conceptions and issues. *Schizophrenia Bulletin*, 2, 30–74.

Garmezy, N., Masten, A. S., & Tellegen, A. (1984). The study of stress and competence in children: A building block for developmental psychology. *Child Development*, 55(1), 97–111.

Gold, J., Sullivan, M. W., & Lewis, M. (2011). The relation between abuse and violent delinquency: The conversion of shame to blame in juvenile offenders. *Child Abuse & Neglect*, 35(7), 459–467.

Green, B. L., Ayoub, C., Bartlett, J. D., Von Ende, A., Furrer, C., Chazan-Cohen, R., Vallotton, C., & Klevens, J. (2014). The effect of Early Head Start on child welfare system involvement: A first look at longitudinal child maltreatment outcomes. *Children & Youth Services Review*, 42(1), 127–135.

Greeson, J. K. P., Briggs, E. C., Kisiel, C. L., Layne, C. M., Ake, G. S., III, Ko, S. J., ... Fairbank, J. A. (2011). Complex trauma and mental health in children and adolescents placed in foster care: Findings from the national child traumatic stress network. *Child Welfare*, 90(6), 91–108.

Groh, A. M., Fearon, R. P., van IJzendoorn, M. H., Bakermans-Kranenburg, M. J., & Roisman, G. I. (2017). Attachment in the early life course: Meta-analytic evidence for its role in socioemotional development. *Child Development Perspectives*, 11(1), 70.

Hackman, D. A., & Farah, M. J. (2009). Socioeconomic status and the developing brain. *Trends in Cognitive Sciences*, 13(2), 65–73. doi:10.1016/j.tics.2008.11.003

Hans, S. L., Bernstein, V. J., & Henson, L. G. (1999). The role of psychopathology in the parenting of drug-dependent women. *Development and Psychopathology*, 11(4), 957–977.

Hawkins, J. D. (2006). Science, social work, prevention: Finding the intersections. *Social Work Research*, 30(3), 137–152.

Herrenkohl, T. I., Sousa, C., Tajima, E. A., Herrenkohl, R. C., & Moylan, C. A. (2008). Intersection of child abuse and children's exposure to domestic violence. *Trauma, Violence, & Abuse*, 9(2), 84–99. doi:10.1177/1524838008314797

Hillis, S. D., Anda, R. F., Dube, S. R., Felitti, V. J., Marchbanks, P. A., & Marks, J. S. (2004). The association between adverse childhood experiences and adolescent pregnancy, long-term psychosocial consequences, and fetal death. *Pediatrics*, 113(2), 320–327.

Hoffman, K. T., Marvin, R. S., Cooper, G., & Powell, B. (2006). Changing toddlers' and preschoolers' attachment classifications: The Circle of Security intervention. *Journal of Consulting and Clinical Psychology*, 74(6), 1017–1026.

Jacobs, F., Easterbrooks, A., Mistry, J., Bumgarner, E., Fauth, R., Goldberg, J., ... Scott, J. (2015). *The Massachusetts Healthy Families Evaluation-2 (MHFE-2): A randomized, controlled trial of a statewide home visiting program for young parents.* Medford, MA: Tufts Interdisciplinary Evaluation Research, Tufts University. Retrieved January 29, 2019 from http://ase.tufts.edu/tier/documents/2015_MHFE2final Report.pdf

Jenson, J. M. (2010). Advances in preventing childhood and adolescent problem behavior. *Research on Social Work Practice*, 20(6), 701–713.

Johnson, S., Hollis, C., Kochhar, P., Hennessey, E., Wolke, D., & Marlow, N. (2010). Autism spectrum disorders in extremely preterm children. *Journal of Pediatrics*, 156(4), 525–531.

Jonson-Reid, M., Kohl, P. L., & Drake, B. (2012). Child and adult outcomes of chronic child maltreatment. *Pediatrics*, 129(5), 839–845.

Kaltenbach, K. (2013). Bio-psychosocial characteristics of parenting women with substance use disorders. In N. E. Suchman, M. Pajulo, & L. M. Mayes (Eds.), *Parenting and substance abuse* (pp. 185–194). New York: Oxford University Press.

Kane, P., & Garber, J. (2004). The relations among depression in fathers, children's psychopathology, and father–child conflict: A meta-analysis. *Clinical Psychology Review*, 24(3), 339–360.

Kaslow, N. J. (2008). Associations of child maltreatment and intimate partner violence with psychological adjustment among low SES, African American children. *Child Abuse & Neglect*, 32(9), 888–896.

Knitzer, J., Theberge, S., & Johnson, K. (2008, January). *Reducing maternal depression and its impact on young children: Toward a responsive early childhood policy framework.* New York: National Center for Children in Poverty Columbia University. Retrieved January 30, 2019 from https://academiccommons.columbia.edu/doi/10.7916/D86T0WCV

Koenig, A. L., Cicchetti, D., & Rogosch, F. A. (2004). Moral development: The association between maltreatment and young children's prosocial behaviors and moral transgressions. *Social Development*, 13, 87–106.

Krieger, F. V., & Stringaris, A. (2015). Temperament and vulnerability to externalizing behavior. In T. P. Beauchaine & S. P. Hinshaw (Eds.), *The Oxford handbook of externalizing spectrum disorders* (pp. 170–183). New York: Oxford University Press.

Krischer, M. K., & Sevecke, K. (2008). Early traumatization and psychopathy in female and male juvenile offenders. *International Journal of Law and Psychiatry*, 31(3), 253–262. doi:10.1016/j.ijlp.2008.04.008

Labella, M. H., & Masten, A. S. (2018). Family influences on the development of aggression and violence. *Current Opinion in Psychology*, 19, 11–16.

Landi, N., Montoya, J., Kober, H., Rutherford, H. J., Mencl, W. E., Worhunsky, P. D., Potenza, N. M., & Mayes, L. C. (2011). Maternal neural responses to infant cries and faces: Relationships with substance use. *Frontiers in Psychiatry*, 2(32), 1–13.

Lansford, J. E., Miller-Johnson, S., Berlin, L. J., Dodge, K. A., Bates, J. E., & Pettit, G. S. (2007). Early physical abuse and later violent delinquency: A prospective longitudinal study. *Child Maltreatment*, 12(3), 233–245. doi:10.1177/1077559507301841

Levendosky, A. A., Bogat, G. A., Bernard, N., & Garcia, A. (2018). The effects of intimate partner violence on the early caregiving system. In M. Muzik & K. L. Rosenblum (Eds.), *Motherhood in the face of trauma: Pathways toward healing and growth* (pp. 39–54). Cham: Springer.

Lieberman, A. F., & Van Horn, P. (2005). *Don't hit my mommy: A manual for child-parent psychotherapy with young witnesses of family violence.* Washington, DC: ZERO TO THREE Press.

Lieberman, A. F., Van Horn, P., & Ippen, C. G. (2005). Toward evidence-based treatment: Child-parent psychotherapy with preschoolers exposed to marital violence. *Journal of the American Academy of Child & Adolescent Psychiatry*, 44(12), 1241–1248.

Lieberman, A. F., Weston, D. R., & Pawl, J. H. (1991). Preventive intervention and outcome with anxiously attached dyads. *Child Development*, 62(1), 199–209.

Light, K. C., Grewen, K. M., Amico, J. A., Boccia, M., Brownley, K. A., & Johns, J. M. (2004). Deficits in plasma oxytocin responses and increased negative affect, stress, and blood pressure in mothers with cocaine exposure during pregnancy. *Addictive Behaviors*, 29(8), 1541–1564.

Lim, Y., & Lee, O. (2017). Relationships between parental maltreatment and adolescents' school adjustment: Mediating roles of self-esteem and peer attachment. *Journal of Child and Family Studies*, 26(2), 393–404. doi:10.1007/s10826-016-0573-8

Love, J., Kisker, E. E., Ross, C., Raikes, H., Constantine, J., Boller, K., ... Vogel, C. (2005). The effectiveness of Early Head Start for 3-year-old children and their parents. *Developmental Psychology*, 41, 885–901.

Lovejoy, M. C., Graczyk, P. A., O'Hare, E., & Neuman, G. (2000). Maternal depression and parenting behavior: A meta-analytic review. *Clinical Psychology Review*, 20(5), 561–592. doi:10.1016/S0272-7358(98)00100-7

Luthar, S. S., Cicchetti, D., & Becker, B. (2000). The construct of resilience: A critical evaluation and guidelines for future work. *Child Development*, 71(3), 543–562.

Lynch, M. (2003). Consequences of children's exposure to community violence. *Clinical Child and Family Psychology Review*, 6(4), 265–274. doi:10.1023/B:CCFP.0000006293.77143.e1

Lyons-Ruth, K., Todd Manly, J., Von Klitzing, K., Tamminen, T., Emde, R., Fitzgerald, H., ... & Watanabe, H. (2017). The worldwide burden of infant mental and emotional disorder: Report of the task force of the world association for infant mental health. *Infant Mental Health Journal*, 38(6), 695–705.

Main, M., & Solomon, J. (1986). Discovery of an insecure-disorganized/disoriented attachment pattern. In T. B. Brazelton & M. W. Yogman (Eds.), *Affective development in infancy* (pp. 95–124). Westport, CT: Ablex Publishing.

Martins, C., & Gaffan, E. A. (2000). Effects of early maternal depression on patterns of infant–Mother attachment: A meta-analytic investigation. *Journal of Child Psychology and Psychiatry*, 41(6), 737–746.

Masten, A., & Garmezy, N. (1985). Risk, vulnerability, and protective factors in developmental psychopathology. In B. Lahey & A. Kazdin (Eds.), *Advances in clinical child psychology* (pp. 1–52). New York: Plenum Press.

McLaughlin, K. A. (2016). Future directions in childhood adversity and youth psychopathology. *Journal of Clinical Child & Adolescent Psychology*, 45(3), 361–382. doi:10.1080/15374416.2015.1110823

McLoyd, V. C. (1998). Socioeconomic disadvantage and child development. *American Psychologist*, 53(2), 185–204. doi:10.1037/0003-066X.53.2.185

Melchior, M., Chastang, J., Falissard, B., Galéra, C., Tremblay, R. E., Côté, S. M., & Boivin, M. (2012). Food insecurity and children's mental health: A prospective birth cohort study. *PloS One*, 7(12), e52615. doi:10.1371/journal.pone.0052615

Melhuish, E. C., Phan, M. B., Sylva, K., Sammons, P., Siraj-Blatchford, I., & Taggart, B. (2008). Effects of the home learning environment and preschool center experience upon literacy and numeracy development in early primary school. *Journal of Social Issues*, 64(1), 95–114. doi:10.1111/j.1540-4560.2008.00550.x

Mendle, J., Leve, L. D., Van Ryzin, M., & Natsuaki, M. N. (2014). Linking childhood maltreatment with girls'internalizing symptoms: Early puberty as a tipping point. *Journal of Research on Adolescence*, 24(4), 689–702. doi:10.1111/jora.12075

Mercer, J. (2015). Examining Circle of Security™: A review of research and theory. *Research on Social Work Practice*, 25(3), 382–392.

Messman-Moore, T. L., Walsh, K. L., & DiLillo, D. (2010). Emotion dysregulation and risky sexual behavior in revictimization. *Child Abuse & Neglect*, 34(12), 967–976. doi:10.1016/j.chiabu.2010.06.004

Michalopoulos, C., Faucetta, K., Warren, A., & Mitchell, R. (2017). *Evidence on the long-term effects of home visiting programs: Laying the groundwork for long-term follow-up in the Mother and Infant Home Visiting Program Evaluation (MIHOPE)*. OPRE Report 2017-73. Washington, DC: Office of Planning, Research and Evaluation, Administration for Children and Families, U.S. Department of Health and Human Services. Retrieved January 13, 2019 from www.mdrc.org/publication/evidence-long-term-effects-home-visiting-programs

Minuchin, P. (1985). Families and individual development: Provocations from the field of family therapy. *Child Development*, 56(2), Family Development and the Child (Apr., 1985), 289–302.

Monk, C., Feng, T., Lee, S., Krupska, I., Champagne, F., & Tycko, B. (2016). Distress during pregnancy: Epigenetic regulation of placental glucocorticoid-related genes and fetal neurobehavior. *American Journal of Psychiatry*, 173, 705–713.

Monk, C., Spicer, J., & Champagne, F. (2012). Linking prenatal adversity to developmental outcomes in infants: The role of epigenetic pathways. *Development and Psychopathology*, 24, 1361–1376.

Murray, D. W., Rosanbalm, K., Christopoulos, C., & Hamoudi, A. (2015). *Self-regulation and toxic stress: Foundations for understanding self-regulation from an applied developmental perspective*. OPRE Report #2015–21, Washington, DC: Office of Planning, Research and Evaluation, Administration for Children and Families, U.S. Department of Health and Human Services. Retrieved January 12, 2019 from www.acf.hhs.gov/opre/resource/self-regulation-and-toxic-stress-foundations-for-understanding-self-regulation-from-an-applied-developmental-perspective

Murray, J., Farrington, D. P., & Sekol, I. (2012). Children's antisocial behavior, mental health, drug use, and educational performance after parental incarceration: A systematic review and meta-analysis. *Psychological Bulletin*, 138(2), 175–210. doi:10.1037/a0026407

National Head Start Association. (2018). *2017 National Head Start profile.* Retrieved January 13, 2019 from https://nhsa.app.box.com/s/z55bxt1zf3ih0cwm65duvwskpijfruiq/file/343254382360

National Home Visiting Resource Center. (2018). *2018 home visiting yearbook.* Arlington, VA: James Bell Associates and the Urban Institute. Retrieved January 31, 2019 from www.nhvrc.org/wp-content/uploads/NHVRC_Yearbook_2018_FINAL.pdf

National Institute of Child Health and Human Development Early Child Care Research Network. (2005). Duration and developmental timing of poverty and children's cognitive and social development from birth through third grade. *Child Development,* 76(4), 795–810. doi:10.1111/j.1467-8624.2005.00878.x

National Research Council & Institute of Medicine [NRC & IOM]. (2009a). *Preventing mental, emotional, and behavioral disorders among young people: Progress and possibilities.* Washington, DC: The National Academies Press. Retrieved January 13, 2019 from www.nap.edu/catalog/12480/preventing-mental-emotional-and-behavioral-disorders-among-young-people-progress

National Research Council & Institute of Medicine [NRC & IOM]. (2009b). *Depression in parents, parenting, and children: Opportunities to improve identification, treatment, and prevention.* Committee on Depression, Parenting Practices, and the Healthy Development of Children. Board on Children, Youth, and Families. Division of Behavioral and Social Sciences and Education. Washington, DC: The National Academies Press.

National Scientific Council on the Developing Child. (2007). *The science of early childhood development.* Retrieved January 30, 2019 from https://46y5eh11fhgw3ve3ytpwxt9r-wpengine.netdna-ssl.com/wp-content/uploads/2015/05/Science_Early_Childhood_Development.pdf

National Scientific Council on the Developing Child. (2014). *Excessive stress disrupts the architecture of the developing brain: Working Paper No. 3.* Updated Edition. Retrieved from www.developingchild.harvard.edu

National Scientific Council on the Developing Child. (2015). *Supportive relationships and active skill-building strengthen the foundations of resilience: Working paper 13.* Retrieved January 12, 2019 from https://developingchild.harvard.edu/resources/supportive-relationships-and-active-skill-building-strengthen-the-foundations-of-resilience/

Olds, D. L., Eckenrode, J., Henderson, C. R., Kitzman, H., Powers, J., Cole, R., ... Luckey, D. (1997). Long-term effects of home visitation on maternal life course and child abuse and neglect: 15-year follow-up of a randomized trial. *Journal of the American Medical Association,* 278(8), 637–643.

Pajulo, M., Pyykkönen, N., Kalland, M., Sinkkonen, J., Helenius, H., Punamäki, R. L., & Suchman, N. (2012). Substance-abusing mothers in residential treatment with their babies: Importance of pre-and postnatal maternal reflective functioning. *Infant Mental Health Journal,* 33(1), 70–81.

Pascoe, J. M., Wood, D. L., Duffee, J. H., & Kuo, A. (2016). Mediators and adverse effects of child poverty in the united states. *Pediatrics,* 137(4), 1.

Paulson, J., Dauber, S., & Leiferman, J. (2006). Individual and combined effects of postpartum depression in mothers and fathers on parenting behavior. *Pediatrics,* 118(2), 659–668.

Peleg-Oren, N., & Teichman, M. (2006). Young children of parents with substance use disorders (SUD): A review of the literature and implications for social work practice. *Journal of Social Work Practice in the Addictions,* 6(1–2), 49–61.

Pollak, S. D., & Sinha, P. (2002). Effects of early experience on children's recognition of facial displays of emotion. *Developmental Psychology,* 38, 784–791.

Ramey, C. T., & Campbell, F. A. (1984). Preventive education for high-risk children: Cognitive consequences of the Carolina Abecedarian Project. *American Journal of Mental Deficiency,* 88, 515–523.

Rosanbalm, K. D., & Murray, D. W. (2017). *Promoting self-regulation in early childhood: A practice brief.* OPRE Brief #2017-79. Washington, DC: Office of Planning, Research, and Evaluation, Administration for Children and Families, US. Department of Health and Human Services. Retrieved January 13, 2019 from https://fpg.unc.edu/sites/fpg.unc.edu/files/resources/reports-and-policy-briefs/PromotingSelf-RegulationIntheFirstFiveYears.pdf

Rose-Jacobs, R., Black, M. M., Casey, P. H., Cook, J. T., Cutts, D. B., Chilton, M., Heeren, T., Levenson, S. M., Meyers, A. F., & Frank, D. A. (2008). Household food insecurity: associations with at-risk infant and toddler development. *Pediatrics,* 121(1), 65–72.

Rosenblum, K. L., Dayton, C. J., & Muzik, M. (2019). Infant social and emotional development. In C. H. Zeanah (Ed.), *Handbook of infant mental health* (4th ed., pp. 80–103). New York: Guilford.

Rothbart, M., Posner, M., & Hershey, K. (1995). Temperament, attention, and developmental psychopathology. In D. Cicchetti & D. Cohen (Eds.), *Developmental psychopathology* (pp. 315–340). New York: Wiley.

Rutherford, H., Potenza, M., & Mayes, L. (2013). The neurobiology of addiction and attachment. In N. E. Suchman, M. Pajulo, & L. M. Mayes (Eds.), *Parenting and substance abuse* (pp. 3–23). New York: Oxford University Press.

Salo, S., & Flykt, M. (2013). The impact of parental addiction on child development. In N. E. Suchman, M. Pajulo, & L. C. Mayes (Eds.), *Parenting and substance abuse: Developmental approaches to intervention* (pp. 195–210). New York: Oxford University Press.

Salo, S., Politi, J., Tupola, S., Biringen, Z., Kalland, M., Halmesmäki, E., ... Kivitie-Kallio, S. (2010). Early development of opioid-exposed infants born to mothers in buprenorphine-replacement therapy. *Journal of Reproductive and Infant Psychology*, 28(2), 161–179.

SAMHSA. (2019). Infants with prenatal substance exposure. Retrieved June 6, 2019 from https://ncsacw.samhsa.gov/resources/substance-exposed-infants.aspx.

Samuelsson, M., Holsti, A., Adamsson, M., Serenius, F., Hagglof, B., & Farooqi, A. (2017). Behavioral patterns in adolescents born at 23 to 25 weeks of gestation. *Pediatrics*, 140(1), e20170199. doi:10.1542/peds.2017-0199

Sanders, M. R., Markie-Dadds, C., Tully, L. A., & Bor, W. (2000). The Triple P-Positive Parenting Program: A comparison of enhanced, standard, and self-directed behavioral family intervention for parents of children with early onset conduct problems. *Journal of Consulting and Clinical Psychology*, 68, 624–640.

Schanzenbach, D. W., & Bauer, L. (2016, August). *The long-term impact of the Head Start program*. Retrieved January 14, 2019 from www.brookings.edu/research/the-long-term-impact-of-the-head-start

Schilling, E. A., Aseltine, J., Robert H, & Gore, S. (2007). Adverse childhood experiences and mental health in young adults: A longitudinal survey. *BMC Public Health*, 7(1), 30. doi:10.1186/1471-2458-7-30

Schwartz, D., & Hopmeyer Gorman, A. (2003). Community violence exposure and children's academic functioning. *Journal of Educational Psychology*, 95(1), 163–173. doi:10.1037/0022-0663.95.1.163

Sedlak, A., United States. Children's Bureau, Fourth National Incidence Study of Child Abuse and Neglect (U.S.), Walter R. McDonald & Associates, Westat, I., & United States. Administration for Children and Families. Office of Planning, Research and Evaluation. (2010). *Fourth national incidence study of child abuse and neglect (NIS-4): Report to congress*. Washington, DC: U.S. Department of Health and Human Services, Administration for Children and Families, Office of Planning, Research and Evaluation and the Children's Bureau.

Shipman, K. L., & Zeman, J. (1999). Emotional understanding: A comparison of physically maltreating and nonmaltreating mother–Child dyads. *Journal of Clinical Child Psychology*, 28, 407–417.

Shonkoff, J. P., Boyce, W. T., & McEwen, B. S. (2009). Neuroscience, molecular biology, and the childhood roots of health disparities: Building a new framework for health promotion and disease prevention. *JAMA*, 301(21), 2252–2259. doi:10.1001/jama.2009.754

Sidebotham, P., & Heron, J. (2006). Child maltreatment in the "children of the nineties": A cohort study of risk factors. *Child Abuse & Neglect*, 30(5), 497–522.

Simms, M. D., Dubowitz, H., & Szilagyi, M. A. (2000). Health care needs of children in the foster care system. *Pediatrics*, 106(4 Suppl), 909.

Slack, K. S., Holl, J. L., McDaniel, M., Yoo, J., & Bolger, K. (2004). Understanding the risks of child neglect: An exploration of poverty and parenting characteristics. *Child Maltreatment*, 9(4), 395–408. doi:10.1177/1077559504269193

Slade, A. (2005). Parental reflective functioning: An introduction. *Attachment & Human Development*, 7(3), 269–281.

Slopen, N., Fitzmaurice, G., Williams, David R., & Gilman, S. E. (2010). Poverty, food insecurity, and the behavior for childhood internalizing and externalizing disorders. *Journal of the American Academy of Child & Adolescent Psychiatry*, 49(5), 444–452. doi:10.1016/j.jaac.2010.01.018

Sousa, C., Herrenkohl, T. I., Moylan, C. A., Tajima, E. A., Klika, J. B., Herrenkohl, R. C., & Russo, M. J. (2011). Longitudinal study on the effects of child abuse and children's exposure to domestic violence, parent–child attachments, and antisocial behavior in adolescence. *Journal of Interpersonal Violence*, 26(1), 111–136. doi:10.1177/0886260510362883

Spatz Widom, C., DuMont, K., & Czaja, S. J. (2007). A prospective investigation of major depressive disorder and comorbidity in abused and neglected children grown up. *Archives of General Psychiatry*, 64(1), 49–56.

Sroufe, L. A. (2005). Attachment and development: A prospective, longitudinal study from birth to adulthood. *Attachment & Human Development*, 7(4), 349–367.

Supplee, L. (2016). *5 things to know about early childhood home visiting*. Bethesda, MD: Child Trends. Retrieved January 13, 2019 from www.childtrends.org/child-trends-5/5-things-to-know-about-early-childhood-home-visiting

Tarullo, A. R. (2012, Winter). Effects of child maltreatment on the developing brain. *Child Welfare 360°: Using a Developmental Approach in Child Welfare Practice*, 11.

Templin, T., Ager, J., Janisse, J., Nordstrom-Klee, B., Covington, C., Ondersma, S. J., ... Delaney-Black, V. (2003). Violence exposure, trauma, and IQ and/or reading deficits among urban children. *Journal of the American Academy of Child and Adolescent Psychiatry*, 42(1), 48.
Thompson, R. (2016). Early attachment and later development: Reframing the questions. In J. Cassidy & P. Shaver (Eds.), *Handbook of attachment: Theory, research and clinical applications* (3rd ed., pp. 330–348). New York: Guilford Press.
Toth, S. L., Rogosch, F. A., Manly, J. T., & Cicchetti, D. (2006). The efficacy of toddler–parent psychotherapy to reorganize attachment in the young offspring of mothers with major depressive disorder: A randomized preventive trial. *Journal of Consulting and Clinical Psychology*, 74(6), 1006–1016.
Tronick, E. Z., & Gianino, A. (1986). Interactive mismatch and repair: Challenges to the coping infant. *Zero to Three*, 6(3), 1–6.
U.S. Department of Health and Human Services. (2010, January). *Head Start Impact Study final report.* Washington, DC: Author. Retrieved January 14, 2018 from www.acf.hhs.gov/sites/default/files/opre/hs_impact_study_final.pdf
U.S. Department of Health & Human Services, Administration for Children and Families, Administration on Children, Youth and Families, Children's Bureau (USDHHS). (2018). *Child maltreatment 2016.* Retrieved June 6, 2019 from https://www.acf.hhs.gov/cb/research-data-technology/statistics-research/child-maltreatment.
Van Horn, P., & Lieberman, A. E. (2012). Early exposure to trauma. In L. Mayes & M. Lewis (Eds.), *The Cambridge handbook of environment in human development* (pp. 466–479). Cambridge: Cambridge University Press.
Vogel, C., Brooks-Gunn, J., Martin, A., & Klute, M. M. (2013). Impacts of Early Head Start participation on child and parent outcomes at ages 2, 3, and 5. *Monographs of the Society for Research in Child Development*, 78(1), 36–63.
Walsh, F. (1996). The concept of family resilience: Crisis and challenge. *Family Process*, 35, 261–281.
Webster-Stratton, C. (1998). Preventing conduct problems in Head Start children: Strengthening parent competencies. *Journal of Consulting and Clinical Psychology*, 66, 715–730.
Weitzman, M., Rosenthal, D. G., & Liu, Y. (2011). Paternal depressive symptoms and child behavioral or emotional problems in the United States. *Pediatrics*, 128(6), 1126–1134.
Weitzman, M., Baten, A., Rosenthal, D. G., Hoshino, R., Tohn, E., & Jacobs, D. E. (2013). Housing and child health. *Current Problems in Pediatric and Adolescent Health Care*, 43(8), 187–224.
Werner, E., & Smith, R. (1977). *Kauai's children come of age.* Honolulu, HI: University of Hawaii Press.
Werner, E. E. (2000). Protective factors and individual resilience. In J. P. Shonkoff & S. J. Meisels (Eds.), *Handbook of early childhood intervention* (pp. 115–132). New York: Cambridge University Press.
Wilhelm, K. (2006). Depression: From nosology to global burden. In C. L. M. Keyes & S. H. Goodman (Eds.), *Women and depression: A handbook for the social, behavior, and biomedical sciences* (p. 3021). New York: Cambridge University Press.
Wulczyn, F., Ernst, M., & Fisher, P. (2011). *Who are the infants in out-of-home care?: An epidemiological and developmental snapshot.* Chicago, IL: Chapin Hall at the University of Chicago.
Young, J. C., & Widom, C. S. (2014). Long-term effects of child abuse and neglect on emotion processing in adulthood. *Child Abuse & Neglect*, 38(8), 1369–1381. doi:10.1016/j.chiabu.2014.03.008
Zeanah, C. H., & Gleason, M. M. (2015). Annual Research Review: Attachment disorders in early childhood–Clinical presentation, causes, correlates, and treatment. *Journal of Child Psychology and Psychiatry*, 56 (3), 207–222.
Zeanah, C. H., & Zeanah, P. D. (2019). Infant mental health: The science of early experience. In C. H. Zeanah (Ed.), *Handbook of infant mental health* (4th ed., pp. 5–24). New York: Guildford Press.

# 18
# MOBILIZING COMMUNITIES TO PREVENT ADOLESCENT SUBSTANCE USE AND DELINQUENCY

*Abigail A. Fagan and C. Cory Lowe*

Although youth substance use and delinquency have declined in recent decades, they remain significant social problems that have short- and long-term adverse effects on health and well-being. According to the Monitoring the Future survey of American high school students, in 2017, 45.3% of 12th graders reported being drunk during their lifetime, 45% reported lifetime marijuana use, 26.6% reported lifetime cigarette use, and 19.5% reported using illicit substances other than marijuana (Johnston et al., 2018). In the U.S., tobacco use is the leading cause of preventable death and disease (U.S. Department Health and Human Services, 2014), and, in 2010, excessive alcohol consumption cost approximately $249 billion in healthcare costs, lost productivity, crime, and accidents (Sacks, Gonzales, Bouchery, Tomedi, & Brewer, 2015). Marijuana use is associated with negative consequences such as cognitive impairment, poor educational outcomes, and cardiovascular and respiratory disease (Volkow, Baler, Compton, & Weiss, 2014).

Substance use is intertwined with delinquency; the two behaviors have common causes and overlap by definition, but youths may commit crimes to procure drugs, because of their pharmacological effects, or because of conflicts related to the drug trade (Bennett, Holloway, & Farrington, 2008; Boles & Miotto, 2003). In 2016, approximately 856,130 juveniles were arrested, and nearly a quarter of these were for serious index offenses (OJJDP, 2018). Furthermore, according to the 2017 Youth Risk Behavioral Surveillance System, 23.6% of participating high school youths had been in a fight in the past year, and 15.7% carried a weapon in the past 30 days (Kann et al., 2018).

In an attempt to reduce the prevalence and consequences of these behaviors, in the past 30 years, researchers have developed numerous evidence-based substance use and delinquency prevention programs, as indicated in registries of interventions such as Crime Solutions and Blueprints for Healthy Youth Development. Most of these programs target the individual, peer, and interpersonal factors that influence delinquency and substance use (i.e., *risk and protective factors*, as described in the next section). Although they have been demonstrated to delay the onset of these behaviors and/or reduce their prevalence and frequency, many interventions have relatively small and short-term effects. In addition, community agencies often struggle to determine which interventions are appropriate for their populations and to successfully implement and sustain these programs.

Community-level interventions have the potential to overcome some of these challenges and have the added benefit addressing community-level factors related to substance use and delinquency. Defined as "individual and environmental change strategies [enacted] across multiple settings" (Wandersman & Florin, 2003, p. 441), community-level interventions have been shown to prevent substance use and delinquency. However, they vary considerably in effectiveness and ease of implementation. This review focuses on one type of community-level intervention, namely community mobilization, and describes the characteristics of effective and ineffective community mobilization efforts, discusses the challenges of enacting this type of approach, and provides suggestions for researchers, policy-makers, and practitioners interested in using community mobilization to prevent youth substance.

## Addressing Risk and Protective Factors via Community Mobilization

As articulated in the relatively new field of prevention science, preventing negative behaviors such as substance use and delinquency is best achieved by reducing risk factors and increasing protective factors. Risk factors increase the likelihood that youths will engage in antisocial behaviors, while protective factors ameliorate the negative effects of risk factors or directly reduce antisocial behaviors (Coie et al., 1993). Research has demonstrated that antisocial behaviors are more likely to occur when youths experience a greater number of risk factors and fewer protective factors; therefore, to have the best chance of success, preventive interventions should target multiple risk and protective factors and provide sufficient dosage and intensity to effect change (Nation et al., 2003).

Risk factors for substance use and delinquency include individual characteristics (e.g., antisocial attitudes), family factors (e.g., poor child management), peer factors (e.g., delinquent peer association), and school factors (e.g., poor school attachment). Protective factors include individuals' prosocial beliefs and attitudes and bonds to conventional individuals (Farrington, Loeber, & Ttofi, 2012; Hawkins, Catalano, & Miller, 1992). Community level risk and protective factors have also been identified. Risk factors include community socio-economic disadvantage, high residential mobility, lack of social ties between residents, and community norms that promote drug use and crime (Pratt & Cullen, 2005). An important community protective factor is collective efficacy, defined as social cohesion among neighbors in conjunction with their willingness to intervene on behalf of the common good (Sampson, Raudenbush, & Earls, 1997).

While there is a large and growing number of evidence-based substance use and delinquency prevention programs, most of these programs only target a few risk and protective factors, and few target community-level risk and protective factors (Fagan & Hawkins, 2015). Community mobilization, on the other hand, attempts to change community risk and protective factors by creating stronger ties among residents, increasing their collective capacity to address local problems like delinquency, and counteracting structural factors by promoting prosocial norms. These efforts include the implementation of multiple prevention programs and practices selected and overseen by broad-based coalitions of community stakeholders, as well as coalition efforts to change local norms, laws, ordinances, and policies. This broad approach enables coalitions to target multiple risk and protective factors, including environmental influences, in multiple settings and for large numbers of youth, which increases their potential to achieve widespread effects (Wandersman & Florin, 2003).

Many of the anticipated benefits of community mobilization are due to its community-wide, collaborative nature and the participation of local residents. Communities differ according to the risk and protective factors faced by youth and the specific behavioral problems committed by youth (Hawkins, Catalano, & Arthur, 2002; Hawkins, Van Horn, & Arthur, 2004). This variation means that a "one size fits all approach," especially one determined by a researcher from outside the community, is not appropriate and is not likely to be effective. In contrast, community mobilization allows community stakeholders to assess the needs of their community and select, implement, evaluate, and sustain appropriate prevention programs, as well as modify prevention efforts as necessary (Hawkins et al., 2002). By relying on local organizations and residents, coalitions are able to build community support for interventions, which should enhance their effectiveness (Nation et al., 2003; Wagenaar & Perry, 1994). Finally, by coordinating prevention efforts and pooling the resources and expertise of their members, coalitions can maximize their ability to faithfully implement a greater number of interventions, reduce service duplication, and secure funding (Hawkins et al., 2002; Rhew, Brown, Hawkins, & Briney, 2012).

## Variation in Community Mobilization Efforts

Community mobilization efforts vary widely in their operation and effectiveness. They range from self-directed coalitions, which develop and implement their own interventions with little outside guidance, to highly structured groups that select evidence-based interventions and receive training and assistance from consultants. Some efforts are narrow in focus (e.g., only implementing environmental change strategies like reducing youth access to alcohol), while others implement multiple interventions that target multiple risk and protective factors. As described next, effective coalitions tend to be well structured, have clear goals, and target a wide range of risk and protective factors with multiple effective prevention programs, while ineffective coalitions do not have these characteristics.

### *Self-Directed Coalitions*

The Chicago Area Project (CAP), begun in 1932, was one of the first community mobilization efforts intended to reduce youth delinquency. The CAP was implemented in several economically disadvantaged and socially disorganized neighborhoods of Chicago, with the goal of motivating residents to create and operate programs to prevent delinquency and improve the welfare of local children (Bursik & Grasmick, 1993). Its creators assumed that, as residents developed autonomy and social ties, they could strengthen conventional institutions and prevent delinquency. While some assistance was provided by researchers at the Institute for Juvenile Research (IJR), the residents were granted considerable autonomy and received little guidance on what to do to prevent delinquency. The primary activities overseen by residents were recreational activities, garbage clean-ups, and property upkeep. They also developed relationships with local agencies that provided counseling and direct interventions for delinquent youths (Bursik & Grasmick, 1993). Despite some success in promoting community mobilization, there was little evidence that the CAP reduced delinquency (Bursik & Grasmick, 1993).

More recently, the Fighting Back initiative (Hallfors, Cho, Livert, & Kadushin, 2002) and the Community Partnership Program (Yin, Kaftarian, Yu, & Jansen, 1997) also provided funding to local coalitions and encouraged them to develop their own programs to reduce youth alcohol and drug use. A four-year evaluation of the Fighting Back Initiative involving 14 coalition communities and 29 demographically matched communities indicated that it did not have a significant effect on youth alcohol use (Hallfors et al., 2002). Likewise, the evaluation of the Community Partnership Program indicated that youths in 24 coalition communities were no less likely to use alcohol than youths in matched communities (Yin et al., 1997).

Evaluations of the CAP and other self-directed efforts suggest that it is not sufficient to simply fund coalitions and ask them to "do their best" to prevent youth substance use and delinquency, probably because community members will gravitate toward activities that are familiar to them, sound promising, and appear to be feasible to implement (Fagan & Hawkins, 2015, p. 345).

However, it is unlikely that community residents will select evidence-based strategies – programs or practices that have been rigorously evaluated and prevent behaviors by reducing risk and promoting protection – because most are unaware that such interventions exist. Reflecting on the Fighting Back initiative, Hallfors et al. (2002) suggested, to be effective, coalitions need: clear, measurable goals: a well-defined structure; knowledge of program development and implementation; and they should implement evidence-based programs and adopt environmental change strategies.

## *Coalitions that Enact Environmental Change Strategies*

Environmental change strategies are policies and practices that reduce opportunities for youth to engage in antisocial behaviors, change social norms, and/or raise community awareness about a particular problem (see Toomey & Lenk, 2011). While these types of changes have some evidence of effectiveness in reducing substance use and related behaviors (e.g., drinking while driving) among adults (Office of the Surgeon General, 2016), there is less evidence that environmental changes alone prevent youth substance use (Fagan & Hawkins, 2012). For example, two coalition-based initiatives, A Matter of Degree (AMOD; Weitzman, Nelson, Lee, & Wechsler, 2004) and Communities Mobilizing for Change on Alcohol (CMCA; Wagenaar et al., 2000), sought to reduce underage alcohol use solely by making environmental changes like enforcing local laws with compliance checks, tracking and registering kegs, and requiring responsible beverage service training. Furthermore, both initiatives restricted alcohol promotion and advertising, organized alcohol-free events, and supported media campaigns to change alcohol-related social norms. A group-randomized trial found that CMCA did not significantly reduce access to alcohol or drinking behaviors among 12th-grade students, although there were marginally significant reductions in DUI arrests and disorderly conduct violations (Wagenaar et al., 2000; Wagenaar, Murray, & Toomey, 2000). AMOD was evaluated in a quasi-experimental study with ten intervention colleges and 32 control colleges. Results indicated that there was no significant reduction in alcohol use or alcohol-related harms (Weitzman et al., 2004).

The Cure Violence model also incorporates environmental change strategies in its efforts to reduce gang violence. In this model, program staff mediate disputes between gang members in order to break the transmission of violence and retaliatory attacks. Program staff also work to change community norms about violence and raise awareness about gangs through media campaigns, billboards, and public events such as antiviolence marches and vigils (Butts, Roman, Bostwick, & Porter, 2015). There is mixed evidence regarding its effectiveness. A review of several evaluations found reduced violence in only one of four cities where the strategy was faithfully implemented, and, even then, several of the sites within the city did not experience reductions in violence. Analyses also indicated that Cure Violence was associated with a reduction in violent events, but an increase in shootings at one of the sites (Butts et al., 2015).

The One Vision One Life (OVOL) initiative involved a highly modified version of the Cure Violence model that included increased gang suppression, social services provision to gang members, and coalition-building activities. Programs for at-risk youth were also delivered, including after-school programming, recreational activities, and close monitoring of school grounds to prevent violence (Wilson, Chermak, & McGarrell, 2010). Results of a quasi-experimental evaluation indicated that OVOL did not significantly reduce violence and the intervention was associated with increased violence in areas adjacent to two of the three evaluation sites (Wilson et al., 2010).

Some policing strategies, such as focused deterrence, problem-oriented, and hot spots policing, have been found to reduce crime in meta-analyses of primarily quasi-experimental evaluations (Weisburd et al., 2017). These strategies are similar to environmental change strategies because they attempt to reduce viable opportunities for crime through deterrence (i.e., increasing surveillance and arrest so that would be offenders will be deterred from crime). However, these efforts usually involve little input from other community stakeholders and cannot, as a result, be considered community mobilization. One exception was the Boston Ceasefire focused deterrence initiative which partnered with the Ten Point Coalition of Black clergy (Braga, Kennedy, Waring, & Piehl, 2001). While police and prosecutors worked to target and prosecute violent gang members to the fullest extent of the law, the Ten Point Coalition worked with community members to stimulate informal social control, raise awareness about youth violence, connect high-risk youth with social services, and provide a strong moral voice regarding youth violence (Pegram, Brunson, & Braga, 2016). In a quasi-experimental evaluation, Boston Ceasefire was associated with a significant reduction in youth homicides, gun assaults, shots-fired calls for service and youth gun assaults in one district (Braga et al., 2001).

The Comprehensive Gang Model also strives to reduce gang activity and gang violence and combines law enforcement strategies with community mobilization (National Gang Center, 2010). It includes five components: (1) organizational change and development activities to ensure community stakeholders are using effective prevention strategies, (2) community mobilization to support gang prevention, (3) provision of educational, training, and employment programs for gang-involved youth, (4) provision of social interventions for at-risk and gang-involved youths, and (5) suppression of violent gang members (Gebo, Bond, & Campos, 2015). While the model provides more structure than some of the efforts discussed so far, the CGM was designed to be flexible and allow local communities to implement the components most needed in their area.

The CGM was initially evaluated in the Little Village Area of Chicago, and then in five other urban areas. The full model proved difficult to enact and only three of the six sites implemented all five components (National Gang Center, 2010). Common implementation problems included poor leadership, a failure to incorporate community organizations in prevention efforts, and a lack of inter-agency and inter-organizational cooperation (Spergel, Wa, & Sosa, 2006). In addition, evidence of CGM effectiveness was mixed. Sites that most faithfully implemented the model experienced reductions in gang violence and/or drug-related offenses in quasi-experimental evaluations, but there was at least one iatrogenic (i.e., harmful) effect in all six sites (Spergel et al., 2006). Subsequent evaluations of the CGM and adaptations have also indicated varying levels of implementation fidelity and effectiveness (see Gebo et al., 2015), prompting the National Gang Center (NGC) to create additional materials to guide implementation, including the selection of evidence-based programs (see National Gang Center, 2010, 2018).

## Coalitions that Enact Environmental Change Strategies and Target Multiple Risk and Protective Factors Using School-Based Prevention Programs

Community mobilization efforts are more likely to be effective when they couple environmental change strategies with prevention programs that target multiple risk and protective factors and reach large numbers of youth with these services (Fagan & Hawkins, 2012). School-based programs are particularly useful because, if they are implemented in all schools of a community, they can saturate the entire community of young people with prevention efforts. Effective school-based prevention curricula typically utilize interactive rather than didactic teaching methods, promote prosocial attitudes and relationships, and foster skills such as effective communication, positive coping strategies, resisting peer influence, setting goals, and making positive decisions (Cuijpers, 2002; Durlak, Weissberg, Dymnicki, Taylor, & Schellinger, 2011).

Project Northland is a multi-year alcohol use prevention program for middle and high school youths that attempts to reduce the supply of alcohol with environmental change strategies and demand for alcohol with school-based interventions (Perry et al., 2002). An evaluation of this program, which took place in 24 school districts in rural Minnesota, involved school-based prevention curricula, parenting programs, peer leadership activities, extracurricular activities, and environmental changes implemented in intervention sites. Results indicated that, at the end of their eighth-grade year, significantly fewer youths in intervention compared to control districts reported past month and past week alcohol use. Youths who had not initiated alcohol use at baseline also reported significantly lower rates of alcohol, marijuana, and cigarette use than baseline abstainers in the control districts (Perry et al., 1996). However, when students were in Grades 9 and 10 and did not received much programming, rates of alcohol use among intervention youths increased at significantly greater rates than youths in the control group. After programming had resumed when students were in Grades 11 and 12, the evaluation indicated that binge drinking increased at a significantly slower rate among youths in intervention districts, as did past month alcohol use, although this effect was only marginally significant. Alcohol retailers were also significantly less likely to sell to minors in intervention compared to control communities by the end of the 12th grade (Perry et al., 2002).

## *Structured Coalitions that Deliver Evidence-Based Programs*

Given the limitations of the self-directed coalitions involved in the Fighting Back initiative and some other coalition efforts, Hallfors et al. (2002) suggested that community mobilization would be more effective when coalitions are structured, have well-defined goals based on the needs of the community, implement evidence-based interventions, and monitor these interventions to ensure they are well implemented and producing desired effects. However, it is not always easy for coalitions to fulfill these edicts, and they are likely to need support to build their capacity to engage in effective community-based prevention (Spoth, Rohrbach, et al., 2013; U.S. Department of Justice and U.S. Department of Health and Human Services, 2011). The four remaining mobilization efforts direct coalitions to implement evidence-based interventions and provide support to do so; moreover, evaluations have shown these coalitions to be well functioning and able to prevent youth substance use and delinquency. The models include two State Incentive Grant initiatives, the PROmoting School-community-university Partnerships to Enhance Resilience (PROSPER) delivery system, and the Communities that Care (CTC) prevention system.

The Substance Use and Mental Health Services Administration (SAMHSA) established the State Incentives Grant (SIG) program to strengthen state and local prevention systems and fund substance use prevention coalitions. Two evaluations of SIG-funded coalitions involved the Kentucky Incentives for Prevention (KIP) Project (Collins, Johnson, & Becker, 2007) and Vermont's New Directions (ND) initiative (Flewelling et al., 2005). The 20 KIP coalitions and 23 ND coalitions all received training and technical assistance through the SIG program, engaged in coalition development, assessed community needs and resources, developed measurable prevention goals, and implemented a mix of evidence-based programs and environmental change strategies that targeted risk and protective factors identified in the needs assessments.

A quasi-experimental evaluation of KIP found that, in the eighth grade, youths in KIP coalition school districts were more likely to use inhalants than youths in control districts. However, by the tenth grade, significantly fewer youths in intervention districts reported past month alcohol use, binge drinking, and cigarette use (Collins et al., 2007). In a quasi-experimental evaluation of the ND coalitions, data from the statewide Youth Risk Behavior Survey showed that, after four years, youth in coalition school districts were significantly less likely to report past month cigarette use and marijuana use compared to those in districts without these coalitions (Flewelling et al., 2005).

PROSPER and CTC have each been evaluated in randomized controlled trials involving long-term follow-up of youth in intervention and control communities, have demonstrated significant reductions in substance use and delinquency, and have proven to be cost-beneficial (WSIPP, 2017a, 2017b). Both provide communities with training and consultation to help them build, high functioning coalitions, learn about effective prevention programs, and select and monitor the implementation of multiple evidence-based interventions.

The PROSPER delivery system leverages existing infrastructure including the Cooperative Extension Service associated with land-grant universities, schools, and community organizations to build coalitions and implement evidence-based programs. University and extension representatives partner with community teams comprised of local community stakeholders. Representatives from the university and extension provide ongoing technical assistance and training to community teams to mobilize the community in support of prevention Then the communities select programs from a limited menu of evidence-based family- and school-based programs targeting youth in early to mid-adolescence (Spoth, Greenberg, Bierman, & Redmond, 2004).

An experimental evaluation of 28 rural and small-town school districts found that, compared to youths in control districts, youths in PROSPER districts reported lower rates of marijuana, inhalant, methamphetamine, and ecstasy initiation. They also had lower rates of past year marijuana and inhalant use 18 months after the start of the study (Spoth et al., 2007). In follow-up studies, youths in PROSPER districts reported significantly lower rates on a variety of substance use measures including cigarette, marijuana, inhalants, and marijuana use, and frequency of drunkenness (Spoth, Redmond, et al., 2013). During high school, youths in PROSPER reported significantly less delinquency (Spoth et al., 2015).

Compared to PROSPER, Communities that Care (CTC) has a less prescribed model for how communities should form coalitions (e.g., all stakeholders who are interested in youth development should participate), requires that coalitions conduct a formal needs assessment, and directs coalitions to implement a wider variety of evidence-based programs. CTC provides training and technical assistance to community stakeholders to help them carry out these activities in a five-phase approach which includes: (1) assessing community readiness to prevent youth antisocial behaviors, (2) developing a coalition to coordinate prevention efforts, (3) using high-quality data to identify elevated risk and depressed protective factors, (4) selecting programs and practices that target these factors from a menu of evidence based programs, and (5) faithfully implementing and evaluating the interventions (Fagan & Hawkins, 2015).

An experimental evaluation of CTC involved 24 rural and small towns randomly assigned to implement CTC or to conduct prevention services as usual, and youth outcomes were assessed by following a longitudinal panel of youth constituted when they were in the 5th grade. During the study, CTC communities enacted 90% of the CTC system on average, and implemented evidence-based programs with high levels of fidelity (Fagan, Hanson, Hawkins, & Arthur, 2009). CTC communities also implemented a significantly greater number of evidence-based interventions than control communities (Fagan, Arthur, Hanson, Briney, & Hawkins, 2011). In terms of youth outcomes, the results indicated that youths in the CTC communities were significantly less likely to engage in delinquency, binge drink, use alcohol, and use smokeless tobacco in the 8th grade compared to youths in control communities. By the 10th grade, CTC youths were less likely to engage in delinquency, use tobacco, or engage in violence, and were less likely to have initiated alcohol or cigarette use (Fagan & Hawkins, 2013). In addition, a quasi-experimental evaluation of CTC that took place across the state of Pennsylvania found that youths in CTC communities reported less risk factors, substance use, and delinquency than youths in control communities (Feinberg, Greenberg, Osgood, Sartorius, & Bontempo, 2007).

## Summarizing the Effectiveness and Challenges of Community Mobilization

Research suggests that effective community mobilization efforts have well-structured coalitions with clearly defined goals, involve implementation of a wide range of evidence-based programs and practices that target elevated risk and depressed protective factors, and link coalitions to expert assistance to help them conduct prevention activities. Self-directed coalitions are unlikely to adhere to these practices, and environmental change strategies alone typically target fewer risk and protective factors and will be less able to reduce youth substance use and delinquency, but when coupled with school-based interventions, they are more effective.

While community mobilization has evidence of effectiveness in preventing youth substance use and delinquency, this approach can be very challenging to implement and evaluate. Coalitions necessarily require active and on-going participation and collaboration by members of the community and ideally will involve a representative and diverse group of stakeholders. Coalition goals, needs, and solutions should be based on group decision-making and consensus. However, diverse groups of community stakeholders will likely have a diverse set of interests. If stakeholders are not able to reconcile their competing interests and coalesce around a shared vision and prevention plan, they will not be able to succeed, and the coalition may then become a source of conflict rather than cooperation (Bursik & Grasmick, 1993).

Coalitions also require some level of infrastructure and resources to succeed. Effective models like PROSPER and CTC strongly recommend a paid (at least half-time) coordinator to lead the initiative and a home institution that can house the coordinator and host coalition meetings. Communities will also require resources to implement evidence-based programs. These human and financial costs are likely to be especially challenging for low socio-economic and socially disadvantaged communities, but these areas are typically most in need of prevention services given their elevated levels of substance use/abuse and crime. If local institutions and organizations are under-funded and there is high population turnover, the community will lack a stable base of support for coalition efforts (Bursik & Grasmick, 1993).

Dating back to the Chicago Area Project, evidence suggests that community mobilization efforts may not be successful in under-resourced communities. As a more recent example, when Project Northland was adapted and implemented in inner-city schools in Chicago, it failed to significantly decrease risk factors, increase protective factors, or reduce alcohol use as it did when implemented in rural Minnesota (Komro et al., 2008). According to the project evaluators, the Chicago youth and communities faced greater socioeconomic disadvantage than youths in the Minnesota trial, as well as more significant local problems such as gang activity (Komro et al., 2008). Komro et al. (2008) suggested that this issue and others may have diverted community residents' attention away from alcohol prevention and toward other social problems that were perceived as more important to address than youth alcohol use.

Despite these discouraging results, coalition efforts have shown some success in inner-city, impoverished communities. For example, the Cure Violence model has reduced violence in some urban areas (Butts et al., 2015). In addition, CTC has been successfully adopted in several under-resourced communities, including Montbello, Colorado, a Denver neighborhood with high rates of poverty and crime, a predominantly African American and Latino population, and few pre-existing evidence-based prevention programs. There was, however, a strong desired among local residents to prevent youth problems and encourage healthy youth development, and they partnered with researchers from the University of Colorado to obtain a violence prevention grant from the Centers for Disease Control. Researchers and community members spent about 18 months to nurture their relationship, build coalition capacity, and enhance community readiness to implement CTC. After several years, they had successfully built a broad-based coalition, conducted a needs assessment, and selected several evidence-based school- and community-based EBIs to address their locally-identified needs (Kingston, Bacallao, Smokowski, Sullivan, & Sutherland, 2016). As this example indicates, community mobilization in disadvantaged areas may require external funding and support, an extended time frame, and strong commitment from all those involved.

Researchers should be aware that evaluating community-level interventions is likely to be costlier and more complex compared to evaluating individual interventions. To evaluate a community-level effort using a randomized controlled trial, randomization must take place at the community level, which means that researchers must gain the participation of a sufficient number of communities to detect statistically significant treatment effects (Koepsell et al., 1992). Quasi-experimental studies may be easier to design, but communities are incredibly diverse and researchers will only be able to statistically control for a limited number of factors when matching intervention and control communities, which can reduce internal validity (Koepsell et al., 1992). Evaluations of community-level interventions will require substantially more data collection than evaluations of individual interventions, including measurement of a range of risk and protective factors, as well as community-level relationships and practices. In addition, implementation will need to be carefully assessed so that challenges can be addressed before they undermine intervention effectiveness.

## Recommendations for Ensuring Effective Community Mobilization Prevention Approaches

Although there is some evidence that community mobilization can prevent adolescent substance use and delinquency, relatively few models have demonstrated effectiveness in rigorous research trials, and there is a need for researchers to develop and evaluate new models of effective community mobilization. It is especially important to design and evaluate community-based interventions in socially disorganized and low-resourced communities, given that such areas are likely to have the highest rates of substance use/abuse and crime and the greatest need for prevention. Community-based participatory research (CBPR) strategies, in which prevention scientists partner with community stakeholders, should be used to develop these new systems to ensure that efforts are culturally relevant (Israel, Eng, Schulz, & Parker, 2012). In CBPR, scientists contribute their understanding of the causes of problem behaviors, program design, data analysis, and program evaluation to the partnership, while community members contribute their understanding of local culture, norms, and practices. These collaborations should help ensure that the community is fully invested in the prevention effort and that prevention actions address locally relevant needs using strategies that are feasible and acceptable to the population.

Another strategy to ensure that community mobilization efforts are culturally relevant is to expand the current menu of individual evidence-based interventions so that communities have more options to select programs and practices that match their demographic characteristics, culture, and resources. Many evidence-based interventions have been developed for a particular population (e.g., high-risk, first-time mothers, in the case of many home visiting programs), have been evaluated only once in a specific context (e.g., rural communities), or have been implemented with diverse participants but have only evaluated effects for the entire sample, not for particular sub-groups. As a result, the generalizability of many evidence-based interventions is unknown, and effects for many under-represented populations have not been adequately examined (Huey & Polo, 2008). Expanding the number of evidence-based interventions available, and the types of populations for whom they are effective, will give communities greater choice when selecting interventions to address their needs and may reduce significant local adaptations made during implementation that can threaten effectiveness (see Elliott & Mihalic, 2004).

This review has indicated that few community mobilization systems to date have adequately ensured strong partnerships between community coalitions and law enforcement, courts, and corrections, and more research is needed to determine if such partnerships will enhance prevention efforts and how they can be feasibly implemented. These efforts would require an expansion of most coalition models from an exclusive focus on prevention efforts to a more comprehensive approach that includes both preventive and reactive strategies. While prevention is an essential and often overlooked component to reducing substance use and crime, communities must also address existing crime and substance use/abuse, and they should do so in a humane, effective way that does not exacerbate problems within the community.

Although the Comprehensive Gang Model includes prevention, deterrence, and suppression strategies, it has focused exclusively on gang activity and has not yet been wholly effective in its implementation or outcomes. As another example, many communities and states are recognizing the need to implement more community-based alternatives to incarceration, and such support should be leveraged to ensure that community stakeholders are actively involved in the selection and implementation of evidence-based prevention approaches. Finally, recent research suggests that hot spots policing may increase community collective efficacy more so than standard police practices, possibly because effective policing leads to greater community confidence in police which results in a greater willingness among residents to exert informal social control (Kochel & Weisburd, 2018). Weisburd and colleagues (2014) suggest that prevention approaches and hot spots policing could be combined to better address crime, but more research is needed to determine how to do so.

All newly developed community mobilization models must be subjected to rigorous evaluations, with research designs that include attention to implementation factors as well as outcomes. As evident in this review, many community-based systems have been evaluated in quasi-experimental designs, but only a few have relied on randomized controlled trials that are better able to ensure that outcomes are due to the intervention itself, and not some other feature of the community. Given that many mobilization strategies involve multiple components (e.g., environmental strategies and school-based interventions), researchers should try to identify the components that are most strongly associated with reductions in problem behaviors. Doing so may help streamline interventions so they are more feasible and less costly to implement.

Last, it is important that policy-makers increase financial support for community-based prevention at the federal, state and local levels. This support includes money for the provision of ongoing training and technical assistance to build coalitions' capacity to engage in effective prevention. As seen in the PROSPER model, community-university partnerships may be an effective means of supporting coalitions, and it is encouraging that the Centers for Disease Control has funded community-university partnerships in its National Centers of Excellence in Youth Violence Prevention (YVPC; formerly Academic Centers of Excellence, see Kingston et al., 2016). Funding should also be increased for grant programs such as the SAMHSA Strategic Prevention Framework State Incentives Grants (SPF SIG) which require recipients to use coalitions and evidence-based interventions to prevent substance use.

## References

Bennett, T., Holloway, K., & Farrington, D. (2008). The statistical association between drug misuse and crime: A meta-analysis. *Aggression and Violent Behavior, 13*(2), 107–118.

Boles, S. M., & Miotto, K. (2003). Substance abuse and violence: A review of the literature. *Aggression and Violent Behavior, 8*(2), 155–174.

Braga, A. A., Kennedy, D. M., Waring, E. J., & Piehl, A. M. (2001). Problem-oriented policing, deterrence, and youth violence: An evaluation of Boston's operation ceasefire. *Journal of Research in Crime and Delinquency, 38*(3), 195–225.

Bursik, R. J., & Grasmick, H. G. (1993). *Neighborhoods and Crime: The Dimensions of Effective Community Control*. New York: Lexington Books.

Butts, J. A., Roman, C. G., Bostwick, L., & Porter, J. R. (2015). Cure violence: A public health model to reduce gun violence. *Annual Review of Public Health*, 36(1), 39–53.

Coie, J. D., Watt, N. F., West, S. G., David, J., Asarnow, J. R., Markman, H. J., … Long, B. (1993). The science of prevention: A conceptual framework and some directions for a national research program. *American Psychologist*, 48(10), 1013–1022.

Collins, D., Johnson, K., & Becker, B. J. (2007). A meta-analysis of direct and mediating effects of community coalitions that implemented science-based substance abuse prevention interventions. *Substance Use & Misuse*, 42(6), 985–1007.

Cuijpers, P. (2002). Effective ingredients of school-based drug prevention programs: A systematic review. *Addictive Behaviors*, 27(6), 1009–1023.

Durlak, J. A., Weissberg, R. P., Dymnicki, A. B., Taylor, R. D., & Schellinger, K. B. (2011). The impact of enhancing students' social and emotional learning: A meta-analysis of school-based universal interventions. *Child Development*, 82(1), 405–432.

Elliott, D. S., & Mihalic, S. (2004). Issues in disseminating and replicating effective prevention programs. *Prevention Science*, 5(1), 47–53.

Fagan, A. A., Arthur, M. W., Hanson, K., Briney, J. S., & Hawkins, J. D. (2011). Effects of Communities that Care on the adoption and implementation fidelity of evidence-based prevention programs in communities: Results from a randomized controlled trial. *Prevention Science*, 12(3), 223–234.

Fagan, A. A., Hanson, K., Hawkins, J. D., & Arthur, M. W. (2009). Translational research in action: Implementation of the Communities that Care prevention system in 12 communities. *Journal of Community Psychology*, 37(7), 809–829.

Fagan, A. A., & Hawkins, J. D. (2012). Community-based substance use prevention. In B. C. Welsh & D. P. Farrington (Eds.), *The Oxford Handbook of Crime Prevention* (pp. 247–268). New York: Oxford University Press.

Fagan, A. A., & Hawkins, J. D. (2013). Preventing substance use, delinquency, violence, and other problem behaviors over the life-course using the Communities that Care system. In C. L. Gibson & M. D. Krohn (Eds.), *Handbook of Life-Course Criminology* (pp. 277–296). New York: Springer.

Fagan, A. A., & Hawkins, J. D. (2015). Enacting preventive interventions at the community level: The Communities that Care prevention system. In L. M. Scheier (Ed.), *Handbook of Adolescent Drug Use Prevention* (pp. 343–360). Washington, DC: American Psychological Association.

Farrington, D. P., Loeber, R., & Ttofi, M. M. (2012). Risk and protective factors for offending. In B. C. Welsh & D. P. Farrington (Eds.), *The Oxford Handbook of Crime Prevention* (pp. 46–69). USA: Oxford University Press.

Feinberg, M. E., Greenberg, M. T., Osgood, D. W., Sartorius, J., & Bontempo, D. (2007). Effects of the Communities that Care model in Pennsylvania on youth risk and problem behaviors. *Prevention Science*, 8(4), 261–270.

Flewelling, R. L., Austin, D., Hale, K., LaPlante, M., Liebig, M., Piasecki, L., & Uerz, L. (2005). Implementing research-based substance abuse prevention in communities: Effects of a coalition-based prevention initiative in Vermont. *Journal of Community Psychology*, 33(3), 333–353.

Gebo, E., Bond, B. J., & Campos, K. S. (2015). The OJJDP comprehensive gang strategy. In S. H. Decker & D. C. Pyrooz (Eds.), *The Handbook of Gangs* (pp. 392–405). Hoboken, New Jersey: Wiley-Blackwell.

Hallfors, D., Cho, H., Livert, D., & Kadushin, C. (2002). Fighting back against substance abuse: Are community coalitions winning? *American Journal of Preventive Medicine*, 23(4), 237–245.

Hawkins, J. D., Catalano, R. F., & Arthur, M. W. (2002). Promoting science-based prevention in communities. *Addictive Behaviors*, 27(6), 951–976.

Hawkins, J. D., Catalano, R. F., & Miller, J. Y. (1992). Risk and protective factors for alcohol and other drug problems in adolescence and early adulthood: Implications for substance abuse prevention. *Psychological Bulletin*, 112(1), 64–105.

Hawkins, J. D., Van Horn, M. L. V., & Arthur, M. W. (2004). Community variation in risk and protective factors and substance use outcomes. *Prevention Science*, 5(4), 213–220.

Huey Jr., S. J., & Polo, A. J. (2008). Evidence-based psychosocial treatments for ethnic minority youth. *Journal of Clinical Child & Adolescent Psychology*, 37(1), 262–301.

Israel, B. A., Eng, E., Schulz, A. J., & Parker, E. A. (2012). *Methods for Community-Based Participatory Research for Health*. San Francisco: Jossey-Bass.

Johnston, L. D., Miech, R. A., O'Malley, P. M., Bachman, J. G., Schulenberg, J. E., & Patrick, M. E. (2018). *Monitoring the Future National Survey Results on Drug Use, 1975–2017: Overview, Key Findings on Adolescent*

*Drug Use*. Ann Arbor, Michigan: Institute for Social Research, The University of Michigan. Retrieved from www.monitoringthefuture.org/pubs/monographs/mtf-overview2017.pdf

Kann, L., McManus, T., Harris, W. A., Lowry, R., Chyen, D., Whittle, L., ... Ethier, K. A. (2018). Youth risk behavior surveillance — United States, 2017. *Morbidity and Mortality Weekly Report Surveillance Summaries*, *67*(8), 1–114.

Kingston, B., Bacallao, M., Smokowski, P., Sullivan, T., & Sutherland, K. (2016). Constructing "packages" of evidence-based programs to prevent youth violence: Processes and illustrative examples from the CDC's Youth Violence Prevention Centers. *The Journal of Primary Prevention*, *37*(2), 141–163.

Kochel, T. R., & Weisburd, D. (2018). The impact of hot spots policing on collective efficacy: Findings from a randomized field trial. *Justice Quarterly*, 1–29. doi: 10.1080/07418825.2018.1465579.

Koepsell, T. D., Wagner, E. H., Cheadle, A. C., Patrick, D. L., Martin, D. C., Diehr, P. H., ... Dey, L. J. (1992). Selected methodological issues in evaluating community-based health promotion and disease prevention programs. *Annual Review of Public Health*, *13*(1), 31–57.

Komro, K. A., Perry, C. L., Veblen-Mortenson, S., Farbakhsh, K., Toomey, T. L., Stigler, M. H., ... Williams, C. L. (2008). Outcomes from a randomized controlled trial of a multi-component alcohol use preventive intervention for urban youth: Project Northland Chicago. *Addiction*, *103*(4), 606–618.

Nation, M., Crusto, C., Wandersman, A., Kumpfer, K. L., Seybolt, D., Morrissey-Kane, E., & Davino, K. (2003). What works in prevention: Principles of effective prevention programs. *American Psychologist*, *58* (6–7), 449–456.

National Gang Center. (2010). *Best Practices to Address Community Gang Problems*. Washington, DC: Office of Juvenile Justice and Delinquency Prevention.

National Gang Center. (2018). Strategic planning tool. Retrieved June 22, 2018, from www.nationalgangcenter.gov/What-Works/#strategic

Office of the Surgeon General. (2016). *The Surgeon General's Report on Alcohol, Drugs, and Health*. Washington, DC: Department of Health and Human Services. Retrieved from https://addiction.surgeongeneral.gov/sites/default/files/surgeon-generals-report.pdf

OJJDP. (2018). Estimated number of juvenile arrests, 2016. Retrieved May 21, 2018, from www.ojjdp.gov/ojstatbb/crime/qa05101.asp?qaDate=2016&text=yes

Pegram, K., Brunson, R. K., & Braga, A. A. (2016). The doors of the church are now open: Black clergy, collective efficacy, and neighborhood violence. *City & Community*, *15*(3), 289–314.

Perry, C. L., Williams, C. L., Komro, K. A., Veblen-Mortenson, S., Stigler, M. H., Munson, K. A., ... Forster, J. L. (2002). Project Northland: Long-term outcomes of community action to reduce adolescent alcohol use. *Health Education Research*, *17*(1), 117–132.

Perry, C. L., Williams, C. L., Veblen-Mortenson, S., Toomey, T. L., Komro, K. A., Anstine, P. S., ... Wolfson, M. (1996). Project Northland: Outcomes of a communitywide alcohol use prevention program during early adolescence. *American Journal of Public Health*, *86*(7), 956–965.

Pratt, T. C., & Cullen, F. T. (2005). Assessing macro-level predictors and theories of crime: A meta-analysis. *Crime and Justice*, *32*, 373–450.

Rhew, I. C., Brown, E. C., Hawkins, J. D., & Briney, J. S. (2012). Sustained effects of the Communities that Care system on prevention service system transformation. *American Journal of Public Health*, *103*(3), 529–535.

Sacks, J. J., Gonzales, K. R., Bouchery, E. E., Tomedi, L. E., & Brewer, R. D. (2015). 2010 national and state costs of excessive alcohol consumption. *American Journal of Preventive Medicine*, *49*(5), e73–e79.

Sampson, R. J., Raudenbush, S. W., & Earls, F. (1997). Neighborhoods and violent crime: A multilevel study of collective efficacy. *Science*, *277*(5328), 918–924.

Spergel, I. A., Wa, K. M., & Sosa, R. V. (2006). The comprehensive, community-wide gang program model: Success and failure. In J. F. Short Jr. & L. A. Hughes (Eds.), *Studying Youth Gangs* (pp. 203–224). Lanham, MD: AltaMira Press.

Spoth, R., Rohrbach, L. A., Greenberg, M., Leaf, P., Brown, C. H., Fagan, A., ... Hawkins, J. D. (2013). Addressing core challenges for the next generation of type 2 translation research and systems: The translation science to population impact (TSci impact) framework. *Prevention Science*, *14*(4), 319–351.

Spoth, R. L., Greenberg, M., Bierman, K., & Redmond, C. (2004). PROSPER community–university partnership model for public education systems: Capacity-building for evidence-based, competence-building prevention. *Prevention Science*, *5*(1), 31–39.

Spoth, R. L., Redmond, C., Shin, C., Greenberg, M., Clair, S., & Feinberg, M. (2007). Substance-use outcomes at 18 months past baseline: The PROSPER community–university partnership trial. *American Journal of Preventive Medicine*, *32*(5), 395–402.

Spoth, R. L., Redmond, C., Shin, C., Greenberg, M., Feinberg, M., & Schainker, L. (2013). PROSPER community–University partnership delivery system effects on substance misuse through 6 1/2years past baseline from a cluster randomized controlled intervention trial. *Preventive Medicine*, *56*(3), 190–196.

Spoth, R. L., Trudeau, L. S., Redmond, C., Shin, C., Greenberg, M. T., Feinberg, M. E., & Hyun, G.-H. (2015). PROSPER partnership delivery system: Effects on adolescent conduct problem behavior outcomes through 6.5 years past baseline. *Journal of Adolescence*, *45*, 44–55.

Toomey, T. L., & Lenk, K. M. (2011). A review of environmental-based community interventions. *Alcohol Research & Health*, *34*(2), 163–166.

U.S. Department Health and Human Services. (2014). *The Health Consequences of Smoking – 50 Years of Progress*. Atlanta, GA: U.S. Department of Health and Human Services, Centers for Disease Control and Prevention, National Center for Chronic Disease Prevention and Health Promotion, Office on Smoking and Health. Retrieved from www.ncbi.nlm.nih.gov/books/NBK294302/

U.S. Department of Justice, U.S. Department of Health and Human Services. (2011). *Evidence-Based Practices for Children Exposed to Violence: A Selection from Federal Databases*. Washington, DC: U.S. Department of Justice, U.S. Department of Health and Human Services.

Volkow, N. D., Baler, R. D., Compton, W. M., & Weiss, S. R. B. (2014). Adverse health effects of marijuana use. *New England Journal of Medicine*, *370*(23), 2219–2227.

Wagenaar, A. C., Murray, D. M., Gehan, J. P., Wolfson, M., Forster, J. L., Toomey, T. L., … Jones-Webb, R. (2000). Communities mobilizing for change on alcohol: Outcomes from a randomized community trial. *Journal of Studies on Alcohol*, *61*(1), 85–94.

Wagenaar, A. C., Murray, D. M., & Toomey, T. L. (2000). Communities Mobilizing for Change on Alcohol (CMCA): Effects of a randomized trial on arrests and traffic crashes. *Addiction*, *95*(2), 209–217.

Wagenaar, A. C., & Perry, C. L. (1994). Community strategies for the reduction of youth drinking: Theory and application. *Journal of Research on Adolescence*, *4*(2), 319–345.

Wandersman, A., & Florin, P. (2003). Community interventions and effective prevention. *American Psychologist*, *58*(6–7), 441–448.

Weisburd, D., Farrington, D. P., Gill, C., Ajzenstadt, M., Bennett, T., Bowers, K., … Wooditch, A. (2017). What works in crime prevention and rehabilitation. *Criminology & Public Policy*, *16*(2), 415–449.

Weisburd, D., Groff, E. R., & Yang, S.-M. (2014). Understanding and controlling hot spots of crime: The importance of formal and informal social controls. *Prevention Science*, *15*(1), 31–43.

Weitzman, E. R., Nelson, T. F., Lee, H., & Wechsler, H. (2004). Reducing drinking and related harms in college. *American Journal of Preventive Medicine*, *27*(3), 187–196.

Wilson, J. M., Chermak, S., & McGarrell, E. F. (2010). *Community-Based Violence Prevention*. Santa Monica, CA: Rand Corporation.

WSIPP. (2017a). Communities that care. Retrieved July 4, 2018, from www.wsipp.wa.gov/BenefitCost/Program/115

WSIPP. (2017b). PROSPER. Retrieved July 4, 2018, from www.wsipp.wa.gov/BenefitCost/Program/652

Yin, R. K., Kaftarian, S. J., Yu, P., & Jansen, M. A. (1997). Outcomes from CSAP's Community Partnership Program: Findings from the national cross site evaluation. *Evaluation and Program Planning*, *20*(3), 345–355.

# 19
# BEHAVIORAL HEALTH AND TREATMENT UTILIZATION AMONG YOUTH INVOLVED IN THE JUVENILE JUSTICE SYSTEM

*Matthew C. Aalsma and Katherine Schwartz*

Youth involved in the juvenile justice system suffer behavioral health problems (i.e., mental health or substance use issues) at significantly higher rates than their peers who have never been arrested or otherwise referred to the justice system (Kessler et al., 2012; Shufelt & Cocozza, 2006). Precise estimates vary (Wasserman, McReynolds, Schwalbe, Keating, & Jones, 2010), but the majority of detained youth meet criteria for a mental health or substance use disorder (40–70%) (Abram et al., 2015; Fazel, Doll, & Långström, 2008; Teplin, Abram, McClelland, Dulcan, & Mericle, 2002). Both externalizing (e.g., conduct disorder) and internalizing disorders, such as major depression, anxiety, and post-traumatic stress disorder, are prevalent among youth involved in juvenile justice (Karnick et al., 2009). In contrast, the prevalence of behavioral health disorders among youth never involved in the justice system is closer to 10–20% (Merikangas et al., 2010; SAMHSA, 2014; Wu, Gersing, Burchett, Woody, & Blazer, 2011).

High rates of mental illness and substance use frequently correspond to both initial involvement in the justice system and criminal recidivism (Chassin, 2008; McReynolds, Schwalbe, & Wasserman, 2010). Substance use disorders (Bennett, Holloway, & Farrington, 2008; Hoeve, McReynolds, Wasserman, & McMillan, 2013; Schubert, Mulvey, & Glasheen, 2011) and comorbid mental health and substance use disorders most consistently predict reoffending (Chassin, 2008; McReynolds et al., 2010). Among mental health disorders alone, a recent meta-analysis found externalizing disorders and comorbid externalizing and internalizing disorders were associated with recidivism, while internalizing disorders were not (Wibbelink, Hoeve, Stams, & Oort, 2017). Existing behavioral health problems may be exacerbated by stress associated with arrest and incarceration (Desai et al., 2006; Holman & Ziedenberg, 2006; Wasserman & McReynolds, 2011), showing how behavioral health and justice system involvement can be harmfully intertwined (Braverman & Murray, 2011; Pajer, Kelleher, Gupta, Rolls, & Gardner, 2007).

Behavioral health interventions designed for youth involved in juvenile justice have been shown to effectively reduce symptoms of mental illness and self-reported substance use, especially if the treatment is administered in the community to address problems holistically. Multisystemic Therapy (MST), Functional Family Therapy (FFT), and Treatment Foster Care

Oregon (TFCO) are among the multi-faceted interventions that have also achieved greater reductions or delays in re-arrest among participants than among comparison groups (Cuellar, McReynolds, & Wasserman, 2006; Dopp, Borduin, White, Mark, & Kuppens, 2017; Foster, Qaseem, & Connor, 2004; Henggeler & Schoenwald, 2011; Pullmann et al., 2006; Sexton & Turner, 2010). These family-based programs generally are designed to address potential sources of delinquent behavior and prevent criminal recidivism by considering the socio-ecological context of youth, including factors related to the individual, the youth's family and peers, and the youth's environment in school or neighborhood (Dopp et al., 2017). These interventions traditionally require parental participation, as family members are a target of treatment.

Despite evidence that successful treatments for youth involved in juvenile justice with behavioral health disorders exist, youth in the juvenile justice system access and utilize behavioral health treatment services at alarmingly low rates (Aalsma, Tong, Lane, Katz, & Rosenman, 2012a; Rawal, Romansky, & Michael Jenuwine, 2004; Teplin, Abram, McClelland, Washburn, & Pikus, 2005). All adolescents, regardless of involvement in the system, tend to underutilize needed treatment for mental health and substance use disorders (Kataoka, Zhang, & Wells, 2002; NSDUH Report, 2014; Wang et al., 2005). Yet, youth involved in juvenile justice are even less likely to receive services; as few as 10% of detained youth are referred to behavioral healthcare upon release to the community (Rogers, Zima, Powell, & Pumariega, 2001). Youth involved in juvenile justice *attend* treatment sessions at similarly low rates (Aalsma et al., 2012a; Abram, Paskar, Washburn, & Teplin, 2008; Teplin et al., 2005). Within a sample of youth involved in juvenile justice in Cook County detention centers, Teplin and colleagues (2005) found that of all youth with demonstrated behavioral treatment needs at intake, only 8% were connected with services within six months of release from detention.

Minority youth, who are overrepresented at all levels of the justice system (Bishop & Frazier, 1996; Iguchi, Bell, Ramchand, & Fain, 2005; Schlesinger, 2005), bear the greatest burden of untreated behavioral health disorders. Black youth are the least likely to receive mental health or substance use treatment services (Rawal et al., 2004) – whether in the form of treatment referrals, outpatient services, or placement in treatment facilities – even after controlling for their need for services, their medical insurance coverage, and other potentially confounding variables (Aalsma et al., 2012a; Alexandre, Younis, Martins, & Richard, 2010; Dalton, Evans, Cruise, Feinstein, & Kendrick, 2009; Garland et al., 2005; LeCook, Barry, & Busch, 2013). When considering youth race and gender together, White females are nearly eight times more likely than Black males, and two and a half times more likely than White males to be placed in mental health treatment facilities rather than detention or prison (Herz, 2001).

## A Focus on Juvenile Probation

The behavioral healthcare needs of *confined* youth are the focus of a significant body of research. There is a good reason for this; there is evidence that the health services and general conditions of juvenile detention centers and secure residential facilities are often lacking in quality, are minimally regulated, and behavioral health services are quite variable (Hockenberry, Sickmund, & Sladky, 2013; Sedlak & McPherson, 2010). It appears that the more secure the facility (i.e., juvenile prisons versus residential placements) the more youth report that the facility is unclean, overcrowded, and isolating (Sedlak, 2016). In a national survey of confined youth, more than 10% of youth held in detention reported having no contact with a family member in the previous 30 days (Sedlak, 2016). It is true that some detention centers provide behavioral health services (i.e., counseling, medication) that youth may not have received if they had remained in the community (Aalsma et al., 2015). However, placement in any system-run facility is likely to interrupt health insurance coverage for mental health services or substance abuse treatment when youth return to the community, preventing continuity of care (Cuellar, Kelleher, Rolls, & Pajer, 2005; Gupta, Kelleher, Pajer, Stevens, & Cuellar, 2005). Calls for improving the conditions of juvenile confinement and facilitating youth reentry into the community are common, yet the majority of youth involved in juvenile justice remain in the community while under court supervision. Of all youth adjudicated delinquent in 2014, 63% were ordered to serve a term of probation (Furdella & Puzzanchera, 2015), so the behavioral health treatment needs of youth probationers also warrant close attention.

Juvenile probation officers play a significant role in the lives of youth involved in juvenile justice; probation officers are involved in screening for and assessing youth needs at system intake, conducting pre-sentence investigations, and monitoring youth adherence to court orders (Corbett, 1999; Leifker & Sample, 2010; Torbet, 1997). Inherent in these duties are the dual, and sometimes conflicting, mandates of (1) youth rehabilitation and (2) enforcement to protect public safety (Clear & Latessa, 1993; Steiner, Purkiss, Kifer, Roberts, & Hemmens, 2004). For example, though one goal of probation is to help youth diagnosed with behavioral health disorders obtain and remain in treatment, probation officers must also fulfill their obligations to respond to the criminal infractions of these youth. Juvenile probation officers have significant discretion to enforce conditions of probation by, for example, determining whether probationers who test positive for illegal drugs on a court-ordered urine screen will be charged with a violation of probation or referred to substance use treatment services. If a youth is so charged, juvenile courts may then order the youth to be placed in a secure facility without directly addressing underlying substance use issues. In sum, a significant proportion of detained youth are held on violations of probation and warrant arrests, charges that can result from JPO discretion (Aalsma et al., 2012a).

While juvenile probation is a common system outcome, a meta-analysis exploring the effectiveness of interventions for youth involved in juvenile justice suggests that supervision alone (i.e., juvenile probation) is not sufficient to reduce the risk of youth recidivism (Lipsey, 2009). Yet, there has been only recent national interest in clarifying how juvenile probation can be leveraged to improve youth outcomes (Mendel, 2018). Researchers have demonstrated that preventing adolescents' repeat system involvement is most likely when the terms of probation match the youth's level of risk for recidivism (Vitopoulos, Peterson-Badali, & Skilling, 2012). Youth at lowest risk for recidivism appear to benefit most from diversion from the justice system altogether (Wilson & Hoge, 2012), while therapeutic interventions (including behavioral health services, skill-building workshops, and restorative justice practices) generally achieve greater reductions in recidivism than supervision alone (Lipsey, 2009).

## Barriers to Behavioral Health Treatment

Youth involved in juvenile justice face a myriad of roadblocks to utilizing behavioral healthcare in the community. First, minor youth lack the legal autonomy to consent for many health services (Kerwin et al., 2015). Social and financial barriers (e.g., stigma regarding treatment or lack of health insurance coverage) may further limit youth's practical access to services. Youth involved in juvenile justice face a shortage of mental health professionals, particularly in programs that administer evidence-based treatments and those that are designed to treat comorbid disorders (Belenko & Dembo, 2003). Probation officers' attitude toward mental health services – or a lack of knowledge about behavioral health issues and available services – also poses problems for youth (Grisso, Barnum, Fletcher, Cauffman, & Peuschold, 2001). In a qualitative study of youth involved in juvenile justice returning to community supervision after detention (Aalsma, Brown, Holloway, & Ott, 2014), youth and their caregivers reported difficulties accessing care related to (1) poor communication from justice system staff while the youth was detained and upon release from detention, (2) long waits between release from detention and initial meetings with a probation officer, and (3) limited coordination efforts among families, the justice system, and behavioral health service providers. Youth also reported that being detained was a type of crisis event that motivated their desire to seek care; once they returned to the community, both the crisis and motivation diminished (Aalsma et al., 2014). See Figure 19.1, depicting components of the reentry process that influence behavioral healthcare utilization.

## A Framework for Improving Behavioral Health Care Utilization: JJ-TRIALS Cascade

A NIDA research cooperative, JJ-TRIALS, has developed a framework for conceptualizing stages of comprehensive, system-level behavioral healthcare for youth involved in juvenile justice: the Juvenile Justice Behavioral Health Services Cascade ("Cascade") (Belenko et al., 2017). Their framework mirrors an established model of the ideal continuum of services to address HIV. Similar to the HIV care continuum, the Cascade indicates optimum components of effective behavioral healthcare and clear treatment gaps to be addressed.

Stages of the Cascade include behavioral health problem identification, care initiation, and care retention. The potential to "lose" individuals at each stage – and interrupt the care continuum – is reflected in distinct activities that must be completed within each stage. For example, identifying behavioral health treatment need requires an initial screening, a comprehensive assessment and/or diagnosis, a detailed case plan, and a specific treatment recommendation. While juvenile justice system personnel may make a referral to a service provider either before or after problem identification, most activities within the continuum are dependent upon completing those that precede them. Treatment initiation is contingent upon problem identification and requires both a referral to a service provider post-assessment and youth participation in the first session of treatment. Treatment engagement requires youth participation within a critical period (i.e., 4–6 weeks) and in continuing care (Belenko et al., 2017). Both initiation and engagement definitions are supported by tested quality care standards associated with positive health outcomes; these standards recommend treatment initiation within 14 days of an assessment (problem identification), at least two treatment visits after treatment initiation (Garnick et al., 2012), and a minimum of three months in care (Hser et al., 2001). The Cascade currently serves as a model for care across a variety of patient populations and care sectors, including use of HIV prevention services by adolescents, community-based treatment of opioid addiction, and treatment of adults suffering major depression in primary care (Pence, O'Donnell, & Gaynes, 2012; Tolou-Shams, Harrison, Conrad, Johnson, & Brown, 2017; Williams et al., 2018).

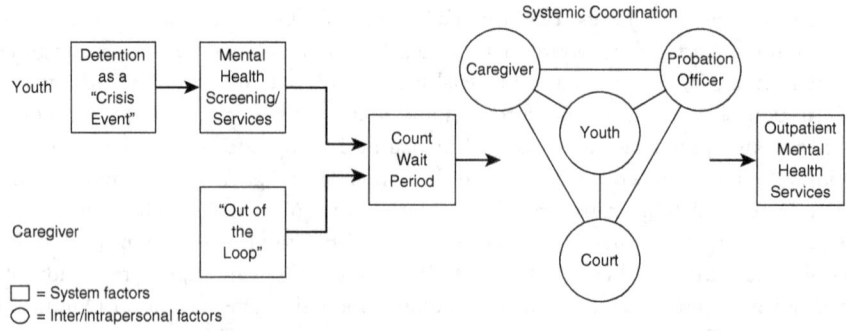

*Figure 19.1* Juvenile mental healthcare reentry model (Aalsma et al., 2014)

Though the Cascade simplifies what can be a convoluted process into a single linear pathway to care, its strength is that it reveals potential missed opportunities to improve care. Likewise, variables positively associated with cascade stage achievement suggest routes for innovative intervention strategies (Belenko et al., 2017). As shown in Figure 19.2, behavioral health screening efforts within the juvenile justice system, which have improved over time (Grisso, 2007; Hoeve, McReynolds, & Wasserman, 2014), may sufficiently capture this population's need for care. However, as visible gaps in the Cascade suggest, there is significant work to be done to increase treatment initiation and engagement. We now provide a brief overview of two promising approaches to improving behavioral health treatment utilization among youth involved in juvenile justice: patient navigation and family engagement.

## Patient Navigation

Patient navigation is an approach that may begin to fill known gaps in behavioral healthcare for youth involved in juvenile justice. Patient navigation – also referred to as care coordination, community case management, and health coaching – is an established intervention designed to supplement professional health services for a variety of diseases and health needs. Patient navigation has gained increasing empirical support for addressing issues such as injury prevention (Kendrick et al., 2012), cancer treatment (Nguyen, Stewart, Nguyen, Bui-Tong, & McPhee, 2015), and infectious disease (Lewin et al., 2010). This type of health intervention traditionally offers patients the assistance of a lay health worker or community member at various points along the continuum of care; patient navigators help their clients with tasks ranging from information gathering about symptom management and community resources, to mobilizing family support, facilitating transportation to medical appointments, and communicating with health insurance and care providers (Flores et al., 2005). Patient navigation models provide a context for helping

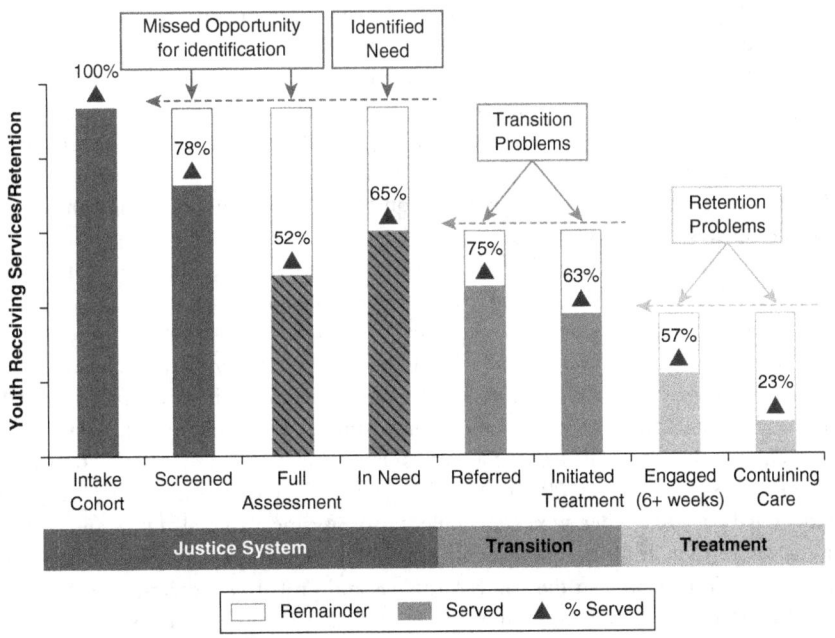

*Figure 19.2* The Juvenile Justice Behavioral Health Services Cascade (Belenko et al., 2017)

patients overcome obstacles to initiating behavior change (Naar-King, Parsons, & Johnson, 2012). Features of the patient navigation model, including its traditional use of lay personnel – staff with usually no more than a relevant bachelor's degree – to provide tailored navigation services to clients, helps minimize intervention costs.

Patient navigation models, however, have rarely been applied to the treatment of behavioral health disorders. In addition, while patient navigation approaches have been applied to adult criminal offenders after their release from prison, this type of intervention has been studied less frequently among adolescents generally or among youth involved in juvenile justice, specifically. One study by Lyons and colleagues (Lyons, Griffin, Quintenz, Jenuwine, & Shasha, 2003) found patient navigators ("liaisons") to be effective in connecting youth involved in juvenile justice with significant mental health needs to community-based services, reducing psychiatric symptoms, and improving overall community function. Other studies of patient navigation for the treatment of behavioral health disorders indicate this may be a promising approach for youth involved in juvenile justice (Gagne, Finch, Myrick, & Davis, 2018; Gopalan, Lee, Harris, Acri, & Munson, 2017; Portillo, Goldberg, & Taxman, 2017).

## Family Engagement

Another promising approach to addressing adolescents' underutilization of behavioral health services has been to improve family participation or engagement in the treatment process, which has special implications for youth involved in juvenile justice. The potential influence of families on youth development and wellbeing cannot be understated. Families often serve as a young person's first cultural context (Patterson, 2004), which educates, nurtures, and socializes youth (Lippold & Jensen, 2017). Note that by "family," we acknowledge its complex and dynamic nature (Brown, Stykes, & Manning, 2016); we use the term to refer to individuals who serve in family- or parent-like roles for youth involved in juvenile justice. The importance of families – of any type – is a common theme throughout research on child-serving systems, including child welfare, education, healthcare, and juvenile justice (Burke, Mulvey, Schubert, & Garbin, 2014; Walker, Bishop, Pullmann, & Bauer, 2015). Across systems, families may be a positive influence on youth outcomes by providing youth with instrumental support (e.g., transportation, funds), emotional support (e.g., empathy, positive identity formation), protection (e.g., advocacy), and cooperation with system-generated care plans (e.g., monitoring) (Lippold & Jensen, 2017). Conversely, when families are not able or willing to provide these positive influences, youth outcomes may suffer. Thus, families are important targets of intervention to maximize the likelihood that their system engagement facilitates youth wellbeing.

The role of families in the juvenile justice system process is not a "uniform construct" (Burke et al., 2014, p. 43). Instead, their involvement tends to be fluid or ever-changing, depending largely on the stage of the system and needs of youth (Paik, 2016). As in other child-serving systems, families of youth involved in juvenile justice have the potential to facilitate the dual purposes of the courts – rehabilitation and public safety – or impede the process and exacerbate the harms of youth reoffending. Indeed, families of youth involved in juvenile justice have often been depicted in research as a cause of youth delinquency or as responsible for the effects of youth offending (Walker et al., 2015). This image is reflected in the legal concepts of *parens patriae* and *in loco parentis*, under which juvenile courts assume parental duties and protection for youth involved in juvenile justice. Unlike in other child-serving systems, the structure of justice system places decision-making in the hands of judges and probation officers, with little opportunity for families' voices to be heard; such a shift in power places the justice system and families at odds, likely testing family willingness to participate in the system process (Burke et al., 2014). Another line of research has shown that families of youth involved in juvenile justice frequently hold unfavorable views of the system, citing a lack of procedural justice (i.e., fairness) and little support for parents' goals for their children (Luckenbill & Yeager, 2009).

Negative parental attitudes correspond to reduced family supervision and increased youth reoffending (Cavanagh & Cauffman, 2015). In turn, both quality parent–child relationships and positive parental views of the system are largely associated with delinquency prevention and criminal desistance (Cavanagh & Cauffman, 2017). We also know that family-based interventions for youth involved in juvenile justice, meaning that parents are a target of intervention along with youth, are among the most likely to reduce youth reoffending (Dopp et al., 2017). Efforts to improve positive family engagement in the justice system process – including court-ordered behavioral health services – have received increasing attention, but tested methods are few. Instead, we look to the behavioral healthcare field to gain insight into what might work to increase utilization of mental health or substance use treatment services by youth involved in juvenile justice.

Parent and family engagement in youth behavioral health services is often included as an outcome of clinical and implementation research trials, since a lack of engagement has been associated with poor outcomes, even for evidence-based treatments (Haine-Schlagel & Walsh, 2015; Ingoldsby, 2010). Families at highest risk for behavioral healthcare needs who also face the most barriers to treatment access, namely racial/ethnic minorities with few financial resources, are also most likely to drop out of treatment (Chacko et al., 2016; Snell-Johns, Mendez, & Smith, 2004), leaving many of the most vulnerable youth underserved. Indeed, the National Institutes of Health (2001) has stated that engagement deficits are a major challenge to implementation and dissemination of evidence-based care. Improving family engagement in adolescent behavioral health treatment has been a pressing public health concern.

Family engagement has been operationalized in various ways, but primarily in terms of treatment attendance or treatment completion/adherence (Nock & Ferriter, 2005). Cognitive and relationship-related definitions of engagement (e.g., treatment acceptability, motivation to change, and therapeutic alliance between provider and client) are studied less frequently (Becker et al., 2015). In a recent review of more than 50 randomized controlled trials to improve family engagement in behavioral health services, authors distilled common components to interventions that successfully increased family engagement when compared to controls (Becker, Boustani, Gellatly, & Chorpita, 2018). Across all measures of family engagement, the successful practice elements that appeared most frequently included the following: assessing client/family strengths; offering psychoeducation about the purpose of the treatment; promoting the accessibility of the treatment (e.g., transportation availability); reviewing and addressing barriers to treatment; and setting measurable goals for treatment (Becker et al., 2018). We know something about how to engage families in behavioral healthcare, but we know less about how to do it for the most vulnerable, high-risk youth – youth who are underrepresented in treatment completion and otherwise disadvantaged (e.g., racial/ethnic minorities). A novel intervention highlighted in a recent review focused on engaging underrepresented parents was "peer pairing" (Pellecchia et al., 2018). Connecting parents of youth with similar needs may reduce isolation and develop supportive networks for families. Youth involved in the juvenile justice system may benefit from unique intervention approaches such as these.

## Summary

Youth involved in the juvenile justice system have significant behavioral healthcare needs. Evidence-based interventions exist for the treatment of common behavioral health disorders among youth involved in the juvenile justice system, including disruptive behavior disorders and substance abuse. Nonetheless, youth involved in the juvenile justice system rarely utilize behavioral health services. In the current article, we highlight innovative interventions for youth involved in juvenile justice that may repair gaps in treatment as identified by the behavioral health services cascade. First, patient navigation may effectively connect youth and their families to care. Second, family engagement techniques have been helpful in increasing the utilization of behavioral health services. However, these two types of interventions need to be adapted for youth involved in juvenile justice. In particular, probation officers, as the "workhorses" of the juvenile justice system, need to be included in any intervention to maximize behavioral health-care utilization. It is our hope that future efforts to adapt successful interventions will improve the wellbeing of youth involved in juvenile justice.

## References

Aalsma, M., Tong, Y., Lane, K., Katz, B., & Rosenman, M. (2012a). Use of outpatient care by juvenile detainees upon community reentry: Effects of mental health screening and referral. *Psychiatric Services*, 63(10), 997–1003.

Aalsma, M. C., Brown, J. R., Holloway, E. D., & Ott, M. A. (2014). Connection to mental health care upon community reentry for detained youth: A qualitative study. *BMC Public Health*, 14, 117.

Aalsma, M. C., Gudonis, L. C., Jarjoura, G. R., Blythe, M. J., Tong, Y., Harezlak, J., & Rosenman, M. B. (2012b). The consequences of juvenile detention reform for mental health and sexually transmitted infection screening among detained youth. *Journal of Adolescent Health*, 50(4), 365–370.

Aalsma, M. C., White, L. M., Lau, K. S., Perkins, A., Monahan, P., & Grisso, T. (2015). Behavioral health care needs, detention-based care, and criminal recidivism at community reentry from juvenile detention: A multisite survival curve analysis. *American Journal of Public Health*, 105(7), 1372–1378.

Abram, K. M., Paskar, L. D., Washburn, J. J., & Teplin, L. A. (2008). Perceived barriers to mental health services among youths in detention. *Journal of the American Academy of Child and Adolescent Psychiatry*, 47(3), 301–308.

Abram, K. M., Zwecker, N. A., Welty, L. J., Hershfield, J. A., Dulcan, M. K., & Teplin, L. A. (2015). Comorbidity and continuity of psychiatric disorders in youth after detention: A prospective longitudinal study. *JAMA Psychiatry*, 72(1), 84–93.

Alexandre, P. K., Younis, M. Z., Martins, S. S., & Richard, P. (2010). Disparities in adequate mental health care for past-year major depressive episodes among white and non-white youth. *Journal of Health Care Finance*, 36(3), 57–72.

Becker, K. D., Boustani, M., Gellatly, R., & Chorpita, B. F. (2018). Forty years of engagement research in children's mental health services: Multidimensional measurement and practice elements. *Journal of Clinical Child and Adolescent Psychology*, 47(1), 1–23.

Becker, K. D., Lee, B. R., Daleiden, E. L., Lindsey, M., Brandt, N. E., & Chorpita, B. F. (2015). The common elements of engagement in children's mental health services: which elements for which outcomes? *Journal of Clinical Child and Adolescent Psychology*, 44(1), 30–43.

Belenko, S., & Dembo, R. (2003). Treating adolescent substance abuse problems in the juvenile drug court. *International Journal of Law and Psychiatry*, 26(1), 87–110.

Belenko, S., Knight, D., Wasserman, G. A., Dennis, M. L., Wiley, T., Taxman, F. S., … Sales, J. (2017). The Juvenile Justice Behavioral Health Services Cascade: A new framework for measuring unmet substance use treatment services needs among adolescent offenders. *Journal of Substance Abuse Treatment*, 74, 80–91.

Bennett, T., Holloway, K., & Farrington, D. (2008). The statistical association between drug misuse and crime: A meta-analysis. *Aggression and Violent Behavior*, 13(2), 107–118.

Bishop, D. M., & Frazier, C. E. (1996). Race effects in juvenile justice decision-making: Findings of a statewide analysis. *The Journal of Criminal Law and Criminology (1973-)*, 86(2), 392–414.

Braverman, P. K., & Murray, P. J. (2011). Health care for youth in the juvenile justice system. *Pediatrics*, 128(6), 1219–1235.

Brown, S. L., Stykes, J. B., & Manning, W. D. (2016). Trends in children's family instability, 1995–2010. *Journal of Marriage and Family*, 78(5), 1173–1183.

Burke, J. D., Mulvey, E. P., Schubert, C. A., & Garbin, S. R. (2014). The challenge and opportunity of parental involvement in juvenile justice services. *Children and Youth Services Review*, 39, 39–47.

Cavanagh, C., & Cauffman, E. (2015). Viewing law and order: Mothers' and sons' justice system legitimacy attitudes and juvenile recidivism. *Psychology, Public Policy, and Law*, 21(4), 432–441.

Cavanagh, C., & Cauffman, E. (2017). The longitudinal association of relationship quality and reoffending among first-time juvenile offenders and their mothers. *Journal of Youth and Adolescence, 46*(7), 1533–1546.

Chacko, A., Jensen, S. A., Lowry, L. S., Cornwell, M., Chimklis, A., Chan, E., ... Pulgarin, B. (2016). Engagement in behavioral parent training: Review of the literature and implications for practice. *Clinical Child and Family Psychology Review, 19*(3), 204–215.

Chassin, L. (2008). Juvenile justice and substance use. *The Future of Children, 18*(2), 165–183.

Clear, T., & Latessa, E. (1993). Probation officers' roles in intensive supervision: Surveillance versus treatment. *Justice Quarterly, 10*(3), 441–462.

Corbett Jr, R. P. (1999). Juvenile probation on the eve of the next millennium. *Federal Probation, 63*(2), 78–86.

Cuellar, A., Kelleher, K. J., Rolls, J. A., & Pajer, K. (2005). Medicaid insurance policy for youths involved in the criminal justice system. *American Journal of Public Health, 95*(10), 1707–1711.

Cuellar, A. E., McReynolds, L. S., & Wasserman, G. A. (2006). A cure for crime: Can mental health treatment diversion reduce crime among youth? *Journal of Policy Analysis and Management, 25*(1), 197–214.

Dalton, R. F., Evans, L. J., Cruise, K. R., Feinstein, R. A., & Kendrick, R. F. (2009). Race differences in mental health service access in a secure male juvenile justice facility. *Journal of Offender Rehabilitation, 48*(3), 194–209.

Desai, R. A., Goulet, J. L., Robbins, J., Chapman, J. F., Migdole, S. J., & Hoge, M. A. (2006). Mental health care in juvenile detention facilities: A review. *Journal of the American Academy of Psychiatry and the Law, 34*(2), 204–214.

Dopp, A. R., Borduin, C. M., White, I. I., Mark, H., & Kuppens, S. (2017). Family-based treatments for serious juvenile offenders: A multilevel meta-analysis. *Journal of Consulting and Clinical Psychology, 85*(4), 335–354.

Fazel, S., Doll, H., & Långström, N. (2008). Mental disorders among adolescents in juvenile detention and correctional facilities: A systematic review and metaregression analysis of 25 surveys. *Journal of the American Academy of Child and Adolescent Psychiatry, 47*(9), 1010–1019.

Flores, G., Abreu, M., Chaisson, C. E., Meyers, A., Sachdeva, R. C., Fernandez, H., ... Santos-Guerrero, I. (2005). A randomized, controlled trial of the effectiveness of community-based case management in insuring uninsured Latino children. *Pediatrics, 116*(6), 1433–1441.

Foster, E. M., Qaseem, A., & Connor, T. (2004). Can better mental health services reduce the risk of juvenile justice system involvement? *American Journal of Public Health, 94*(5), 859–865.

Furdella, J., & Puzzanchera, C. (2015). Delinquency cases in juvenile court, 2013. *Juvenile Offenders and Victims: National Report Series, October.*

Gagne, C. A., Finch, W. L., Myrick, K. J., & Davis, L. M. (2018). Peer workers in the behavioral and integrated health workforce: Opportunities and future directions. *American Journal of Preventive Medicine, 54*(6, Supplement 3), S258–S266.

Garland, A. F., Lau, A. S., Yeh, M., McCabe, K. M., Hough, R. L., & Landsverk, J. A. (2005). Racial and ethnic differences in utilization of mental health services among high-risk youths. *American Journal of Psychiatry, 162*(7), 1336–1343.

Garnick, D. W., Lee, M. T., O'Brien, P. L., Panas, L., Ritter, G. A., Acevedo, A., ... Godley, M. D. (2012). The Washington Circle engagement performance measures' association with adolescent treatment outcomes. *Drug and Alcohol Dependence, 124*(3), 250–258.

Gopalan, G., Lee, S. J., Harris, R., Acri, M. C., & Munson, M. R. (2017). Utilization of peers in services for youth with emotional and behavioral challenges: A scoping review. *Journal of Adolescence, 55*, 88–115.

Grisso, T. (2007). Progress and perils in the juvenile justice and mental health movement. *Journal of the American Academy of Psychiatry and the Law, 35*(2), 158–167.

Grisso, T., Barnum, R., Fletcher, K. E., Cauffman, E., & Peuschold, D. (2001). Massachusetts Youth Screening Instrument for mental health needs of juvenile justice youths. *Journal of the American Academy of Child and Adolescent Psychiatry, 40*(5), 541–548.

Gupta, R. A., Kelleher, K. J., Pajer, K., Stevens, J., & Cuellar, A. (2005). Delinquent youth in corrections: Medicaid and reentry into the community. *Pediatrics, 115*(4), 1077–1083.

Haine-Schlagel, R., & Walsh, N. E. (2015). A review of parent participation engagement in child and family mental health treatment. *Clinical Child and Family Psychology Review, 18*(2), 133–150.

Henggeler, S., & Schoenwald, S. J. (2011). Evidence-based interventions for juvenile offenders and juvenile justice policies that support them. *Social Policy Report, 25*(1), 1–20.

Herz, D. C. (2001). Understanding the use of mental health placements by the juvenile justice system. *Journal of Emotional and Behavioral Disorders, 9*(3), 172–181.

Hockenberry, S., Sickmund, M., & Sladky, A. (August 2013). Juvenile residential facility census, 2010: Select findings. *Juvenile Offenders and Victims: National Report Series.*

Hoeve, M., McReynolds, L., & Wasserman, G. (2014). Service referral for juvenile justice youths: Associations with psychiatric disorder and recidivism. *Administration & Policy in Mental Health & Mental Health Services Research, 41*(3), 379–389.

Hoeve, M., McReynolds, L. S., Wasserman, G. A., & McMillan, C. (2013). The influence of mental health disorders on severity of reoffending in juveniles. *Criminal Justice and Behavior, 40*(3), 289–301.

Holman, B., & Ziedenberg, J. (2006). *The dangers of detention: The impact of incarcerating youth in detention and other secure facilities.* Washington, DC: Justice Policy Institute.

Hser, Y. I., Grella, C. E., Hubbard, R. L., Hsieh, S. C., Fletcher, B. W., Brown, B. S., & Anglin, M. D. (2001). An evaluation of drug treatments for adolescents in 4 US cities. *Archives of General Psychiatry, 58*(7), 689–695.

Iguchi, M. Y., Bell, J., Ramchand, R. N., & Fain, T. (2005). How criminal system racial disparities may translate into health disparities. *Journal of Health Care for the Poor and Underserved, 16*, 48–56.

Ingoldsby, E. M. (2010). Review of interventions to improve family engagement and retention in parent and child mental health programs. *Journal of Child and Family Studies, 19*(5), 629–645.

Karnick, N. S., Soller, M., Redlich, A., Silverman, M., Kraemer, H. C., Haapanen, R., & Steiner, H. (June 2009). Prevalence of and gender differences in psychiatric disorders among juvenile delinquents incarcerated for nine months. *Psychiatric Services, 60*(6), 838–841.

Kataoka, S. H., Zhang, L., & Wells, K. B. (2002). Unmet need for mental health care among U.S. children: Variation by ethnicity and insurance status. *American Journal of Psychiatry, 159*(9), 1548–1555.

Kendrick, D., Young, B., Mason-Jones, A. J., Ilyas, N., Achana, F. A., Cooper, N. J., ... Coupland, C. (2012). Home safety education and provision of safety equipment for injury prevention. *Cochrane Database of Systematic Reviews, 9*, Cd005014.

Kerwin, M. E., Kirby, K. C., Speziali, D., Duggan, M., Mellitz, C., Versek, B., & McNamara, A. (2015). What can parents do? A review of state laws regarding decision making for adolescent drug abuse and mental health treatment. *Journal of Child & Adolescent Substance Abuse, 24*(3), 166–176.

Kessler, R. C., Avenevoli, S., Costello, E. J., Georgiades, K., Green, J. G., Gruber, M. J., ... Merikangas, K. R. (2012). Prevalence, persistence, and sociodemographic correlates of DSM-IV disorders in the National Comorbidity Survey Replication Adolescent Supplement. *Archives of General Psychiatry, 69*(4), 372–380.

LeCook, B., Barry, C. L., & Busch, S. H. (2013). Racial/ethnic disparity trends in children's mental health care access and expenditures from 2002 to 2007. *Health Services Research, 48*(1), 129–149.

Leifker, D., & Sample, L. L. (2010). Probation recommendations and sentences received: The association between the two and the factors that affect recommendations. *Criminal Justice Policy Review, 22*(4), 494–517.

Lewin, S., Munabi-Babigumira, S., Glenton, C., Daniels, K., Bosch-Capblanch, X., van Wyk, B. E., ... Scheel, I. B. (2010). Lay health workers in primary and community health care for maternal and child health and the management of infectious diseases. *Cochrane Database of Systematic Reviews*, (3), Cd004015. doi: 10.1002/14651858.CD004015.pub3

Lippold, M. A., & Jensen, T. M. (2017). Harnessing the strength of families to prevent social problems and promote adolescent well-being. *Children and Youth Services Review, 79*, 432–441.

Lipsey, M. W. (2009). The primary factors that characterize effective interventions with juvenile offenders: A meta-analytic overview. *Victims and Offenders, 4*(2), 124–147.

Luckenbill, W., & Yeager, C. (2009). Family involvement in Pennsylvania's juvenile justice system. *Models for Change.* Retrieved from www.modelsforchange.net/publications/238

Lyons, J. S., Griffin, G., Quintenz, S., Jenuwine, M., & Shasha, M. (2003). Clinical and forensic outcomes from the Illinois mental health juvenile justice initiative. *Psychiatric Services, 54*, 1629–1634.

McReynolds, L. S., Schwalbe, C. S., & Wasserman, G. A. (2010). The contribution of psychiatric disorder to juvenile recidivism. *Criminal Justice and Behavior, 37*(2), 204–216.

Mendel, R. A. (2018). *Transforming juvenile probation: A vision for getting it right.* Retrieved from www.aecf.org/m/resourcedoc/aecf-transformingjuvenileprobation-2018.pdf

Merikangas, K. R., He, J. P., Brody, D., Fisher, P. W., Bourdon, K., & Koretz, D. S. (2010). Prevalence and treatment of mental disorders among US children in the 2001–2004 NHANES. *Pediatrics, 125*(1), 75–81.

Naar-King, S., Parsons, J. T., & Johnson, A. M. (2012). Motivational interviewing targeting risk reduction for people with HIV: A systematic review. *Current HIV/AIDS Reports, 9*(4), 335–343.

National Institutes of Health. Blueprint for Change: Research on child and adolescent mental health. (2001). *Report of the National Advisory Mental Health Council's Workgroup on Child and Adolescent Mental Health Intervention Development and Deployment.* Retrieved from https://catalog.hathitrust.org/Record/003898239

Nguyen, B. H., Stewart, S. L., Nguyen, T. T., Bui-Tong, N., & McPhee, S. J. (2015). Effectiveness of lay health worker outreach in reducing disparities in colorectal cancer screening in vietnamese americans. *American Journal of Public Health, 105*(10), 2083–2089.

Nock, M. K., & Ferriter, C. (2005). Parent management of attendance and adherence in child and adolescent therapy: A conceptual and empirical review. *Clinical Child and Family Psychology Review, 8*(2), 149–166.

NSDUH Report. (September 4, 2014). *The NSDUH report: Substance use and mental health results from the 2013 National Survey on Drug Use and Health: Detailed tables*. Retrieved from www.samhsa.gov/data/NSDUH/2013SummNatFindDetTables/DetTabs/NSDUH-DetTabsTOC2013.htm

Paik, L. (2016). Good parents, bad parents: Rethinking family involvement in juvenile justice. *Theoretical Criminology, 21*(3), 307–323.

Pajer, K. A., Kelleher, K., Gupta, R. A., Rolls, J., & Gardner, W. (2007). Psychiatric and medical health care policies in juvenile detention facilities. *Journal of the American Academy of Child and Adolescent Psychiatry, 46*(12), 1660–1667.

Patterson, J. M. (2004). Integrating family resilience and family stress theory. *Journal of Marriage and Family, 64*(2), 349–360.

Pellecchia, M., Nuske, H. J., Straiton, D., McGhee Hassrick, E., Gulsrud, A., Iadarola, S., … Stahmer, A. C. (2018). Strategies to engage underrepresented parents in child intervention services: A review of effectiveness and co-occurring use. *Journal of Child and Family Studies, 27*(10), 3141–3154.

Pence, B. W., O'Donnell, J. K., & Gaynes, B. N. (2012). The depression treatment cascade in primary care: A public health perspective. *Current Psychiatry Reports, 14*(4), 328–335.

Portillo, S., Goldberg, V., & Taxman, F. S. (2017). Mental health peer navigators: Working with criminal justice–involved populations. *The Prison Journal, 97*(3), 318–341.

Pullmann, M. D., Kerbs, J., Koroloff, N., Veach-White, E., Gaylor, R., & Sieler, D. (2006). Juvenile offenders with mental health needs: Reducing recidivism using wraparound. *Crime & Delinquency, 52*(3), 375–397.

Rawal, P., Romansky, J., & Michael Jenuwine, J. (2004). Racial differences in the mental health needs and service utilization of youth in the juvenile justice system. *Journal of Behavioral Health Services and Research, 31*(3), 242–254.

Rogers, K. M., Zima, B., Powell, E., & Pumariega, A. J. (2001). Who is referred to mental health services in the juvenile justice system? *Journal of Child and Family Studies, 10*(4), 485–494.

SAMHSA Estimates from the 2013 National Survey on Drug Use and Health: Overview of Findings. (September 4, 2014). *The NSDUH Report.*

Schlesinger, T. (2005). Racial and ethnic disparity in pretrial criminal processing. *Justice Quarterly, 22*(2), 170–192.

Schubert, C. A., Mulvey, E. P., & Glasheen, C. (2011). Influence of mental health and substance use problems and criminogenic risk on outcomes in serious juvenile offenders. *Journal of the American Academy of Child and Adolescent Psychiatry, 50*(9), 925–937.

Sedlak, A. J. (2016). *Survey of youth in residential placement: Conditions of confinement*. SYRP Report. Rockville, MD: Westat.

Sedlak, A. J., & McPherson, K. S. (May 2010). Conditions of confinement: Findings from the survey of youth in residential placement. *Juvenile Justice Bulletin*. Retrieved from www.ncjrs.gov/pdffiles1/ojjdp/227729.pdf

Sexton, T., & Turner, C. W. (2010). The effectiveness of Functional Family Therapy for youth with behavioral problems in a community practice setting. *Journal of Family Psychology, 24*(3), 339–348.

Shufelt, J., & Cocozza, J. (June 2006). Youth with mental health disorders in the juvenile justice system: results from a multi-state prevalence study. Retrieved from www.ncmhjj.com/pdfs/publications/PrevalenceRPB.pdf

Snell-Johns, J., Mendez, J. L., & Smith, B. H. (2004). Evidence-based solutions for overcoming access barriers, decreasing attrition, and promoting change with underserved families. *Journal of Family Psychology, 18*(1), 19–35.

Steiner, B., Purkiss, M., Kifer, M., Roberts, E., & Hemmens, C. (2004). Legally prescribed functions of adult and juvenile probation officers – worlds apart? *Journal of Offender Rehabilitation, 39*(4), 47–67.

Teplin, L. A., Abram, K. M., McClelland, G. M., Dulcan, M. K., & Mericle, A. A. (2002). Psychiatric disorders in youth in juvenile detention. *Archives of General Psychiatry, 59*(12), 1133–1143.

Teplin, L. A., Abram, K. M., McClelland, G. M., Washburn, J. J., & Pikus, A. K. (2005). Detecting mental disorder in juvenile detainees: Who receives services? *American Journal of Public Health, 95*(10), 1773–1780.

Tolou-Shams, M., Harrison, A., Conrad, S. M., Johnson, S., & Brown, L. K. (2017). Challenges to conducting adolescent HIV prevention services research with court-involved youth. *Children and Youth Services Review, 83*, 201–208.

Torbet, P. (1997). Juvenile probation: The workhorse of the juvenile justice system. *Juvenile Probation Administrators Desktop Guide, 13*.

Vitopoulos, N. A., Peterson-Badali, M., & Skilling, T. A. (2012). The relationship between matching service to criminogenic need and recidivism in male and female youth: Examining the RNR principles in practice. *Criminal Justice and Behavior, 39*(8), 1025–1041.

Walker, S. C., Bishop, A. S., Pullmann, M. D., & Bauer, G. (2015). A research framework for understanding the practical impact of family involvement in the juvenile justice system: The juvenile justice family involvement model. *American Journal of Community Psychology, 56*(3–4), 408–421.

Wang, P. S., Lane, M., Olfson, M., Pincus, H. A., Wells, K. B., & Kessler, R. C. (2005). Twelve-month use of mental health services in the united states: Results from the National Comorbidity Survey Replication. *Archives of General Psychiatry, 62*(6), 629–640.

Wasserman, G. A., & McReynolds, L. S. (2011). Contributors to traumatic exposure and posttraumatic stress disorder in juvenile justice youths. *Journal of Traumatic Stress, 24*(4), 422–429.

Wasserman, G. A., McReynolds, L. S., Schwalbe, C. S., Keating, J. M., & Jones, S. A. (2010). Psychiatric disorder, comorbidity, and suicidal behavior in juvenile justice youth. *Criminal Justice and Behavior, 37*(12), 1361–1376.

Wibbelink, C. J. M., Hoeve, M., Stams, G. J. J. M., & Oort, F. J. (2017). A meta-analysis of the association between mental disorders and juvenile recidivism. *Aggression and Violent Behavior, 33*, 78–90.

Williams, A. R., Nunes, E. V., Bisaga, A., Pincus, H. A., Johnson, K. A., Campbell, A. N., ... Olfson, M. (2018). Developing an opioid use disorder treatment cascade: A review of quality measures. *Journal of Substance Abuse Treatment, 91*, 57–68.

Wilson, H. A., & Hoge, R. D. (2012). The effect of youth diversion programs on recidivism: A meta-analytic review. *Criminal Justice and Behavior, 40*(5), 497–518.

Wu, L. T., Gersing, K., Burchett, B., Woody, G. E., & Blazer, D. G. (2011). Substance use disorders and comorbid Axis I and II psychiatric disorders among young psychiatric patients: Findings from a large electronic health records database. *Journal of Psychiatric Research, 45*(11), 1453–1462.

# 20
# RESTORATIVE JUSTICE IN K-12 SCHOOLS AS A STRUCTURAL HEALTH EQUITY INTERVENTION

*Jelena Todic, Catherine Cubbin, and Marilyn Armour*

Over the past decade, restorative justice in K-12 schools has gained national prominence because of its documented potential to interrupt the school-to-prison pipeline—a U.-S. phenomenon resulting from the widespread use of zero-tolerance discipline policies that push students out of the classrooms and into the criminal justice system (Rodríguez Ruiz, 2017). In contrast, restorative justice relies on a "whole school relational approach to building school climate and addressing student behavior through fostering belonging over exclusion, social engagement over control, and meaningful accountability over punishment" (Armour, 2014b, n.p.). Surprisingly, despite its simultaneous positive impact on factors associated with adolescent and adult health—academic success, school safety, connectedness, and social support—most scholars and practitioners do not associate restorative justice with population health (Todic, 2018). In the United States, this is especially important because the school-to-prison pipeline disproportionately impacts African Americans, Latinos, Native Americans, and youth with disabilities, who also experience health inequities. Consequently, implementing restorative justice in K-12 schools has the potential to not only interrupt the school-to-prison pipeline, but to also improve educational outcomes for the most marginalized communities in the US and reduce closely associated health inequities (Todic, 2018).

## Education as a Social Determinant of Health

Health inequities or health disparities are the persistent, avoidable, unnecessary, and unjust differences in health outcomes closely associated with economic, social, or environment disadvantage (Walters et al., 2016; Whitehead, 1992). Health equity, on the other hand, refers to the "absence of systemic inequalities in health" (Farrer, Marinetti, Cavaco, & Costongs, 2015, p. 394) and the "right to the highest attainable standard of health as indicated by the health status of the most socially advantaged group" (Braveman & Gruskin, 2003). Evidence overwhelmingly indicates that factors beyond genes, biology, health behaviors, and healthcare have a critical impact on health outcomes and health inequities (The US Department of Health and Human Services, 2016; Walters et al., 2016). These conditions, also called social determinants of health, include differential access to social and economic opportunities; resources available in homes, neighborhoods, and communities; quality of education; workplace safety; cleanliness of water, food, and air; and the quality of social interactions and relationships (HHS, 2016). Intersecting systems of oppression, which grant access to power by social group (e.g., gender, ethnicity, socioeconomic status, sexual orientation) membership, structure these social and physical conditions through current and historical processes (Andersen & Collins, 2015). In turn, social and physical conditions impact health through biological wear-and-tear resulting from repeated experiences with social or economic adversity (Geronimus, 1992), early-life exposure to adverse events, and epigenetic processes that regulate gene expression (Braveman & Gottlieb, 2014). Although the existing evidence does not offer the precise contributions of each determinant of health, it suggests that the social environment may explain up to 40% of population health outcomes (McGovern, Miller, & Hughes-Cromwick, 2014).

According to the World Health Organization (WHO) and Healthy People 2020, education is a critical social determinant of health. More than 30 years of research provides consistent evidence for a strong relationship between education and health, with more educated adults living longer and healthier lives, even after controlling for income and occupation (Braveman, Cubbin, Egerter, Williams, & Pamuk, 2010; Cubbin, Heck, Powell, Marchi, & Braveman, 2015; Kitagawa & Hauser, 1973; Lleras-Muney, 2005; Montez & Hayward, 2014; Rogers, Hummer, Nam, & Peters, 1996). The association between education and health generally has a strong gradient pattern: each educational group has better health outcomes and engages in more health-promoting behaviors than the group below in the educational hierarchy. For example, according to the most recent National Center for Health Statistics' (2018) analysis of the 2016 National Health Interview Survey data, 74% of those with a college degree, 59% of those with some college, and 52% of those with a high school diploma or GED reported excellent or very good health compared to only 41% of those who have not finished high school. Similarly, 6% of those with a college degree, 18% of those with some college, and 24% of those with a high school diploma or GED smoked cigarettes—the leading cause of preventable death in the U.S. according to the Centers for Disease Control and Prevention (2017)–compared to 26% among those who have not finished high school. Generally, more years of education imply better health-related behaviors and health outcomes.

Current research suggests that multiple and interrelated pathways link education with health (Figure 20.1). Education may impact health through increasing health literacy and changing health-related behaviors, increasing a person's sense of control and empowerment, improving life chances through employment opportunities and higher income, and increasing access to health insurance and healthcare (Egerter, Braveman, Sadegh-Nobari, Grossman-Kahn, & Dekker, 2011; Klebanoff Cohen & Syme, 2013). While only a small number of studies demonstrate causality (Amin, Behrman, & Kohler, 2015; Link, Lennon, & Dohrenwend, 1993; Lleras-Muney, 2005; Montez & Hayward, 2014), the 12-year difference in life expectancy between those who have finished high school with a diploma and those with an advanced degree highlights the power of the effect (Braveman, Egerter, & Williams, 2011; Montez & Hayward, 2014). Evidence further suggests that improving overall levels of education can be beneficial not only for individual wellbeing but also for collective wellbeing. A report by the University of California, San Francisco Center on Social Disparities in Health (2008) estimates that the cost of the poorer health of Americans who do not complete high school is $390 billion annually. This number represents a combined cost of $217 billion economic loss due to premature deaths and $173 billion due to poor health, relative to college graduates. Furthermore, if mortality and health status of high school graduates and

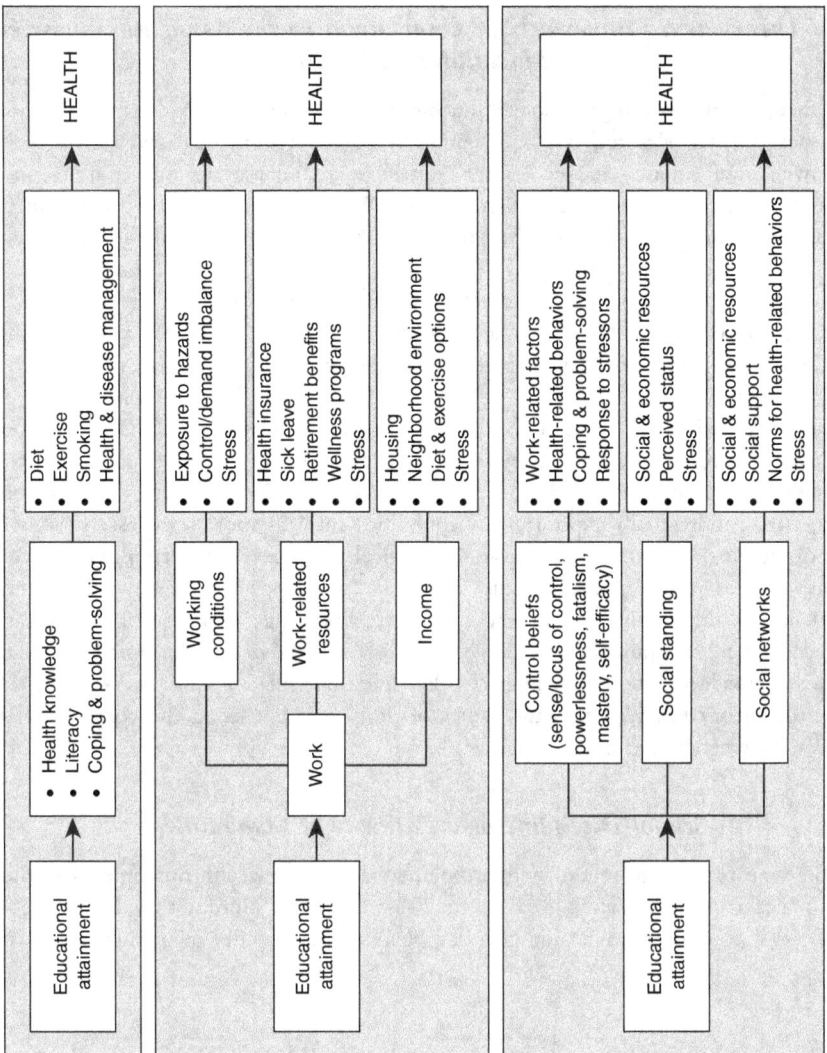

*Figure 20.1* Pathways Linking Education and Health. Source: Egerter, S., Braveman, P., SadeghNobari, T., GrossmanKahn, R., & Dekker M.. (2011). *Education matters for health*. Exploring the social determinants of health (Issue Brief No. 6). Princeton, NJ: Robert Wood Johnson Foundation. Note: Figure 20.1 is publicly available via the Robert Wood Johnson Foundation. See: www.commissiononhealth.org/PDF/c270deb3-ba42-4fbd-baeb-2cd65956f00e/Issue%20Brief%206%20Sept%2009%20-%20Education%20and%20Health.pdf

those who have not completed college matched those of college graduates, the estimated economic benefits would total an additional $618 billion, $264 billion as a result of reduced death rates and $354 billion as a result of improved health status. Combined, the cost amounts to more than one trillion dollars each year. These findings provide a clear direction for intervention and policy priorities: if all Americans finished high school and enjoyed access to quality and affordable higher education, overall population health could improve significantly, saving billions of dollars.

## Ecosocial Theory as a Framework for Understanding the Association between K-12 Education and Health

Ecosocial theory seeks to integrate social and biological reasoning with dynamic, historical, and ecological perspectives (Krieger, 2011). It considers how our individual and collective histories, societal power arrangements, and ecological context "get under our skin," resulting in a literal embodiment of social conditions. The theory asks: "Who and what drives current and changing patterns of social inequalities in health?" (Krieger, 2011, p. 214). While it calls attention to biological processes, it relies on the analysis central to "social production of disease" and "political economy of health" to explain how societal structures, like schools or the economy, impact health. It, therefore, rejects the biomedical perspective, which attributes causes of disease to biological, chemical, and physical phenomena and relies on a single primary principle to explain disease (Krieger, 2011).

The idea of *embodiment* is central to ecosocial theory's explanation of health outcomes and health disparities. Embodiment advances the notion that human bodies exist in the context of social conditions, which leave marks on the body (Krieger, 2005). It represents a cumulative interplay between individual's exposure, susceptibility, and resistance to disease; various contexts (e.g., school, public settings, and work); and ecological resources. For example, social conditions such as paid sick leave, living wage, quality healthcare, access to clean water, and safe neighborhood mark bodies differently than unpaid sick leave, low wage, poor quality healthcare, toxic exposure, and unsafe neighborhoods (Krieger, 2005). Ultimately, it is the human body that tells a story of the broader context in which one has lived, attended school, worked, and aged. In that sense, the theory provides a useful framework for conceptualizing the complex relationship between K-12 education and health (Figure 20.2).

### School Discipline as a Pathway of Embodiment

While those who finish high school with a diploma have better health outcomes than those who drop out or get a GED (Zajacova & Everett, 2014; Zajacova, Hummer, & Rogers, 2012), the impact of K-12 education on health goes far beyond the benefits of a high school diploma.

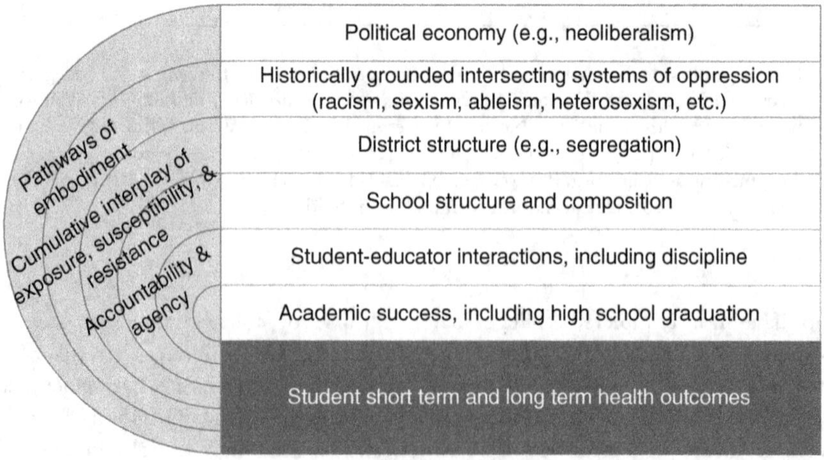

*Figure 20.2* Application of Krieger's (2011) ecosocial theory to understanding factors impacting High school graduation and ultimately health outcomes

Given that K-12 students spend nearly half of their waking weekday hours in school, it is important to also view K-12 schools as essential social structures impacting students' well-being (Farmer & Farmer, 1999). A study using the National Longitudinal Study of Adolescent Health found that school connectedness—the student's belief that adults and peers in the school care about them and their learning—was the strongest predictor of decreased school absenteeism, substance abuse, early sexual initiation, violence, and risk of unintended injury (e.g., drinking and driving; CDC, 2009). School connectedness was the second strongest—after family connectedness—protective factor against emotional distress, eating disorders, and suicidal ideation and attempts (CDC, 2009). Furthermore, a study examining the school and neighborhood effects on depression among adolescents found that the school-level effect was more than three times the neighborhood-level effect, even after controlling for individual-level characteristics (Dunn, Milliren, Evans, Subramanian, & Richmond, 2015).

The overall US high school graduation rate has improved over time; however, graduation outcomes vary (91% for Asian/Pacific Islander students, 88% for Whites, 79% for Latinos, 76% for Blacks, and 72% for American Indians/Alaska natives; National Center for Education Statistics, 2017), reflecting health disparities by race/ethnicity (Centers for Disease Control and Prevention [CDC], 2015). Evidence suggests that a number of interrelated structural and individual factors contribute to school dropout and academic achievement. Rumberger (2011), after reviewing the theoretical literature and almost 300 empirical studies, concluded that dropping out of school was a complicated process, beginning as early as the first grade. Academic failure played a central role in the process, with academic failure in high school as the most powerful predictor of high school graduation. Failing classes in ninth grade appeared to be especially important. High absenteeism and misbehavior also contributed to the process of dropping out. Furthermore, a student's life context was highly influential, with families having the most powerful influence. Lastly, some groups of students, notably Black, Latino, and Native American, students with disabilities, and low-income students, were at high risk for dropping out as a result of structural barriers and injustices they faced at home, at school, and in the community.

A substantial body of evidence suggests that harsh school discipline practices are a powerful example of structural barriers and injustices contributing to high school dropout and negative school climate. Over the past several decades, school discipline trends have dramatically shifted towards retributive practices and criminalization of youth behavior. The roots of these trends date back to the 1980s, when schools adopted zero-tolerance policies (initially developed by the U.S. Customs Agency to target the expanding drug trade) to discourage drug use among students (Curtis, 2014; Skiba & Rausch, 2006). The Gun-Free Schools Act (GFSA) of 1994 furthered the criminalizing trend by requiring states to pass laws that mandated schools to expel students who brought a weapon to school (Martinez, 2009). Most communities across the country fully embraced zero-tolerance policies and expanded policies far beyond the required response to firearms on school property. By the 1996–1997 school year, 94% of public schools had zero-tolerance policies for firearms, 91% for weapons other than firearms, 88% for drugs, 87% for alcohol, and 79% for violence (Curtis, 2014).

Today, the use of security measures in American public schools is pervasive, despite the fact that decades of data (Curtis, 2014; Poulin Carlton, 2017) tend to suggest that, overall, school violence has remained stable or decreased. The percentage of schools with a police officer on site has increased from less than 1% of schools in 1975 to 40% of schools by 2008 (Na & Gottfredson, 2013). During the 2015–2016 school year, 77% of schools with 1,000 or more enrolled students reported having one or more school resource officers present at least one day per week, compared to 47% of schools with 500–999 enrolled students, 36% of schools with 300–499 students, and 24% with less than 300 students (Diliberti, Jackson, & Kemp, 2017). Furthermore, approximately half of high schools perform random inspections using drug-sniffing dogs and a quarter use security cameras and perform random contraband checks (Finn & Servoss, 2014). Although the most recent Summary of School Safety Statistics (Poulin Cartlon, 2017) suggests that violent crime against students increased from 2010 to 2013 (from 17 to 37 per 1,000 students), the violent crime rate in 2013 was still lower than the rate in 1992 (68 per 1,000 students). Students' fear of being harmed has also decreased, with the percentage of students who reported being afraid of attack or harm at or on the way to and from school decreasing from 12% in 1995 to 3% in 2013. Finally, school homicide—frequently cited as the reason for zero-tolerance policies—has remained relatively constant between 1992 and 2011, constituting less than 3% of all youth homicides (Curtis, 2014; Poulin Carlton, 2017). While high-profile incidents of violence at U.S. schools justifiably raise concerns about school safety and contribute to increased attention to discipline, it is important to note that current scientific evidence does not suggest an epidemic of school violence in need of severe school discipline or safety measures.

However, scientific evidence does suggest that zero tolerance policies, which were instituted to increase school safety and maintain school norms, have an alarmingly negative impact on academic success, including high school graduation, and school climate. While causality cannot be concluded, empirical evidence indicates a strong relationship between the zero tolerance policies, which include suspensions and expulsions, on the one hand and dropout rates and juvenile justice involvement on the other. A suspension is frequently the first step in a chain of events leading to academic disengagement, academic failure, dropout, and delinquency (American Psychological Association, 2008; Balfanz, Byrnes, & Fox, 2015; Skiba, Arredondo, & Rausch, 2014). A longitudinal study following one million Texas seventh graders found that students who were suspended or expelled, and especially those who experienced repeated suspensions and expulsions, were more likely to repeat a grade or to drop out than students who did not have disciplinary system experiences (Fabelo et al., 2011). Moreover, Perry and Morris (2014) found that schools with high rates of exclusionary discipline over time generate "collateral damage," also negatively affecting the reading and math achievement of students who are not suspended.

Finally, a recent study points to the long-term negative implications of school suspensions for adult outcomes. According to a recent study that compared the educational and criminal justice outcomes of 480 youth suspended for the first time with those of 1,193 matched nonsuspended youth, suspended youth were less likely to have graduated from high school or college and were more likely to have been arrested and on probation than matched nonsuspended youth twelve years after suspension (ages 25–32; Rosenbaum, 2018). Students who are excluded from class or placed in alternative education programs miss essential instruction time and, as a result, fall behind (Advancement Project, 2014; Armour, 2016; Rausch & Skiba, 2017). Opportunity to learn is the strongest predictor of academic achievement; thus, it is not surprising that suspensions and expulsions lead to course failure, academic disengagement, and eventually school dropout (Skiba, Arredondo, & Rausch, 2014). Given this dynamic, the Advancement Project (2010) suggested referring to student attrition in schools employing criminalizing policies as schools "pushing out" students rather than students "dropping out" of schools.

Contrary to their intention, the zero-tolerance policies also do not appear to improve school climate. The American Psychological Association's (2008) extensive literature review found that the limited available data on the impact of zero-tolerance policies tended to contradict the assumption that the removal of disruptive students will result in a safer climate for others more conducive to learning. Instead, higher rates of suspensions and expulsions decrease feelings of safety (Skiba, Mediratta, & Rausch, 2016) and lead to less satisfactory ratings of school climate (American Psychological Association Zero Tolerance Task Force, 2008; Skiba, Mediratta, & Rausch, 2016). Additionally, these policies have resulted in criminalization of student misbehavior (e.g., ticketing, arrests) that schools commonly handled internally in the past (Fowler,

Lightsey, Monger, & Aseltine, 2010). Most recently, the American Academy of Pediatrics (2013) issued a policy statement warning about the ineffectiveness of zero-tolerance policies, outlining negative life outcomes associated with punitive discipline such as involvement with the criminal justice system and high school dropout, and highlighting the short- and long-term harms of such policies to students, families, and communities. Indeed, the long term fallout from these policies has strong implications for individuals and society.

*The Disproportionate Impact of Punitive Discipline on Students of Color and Students with Disabilities*

While harsh school discipline practices negatively impact all students, they have profoundly negative implications for academic, and ultimately health outcomes, of students of color and students with disabilities. Youth of color do not misbehave more than their White peers (Anyon et al., 2014; Bradshaw, Mitchell, O'Brennan, & Leaf, 2010; Payne & Welch, 2010); yet, race remains a significant predictor of out-of-school suspension regardless of the severity of behavior (Skiba et al., 2011). Punitive discipline disproportionately impacts African American, Latino, and Native American youth, boys, youth with disabilities, and LGBT youth (Fabelo et al., 2011; Himmelstein & Brückner, 2011; Losen & Martinez, 2013; Skiba, Mediratta, & Rausch, 2016; U.S. Department of Education Office of Civil Rights, 2014; Whitford & Levine-Donnerstein, 2014). Black students are the most vulnerable. According to the U.S. Department of Education Office of Civil Rights (2014), on average, 5% of White students are suspended, compared to 16% of Black students. Black students are also more likely to get arrested, be referred to law enforcement, and be restrained at school through the use of mechanical devices or equipment designed to restrict the freedom of movement than White students (U.S. Department of Education Office of Civil Rights, 2014). Studies demonstrate that, compared to White students, Black students are more likely to receive every type of discipline, from minor office referrals to suspensions and expulsions, for the same or lesser offenses (Anyon et al., 2014; Schollenberger, 2015). Even more alarming is that the use of punitive discipline begins as early as preschool, with African American children being the most likely to get suspended (United States Department of Eduction, Office for Civil Rights, 2014). The pattern continues through elementary and middle school (Skiba et al., 2011). Given the overlap of race and poverty in the U.S., it is also important to highlight that studies controlling for socioeconomic status, consistently found that being Black is an independent predictor of disproportionality in school discipline (Rausch & Skiba, 2017), although it is not possible to completely "control" for socioeconomic status (Braveman et al., 2015)

African American boys bear most of the harsh school discipline burden; however, they are not alone. Fabelo et al. (2011) found that, compared to 59% of White male students, 83% of African American and 74% of Hispanic male students had at least one discretionary violation. Other studies have also revealed that Latino students are at increased risk of school punishment (Kupchik, 2010; Kupchik & Ellis, 2008; Peguero & Shekarkhar, 2011). American Indian and Native-Alaskan students, including American Indian students in special education, are also disproportionately suspended and expelled (Whitford, 2017; Whitford & Levine-Donnerstein, 2014). They represent 2% of out-of-school suspensions and 3% of expulsions, but less than 1% of the student population (U.S. Department of Education Office of Civil Rights, 2014). Finally, students with disabilities across all racial groups are twice as likely (13%) to get suspended as their peers who do not have a disability (Carter, Fine, & Russell, 2014).

While the disproportionate impact of punitive school discipline on boys has been well established in the literature, researchers have notably paid less attention to the experiences of girls, and girls of color in particular. According to the Department of Education 2011–2012 data, Black males were suspended at an alarming rate—more than three times as often as their White peers; however, Black girls were suspended six times as often as White girls (Crenshaw, Ocen, &

Nanda, 2015). Compared to White girls, Black girls receive disproportionately more referrals for disruptive behavior, dress code violations, disobedience, and aggressive behavior (Morris & Perry, 2017). Black girls with darker complexions appear to be especially at risk, compared to Black girls with lighter skin complexions (Blake, Keith, Luo, Le, & Salter, 2017). American Indian and Native-Alaskan girls (7%) are also suspended at higher rates than White boys (6%) or girls (2%; U.S. Department of Education Office of Civil Rights, 2014). In fact, they are actually more likely than Native American boys to receive in-school suspension, out-of-school suspension, expulsion either with or without educational services, and a referral to law enforcement (Martin, Sharp-Grier, & Smith, 2016). Finally, among LGBT students, girls had the highest risk of being stopped by a police officer (Himmelstein & Brückner, 2011). Crenshaw, Ocen and Nanda (2015) refer to this lack of attention to the experiences of girls of color in research, policy, and practice as "the multidimensional and cross-institutional silence." This silence produces undereducated activists, community members, and educators who, in turn, ignore the 'consequences of punitive discipline on girls as well as the distinctly gendered dynamics of zero-tolerance environments that limit their educational achievement' (p. 11).

## Bias and Disproportionality in Discipline

While the studies document a nationwide use of harsh zero-tolerance policies, it must be noted that their implementation is largely a choice controlled by individual schools and districts. In fact, school-level characteristics such as school composition, combined with the individual-level factors such as educator's beliefs, are important predictors of how schools may approach responding to student misconduct. For instance, schools with larger proportion of enrolled Black, Hispanic, and low-income students are more likely to use harsh discipline than schools with schools with smaller proportion (Payne & Welch, 2010, 2015, 2018). Students attending these schools have a higher risk for suspension after accounting for student-level demographic and behaviors, than students attending schools with smaller proportion of low income or students of color (Anyon et al., 2014; Hannon, DeFina, & Bruch, 2013; Skiba et al., 2011, 2014). Other school variables such as mean school achievement and self-reported principal perspectives toward school discipline appear to be the strongest predictors of racial disparities in discipline (Skiba et al., 2014).

In addition to these school-level predictors, individual teachers' biases at the classroom level (Girvan, Gion, McIntosh, & Smolkowski, 2017) and administrators' biases during the disciplining processes significantly contribute to the disproportionality in school discipline outcomes (Skiba et al., 2011). A large body of empirical evidence documents the harmful effects of racial bias on people of color in diverse contexts, including educational settings. While a number of factors may contribute to discipline disparities, school personnel's internalized beliefs—reflective of the stereotypical and usually negative views of people of color, women, people with disabilities, and LGBT individuals—play a powerful role (Carter, Skiba, Arredondo, & Pollock, 2017; Gregory & Roberts, 2017). Data indicate that the types of referrals resulting in disproportionality are most likely to be in categories that are discretionary, such as defiance and disrespect (Girvan, Gion, McIntosh, & Smolkowski, 2017). These discretionary categories do not have clear guidelines such as suspending any student who brings a firearm to the school grounds and educators' internalized beliefs especially matter because they influence the subjective interpretation of the situation.

The ongoing process of implicit bias, micro-aggression and colorblindness continue to reinforce "race"—a socially constructed consequence of slavery and conquest—and shape school discipline patterns (Carter, Skiba, Arredondo, & Pollock, 2017), which have long-range consequential health implications for students. For example, American schools and districts remain segregated by race and income (Bohrnstedt, Kitmitto, Ogut, Sherman, & Chan, 2015; Orfield, Kuscera, & Siegel-Hawley, 2012; Reardon & Owens, 2014) often resulting in limited educational opportunities for low income and youth of color, as well as limited meaningful interactions across racial and ethnic social group boundaries. Furthermore, the majority of U.S teachers are still White, middle-class women (Villegas, Strom, & Lucas, 2012). To that point, Marchbanks, Peguero, Varela, Blake, and Eason (2018) found that juvenile justice referral rates in urban schools increased as the student–teacher racial and ethnic incongruence increased.

Another example of the power of internalized narratives about race to shape discipline practices is adultification. In the context of school discipline practices, adultification refers to the cultural stereotype based on adults' view of children, in part due to their race (Blake, Keith, Luo, Le, & Salter, 2017; Epstein, Blake, & González, 2017; Goff et al., 2014). For instance, research has shown that adults see Black boys, beginning at the age of ten, as older and less innocent (Goff et al., 2014). As a result, adults are less likely to grant them the protections of childhood they give to their White peers and view them as guilty of suspected crime. Similarly, a recent study found that adults perceived that Black girls needed less nurturing, protection, support, and comfort, viewing them as more independent and more knowledgeable about adult topics and sex compared to White girls of the same age (Epstein, Blake, & González, 2017). Overall, the evidence points to the alarming need to address racism explicitly in teacher training, school-based interventions design, and policy development; yet, despite the need, these processes often remain colorblind, treating racism and other structural inequities as extraneous factors (Carter, Skiba, Arredondo, & Pollock, 2017; Gregory & Roberts, 2017).

## Schools as Sites of Structural Interventions

School discipline policies and practices are an excellent example of how social structures impact health and affect individual choices, risks, and ultimately health, as described above in the review of zero tolerance policies and their consequences. Structural public health interventions promote health by altering the structural context within which heath is produced and reproduced (Blankenship, Friedman, Dworkin, & Mantell, 2006). Rather than focusing on how characteristics of individuals affect their health and risk behaviors, structural interventions target contextual or environmental factors that influence those outcomes and behaviors. Structural interventions assume a degree of social causation and, in that sense, recognize that social structures limit individual autonomy, placing constraints on individual agency (Blankenship, Friedman, Dworkin, & Mantell, 2006).

Given the abundance of evidence documenting the negative effects of school discipline policies and practices on academic achievement, especially the academic achievement of students of color and students with disabilities, it is necessary to conceptualize these dynamics as a structural failure in need of structural interventions. Despite this need, a recent systematic review of 25 experimental or quasi-experimental studies aiming to improve high school completion rates found that most of these interventions (79%) were limited to a single school component, individual students, or small groups of students (Freeman & Simonsen, 2015). The authors also noted a "surprising lack of emphasis" in the literature on developing structural interventions that address broader community issues such as poverty and structural racism (Freeman & Simonsen, 2015). They urged intervention researchers to (1) go beyond the typical school boundaries, and (2) form meaningful and effective partnerships with community agencies, community mental health supports, and other public health initiatives to address the effects of poverty and racism. Similarly, while health researchers are paying increasing attention to the impact of school on health outcomes (American Public Health Association,

2018; Hale et al., 2014), most still approach intervention research from only the biomedical and lifestyle perspectives, which emphasize the role of individuals and minimize the effect of social structures on population health (Krieger, 2011). The health intervention research still primarily focuses on schools as sites for treatment or individual behavioral change such as healthy eating or exercise. As discussed earlier, it is critical that researchers and practitioners broaden their perspective so they can begin to view K–12 schools as essential structures with significant consequences for both educational and health outcomes.

## *School-Based Restorative Justice as a Structural Intervention*

Restorative justice, rooted in the traditional practices of the indigenous people of North America and New Zealand as well as peace philosophy of the U.S. Mennonite community, seeks to involve all impacted by an offense to collectively repair harms and "put things as right as possible" (Zehr, 2002, p. 37). According to restorative justice philosophy, any misconduct is a violation of people and relationships rather than a violation of the law or rules (Zehr, 2002). As a result, violations create obligations to address the needs of those who have been harmed, the wrongdoer(s), and the community. Providing an opportunity for those most directly impacted by the harm to be involved in responding to and repairing the harm is a central feature of the restorative process (Zehr, 2002). In that sense, restorative justice is a relational process that integrates support with accountability (Morrison & Vaandering, 2012, p. 141).

Over the past several decades, schools and districts across the United States adopted restorative justice to address youth misconduct and build supportive school communities. In schools, restorative justice philosophy translates into building a relational ecology, which relies on relationships and belonging as a motivator for change rather than fear (Morrison & Vaandering, 2012). Within the relational ecology context, members of the school community make changes because they care about each other rather than fear punitive consequences. Unlike most institutional responses, which focus on establishing the facts (e.g., the criminal justice system), restorative practices work with "social, emotional, and spiritual dimensions that make up the rich motivational ecologies within the lives of individuals and communities" (Morrison & Vaandering, 2012, p. 141).

While schools implement restorative justice in different ways, scholars and practitioners emphasize that the most successful approach is to focus on the whole school and building a caring school community (Armour & Todic, 2016; González, 2015; McCluskey et al., 2011; Riestenberg, 2012; Thorsborne & Blood, 2013). Blood and Thorsborne's (2005) three-tier model (Figure 20.3) outlines the components of relational ecology at each level of the model. Primary or Tier 1 practices (e.g., classroom circles to "check in" with students at the beginning or develop classroom values) are central to the whole school approach because they focus on developing social and emotional skills essential for building relational ecology. Tier 1 practices strengthen and reaffirm relationships among the community members. They assist with identifying common values and guidelines and promote and strengthen a sense of belonging and ownership. When the whole school community rests on a foundation of restorative principles, the caring and supportive culture is always present (Kidde & Alfred, 2011). Consequently, responding to difficulties and harmful incidents in a supportive rather than a punitive way is just another manifestation of the culture in which everyone belongs and is worthy of other's compassion (Gardella, 2015). Secondary or Tier 2 practices (e.g., problem-solving circles, hallway conferences, restorative conversations, and peer mediation) build on the Tier 1 practices and focus on managing difficulties. Tier 2 practices aim to prevent harm, resolve differences, and build social–emotional capacity. Finally, Tier 3 practices (e.g., intervention circles, restorative conferencing) repair and reintegrate after harm occurs, focus on accountability, and rebuild relationships through intensive practices such as conferencing. Together, these three practices enable

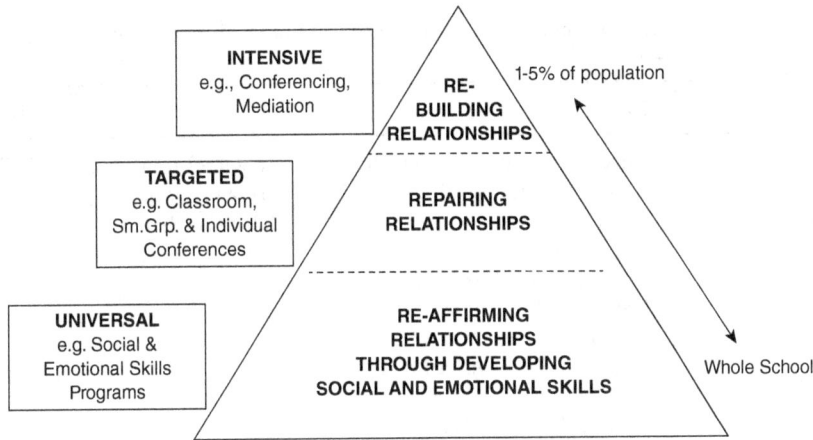

*Figure 20.3* Hierarchy of restorative responses, Blood and Thorsborne (2005). Note: The authors received permission to use this image that was initially included in a doctoral dissertation.

a community affected by harm or wrongdoing to address it through "nurturing the human capacity for restitution, resolution, and reconciliation" (Morrison & Vaandering, 2012, p. 140). Restitution repairs harm, resolution reduces the risk of its reoccurrence, and reconciliation brings emotional healing (Morrison & Vaandering, 2012). As a result, restorative justice transforms the school from a social structure in which adults do things 'to' students, diminishing their agency, to a social structure in which adults do things 'with' students, building their capacity for agency. In turn, students feel included and are an active part of the decision-making that affects the outcome or consequence of their behavior and the behavior of their peers.

School-based restorative justice is a structural intervention because it aims to fundamentally transform schools as social structures within which heath is produced and reproduced. Unlike punitive zero-tolerance policies, which exclude students from the school community, circles and other restorative practices reintegrate an offending student as a productive member of the community, thereby decreasing the potential for separation, resentment, recidivism (González, 2012), and ultimately dropout. The community recognizes the undesirable behavior as harmful, while also treating the person engaging in harm as a valued member who can make different choices in the future (Riestenberg, 2012). As such, restorative justice targets the community and how students belong rather than their misconduct *per se*. Ultimately, it recognizes that the institutionalized and socially acceptable punitive approach to discipline is a contextual factor that negatively influences individual student outcomes and aims to replace it with a context that produces positive short- and long-term outcomes, including health.

While more rigorous studies are needed, early evidence suggests that restorative practice in schools can (1) reduce office referrals, suspensions, and expulsions; (2) improve attendance; (3) improve academic achievement; (4) reduce violence, offenses, and repeated misbehaviors; (5) improve parental engagement and parent–child relationships; (6) improve school climate; (7) improve social and emotional skills and wellbeing; and reduce racial disparities in discipline. Table 20.1 presents outcomes from 25 studies, dissertations, and evaluation reports conducted in the U.S., Canada, Australia and the U.K. between 2000 and 2018. In the educational literature, these conditions are associated with academic success (Morgan, Salomon, Plotkin, & Cohen, 2014), dropout prevention (Freudenberg & Ruglis, 2007), and adolescent health (CDC, 2009). For example, evidence suggests that having the opportunity to learn is

*Table 20.1* Review of literature examining the association between restorative justice in schools and health-associated outcomes, 2000–2018

| Outcome | Positive | Negative | No Change |
|---|---|---|---|
| Reduce Office Referrals, Suspensions and Expulsions | Anyon et al. (2014) Anyon (2016) Armour (2013, 2014a [ISS], 2015a [overall]) Baker (2008) Gregory, Allen, Mikami, Hafen and Pianta (2014) González (2015) Jain, Bassey, Brown, & Kalra, (2014) Mansfield, Fowler, & Rainbolt (2018) Reistenberg (2003) Sumner, Silverman and Frampton (2010) | Armour (2014a [OSS], 2015a [some grades]) Baker (2008) one school | Todic (2018) |
| Improve Attendance | Armour (2014a) Baker (2008, 2009) McMorris, Beckman, Baumgartner and Eggert (2014) Jain, Bassey, Brown and Kalra (2014) Rideout, Karen, Salinitri and Marc (2010 [HS only]) Todic (2018) | Todic (2018) | Todic (2018) |
| Improve Academic Achievement | Armour (2014a) Baker (2008) González (2015) Jain, Bassey, Brown and Kalra (2014) McMorris, Beckman, Baumgartner and Eggert (2014) Rideout, Karen, Salinitri and Marc (2010 [elementary only]) Todic (2018) | Armour (2015a) Todic (2018) | Norris (2009) |
| Reduction in Violence, Offenses, and Repeated Misbehavior | Kelly (2017) Lewis (2009) Mansfield et al. (2018) McCold (2002, 2008) McMorris, Beckman, Baumgartner and Eggert (2014) Mirsky (2007) Sumner, Silverman and Frampton (2010) | Armour (2014) | |

(Continued)

Table 20.1 (Cont.)

| Outcome | Positive | Negative | No Change |
| --- | --- | --- | --- |
| Improve Parental Engagement or Parent–Child Relationships | Baker (2008, 2009)<br>Sumner, Silverman and Frampton (2010)<br>McMorris, Beckman, Baumgartner and Eggert (2014) | | |
| Improve Climate | Armour (2015a)<br>Gregory, Allen, Mikami, Hafen and Pianta (2014)<br>Jain, Bassey, Brown and Kalra (2014)<br>Mirsky (2007)<br>Sumner, Silverman and Frampton (2010) | Armour (2014a, 2015a)<br>Todic (2018) | Todic, 2018 |
| Improve Social and Emotional Skills and Wellbeing | Armour (2014a)<br>Jain, Bassey, Brown and Kalra (2014)<br>McCold (2002) (2008)<br>McMorris, Beckman, Baumgartner and Eggert (2014)<br>Mirsky (2007a, 2007b)<br>Sumner, Silverman and Frampton (2010) | | |
| Reduce Racial Disparities | Gregory, Allen, Mikami, Hafen and Pianta (2014)<br>González (2015)<br>Jain, Bassey, Brown and Kalra (2014)<br>Mansfield et al. (2018) | Armour (2015a [Latino students]) | Anyon (2016)<br>Armour (2015a) |

the strongest predictor of academic achievement (Skiba, Arredondo, & Rausch, 2014). Missing 10% or more of the school year predicts poor academic performance in middle school and increased likelihood of dropping out from high school (Allensworth & Easton, 2007). At risk populations are particularly vulnerable. Specifically, students living in poverty, students of color, and students with disabilities have disproportionately higher rates of chronic absenteeism (Ready, 2010) which concomitantly impacts performance.

School-based restorative justice is still a developing approach to building a positive school climate and responding to misbehavior. The majority of studies we reviewed (Table 20.1) are descriptive or use a pre-post evaluation design without randomization/control groups, making it difficult to conclude that generally positive outcomes listed in Table 20.1 are in fact a result of restorative justice implementation. At the same time, these studies establish a foundation for further investigating the effects of restorative practices through more rigorous research designs. Currently, there are three randomized control trials underway in the U.S., one funded by the National Institute of Health and two supported by the National Institute of Justice (Fronius, Persson, Guckenburg, Hurley, & Petrosino, 2016).

## Approach to Implementation to Ensure Structural Transformation

Despite its powerful emphasis on interdependence, intentional examination of power, and meaningful response to harm, restorative justice as a field is most often associated with individual behavior changes such as reduction in misbehavior, recidivism, and crime. Indeed, school-based restorative justice offers a blueprint for structural transformation of individual and systemic harms such as health or educational inequities, but teams implementing it must ensure two conditions: they must target the whole school and incorporate structural analysis of complex social conditions that result in discipline disproportionality.

Scholars and practitioners agree that the whole school approach to restorative practices is necessary to ensure positive student and climate outcomes, which is consistent with the structural health equity intervention. Morrison, Blood, and Thorsborne (2006) insist that successful implementation requires a paradigm shift away from restorative practices as a program and towards understanding restorative practices as a philosophy that needs to be integrated it into all aspects of the school structure. As is true for any practice that targets fundamental shifts in core beliefs and institutional structures, this long-term nonlinear process requires time—between three and six years (Armour, 2016; González, 2015; Morrison, Blood, & Thorsborne, 2006). Table 20.2 outlines the timeframe. A number of U.S.-based case studies—Oakland Unified School District, Los Angeles Unified School District, San Francisco Unified School District, and Denver Public Schools, for example—also highlight the importance of district-wide implementation. Based on the success of the Denver Public Schools' implementation of restorative practices, González (2015)—in addition to affirming many of the strategies Thorsborne and Blood (2013) outline—emphasizes the importance of adopting district-wide disciplinary policy and practices that integrate restorative principles and philosophy. Furthermore, Gardella (2015) points to the relevance of Bryk, Sebring, Allensworth, Luppescu, and Easton (2010) evidence-based Framework of Essential Supports and Contextual Resources for School Improvement for successful implementation of restorative justice in schools. The framework emphasizes transformative leadership powered by capable staff, high academic expectations, and strong school-community ties as necessary elements of any successful school improvement efforts.

While school-based restorative justice holds promise as a structural health intervention, the evidence on its ability to reduce racial disparities in discipline is mixed. Emerging literature suggests that restorative justice can reduce disparities in discipline disproportionality (González, 2015; Gregory, Allen, Mikami, Hafen, & Pianta, 2014; Jain, Bassey, Brown, & Kalra, 2014; Mansfield, Fowler, & Rainbolt, 2018), but that this is not always the case (Anyon et al., 2016; Armour, 2015b; see Table 20.1). Anyon et al. (2016) found that a district-wide implementation

*Table 20.2* Timeframe and indicators of change, Morrison, Blood, and Thorsborne (2006)

| | |
|---|---|
| 12–18 months | Gaining commitment. Changing dialogue. Pockets of practice. Improved statistics. Increased options for managing behavior. |
| 12–24 months | Altered dialogue and processes. Alignment of policy and procedure. Increased skill development. School community commitment. |
| 24–36 months | Embedding of practice at all levels. Altered operating framework. Reviewing policy and procedure. Creative solutions emerge. |
| 4–5 years | Best practice. Behavior change embedded. Cultural change across school community. |

of restorative justice reduced the overall odds of receiving office discipline referrals and suspensions. At the same time, the suspension gap between Black and White students persisted. Similarly, Armour (2015b) found that, after three years of restorative practices implementation in one middle school, the overall in-school suspensions decreased by 66% compared to the baseline; however, the disparities between Black and White students in disciplinary office referrals persisted in the third year of implementation. Furthermore, the proportion of Latino students receiving disciplinary office referrals increased by more than 4%. Overall implementation challenges during the third year may in part explain these changes. Even more troubling is the body of evidence that demonstrates that the school's composition predicts the likelihood of implementing restorative practices. Students attending schools with higher proportions of Black and Latino students are at higher risk for suspension after accounting for student-level demographic and behaviors (Marchbanks, Peguero, Varela, Blake, & Eason, 2018; Anyon, 2014; Hannon, DeFina, & Bruch, 2013; Skiba et al., 2011). Unfortunately, schools with large percentages of Black, Hispanic, and low-income students are more likely to use harsh discipline and less likely to implement restorative practices (Payne & Welch, 2010, 2015, 2018).

In many instances, restorative justice regrettably remains focused on individual student behaviors. The approach gets applied alongside retributive discipline policies and with little regard for the effects of implicit bias or the consequences of historically grounded structural inequities that are embedded in schools as well as other U.S. institutions. As such, some scholars suggest that school-based restorative justice may be failing the marginalized communities they are meant to support. Indeed, if restorative practices are implemented without regard to implicit biases, subtle forms of power and intimidation, the current culture of high-stakes accountability, and the ominous replication of larger social and economic inequities, a promising option could miss the mark. Restorative justice could become just another tool of social control undermining authentic interpersonal engagement and the transformative power of restorative justice (Lustick, 2017).

There is, however, growing recognition about the importance of explicitly addressing structural inequities, and institutionalized racism in particular, to improve educational outcomes. For example, widely used behavioral interventions such as Positive Behavioral Interventions and Supports (PBIS) or Social Emotional Learning (SEL) programs reduce overall office referrals. They do not necessarily, however, reduce disparities in discipline (Rausch & Skiba, 2017). In their comprehensive review of school discipline literature, Rausch and Skiba (2017) highlight that any effort to minimize disparities in school discipline must desegregate data to monitor the reduction in disproportionality and explicitly focus on cultural responsiveness by centering equity. In another paper, Gregory and Fergus (2017) discuss why the prevailing "colorblind" approaches to SEL hold limited promise for reducing disparities in discipline. Specifically, SEL focuses only on students and ignores the role of adults thereby reducing its ability to impact the social structure of the school. Alternatively, the authors describe SEL efforts in one school, which stresses equity and promotes both adults' and students' SEL competencies. In another paper, Gregory, Skiba, and Mediratta (2017) synthesize available research and recommend a framework for culturally conscious implementation of reform, warning against the typical approaches, which ignore power, privilege, and cultural difference. Furthermore, Lustick (2017) recommends the use of culturally responsive pedagogy and a Foucauldian lens to construct spaces in which students and staff can bring their authentic selves to the restorative process. As a result, they may be able to reflect on their actual contributions to the conflict and have a chance of repairing authentic relationships, rather than "the traditional power structures of schools" (p. 308). Others, like Vaandering (2010), Anyon et al. (2018), and Wadhwa (2010, 2017) recommend the use of critical theory and critical race theory in restorative work in schools. This emphasis, in the broadest sense of the term, aims to explain and transform all the circumstances that enslave and dehumanize people. Indeed, these scholars suggest that critical theory can inform the process of analyzing issues prior to deciding to implement restorative practices and throughout the implementation process to ensure implementation actually reduces disparities. Finally, Crenshaw and colleagues (2015) make a strong case for the importance of intersectional feminist critical analysis to ensure human rights of all youth disproportionately impacted by punitive discipline practices. Consequently, restorative practices, enhanced by these critical lenses, could indeed come closer to fulfilling its potential to transform unjust school structures and, as a result, reduce inequities in education, health, and incarceration.

## Conclusion

After reviewing the early evidence on the effects of restorative practices in schools in light of transdisciplinary empirical evidence, we suggest that restorative practices may be not only effective as an alternative to zero-tolerance policies, but also as a structural intervention with significant implications for population health. Considering that last year 50.4 million students attended 98,300 public schools, the size of that effect is of enormous importance. More evidence utilizing nationally representative samples, randomized control trials, multilevel modeling, and qualitative methods to understand the impact of restorative practices on health is needed.

While we encourage researchers–practitioner partnership to generate more sound evidence for school-based restorative justice association, we find that analyzing the current evidence through the ecosocial theoretical framework is instructive. *Healthy People 2020*, the science-based ten-year national objectives for improving Americans' health, recognizes that social conditions such as economic opportunities, neighborhoods and community resources, and the nature of social relationships explain in part why some people are healthier than others (The US Department of Health and Human Services, 2016). Consequently, it supports policies and interventions that positively influence social and economic circumstances, such as education, as a strategy to improve health for large numbers of people.

Restorative practices in schools hold the potential to simultaneously interrupt the school-to-prison pipeline, improve educational outcomes, and address health inequities at a root-level. Given this, public health professionals, social workers, educators, criminologists, and policymakers should collectively advocate for this structural intervention and policies that support implementation and rigorous evaluation of restorative practices in K-12 schools.

## References

Advancement Project. (2010). Test, punish, and push out: How "zero tolerance" and high-stakes testing funnel youth into the school-to-prison pipeline (revised). Retrieved from www.ushrnetwork.org/sites/ushrnetwork.org/files/test_punsih_push_out.pdf

Advancement Project. (2014). Restorative practices: Fostering healthy relationships & promoting positive discipline in schools. Retrieved from https://advancementproject.org/resources/restorative-practices-fostering-healthy-relationships-promoting-positive-discipline-in-schools/

Allensworth, E. M., & Easton, J. Q. (2007). What matters for staying on-track and graduating in Chicago public high schools: A close look at course grades, failures, and attendance in the freshman year. Consortium on Chicago School Research at The University of Chicago. Retrieved from https://consortium.uchicago.edu/sites/default/files/publications/07%20What%20Matters%20Final.pdf

American Academy of Pediatrics, Council on School Health. (2013). Out-of-school suspensions and expulsions. Retrieved from http://pediatrics.aappublications.org/content/early/2013/02/20/peds.2012-3932

American Psychological Association Zero Tolerance Task Force. (2008). Are zero tolerance policies effective in the schools?: An evidentiary review and recommendations. *The American Psychologist*, *63*(9), 852.

American Public Health Association. (2018). Chronic stress and the risk of high school dropout. Retrieved from www.schoolbasedhealthcare.org/-/media/files/pdf/sbhc/chronic_stress.ashx?la=en&hash=F5FB7AF535D2CDA4CBC81236DBCE6580B53607E4

Amin, V., Behrman, J. R., & Kohler, H.-P. (2015). Schooling has smaller or insignificant effects on adult health in the US than suggested by cross-sectional associations: New estimates using relatively large samples of identical twins. *Social Science & Medicine*, *127*(0), 181–189.

Andersen, M., & Collins, P. H. (2015). *Race, class, & gender: An anthology*. Boston, MA: Cengage Learning.

Anyon, Y. (2016). *Taking restorative practices school-wide: Insights from three schools in Denver*. Denver, CO: Denver School-Based Restorative Justice Partnership.

Anyon, Y., Jenson, J. M., Altschul, I., Farrar, J., McQueen, J., Greer, E., Downing, B., & Simmons, J. (2014). The persistent effect of race and the promise of alternatives to suspension in-school discipline outcomes. *Children and Youth Services Review*, *44*, 379–386.

Anyon, Y., Gregory, A., Stone, S., Farrar, J., Jenson, J. M., McQueen, J., … Simmons, J. (2016). Restorative interventions and school discipline sanctions in a large urban school district. *American Educational Research Journal*, *53*(6), 1663–1697.

Anyon, Y., Jenson, J. M., Altschul, I., Farrar, J., McQueen, J., Greer, E., … Simmons, J. (2014). The persistent effect of race and the promise of alternatives to suspension in school discipline outcomes. *Children and Youth Services Review*, *44*, 379–386.

Anyon, Y., Lechuga, C., Ortega, D., Downing, B., Greer, E., & Simmons, J. (2018). An exploration of the relationships between student racial background and the school sub-contexts of office discipline referrals: A critical race theory analysis. *Race, Ethnicity & Education*, *21*(3), 390–406.

Armour, M. (2013). *Ed White Middle School restorative discipline evaluation: 2012/2013*. Austin, TX: Institute for Restorative Justice and Restorative Dialogue, The University of Texas at Austin.

Armour, M. (2014a). *Ed White Middle School restorative discipline evaluation: 2013/2014*. Austin, TX: Institute for Restorative Justice and Restorative Dialogue, The University of Texas at Austin.

Armour, M. (June 25, 2014b). *Restorative disciple: A whole school approach*. Paper presented at the 10th annual Texas Behavior Support State Conference, Houston, TX.

Armour, M. (2015a). Restorative practices: Righting the wrongs of exclusionary school discipline. *University of Richmond Law Review*, *50*, 999.

Armour, M. (2015b). *Ed White Middle School restorative discipline evaluation: 2014/2015*. Austin, TX: Institute for Restorative Justice and Restorative Dialogue, The University of Texas at Austin.

Armour, M. (2016). Restorative practices: Righting the wrongs of exclusionary school discipline. *University of Richmond Law Review*, *50*, 999–1037.

Armour, M., & Todic, J. (2016). *Restorative practices at a charter K-3 elementary school first year implementation evaluation*. Austin, TX: Institute for Restorative Justice and Restorative Dialogue, The University of Texas at Austin.

Baker, M. (2009). *DPS restorative justice project: Year three*. Denver, CO: Denver Public Schools.

Baker, M. L. (2008). DPS restorative justice project: Executive summary 2007–2008. Denver, CO. Retrieved from http://restorativesolutions.us/wp-content/uploads/2013/11/RestorativeSolutions-DPSRJ-ExecSum07-08.pdf

Balfanz, R., Byrnes, V., & Fox, J. H. (2015). Sent home and put off track. In Losen, D. (Ed.), *Closing the school discipline gap: Equitable remedies for excessive exclusion* (pp. 17–30). New York: Teachers College Press.

Blake, J. J., Keith, V. M., Luo, W., Le, H., & Salter, P. (2017). The role of colorism in explaining African American females' suspension risk. *School Psychology Quarterly*, *32*(1), 118–130.

Blankenship, K. M., Friedman, S. R., Dworkin, S., & Mantell, J. E. (2006). Structural interventions: Concepts, challenges and opportunities for research. *Journal of Urban Health*, *83*(1), 59–72.

Blood, P., & Thorsborne, M. (2005). The challenge of culture change: Embedding restorative practice in schools. In *6th International Conference on Conferencing, Circles and other Restorative Practices, Building a Global Alliance for Restorative Practices and Family Empowerment*, 1–18. Retrieved from www.thorsborne.com.au/conference_papers/Challenge_of_Culture_Change.pdf

Bohrnstedt, G., Kitmitto, S., Ogut, B., Sherman, D., & Chan, D. (2015). School composition and the Black–White achievement gap: Methodology companion (NCES 2015-032). U.S. Department of Education, Washington, DC: National Center for Education Statistics. Retrieved from https://nces.ed.gov/nationsreportcard/subject/studies/pdf/school_composition_and_the_bw_achievement_gap_2015_methodology.pdf

Bradshaw, C. P., Mitchell, M. M., O'Brennan, L. M., & Leaf, P. J. (2010). Multilevel exploration of factors contributing to the overrepresentation of black students in office disciplinary referrals. *Journal of Educational Psychology*, *102*(2), 508–520.

Braveman, P., Egerter, S., & Williams, D. R. (2011). The social determinants of health: Coming of age. *Annual Review of Public Health, 32*, 381–398. doi:10.1146/annurev-publhealth-031210-101218.

Braveman, P., & Gottlieb, L. (2014). The social determinants of health: It's time to consider the causes of the causes. *Public Health Reports, 129*, 19–31.

Braveman, P., & Gruskin, S. (2003). Defining equity in health. *Journal of Epidemiology & Community Health, 57*(4), 254–258.

Braveman, P. A., Cubbin, C., Egerter, S., Williams, D. R., & Pamuk, E. (2010). Socioeconomic disparities in health in the United States: What the patterns tell us. *American Journal of Public Health, 100*(S1), S186-S196.

Braveman, P. A., Heck, K., Egerter, S., Marchi, K. S., Dominguez, T. P., Cubbin, C., ... & Curtis, M. (2015). The role of socioeconomic factors in black–White disparities in preterm birth. *American Journal of Public Health, 105*(4), 694–702.

Bryk, A., Sebring, P. B., Allensworth, E., Luppescu, S., & Easton, J. Q. (2010). *Organizing schools for improvement: Lessons from Chicago*. Chicago and London: The University of Chicago Press.

Carter, P., Fine, M., & Russell, S. (2014). *Discipline disparities series: Overview*. Bloomington, IN: Center for Evaluation and Education Policy. https://safesupportivelearning.ed.gov/sites/default/files/Discipline_Disparities_Overview.pdf.

Carter, P. L., Skiba, R., Arredondo, M. I., & Pollock, M. (2017). You can't fix what you don't look at: Acknowledging race in addressing racial discipline disparities. *Urban Education, 52*(2), 207–235. doi:10.1177/0042085916660350

Centers for Disease Control and Prevention (CDC). (2009). *School connectedness: Strategies for increasing protective factors among youth*. Atlanta, GA: U.S. Department of Health and Human Services.

Centers for Disease Control and Prevention (CDC). (2015). Health disparities. Retrieved from www.cdc.gov/healthyyouth/disparities/index.htm

Centers for Disease Control and Prevention (CDC). (2017) Tobacco-related mortality. Retrieved from www.cdc.gov/tobacco/data_statistics/fact_sheets/health_effects/tobacco_related_mortality/index.htm

Crenshaw, K., Ocen, P, & Nanda, J. (2015). Black girls matter: Pushed out, overpoliced, and underreported. Retrieved from www.law.columbia.edu/sites/default/files/legacy/files/public_affairs/2015/february_2015/black_girls_matter_report_2.4.15.pdf

Cubbin, C., Heck, K., Powell, T., Marchi, K., & Braveman, P. (2015). Racial/ethnic disparities in depressive symptoms among pregnant women vary by income and neighborhood poverty. *AIMS Public Health, 2*(3), 411.

Curtis, A. J. (2014). Tracing the school-to-prison pipeline from zero-tolerance policies to juvenile justice dispositions. *Georgetown Law Journal, 102*(4), 1251.

Diliberti, M., Jackson, J., Kemp, J., & National Center for Education. (2017). *Crime, violence, discipline, and safety in U.S. Public Schools: Findings from the school survey on crime and safety: 2015–16. First Look*. NCES 2017-122. Retrieved from http://ezproxy.lib.utexas.edu/login?url=http://search.ebscohost.com/login.aspx?direct=true&db=eric&AN=ED574956&site=ehost-live

Dunn, E. C., Milliren, C. E., Evans, C. R., Subramanian, S. V., & Richmond, T. K. (2015). Disentangling the relative influence of schools and neighborhoods on adolescents' risk for depressive symptoms. *American Journal of Public Health, 105*(4), 732–740. doi:10.2105/AJPH.2014.302374

Egerter, S., Braveman, P., Sadegh-Nobari, Y., Grossman-Kahn, R., & Dekker, M. (2011). Education and health. Robert Wood Johnson Foundation. Retrieved from www.rwjf.org/en/library/research/2011/05/education-matters-for-health.html

Epstein, R., Blake, J., & González, T. (2017). Girlhood interrupted: The erasure of black girls' childhood. Center on Poverty and Inequality, Georgetown Law. Retrieved from https://ssrn.com/abstract=3000695 or http://dx.doi.org/10.2139/ssrn.3000695

Fabelo, T., Thompson, M. D., Plotkin, M., Carmichael, D., Marchbanks, M. P., & Booth, E. A. (2011). *Breaking schools rules: A statewide study of how school discipline relates to students' success and juvenile justice involvement* (pp. 1–124). New York: Council of State Governments Justice Center.

Farmer, E. M. Z., & Farmer, T. W. (1999). The role of schools in outcomes for youth: Implications for children's mental health services research. *Journal of Child & Family Studies, 8*(4), 377–396.

Farrer, L., Marinetti, C., Cavaco, Y. K., & Costongs, C. (2015). Advocacy for health equity: A synthesis review. *Milbank Quarterly, 93*(2), 392–437.

Finn, J. D., & Servoss, T. J. (2014). Misbehavior, suspensions, and security measures in high school: Racial/ethnic and gender differences. *Journal of Applied Research on Children: Informing Policy for Children at Risk, 5*(2), 11.

Fowler, D., Lightsey, R., Monger, J., & Aseltine, E. (2010). Texas' school-to-prison pipeline: School expulsion—The path from lockout to dropout. Retrieved from www.njjn.org/uploads/digital-library/Texas-School-Prison-Pipeline-School-Expulsion_Texas-Appleseed_Apr2010.pdf

Freeman, J., & Simonsen, B. (2015). Examining the impact of policy and practice interventions on high school dropout and school completion rates: A systematic review of the literature. *Review of Educational Research*, *85*(2), 205–248.

Freudenberg, N., & Ruglis, J. (2007). Reframing school dropout as a public health issue. *Preventing Chronic Disease*, *4*(4), A107.

Fronius, T., Persson, H., Guckenburg, S., Hurley, N., & Petrosino, A. (2016). Restorative justice in US schools: A research review. *Justice & Prevention Research Center*, WestEd, 1–33. Retrieved from www.antoniocasella.eu/restorative/Fronius_feb16.pdf

Gardella, J. H. (2015). Restorative practices: For school administrators considering implementation. Retrieved from https://my.vanderbilt.edu/tn-s3-center-vanderbilt/files/2014/05/Restorative-practices-booklet-9.26.15-copy.pdf

Geronimus, A. T. (1992). The weathering hypothesis and the health of African-American women and infants: Evidence and speculations. *Ethnicity & Disease*, *2*(3), 207–221.

Girvan, E. J., Gion, C., McIntosh, K., & Smolkowski, K. (2017). The relative contribution of subjective office referrals to racial disproportionality in school discipline. *School Psychology Quarterly*, *32*(3), 392–404. doi:10.1037/spq0000178.

Goff, P. A., Jackson, M. C., Leone, D., Lewis, B. A., Culotta, C. M., & DiTomasso, N. A. (2014). The essence of innocence: Consequences of dehumanizing Black children. *Journal of Personality and Social Psychology*, *106*(4), 526–545.

González, T. (2012). Keeping kids in schools: Restorative justice, punitive discipline, and the school to prison pipeline. *The Journal of Law and Education*, *41*(2), 281.

González, T. (2015). Socializing schools: Addressing racial disparities in discipline through restorative justice. In Losen, H. J. (Ed.), *Closing the school discipline gap: Equitable remedies for excessive exclusions (disability, equity, and culture)*. New York: Teachers College Press. Retrieved from https://papers.ssrn.com/sol3/papers.cfm?abstract_id=2728960

Gregory, A., Allen, J. P., Mikami, A. Y., Hafen, C. A., & Pianta, R. (2014). Eliminating the racial disparity in classroom exclusionary discipline. *Journal of Applied Research on Children*, *5*(2), 1–22.

Gregory, A., & Fergus, E. (2017). Social and emotional learning and equity in school discipline. *The Future of Children*, *27*(1), 117–136.

Gregory, A., & Roberts, G. (2017). Teacher beliefs and the overrepresentation of Black students in classroom discipline. *Theory into Practice*, *56*(3), 187–194. doi:10.1080/00405841.2017.1336035

Gregory, A., Skiba, R. J., & Mediratta, K. (2017). Eliminating disparities in school discipline: A framework for intervention. *Review of Research in Education*, *41*(1), 253–278.

Hale, D. R., Patalay, P., Fitzgerald-Yau, N., Hargreaves, D. S., Bond, L., Görzig, A., ... Viner, R. M. (2014). School-level variation in health outcomes in adolescence: Analysis of three longitudinal studies in England. *Prevention Science*, *15*(4), 600–610. doi:10.1007/s11121-013-0414-6

Hannon, L., DeFina, R., & Bruch, S. (2013). The relationship between skin tone and school suspension for African Americans. *Race and Social Problems*, *5*(4), 281–295.

Himmelstein, K. E. W., & Brückner, H. (2011). Criminal-justice and school sanctions against nonheterosexual youth: A national longitudinal study. *Pediatrics*, *127*(1), 49–57. doi:10.1542/peds.2009-2306.

Jain, S., Bassey, H., Brown, M., & Kalra, P. (2014). *Restorative justice in Oakland schools: An effective strategy to reduce racially disproportionate discipline, suspensions, and improve academic outcomes*. Oakland Unified School District. Oakland, CA: Data In Action, LLC. Retrieved from https://www.ousd.org/cms/lib07/CA01001176/Centricity/Domain/134/OUSD-RJ%20Report%20revised%20Final.pdf

Kelly, D. R. (2017). *Predicting violent incidence and disciplinary actions in schools: Use of the National Center for Educational Statistics to Examine School Violence Interventions*. (Doctoral dissertation, The University of Texas at Arlington).

Kidde, J., & Alfred, R. (2011). *Restorative justice: A working guide for our schools*. San Leandro, CA: Alamada County School Health Services Coalition.

Kitagawa, E. M., & Hauser, P. M. (1973). *Differential mortality in the United States: A study in socioeconomic epidemiology*. Cambridge, MA: Harvard University Press.

Klebanoff Cohen, A., & Syme, S. L. (2013). Education: A missed opportunity for public health Intervention. *American Journal of Public Health*, *103*(6), 997–1001. doi:10.2105/AJPH.2012.300993

Krieger, N. (2005). Embodiment: A conceptual glossary for epidemiology. *Journal of Epidemiology and Community Health*, *59*(5), 350–355. doi:http://doi.org/10.1136/jech.2004.024562

Krieger, N. (2011). *Epidemiology and the people's health: Theory and context*. New York: Oxford University Press. Journal of School Health, 85(5), 318–326.

Kupchik, A. (2010). *Homeroom security: School discipline in an age of fear*. New York: NYU Press.

Kupchik, A., & Ellis, N. (2008). School discipline and security: Fair for all students? *Youth & Society, 39*(4), 549–574.

Lewis, S. (2009). *Improving school climate: Findings from schools implementing restorative practices*. Bethlehem, PA: International Institute for Restorative Practices.

Link, B. G., Lennon, M. C., & Dohrenwend, B. P. (1993). Socioeconomic status and depression: The role of occupations involving direction, control, and planning. *American Journal of Sociology, 98*(6), 1351.

Lleras-Muney, A. (2005). The relationship between education and adult mortality in the United States. *The Review of Economic Studies, 72*(1), 189–221.

Losen, D. J., & Martinez, T. E. (2013). Out of school and off track: The overuse of suspensions in American middle and high schools. The UCLA Civil Rights Project. Retrieved from www.civilrightsproject.ucla.edu/resources/projects/center-for-civil-rights-remedies/school-to-prison-folder/federal-reports/out-of-school-and-off-track-the-overuse-of-suspensions-in-american-middle-and-high-schools

Lustick, H. (2017). Administering discipline differently: A Foucauldian lens on restorative school discipline. *International Journal of Leadership in Education, 20*(3), 297–311.

Mansfield, K. C., Fowler, B., & Rainbolt, S. (2018). The potential of restorative practices to Ameliorate discipline gaps: The story of one high school's leadership team. *Educational Administration Quarterly, 54*(2), 303–323. doi:10.1177/0013161X17751178

Marchbanks, M. P., Peguero, A. A., Varela, K. S., Blake, J. J., & Eason, J. M. (2018). School strictness and disproportionate minority contact: Investigating racial and ethnic disparities with the "school-to-prison pipeline". *Youth Violence and Juvenile Justice, 16*(2), 241–259. doi:10.1177/1541204016680403

Martin, J. L., Sharp-Grier, M., & Smith, J. B. (2016). Alternate realities: Racially disparate discipline in classrooms and schools and its effects on Black and Brown students. *Leadership and Research in Education, 3*(1), 16–33.

Martinez, S. (2009). A system gone berserk: How are zero-tolerance policies really affecting schools? *Preventing School Failure: Alternative Education for Children and Youth, 53*(3), 153–158.

McCluskey, G., Kane, J., Lloyd, G., Stead, J., Riddell, S., & Weedon, E. (2011). "Teachers are afraid we are stealing their strength": A risk society and restorative approaches in school. *British Journal of Educational Studies, 59*(2), 105–119. doi:10.1080/00071005.2011.565741

McCold, P. (2002). *Evaluation of a restorative milieu: CSF Buxmont School/Day Treatment Programs 1999–2001*. Bethlehem, PA: IIRP E-Forum.

McCold, P. (2008). Evaluation of a restorative milieu: Restorative practices in context. *Sociology of Crime, Law and Deviance, 11*, 99–137.

McGovern, L., Miller, G., & Hughes-Cromwick, P. (2014, August 21). The relative contribution of multiple determinants to health outcomes. Health Policy Briefs. *Health Affairs*. Retrieved from www.healthaffairs.org/healthpolicybriefs/brief.php?brief_id=123

McMorris, B. J., Beckman, K. J., Baumgartner, J., & Eggert, R. C. (2014). Applying restorative justice practices to Minneapolis public school students recommended for possible expulsion: A pilot program evaluation of the family and youth restorative conference program. Minneapolis, MN: School of Nursing and the Healthy Youth Development. Prevention Research Center, Department of Pediatrics, University of Minnesota.

Mirsky, L. (2007a). Safer saner schools: Transforming school culture with restorative practices. *Reclaiming Children and Youth, 16*(2), 5–12.

Mirsky, L., & Watchel, T. (2007b). The worst school I've ever been to: Empirical evaluations of a restorative school and treatment milieu. *Reclaiming Children and Youth, 16*(2), 13–16.

Montez, J. K., & Hayward, M. D. (2014). Cumulative childhood adversity, educational attainment, and active life expectancy among U.S. adults. *Demography, 51*(2), 413–435. doi:http://link.springer.com/journal/volumesAndIssues/13524

Morgan, W., Salomon, M., Plotkin, M., & Cohen, R. (2014). *The school discipline report: Strategies from the field to keep students engaged in school and out of the juvenile justice system*. New York: Council of State Governments Justice Center.

Morris, E. W., & Perry, B. L. (2017). Girls behaving badly? Race, gender, and subjective evaluation in the discipline of African American girls. *Sociology of Education, 90*(2), 127–148.

Morrison, B. E., & Vaandering, D. (2012). Restorative justice: Pedagogy, praxis, and discipline. *Journal of School Violence, 11*(2), 138–155. doi:10.1080/15388220.2011.653322.

Morrison, B., Blood, P., & Thorsborne, M. (2006). Practicing restorative justice in school communities; The challenge of culture change. *Public Organization Review: A Global Journal, 5*, 335–367.

Na, C., & Gottfredson, D. C. (2013). Police officers in schools: Effects on school crime and the processing of offending behaviors. *Justice Quarterly, 30*(4), 619–650.

National Center for Education Statistics. (2017). *Public high school graduation rates.* Retrieved from https://nces.ed.gov/programs/coe/indicator_coi.asp
National Center for Health Statistics. (2018). *Quick stats from the National Health Interview Survey.* Retrieved from www.cdc.gov/nchs/nhis/nhis_quickstats.htm
Norris, A. (2009). Gender and race effects of a restorative justice intervention on school effects. *Paper presented at the annual meeting of the ASC Annual Meeting, Philadelphia Marriott Downtown, Philadelphia, PA.*
Orfield, G., Kuscera, J., & Siegel-Hawley, G. (2012). *E Pluribus ... separation: Deepening double segregation for more students.* Cambridge, MA: The Civil Rights Project Harvard University. Retrieved from www.civilrightsproject.ucla.edu/research/k-12-education/integration-and-diversity/mlk-national/e-pluribus.separation-deepening-double-segregation-for-more-students/orfield_epluribus_revised_omplete_2012.pdf
Payne, A. A., & Welch, K. (2010). Modeling the effects of racial threat on punitive and restorative school discipline practices. *Criminology: An Interdisciplinary Journal, 48*(4), 1019–1062. doi:10.1111/j.1745-9125.2010.00211.x
Payne, A. A., & Welch, K. (2015). Restorative justice in schools: The influence of race on restorative discipline. *Youth & Society, 47*(4), 539–564. doi:10.1177/0044118X12473125
Payne, A. A., & Welch, K. (2018). The effect of school conditions on the use of restorative justice in schools. *Youth Violence & Juvenile Justice, 16*(2), 224–240. doi:10.1177/1541204016681414
Peguero, A. A., & Shekarkhar, Z. (2011). Latino/a student misbehavior and school punishment. *Hispanic Journal of Behavioral Sciences, 33*(1), 54–70. doi:10.1177/0739986310388021.
Perry, B. L., & Morris, E. W. (2014). Suspending progress: Collateral consequences of exclusionary punishment in public schools. *American Sociological Review, 79*(6), 1067–1087.
Poulin Carlton, M. (2017). *Summary of school safety statistics.* National Institute of Justice report. retrieved from www.ncjrs.gov/pdffiles1/nij/250610.pdf
Rausch, M. K., & Skiba, R. J. (2017). Addressing disproportionately high rates of disciplinary removal for students of color: The need for systemic interventions. In E. C. Lopez, S. G. Nahari, & S. L. Proctor (Eds.), *Handbook of multicultural school psychology: An interdisciplinary perspective* (pp. 276–290). New York: Routledge/Taylor & Francis Group.
Ready, D. D. (2010). Socioeconomic disadvantage, school attendance, and early cognitive development: The differential effects of school exposure. *Sociology of Education, 83*(4), 271–286.
Reardon, S. F., & Owens, A. (2014). 60 years after Brown: Trends and consequences of school segregation. *Annual Review of Sociology, 40*, 199–218.
Reistenberg, N. (2003). *In-school behavior intervention grants: A three year evaluation of alternative approaches to suspensions and expulsions.* Roseville, MN: Minnesota Department of Children, Families & Learning.
Rideout, G., Karen, R., Salinitri, G., & Marc, F. (2010). Measuring the impact of restorative justice practices: Outcomes and contexts. *Journal of Educational Administration and Foundations, 21*(2), 35.
Riestenberg, N. (2012). *Circle in the square: Building community and repairing harm in schools.* St. Paul, MN: Living Justice Press.
Rodríguez Ruiz, R. (2017). School-to-prison pipeline: An evaluation of zero tolerance policies and their alternatives. *Houston Law Review, 54*(3), 803–837.
Rogers, R. G., Hummer, R. A., Nam, C. B., & Peters, K. (1996). Demographic, socioeconomic, and behavioral factors affecting ethnic mortality by cause. *Social Forces, 74*(4), 1419–1438.
Rumberger, R. W. (2011). *Dropping out: Why students drop out of high school and what can be done about it.* Cambridge, MA: Harvard Press.
Schollenberger, T. L. (2015). Racial disparities in school suspension and subsequent outcomes: Evidence from the National Longitudinal Survey of Youth 1997. In Losen, D. J. (Ed.), *Closing the school discipline gap: Equitable remedies for excessive exclusion* (pp. 31–44). New York: Teachers College Press.
Skiba, R., & Rausch, M. K. (2006). School disciplinary systems: Alternatives to suspension and expulsion. In G. G. Bear & K. M. Minke (Eds.), *Children's needs III: Development, prevention, and intervention* (pp. 87–102). Washington, DC: National Association of School Psychologists.
Skiba, R. J., Arredondo, M. I., & Rausch, M. K. (2014). *New and developing research on disparities in discipline. Discipline Disparities: A Research-to-Research Collaborative.* Retrieved from www.indiana.edu/~atlantic/wp-content/uploads/2014/04/Disparity_NewResearch_Full_040414.pdf
Skiba, R. J., Chung, C.-G., Trachok, M., Baker, T. L., Sheya, A., & Hughes, R. L. (2014). Parsing disciplinary disproportionality: Contributions of infraction, student, and school characteristics to out-of-school suspension and expulsion. *American Educational Research Journal, 51*(4), 640–670. doi:10.3102/0002831214541670.
Skiba, R. J., Horner, R. H., Chung, C.-G., Rausch, M. K., May, S. L., & Tobin, T. (2011). Race is not neutral: A national investigation of African American and Latino disproportionality in school discipline. *School Psychology Review, 40*(1), 85.

Skiba, R. J., Mediratta, K., & Rausch, M. K. (2016). *Inequality in school discipline: Research and practice to reduce disparities*. New York: Palgrave Macmillan.

Sumner, M. D., Silverman, C. J., & Frampton, M. L. (2010). School-based restorative justice as an alternative to zero tolerance policies: Lessons from West Oakland. University of California, Berkeley, School of Law: Thelton E. Henderson Center for Social Justice. Retrieved from https://www.law.berkeley.edu/files/thcsj/10-2010_School-based_Restorative_Justice_As_an_Alternative_to_Zero-Tolerance_Policies.pdf

Thorsborne, M., & Blood, P. (2013). *Implementing restorative practices in schools: A practical guide to transforming school communities*. Philadelphia, PA: Jessica Kingsley Publishers.

Todic, J. (2018). Towards health equity through restorative justice in schools. (Doctoral dissertation, The University of Texas at Austin).

United States Department of Education, Office for Civil Rights. (2014). Data snapshot: School discipline. Retrieved from https://ocrdata.ed.gov/downloads/crdc-school-discipline-snapshot.pdf

University of California, San Francisco Center for Social Disparities in Health. (2008). *Overcoming obstacles to health: Report from the Robert Wood Johnson foundation to the commission to build a healthier America*. Princeton, NJ: Robert Wood Johnson Foundation.

US Department of Health and Human Services. (2016). *Healthy people 2020*. Retrieved from www.healthypeople.gov/2020/topics-objectives/topic/social-determinants-of-health

Vaandering, D. (2010). Critical relational theory. In Hopkins, B. (Ed.), *Restorative theory in practice: Insights into what works and why* (pp. 63–76). London and Philadelphia: Jessica Kingsley Publishers.

Villegas, A. M., Strom, K., & Lucas, T. (2012). Closing the racial/ethnic gap between students of color and their teachers: An elusive goal. *Equity & Excellence in Education, 45*(2), 283–301.

Wadhwa, A. K. (2010). "There has never been a glory day in education for non-whites": Critical race theory and discipline reform in Denver. *International Journal on School Disaffection, 7*(2), 21–28.

Wadhwa, A. K. (2017). *Restorative justice in urban schools: Disrupting the school-to-prison pipeline*. New York: Routledge.

Walters, K., Spencer, M. S., Smukler, M., Allen, H. L., Andrews, C., Browne, T., ... Uehara, E. (2016). *Health equity: Eradicating health inequalities for future generations. Grand Challenges for Social Work Initiative*. (Working Paper, No. 19). Baltimore, MD: American Academy of Social Work and Social Welfare. Retrieved from http://aaswsw.org/wp-content/uploads/2016/01/WP19-with-cover2.pdf

Whitehead, M. (1992). The concepts and principles of equity and health. *International Journal of Health Services, 22*(3), 429–445. doi:10.2190/986l-lhq6-2vte-yrrn

Whitford, D. K. (2017). School discipline disproportionality: American Indian students in special education. *The Urban Review, 49*(5), 693–706. doi:10.1007/s11256-017-0417-x

Whitford, D. K., & Levine-Donnerstein, D. (2014). Office disciplinary referral patterns of American Indian students from elementary school through high school. *Behavioral Disorders, 39*(2), 78–88. doi:10.1177/019874291303900204

Zajacova, A., & Everett, B. G. (2014). The nonequivalent health of high school equivalents. *Social Science Quarterly (Wiley-Blackwell), 95*(1), 221–238. doi:10.1111/ssqu.12039

Zajacova, A., Hummer, R. A., & Rogers, R. G. (2012). Education and health among U.S. working-age adults: A detailed portrait across the full educational attainment spectrum. *Biodemography and Social Biology, 58*(1), 40–61. doi:10.1080/19485565.2012.666122

Zehr, H. (2002). *The little book of restorative justice*. Intercourse, PA: Good Books.

# 21
# THE ROLE OF OCCUPATIONAL SCIENCE AND OCCUPATIONAL THERAPY IN THE JUVENILE JUSTICE SYSTEM

*Lisa A. Jaegers, Karen F. Barney, and Rebecca M. Aldrich*

## Introduction

Scholars and practitioners in the criminal justice arena may know little about occupational therapy unless they work in forensic settings that house people with serious mental illness (Farnworth & Muñoz, 2009). The proportion of occupational therapists working in criminal justice settings is low (Muñoz, Moreton, & Sitterly, 2016), but there is growing recognition that an occupational perspective can make a distinct and significant contribution within these settings. The purpose of this chapter is to introduce readers to the occupational perspective and the ways in which it grounds occupational therapy practice in the criminal justice arena. We will provide examples of how this perspective has shaped occupational therapists' work with juveniles internationally, within the justice system in California for over 20 years, and with adults inside and outside correctional facilities in Missouri. Based on those examples, we will suggest how occupational scientists and occupational therapists can be engaged by a range of disciplines and professions as partners in preventing juvenile suspension and detention, as well as promoting optimal outcomes within juvenile justice systems.

## An Occupational Perspective of Health

A unique perspective – the occupational perspective – grounds the discipline of occupational science and profession of occupational therapy. An occupational perspective of health privileges the relationship between everyday human activities, such as work, parenting, self-care, and healthy survival (Wilcock & Hocking, 2015). These activities, or "occupations," are the subject of inquiry for occupational scientists (Dickie, 2010; Hocking, 2009) and also the means and ends of occupational therapy practice (Gray, 1997). Occupational scientists and occupational therapists see occupations as complex phenomena that encompass people's doing, being, becoming, and belonging (Hitch, Pépin, & Stagnitti, 2014; Wilcock, 1998). People who take up the occupational perspective in research and practice acknowledge the situated nature of everyday doing and try to discern how occupations help develop meaning, identity, purpose, and community (Laliberte Rudman, & Aldrich, 2017). This perspective aims to take a holistic approach (Aldrich, 2008) to inquiring about occupation and employing it as a therapeutic medium and outcome. An occupational perspective thus examines the diverse ways in which personal and contextual factors transact to produce occupation (Dickie, Cutchin, & Humphry, 2006) on both individual and community levels (Cutchin, Dickie, & Humphry, 2017; Lavalley, 2017).

Since the inception of occupational therapy in 1917 and the formalization of occupational science in 1989, scholars have worked to articulate how research and practice can be more occupation-focused (Fisher, 2014) and thus more reflective of human experience. As part of those efforts, there has been increasing attention to the ways in which occupational engagement reveals and is related to conditions of justice or injustice (Aldrich, 2018; Bailliard, 2016; Wilcock & Hocking, 2015). An occupational perspective links the conditions of everyday life that promote or inhibit occupational engagement (Durocher, Gibson, & Rappolt, 2014) to the equitable or inequitable outcomes that constitute social problems (Wilcock & Hocking, 2015). Aside from this focus on conditions, the view of occupation as a human right is central to an occupational justice perspective of health (Hammell & Beagan, 2016; Hocking, 2017). Given the belief that people are occupational beings who have a right to facilitate their health and survival through occupations, the pursuit of occupational justice is increasingly seen as an inherent aspect of occupational therapy practice (Aldrich, Boston, & Daaleman, 2016; Bailliard & Aldrich, 2016).

Within this focus on justice, much attention has been paid to occupational deprivation (Durocher, Gibson, & Rappolt, 2014), which Whiteford (2000) defined as "a state in which a person or group of people are unable to do what is necessary and meaningful in their lives due to external restrictions" (p. 200). Incarceration is the most frequently referenced example of occupational deprivation in the occupational justice literature. Whiteford (2010) noted that

> from an occupational perspective, incarceration deliberately withdraws opportunities to participate in or choose occupational pursuits … such a sanction represents a powerful reminder that the right to *do* what one chooses, when, and where (within the confines of the law) is considered to be so central to our cultural understandings of what it is to be human, that to remove that freedom of choice and participation in occupations is considered the most severe punishment.
>
> (p. 312)

Whiteford went on to suggest that "severe forms of occupational deprivation actually mitigate against inmates' future abilities to reintegrate successfully into communities" (p. 314). As a form or outcome of occupational injustice, occupational deprivation provides a conceptual anchor for addressing occupation from a structural level within education and justice systems, allowing occupational therapists to both enrich and move beyond the individual-level interventions that have long characterized their profession.

Beyond the specific focus on occupational deprivation, the increased uptake of critical theoretical perspectives has engendered a spirit of questioning the status quo among some occupational scientists and occupational therapists (Farias & Laliberte Rudman, 2016). One outcome of this emphasis is the reconceptualization of occupation itself among scholars and practitioners. Despite the predominant emphasis on the health-promoting aspects of occupation, there is recognition that not all occupations promote health and that some occupations labeled as socially deviant may have beneficial attributes and effects (Twinley, 2013). In understanding these so-called, nonsanctioned sides of occupation (Kiepek, Beagan, Laliberte Rudman, & Phelan, 2018; Twinley & Addidle, 2012), occupational scientists have joined with criminologists to advocate for a more holistic, community-focused view of occupation (Aldrich & White, 2012) informed by the late Dr. Norman White's (2013) work on risk immersion. Dr. White, a developmental criminologist, was a champion of the occupational perspective in his work with communities. In his many conversations and collaborations with the third author of this chapter, he admitted to incorporating the notion of occupation into both his teaching and research, describing the benefits of focusing on the "activities of people's lives" (N. White, personal communication, 2012). Dr. White's ardent support of the occupational perspective signals its potential contribution to the wider conversation about juvenile justice issues. As a tribute to his work and means of honoring his legacy, this chapter will delve further into the contributions that an occupational perspective can make through research and practice to understanding the conditions and outcomes of juvenile delinquency.

## Occupational Therapy Practice Perspective and Process

A conceptual model known as the *Occupational Therapy Practice Framework* (OTPF) guides Occupational Therapy (OT) practice in the United States. Within the OTPF, *occupational therapy* is defined as striving to "achieve health, well-being, and participation in life through engagement in occupation" (AOTA, 2014, p. S2), guided by World Health Organization definitions for each of these terms (WHO, 2014). Occupational therapists (OTs) use everyday life activities (occupations) with individuals, groups, systems, or populations for the purpose of enhancing or enabling participation in roles, habits, and routines in home, school, workplace, community, and other settings (AOTA, 2014).

Occupational therapy services are provided throughout the lifespan for prevention, habilitation, rehabilitation, life transitions, and promotion of health and wellness for clients who are at risk for or with disability-and non-disability-related needs, as well as their family, friends, and communities. These services include acquisition and preservation of occupational identity for those who have or are at risk for developing an illness, injury, disease, disorder, condition, impairment, disability, activity limitation, or *participation restriction,* [as in suspension, detention, incarceration, or supervision] (AOTA, 2014). Knowledge of the transactional relationship and the significance of meaningful and productive occupations form the basis for the use of occupations as both the means and the ends of OT interventions (Trombly, 1995). This knowledge sets occupational therapy apart as distinct and has been shown to make significant differences in preventing pathological outcomes (Case-Smith, 2015; Dunn, 2011; Fingerhut et al., 2013; Rogers, Bai, Lavin, & Anderson, 2017; Shea & Siu, 2016).

Figure 21.1 describes the transactional relationship between the person, her or his participation in occupations (activities), also known as *occupational performance,* and the individual's health related quality of life, as follows:

- **Person/Client:** How are intrinsic factors uniquely expressed in this individual/group/population; how may functional performance of activities/occupations be different now compared with the past or future?
- **Contexts/Environment:** What are the contexts (e.g. social, cultural, personal, temporal, and virtual), environments (e.g. physical terrain, built, neighborhoods), and other social determinants of health (e.g. health care, education, economic stability, and community) in which actual and potential occupational (activity) options are grounded?
- **Occupational Options:** What are the activity participation possibilities (e.g. self-care, education, play/leisure, social, work, rest/sleep)? What activities does this child/youth/parent/group/population want or need to do; what are current priorities and goals (e.g. ideally determined by the individual or family/group/population and OT)?

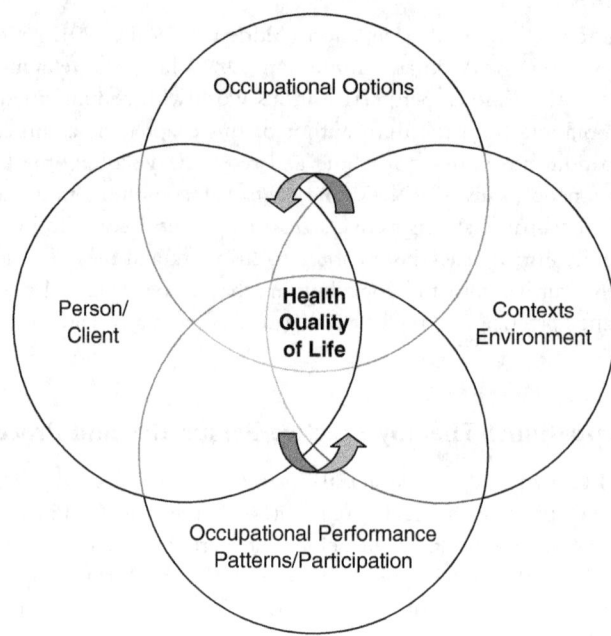

Adapted from Person-environment-occupation-performance/participation (PEOP) model (Christiansen et al., 2005).

*Figure 21.1* Occupational therapy conceptual process for health promotion

- **Occupational Performance/Participation:** What comprises enactment of activities (e.g. performance patterns and skills) within the individual's/group's context? Where non-sanctioned activities represent meaningful participation for the child/youth/parent/group/population, these become foci for occupational therapy interventions.
- **Outcome Goal for OT Intervention:** What will enable performance of and engagement in priority activities to support the individual's/group's/population's overall health, well-being and quality of life?

Occupational therapy practitioners use their knowledge of the transactional relationship among the client, his or her engagement in valued occupations, and the context to collaboratively assess the client, design and implement occupation-based intervention plans; and perform periodic re-evaluation to determine continuation and/or discontinuation and referral to other services. Planning includes close collaboration with the client and other relevant professionals, services and resources. Occupational therapy assessment focuses on the client's performance of the occupations (activities) that are needed, motivating to the client, and expected within the individual's community and society. Client strengths, as well as gaps in development and occupational performance reflected in the individual's or significant others' account of personal history, as well as records (e.g. educational, medical, justice-system related) are identified. Occupational therapy practitioners' education foundation includes social, neurological, human anatomical, physiological, psychological, social and occupational sciences, as well as extensive fieldwork, all of which prepare OTs in applying thorough assessment, evaluation and intervention skills.

Standardized assessments, as well as input from parents and/or all relevant sources are typically included in the evaluation process, prior to intervention planning. First, an *occupational profile* is finalized, providing an understanding of the client's background and perspective, and summarizes the client's occupational history, daily living routines and performance in related activities, interests, values and needs. Next, an *intervention plan* is collaboratively developed with the client, in order to facilitate change or growth in client factors (body functions, body structures, values, beliefs, and spirituality) and skills (functional cognition, motor, social interaction, and daily living) needed for successful participation within society. Occupational therapy practitioners are concerned with the participatory process and end result, and thus enable the client's engagement through interventions that focus on improving behaviors, habits, roles, routines, and functional status, as well as adaptations and modifications to the environment or objects within the environment, wherever needed (AOTA, 2014).

## Occupational Therapy Intervention

Interventions follow the plan developed collaboratively with the client or proxies, including parents, and describe the OT approaches and interventions to be utilized in addressing the client's needs and measurable occupation-focused goals. Collaboration occurs with other disciplines and relevant individuals (e.g. parents, early intervention, daycare and/or school or justice system personnel), to determine methods of service delivery, types of intervention to be used, and related personnel. Relevant referrals are made, as well as addressing potential discharge needs and plans. This planning is repeatedly reviewed and updated, as indicated. Additional evaluation may ensue, if prior unidentified needs or problems are observed during the OT intervention process.

A focus on outcomes, is included throughout the occupational therapy process during the evaluation and intervention phases, and renegotiated as indicated. Outcomes are documented, evaluated, and reported to all relevant parties. They are directly related to the interventions provided and to the targeted occupations, client intrinsic factors, performance skills and patterns, as well as their contexts and environments. Additionally, the client's subjective impressions (e.g. improvements in outlook, confidence, resilience, achievement of greater balance of activities, resilience and sense of health and well-being) may be included as targeted outcomes (AOTA, 2014). Outcomes for groups, organizations, and populations may include improved social interaction, use of leisure time, peer support, health promotion, sense of well-being, and quality of life, or productivity and purpose/meaningfulness of work roles.

## Lifespan Approach: Holistic Assessment and Intervention Process

Occupational therapy practitioners promote health and quality of life by promoting the establishment of healthy roles, habits and routines that lead to active participation across the life span via the following:

- Adapting activities and environments to enhance participation in meaningful roles and routines (AOTA, 2014; Doll, 2014).
- Enhancing development and skill acquisition in fine and gross motor coordination, social interaction, problem solving, and self-advocacy (Case-Smith, 2015; Cohn & Lew, 2010; Doll, 2014).
- Facilitating independence across the spectrum of occupational routines in feeding, bathing, dressing, and other self-care and school-related activities (Cohn & Lew, 2010).

Occupational therapists work in a variety of settings that serve infants, children, their parents and extended families, including clinics, hospitals, daycare settings, detention centers, other juvenile justice settings, homeless shelters, homes, schools, and wellness centers, as well as other settings in communities throughout the world.

## International Application of Occupational Therapy Interventions

Globally occupational therapists have historically recognized the uniquely effective role of occupational therapy in the rehabilitation of individuals who are at risk for or involved with criminal justice systems (Muñoz, Moreton, & Sitterly, 2016; O'Connell & Farnworth, 2007; Penner, 1978). Occupational therapy's worldwide presence in providing interventions to prevent or mitigate juvenile dysfunction has been broad. From work in Central and South America with marginalized families and children, Sierra Leon with child soldiers, Gaza, Cambodia and other parts of Asia, throughout Europe, and South Africa, the discipline utilizes age-appropriate, culturally relevant interventions based upon individual, group, and population needs. In Japan, where norms for culturally appropriate occupational behavior are highly defined, 20% of the occupational therapy profession works with persons at risk for detention or who are incarcerated (Tomoko Kondo, personal communication, 2014).

Since spiritual qualities such as hope, courage, and trust are integral to children's abilities to achieve their highest potential throughout their lives, intervention plans are developed collaboratively and grounded in the participants' cultural experience (Townsend & Polatajko, 2007). Following are examples of international occupational therapy programs for children and youth.

*Argentina:* Occupational therapy via a "Coming Back to School" program has been utilized with teenagers from large marginalized families to prevent and mitigate the impact of parental chronic poverty and unemployment, resulting in limited food, health supports, education, homes, work, and overall occupational development. Many of the teenagers and their parents have a history of encounters with law enforcement and have dropped out of their education programs (Kielhofner, 2004). Different strategies to support the teens, despite pregnancy, delinquency or addictions have been developed, in collaboration with social workers and their community (Duschatzky & Corea, 2007). These approaches have included strengthening individual skills, identifying leisure activities and work with economic incentives that is motivating to the participant. In this program >86% of the teenagers completed the school year. Additional notable outcomes were that some of these youth reported no longer being treated as "criminals" and valued socializing in healthier daily life experiences (Benassi & Fraile, 2011).

*Brazilian* occupational therapists have developed territorial interventions to address societal needs. Evidenced by statistical indicators, in Brazil violence experienced by adolescents from working-class groups had escalated to alarming levels, due to inadequate public policies. As a result, the following projects were developed by occupational therapists:

1 *School Violence and Educational Initiatives*: Contributing to the participation and effective inclusion of working-class youth who attended or dropped out of schools.
2 *Urban Violence and Territory*: Youth identification of needs and organizing discussion groups regarding violence while training human resources support among partnering institutions (Barros, Garcez Ghirardi, Lopes, & Galheigo, 2011).

In *Mexico and Guatemala,* Frank Kronenberg, an occupational therapist from the Netherlands, tackled complex contextual conditions that deprived children and youth living on the streets. These youth were alienated from and would not attend established rehabilitation programs. Their sense of isolation, powerlessness, frustration, loss of control and estrangement [occupational alienation] was derived from participating in activities that didn't motivate them. Thus, he created a variety of occupational forms that had the potential to reach them and to achieve the following:

- Building self-confidence and a (new) sense of belonging
- Learning to listen to, express, and make sense of personal experiences
- Learning about and confronting their occupational apartheid experience (participation restriction on the margins of society)
- Working to establish a new structure of habits and roles that would enable them to shape their destinies (Kronenberg, 2005).

## United States: Opportunities for Promoting Optimal Occupational Performance

In the U.S., outcomes of prenatal alcohol and drug exposure, as well as abuse, neglect, and trauma have been studied for decades and been identified as precursors to physical and behavioral abnormalities in infants, toddlers, children, and incarceration for youth and adults (Bandstra, Morrow, Mansoor, & Accornero, 2010; Wolff & Shi, 2012). Occupational therapists (OTs) working in primary care and community settings serve as members of interdisciplinary teams with physicians and other health care and social service providers to identify and work with those at risk for substance use or alcohol use or abuse during pregnancy (Farmer, Lamb, Muir, & Siebert, 2014). Within the medical team, OTs work with parents to prevent alcohol and substance abuse, neglect and trauma, by assisting in educating them on potential risks and identifying and substituting meaningful leisure activities, routines, and relationships for those that are triggers for alcohol or substance use. Additionally, OTs work with parents to promote positive, functional parenting skills. Occupational therapists also work in daycare settings and homeless shelters that include children, assessing development and determining delays and factors that place children at risk for future behavioral problems if left untreated (Bruder, 2010; Rybski & Wilder, 2008; Thomas, Gray, & McGinty, 2011).

Occupational therapy intervention between the ages of 0 to 5 years has been demonstrated to be effective with infants and children affected by alcohol or substance use. Occupational therapy practitioners provide services to children and youth in order to promote the following:

- Enhancing play and leisure skills by assisting children in adapting to the environment, negotiate barriers, establish functional routines, habits and behaviors, and find supports in friends, pets, neighbors, and teachers (Harding et al., 2009).
- Supporting children's interests and abilities to create positive vs disruptive experiences in play and leisure (Frolek Clark & Kingsley, 2013; Harding et al., 2009).
- Providing family-centered service delivery that incorporates support to strengthen the family to improve satisfaction, well-being, social support, child performance (e.g., cognitive, motor, self-care, socially sanctioned behaviors), and parenting skills (Frolek Clark & Kingsley, 2013).
- Using a variety of interventions such as modeling, play-based activities, cognitive-behavioral strategies, and social toys to promote cooperative play and positive social outcomes (Frolek Clark & Kingsley, 2013).
- Improving social interactions, and physical, cognitive, communication, emotional, and sensory processing skills (Frolek Clark & Kingsley, 2013; Harding et al., 2009).

From ages 3 to 21 years, preschools and K-12 systems focus on learning academic, non-academic, and functional skills. Occupational therapists enhance participation in daily life activities in school for children with disabilities *or at risk for disabilities* including *behavioral,* as follows:

- Assisting the child designated with behavioral, physical, or psychosocial challenges to benefit from his or her educational program (Yell, Shriner, & Katsiyannis, 2006) by focusing on developing routines in activities of daily living (e.g., dressing, hygiene, eating, rest and sleep), instrumental activities of daily living (e.g., community mobility, safety), learning (e.g., handwriting, computer use, attention), *play and leisure, social participation, and work* (Doll, 2014; Elbaum & Vaughn, 2001; Frolek Clark & Chandler, 2013).
- Providing services in the least restrictive environment and assisting in transition planning to prepare children for further education, employment, and independent lives (Landmark, Ju, & Zhang, 2010).
- Working with the student as well as their family, educational staff, and community members to promote societally sanctioned educational, physical, and social choices and skills of participation in society (Frolek Clark & Chandler, 2013).
- Enhancing access to the school environment through modifications and supports (e.g. socio-emotional self-regulation strategies for at-risk children, appropriate socializing and playing on playgrounds) (Barnes, Vogel, Beck, Schoenfeld, & Owen, 2008; Bazyk & Arbesman, 2013; Frolek Clark & Chandler, 2013).
- Promoting evidence-based initiatives such as Early Intervening Services (multi-tiered system of services), Family Centered Practice (FCP), Universal Design for Learning, and School Health and Wellness (e.g., nutritional foods, activity to increase health and decrease obesity, *coping with neglect, abuse or other trauma, stopping school bullying and other socially deviant behaviors*) (Frolek Clark & Chandler, 2013).

Early intervention, school-based, and juvenile detention services, where identification of client needs *as well as strengths and occupational performance skills* are not included in typical assessment and programming, omit addressing fundamental occupational performance needs for sanctioned functioning within society, especially for those living in poverty on the margins of society.

An historical focus on behavioral interventions that suspend or remove juvenile offenders from school and/or place them in jail or prison has prevailed since the 1980s, when a shift in legislation from nurturing and educating incarcerated youth toward punishment took place (Listwan, Sullivan, Agnew, Cullen, & Colvin, 2013; Seiter, 2011). Infusing an occupational perspective in policy, justice system design and culture, collaborative practice, and community education has the potential to change the punitive nature of juvenile delinquency to a transformative process (Henderson, Batten, & Richmond, 2015). This client-centered and occupation-based therapy uses a non-prescriptive approach that validates the client and has been shown to be especially effective with youth who are at-risk and participating in urban programs in California that were established to serve vulnerable youth ages 5–24 years (Shea & Jackson, 2015; Snyder, Clark, Masunaka-Noriega, & Young, 1998).

For 43 years, the Los Angeles based program has operated, funded by the U.S. Department of Labor; and for 19 years, the San Francisco Bay Area Occupational Therapy Treatment Program (OTTP), funded by the City of San Francisco, has served vulnerable youth with mental health challenges, learning, social, and/or emotional disabilities, special education status, economically disadvantaged, on probation or detained, pregnant or parenting, placement in foster care system, and developmental delays. The ultimate goal of OTTP services is to decrease risk behaviors by engaging youth in meaningful, purposeful activities that result in positive future orientation and goal fulfillment. The youth in these programs build skills necessary for optimal performance in school, vocational, home, and community settings; and are empowered to maximize their potential to achieve personal, educational, and vocational goals (Shea & Jackson, 2015).

The OTTP organization provides 14 interprofessional programs that are client-centered, strengths-based, and customized to meet the individual youth's needs. Each program addresses different needs of the adolescent population served via the OTTP approach, which includes the following:

- Approaching each youth holistically
- Facilitating opportunities to cultivate each youth's strengths
- Identifying and honoring their interests and priorities
- Facilitating utilization of community resources that match strengths and interests
- Empowering youth to select intervention options
- Providing trauma-informed care
- Addressing social skills, healthy decision-making, problem-solving, healthy risk-taking, effective communication, vocational skills and experience, as well as educational pursuits.

*Occupational therapy services* at OTTP include screenings, assessments including vocational strengths and deficits, and individual or group interventions (Haworth & Cyrs, 2017). Their *vocational preparation* services includes vocational assessments, job readiness, skill building, job referrals, and placement. *Transition Planning* supports youth as they navigate the next steps after turning 18 years of age. *Case Management* provided by social workers, *Psychotherapy, Family Therapy, Resource Development,* and *After-care Services* provide additional supports to youths to promote optimal outcomes.

Play as occupation is critical for children through adolescence, and is particularly important for youth in detention. Since their environment limits daily occupations, incarcerated youth typically experience few opportunities for play activities or engagement in personally chosen meaningful occupations (Shea & Siu, 2016). Routine life in detention represents restriction to a jail cell or similar circumstances, with external activities primarily involving bathing, grooming, dressing, eating, formal education, and occasional court appearances. More available for youths in detention are unstructured activities that are more passive (e.g. watching television, talking and listening to music); these provide some alternatives to boredom. Structured leisure occupations, such as crafts, games, and sports are more meaningful but less available for detained youths (Farnworth, 2000). The lack of structured play opportunities for youth in detention deepens their isolation, thus impeding their healthy growth and development (Farnworth, 2000; Shea & Siu, 2016).

Basic living skills are also fundamental to successful youth transitions to adulthood. Studies by Arnett (2001, 2014) and Schwartz, Côté, and Arnett (2005) demonstrated that adolescents strive to accept personal responsibilities, formation of mature relationships with adults, maturation of personal beliefs, values, and financial independence as the most important elements of successful adulthood. However, youth in detention have limited opportunities to develop healthy relationships, strong self-identities, and employment skills (Arnett, 2001, 2014; Schwartz, Côté, & Arnett, 2005).

Occupational therapists in the community-based Occupational Therapy Training Program (OTTP), conducted a study exploring the extent of engagement of male and female youth in detention, aged 14 to 18 years old, in structured play activities on topics such as interpersonal relationships, self-awareness, cultural celebrations and the transition to community. Retrospective analysis of data collected from surveys using the Engagement in OTTP Activities Questionnaire (EOAQ), completed by youth participants at the end of each group session, was used to measure the extent of occupational engagement. Additional activity related data (e.g. worksheets and art projects) were also analyzed (Shea & Siu, 2016).

Participants reported very high engagement in OTTP; scores for males were higher than those for female participants, and both genders had higher engagement scores for different activities. Over 90% of the worksheets and artworks were found to be complete and relevant to the topic of the session. These results indicate that play activities may facilitate acquisition of life skills for youth in detention. Future studies examining the potential gender-related preferences for specific topics deserve further investigation as well as research comparing the youth's engagement in OTTP interventions using play activities to other group interventions (Shea & Siu, 2016).

## Transformative Justice Initiative

### *Historical Overview*

Since 2010, the second author of this chapter, Dr. Karen F. Barney, has shaped an innovative model for facilitating successful community reentry. Barney initially worked with the Saint Louis University (SLU) Prison Program founder, Dr. Kenneth Parker, who built a unique higher education program for both staff and individuals incarcerated within the Missouri Department of Corrections prisons. Barney's vision for re-entry included capitalizing upon the presence of many professions at SLU in providing pre- and post-release seamless habilitation and rehabilitation supports, utilizing occupational therapy as a core discipline, while collaborating with justice systems. The interprofessional process invited professionals in social work, medicine, nursing, psychology, business, law, nutrition, career services, English as a second language faculty, and the Workforce Development Center to provide all indicated areas of expertise to support reentry and long-term successful return to society from incarceration. Occupational therapy provides evidence-informed assessment and one-one, as well as small group, occupation-based interventions. The process is guided by the presenting needs of clients, including high school equivalency preparation and completion, higher education, and ongoing pre-release preparation and post-release facilitation of occupation-based and interprofessional services supported by many related community agencies, to encourage successful reentry.

In 2014, the first author of this chapter, Dr. Lisa Jaegers, proposed widening the scope of reentry services by including justice system organizational needs assessment and workplace health along with Barney's model for collaborative and bridged transition services. The Transformative Justice Initiative (TJI) was formed to include partnerships with city, state, and federal justice settings that work strategically towards organizational change and implementation of evidence-informed transition services. The Initiative's core is a combination of systems, community, university, and individual action to address incarceration and justice system needs; in essence, a transformative justice model.

Implementation of TJI programs began with correctional staff. The work of correctional officers is dangerous and has a negative impact on their health (Brower, 2013). Correctional officers often lack freedom to engage in meaningful work activities in cultural environments that promote punitive, punishment as opposed to positive, skill building and encouragement (Brower, 2013). Through a community-based participatory research study using a Total Worker Health® approach at urban and rural jails, we learned that officers experience serious mental and physical health issues (Jaegers et al., under review-a). Officers agreed with the need for resident treatment and rehabilitation programs, and agreed with the importance of having compassion for jail residents. The project identified specific workplace health promotion and protection interventions and the implementation process has been in progress since 2016. We recognize that unmet correctional worker health needs, combined with a highly stressful work environment, likely contribute to limitations in performing quality work with residents. Programming to improve workplace health and culture are necessary for potentially improving the identification, implementation, and delivery of services for individuals including juveniles interacting with the justice system.

The Occupational Therapy Transition and Integration Services (OTTIS) through TJI apply Barney's pre- and post-release model in an urban jail. Through a 16-month process evaluation, we've learned the participating jail was not designed to provide rehabilitation and transition or reentry programming and there were major barriers to resident participation due to the unknown nature of being held pre-sentenced (Jaegers et al., under review-b). Despite many challenges, it was feasible to implement OTTIS in an urban jail largely due to solid partnerships with correctional officers and staff that were developed through our workplace health project. Our study findings informed program modifications to work more directly with attorneys and courts who, after learning about the benefits of occupational therapy, have referred clients to our pre-release services. By working with individuals during the pre-sentencing period, we explore their occupational goals, begin therapeutic activities towards those goals, and share progress with the court during sentencing. Our advocacy work has resulted in lower sentence duration and community release where post-release occupational therapy interventions continue.

## Conclusion

This chapter provided an introduction to the application of criminal justice-based occupational perspectives and occupational therapy practice for work with juveniles. We have explored examples of occupational therapy practice across prevention of juvenile detention and intervention within the justice system. Our formative research gives practical details to inform correctional workplace health and transition and integration (reentry) program development to potentially impact system change and engage individuals in health-promoting, meaningful occupations.

## References

Aldrich, R. (2018). Strengthening associated living: A Deweyan approach to occupational justice. *Journal of Occupational Science, 25*, 337–345. doi: 10.1080/14427591.2018.1484386.

Aldrich, R., Boston, T. L., & Daaleman, C. E. (2016). The issue is ... Justice and US occupational therapy practice: A relationship 100 years in the making. *American Journal of Occupational Therapy, 71*, 7101100040p1–7101100040p5. doi: 10.5014/ajot.2017.023085.

Aldrich, R., & White, N. (2012). Re-considering violence: A response to Twinley and Addidle (2012) and Morris (2012). *British Journal of Occupational Therapy, 75*, 527–529.

Aldrich, R. M. (2008). From complexity theory to transactionalism: Moving occupational science forward in theorizing the complexities of behavior. *Journal of Occupational Science, 15*, 147–156. doi: 10.1080/14427591.2008.9686624.

AOTA – American Occupational Therapy Association. (2014). Occupational therapy practice framework: Domain and process (3rd ed.). *American Journal of Occupational Therapy, 68*, S1–S48.

Arnett, J. J. (2001). Conceptions of the transition to adulthood: Perspectives from adolescence through midlife. *Journal of Adult Development, 8*, 133–143. 2014.

Arnett, J. J. (2014). *Adolescence and emerging adulthood*. Boston, MA: Pearson.

Bailliard, A. (2016). Justice, difference, and the capability to function. *Journal of Occupational Science, 23*, 3–16. doi: 10.1080/14427591.2014.957886.

Bailliard, A., & Aldrich, R. (2016). Occupational justice in everyday occupational therapy practice. In D. Sakellariou & N. Pollard (Eds.), *Occupational therapies without borders: Integrating justice with practice* (pp. 83–94). Oxford, UK: Elsevier.

Bandstra, E. S., Morrow, C. E., Mansoor, E., & Accornero, V. H. (2010). Prenatal drug exposure: Infant and toddler outcomes. *Journal of Addictive Diseases, 29*, 245–258. doi: 10.1080/10550881003684871.

Barnes, K. J., Vogel, K. A., Beck, A. J., Schoenfeld, H. B., & Owen, S. V. (2008). Self-regulation strategies of children with emotional disturbance. *Physical & Occupational Therapy in Pediatrics, 28*, 369–387.

Barros, D. D., Garcez Ghirardi, M. I., Lopes, R. E., & Galheigo, S. M. (2011). Brazilian experiences in social occupational therapy. In F. Kronenberg, N. Pollard, & D. Sakellariou (Eds.), *Occupational therapies without borders* (Vol. 2, pp. 209–216). London: Churchill Livingstone Elsevier.

Bazyk, S., & Arbesman, M. (2013). *Occupational therapy practice guidelines for mental health promotion, prevention, and intervention for children and youth*. Bethesda, MD: AOTA Press.

Benassi, J., & Fraile, M. (2011). Daytime activities device (DAD) for children and teenagers in a psychosocially vulnerable situation. In F. Kronenberg, N. Pollard, & D. Sakellariou (Eds.), *Occupational therapies without borders* (Vol. 2, pp. 232–233). London: Churchill Livingstone Elsevier.

Brower, J. (2013). *Correctional officer wellness and safety literature review.* Washington, DC: U.S. Department of Justice Office of Justice Programs Diagnostic Center. Retrieved from https://nicic.gov/correctional-officer-wellness-and-safety-literature-review.

Bruder, M. B. (2010). Early childhood intervention: A promise to children and families for their future. *Exceptional Children, 76,* 339–355.

Case-Smith, J. (2015). An overview of occupational therapy for children. In Case-Smith, J., & O'Brien, J. C. (Eds.), *Occupational therapy for children and adolescents* (7th ed., pp. 1–26). St. Louis, MO: Elsevier.

Cohn, E., & Lew, C. (2010). Occupational therapy's perspective on the use of environments and contexts to support health and participation in occupations. *American Journal of Occupational Therapy, 64,* S57–S69. doi: 10.5014/ajot.2010.64S57.

Cutchin, M. P., Dickie, V. A., & Humphry, R. (2017). Foregrounding the transactional perspective's community orientation. *Journal of Occupational Science, 24,* 434–445. doi: 10.1080/14427591.2017.1365750.

Dickie, V. A. (2010). Are occupations 'processes too complicated to explain'? What we can learn by trying. *Journal of Occupational Science, 17,* 195–203. doi: 10.1080/14427591.2010.9686696.

Dickie, V. A., Cutchin, M., & Humphry, R. (2006). Occupation as transactional experience: A critique of individualism in occupational science. *Journal of Occupational Science, 13,* 83–93. doi: 10.1080/14427591.2006.9686573.

Doll, J. (2014). Establishing routines for the healthy development of children. *OT Practice, 19,* 15–17.

Dunn, W. (2011). *Best practice occupational therapy for children and families in community settings* (2nd ed.). Thorofare, NJ: Slack.

Durocher, E., Gibson, B. E., & Rappolt, S. (2014). Occupational justice: A conceptual review. *Journal of Occupational Science, 21,* 418–430. doi: 10.1080/14427591.2013.775692.

Duschatzky, S., & Corea, C. (2007). *Chicos en banda. Los Caminos de la Subjetividad en el Declive de las Instituciones.* Buenos Aires, Argentina: Paidos.

Elbaum, B., & Vaughn, S. (2001). School-based interventions to enhance the self-concept of students with learning disabilities: A meta-analysis. *Elementary School Journal, 101,* 303–329. doi: 10.1086/499670.

Farias, L., & Laliberte Rudman, D. (2016). A critical interpretive synthesis of the uptake of critical perspectives in occupational science. *Journal of Occupational Science, 23,* 33–50. doi: 10.1080/14427591.2014.989893.

Farmer, M. E., Lamb, A. J., Muir, S., & Siebert, C. (2014). The role of occupational therapy in primary care. *American Journal of Occupational Therapy, 68,* S25.

Farnworth, L. (2000). Time use and leisure occupations of young offenders. *American Journal of Occupational Therapy, 54,* 315–325.

Farnworth, L., & Muñoz, J. P. (2009). An occupational and rehabilitation perspective for institutional practice. *Psychiatric Rehabilitation Journal, 32,* 192–198. doi: 10.2975/32.3.2009.192.198.

Fingerhut, P. E., Piro, J., Sutton, A., Campbell, R., Lewis, C., Lawji, D., & Martinez, N. (2013). Family-centered principles implemented in home-based, clinic-based, and school-based pediatric settings. *American Journal of Occupational Therapy, 67,* 228–235. doi: 10.5014/ajot.2013.006957.

Fisher, A. G. (2014). Occupation-centred, occupation-based, occupation-focused: Same, same or different? *Scandinavian Journal of Occupational Therapy, 21,* 96–107. doi: 10.3109/11038128.2014.952912.

Frolek Clark, G., & Chandler, B. E. (Eds.). (2013). *Best practices for occupational therapy in schools.* Pittsburgh, PA: AOTA Press.

Frolek Clark, G., & Kingsley, K. (2013). *Occupational therapy practice guidelines for early childhood: Birth through 5 years.* Bethesda, MD: AOTA Press.

Gray, J. M. (1997). Application of the phenomenological method to the concept of occupation. *Journal of Occupational Science, 4,* 5–17. doi: 10.1080/14427591.1997.9686416.

Hammell, K. W., & Beagan, B. (2016). Occupational injustice: A critique. *Canadian Journal of Occupational Therapy, 84,* 58–68. doi: 10.1177/0008417416638858.

Harding, J., Harding, K., Jamieson, P., Mullally, M., Politi, C., Wong-Sing, E., … Petrenchik, T. M. (2009). Children with disabilities' perceptions of activity participation and environments: A pilot study. *Canadian Journal of Occupational Therapy, 76,* 133–144. doi: 10.1177/000841740907600302.

Haworth, C., & Cyrs, G. (2017). Supporting transitions to the workforce for at-risk youth: Developing and using an occupation-based work skills assessment. Retrieved from www.ottp-sf.org/programs

Henderson, P., Batten, R., & Richmond, J. (2015). Perceptions of the role of occupational therapy in community child and adolescent mental health services. *Occupational Therapy in Mental Health, 31,* 155–167. doi: 10.1080/0164212X.2015.1035475.

Hitch, D., Pépin, G., & Stagnitti, K. (2014). In the footsteps of Wilcock, part one: The evolution of doing, being, becoming, and belonging. *Occupational Therapy in Health Care, 28,* 231–246. doi: 10.3109/07380577.2014.898114.

Hocking, C. (2009). The challenge of occupation: Describing the things people do. *Journal of Occupational Science, 16*, 140–150. doi: 10.1080/14427591.2009.9686655.

Hocking, C. (2017). Occupational justice as social justice: The moral claim for inclusion. *Journal of Occupational Science, 24*, 29–42. doi: 10.1080/14427591.2017.1294016.

Jaegers, L. A., Ahmad, S. O., Scheetz, G., Bixler, E., Nadimpalli, S., Barnidge, E., Katz, I. M., Vaughn, M. G., & Matthieu, M. (under review-a). Total Worker Health® needs assessment to identify workplace mental health interventions in rural and urban jails.

Jaegers, L. A., Skinner, E., Conners, B., Hayes, C., West-Bruce, S., Vaughn, M. G., & Barney, K. F. (under review-b). Implementation evaluation of the jail-based Occupational Therapy Transition and Integration Services (OTTIS) program.

Kielhofner, G. (2004). *Terapia Ocupacional. Modelo de la Ocupacion Humana: Teoria y Aplicacion*. Buenos Aires, Argentina: Panamericana.

Kiepek, N. C., Beagan, B., Laliberte Rudman, D., & Phelan, S. (2018). Silences around occupations framed as unhealthy, illegal, and deviant. *Journal of Occupational Science*. doi: 10.1080/14427591.2018.1499123.

Kronenberg, F. (2005). Occupational therapy with street children. In F. Kronenberg, S. Simó Algado, & N. Pollard (Eds.), *Occupational therapy without borders: Learning from the spirit of survivors* (pp. 261–276). London: Elsevier.

Laliberte Rudman, D., & Aldrich, R. M. (2017). Discerning the social in individual stories of occupation through critical narrative inquiry. *Journal of Occupational Science, 24*, 470–481. doi: 10.1080/14427591.2017.1369144.

Landmark, L. J., Ju, S., & Zhang, D. (2010). Substantiated best practices in transition: Fifteen plus years later. *Career Development for Exceptional Individuals, 33*, 165–176. doi: 10.1177/0885728810376410.

Lavalley, R. (2017). Developing the transactional perspective of occupation for communities: "How well are we doing together?". *Journal of Occupational Science, 24*, 458–469. doi: 10.1080/14427591.2017.1367321.

Listwan, S. J., Sullivan, C. J., Agnew, R., Cullen, F. T., & Colvin, M. (2013). The pains of imprisonment revisited: The impact of strain on inmate recidivism. *Justice Quarterly, 30*, 144–168. doi: 10.1080/07418825.2011.597772.

Muñoz, J., Moreton, E. M., & Sitterly, A. M. (2016). The scope of practice of occupational therapy in U.S. criminal justice settings. *Occupational Therapy International, 23*, 241–254. doi: 10.1002/oti.1427.

O'Connell, M., & Farnworth, L. (2007). Occupational therapy in forensic psychiatry: A review of the literature and a call for a united and international response. *British Journal of Occupational Therapy, 70*, 184–191. doi: 10.1177/030802260707000502.

Penner, D. A. (1978). Correctional institutions: An overview. *The American Journal of Occupational Therapy: Official Publication of the American Occupational Therapy Association, 32*, 517–524.

Rogers, A. T., Bai, G., Lavin, R. A., & Anderson, G. F. (2017). Higher hospital spending on occupational therapy is associated with lower readmission rates. *Medical Care Research and Review, 74*, 668–686.

Rybski, D. A., & Wilder, E. (2008). A pilot study to identify developmental delay in children in underserved urban community child care settings. *Journal of Allied Health, 37*, e34–49.

Schwartz, S. J., Côté, J. E., & Arnett, J. J. (2005). Identity and agency in emerging adulthood: Two developmental routes in the individualization process. *Youth & Society, 37*, 201–229. doi: 10.1177/0044118X05275965.

Seiter, R. P. (2011). *Corrections: An introduction* (3rd ed., pp. 249–277). Boston, MA: Prentice Hall.

Shea, C. K., & Jackson, N. (2015). Client perception of a client-centered and occupation-based intervention for at-risk youth. *Scandinavian Journal of Occupational Therapy, 22*, 173–180. doi: 10.3109/11038128.2014.958873.

Shea, C. K., & Siu, A. M. H. (2016). Engagement in play activities as a means for youth in detention to acquire life skills. *Occupational Therapy International, 23*, 276–286. doi: 10.1002/oti.1432.

Snyder, C., Clark, F., Masunaka-Noriega, M., & Young, B. (1998). Los Angeles street kids: New occupations for life program. *Journal of Occupational Science, 5*, 133–139.

Thomas, Y., Gray, M., & McGinty, S. (2011). A systematic review of occupational therapy interventions with homeless people. *Occupational Therapy in Health Care, 25*, 38–53. doi: 10.3109/07380577.2010.528554.

Townsend, E. A., & Polatajko, H. J. (2007). *Enabling occupation II: Advancing an occupational therapy vision for health, well-being, and justice through occupation*. Ottawa, ON: CAOT Publications.

Trombly, C. A. (1995). Occupation: Purposefulness and meaningfulness as therapeutic mechanisms. *American Journal of Occupational Therapy, 49*, 960–972. doi: 10.5014/ajot.49.10.960.

Twinley, R. (2013). The dark side of occupation: A concept for consideration. *Australian Occupational Therapy Journal, 60*, 301–303. doi: 10.1111/1440-1630.12026.

Twinley, R., & Addidle, G. (2012). Considering violence: The dark side of occupation. *British Journal of Occupational Therapy, 75*, 202–204. doi: 10.4276/030802212X13336366278257.

White, N. (2013). The third world near you: The challenge of urban America. In C. Camp-Yeakey, V. L. Sanders Thompson, & A. Wells (Eds.), *Urban ills: Post-recession complexities of urban living in global contexts* (pp. 407–432). Lanham, MD: Lexington Books.

Whiteford, G. (2000). Occupational deprivation: Global challenge in the new millennium. *British Journal of Occupational Therapy, 63*, 200–204. doi: 10.1177/030802260006300503.

Whiteford, G. (2010). Occupational deprivation: Understanding limited participation. In C. Christiansen, & E. Townsend (Eds.), *Occupation: The art and science of living* (pp. 303–328). Upper Saddle River, NJ: Prentice Hall.

Wilcock, A. A. (1998). Reflections on doing, being, and becoming. *Canadian Journal of Occupational Therapy, 65*, 248–256. doi: 10.1177/000841749806500501.

Wilcock, A. A., & Hocking, C. (2015). *An occupational perspective of health* (3rd ed.). Thorofare, NJ: Slack.

Wolff, N., & Shi, J. (2012). Childhood and adult trauma experiences of incarcerated persons and their relationship to adult behavioral health problems and treatment. *International Journal of Environmental Research and Public Health, 9*, 1908–1926.

World Health Organization. (2014). *Constitution of the World Health Organization* (45th ed.). Retrieved from http://apps.who.int/gb/bd/PDF/bd47/EN/constitution-en.pdf?ua=1

Yell, M. L., Shriner, J. G., & Katsiyannis, A. (2006). Individuals with disabilities education improvement act of 2004 and IDEA regulations of 2006: Implications for educators, administrators, and teacher trainers. *Focus on Exceptional Children, 39*, 1–24.

# 22
# QUALITATIVE RESEARCH AT THE INTERSECTIONS OF YOUTH JUSTICE AND HEALTH

*Laura S. Abrams and Elizabeth S. Barnert*

In this chapter, we will provide reflections on conducting team-driven, qualitative research at the intersection of youth justice and health. Brought together by a mutual interest in youth reentry from incarceration, we are a social work professor (Laura) and an academic pediatrician (Liz) who bring diverse disciplinary and methodological perspectives to our partnership. Over the past three years, we have worked on a variety of funded and unfunded projects, including large-scale secondary data analyses on the association of child incarceration with adult health outcomes; a mixed methods policy project on setting a minimum age of juvenile justice jurisdiction in California; and mostly qualitative, mixed methods project on youth reentry into medical and behavioral healthcare settings. In related projects, we have also studied the health needs of specialized populations, such as commercially and sexually exploited young women. While we have collaborated with additional faculty, students, community advocates, youth justice leaders, and policymakers, together we have maintained a core focus on improving systems of care for youth who are transitioning out of juvenile justice settings, including detention and long-term incarceration.

Our partnership coupling academic social work (with social science PhD training) and medicine (with medical school, MD training) ushers in distinct, yet complementary perspectives. Laura tends to focus on building theory through qualitative methodology and views "health" under a broad umbrella; Liz often views issues through a more medical view of "health" and healthcare access, and pushes us as a team to ensure that the work has a practical, real world impact. With our different perspectives, our partnership has been aligned in our use of a range of qualitative methods in order to capture the complexity and nuances of youth reentry and health, with health broadly defined as "well-being."

## Why Qualitative Methods?

As authors, scholars, and practitioners, we continue to be drawn to qualitative methods to study the intersection of justice-involved youth and health. We use these methods for a variety of reasons, as be briefly summarize below.

1. **Understanding barriers in a deeper way.** Youth reentry incarceration is a complex phenomenon with numerous forces- positive, negative, and neutral-interacting with the young person who is experiencing reintegration (Abrams, 2006). We have found that in order to more deeply understand the linkages between youth justice and well-being, it is not sufficient to simply list or identify these barriers. There are a range of complex connections between reentry barriers that young people experience, and so much of our work has tried to disentangle, qualify, and illustrate these barriers in a deeper way.
2. **Looking at pathways.** Just as it is important to look at barriers, it is also key to view pathways to successful medical and behavioral healthcare following incarceration. Qualitative research allows us to hone in on typologies of successful healthcare utilization and well-being in a way that we hope can lead to interventions. Without this qualitative data, we might be limited in our focus on the negative outcomes or low health-care utilization rates, rather than able to cull out solutions.
3. **Person in environment.** Particularly from the social work standpoint, we find that the person-in-environment (Bronfenbrenner, 1979) perspective is best illustrated through qualitative methods. Reentry itself is particularly well suited to being approached from multiple levels of interaction (Abrams & Snyder, 2010). As such, we do not view a young person's situation in isolation of the micro-system (family), the mezzo system (school and other neighborhood resources), or the macro systems of criminalization, racism, and poverty. Rather, with qualitative methodology, aim situate their experiences and world-views in the contexts of surrounding environments.
4. **Gives voice to marginalized youth and families.** We have found, like other scholars, that young people in the juvenile justice system are among the most vulnerable adolescents in American society (Cox, 2017). Qualitative research allows researchers to bring direct quotes from youth and their families to the academy, to community members, and to policymakers, so that youth and family perspectives can be more central to the discussion of solutions.
5. **Provides key policy recommendations.** While policymakers often appreciate on hard data, they often stories for persuasion (Shonkoff & Bales, 2011). We have found that our arsenal of research stories, quotes, and real-life situations has provided policymakers with just as much sway as the numbers when pushing for legislative reform in youth justice.

## *Navigating Barriers*

Despite these aforementioned benefits, there are numerous challenges involved in conducting research with incarcerated and formerly incarcerated youth. Interestingly, there is a not a great deal of prior research the specifically lists these barriers or discusses ways around them. However, the combination of more general strategies for conducting qualitative field work (Maxwell, 2013) as well as some literature on conducting research in carceral or probation settings, and research with children, contributes to the literature base in this area.

Qualitative fieldwork with vulnerable groups, including children, always involves issues of access. With incarcerated youth (particularly under age 18) the gatekeeping can be even more layered and complex to navigate. Children have privacy rights as does protected health and court information, and are generally viewed as a vulnerable population by institutional review boards (Kirk, 2006). Additionally, obtaining permission for research with individuals who are "prisoners" involves additional safeguards and protections. Thus, access to minors who are incarcerated, on probation, or wards of the court often has to pass through many gatekeepers including, but not limited to: IRB regulations, court, and parents/guardians, and the setting itself (Abrams & Anderson-Nathe, 2013; Cox, 2017). For example:

- IRB requires specific assurances and permissions for minors, for wards of the court, and for incarcerated persons, and/or persons with cognitive impairment (National Institute of Health, 2018). The IRB may also want to have extra scrutiny around the questions that are asked to minors and ensure that the researchers are trained in mandatory reporting, when applicable (Sieber, 1994).
- Juvenile court judges often need to approve any research study conducted with a court supervised population, including foster youth, youth in custody, or youth in court ordered care of any type (Varma & Wendler, 2008). From our own experiences, requirements can hard to navigate and petitions may take time to be reviewed. Judges can deny research petitions or delay the process seeking additional information or approvals from various county or state entities.
- Even if the child is in custody, the court and/or IRB may not waive parental or guardian consent. This means that in addition to the layer of court approval, the researcher will also have to contact parents/caregivers (c.f. Abrams & Anderson-Nathe, 2013, methods appendix for an example).
- Even once all permissions have been obtained, the juvenile justice setting might impose restrictions on aspects such as timing of recruitment or data collection, offering a confidential space to conduct the study, or even at times, may not want certain youth to participate or might discourage youth to take part in the study, introducing restrictions or parameters that might run counter to IRB regulations (Abrams, 2010). In other instances, the justice system may actively facilitate the data collection progress. Essentially, they have power to ease or smooth the research project, or effectively, to limit feasibility.

It is clear to us, as is the case with many other researchers, that negotiating gatekeeping is really key to field work success. Later in this chapter, we provide an example and some advice on working with gatekeepers, planning for obstacles, and taking the "long view" that this work takes time, care, and building relationships for it to succeed.

In addition to gatekeeping, there are some particular issues concerning sampling and retention for this population. As Laura has detailed in a prior publication (Abrams, 2010), studying incarcerated youth often turns into a form of convenience sampling due to these layers of barriers noted above. Hence the researcher or team is often quite content to secure a robust sample even when the initial goals of the sampling were not attained. Moreover, difficulties in recruiting, and the nature of a high rate of attrition among vulnerable populations necessitates, at times, knowing that the sample will not meet ideal publishing standards for rigorous qualitative research (Sandelowski, 1989). Hence the researcher often goes through a process of "trial and error" in order to recruit, consent, and attain a sample that is diverse, not "creaming" only the most successful incarcerated or formerly incarcerated youth, and that will remain engaged in a longitudinal study. We have not located a specific literature that articulates these strategies for a youth reentry population, which has been the focus of much of our research, so we hope to provide you with some examples in this chapter.

## Example of a Qualitative Youth Reentry and Health Study

Here we present the qualitative research process, focusing on of one of our studies on the health status and healthcare needs of youth return homing from incarceration. We fielded a mixed methods study within Los Angeles County with the probation department and county health department serving collaborators. The overall goal of the study was to understand longitudinal healthcare access and utilization among young people who were returning home from local probation camps back to the Los Angeles area. The specific research questions were:

1 What are youths' health needs and healthcare access during reentry?
2 How do youth experience change across a six-month reentry period?
3 What is the role of caregiver engagement in promoting youths' health and healthcare access after incarceration?

Data collection included a one-time, close-ended quantitative survey conducted with youth at one-month post-release from incarceration. A sub-set of youth participants and their parents/caregivers subsequently completed one-on-one qualitative interviews at one, three, and six-months post-release. The quantitative survey measured youths' health status and healthcare access during reentry. The youth and caregiver interviews provided a longitudinal, in-depth view of youths' health needs and experiences with health and healthcare throughout reentry. These instruments asked about youths' health, in terms of their physical, reproductive, and mental health, and substance use. Interviews also explored youths' healthcare experiences during reentry, including barriers and facilitators to care, and youths' interactions with caregivers and other members of their social network that influence care access.

In addition to the youth and caregivers, we also interviewed a purposive sample of county stakeholders with expertise in juvenile justice to identify their perspectives on strategies for improving youths' access to care during reentry. Participants included juvenile justice, health, and education systems leaders, and health providers, both in the correctional and community setting. Data collection occurred from 2017–2018. The study was funded by an NIH Career Development Award received by Liz, with Laura serving as one of three mentors on the project.

## *Community Buy-In*

Successful execution of the project required close partnership with juvenile justice partners, especially with the probation department, as well as with the county correctional pediatric and mental health leaders. Prior collaborations with these partners formed the basis for the trust necessary to mutually develop the study protocol, submit grant proposals (including community partner letters of support), and to obtain the necessary approvals. The reentry study built off of relationships Liz had established while a research fellow at UCLA. During the study, an alum of her same fellowship program, Dr. Ray Perry, served as medical director of Los Angeles County's Juvenile Court Health Services programs, which provides medical care to detained youth in the County. Ray, also a pediatrician, became an exceptional community partner for Liz's fellowship project, introducing her to key stakeholders within probation and the juvenile hall clinics, to launch her study. The trust Ray had developed with his juvenile justice colleagues extended to Liz for her first introductions. Subsequently, timely, efficient, and useful research by Liz with the justice partners built trust over time that formed by the basis for her career development award reentry study.

When developing the career development award proposal, it was Ray, as chief pediatrician, who had suggested that a focus on reentry would be helpful. Ray than connected Liz to a probation gatekeeper who oversaw reentry services. Periodic communication with the key probation gatekeeper over a period of two years ultimately led to the development of the recruitment plan, which entailed probation providing the research team a spreadsheet, each week, with the names and phone numbers of youth newly released from custody. As the study was launching, our research team attended meetings of probation officers so that they were aware of the study and would distribute a study flyer.

The team maintained regular and as needed communication with the probation partners and collaborating correctional health leaders. Community buy-in, in the case of this study, was essential. Without this level of buy-in and cooperation, we would not have been able to develop our study plan, obtain funding and permissions, and carryout the study. Community buy-in was based on the partners trusting our ethical, scientifically grounded approach, as well as our intentions—to contribute to research that could potentially benefit justice-involved youth and the larger system surrounding these young people. A few youth even called our study phone number saying that their probation officer had encouraged them to do so, an approved procedure and welcome surprise when it occurred.

## *Permission*

Obtaining permission for the study was challenging but provided a key learning experience. In Liz's whole career, this was only time she has ever met with an Institutional Review Board (IRB) administrator in person to discuss the necessary elements of the IRB protocol. Permission for the study was pursued in a sequential fashion. First, we obtained IRB approval from our university's IRB, the University of California, Los Angeles. Subsequently, we obtained approval from the county health department, whose IRB provided a reliance on our university's IRB. We also had a telephone conversation and documented e-mail communication confirming that the study did not also require approval from the county mental health department's IRB. Finally, we obtained formal permission for research from the county juvenile court. We had spoken early in the process with stakeholders involved in the juvenile court's research approval process, including officials within the juvenile court and in probation, to anticipate and adjust to any anticipated snags. Our prior experience had taught us that the court only likes to see the study protocol once—and needs to review the exact questions being asked of the youth. Unlike the IRB amendment process, which can be fairly interactive and iterative, the materials needed to be in their true final form once they got to the court. After the presiding juvenile court judge officially approved the study, which included a required review process by over 20 relevant stakeholders, including district attorneys, public defenders, and probation leadership, we began data collection.

The permissions process was lengthy—it took roughly one year. However, the payoff was great as we had permission to access the youth at home, either via telephone or in person, depending on their preference, and to receive from probation the names and names of youth released each week, and updated phone numbers, should we lose contact. We had planned for a long timeline for the approvals and the process allowed us to hone the study materials and procedure. IRB protocols involving "prisoners" and "minors" are flagged as involving vulnerable populations. Although the study was minimal risk, based on our prior experience conducting research with justice-involved youth, we were aware this would be a lengthy process and had prior experience to tell us to request the court approval last, so that all the materials the court was receiving were in the final form.

## *Recruitment and Consent*

Recruiting high-risk youth for research studies in community settings is often challenging; this is especially true in the case of youth transitioning home after incarceration. We had to overcome several barriers to recruitment and assent/consent. The first contact the youth received from our study team, occurring at approximately two to three weeks after a youth's release, was essentially experienced by families as a "cold call," as most had not viewed the study flyer. When we made telephone calls from a university landline, potential participants read "UCLA" as the caller identification, which caused potential participants to perceive we were part of "a system." Many hung up after a few seconds on a call. Potential participants had many reasons not to trust "official" systems, including medical or educational systems. Our independence from probation was likely difficult for families to understand, especially since probation had provided youths' phone numbers to the team. Some families misunderstood and thought we wanted to provide healthcare. There were also many families we could not reach or who indicated constrained schedules and thus limited time to talk. Youth were frequently not available or reachable because they were in school or on the run. We had one youth answer our call while in class! We told him we would call him later. Also, frequently caregivers were busy, juggling young children and jobs; we had several mothers tell us they were busy cooking and doing other tasks, and we could hear young children in the background. Phone numbers changed and even probation officers lost track of some of the youth within one to two weeks of a youth's release. In several instances, parents told us that they did not know where their child was.

We developed several strategies to overcome barriers related to mistrust and "outsider" identity that can create challenges for recruitment of racial and ethnic minority study participants (Rivas-Drake, Camacho, & Guillaume, 2016). These barriers are likely heightened for justice-involved individuals. Strategies to overcome the barriers included:

- Carefully timing recruitment calls. We targeted times when youth were not in school and that caregivers indicated were convenient.
- Flexibility in the timing of the consent process. We called families back at the time they indicated most convenient, to have the lengthier consent discussion.
- We utilized a study cell phone. This allowed for the Caller ID to not read "UCLA" for families receiving a call and also gave families a convenient way to reach us.
- We honed our pitch. Our team actively discussed what did and did not work in the recruitment process. We adjusted accordingly.
- We maximized our cultural and linguistic fluency. Native Spanish speakers on the study team conducted outreach to the Latino families. We guessed race and ethnicity by participant name. We also outreached to medical students and other graduate students from racial and ethnic minority backgrounds. Liz approached one African-American student who she had a good mentorship relationship with and the student declined to assist, saying "I sound White on the phone." Ultimately, what worked was overtly seeking students who could "code switch" during the recruitment and consent procedure, communicating in a tone, vocabulary, and manner that felt familiar and trustworthy to families. One particular medical student was with our team for an entire summer and we had several families who only wanted to do the longitudinal follow-up only if she was the interviewer.
- We were patient. Recruitment remained open for months. (Laura guided Liz to remember to be patient, since the medical model and grant pressures can make patience hard to come by.)
- We communicated with field probation officers to receive assistance in obtaining new phone numbers for the youth and to maintain their buy-in for the study. A few youth contacted us based on their probation officer's recommendation. We were pleased with the support from the probation officers, who understood our main goal was to develop knowledge that could improve reentry healthcare services.
- We provided incentives. Monetary incentives in the form of Target gift cards were provided. We offered as much as we were able to provide logistically and ethically. Families who completed data collection could earn up to $150. It was clear that many of the youth we interviewed gave the gift cards to their parents; it was nice to be able to give them a way to contribute to their families monetarily, and also to give them the opportunity to share their experiences.

In short, by employing the above strategies, many of which are likely relevant to qualitative research with justice-involved youth in other areas, we overcame obstacles inherent to recruitment of these transient youth.

The response rate for this study was overall low, which is not uncommon for this population. Our goal was to survey 50 youth. To do so, our study team obtained the names of phone numbers of 427 potential youth participants before we reached our goal sample size for the quantitative portion of the study. Of these 427 youth, 51 completed surveys, 25 were not eligible (included 23 who had returned to juvenile hall by one-month post-release), 41 declined, 138 were not reached by the study team, and 172 were reached but did not complete the consent and data collection procedures. Youth who completed the quantitative survey and who were invited for interviews generally agreed to participate in the qualitative interviews. These numbers are similar to Laura's prior phone survey of formerly incarcerated youth (Abrams, Terry, & Franke, 2011), out of 550 on a list, only 73 interviews were completed. Overall, it is easier to recruit youth while they are incarcerated, rather than in the community. For example, in Liz's fellowship study, conducted with 20 youth detained at juvenile hall, only three youth declined participation (Barnert et al., 2015).

## Data Collection

We successfully recruited a purposive sample of 27 youth and 34 caregivers for the longitudinal, qualitative component of the study. The study also included 20 expert stakeholders. Although we did not achieve the youth and caregiver enrollment numbers as quickly as we would have liked, by extending the enrollment period to 1 year, we exceeded our goal and believe that we reached thematic saturation regarding our qualitative findings. Retention of youth in the longitudinal interviews was an issue. We found that several caregivers wanted to stay involved even if youth declined or were re-incarcerated, although retention was an issue for the caregivers. Specifically, 27 youth participated in the baseline (one-month post-release interview), 10 in the 3-month post-release interview, and 4 in the 6-month post-release interview. Among parents, 34 parents participated in the one-month post-release interviews, 13 in the three-month post-release interviews, and 5 in the six-month post-release interviews.

A key element of successful data collection entailed offering to meet families at the time and location of their preference. This included the option to meet in person versus at participants' homes or a designated community organization, such as a library or community building. At one of the local libraries, a librarian would offer our team a conference room for the interviews. We navigated around youth and caregiver schedules. We confirmed interviews before heading out to the field, and identified safe locations for interviews. One youth was high on marijuana at the time of her three-month interview; we believe that she had gotten high while we were interviewing her mother. Participants also varied in the extent to which they felt engaged or rushed during the data collection process. Youth were more likely to seem rushed during interviews conducted over the telephone, rather than in person. We did our best to cultivate trust and meet participants where they were at in order to obtain the highest quality data. This is a similar strategy that Laura used when she studied reentry youth for her book *Everyday Desistance* (2017), essentially meeting youth where they wanted to meet, providing several follow-up texts and reminders, and being constantly aware that one missed appointment did not mean that they were dropping out of the study.

It is notable that for other studies our team has conducted, we have recruited youth detained in juvenile hall or probation campus and completed data collection on site in the detention setting (Barnert et al., 2015; Fields & Abrams, 2010). In these studies, although locating the youth was not a problem, we had to navigate the probation rules and schedules, which is often filled with classes and other scheduled activities. Pros and cons of conducting research with justice-involved youth in the community versus when in detention merit consideration by a researcher in the early stages of developing a study question and design.

## Additional Ethical Concerns

Fear of triggering mandatory reporting requirements was a concern actively raised during the permissions process and by several youth study participants. Our study materials were designed to avoid questions deemed highly likely to trigger mandatory reporting. A Certificate of Confidentiality was automatically in place as the study was funded by the National Institutes of Health (NIH).

Since this was a health study, asking participants about the health status and healthcare needs revealed unmet health issues. In cases when healthcare was needed, the interviewer, most often a research assistant, assessed the acuity and severity of the problem in conjunction with Liz, a pediatrician. When appropriate, referrals to mental health, medical care, or insurance enrollment services were provided. Several families expressed gratitude for the referrals; although this had a slight influence on our study, as we sought to understand pathways to care services, it was gratifying to be able to offer assistance. The study had a detailed emergency response protocol in place. We did have to assess a few youth participants for immediate danger to self or others; in the few instances this came up, emergency services were deemed not necessary, but we had a plan in place should we need to do so.

## Analysis: Making It Meaningful

Completing qualitative analyses to yield meaningful results was both a challenge and, in some senses, we had an advantage. Because the youth were high risk and difficult to reach (for the reasons outlined above related to obtaining research permissions as well as recruitment and retention challenges), the data we obtained were novel and interesting. However, our challenge in interpreting the data in a meaningful way was in disentangling the interrelated factors that influence youths' health and healthcare access, and identifying salient facets specific to reentry and not just general adolescent health issues. Additionally, describing challenges faced by justice-involved youth is not completely helpful for creating change. For our work to have maximum relevance, the goal of identifying solutions for improving youths' health and healthcare access during reentry guided our analyses. This was particularly important to Liz, who as mentioned, keeps her eye on the practical implications of all of this work.

## Dissemination: Translating Findings to Multiple Audience

Given the interdisciplinary nature of the work, and the social justice and public health relevance of youth reentry, we translated our study findings to multiple audiences. For academic dissemination, we presented findings at national academic conferences and prepared peer-reviewed publications, both for the medical and social sciences literatures, depending on which target audience best suited various aspects of the data. We also shared study findings with our community partners, other community leaders, and leadership in the mayor's office and the county juvenile justice and health agencies. Our community dissemination strategy focused on describing the solvable problems (such as gaps in Medicaid reinstatement during reentry) and highlighting recommendations (e.g., strategies to eliminate gaps in Medicaid coverage during reentry). In addition to gaps in Medicaid coverage, the other issue that emerged as most solvable, and thus a focus for dissemination, was transportation. Findings from the youth, caregiver, and county expert interviews, as well as the quantitative surveys, all identified lack of transportation to healthcare appointments as a solvable barrier that could eliminate gaps in care. Conservations with community partners, including the county and city leadership, to address these issues, are in process. Policymaker discussions involved conversations to identify policy windows for tacking the solvable issues for improving healthcare access and health outcomes during reentry. Multiple audiences are needed to affect change that improves health outcomes for justice-involved youth and thus, our outreach strategy was multi-focal. To protect the confidentiality of our participants, our protocol entailed destroying the study team's access to participant personal identifiers and contact information as soon as we had completed data collection. Thus, we did not have permission to re-contact participants to share findings with them. When possible, however, doing so can be a valuable shared goal.

## Conclusion

There are numerous benefits to conducting qualitative field work around health issues with youth who are incarcerated or on probation/parole. The complexities of reentry for this population require complex research designs, protocols that truly "get at" the root experiences, and creative researchers who are willing to go the extra mile to recruit and follow subjects to obtain meaningful data. As both of us have experienced in various studies numerous layers of bureaucracy and obstacles to conducting this type of research, we hope to leave the reader with a few sage pieces of wisdom from this example.

First and foremost, it is important to set out with the expectation that this type of qualitative fieldwork will not be easy to launch. One must expect some layers of red tape and what appear to be insurmountable hoops in order to even start the research process. Having someone experienced on the team, who has been through this before as a mentor is key to setting a realistic timeline and expectations for success the first time around.

At the onset of the study, one must make inroads with the gatekeepers that have the power to turn you away. This is best accomplished through established connections in the community with people who can vouch for the integrity and importance of the research. It is important to begin outreach to those gatekeepers early on in the process and to keep them in the loop throughout the study and beyond. Keeping them apprised of the research process findings, and implications for the study will hopefully also pave the way for future studies or opportunities for dissemination and input.

It is important not to be discouraged by poor recruitment results, particularly when recruiting in the community. Transience, language barriers, distrust, and parental consent will all play a role in limiting your pool of willing participants. As we noted in the above example, it may take shifting gears, and using different approaches in order to recruit and retain the necessary sample. Community presence and belonging is also important; as often the "academic" title can be off putting for not only the potential participants, but the recruiting organization or agency. One must learn to balance persistence with respecting other people's time commitments and unpaid efforts to help you recruit. All in all, the researcher has to work to find a way to "nudge" recruitment without tipping the scales toward being perceived as a burden.

Last but not least, we think it is important to give back to the community as a part of this process. Whether that be dissemination or other forms of giving, as researchers we are most often still "outsiders" and we must thank the courts, probation officers, and the families who let us "in" to their offices and homes. While the IRB may place stipulations on incentives to incarcerated persons or minors, there are ways to provide groups gifts such as pizza parties or book donations to convey a sense of appreciation for partnering with the study. Ultimately, we have learned that youth we have interacted with are young people wanting to do their best—they are motivated by the idea of contributing to something that may help other youth. Giving their trauma histories and social marginalization, they also often appreciate being listened to—or take part in the research for the incentives or out of respect or a feeling of duty. Regardless of their reasons for participating, qualitative researchers who interact with justice-involved youth at the intersection of health have a responsibility and shared commitment to improve health outcomes for these youth. This is an admirable goal and well worth pursuing. While there are numerous challenges to overcome, the rewards and opportunities are great.

## References

Abrams, L. S. (2006). From corrections to community: Youth offenders' perceptions of the challenges of transition. *Journal of Offender Rehabilitation*, *44*(2–3), 31–53. doi:10.1300/j076v44n02_02

Abrams, L. S. (2010). Sampling 'hard to reach' populations in qualitative research: The case of incarcerated youth. *Qualitative Social Work: Research and Practice*, *9*(4), 536–550. doi:10.1177/1473325010367821

Abrams, L. S., & Anderson-Nathe, B. (2013). *Compassionate confinement: A year in the life of Unit C*. New Brunswick, NJ: Rutgers University.

Abrams, L. S., & Snyder, S. M. (2010). Youth offender reentry: Models for intervention and directions for future inquiry. *Children and Youth Services Review*, *32*(12), 1787–1795. doi:10.1016/j.childyouth.2010.07.023

Abrams, L. S., Terry, D., & Franke, T. M. (2011). Community-based juvenile reentry services: The effects of service dosage on juvenile and adult recidivism. *Journal of Offender Rehabilitation*, *50*(8), 492–510. doi:org/10.1080/10509674.2011.596919

Barnert, E. S., Perry, R., Azzi, V. F., Shetgiri, R., Ryan, G., Dudovitz, R., … Chung, P. J. (2015). Incarcerated youths' perspectives on protective factors and risk factors for juvenile offending: A qualitative analysis. *American Journal of Public Health*, *105*(7), 1365–1371. doi:10.2105/AJPH.2014.302228

Bronfenbrenner, U. (1979). *The ecology of human development: Experiments by nature and design*. Cambridge, MA: Harvard University.

Cox, A. (2017). *Trapped in a vice: The consequences of confinement for young people*. New Brunswick, NJ: Rutgers University.

Fields, D., & Abrams, L. S. (2010). Gender differences in the perceived needs and barriers of youth offenders preparing for community reentry. *Child and Youth Care Forum*, *39*, 253–269.

Kirk, S. (2006). Methodological and ethical issues in conducting qualitative research with children and young people: A literature review. *International Journal of Nursing Studies*, *44*(7), 1250–1260. doi:10.1016/j.ijnurstu.2006.08.015

Maxwell, J. A. (2013). *Qualitative research design: An interactive approach* (3rd ed.). Thousand Oaks, CA: Sage.

Nation Institute of Health. (2018, January 29). Research involving vulnerable populations: Research involving prisoners. Retrieved from https://humansubjects.nih.gov/prisoners

Rivas-Drake, D., Camacho, T. C., & Guillaume, C. (2016). Just good developmental science: Trust, identity, and responsibility in ethnic minority recruitment and retention. *Equity and Justice in Developmental Science: Theoretical and Methodological Issues*, *50*, 161–188. doi:10.1016/bs.acdb.2015.11.002

Sandelowski, M. (1989). The problem of rigor in qualitative research. *Advances in Nursing Science*, *8*(3), 27–37.

Shonkoff, J. P., & Bales, S. N. (2011). Science does not speak for itself: Translating child development research for the public and its policymakers. *Child Development*, *82*(1), 17–32. doi:10.1111/j.1467-8624.2010.01538.x

Sieber, J. E. (1994). Issues presented by mandatory reporting requirements to researchers of child abuse and neglect. *Ethics & Behavior*, *4*(1), 1–22. doi:10.1207/s15327019eb0401_1

Varma, S., & Wendler, D. (2008). Research involving wards of the State: Protecting particularly vulnerable children. *The Journal of Pediatrics*, *152*(1), 9–14. doi:10.1016/j.jpeds.2007.07.039

# 23
# DRUGS, HEALTH AND JUVENILE DELINQUENCY IN LATIN AMERICA

Trends, Policies and Actions

*Augusto Pérez-Góme, Juliana Mejía-Trujillo, Mónica Pérez-Trujillo, and Jessica Orr*

## Introduction

The relationships between drugs and crime are complicated. For a long time, Goldstein's (1985) early conceptualization of three basic types of relationships: the pharmacologically driven crime, the systemic crime, and the economically compulsive crime, was widely accepted (Bartol & Bartol, 1994). Since then, empirical studies have added to its complexity by identifying that drugs are also used by offenders to commit and justify many different types of crimes (e.g., theft, domestic violence and sexual abuse), that crimes related to drug trafficking and distribution are numerous and have various dynamics (Pernanen, Cousineau, Brochu, & Sun, 2002; Siegel & Welsh, 2012) and that economically compulsive crimes may vary dramatically across countries depending on the drugs used (Pernanen et al., 2002). In Latin America, drugs are also associated with phenomena like rituals of acceptance into drug-trafficking gangs (killing an unknown passerby), emulation of great criminal figures (children wanting to be like a well-known "narco" and openly misbehaving), or reducing someone to a vulnerable situation with the purpose of committing robbery (Alape, 1995; Mesa, 2016; Salazar, 1990, 2012).

The academic community has reached some consensus regarding the relationship between drugs and juvenile delinquency. Drugs are no longer viewed as a cause of delinquency but rather delinquency tends to precede the use of drugs (Bartollas & Schmalleger, 2011). Even if there are no formal studies confirming this in Latin America, anecdotal evidence provided from the Maras in Central America, from the Comunas in Medellín, Colombia, or the favelas from Rio de Janeiro in Brazil, tend to confirm this hypothesis (Mesa, 2016; Pérez-Gómez, Bodnar, Guevara, & Rodríguez, 2004; Sperberg & Happe, 2000). However, one important difference has to be mentioned: the use of drugs in the US is considered by itself a delinquent behavior, and this is not the case in most LA countries.

The use of substances and involvement in delinquency change in a similar pattern over time, but there is not a clear progression from one to another (Mulvey, Schubert, & Chassin, 2010). Also, there is an overlap of drug abuse and other problem behaviors such as violence, school drop-out and adolescent pregnancy (Hawkins, Catalano, & Brewer, 1995). Usually, youth who engage in substance abuse and have problems with it are more likely to engage in serious juvenile delinquency; actually, both substance use and delinquency decrease in late adolescence, related to reaching maturity and having new perspectives on life (Mulvey et al., 2010).

However, while some of these trends are similar in many countries, others are not. For example, Bartollas and Schmalleger (2011) identified that, in the United States, alcohol use follows a pattern of minor delinquency and exposure to parents and friends who drink; such is not the case in many parts of Latin America, where minors begin to drink alcohol at a very early age (between 11 and 13 years old), and this is considered very "normal" and is culturally accepted (Mejía-Trujillo, 2017). In fact, the use of drugs in most LA countries is not a crime. Ford (2005) and Pérez-Gómez, Lanziano, Reyes-Rodríguez, Mejía-Trujillo & Cardozo (2018) also found that alcohol and drug abusers are more likely than non-abusers to become delinquents.

Facing the challenges associated with these relationships and improving the strategies of crime control requires examining both patterns of crime and the policies implemented within and across countries. The purpose of this chapter is to present patterns of drug abuse and delinquency in Latin America, as well as the main trends on related policies. This analysis shows that developments in the region are not isomorphic: whilst many advances have been accomplished on drugs and health, policies on juvenile delinquency are still weak and lack systematic research.

## Drug Use and Abuse in Latin American Adolescents: Trends, Policies and Actions

Despite having multiple problems associated with drug production and trafficking, most countries in Latin America have relatively reduced levels of drug abuse as compared with the United States, Canada and some European countries. The exceptions are the so-called Southern Cone countries, with Chile and Argentina displaying the highest rates of marijuana and cocaine use; currently, regarding consumption among adolescents, Chile has higher rates of marijuana use than the United States (see Table 23.1).[1]

Table 23.1 shows the results of the most recent studies in several LA countries. We chose to present the data related to the most commonly used substances in order to give a general idea of the situation. Heroin is not included because the number of users is too low, and the same is true for opiates; heroin use had a rapid but transient increase in a few years in some countries, and this was particularly true in Brazil, Argentina, Chile and Colombia. However, currently the percentages are very low and difficult to assess with conventional household or school-based survey strategies. In addition to the Southern Cone countries, Central America also has a high percentage of marijuana users, whilst Bolivia and Ecuador have the lowest number of drug users. Data also shows that Argentina has high rates of early consumption of alcohol and use of tranquilizers.

However, the analysis of multiple studies carried out in the subcontinent (CICAD/OAS, 2015; UNODC, 2018), as well as local investigations and national observatories on drugs also show that there is a high level of drug use among adolescents in the hemisphere, and a very low perceived risk of the occasional use of drugs. High levels of drug use seem to be associated with a high level of perceived ease of access to drugs as well as significant volumes of drugs offered to adolescents.

There is a constant tendency for the consumption of all substances, both legal and illegal, to increase among women. Indeed, while the proportion of men and women who consume alcohol is often virtually the same, the proportion of consumers of illegal substances, which 20 years ago

Table 23.1 Prevalence of Drug Use among Minors in Latin America

| Country | Year | Age Rank | Substance | Life | Last Year | Last Month |
|---|---|---|---|---|---|---|
| Argentina | 2014 | 13 to 17 | Alcohol | 70,05 | 62,2 | 50,1 |
| | | | Marijuana | 15,9 | 11,8 | 7,6 |
| | | | Cocaine | 3,70 | 2,00 | 1,00 |
| | | 15 to 16 | Marijuana | 18,30 | 13,60 | 8,80 |
| | | | Coca Paste | 1,80 | 0,90 | 0,40 |
| | | | Ecstasy | 2,40 | 1,60 | 1,00 |
| | 2016 | 13 to 17 | Marijuana | 15,90 | 11,80 | 7,60 |
| Bolivia | 2013 | 12 to 17 | Coca Paste | 0,02 | 0,02 | 0,02 |
| | | | Ecstasy | 0,02 | 0,02 | |
| | | 15 to 16 | Marijuana | 1,11 | 0,71 | 0,34 |
| Costa Rica | 2015 | 1516 | Marijuana | 13,31 | 7,30 | 1,80 |
| | | | Ecstasy | 1,66 | 1,66 | |
| | | 13,15,17 | Marijuana | 34,89 | 28,35 | 17,13 |
| | 2013 | 15 to 16 | Marijuana | 38,96 | 32,87 | 19,98 |
| Chile | | 15 to 16 | Coca Paste | 4,15 | 2,25 | 1,13 |
| | | | Marijuana | 43,83 | 34,79 | 20,00 |
| | | | Coca Paste | 4,70 | 2,63 | 1,23 |
| | 2015 | 15 to 16 | Ectasy | 4,73 | 2,57 | 1,11 |
| Ecuador | 2012 | 12 to 17 | Marijuana | 7,19 | 3,10 | 1,37 |
| | | | Ectasy | 1,10 | 0,50 | 0,20 |
| El Salvador | 2016 | 13 to17 | Marijuana | 15,40 | 7,30 | 4,00 |
| | | | Coca Paste | 4,70 | 1,40 | 0,80 |
| Guatemala | 2014 | 11 to22 | Marihuana | 11,31 | 5,69 | 3,08 |
| | | | Coca Paste | 6,44 | 2,34 | 1,37 |
| | | | Marijuana | 14,70 | 6,80 | 1,10 |
| Honduras | 2015 | 14 to 17 | Cocaine | 6,80 | 3,40 | 1,10 |
| | 2014 | 15 to 16 | Cocaine | 10,00 | 3,20 | 1,60 |
| Perú | 2012 | 13, 15, 17 | Marijuana | 5,02 | 2,53 | 1,55 |
| | | 14 to 16 | Cocaine | 2,14 | 1,02 | 0,81 |
| | | | Coca Paste | 2,22 | 1,00 | 0,79 |
| | | | Marijuana | 20,10 | 17,00 | 9,50 |
| Uruguay | 2014 | 13 to 17 | Cocaine | 3,00 | 2,30 | 0,90 |
| | | | Coca Paste | 0,90 | 0,50 | 0,10 |
| | | | Ecstasy | 1,00 | 0,80 | 0,20 |
| | | | Alcohol | 68,06 | 57,89 | 36,13 |
| | | | Marijuana | 11,70 | 7,97 | 5,19 |
| Colombia | 2016 | 12 to 18 | Cocaine | 3,90 | 2,65 | 1,50 |
| | | | Ecstasy | 2,12 | 1,34 | 0,73 |
| | | | Tranquilizers | 2,96 | 1,97 | 1,02 |

was about 10 men for every woman, is currently just over 2:1. With regard to tobacco use, there is currently a slightly higher proportion of women than men users, especially among adolescents.

As in other parts of the world (UNODC, 2018), the consumption of synthetic substances such as Poppers, GHB, Ketamine, and methamphetamine has increased in large cities. Additionally, the emergence of new psychoactive substances (NPS) has changed traditional patterns of illicit drug production by simplifying procedures to such an extent that NPS may potentially be produced anywhere in any country. Although epidemiologically these substances do not constitute a serious threat at the moment, it is important to carry out monitoring to see how the situation evolves.

There has been a significant decrease in the consumption of coca paste in all Andean countries, where use is increasingly limited to marginalized populations. However, in Argentina and Uruguay, as well as in Honduras and Guatemala, there has been an important increase in recent years.

The need to develop preventive systems, within which programs and preventive campaigns are inserted, is becoming increasingly acute. At the present time there is a great disorder in this field, a lack of defined criteria to intervene and a lack of evaluative strategies that allow making decisions based on the evidence. Likewise, there is a need to thoroughly evaluate the treatment centers, which in many cases continue to act with strategies that have been abandoned in most countries of the world due to their inefficiency, their excessive costs or because of their use of ethically unacceptable technique.

## Policies and Actions on Drugs and Health in LA

Even though important advances have been made in recent years in terms of drug policy, in most Latin American countries there is still an open contradiction between what the laws say and what happens in reality. In fact, in most countries of the continent, the repressive approach towards the consumers of substances has been gradually abandoned, especially in the last ten years, and replaced by a public health approach; however, investments in the four major fields that constitute the area of demand (prevention, treatment, mitigation and harm reduction) are usually very small in most countries, and the situation is even worse when it comes to investments on evaluation and research (Pérez-Gómez, Mejía-Trujillo, & Becoña-Iglesias, 2015).

## Advances in International Policies

With regard to drug policies, almost all countries of the world are governed by the successive conventions of the United Nations, the last of which took place in 1988. In terms of trafficking, the agreements are totally clear and of obligatory fulfillment; but in the field of consumption, the conventions leave countries free to adopt the decisions they consider appropriate, ranging from extreme repression (in some cases the death penalty is considered) to the decriminalization of consumers.

In 2009, the Heads of State, ministers and government representatives of 132 countries met to conduct an evaluation of progress in meeting the goals established at the Twentieth special session of the Assembly General, dedicated to the "global problem of drugs." From these special high-level sessions, a Political Declaration and Action Plan on International Cooperation was derived in favor of a comprehensive and balanced strategy to counteract the world drug problem; it was concluded that, in spite of efforts and progress in many countries, drug abuse continues to be a serious threat to the integral welfare of society, especially youth (UNODC, 2009). Some of the main recommendations of this document were to strengthen policies and to carry out prevention programs based on scientific evidence, aimed at both the general public and specific groups, in various environments, especially targeted at young people and children.

In 2009, the members of the Latin American Commission on Drugs and Democracy, composed of several former presidents and scholars of the region, made an analysis about the deficiencies of the current policy to tackle drugs, and invited a reevaluation of the prohibition as approach, based on the repression of production and interdiction of trafficking and distribution, and the criminalization of consumption. From their point of view, this policy has brought disastrous consequences for society, specifically for Latin America, which has had to face them more directly.

According to the Commission, the so-called "War on Drugs" led by the United States in recent decades has contributed to the increase of violence and organized crime, and has meant social and human costs of very high proportions for the region, without achieving the expected outcomes. Latin America continues to be the world's largest exporter of cocaine, and the production of opium and heroin has been increasing. Consumption in the region has increased, while in North America and Europe it tends to stabilize. The criminalization has led to the infiltration of organized crime into democratic institutions, generating an increase in "the corruption of public officials, the judicial system, governments, the political system and, in particular, the police forces in charge to maintain law and order" (Comisión Latinoamericana sobre Drogas y Democracia, 2009).

From this basis, the Commission proposed "a new paradigm" based on treating drug use as a public health issue, reducing consumption through information and prevention actions, and focusing the repression on organized crime. The first one has been adopted by almost all LA countries, which decriminalized drug possession; but the second one is hardly developed in a proper way: the evaluations are, very often, more focused on the acceptability of the programs among the beneficiaries, than on the efficacy of the interventions.

The Pan American Health Organization (2010) proposed to focus on early interventions based in the immediate social environment, also addressing social development and behaviors which positively affect problems other than the use of drugs (PAHO, 2010). This is the reason why more strategies created to address consumption problems are integrated with strategies against micro-trafficking, violence and gangs (Ministerio de Justicia y del Derecho, 2016).

## National Policies and Actions

Probably the most remarkable change in Latin America regarding alcohol and drug use and abuse, is the massive movement toward a public health approach. Many countries in the Hemisphere assumed for decades a repressive and criminal approach towards drug users, but this began to change in the first years of the XXI century, and in less than 20 years all seem to be reading the same page: repression is all right with dealers, traffickers and producers, but not with consumers or addicts. On the other hand, for a long time many countries gave precedence to treatment; with the assumption of a public health approach the accent had to shift, necessarily, toward prevention. Because of the increase of drug use in LA since the middle of the 1980s, and the growing preoccupation among the local authorities as well as among the general population, all countries created at least one governmental institution in charge of the issues related to alcohol and drug consumption and abuse; in some cases, several institutions exist depending on different Ministries (health, education, internal affairs). All countries have developed national policies on prevention, and international institutions (for instance, United Nations, CICAD/OAS, European Union) have supported these initiatives. In most countries, universities and nonprofit organizations also support governmental initiatives, or even develop their own (Pérez-Gómez & Mejía-Trujillo, 2017).

With some exceptions, programs focused only on information dissemination and attitude change have lost credibility. Little by little countries are looking for evidence-based strategies, even if the concept is not always used in the right way. In many places foreign prevention programs are still largely in use, but very often they have not been validated with local populations, and the local governments require validations and adaptations in order to fund them. There is also a notable interest in developing local programs that more directly consider a country's needs, and one of the first to do so was Chile. This is also happening in Mexico, Colombia and Peru, where not only local initiatives have been developed but at least some of them are under strict processes of evaluation, including randomized controlled trials. Costa Rica has just one program, but with a national coverage and positive effectiveness evaluations over several years. Brazil is developing several prevention initiatives, but because of its huge population, it will need several years before reaching sufficient coverage throughout the country (Pérez-Gómez et al., 2015). While there are important differences among countries, most of them have developed research and evaluation structures, although in many cases these structures are weak and poorly funded. In this context, evaluation and assessment agencies must become a priority to advance the prevention field, and the universities have to become the nucleus of this effort; this is already happening in Mexico, Brazil, Chile, Peru and Colombia, and to a lesser extent in Central America, Ecuador and Paraguay. It is essential that academic institutions, and particularly universities, become involved in the construction, development and implementation of preventive programs, as well as in the evaluation processes aimed at demonstrating their effectiveness.

One of the main difficulties in LA is the lack of formal academic training programs on prevention. Those interested in becoming proficient in this area of knowledge must attend universities or specialized institutions in countries like the US, Canada or Spain. However, in several LA countries, symposia, conferences and workshops are provided as a means to educate about prevention and share information and research. Unfortunately, there are still many people who think that lectures, simple interventions and "good intentions" are all that is needed to prevent drug and alcohol abuse. In addition, the poor knowledge of those in charge of political decisions about the meaning of "prevention" has provoked, among other things, sudden changes in decisions, in the orientation of strategies and has made "going back to square zero" a norm. Finally, the irregular funding of prevention initiatives makes failure more likely because prevention initiatives have to be, by definition, a long-term endeavor.

It is of the utmost importance to articulate all the components of preventive strategies, including developing mass media messages linked to community interventions, developing new skills among children and adolescents, reducing school drop-outs, promoting healthy and creative use of leisure time, and promoting youth participation in the planning and implementation of activities that affect their everyday lives. This articulation has hardly been done in any LA country, but at least some of the above suggested strategies are taking place in different regions of the subcontinent.

## Policies and Actions on Juvenile Crime and Gangs in LA

While crime rates are continuing to rise on a regional level in Latin America, the treatment of adolescents in the juvenile justice system is undergoing changes, and national governments are addressing adolescent involvement in drug related crimes. Mexico, Colombia, Peru, and Brazil are some of the largest economies in Latin America, while they are also home to cities marked by violence associated with drug trafficking (OECD/ECLAC/CAF, 2016).

Within the framework of public youth policies in Latin America, the intervention of the state in issues of social, economic and political integration of young people takes various expressions, ranging from strategies of control and prevention of youth violence, to the re-socialization of youth in conflict with the law. This has made it easier for international cooperation agencies to establish public and private forms of action to guarantee, restore and fulfill the rights of young people. ECLAC and the Ibero-American Youth Organization in 2015 carried out an analysis of the policies related to juvenile delinquency in the region and provided intervention elements for young people in vulnerable and unprotected environments (Ministerio de Justicia y del Derecho, 2017). However, one of the difficulties in approaching this issue in Latin America lies in the delimitation of the population targeted for intervention: in LA there is no homogeneous definition of "youth" and this means that the approaches and levels of prioritization and attention vary. Therefore, one way to understand the magnitude of public policy in the region is through investment levels: high, medium or low investment in youth, with Ecuador, Bolivia, Cuba and Paraguay presenting high investment, followed by Peru, the Dominican Republic, Mexico, Guatemala and Chile with medium-sized investments, and finally, Costa Rica, Uruguay, Colombia, El Salvador, Argentina and Brazil, which present the lowest levels of investment (Ministerio de Justicia y del Derecho, 2017).

There are three types of youth public policies: (a) direct impact on the young population, such as employment programs, job training or higher education; (b) indirect impact on young population, as members of households and families, which includes issues of social security, education or justice; and (c) impact on broad sectors of the population and, by extension, on youth, such as improving access to public services, access to housing, security and transport (Ministerio de Justicia y del Derecho, 2017). According to this ECLAC document, the areas where there have been the most allocation of resources in the region are education, health, and leisure time. However, investment has been lesser in labor insertion, prevention of violence, overcoming poverty, social assistance and citizen participation of this population (Ministerio de Justicia y del Derecho, 2017). Taking into account the scale of investment and the lack of resources to address the problem of gangs, the infraction of criminal law by adolescents and young people becomes evident.

The International Covenant on Civil and Political Rights (Human Rights of the United Nations, 1966) in article 10 mentions the differential nature of sanctions and judicial proceedings for adults and minors, given the vulnerability of adolescents, their stage of development and personal growth; a pact that is reaffirmed in the Convention on the Rights of the Child (UNICEF, 2015), which all LA countries signed and ratified, especially as foreseen in articles 37 and 40, where states committed to the deprivation of freedom were the exception, and where each country would ensure the protection of rights even in its capacity as criminally responsible. In 2015, the Inter-American Commission on Human Rights recommended the use of Restorative Justice in criminal proceedings for adolescents, given the damage caused by custodial measures.

Based on these international commitments, beginning in 2003 and following resolution 2000/14 of the Economic and Social Council of the United Nations (2000), programs of adolescent criminal responsibility with a restorative approach involve the active participation of victims, victimizers and members of the community, in order to provide reparation to the victim and the community and encourage the reintegration of the offender and the restoration of links with society. Restorative programs have been implemented in different countries of LA. The Restorative Juvenile Justice Project in Peru, framed in the Children's Code and Adolescents (Law 27337 of 2000), has been carried out since 2003 in the districts of Lima and Chiclayo, with the support of two private organizations that incorporate programs in the open environment with alternative sanctions that involve community actions to repair damage to the victims and the reestablishment of adolescent bonds (Ministerio de Justicia y del Derecho, 2018).

In Brazil, in 2005, the Justice, Education and Community Pilot Project: Partnerships for Citizenship was launched, where through the Community Circles methodology suggested by the Economic and Social Commission (Ministerio de Justicia y del Derecho, 2018), it began to apply restorative justice for the resolution of conflicts. In Chile, as of 2007, the Program for the Repair of Harm and Services for the Benefit of the Community (Law 20084 of 2007) has been developed for adolescents with criminal responsibility, including non-custodial measures such as work with the community. Finally, in Costa Rica, since 2011, although with progress since the mid-1990s, the Restorative Justice Program of the Judiciary was created, including all the actors involved in the judicial process of adolescents, regarding the repair and restoration of the victims.

In Mexico, 1990 marked the ratification of the UN Convention on the Rights of the Child, at which point the government adopted a doctrine to protect juvenile offenders (Centro de Investigación para el Desarrollo, 2016). Previously, as a result of public perception in the 1980s regarding increase in violent crimes, punitive measures were enforced in an effort to maintain public safety, with extreme cases treating adolescent offenders as adults, resulting in increased police aggression towards juvenile offenders and an increase in detention rates of adolescents (Centro de Investigación para el Desarrollo, 2016). Further change began in December 2005, when Article 18 of the Mexican Constitution was reformed to establish a juvenile justice doctrine based on comprehensive protection, and establishing a federally integrated system rather than statewide systems.

In tracing some of the risk factors associated with juveniles in detention in Mexico, the Institute of Judicial Investigations-UNAM cites a National Human Rights Commission report; of all detained juveniles, 71% of cases had parents that were dependent on substances, while 36% had incarcerated family members, 25% of these adolescents were part of gangs, and 18% were victims of family violence (Calero-Aguilar, 2010). In 2016, a new law was presented in Mexico, the "Ley Nacional del Sistema Integral de Justicia Penal para Adolescentes" (The national law on Integral penal justice for adolescents). This law significantly limits sentencing times, establishing that sentences for children between twelve and under fourteen may not exceed one year; sentences for children between fourteen and under sixteen may not exceed three years; sentences for children between sixteen and under eighteen may not exceed five years. Additionally, detention will be considered the most extreme measure for punishing adolescent crimes, and restorative justice should be explored prior to jail sentences.

## Colombia as a Paradigmatic Case

The Colombian accusatory criminal system for adults extends to adolescents between 14 and 18 years of age who commit crimes. However, the sanctions imposed, as well as the entire process of justice, must have a pedagogical objective, be differentiated from adults and have special programs and institutions that guarantee the total protection of juveniles´ rights and the restoration of them when they are vulnerable (Congress of the Republic of Colombia, 2006), following the international instruments cited above.

The second book of the law 1098 of 2006 discusses the criminal responsibility of teenagers from 14 to 18 years of age in Colombia. Although it is a law that sanctions, under the principle of "comprehensive protection," a special population group, it also becomes lax when it comes to imposing the necessary corrective measures for crimes committed by young people and is almost nil compared to crimes committed by children under 14 years of age. Although the outlook is not flattering, it is better than either of the two extremes that were previously proposed to reduce crime: judging those over 15 years as adults, without recognizing their special status; or considering any minor as unimpeachable appealing to the status of victims because the State had not guarantee their rights, and for that reason the youth had no other way to survive than to commit a crime. The reason for this idea was based on the fact that crimes against property were those with the highest rate (60%) of commission by minors and it was understood that the poverty lived by adolescents drove them to commit certain crimes. Nonetheless, the data from the System of Criminal Responsibility for Adolescents in Colombia show that, in the last ten years, the main offences committed by adolescents are theft and aggravated theft (with guns or knives, or in group), but the trend is towards a substantial decrease (20 percentage points, or 33%) followed by possession, traffic and manufacture of psychoactive substances (30%) (Instituto Colombiano de Bienestar Familiar, 2018).

The global balance of the impact of the System of Criminal Responsibility for Adolescents in Colombia shows that from March 2007 to May 2018, 88% of the offences were committed by men and 12% by women; the age when the largest number of offences occur is between 15 and 17 years, and 37% of those who break the criminal law are 17 years old, 60% are 14 to 16, 2%, 1% under 14 and 2% over 18.

As can be seen in Figure 23.1, 71% of the crimes were related to drugs or to theft; 7% to fire arms (which is surprising because in Colombia guns are very expensive); 18% to violent behavior at home, to other people or against property; 2% homicide and 2% sexual acts against minor under 14.

Other characteristics of this system for adolescents refer to the joint responsibility of the family of the criminally responsible, and to the repair and restoration of the damage caused. Although

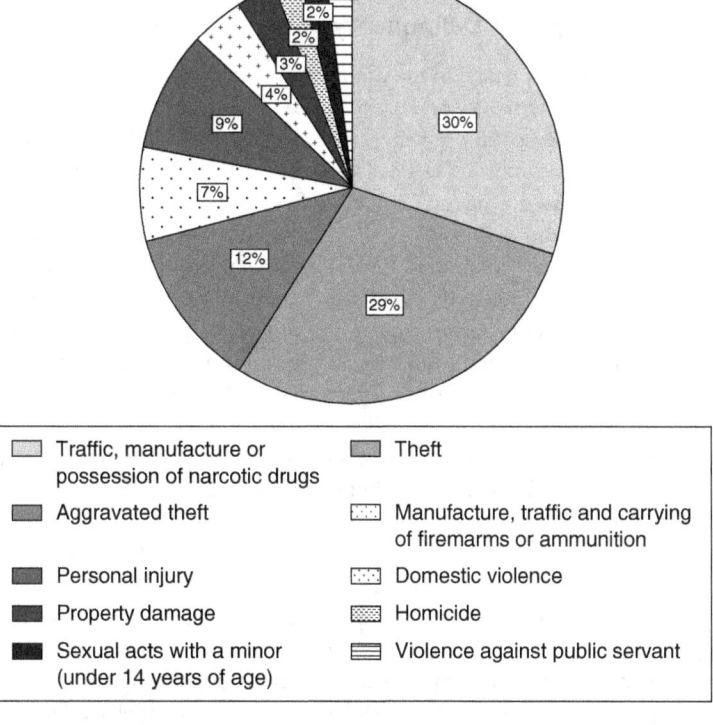

*Figure 23.1* Offences committed by adolescents in Colombia 2007–2018

the intention is valid and pertinent given the pedagogical and formative nature of the law, the sanctions do not help to develop these principles. Thus, of the six sanctions contemplated for adolescents (deprivation of freedom, internment in a semi-closed environment, supervised freedom, provision of services to the community, imposition of rules of conduct and reprimand), the only one that can generate symbolic reparation is that of provision of services to the community, which allows adolescents to take responsibility for the offence committed and to exert an action to restore society. However, the family co-responsible for the crime of the adolescent has no place in this or in any sanction, and in addition, since the creation of the System in 2007, only 5.2% of the 250,000 sanctioned adolescents have received this measure, while 26.2% have been incarcerated (Instituto Colombiano de Bienestar Familiar, 2018), although the reasons for this are clear and exceptional homicide, extortion or kidnapping (Congreso de la República de Colombia, 2006).

The restorative character of the system of criminal responsibility for adolescents is a complex process that has not yet been widely developed and that is implemented only in some centers serving this population. When it happens, the sanction imposed by the judge takes place in nursing homes, orphanages, aid collection centers, etc., where it is possible to help vulnerable or disadvantaged populations.

Many people have been critical of the adolescent and community reparation approaches, insofar as the adolescent is the perpetrator and reparation must be personal, addressed to the victim and not to the community. Although there are normative bases to develop programs of juvenile restorative justice (Ministerio de Justicia y del Derecho, 2018), there is no institutional, social or community structure that allows for obtaining the maximum benefit of this tools.

## Drugs and Delinquency among Adolescents

The correlation between delinquency and psychoactive substance use among adolescents is challenging to measure. However, in 2016, 28.1% of the minors surveyed in Mexico committed a crime while under the influence of a psychoactive substance, of which 94.1% were male (Instituto Nacional de Psiquiatría Ramon de la Fuente Muñiz, 2017). The survey also reports that the substances most frequently used while under the influence were alcohol (34.8%), followed by marijuana (31.5%), and inhalants (15.1%).

Given the incidence of crimes committed under the influence of psychoactive substances among adolescents, the Mexican government recognizes the demand for universal prevention programs. CONADIC (National Commission against Addictions) runs several national programs, one of which is Crianza Positiva (Positive upbringing); this program focuses on training parents of young children ages 8–13 years old, teaching and reinforcing parenting skills that prevent adolescent anti-social behavior (Morales Chainé, 2013).

In Colombia, the last study on drug use among adolescents in conflict with law, and under the System of Adolescent Criminal Responsibility, showed that those youngsters' use of drugs was considerably higher than among their counterparts of similar ages, but inserted into the regular educational system (see Table 23.2) (Observatorio de Drogas de Colombia, 2018). Their life prevalence of marijuana, tranquillizers, cocaine and coca paste was between 10 and 12 times higher and their life prevalence of inhalants and ecstasy between five and seven times higher. Similarly, last year prevalence was between nine and five times higher; and last month (which means that they are consuming in correctional or under vigilance measures), between six and three times higher than youth that were not involved in the criminal justice system.

In Brazil, changes in drug policies in recent decades include the 2004 Policy of Integral Assistance to alcohol and drug users; this policy factors in public health effects of PSA use to society, and focuses on "recovery, social reintegration, and community psychosocial services

*Table 23.2* Drug Use in Adolescents in Conflict with Law, Colombia 2018

| Drug | Juvenile Delinquents (2018) | | | School students (2016) | | | Comparison | | |
|---|---|---|---|---|---|---|---|---|---|
| | Life | Last year | Last month | Life | Last year | Last month | Life | Last year | Last month |
| Alcohol | 86.3 | 74.1 | 30.6 | 69.3 | 60 | 37 | 24%+ | 23%+ | 17%< |
| Marijuana | 84.4 | 54.4 | 28.4 | 11.7 | 8 | 4.3 | x12+ | x6+ | x6.5+ |
| Tranquillizers | 32.4 | NA* | NA | 3 | 2 | 1 | x11+ | NA | x3+ |
| Cocaine | 45,8 | 19.1 | 4.9 | 3.9 | 2.65 | 1.5 | x11+ | x6+ | x3+ |
| Inhalants | 28,5 | 10,2 | NA | 4 | 2.2 | 1.2 | x7+ | x9+ | NA |
| Coca paste | 13.1 | 3.8 | NA | 1.3 | 1 | 0.6 | x10+ | x6+ | NA |
| Ecstasy | 11,7 | 3,5 | NA | 2.12 | 1.34 | 0.73 | x5+ | x5+ | NA |

* NA: Not available. At the time of writing this chapter (August 2018), not all the results of the study had been published.

for users" (de Souza, Fiorati, Macedo, & de Macedo, 2018). In a documental analysis of the structure of drug policies in Brazil by de Souza et al, findings showed that Brazilian public health policies prioritize corrective actions that address current problems more than health promotion. The study also reveals that recommended prevention strategies in Brazil include participatory approaches, and consideration of social determinants of health (de Souza et al., 2018).

Conditional Cash Transfer programs (CCT) have been implemented in Brazil to meet various national objectives related to poverty reduction, increase in school enrollment rates, and reduction in social inequalities (Chioda, 2017). Chioda mentions a 2016 study by Chioda, De Mello and Soares that found that the expansion of the Bolsa Familia CCT program to 16 and 17 years old lowered crime in school neighborhoods, with statistically significant results for violent crimes, drug related crimes, and robberies (Chioda, 2017).

An example of a regional trend in Latin America in legal processes for drug related proceedings is the gradual adaptation of the United States-based Drug Court (Social Science Research Council, 2018). In the LA region drug courts are commonly known as Drug Treatment Centers, and CICAD (Organization of American States' Inter-American Drug Abuse Control Commission) has been a key proponent of this expansion. Currently, drug courts are operating in Chile, Mexico, and Costa Rica; they are in a "pilot phase" in Argentina, Panama, Dominican Republic, and Colombia; they are currently under consideration of Ecuador and Peru (Social Science Research Council, 2018). These courts are particular programs within the legal system, rather than special drug courts. Some of the findings report that these courts deal with mostly with possession of drugs and graduate few participants in treatment programs (Social Science Research Council, 2018). So far there is not a clear evaluation of these initiatives, and its implementation is expensive. Furthermore, their insertion into the legal system of the different countries where they are currently in use in LA is far from being clear.

## Conclusions and Suggestions

Juvenile delinquency and drug use in LA are closely related in different ways, but there are big differences among countries, and the relationship is not obvious. Countries like Chile, Uruguay and Argentina, with the highest rates of drug use in the subcontinent, do not present high rates of juvenile delinquency; on the other hand, countries in a medium range of drug use (El Salvador, Honduras, Guatemala), present high rates of delinquency, including phenomena like the "maras"; huge gangs with several thousand members at the service of narcotrafficking. Other countries, like Colombia, heavily involved in production and trafficking of cocaine, show a medium level of juvenile delinquency, frequently focused in specific areas of the larger cities, and a medium range of drug use.

Policies and actions have shown important advancements in the last two decades, particularly regarding drugs. The adoption in most countries of a public health approach has allowed to give (at least on paper) preeminence to prevention and treatment for drug users, but there is still a long way to go: in many countries there is a lack of unity, and the interventions are limited to "one-shot" because the legal norms order that everyone must receive attention. Even if the concept is valid, this ensures the failure of the intervention. In addition, the treatment systems are the same than the ones used for adults, and the facilities are in most cases inadequate and operate more like prisons than genuine treatment centers. In the field of delinquency, many countries have adopted the restorative justice approach, but its implementation is not easy and there are still several divergent interpretations and gaps, which may even contribute to increase the commission of crimes.

The following are some suggestions that may be useful in more LA countries:

1. It is essential to improve the training of the institutions and people in charge of carrying out prevention and treatment programs. So far there are still serious deficiencies at the conceptual level and a lack of updating of those responsible for these programs.
2. It is necessary to give continuity to the programs and increase their scope as much as possible. In most countries of the hemisphere there are no consistent state policies with a long-term vision, despite the efforts made in this regard by organizations such as CICAD.
3. The development of permanent evaluation systems is a basic requirement to achieve greater investments on behalf of the states, to correct errors, and to update procedures when necessary.
4. A priority should be the creation of preventive systems clearly adapted to the cultural characteristics of each country. Even if some changes are happening, it is still very common that developing countries take what has already been tried in the industrialized countries and apply it without taking into account the enormous differences that exist in the conditions of each of them.
5. Creativity in this field has to be stimulated, but without neglecting the theoretical and conceptual support of the programs that are developed.
6. In the case of schools, prevention should be part of the training of teachers, in order to avoid having to invest huge resources in these processes; if this were achieved, it would be enough to carry out reinforcements and periodic updates. This requires that governments have a clear vision of the situation and know how to give it the importance it deserves; unfortunately, this is not the case in a significant proportion of the South American countries.
7. It will be necessary to strengthen the family and community programs; the involvement of parents and representatives of the civil society in these procedures can become a fundamental support for the sustainability of prevention strategies.
8. It will be necessary to develop specific harm reduction policies and interventions for youth involved in drug use and delinquency. Harm reduction is, internationally, a measure to be implemented with adult populations at high risk and reluctant to abandon their drug use, but

this doesn't seem to be a reasonable policy with minors: the youth must be helped, through all available means, to stop consumption.
9. Preventive programs need to be constantly updated, which creates some difficulties with regard to evaluations; when the concept of "fidelity" is too rigid, the programs become frozen and in a few years become obsolete. It is then necessary to develop preventive programs that are easily modifiable without altering their nuclear structure. They must also include flexible and reliable evaluation processes.
10. It seems of the paramount importance to develop in-depth policies for preventing juvenile delinquency. This is probably the most serious gap, currently, in the whole of Latin America.

## Note

1  For this table we consulted three sources: the World Drug Report (UNODC, 2018); the document on drug use in the Americas published by CICAD/OAS in 2015; and recent data provided by National Observatories on Drugs, supported by CICAD/OAS, and not published in the two previously quoted reports. Surprisingly, Mexico and Brazil do not have recent published information on drug use among adolescents.

## References

Alape, A. (1995). *La hoguera de las ilusiones.* Bogotá, Colombia: Planeta.
Bartol, C. R., & Bartol, A. M. (1994). *Psychology and Law: Research and Application* (2nd ed.). Belmont, CA: Thomson Brooks/Cole Publishing Co.
Bartollas, C., & Schmalleger, F. (2011). *Juvenile Delinquency* (8th ed.). Upper Saddle River, NJ: Prentice Hall.
Calero-Aguilar, A. (2010). El Nuevo Sistema de Justicia para adolescentes en México. *Biblioteca Jurídica Virtual del Instituto de Investigaciones Jurídicas de la UNAM,* 19. Retrieved on August 3, 2028, from archivos.juridicas. unam.mx/www/bjv/libros/6/2758/9.pdf
Centro de Investigación para el Desarrollo. (2016). *Justicia para Adolescentes en Mexico: ¿Se garantizan los derechos de los jóvenes?* México, D.F: Embajada de Finlandia.
Chioda, L. (2017). *Stop the Violence in Latin America: A look at Prevention from Cradle to Adulthood.* Washington, DC: International Bank for Reconstruction and Development/The World Bank.
CICAD/OAS. (2015). *Report on Drug Use in the Americas 2015.* Washington, DC: CICAD/OAS.
Comisión Latinoamericana sobre Drogas y Democracia. (2009). *Drogas y democracia: Hacia un cambio de paradigma.* Retrieved from www.cicad.oas.org/fortalecimiento_institucional/planesnacionales/docs/Drogas% 20y%20Democracia.%20Hacia%20un%20cambio%20de%20paradigma.pdf
Congress of the Republic of Colombia. (2006). *Law 1098.* Bogotá, Colombia: Congreso de la República.
de Souza, J., Fiorati, R. C., Macedo, M. M., & de Macedo, J. Q. (2018). Brazilian public policies on drugs: An analysis considering the aspects of assistance, prevention, and supply control. *Journal of Addictions Nursing,* 29(1), 50–56.
Economic and Social Council of the United Nations (2000). *Resolution 2000/14.* Retrieved from https://documents-dds-ny.un.org/doc/UNDOC/GEN/N01/487/49/IMG/N0148749.pdf?OpenElement
Ford, J. A. (2005). The connection between heavy drinking and juvenile delinquency during adolescence. *Sociological Spectrum,* 25, 629–650.
Goldstein, P. J. (1985). The drugs/violence nexus: A tripartite conceptual framework. *Journal of Drug Issues,* 15, 493–506.
Hawkins, D., Catalano, R., & Brewer, D. (1995). Preventing serious, violent and chronic offending: Effective strategies from conception to age 6. In J. C. Howell, et al. (eds.), *Serious, Violent, and Chronic Juvenile Offenders: A Sourcebook.* Thousands Oaks, CA: Sage, pp. 47–60.
Human Rights of the United Nations. (1966). *International Covenant on Civil and Political Rights.* Retrieved from www.ohchr.org/en/professionalinterest/pages/ccpr.aspx
Instituto Colombiano de Bienestar Familiar. (2018). *Sistema de Responsabilidad Penal para Adolescentes: consolidado nacional.* Bogotá, Colombia: ICBF.
Instituto Nacional de Psiquiatria Ramon de la Fuente Muñiz. (2017). *Encuesta Nacional de Consumo de Drogas, Alcohol y Tabaco 2016-2017.* Ciudad de Mexico, Mexico: INPRFM.

Mejía-Trujillo, J. (2017). Distintas familias, distintos consumos: relación de las dinámicas familiares con el consumo de alcohol en adolescentes en Colombia. *Hallazgos, 28*, 63–82.

Mesa, G. (2016). *La cuadra*. Bogotá, Colombia: Penguin Random Hose.

Ministerio de Justicia y del Derecho. (2016). *Microtráfico y comercialización de sustancias psicoactivas en pequeñas cantidades en contextos urbanos*. Bogotá, Colombia: Ministerio de Justicia y del Derecho – Observatorio de Drogas de Colombia.

Ministerio de Justicia y del Derecho. (2017). *Pandillas juveniles en Colombia: aproximaciones conceptuales, expresiones urbanas y posibilidades de intervención*. Bogotá, Colombia: Ministerio de Justicia y del Derecho – Observatorio de Drogas de Colombia.

Ministerio de Justicia y del Derecho. (2018). *Diagnóstico y Lineamientos de Política para la aplicación de la Justicia Juvenil Restaurativa en Colombia*. Bogotá, Colombia: Ministerio de Justicia y del Derecho – Observatorio de Drogas de Colombia.

Morales Chainé, S. (2013). *Prevención de las Conductas Adictivas a través de la Atención del Comportamiento Infantil para la crianza positiva*. México DF: Secretaría de Salud.

Mulvey, E. P., Schubert, C. A., & Chassin, L. (2010). *Substance Use and Delinquent Behavior amongst Serious Adolescent Offenders*. Juvenile Justice Bulletin (December). Washington, DC: Office of Juvenile Justice and Delinquency Prevention.

Observatorio de Drogas de Colombia. (2018). *Estudio de consumo de sustancias psicoativas en el Sistema de Responsabilidad Penal para Adolescentes*. Bogotá, Colombia: ODC.

OECD/ECLAC/CAF. (2016). *Latin American Economic Outlook 2017: Youth, Skills and Entrepreneurship*. Paris: OECD Publishing, p. 313.

Pan American Health Organization (PAHO). (2010). *Drug Policy and the Public Good*. Retrieved from www.cicad.oas.org/fortalecimiento_institucional/planesnacionales/docs/La%20politica%20 de%20drogas%20y%20el%20bien%20publico.pdf

Pérez-Gómez, A., Bodnar, G, Guevara, A., & Rodríguez, K. (2004). Relación entre drogas y violencia: estudio comparativo. In Consejo Nacional de Seguridad Pública/PNUD, *El impacto de las drogas en la violencia*. San Salvador, El Salvador: CNSP/PNUD, pp. 7–90.

Pérez-Gómez, A., Lanziano, C., Reyes-Rodríguez,M. F., Mejía-Trujillo, J., & Cardozo-Macías, F. (2018). Profiles associated with alcohol consumption in Colombian adolescents. *Acta Colombiana de Psicología, 21*(2), 268–279.

Pérez-Gómez, A., & Mejía-Trujillo, J. (2017). The evolution of drug and alcohol prevention strategies in Latin America. In J. Romano & M. Israelashvili (eds.), *International Handbook of Prevention Science*. New York: Cambridge University Press. Cap. 2, pp. 753–779.

Pérez-Gómez, A., Mejía-Trujillo, J., & Becoña-Iglesias, E. (2015). *De la Prevención y otras Historias*. Bogotá, Colombia: California-edit.

Pernanen, K., Cousineau, M., Brochu, S., & Sun, F. (2002). *Proportion des crimes associés à l'alcool et aux drogues au Canada*. Ottawa, ON: Centre Canadien de Lutte contre l'Alcoolisme et les Toxicomanies.

Salazar, A. (1990). *No nacimos pa' semilla*. Bogotá, Colombia: CINEP.

Salazar, A. (2012). *La parábola de Pablo*. Bogotá, Colombia: Planeta.

Siegel, L. J., & Welsh, B. C. (2012). *Juvenile Delinquency: Theory, Practice and Law* (11th ed.). Belmont, CA: Wadsworth.

Social Science Research Council. (2018). *Drug Courts in the Americas*. New York: SCRC.

Sperberg, J., & Happe, B. (2000). Violencia y delincuencia en barrios pobre de Santiago de Chile y Rio de Janeiro. *Nueva Sociedad, 169*, 44–60.

UNICEF. (2015). *Convention on the Rights of the Child*. Retrieved from www.unicef.es/sites/unicef.es/files/comunicacion/ConvencionsobrelosDerechosdelNino.pdf

UNODC. (2009). *Political Declaration and Plan of Action on International Cooperation towards an Integrated and Balanced Strategy to Counter the World Drug Problem*. Vienna, Austria: UNODC.

UNODC. (2018). *World Drug Report*. Vienna, Austria: UNODC.

# 24
# DELINQUENCY AND HEALTH IN AUSTRALIAN YOUTH

*Sheryl A. Hemphill and Jessica A. Heerde*

Youth antisocial behavior (e.g., violence, stealing, truancy) and delinquency (antisocial behavior that is a crime) are both prevalent and costly phenomena in Western countries including Australia. The prevalence of antisocial behavior peaks in adolescence (Baker, 1998; Bond, Thomas, Toumbourou, Patton, & Catalano, 2000) and is estimated to be 5% to 17% (depending on how it is defined) in Australia; this is similar to rates in the United States of America and the United Kingdom (Costello, Mustillo, Erklanli, Keeler, & Angold, 2003; Sawyer et al., 2001). The costs associated with youth antisocial behavior and delinquency are extensive and include those associated with physical and mental health services for youth, law enforcement and youth justice services (Hemphill, 1996; Smith, Jorna, Sweeney, & Fuller, 2014). Indeed, the cost of crime has been estimated to be $47 billion per year in Australia (Smith et al., 2014), with youth engaging in the bulk of these criminal acts and therefore contributing strongly to the costs associated with crime.

During adolescence, a range of mental health problems (e.g., depression, self-harm), physical health problems (e.g., injuries to the brain and other physical injuries due to traffic or other accidents), and health risk behaviors (e.g., substance misuse and abuse, risky sexual behaviors) tend to emerge. Youth engaging in delinquent behavior are known to be particularly vulnerable to these mental health and physical health problems and to engaging in health risk behaviors. In addition, youth engaging in delinquent behavior tend to have multiple problems; that is co-occurring mental and physical health problems and health risk behaviors (Australian Institute of Health and Welfare [AIHW], 2018a) and these youth may also experience social problems (e.g., homelessness) that impact on their health (AIHW, 2018a). Any approaches that aim to address the health problems and health risk behaviors of youth engaging in delinquent behavior need to work across sectors and be multi-faceted to address their complex needs. Public health approaches lend themselves well to addressing the health needs of youth engaging in delinquent behavior.

## Public Health Approaches

Traditionally, the medical model of health was the main approach applied to health problems. In more recent times, public health approaches have emerged. The public health approach has as its focus the prevention of harm to entire populations (Krug, Dahlberg, Mercy, Zwi, & Lozano, 2002) through the use of evidence-based approaches that are interdisciplinary (Rutherford, Zwi, Grove, & Butchart, 2007a). Public health approaches draw on social-ecological models of the development of health problems and health risk behaviors. In these models, it is recognized that the different environments in which youth live impact their development. These environments include those closest to youth (e.g., families, peer groups), those less proximal to youth (e.g., schools, neighborhoods), and those distal to youth (e.g., social and political environments). Public health approaches identify core social determinants of health (e.g., access to education and employment) and also take into account the impact of lifestyle and lifestyle choices on health.

A focus of public health approaches is the factors that influence health and health risk behaviors that are modifiable; risk factors and protective factors. Risk factors are influences that increase the likelihood of delinquent behavior (National Crime Prevention, 1999) and protective factors reduce the likelihood of delinquent behavior or mediate or moderate the effect of risk factors on delinquency (Jessor, Turbin, & Costa, 1998; Jessor, Van Den Bos, Vanderryn, Costa, & Turbin, 1995). Although delinquent behavior tends to be considered a criminal justice issue, public health models have been applied to the prevention of these behaviors. For example, the Social Development Model (Catalano & Hawkins, 1996) has been applied to the development of youth antisocial behavior. In this Model, it is recognized that risk and protective factors can occur in multiple domains in a youth's life; within the youth him or herself, the peer group, family, school environment, or local community (Catalano & Hawkins, 1996). Youth engaging in delinquent behavior are known to experience multiple risk factors and to be lacking protective factors. A number of the risk and protective factors for delinquent behavior also predict mental health problems, health risk behaviors, and to a lesser extent physical health problems. Therefore, youth engaging in delinquent behavior are vulnerable to mental health problems, physical health problems, and health risk behaviors.

Prevention activities can be classified according to the timing of the activity: primary prevention (before a problem emerges); secondary prevention (early in the development of the problem); and tertiary prevention (after the problem has emerged) (Rutherford, Zwi, Grove, & Butchart, 2007b). Prevention activities can also be distinguished by the population receiving the activity: universal prevention (for the general population or specific groups within the population such as gender); selected or targeted prevention (for populations at increased risk of the problem); and indicated intervention (for populations that are at high-risk and already showing the problem) (Rutherford et al., 2007b). The distinctions made between these prevention activities are relevant given that delinquent behavior may occur within the general population (and remain undetected by law enforcement), in groups at risk of delinquent behavior, and in young offenders apprehended for delinquent behaviors.

## Youth Engaging in Delinquent Behavior in Australia

In the present chapter, the mental and physical health problems and health risk behaviors of youth engaging in delinquent behavior in Australia in the general population, in the youth justice population, and in homeless youth will be described. It is recognized that youth engaging in delinquent behavior in each of these population groups are vulnerable to the typically emerging mental and physical health problems and health risk behaviors in adolescence (AIHW, 2018a; The Royal Australasian College of Physicians [RACP], 2011). Some of the associations between risk and protective factors that are specifically linked to the vulnerability of youth engaging in delinquent behavior are those between engaging in delinquent behavior and socioeconomic disadvantage and the range of health problems often experienced by people from socioeconomically disadvantaged backgrounds (AIHW, 2018a). In addition, youth engaging in delinquent behavior are at greater risk than their peers of participating in health risk behaviors (such as the misuse of licit drugs, the use of illicit drugs, and risky sexual behavior; AIHW, 2018a; RACP, 2011). This is likely due to the tendency for youth engaging in delinquent behavior to also obtain high scores on sensation-seeking and impulsivity (e.g., Higgins, Kirchner, Ricketts, & Marcum, 2013), suggesting they are drawn to situations that include engaging in health risk behaviors. Further, the situations in which youth engaging in delinquent behavior find themselves can place them more at risk of being injured or compromising their health (Shepherd, Farrington, & Potts, 2004).

## Youth Justice Population

Youth who comprise the Australian youth justice population are particularly vulnerable to health problems. Children can be charged with a criminal offence if they are ten years of age or older. In Australia, the justice systems for youth (and adults) are separate in each of the seven States and Territories, each with their own legislation. Within each State and Territory, there are two major forms of youth justice contact; supervised contact in the community or being held in custody in a youth detention facility. The detention of youth in a facility is used as a last resort in Australia. Hence, in 2016/17, of the 5,359 youth under the supervision of youth justice, 4,473 were located in the community and 913 in detention (AIHW, 2018b).

Youth in contact with youth justice in Australia are known to be drawn from our most vulnerable communities. For example, on an average day in 2016/17 indigenous youth aged 10 to 17 years comprised 50% of the youth under the supervision of youth justice, even though they only comprise 5% of the youth population in Australia (AIHW, 2018b). There are other immigrant groups (particularly Maori, Pacific Islander, South Sudanese) strongly represented in the youth justice population (Armytage & Ogloff, 2017). Reports also show that youth with an intellectual disability comprise a high percentage of the youth justice population. For example, the Victorian Youth Parole Board Annual Report 2016–2017 surveyed 176 male and 8 female youth detained on sentence or remand on 28 September 2016 and found that 11% were registered with Disability Services and 26% presented with issues in relation to their intellectual functioning (Department of Justice, 2017). Other notable signs of vulnerability were that 71% had been victims of abuse, trauma, or neglect, for 22% of respondents, English was a second language, and 13% were homeless before being taken into custody (i.e., had no fixed address or were living in insecure housing) (Department of Justice, 2017).

## Homeless Youth

Homelessness among youth is a multifaceted and significant social problem in Australia. These youth include those who are without suitable accommodation and their current living arrangement: is in an inadequate dwelling; or has no tenure or the tenure is short and not extendable; or does not permit the individual to have control of, and access to space for social interactions (Australian Bureau of Statistics, 2012). It was estimated 27,680 young Australians (12–24 years old) were homeless in 2016 (Australian Bureau of Statistics, 2016), not including accompanied youth who were with parental or adult care within homeless families. With one in six Australian youth having experienced homelessness (Fildes, Perrens, & Plummer, 2018), this issue is directly and indirectly responsible for high levels of health and social problems for these youth. The annual cost of health and justice services to youth experiencing homelessness in Australia is estimated at $747 million annually (Mackenzie, Flatau, Steen, & Thielking, 2016). The short- and long-term health outcomes associated with homelessness are well-documented and include mental health problems (e.g., depression), substance use and abuse, physical health problems (e.g., malnutrition, effects of the cold) and sexual health concerns (e.g., sexually transmitted infections) (Bearsley-Smith, Bond, Littlefield, & Thomas, 2008; Ensign & Bell, 2004; Farrow, Deisher, Brown, Kulig, & Kipke, 1992).

Experiencing homelessness embeds youth within a social context where subcultures of violence that normalize and enable forms of antisocial and delinquent behaviors are ubiquitous (Heerde & Pallotta-Chiarolli, 2018; Kipke, Simon, Montgomery, Unger, & Iversen, 1997). Such subcultures of violence result in engagement in antisocial behaviors being required and accepted as a normal and regular occurrence (Baron & Hartnagel, 1998; Heerde & Pallotta-Chiarolli, 2018; Kipke et al., 1997). However, these behaviors are prohibited under conventional laws and regulations within the Australian context and can result in criminal charges. In an Australian study, antisocial and delinquent behaviors were engaged in as a response to individual vulnerability (i.e., self-protection), threats from other homeless persons and members of the general public, in response to violent victimization and to obtain commodities such as money, food or shelter (Heerde & Pallotta-Chiarolli, 2018). Australian research examining strategies to reduce violence and crime (including antisocial and delinquent behaviors) among disadvantaged and homeless youth estimated rates of community-based orders for these youth were as high as 72%, while estimated rates of custodial sentences were approximately 44% (Garton, 1999).

## Mental Health Problems Experienced by Youth Engaging in Delinquent Behavior in Australia

Mental health problems can be divided into externalizing behaviors (i.e., aggression, delinquency) and internalizing problems (i.e., anxiety, depression). In this section, the main mental health problems that are reported in youth engaging in delinquent behavior in Australia are described. Although these problems will be described independently where possible, it is important to recognize that youth engaging in delinquent behavior, particularly those in contact with youth justice, show multiple, co-occurring (co-morbid) mental health problems. General statistics from the Youth Parole Board Annual Report in Victoria, demonstrate the mental health needs of youth in custody, with 40% of youth detained on sentence or remand on 28 September 2016 presenting with mental health issues (Department of Justice, 2017).

### *Depression*

Although youth engaging in delinquent behavior tend to draw attention to themselves with their externalizing behaviors, they often also experience a range of other mental health problems including internalizing problems such as depression. In analyses of data from a state-representative sample of students in Victoria, Australia and Washington State, US (the International Youth Development Study), Heerde et al. (in press) found that Grade 7 antisocial behavior predicted Grade 8 depressive symptoms in bivariate analyses but there were no statistically significant associations between Grade 8 antisocial behavior and Grade 9 depressive symptoms or between Grade 7 antisocial behavior and Grade 9 depressive symptoms. The one bivariate association found did not remain once other established risk factors were added to the models. Grade 7 depressive symptoms were associated with Grade 8 and Grade 9 antisocial behavior in bivariate associations. However, again once other established risk and protective factors were added to the models, the associations did not remain. These findings suggest that other risk and protective factors are more strongly associated with antisocial behavior and depressive symptoms than the two behaviors are with each other during adolescence in this Victorian (and Washington State) sample.

### *Deliberate Self-Harm*

Deliberate self-harm (DSH), defined in general population studies as self-inflicted behavior that is intended to cause physical harm but without suicide intent and having a nonfatal outcome

(National Collaborating Centre for Mental Health, 2004), is of clinical concern due to its serious health and social implications. DSH is known to peak in mid-adolescence before declining into young adulthood (Klonsky, Oltmanns, & Turkheimer, 2003; Patton et al., 2007). In Australia and the United Kingdom, rates of DSH have been estimated at approximately 5% in the general population (Hawton & James, 2005; Heerde et al., 2015; Patton et al., 2007), while higher rates of 12–13% have been reported in the United States (Evans, Hawton, & Rodham, 2004).

Researchers internationally have consistently identified correlations between DSH and antisocial behaviors, including traditional bullying perpetration, as well as other social and behavioral problems (e.g. mental health problems, substance use, family conflict) (Evans et al., 2004; Fliege, Lee, Grimm, & Klapp, 2009; Heerde & Hemphill, 2018; Heerde et al., 2015; Portzky & van Heeringen, 2007). A recent meta-analysis showed traditional bullying perpetration (including aggressive conduct towards others) was associated with increased likelihood of DSH (Heerde & Hemphill, 2018). Other researchers have found similar results in relation to suicidal behaviors (e.g. ideation, thoughts, self-injury, suicide attempts) (Hinduja & Patchin, 2010; Kowalski & Limber, 2013; Schneider, O'Donnell, Stueve, & Coulter, 2012) internationally. A possible explanation of the association between delinquent behavior and DSH is that emotional dysregulation underlies both engagement in antisocial behavior and DSH, such that dysregulation in one's ability to manage anger and other aggression-based emotions is associated with acts of physical aggression towards others (Barker, Arseneault, Brendgen, Fontaine, & Maughan, 2008). Elsewhere, self-harm has been posited as behavior used by youth to manage and alleviate feelings of depression and anxiety (Moran et al., 2012).

In the youth justice population in Victoria, the Youth Parole Board Annual Report found that 22% of young offenders had a history of self-harm (this definition may differ to that outlined above) or suicidal ideation (Department of Justice, 2017). Analyses of data from 242 youth on community-based orders and 273 youth in custody in Victoria showed rates of self-harm in the previous six months of 12% and 19%, respectively (Borschmann et al., 2014). Moore, Gaskin, and Indig (2015) reported on data from 313 participants in the 2009 New South Wales Young People in Custody Survey. It was found that rates of a suicide attempt and reported self-harm in their lifetimes were 10% and 16% respectively. During the previous year, 12% of participants had thoughts of self-harm, 5% had a plan for self-harm, and 11% had actually self-harmed (Moore et al., 2015). In addition, 25% of youth in detention who had reported previous suicidal behavior reported that their suicidal thoughts had increased entering custody (Moore et al., 2015). This is concerning since one of the main aims of health care in custody is to ensure that the experience does not worsen health (RACP, 2011).

## *Other Mental Health Issues*

In a paper on a cross-sectional survey of 242 youth on community-based orders and 273 youth in custody in Victoria in 2002–2003, Kinner et al. (2014) reported that 23% of those on community-based orders and 39% in custody had depressive symptoms. The same paper reported that 10% of youth on community-based orders compared with 17% of youth in custody had screened positive for psychosis and 10% on community-based orders versus 22% in custody had self-harmed in the past 6 months (Kinner et al., 2014).

For homeless youth living within subcultures of violence, psychological health concerns are a pervasive reality in the aftermath of engaging in antisocial and delinquent behaviors. These youth commonly dissociate and express emotional detachment, discomfort, and shame in recounting their engagement in antisocial and delinquent behaviors (Heerde & Pallotta-Chiarolli, 2018). These reactions are trauma-based psychological responses and coping mechanisms (Davies & Allen, 2017; Herman, 1992). Understanding the duality between youth's normative acceptance of antisocial and delinquent behaviors (including resultant injury) and their psychological detachment from these experiences is important within the context of short- and long-term psychological trauma (Heerde & Pallotta-Chiarolli, 2018).

## Physical Health Problems Experienced by Youth Engaging in Delinquent Behavior in Australia

There is limited information about the physical health problems of youth engaging in delinquent behavior in Australia. Using data from the United Kingdom's longitudinal Cambridge Study of Delinquent Development, Shepherd et al. (2004) found strong associations between injuries (e.g., road, home, and self-injuries) and antisocial behavior 16–18 years of age and these were maintained until at least age 32 years. However, in the same study, participants engaging in antisocial behavior had low rates of illnesses (e.g., respiratory infections, organic illnesses). It is well known in American detention centers that youth in custody have a range of oral health problems (e.g., Bolin & Jones, 2006) and this seems likely to be the case in Australia as well (RACP, 2011).

Few studies have investigated health concerns associated with injuries sustained as a consequence of homeless youths' engagement in antisocial and delinquent behaviors (Heerde & Pallotta-Chiarolli, 2018; Kipke et al., 1997). The injuries that have been identified include general soreness, bruises, cuts, suspected cracked or broken bones, head trauma, and joint dislocations (Baron & Hartnagel, 1998; Heerde & Pallotta-Chiarolli, 2018).

## Health Risk Behaviors of Youth Engaging in Delinquent Behavior in Australia

### Substance Misuse and Abuse

The defining features of delinquent behavior include not only illicit (e.g., cannabis, cocaine, methamphetamine) substances but also using licit (alcohol, tobacco) substances since such use is not permitted at this age. Youth engaging in delinquency not only *use* licit substances as part of this behavior but also engage in excessive use, placing them at risk of a range of health problems. In an analysis of longitudinal data of Victorian and Washington State students enrolled in the state-representative sample of the International Youth Development Study, Hemphill et al. (2014) examined associations between alcohol use and misuse in Grade 7 students and Grade 8 and Grade 9 antisocial behavior. There were bivariate associations between each measure of Grade 7 alcohol use and misuse (lifetime alcohol use, current alcohol use, heavy episodic use, and frequent use) and each indicator of antisocial behavior (carrying a weapon, threatening someone with a weapon, stealing, violent behavior, and being arrested by police) in Grades 8 and 9. However, once the analyses controlled for established risk and demographic factors for antisocial behavior, only a few associations remained between Grade 7 alcohol use and misuse and later antisocial behavior, except that Grade 7 lifetime use predicted Grade 9 carrying a weapon; Grade 7 current use was associated with Grade 8 police arrests and stealing and Grade 9 carrying a weapon and stealing; and Grade 7 heavy episodic use predicted Grade 8 and Grade 9 police arrests. Associations in the reverse direction (early antisocial behavior to later alcohol use) were not examined in this study.

However, in another analysis of International Youth Development Study data Victorian students in Grades 7 to 11, Scholes-Balog, Hemphill, Kremer, and Toumbourou (2013) found that the frequency of alcohol use from early (Grade 7) and mid-adolescence (Grade 9) predicted violence two years later (Grade 11) and there was a bi-directional relationship between heavy episodic drinking and violence. Similar to the results of Hemphill et al. (2014), some of these relationships did not remain statistically significant after the analyses were adjusted for established risk factors. The findings of the International Youth Development Study suggest that there are links between youths' engagement in antisocial behavior and alcohol use and misuse and vice versa but that these associations may be due to risk factors common to both of these behaviors.

In another longitudinal study of over 30-years duration, the Australian Temperament Project, Miller et al. (2016) examined longitudinal associations between delinquent behavior and heavy episodic drinking from adolescence (age 13–18 years) to young adulthood (age 19–24 years) for 1,650 participants. The findings of this study were that adolescent delinquent behavior was associated with heavy episodic drinking at each subsequent adolescent time-point but not in young adulthood. Heavy episodic drinking at 17–18 years of age was associated with delinquent behavior in young adulthood. Given this latter finding, Miller et al. (2016) concluded that increased access to alcohol at the legal drinking age of 18 years increases youth engagement in delinquent behavior.

Within the youth justice population, Victoria's Youth Parole Board reported in their annual report of 2016/16 that 4% had a history of alcohol misuse, 18% had a history of drug misuse, and 65% had a history of both alcohol and drug misuse (Department of Justice, 2017). Often, youth have offended while using alcohol and/or drugs. The Youth Parole Board in Victoria found that 8% had offended while under the influence of alcohol but not drugs, 20% had offended while under the influence of drugs but not alcohol, and 54% had offended while under the influence of alcohol and drugs (Department of Justice, 2017).

The results of a cross-sectional survey of 242 young offenders on community-based orders and 273 youth in custody in Victoria in 2002–2003 showed that both groups reported regular tobacco use (Kinner et al., 2014). The youth on community-based orders also reported hazardous alcohol consumption and a third of them were dependent on another substance, usually cannabis (Kinner et al., 2014). Youth in custody were more likely than those on community-based orders to be dependent on cannabis, heroin, amphetamine and sedatives, and were also more likely to have injected drugs (Kinner et al., 2014).

## Risky Sexual Behavior

In the analysis of the data from a cross-sectional survey of youth in contact with youth justice in Victoria in 2002–2003, Kinner et al. (2014) reported that youth on community-based orders ($N = 242$) and in custody ($N = 273$) engaged in a range of risky sexual behaviors including having had sex for the first time under the age of 15 years (68% on community-based orders; 85% in custody), having had more than five partners in the past 6 months (9% on community-based orders; 14% in custody), and having had a sexual partner who has injected drugs (17% on community-based orders; 39% in custody). There are reports of an increase in the prevalence of sexually transmitted diseases in the youth justice population (Templeton, 2006).

## Challenges to Knowledge about the Mental and Physical Health Problems and Health Risk Behaviors of Youth Engaging in Delinquent Behavior in Australia

There are relatively few population studies in Australia that can provide information on the connections between delinquency and health. Further, even though there is now a national dataset on the health of adult Australian prisoners, there is no equivalent dataset for youth. A limited amount of information is collected about youth under youth justice supervision in Australia through the Juvenile Justice National Minimum Data Set (JJ NMDS) and there is an agreement with the Australasian Juvenile Justice Administrators to ensure that each state and territory government department responsible for youth justice provides data each year for the Data Set (AIHW, 2018a). This data is then compiled and analyzed by the Australian Institute of Health and Welfare (AIHW), Australia's leading government institute on health and welfare. The AIHW conducted a study in 2016–2017 to explore the feasibility of developing a national data set for young offenders in Australia (AIHW, 2018a). Steps are being taken in 2018 to continue to make progress towards the collection of data on the health of youth in contact with youth justice nationally. It is likely that the first step towards this will be to integrate data that is currently collected by government departments and youth detention centers (AIHW, 2018a).

## Approaches and Policies to Prevent Health Problems and Health Risk Behaviors in Youth Engaging in Delinquency and the Impact of Social Problems on Their Health

Without adequate data on the health needs of youth engaging in delinquent behavior, including those contact with the youth justice system, it is difficult to make recommendations for appropriate approaches and policies to address these health needs. Better monitoring systems are needed to collect data on young Australian's health and behavior (including delinquent behavior) in the general population. Further, the AIHW (2018a) feasibility study recommended that national data collection on the health of youth under youth justice supervision (in detention and in the community) be developed, using a combination of data linkage with the Juvenile Justice National Minimum Data Set and administrative data available from youth detention centers. In the AIHW (2018a) report, it was acknowledged that the set of indicators available may be less comprehensive than data collected on the health of adult prisoners in terms of health status and heath behaviors, but could provide more complete information on service usage and health changes before and after detention, and on the continuity of care for youth.

Using the information available in Australia, and also what we know from other similar Western countries, the following approaches and policies are warranted. First, a multidisciplinary approach is required to address effectively the health needs of youth engaging in delinquent behavior. Shepherd et al. (2004) similarly recommended that an integrated approach to prevention is needed that brings together a focus on the prevention of offending behavior and the prevention of injury and illness. They noted that often staff in criminal justice work separately from public health workers; however, these staff need to collaborate to ensure an integrated approach to meeting the health needs of youth engaging in delinquent behavior.

Second, findings from studies such as the International Youth Development Study and more broadly in public health (Rutherford et al., 2007a) have shown that there are risk and protective factors that are common to a range of health problems and health risk behaviors. By focusing prevention and early intervention efforts on these common factors, multiple health outcomes are likely to be reduced. Such approaches need to be implemented early in the development pathway for these health problems, not only early in life.

Consistent with a public health perspective, the approaches implemented to address health problems need to evidence-based and it is essential that the effects of such approaches are monitored and evaluated. The approaches used to improve the health of youth engaging in delinquent behavior should target multiple risk and protective factors and may need to include multiple components (e.g., for the young person, parents, and teachers) to address the main factors that influence the development of youth's delinquent behavior and health problems. Given that youth engaging in delinquent behavior are often vulnerable members of our community, care needs to be taken to ensure that the approaches used are socially and culturally appropriate for the participants. Also consistent with a public health approach, efforts to prevent delinquent behavior and related health problems need to address the social determinants of health, as well as take into account the effect of lifestyles and lifestyle choices on behavior and health.

For youth in contact with youth justice specifically, the need to provide services that optimize the health of these youth has been recognized in Standard 10 of the Australasian Juvenile Justice Administrators (AJJA) in the *Juvenile Justice Standards 2009* (AIHW, 2018a). The services described in Standard 10 include conducting health assessments on admission to custody; access to a continuum of health care; and access to a range of programs that promote development and wellbeing. The Royal Australian College of Physicians (RACP, 2011) has also emphasized that services be provided by non-custodial health staff and the importance of following up on these once youth their sentences. The implementation of the latter may be difficult given the complex needs, and often ever-changing life circumstances, of these youth, as well as the potential reluctance of these youth to attend health services in their local community.

The World Health Organization (2003) has set out seven principles for the health and wellbeing for youth in custody and the policies and practices to support these principles. These principles could be extended to apply to youth in contact with youth justice in the community. The principles cover ensuring that youth: have opportunities for health physical, mental, and social development; have access to good quality health services of similar quality to those available in the community; can live in a positive care environment that promotes their health and development; are consulted and listened to in relation to their health needs; can develop and maintain relationships with at least one suitable adult from the community in which they will live; are shown respect in terms of their culture and identity and are therefore able to construct their own positive self-perceptions and self-esteem; and have opportunities for education, training, and healthy lifestyle and work skills. It is essential that principles like these are at the forefront of planning for the health care of youth in contact with youth justice.

The research by Kinner et al. (2014) identified that the needs of the large group of youth on community-based orders were unmet. One of their recommendations was to expand coordinated health and welfare services for youth on community-based orders to service not only youth on these orders but also youth released from custody and transitioning back into the community. To ensure quality transitional care, Kinner et al. (2014) suggested that this would need to include the identification of needs through routine screening, along with case management that covers both custodial and community health and welfare services.

Youth experiencing homelessness often report having had contact with police and, in some cases, the youth justice system. These youth have complex and multiple health needs. Experiencing homelessness does not afford youth the opportunity for rest and recuperation from physical injury, seek medical care for physical injury, or obtain counselling for psychological trauma. In Australian research, Heerde and Pallotta-Chiarolli (2018) reported feelings of shame, stigma, and unequal power relationships are described by youth in their interactions with health professionals; these feelings often arise as a result of non-conformity to and non-compliance with broader social norms (e.g. cleanliness, substance use, social language), distrust in health professionals and perceived discrimination by health professionals. Furthermore, the transient nature of homelessness and associated financial instability often impedes youth's ability to attain medical and psychological health care in the community. Intervention and prevention programming that acknowledges the social context and subcultures of violence within which youth experiencing homelessness are located, and those that maintain neutrality in providing physical and psychological support, are important in the delivery of health care to homeless youth (Heerde & Pallotta-Chiarolli, 2018).

## Conclusions

Youth engaging in delinquent behavior in Australia are vulnerable to experiencing multiple and complex health problems. The extent of these problems in both the general population and the youth justice population in Australia is unclear since there is currently no regular data collection for the former and no national database for the latter. There is a clear need in Australia to develop a national database on the health problems and needs of youth in contact with the youth justice system. There is also a need for regular monitoring systems in the community to monitor the health needs of youth in the general population. It is only by having data available that we can begin to understand the health problems of this group and develop programs and policies to address these problems where they are most needed.

To address the health needs of youth engaging in delinquent behavior, multiple risk factors need to be addressed across the multiple domains of a young person's life (the young person, peer group, family, school, and community). There are risk and protective factors that are common to multiple health problems; targeting these factors may offer efficiencies in reducing a range of health problems. A continuum of health care from prevention to intervention needs to be available to all youth engaging in delinquent behavior, including those in contact with youth justice. It is essential that any approaches that are implemented are monitored and evaluated to ensure they are addressing youth's health needs, and that when necessary, approaches are adjusted to better meet health needs. Addressing the health problems of youth engaging in delinquent behavior provides a valuable opportunity to integrate the work of a range of health professionals, public health workers, and youth justice staff. Making the effort to address the health needs of youth engaging in delinquent behavior while they are young will reduce health costs in the future.

## References

Armytage, P., & Ogloff, J. (2017). *Youth justice review and strategy: Meeting needs and reducing offending – Executive summary*. Melbourne, Victoria: Victorian Government.

Australian Bureau of Statistics. (2012). 4922.0 – Information paper – A statistical definition of homelessness, 2012. www.abs.gov.au/AUSSTATS/abs@.nsf/DetailsPage/4922.02012?OpenDocument

Australian Bureau of Statistics. (2016). 2049.0 – Census of Population and Housing: Estimating homelessness, 2016. www.abs.gov.au/AUSSTATS/abs@.nsf/DetailsPage/2049.02016?OpenDocument

Australian Institute of Health and Welfare. (2018a). *National data on the health of justice-involved young people: A feasibility study 2016–17*. Cat. no. JUV 125. Canberra, Australia: AIHW.

Australian Institute of Health and Welfare. (2018b). *Youth justice in Australia 2016–17*. Cat. no. JUV 116. Canberra, Australia: AIHW.

Baker, J. (1998). *Juveniles in crime Part 1: Participation rates and risk factors*. Sydney, Australia: New South Wales Bureau of Crime Statistics and Research.

Barker, E. D., Arseneault, L., Brendgen, M., Fontaine, N., & Maughan, B. (2008). Joint development of bullying and victimization in adolescence: Relations to delinquency and self-harm. *Journal of the American Academy of Child and Adolescent Psychiatry, 47*(9), 1030–1038.

Baron, S. W., & Hartnagel, T. F. (1998). Street youth and criminal violence. *Journal of Research in Crime and Delinquency, 35*(2), 166–192.

Bearsley-Smith, C. A., Bond, L. M., Littlefield, L., & Thomas, L. R. (2008). The psychosocial profile of adolescent risk of homelesssness. *European Child & Adolescent Psychiatry, 17*(4), 226–234. doi:10.1007/s00787-007-0657-5

Bolin, K., & Jones, D. (2006). Oral health needs of adolescents in a juvenile detention facility. *Journal of Adolescent Health, 38*, 755–757.

Bond, L., Thomas, L., Toumbourou. J., Patton, G., & Catalano, R. (2000). *Improving the lives of Young Victorians in Our Community: A survey of risk and protective factors*. Melbourne, Australia: Centre for Adolescent Health. Report prepared for Community Care Division, Department of Human Services.

Borschmann, R., Coffey, C., Moran, P., Hearps, S., Degenhardt, L., Kinner, S., & Patton, G. (2014). Self-harm in young offenders. *Suicide and Life-Threatening Behavior, 44*(6):641–652.

Catalano, R. F., & Hawkins, J. D. (1996). The social development model: A theory of antisocial behavior. In J. D. Hawkins (Ed.), *Delinquency and crime: Current theories* (pp. 149–197). New York: Cambridge University Press.

Costello, E. J., Mustillo, S., Erklanli, A., Keeler, G., & Angold, A. (2003). Prevalence and development of psychiatric disorders in childhood and adolescence. *Archives of General Psychiatry, 60*, 837–844.

Davies, B. R., & Allen, N. B. (2017). Trauma and homelessness in youth: Psychopathology and intervention. *Clinical Psychology Review, 54*, 17–28.

Department of Justice. (2017). *Youth Parole Board Annual Report*. Melbourne, Australia: Department of Justice.

Ensign, J., & Bell, M. (2004). Illness experiences of homeless youth. *Qualitative Health Research, 14*(9), 1239–1254.

Evans, E., Hawton, K., & Rodham, K. (2004). Factors associated with suicidal phenomena in adolescents: A systematic review of population-based studies. *Clinical Psychology Review, 24*(8), 957–979.

Farrow, J. A., Deisher, R. W., Brown, R., Kulig, J. W., & Kipke, M. D. (1992). Health and health needs of homeless and runaway youth: A position paper of the Society for Adolescent Medicine. *Journal of Adolescent Health, 13*(8), 717–726.

Fildes, J., Perrens, B., & Plummer, J. (2018). *Young people's experiences of homelessness: Findings from the Youth Survey 2017*. Sydney, Australia: Mission Australia.

Fliege, H., Lee, J.-R., Grimm, A., & Klapp, B. F. (2009). Risk factors and correlates of deliberate self-harm behavior: A systematic review. *Journal of Psychosomatic Research, 66*(6), 477–493.

Garton, K. (1999). *Living rough: Preventing crime and victimisation among homeless young people*. Canberra, Australia: National Crime Prevention Unit.

Hawton, K., & James, A. (2005). Suicide and deliberate self harm in young people. *BMJ: British Medical Journal, 330*(7496), 891–894.

Heerde, J. A., Curtis A., Bailey, J. A., Smith, R., Hemphill, S. A., & Toumbourou, J. W. (in press, accepted 1 September 2018). Reciprocal associations between early adolescent antisocial behavior and depressive symptoms: A longitudinal study in Victoria, Australia and Washington State, United States. *Journal of Criminal Justice*, doi:10.1016/j.jcrimjus.2018.09.003

Heerde, J. A., & Hemphill, S. (2018). Are traditional- and cyber- bullying perpetration and victimization associated with adolescent deliberate-self harm? A meta-analysis. *Archives of Suicide Research, accepted 2 May 2018*. doi:10.1080/13811118.2018.1472690

Heerde, J. A., & Pallotta-Chiarolli, M. (2018). "The longer you spend homeless the more damaged you become ...": An introduction to the study of exposure to physical violence among young people experiencing homelessness. *Unpublished manuscript*.

Heerde, J. A., Toumbourou, J. W., Hemphill, S. A., Herrenkohl, T. I., Patton, G. C., & Catalano, R. F. (2015). Incidence and course of adolescent deliberate self-harm in Victoria, Australia, and Washington State. *Journal of Adolescent Health, 57*(5), 537–544. doi:10.1016/j.jadohealth.2015.07.017

Hemphill, S. A. (1996). Characteristics of conduct-disordered children and their families: A review. *Australian Psychologist, 31*, 109–118.

Hemphill, S. A., Heerde, J. A., Scholes-Balog, K. E., Smith, R., Herrenkohl, T. I., Toumbourou, J. W., & Catalano, R. F. (2014). Reassessing the effects of early adolescent alcohol use on later antisocial behavior: A longitudinal study of students in Victoria, Australia, and Washington State, United States. *The Journal of Early Adolescence, 34*(3), 360–386. doi:10.1177/0272431613491830.

Herman, J. (1992). *Trauma and recovery: The aftermath of violence – from domestic abuse to political terror*. New York: Basic Books.

Higgins, G. E., Kirchner, E. E., Ricketts, M. L., & Marcum, C. D. (2013). Impulsivity and offending from childhood to young adulthood in the United States: A developmental trajectory analysis. *International Journal of Criminal Justice Sciences, 8*(2), 182–187.

Hinduja, S., & Patchin, J. W. (2010). Bullying, cyberbullying, and suicide. *Archives of Suicide Research, 14*(3), 206–221.

Jessor, R., Turbin, M. S., & Costa, F. M. (1998). Protective factors in adolescent health behavior. *Journal of Personality & Social Psychology, 75*, 788–800.

Jessor, R., Van Den Bos, J., Vanderryn, J., Costa, F. M., & Turbin, M. S. (1995). Protective factors in adolescent problem behavior: Moderator effects and developmental change. *Developmental Psychology, 31*, 923–933.

Kinner, S. A., Degenhardt, L., Coffey, C., Sawyer, S., Hearps, S., & Patton, G. (2014). Complex health needs in the youth justice system: A survey of community-based and custodial offenders. *Journal of Adolescent Health, 54*, 521–526.

Kipke, M. D., Simon, T. R., Montgomery, S. B., Unger, J. B., & Iversen, E. F. (1997). Homeless youth and their exposure to and involvement in violence while living on the streets. *Journal of Adolescent Health, 20*(5), 360–367.

Klonsky, E. D., Oltmanns, T. F., & Turkheimer, E. (2003). Deliberate self-harm in a nonclinical population: Prevalence and psychological correlates. *American Journal of Psychiatry, 160*(8), 1501–1508.

Kowalski, R. M., & Limber, S. P. (2013). Psychological, physical, and academic correlates of cyberbullying and traditional bullying. *Journal of Adolescent Health, 53*(1), S13–S20.

Krug, E. G., Dahlberg, L. L., Mercy, J. A., Zwi, A. B., & Lozano, R., eds. (2002). *World report on violence and health*. Geneva: World Health Organization.

Mackenzie, D., Flatau, P., Steen, A., & Thielking, M. (2016). *The cost of youth homelessness in Australia*. Victoria, Australia: Swinburne Institute for Social Research.

Miller, P. G., Butler, E., Richardson, B., Staiger, P. K., Youssef, G. J., Macdonald, J. A., Sanson, A., Edwards, B., & Olsson, C. A. (2016). Relationships between problematic alcohol consumption and delinquent behaviour from adolescence to young adulthood. *Drug & Alcohol Review, 35*, 317–325.

Moore, E., Gaskin, C., & Indig, D. (2015). Attempted suicide, self-harm and psychological disorder among young offenders in custody. *Journal of Correctional Health Care, 21*(3), 243–254.

Moran, P., Coffey, C., Romaniuk, H., Olsson, C., Borschmann, R., Carlin, J. B., & Patton, G. C. (2012). The natural history of self-harm from adolescence to young adulthood: A population-based cohort study. *The Lancet, 379*(9812), 236–243.

National Collaborating Centre for Mental Health. (2004). *Self-harm: The short-term physical and psychological management and secondary prevention of self-harm in primary and secondary care* (1854334093). Leicester, UK: National Collaborating Centre for Mental Health.

National Crime Prevention. (1999). *Pathways to prevention: Developmental and early intervention approaches to crime in Australia*. Canberra, Australia: Commonwealth Attorney Generals Department.

Patton, G. C., Hemphill, S. A., Beyers, J. M., Bond, L., Toumbourou, J. W., McMorris, B. J., & Catalano, R. F. (2007). Pubertal stage and deliberate self-harm in adolescents. *Journal of the American Academy of Child and Adolescent Psychiatry, 46*(4), 508–514. doi:10.1097/chi.0b013e31803065c7

Portzky, G., & van Heeringen, K. (2007). Deliberate self-harm in adolescents. *Current Opinion in Psychiatry, 20*(4), 337–342.

The Royal Australasian College of Physicians. (2011). *The health and well-being of incarcerated adolescents*. Sydney, Australia: The Royal Australasia College of Physicians.

Rutherford, A., Zwi, A. B., Grove, N. J., & Butchart, A. (2007a). Violence: A priority for public health? (part 2). *Journal of Epidemiology and Community Health, 61*, 764–770. doi:10.1136/jech.2006.049072

Rutherford, A., Zwi, A. B., Grove, N. J., & Butchart, A. (2007b). Violence: A Glossary. *Journal of Epidemiology and Community Health, 61*, 676–680. doi:10.1136/jech.2005.043711

Sawyer, M. G., Arney, F. M., Baghurst, P. A., Clark, J. J., Graetz, B. W., Kosky, R. J., Nurcombe, B., Patton, G. C., Prior, M. R., Raphael, B., Rey, J. M., Whaites, L. C., & Zubrick, S. R. (2001). The mental health of young people in Australia: Key findings from the child and adolescent component of the national survey of mental health and well-being. *Australian and New Zealand Journal of Psychiatry, 35*, 806–814.

Schneider, S. K., O'Donnell, L., Stueve, A., & Coulter, R. W. (2012). Cyberbullying, school bullying, and psychological distress: A regional census of high school students. *American Journal of Public Health, 102*(1), 171–177.

Scholes-Balog, K. E., Hemphill, S. A., Kremer, P., & Toumbourou, J. W. (2013). A longitudinal study of the reciprocal effects of alcohol use and interpersonal violence among Australian young people. *Journal of Youth and Adolescence, 42*(12), 1811–1823. doi:10.1007/s10964-013-9910-z

Shepherd, J., Farrington, D., & Potts, J. (2004). Impact of antisocial lifestyle on health. *Journal of Public Health, 26*(4), 347–352.

Smith, R., Jorna, P., Sweeney, J., & Fuller, G. (2014). *Counting the costs of crime in Australia: A 2011 estimate. Research and public policy series no. 129*. Canberra, Australia: Australian Institute of Criminology.

Templeton, D.J. (2006). Sexually transmitted infection and blood-borne virus screening in juvenile correctional facilities: A review of the literature and recommendations for Australian centres. *Journal of Clinical Forensic Medicine, 13*, 30–36.

World Health Organization. (2003). *Promoting the health of young people in custody*. Copenhagen, Denmark: World Health Organization.

# 25
# DELINQUENCY AND HEALTH
## Future Directions

*Michael G. Vaughn, Christopher P. Salas-Wright, and Dylan B. Jackson*

The chapters in this volume exemplify the tremendous intellectual diversity present when the study of juvenile delinquency is linked to health. The fruitful intersections of what some have variously referred to as health and justice, health and criminal justice or what we term − health criminology − is a rich and exciting interdisciplinary area poised for growth. For instance, if we execute a Google Scholar search of the term "health criminology", we see a quadrupling of citation hits from 2000 to 2018. Part of this growth is certainly tied to the broadening of the concept of health and the attendant rise in interdisciplinary or what is more fad to say transdisciplinary research. But, what is also clear is that individuals in the criminal justice system − and those on a life course trajectory to encounter the justice system − are at greater odds of behavioral, mental, and physical health problems. This, of course, is unsurprising given the pronounced disadvantage of persons who encounter the justice system. However, where there are unique changes under way is with respect to the convergence of disciplines that have traditionally studied crime and justice and health in previous isolation. For instance, the tradition of criminological training is social science based and has been somewhat avoidant, conceited or even skeptical of what could be viewed as a "biomedical" approach to traditional areas of social science theory and research. Conversely, health and medical researchers are not typically trained in social science approaches, let alone criminological theory.

The goal of the present chapter is to highlight some areas that are especially fertile intersectional research grounds and discuss major research topics that need to be pursued to realize the potential of the health criminology paradigm. The areas that we highlight are not meant to be a comprehensive list as there are a multitude of important and interesting studies that could be carried forth. However, we think these areas highlighted have been neglected by criminologists at-large and are fruitful for building partnerships with health researchers and moving investigation of delinquency and health forward.

### Maternal Child Health Research and Antisocial Behavior

The roots of both delinquency and poor health often have their genesis at earlier stages of the life course. As such, greater attention to maternal child health research by criminologists is critical. Focusing on this time period may also prove advantageous for prevention. For instance, Olds and colleagues (1998) followed up with adolescents and their mothers 15 years after a randomized trial involving prenatal and early childhood nurse home visitations to investigate the long-term effects of these visits on children's antisocial behavior. Findings suggest that adolescents whose mothers received nurse home visits had a lower incidence of running away, fewer arrests, fewer lifetime sex partners, fewer convictions and violations of probation, lower alcohol and tobacco usage and fewer behavioral problems compared to those whose mothers did not receive home nurse visits. The cost savings in well-being and monetary terms are enormous if trajectories can be diverted at these early stages. While there have been several studies in this area, substantially more is needed. Raine (2002) reviewed biosocial studies of antisocial behavior in children and adults finding that obstetric influences demonstrate the most compelling evidence of biosocial interactions. Raine categorizes the obstetric studies in three domains, minor physical anomalies, prenatal nicotine exposure, and birth complications. Raine finds that at least six studies exhibit a relationship between increased minor physical anomalies associated with disorders of pregnancy (low-seated ears, adherent ear lobes, and furrowed tongue) and increased antisocial behavior in children. Raine also finds that recent studies have established a significant link between prenatal exposure to nicotine and later conduct disorder beyond reasonable doubt. Further, several studies show that birth complications interact with psychosocial risk factors related to adult violence, including a disruptive family environment, to predispose offspring to delinquency. Beck and Shaw (2005) tested Raine's (2002) biosocial model through an investigation of the interactive effects of perinatal complications and environmental adversity on the development of early-onset antisocial behavior among 310 low-income boys followed from birth to age ten. Results from maternal report suggest that boys with high levels of perinatal complications, measured using a weighted-severity scale for 22 potential complications, exhibited high levels of antisocial behavior in the context of rejecting parenting and family adversity. These results were partially corroborated by youth self-report, revealing that boys experiencing high levels of perinatal complications and family adversity reported increased antisocial activity compared to boys with no risk or only one environmental risk. Interesting questions remain such as do birth complications prospectively predict contact with the criminal justice system? What is the empirical status of the relationship between birth complications and psychopathy?

Several important studies have examined the role of maternal health behaviors and its association with conduct problems later. The case of smoking during pregnancy is illustrative. Brennan, Grekin, and Mednick (1999) examined the relationship between prenatal smoking and adult criminal outcomes in a longitudinal birth cohort study of 4,169 males born in Denmark. Criminal outcomes were measured using arrest histories at age 34. Results suggested a dose-response relationship between maternal smoking during pregnancy and arrests for both nonviolent and violent crime, particularly for persistent criminal behavior past adolescence, after controlling for demographic, parental, and other perinatal risk factors. Cornelius and Day (2009) reviewed results of studies examining the link between prenatal tobacco exposure (PTE) and neurodevelopmental outcomes in offspring. Consequences of PTE in early childhood were primarily behavioral and included conduct disorder and antisocial behavior. For example, Gatzke-Kopp and Beauchaine (2007) found increased conduct disorder symptoms among offspring ages 7–15 years of mothers with second-hand exposure to tobacco smoking during pregnancy, after controlling for income, prematurity, parental antisocial tendencies, parenting practices and birthweight. Huijbregts and colleagues (2008) examined the interaction between PTE, childhood physical aggression, and parental antisocial behaviors in children ages 17–42 months finding a direct effect of PTE on child aggression. Increased aggression in children was also related to both an interaction between PTE and maternal history of antisocial behavior as well as the interaction of PTE and lower family income. Among children with ADHD, Langley et al. (2007) found that those with PTE had increased conduct disorder and hyperactive-impulsive symptoms compared to children without PTE. In a study involving genetic testing, Wakschlag and colleagues (2010) examined the effects of a polymorphism of the MAOA and PTE on antisocial behavior in adolescents finding that males with PTE and low activity MAOA 5′ exhibited increased risk of conduct disorder symptoms, however, this relationship was not found among females. Interestingly, Gilman and colleagues (2008) examined over 52,000 children from birth to age seven, finding that PTE was not associated with PTE and argued that effects of PTE may not be discernible from the range of familial factors associated with PTE. Gaysina and colleagues (2013) conducted three studies to assess the association between prenatal smoking and conduct problems among biological and adopted offspring. The study revealed a significant relationship between prenatal smoking and offspring conduct problems regardless of whether the child was reared by a genetically related mother or genetically unrelated mother. Other studies of maternal health behaviors are needed including investigations of diet, sleep, and exercise and their empirical relations to delinquency etiology and related juvenile offender outcomes.

One additional line of research that has yielded meaningful findings is the role of maternal depression and offspring outcomes. In a longitudinal study of 842 adolescents ages 11–16 at baseline and 15–20 at follow-up, Rice and colleagues (2007) found that maternal and adolescent-rated depressive symptoms predicted future antisocial behavior, depression, health service use, regular tobacco use, and impairment in the adolescents. A study using data on 1,116 twin pairs assessed at ages five and seven revealed that maternal depression occurring after birth, but not before birth, was related to child antisocial behavior (ASB) (Kim-Cohen et al., 2005). Avan and colleagues (2010) assessed the association between maternal postnatal depression and child behavior problems at age two in a longitudinal birth cohort study. Results revealed that maternal depression was significantly associated with child behavior problems measured by hyperactivity, poor relationships, lack of concentration, tempers, soiling, sleep disturbances, and eating problems, after accounting for socioeconomic status. In a study involving 108 children diagnosed with ADHD, Chronis and colleagues (2007) found that maternal depression assessed at Wave 1 predicted conduct problems 2–8 years later, after controlling for demographic variables and baseline ADHD and conduct problems. In total, these maternal health findings link up nicely with long-standing programs of research on children exhibiting aggression and conduct problems (e.g., Loeber et al., 2000). However, most of these studies do not fully engage the question, what does research tell us about the *early health* of children exhibiting aggression and conduct problems? What are the early health histories of severe 5% (Vaughn et al., 2014) or chronic offenders? Collaboration between developmental psychologists, pediatricians, and criminologists could lead to some important new findings with respect to this question.

## Physical Health of Juvenile Offenders

While a substantial body of research has accrued with respect to the mental health of juvenile offenders (Abram et al., 2003; Vaughn et al., 2007, 2008), far less attention has been focused on physical health. It is well-established that psychiatric disorders are more prevalent among juvenile offenders. For instance, using nationally representative data, Vaughn and colleagues (2015) explored the psychiatric status of adults with a history of juvenile offending, finding that almost half meet criteria for at least one psychiatric disorder in the past year and nearly two-thirds meet criteria for a personality disorder. Compared to the general population, former juvenile detainees were more likely to meet criteria for MDD, bipolar disorder, PTSD, ASPD, and several personality disorders, including borderline, histrionic, narcissistic, and schizotypal. In a longitudinal study, Abram and colleagues (2015) examined the comorbidity and continuity of psychiatric disorders of youth ages 14–24 five years after detention. Results indicate that nearly 27% of males and 14% of females had comorbid psychiatric disorders after leaving detention. Interestingly, while females had significantly higher rates of comorbidity while detained, males had significantly higher rates following detention. Among males, the most common comorbidities were substance use and behavioral disorders (CD, ODD, or APD). The more disorders one had at baseline, the more likely they were to have a disorder at follow-up five years later. Far less is known about physical health of juvenile offenders. Extant studies, few in number, suggest additional research may be critically important. Perry and Morris (2014) reviewed existing literature on health care for youth involved with the correctional system finding that health disparities affecting these youths include sexually transmitted infections, teenage pregnancy and parenthood, chronic conditions (e.g., asthma, type II diabetes, sickle cell disease), ADHD and learning disorders, behavioral problems (e.g., conduct disorder, anger management), posttraumatic stress disorder, mood disorders, substance abuse, and suicidality. The authors noted several barriers to providing health care in juvenile detention facilities including conflicting priorities (e.g., school, court), security concerns, transportation challenges, lack of parental presence during the visit, youths' perceptions of relationship between health care providers and correctional system, availability of subspecialty care, and recruitment of providers. The authors suggested that community providers can help formerly detained youth through requesting medical records from the detention facility, determining need for referral for mental health or substance abuse treatment, asking youth about risk behaviors, communication with the probation officer and understanding probation requirements, continuing screening for sexually transmitted diseases, and assisting with academic needs. Winkelman et al. (2017) compared the physical and mental health of justice-involved adolescents and those without justice involvement in the past year. Results indicated that adolescents involved in the justice system had a significantly higher prevalence of asthma, hypertension, substance use disorders, mood disorders, and sexually transmitted infections. With regard to racial differences, compared to white and Hispanic justice-involved adolescents, African-American adolescents were less likely to have a substance use or mood disorder, however, they were more likely to have a physical health disorder. We know very little about the physical health of juvenile offenders. While the knowledge base would greatly benefit from the inclusion of health-related variables in ongoing studies with juvenile offenders, new investigations are needed that engage the treatment professional at juvenile facilities. Most states use pediatric and adolescent medicine professionals or nurses for the care of youthful offenders. Engaging these professional in research projects to assess the basic prevalence of acute and chronic health conditions and track the course of these conditions upon release are needed. Health promotion research could also be undertaken that involve nutrition, exercise, sleep hygiene, oral health screening and pain assessment.

## Program of Policy Research on the Intertwined Nature of Health and Criminal Justice Policy

New investigations that examine health and criminal justice policy would be advantageous. Linking policy changes to the systematic study of multiple dimensions of health risk (i.e., high-risk health conditions, behaviors, and resources) across the early life course (i.e., prenatal/perinatal, infancy, and early childhood) in the development of problem behaviors and the early onset of offending behaviors would be powerful. Moreover, the exploration of these health risks as potential mediators of the links between health disparities based on race/ethnicity, and SES delinquent behaviors would simultaneously advance the public health paradigm of health disparities research and add new lines to traditional delinquency research. The governing concept behind these line of research is that health policy and criminal justice policy are inextricably linked and when one area of policy advances it helps the other.

In order to meet the research needs of health and criminal justice policy, improvements in extant data are required. Expanding the inclusion of health and justice-related variables in major data collections would be easy. For example, health studies that include just a few items that tap whether an individual had been in formal custody as a juvenile would open the door for many comparisons. Conversely, criminological studies on juveniles often include measurement of mental health but not much in the way of physical health conditions. Further, research on delinquency and health is gained by building a cross-national storehouse on comparative findings and many nations do not collect such data. Where opportunities permit, we encourage researchers to include health and delinquency variables for analysis and reach out to pediatricians, nursing research or other health professionals that are interested in the child and adolescent outcomes. On the horizon, the landmark Adolescent Brain Cognitive Development (ABCD) longitudinal study (see Barch et al., 2018) includes a rich comprehensive set of mental and physical health assessments with data that will include delinquent acts. This study should be of value to criminologists with are interested in the intersectional genesis of delinquency and poor health.

## Conclusions

We envision a bright future for the health criminology paradigm. However, this future is dependent on strengthening delinquency and health research across several fronts. One of these agenda items involves expanding beyond mental health into physical health conditions. There is a dearth of studies on the physical health of juvenile offenders. Another is to more full examine the life course of the co-relationships between poor health and delinquency. Linked to this is the critical need for research collaborations between criminologists and medical/health science researchers. Unfortunately, most criminology programs and faculty are located at universities that either do not have a medical school or extensive health science research infrastructure. This will necessitate greater intentionality to reach out where these collaborations are feasible. Another major area of need is the inclusion of basic criminological data in health science data collections and vice versa. Doing so would open the door to numerous opportunities to test hypotheses in extant data sources. Despite some of these challenges, it is clear to us that the research footprint at this intersection will increase and volumes such as the present one are useful as initial platforms for growth and idea generation.

## References

Abram, K.M., Teplin, L.A., McClelland, G.M., & Dulcan, M.K. (2003). Comorbid psychiatric disorders in youth in juvenile detention. *Archives of General Psychiatry, 60*(11), 1097–1108.

Abram, K.M., Zwecker, N.A., Welty, L.J., Hershfield, J.A., Dulcan, M.K., & Teplin, L.A. (2015). Comorbidity and continuity of psychiatric disorders in youth after detention: a prospective longitudinal study. *JAMA Psychiatry, 72*(1), 84–93.

Avan, B., Richter, L.M., Ramchandani, P.G., Norris, S.A., & Stein, A. (2010). Maternal postnatal depression and children's growth and behaviour during the early years of life: exploring the interaction between physical and mental health. *Archives of Disease in Childhood, 95*(9), 690–695.

Barch, D.M., Albaugh, M.D., Avenevoli, S., Chang, L., Clark, D.B., Glantz, M.D., Hudziak, J.J., Jernigan, T. L., Tapert, S.F., Yurgelun-Todd, D., Alia-Klein, N., Potter, A.S., Paulus, M.P., Prouty, D., Zucker, R. A., & Sher, K.J. (2018). Demographic, physical and mental health assessments in the adolescent brain and cognitive development study: Rationale and description. *Developmental Cognitive Neuroscience, 32*, 55–66.

Beck, J.E., & Shaw, D.S. (2005). The influence of perinatal complications and environmental adversity on boys' antisocial behavior. *Journal of Child Psychology and Psychiatry, 46*(1), 35–46.

Brennan, P.A., Grekin, E.R., & Mednick, S.A. (1999). Maternal smoking during pregnancy and adult male criminal outcomes. *Archives of General Psychiatry, 56*(3), 215–219.

Chronis, A.M., Lahey, B.B., Pelham, W.E. Jr, Williams, S.H., Baumann, B.L., Kipp, H., … Rathouz, P.J. (2007). Maternal depression and early positive parenting predict future conduct problems in young children with attention-deficit/hyperactivity disorder. *Developmental Psychology, 43*(1), 70–82.

Cornelius, M.D., & Day, N.L. (2009). Developmental consequences of prenatal tobacco exposure. *Current Opinion in Neurology, 22*(2), 121–125.

Gatzke-Kopp, L.M., & Beauchaine, T.P. (2007). Direct and passive prenatal nicotine exposure and the development of externalizing psychopathology. *Child Psychiatry and Human Development, 38*(4), 255–269.

Gaysina, D., Fergusson, D.M., Leve, L.D., Horwood, J., Reiss, D., Shaw, D.S., ... Harold, G.T. (2013). Maternal smoking during pregnancy and offspring conduct problems: evidence from 3 independent genetically sensitive research designs. *JAMA Psychiatry, 70*(9), 956–963.

Gilman, S.E., Gardener, H., & Buka, S.L. (2008). Maternal smoking during pregnancy and children's cognitive and physical development: a causal risk factor? *American Journal of Epidemiology, 168*(5), 522–531.

Huijbregts, S.C., Séguin, J.R., Zoccolillo, M., Boivin, M., & Tremblay, R.E. (2008). Maternal prenatal smoking, parental antisocial behavior, and early childhood physical aggression. *Development and Psychopathology, 20*(2), 437–453.

Kim-Cohen, J., Moffitt, T.E., Taylor, A., Pawlby, S.J., & Caspi, A. (2005). Maternal depression and children's antisocial behavior: nature and nurture effects. *Archives of General Psychiatry, 62*(2), 173–181.

Langley, K., Holmans, P.A., van Den Bree, M.B., & Thapar, A. (2007). Effects of low birth weight, maternal smoking in pregnancy and social class on the phenotypic manifestation of Attention Deficit Hyperactivity Disorder and associated antisocial behaviour: Investigation in a clinical sample. *BMC Psychiatry, 7*(1), e26.

Loeber, R., Burke, J.D., Lahey, B.B., Winters, A., & Zera, M. (2000). Oppositional defiant and conduct disorder: A review of the past 10 years, part I. *Journal of the American Academy of Child & Adolescent Psychiatry, 39*(12), 1468–1484.

Olds, D., Henderson, C.R. Jr, Cole, R., Eckenrode, J., Kitzman, H., Luckey, D., ... Powers, J. (1998). Long-term effects of nurse home visitation on children's criminal and antisocial behavior: 15-year follow-up of a randomized controlled trial. *JAMA, 280*(14), 1238–1244.

Perry, R.C., & Morris, R.E. (2014). Health care for youth involved with the correctional system. *Primary Care: Clinics in Office Practice, 41*(3), 691–705.

Raine, A. (2002). Biosocial studies of antisocial and violent behavior in children and adults: a review. *Journal of Abnormal Child Psychology, 30*(4), 311–326.

Rice, F., Lifford, K.J., Thomas, H.V., & Thapar, A. (2007). Mental health and functional outcomes of maternal and adolescent reports of adolescent depressive symptoms. *Journal of the American Academy of Child & Adolescent Psychiatry, 46*(9), 1162–1170.

Vaughn, M.G., DeLisi, M., Salas-Wright, C., & Maynard, B.R. (2014). Examining violence and externalizing behavior among youth in the United States: Is there a severe 5%? *Youth Violence and Juvenile Justice, 12*, 3–21.

Vaughn, M.G., Freedenthal, S., Jenson, J.M., & Howard, M.O. (2007). Psychiatric symptoms and substance use among juvenile offenders: A latent profile investigation. *Criminal Justice and Behavior, 34*, 1296–1312.

Vaughn, M.G., Salas-Wright, C.P., DeLisi, M., Maynard, B.R., & Boutwell, B. (2015). Prevalence and correlates of psychiatric disorders among former juvenile detainees in the United States. *Comprehensive Psychiatry, 59*, 107–116.

Vaughn, M.G., Wallace, J., Davis, L.E., Fernandes, G., & Howard, M.O. (2008). Variations in mental health problems, substance use and delinquency between African-American and White juvenile offenders: Implications for reentry services. *International Journal of Offender Therapy and Comparative Criminology, 52*, 311–329.

Wakschlag, L.S., Kistner, E.O., Pine, D.S., Biesecker, G., Pickett, K.E., Skol, A.D., ... Burns, J.L. (2010). Interaction of prenatal exposure to cigarettes and MAOA genotype in pathways to youth antisocial behavior. *Molecular Psychiatry, 15*(9), 928–937.

Winkelman, T.N., Frank, J.W., Binswanger, I.A., & Pinals, D.A. (2017). Health conditions and racial differences among justice-involved adolescents, 2009 to 2014. *Academic Pediatrics, 17*(7), 723–731.

# INDEX

A Matter of Degree (AMOD) 247
Aalsma, Matthew C. 257–268
ABC *see* Attachment and Biobehavioral Catch-up
ABCD study *see* Adolescent Brain Cognitive Development longitudinal study
Abram, K. M. 343
Abrams, Laura S. 305–314
abuse 40, 53, 67, 99, 185, 226–227, 229; academic performance 228; ACE score 90–91; Australia 331; family as source of stress 77; human trafficking 96; impact on mental health 186; impact on the brain 188; occupational therapy 297; preventive interventions 230; psychological 199–200, 201; psychosocial risk factors 52; teenage pregnancy 228; temperamental deficits 62; two-generation programs 231; *see also* sexual abuse
academic performance: adverse childhood experiences 228; bullying impact on 148; community violence 224; lead exposure 210–211; poor housing 224; restorative justice 279–281; school dropout 273, 274; sleep 132, 138; substance use 152; teenage pregnancy 151; *see also* education; schools
Accornero, V. H. 19
ACEs *see* adverse childhood experiences
Ackerman, J. P. 19–20
active coping style 79–80, 125–126
Add Health *see* National Longitudinal Study of Adolescent to Adult Health
ADHD *see* attention deficit/hyperactivity disorder
adolescence: adolescence-limited offenders 3–4; adverse childhood experiences 93, 94–96, 227–228; alcohol and drug misuse 160–168, 316; behavioral health interventions 258; depression 169, 172–173; early prevention 234; health disparities 6, 34–35; Latin America 320–325; mental health problems 329; nutritional deficits during childhood 54–55; occupational therapy 296, 298–299; Omega-3 supplements 56; parental incarceration 110; peer victimization 187; prenatal health risks 17–18, 19, 20–23, 24; psychopathic traits 145–146, 148–149; psychopathology 222; sleep 132–133, 135, 140; stress 74, 75, 77–85, 191; substance use disorders 169, 170–171; teen dating violence 197–208; temperament 62–63, 64–65, 67–68; traumatic brain injury 120; treatment of co-occurring disorders 179; understanding of adolescent brain development 119
Adolescent Brain Cognitive Development (ABCD) longitudinal study 345
adultification 277
Advancement Project 274
adverse childhood experiences (ACEs) 40, 42, 90–103, 227–228; alcohol and drug misuse 161; depression 173; sleep problems 139; substance use and depression co-morbidity 175, 176; *see also* abuse; neglect
affectivity 21
Afifi, T. O. 186
African Americans: community mobilization 251; Head Start 231; health disparities 6, 33–35, 40; incarceration 36, 37, 40, 41, 42, 110; physical health disorders 344; poverty 37; qualitative research 310; racial discrimination 38; school discipline 275; school-to-prison pipeline 36, 269; sleep 140; traumatic brain injury 121; *see also* Black people; ethnicity; race
Agarwal, S. 53
Age-Graded Theory of Informal Social Control 3, 4, 9
agency 277, 279
aggression: adverse childhood experiences 95, 98; angry rumination 65; attachment theory 202; Conflict Tactics Scale-2 203–204; early health risk factors 52; emotional dysregulation 333; exposure to family violence 223; gender differences 139;

general strain theory 76; interventions 57; malnutrition 54–55, 57; maternal health risks 39–40; maternal stress during pregnancy 21; mental health problems 332; Omega-3 interventions 56; parental incarceration 109; peer influence 148; prenatal drug exposure 19, 20; prenatal tobacco exposure 342; prevention programs 165; psychopathic traits 145, 148, 152; as public health issue 50; self-control theory 38; sleep 135, 136, 139; teen dating violence 197–198, 199, 200; temperament 63, 64, 66; traumatic brain injury 123; *see also* violence

Agnew, R. 81, 83

AIDS 41, 146; *see also* HIV

Ainsworth, M. D. S. 222–223

alcohol use 51, 160–168; adolescence-limited offenders 4; adverse childhood experiences 91, 94; Australia 334–335; benefits of home visits 341–342; community mobilization 246, 247, 249–250; depression co-morbidity 174, 175; high-school students 244; impact of violence 50; incarceration 108; Latin America 317, 324, 325; low self-control 65; occupational therapy 297; parental 62; prenatal exposure 17–18, 20, 25, 51, 297; psychopathic traits 148; school-based prevention programs 248–249; sleep 134–135; stress 105; substance use disorders 170, 171; teen dating violence 201, 202; temperament 66; traumatic brain injury 121, 122; *see also* substance use

Aldrich, Rebecca M. 291–304

Allensworth, E. 282

allostasis 74–75, 224

Althoff, R. R. 63–64

American Academy of Pediatrics 140, 274–275

American Indians *see* Native Americans

American Medical Association 132

American Psychological Association 274

AMOD *see* A Matter of Degree

amygdala 176, 188, 189, 190

anger: adverse childhood experiences 98; angry rumination 65; child abuse and neglect 229; cognitive-behavioral therapy 192; emotional dysregulation 333; general strain theory 75; stress appraisal 78; teen dating violence 201; teenage pregnancy 95–96; temperament 62, 64, 65, 67, 68; victimization 186

Anson, K. 126

anti-depressants 24

antisocial behavior: ADHD 212; adverse childhood experiences 91, 97, 228; Australia 329, 332, 333–334; community mobilization 250; deliberate self-harm 333; early health model 51–53; environmental change strategies 247; executive functioning 122; homelessness 332; lead exposure 211; life-course persistent offenders 3; malnutrition 50, 53–55, 57; maternal child health research 341–343; maternal depression 343; maternal prenatal smoking 18, 25; Omega-3 interventions 55–56; physical health 334; prenatal and perinatal health risks 16–17, 21, 342; psychopathic traits 146; risk factors 245; sleep 139; teen dating violence 202; temperament 61, 62, 63, 67, 123; traumatic brain injury 121, 123; *see also* behavioral problems; delinquency

Antisocial Personality Disorder 63, 343

anxiety 257, 332; abused children 186; adverse childhood experiences 228; amygdala 189; dysregulated temperament 64; epigenetics 190; life-course persistent offenders 65; parents 225; prenatal drug exposure 20; preventive interventions 230; self-harm 333; stress 78; teen dating violence 198, 202; traumatic brain injury 121, 125, 126; victimization 148, 186

Anyon, Y. 282–283

Ard, K. 6

Argentina 296, 316, 317, 318, 321, 325–326

Armour, Marilyn 269–290

Arnett, J. J. 299

arousal 76, 133

Asian Americans: depression 172; high school graduation rates 273; poverty 37; racial disparities 33–34; substance use disorders 170

assessment: occupational therapy 294, 300; traumatic brain injury 124–125, 127

asthma 5, 110, 344

Attachment and Biobehavioral Catch-up (ABC) 233

attachment theory 202, 222–223, 226, 233–234

attention: lead exposure 210, 211; Neonatal Abstinence Syndrome 226; prematurity and low birth weight 222; prenatal alcohol exposure 17; prenatal cocaine exposure 19; traumatic brain injury 119

attention deficit/hyperactivity disorder (ADHD): adverse childhood experiences 94; health disparities 344; lead exposure 212, 214; malnutrition 54, 55; parental incarceration 109; prenatal drug exposure 20; prenatal tobacco exposure 342; *see also* hyperactivity

Augustyn, Megan Bears 169–184

Australia 6, 329–340

Australian Temperament Project 335

Avan, B. 343

avoidant coping style 79–80, 125–126

Backman, H. 135, 136

Baglivio, Michael 62, 90–103

Bandura, Albert 202–203

Banyard, V. L. 186

Barnert, Elizabeth S. 305–314

Barnes, J. C. 134, 140

Barnett, G. D. 192

Barney, Karen F. 291–304

Baron, S. W. 82

Bartlett, Jessica Dym 221–243

Bartollas, C. 316

# Index

Beauchaine, T. P. 342
Beaugard, Corinne 221–243
Beck, J. E. 342
behavioral health interventions 192, 257–268
behavioral problems: adverse childhood experiences 40; benefits of home visits 341–342; dysregulated temperament 64; health care disparities 344; malnutrition 55; parental incarceration 41, 109; as precursor to delinquency 17; prematurity and low birth weight 22, 222; prenatal cocaine exposure 20; preventive interventions 230; problem behavior theory 161–162; temperament 64; *see also* antisocial behavior; conduct problems
belief systems 82
Bender, Annah K. 197–208
binge drinking 122, 161, 249, 250
biological risk factors 51, 52, 175–176
biomedical perspective 272, 341
biosocial life course perspective 164, 165
biosocial model 342
bipolar disorder 108, 343
birth complications 9, 23, 51, 52, 53, 222, 342
Black, M. M. 19–20
Black people: adultification 277; adverse childhood experiences 94; behavioral health interventions 258; depression 172; high school graduation rates 273; incarceration 99, 105; school discipline 275–276, 283; school dropout 273; self-control theory 39; substance use disorders 170; teen dating violence 201; *see also* African Americans; ethnicity; race
Blake, J. J. 277
Blood, P. 278–279, 282
Boddy, L. E. 65
body mass index (BMI) 38–39, 110
Bogen, Katherine W. 145–159
Bogg, T. 66
Bogner, J. 124
Bolivia 316, 317, 321
Bolton, J. M. 177
Bond, G. R. 175
Boston Ceasefire 248
Boutwell, Brian B. 209–217
Bower, C. 18
Bowlby, J. 222
Boyle, M. H. 78
brain development 21, 119, 198; adverse childhood experiences 91; early childhood 221; epigenetic factors 52; gender differences 55; lead exposure 210; malnutrition 53–54, 57; maternal prenatal smoking 18; prenatal alcohol exposure 17; stress 75; substance use 151; *see also* traumatic brain injury
brain structure and function 222, 226; brain dysfunction 56–57; substance use and depression co-morbidity 175–176; victimization 187, 188–190, 191

Braveman, P. 269
Brazil 296, 315, 320, 321–322, 324–325
Breivik, Anders 150
Brennan, P. A. 18, 342
Bridgett, D. J. 65
Bronfenbrenner, Urie 147, 203
Brooks-Gunn, J. 84
Brooks, J. R. 53
Bryk, A. 282
bullying 77, 148, 187, 333
Burt, N. M. 65
Byers, R. K. 211

CADRI *see* Conflict in Adolescent Dating Relationships Inventory
Cale, Jesse 16–32
callous-unemotional (CU) traits 145–146, 149
Cambridge Study in Delinquent Development 93, 334
Canada 23, 121, 122
cancer 50, 91, 162, 213, 261
cannabis 170, 171, 334, 335; *see also* marijuana
CAP *see* Chicago Area Project
capital punishment 119
cardiovascular disease 50, 152, 244; *see also* heart disease/heart problems
Cardozo-Macías, F. 316
care coordination 261–262
Cascade framework 260–261
Caspi, A. 63
Catrett, C. D. 136
Cavaco, Y. K. 269
CBPR *see* community-based participatory research
CBT *see* cognitive-behavioral therapy
CCT *see* Conditional Cash Transfer programs
Centers for Disease Control and Prevention (CDC) 34–35, 90, 169; community mobilization 251; community-university partnerships 253; smoking 270; teen dating violence 197, 199
Central America 315, 316, 320
cerebral cortex 188, 189
CGM *see* Comprehensive Gang Model
Chan, R. C. 122
Chan, S. F. 186–187
Chang, L.-Y. 136
Chassin, L. 63
Chicago Area Project (CAP) 246–247, 251
Child-Parent Psychotherapy (CPP) 232–233
children: early childhood development 221–243; early intervention 25; exposure to violence 185; malnutrition 54–55; mental health impacts of abuse 186; occupational therapy 297–298; Omega-3 interventions 56; parental incarceration 8, 41, 105, 109–110, 229; peer victimization 187; pre-school health lifestyles 11; psychopathic traits 145–146, 148; qualitative research 306; sleep 132; social learning theory 202–203; street children 296–297; stress proliferation 106; traumatic brain

injury 120; victimization 186; *see also* adolescence; adverse childhood experiences
Chile 55, 316, 317, 320, 321, 322, 325–326
Chioda, L. 325
Chitsabesan, P. 121–122
cholesterol 5, 51, 110
Chronis, A. M. 343
circadian rhythms 133
Circle of Security (COS) 233–234
Clinkinbeard, Samantha S. 132–144
CMCA *see* Communities Mobilizing for Change on Alcohol
coalitions 245, 246–250, 251, 253
coca paste 317, 318, 324, 325
cocaine: Latin America 316, 317, 319, 324, 325, 326; prenatal exposure 19–20; substance use disorders 170
cognitive-behavioral therapy (CBT) 97, 126, 179, 192
cognitive coping style 79–80
cognitive development: ABCD study 345; adolescence 75; child abuse and neglect 226; Head Start 231; maternal stress during pregnancy 21; substance use and depression co-morbidity 169
cognitive functioning: lead exposure 210; prenatal health risks 16, 21; substance use impact on 151–152, 244; traumatic brain injury 120, 122–123, 125; *see also* executive functioning
cognitive rehabilitation 126
Cohen, G. L. 148
collective efficacy 245, 253
college campuses 192
Colman, I. 20–21
Colombia 55, 315, 316–317, 320–321, 322–324, 325, 326
Columbine high school massacre (1999) 149
Colvin, M. 82
Comfort, Megan 108
common cause theories 37–39
Communities Mobilizing for Change on Alcohol (CMCA) 247
Communities that Care (CTC) 249, 250, 251–252
community-based participatory research (CBPR) 252
community buy-in 308–309
community case management 261–262
community mobilization 244–256
Community Partnership Program 246
community protective factors 230
community violence 52, 191, 202, 224, 232–233
Comprehensive Gang Model (CGM) 248, 253
Conditional Cash Transfer programs (CCT) 325
conduct problems: coping styles 80; health care disparities 344; malnutrition 55, 57, 68n2; maternal prenatal smoking 18, 19, 342–343; maternal stress during pregnancy 20–21; parental incarceration 109; as precursor to delinquency 17; preventive interventions 230; temperament 62, 63–64, 65, 67; *see also* behavioral problems
Conflict in Adolescent Dating Relationships Inventory (CADRI) 204
Conflict Tactics Scale-2 (CTS-2) 203–204
conscientiousness 65–66
consent 307, 309–310
Consortium for Longitudinal Studies of Child Abuse and Neglect (LONGSCAN) 95
Convention on the Rights of the Child 321, 322
coping styles/strategies 76, 79–80, 84, 105, 107; impact of incarceration on families 111; school-based prevention programs 248; traumatic brain injury 125–126
Cornelius, M. D. 342
correctional officers 300–301
Corrigan, J. D. 124
COS *see* Circle of Security
Costa Rica 317, 320, 321, 322, 325
Costongs, C. 269
costs 329, 338; community mobilization 251, 253; early interventions 342; homeless youth in Australia 331; patient navigation 262; of poor health 270–271
Côté, J. E. 299
CPP *see* Child-Parent Psychotherapy
Craig, J. M. 98
Crenshaw, K. 276, 284
criminal justice system: ADHD 212; depression 173–174; health problems 341; occupational therapy 296; racial disparities 36–42, 105; substance use and mental health disorder co-morbidity 169, 177–178, 179; substance use disorders 171; temperament 62, 66; traumatic brain injury 121, 123, 124–125, 127; understanding of adolescent brain development 119; *see also* incarceration; juvenile detention; juvenile justice system
criminal propensity 82
criminology: early health predictors 16, 25–26; health criminology 209–210, 212, 214, 341, 345; life-course 3, 5, 8–11; policy research 344–345; prenatal and perinatal health risks 16
critical theory 283–284, 292
Crossover Youth Practice Model (CYPM) 99
CTC *see* Communities that Care
CTS-2 *see* Conflict Tactics Scale-2
CU traits *see* callous-unemotional traits
Cuba 321
Cubbin, Catherine 269–290
Cullen, F. T. 38
cultural responsiveness 283
Cure Violence model 247, 251
cyber dating violence 200
CYPM *see* Crossover Youth Practice Model

Dams-O'Connor, K. 120
data collection: Australia 336, 337–338; collaboration in criminology and health research 345; policy research 344–345; qualitative research 307, 308, 311–312; self-reports 137, 204, 206; stress 84; *see also* research designs
dating violence 197–208
Day, N. L. 19, 342
deception 145
decision-making: alcohol intoxication 163; cerebral cortex 189; occupational therapy 299; sleep/delinquency relationship 139
DeKeseredy, W. 203
Del Vecchio, T. 63
deliberate self-harm (DSH) 332–333; *see also* self-harm
delinquency: adverse childhood experiences 93; alcohol and drug misuse 160–168; Australia 330–338; child abuse and neglect 226–227, 229; community mobilization 244–256; drugs linked to 315–316; early health risk factors 52; early-onset 5, 10; family engagement 263; general strain theory 82; health disparities 9–10; Latin America 320–322, 325–326; lead exposure 40, 211; Life Skills Training 192; malnutrition 54–55; maternal child health research 341–343; mental health problems 329; occupational therapy 298; parental incarceration 109; peer exposure 68; policy research 344–345; poor health as a stressor 83; prenatal health risks 16–32; psychopathic traits 146; public health approaches 330; racial disparities 38; self-efficacy 81; self-esteem 80; sleep related to 132, 133–141; stress 76; temperament 62, 66, 67, 68; traumatic brain injury 122; *see also* antisocial behavior
DeLisi, Matthew 61–73, 123, 161
DeLongis, A. 125
Denmark 342
depression 171–174, 257, 329; abused children 186; adverse childhood experiences 94, 228; Australia 332, 333; child abuse and neglect 227; diagnostic criteria 180n2; dysregulated temperament 64; epigenetics 190; first-responders 150; general strain theory 75; homelessness 331; impact of violence 50; incarceration 7, 108, 110; Juvenile Justice Behavioral Health Services Cascade 260; life-course persistent offenders 65; malnutrition prevention 57; maternal 21, 53, 225, 343; prenatal drug exposure 20; preventive interventions 230; racial disparities 35; school connectedness 273; self-control theory 38–39; self-harm 333; sleep 140; socioeconomic disparities 5; stress 78, 105; substance use co-morbidity 169, 174–179; teen dating violence 198, 201, 202; temperament 63, 66, 67; traumatic brain injury 121, 125, 126; victimization 148, 186, 187
deprivation: deprivation theory 37; occupational 292
desensitization 150, 151, 152

deterrence 247–248, 253
developmental taxonomy of offenders 3–4, 16
diabetes 8, 34–35, 50, 224, 344
Diaz, S. 20
diet 6, 9, 11, 23–24, 66; *see also* nutrition
Dietrich, K. N. 211
Dilts, Caroline 197–208
disability: Australia 331; occupational therapy 293, 297–298; risk factors 222; school absenteeism 281; school discipline 275; school dropout 273; school-to-prison pipeline 269
discipline in schools 273–277, 279, 282–283, 284
discrimination 37–38, 40, 77, 337; *see also* racism
diseases: biomedical perspective 272; deprivation theory 37; educational attainment 152; impact of violence 50; incarceration effects on health 41, 42, 108; patient navigation 261; prenatal exposure 24; public health model 146; racial disparities 34–35
disinhibition 123, 163
dissemination of research 312–313
divorce 77, 227
DNA 190
domestic violence 77, 90, 185; adverse childhood experiences 228; Colombia 323; drugs linked to 315; family intervention programs 192; Latin America 322; parental substance misuse 226; *see also* intimate partner violence; teen dating violence
Dominican Republic 321, 325
D'Onofrio, B. M. 18–19
dopamine 56–57, 175–176, 226
Drake, R. E. 175, 179
drinking *see* alcohol use
drug courts 325
drug use 8, 160–168; Australia 330; dysregulated temperament 64; Fetal Alcohol Spectrum Disorder 18; general strain theory 76; impact of violence 50; incarceration 108; juvenile probation 259; Latin America 315–328; low self-control 65; parental 62; prenatal exposure 19–20, 24, 51, 53, 226, 297; racial disparities 38; school dropout 68; sleep 134–135; temperament 66, 68; traumatic brain injury 121, 122; victimization 187; *see also* substance use
drunk driving 162, 163
dysthymia 67, 108

Early Child Longitudinal Study 68n2
Early Head Start (EHS) 231, 232
Eason, J. M. 277
Easton, J. Q. 282
eating disorders: parental incarceration 8; school connectedness 273; teen dating violence 202; temperament 65, 67; victimization 187–188
Eckenrode, J. 192
ecological framework 203; *see also* social ecological model
ecosocial theory 272, 284
ecstasy 250, 317, 324, 325

## Index

Ecuador 316, 317, 320, 321, 325
education 10–11; adverse childhood experiences 91; community mobilization 248; community protective factors 230; early childhood 221, 230; Latin America 321; parental incarceration 105; racial disparities 33; as social determinant of health 147, 152, 269–271; substance use 152; teenage pregnancy 151; WHO principles 337; *see also* academic performance; schools
effortful control 61–68, 123; *see also* self-control
EHS *see* Early Head Start
Eisenberg, N. 63
Eitle, D. 40
El Salvador 317, 321, 326
Elder, Glen 4, 164
embodiment 272
Emond, A. 17
emotional regulation: adolescence 133; cerebral cortex 189; child abuse and neglect 226; deliberate self-harm 333; neurotransmitters 175–176; prenatal health risks 21; sleep problems 132; temperament 61; traumatic brain injury 123; *see also* self-regulation
employment: adverse childhood experiences 91; education relationship 270, 271; impact of incarceration 41; informal social control 4; Latin America 321; racial disparities 33; teenage pregnancy 95–96
environmental change strategies 247–248, 251
environmental risk factors 176–177, 209–210, 213–214, 224
Environmental Risk (E-Risk) Longitudinal Twin Study 63
epidemiological research 212–214
epigenetics 52, 190, 222, 270
Epps, N. 91
equifinality 222, 234
equity 269, 282
ethical issues 213, 312
ethnicity: adolescent status characteristics 82; adverse childhood experiences 94, 99, 227; behavioral health interventions 263; depression 172; health disparities 6, 9–10; high school graduation rates 273; as moderating factor 4; oppression 270; policy research 344; teen dating violence 202; violent crime 5, 8; *see also* African Americans; Asian Americans; Black people; Hispanics; Native Americans; race; White people
Evans, J. 20–21
executive functioning: adolescent development 133; cerebral cortex 189; lead exposure 210; prenatal health risks 17, 19, 21; protective factors 229; sleep deprivation 139; traumatic brain injury 122–123, 126; *see also* cognitive functioning
exercise 38–39
experimental designs 138, 141
externalizing behaviors 257, 332; adverse childhood experiences 94, 228; chronic health conditions 83; clinical focus on 173; community violence 224; early risk health factor framework 51, 52; executive functioning 122; food insecurity 224; interventions 57; malnutrition 54, 55, 56, 57; maternal health risks 39–40; maternal prenatal smoking 18, 19; maternal stress during pregnancy 20; Omega-3 interventions 56; parental incarceration 109; physical abuse 229; as precursor to delinquency 17; pregnancy and birth complications 23; prenatal drug exposure 19, 20; problem behavior theory 161–162; racial disparities 38; temperament 63, 64, 65, 66; Trauma-Focused CBT 97
Eze, N. 20

Fabelo, T. 275
Fagan, Abigail A. 244–256
family: adverse childhood experiences 95; drug use and delinquency in Latin America 326; early childhood risk factors 222–223; family breakdown 37; family engagement 262–263, 264; family intervention programs 98, 192; health consequences of incarceration 104–115; protective factors 230; risk factors for substance use 245; stress 77; treatment of co-occurring disorders 179; *see also* parents
Fanti, K. A. 64
Farrer, L. 269
Farrer, T. J. 121
FASD *see* Fetal Alcohol Spectrum Disorder
fatigue 186
Fazel, S. 173
fear 75, 152, 185, 189, 274
Feigenbaum, J. J. 211
Felitti, V. J. 91
feminism 284
Fergus, E. 283
Ferro, M. A. 78
Fetal Alcohol Spectrum Disorder (FASD) 17–18, 25
fetal death 95–96
FFT *see* Functional Family Therapy
Fighting Back initiative 246–247, 249
financial insecurity 106, 173, 337
financing of interventions 251, 253; *see also* costs
Finland 6, 21, 136
first-responders 150
Florin, P. 245
Folkman, S. 125
food insecurity 9, 62, 68n2, 224
Ford, J. A. 316
foster care 228, 231
Foster, H. 84
Fragile Families and Child Wellbeing Study 68n2, 94, 108–109, 135
Frick, P. J. 148
Fried, P. 19
frustration 67, 75, 198

Fujimoto, K. 148
Fulgoni III, V. L. 53
Functional Family Therapy (FFT) 98, 257–258

Galton, Francis 213
gangs: community mobilization 247, 248, 251, 253; Latin America 315, 319, 322, 326
Gardella, J. H. 282
Gaskin, C. 333
gatekeepers 306–307, 308, 313
Gatzke-Kopp, L. M. 342
Gaultney, J. F. 134, 136, 139
Gaysina, D. 343
gender differences: adolescent status characteristics 82; adverse childhood experiences 94, 96; behavioral health interventions 258; depression 172–173; drug use in Latin America 316–318; hippocampal structure 189; HPA functioning 191; human trafficking 96; malnutrition 55; parental incarceration 110; school discipline 275–276; sexual abuse treatment 186; sleep 139–140; substance use disorders 170; teen dating violence 197–198, 201
gender oppression 270
general strain theory 74, 75–76, 78–79, 82
genetics 209–210; ADHD 212; alcohol and drug misuse 161; antisocial behavior 63; biosocial life course perspective 164; early childhood development 221, 222; hippocampal structure 189; nutrition 68n8; parental mental illness 225; sleep 140–141; substance use and depression co-morbidity 175, 176; twin studies 213–214
Gesch, C. 56
Gilman, S. E. 343
Goal Management Training (GMT) 126
Golding, J. 17
Goldman, A. W. 8
Goldschmidt, L. 19
Goldstein, P. J. 315
González, T. 282
Goodman, R. 63
Goodnight, J. A. 18–19
Gorman, S. 123
Gottfredson, M. R. 38, 39
gratification delay 210
Green, B. 150
Green Dot initiative 192
Greenfield, S. 174
Greenland, S. 212–213
Gregory, A. 283
Grekin, E. R. 18, 342
Griffin, G. 262
Gruen, R. 125
Gruenfelder, Kalynn 185–196
Gruskin, S. 269
Guatemala 296–297, 317, 318, 321, 326
gun violence 146, 149–151

Hallfors, D. 247, 249
hallucinogens 170
harm reduction 326–327
Harris, Eric 149
Harvey, A. G. 134–135, 141n1
Hawkins, E. H. 179
head injury 53; *see also* traumatic brain injury
Head Start (HS) 231
health: adverse childhood experiences 91, 94–96, 227–228; alcohol and drug misuse 160–168, 244; Australia 330, 332–338; behavioral 257–268; ecosocial theory 272; education relationship 270–271; health consequences of crime 7–8; impact of stress on 75, 83, 84; incorporation of health disparities research into crime prevention 8–10, 11; interventions 85; occupational perspective 291–293, 294; policy research 344–345; poor health as a stressor 83; public health model 146–147, 153, 318, 319, 326, 329–330, 336, 344; qualitative research 305, 307–313; racial disparities 6, 33–49; restorative justice 279–281; schools 277–278; social and financial 68; social determinants of 147, 151–152, 227, 269–271, 284, 330, 336; socioeconomic disparities 5–6; temperament 64–67; victimization 148, 185–196; *see also* mental health; prenatal health risks; well-being
health care: access to 35, 42, 85; continuum 338; incarceration 107; juvenile detention 344; social determinants of health 147
health coaching 261–262
health criminology 209–210, 212, 214, 341, 345
health equity 269, 282
Healthy Families America 232
*Healthy People 2020* 284
heart disease/heart problems 8, 186; adverse childhood experiences 91; heart attacks 110; racial disparities 34; substance use 162; victims of violence 148; *see also* cardiovascular disease
Heerde, Jessica A. 329–340
helicobacter pylori 34
Hemphill, Sheryl A. 329–340
Henrich, C. C. 64
hepatitis 7, 163
Herge, W. M. 186–187
heritability 209, 212
Hernandez, Martha Morales 104–115
heroin 170, 316, 319, 335
Heron, J. 17
Herrenkohl, T. I. 186
high blood pressure 51, 186
hippocampus 187, 188–189
Hirschi, T. 38, 39
Hispanics/Latinos: adverse childhood experiences 94; community mobilization 251; depression 172; Head Start 231; health disparities 6, 34–35; high school graduation rates 273; incarceration 36, 37, 105; physical health disorders 344; qualitative

research 310; school discipline 275, 283; school dropout 273; school-to-prison pipeline 269; substance use disorders 170; teen dating violence 201; *see also* ethnicity; race
HIV 8, 110, 146, 164, 260; *see also* AIDS
home visiting 97, 230, 232, 341–342
homelessness: Australia 331–332, 333, 337; depression 173–174; Head Start 231; injuries 334; life-course persistent offenders 65
homicide: Colombia 323, 324; lead exposure correlation 211; prevalence 185; racial disparities 38; school 274
Honduras 317, 318, 326
Hong Kong 24
Horel, T. 150
hospitalization 65
household dysfunction 90, 99
housing: access to 42; health disparities 5; insecurity 224; Latin America 321; parental substance misuse 226; social determinants of health 147
Howard, F. F. 192
HPA *see* hypothalamic-pituitary-adrenocortical axis
HS *see* Head Start
Hudziak, J. J. 63–64
Hughes, N. 121
Huijbregts, S. C. 342
human trafficking 96
Hux, K. 119
hyperactivity: early health risk factors 52; food insecurity 224; malnutrition 54–55; maternal depression 343; maternal prenatal smoking 18; maternal stress during pregnancy 20–21; Neonatal Abstinence Syndrome 226; *see also* attention deficit/hyperactivity disorder
hypertension 5, 8, 39–40, 344
hypothalamic-pituitary-adrenocortical (HPA) axis 74, 190, 191

IDEAL study 20
Ilie, Gabriela 121
impulsivity: adolescence 172; alcohol intoxication 163; health risk behaviors 330; iron deficiency 56–57; lead exposure 210, 211; life-course persistent offenders 3; maternal health risks 39–40; psychopathic traits 145; teen dating violence 198; temperament 63; traumatic brain injury 119, 121, 123
*in loco parentis* 262
inattention 18
incarceration: adverse childhood experiences 91, 92, 227; children with incarcerated parents 8, 41, 77, 105, 109–110, 229; Colombia 324; Fetal Alcohol Spectrum Disorder 18; health consequences for families 104–115; health consequences for individuals 7, 41, 42, 107–108; health effects on 39–40; Latin America 322; occupational perspective 292; qualitative research 305, 306–307; racial disparities 36, 37, 38, 40, 41, 42, 99, 105;

stress of 257; substance use and mental health disorder co-morbidity 177–178; *see also* criminal justice system; juvenile detention
incentives for research participants 310, 313
Indig, D. 333
indigenous people 278, 331
inequalities 5–6, 269; Brazil 325; impact of incarceration on families 111; racial 33, 37–38, 42; restorative justice 284; societal 203; stress 75, 76, 105; structural 82
Infant Development, Development, Environment, and Lifestyle (IDEAL) study 20
inflammation 187
informal social control 3, 4, 9, 248, 253
inhalants 250, 324, 325
inhibition 20, 189, 210, 224; *see also* disinhibition
injuries 334
insomnia 108, 135, 136
Institute of Medicine (IOM) 230, 232
Institutional Review Boards (IRBs) 306–307, 309, 313
intelligence 17, 210–211, 222, 229; *see also* IQ
internalizing behaviors 257, 332; adverse childhood experiences 94, 228; allostatic load 224; chronic health conditions 83; community violence 224; food insecurity 224; lack of clinical focus on 173; low birth weight 22; maternal stress during pregnancy 20; parental depression 225; parental incarceration 109; prenatal drug exposure 20; temperament 65, 66; Trauma-Focused CBT 97
International Covenant on Civil and Political Rights 321
International Youth Development Study 335, 336
intersectionality 284
interventions: adverse childhood experiences 97, 98, 99; alcohol and drug misuse 164–165; behavioral health 192, 257–268; biosocial life course perspective 164; community-level 244–256; continuum of health care 338; early childhood 221, 230–234; evidence-based 5, 98, 126, 127, 246–252, 259, 298, 336; homeless youth 337; intensive and multimodal 25; lead exposure 210; malnutrition 57–58; occupational therapy 295, 298–301; Omega-3 interventions 55–56; positive goals 85; psychopathy 152–153; schools as sites of structural interventions 277–284; sleep 141; substance use and delinquency 244; teen dating violence 205, 206; traumatic brain injury 125–126, 127; victimization 191–192; *see also* treatment
intimate partner violence (IPV) 50, 198, 223; child abuse and neglect 226–227; impact on physical health 186; policies 205; psychosocial risk factors 52; public health model 146–147; services 205–206; *see also* domestic violence
IOM *see* Institute of Medicine
IQ 20, 53, 55, 210–211, 224; *see also* intelligence
IRBs *see* Institutional Review Boards
iron deficiency 54–55, 56–57

Jackson, Dylan B. 3–15, 341–346; maternal health risks 39–40; nutrition 68n2; sleep 135, 136
Jaegers, Lisa A. 291–304
Japan 296
Jenuwine, M. 262
JJ-TRIALS 260–261
Johnson, Abby K. 169–184
Johnson, R. C. 41
judges 307, 309
juvenile detention 36, 67, 68; access to health care 85; adverse childhood experiences 92, 93–94; alcohol and drug misuse 161, 163; Australia 331, 332; behavioral health interventions 258–260; health care 344; Latin America 322; occupational therapy 299, 300–301; psychiatric disorders 343–344; qualitative research 305; WHO principles 337; *see also* criminal justice system; incarceration
Juvenile Justice Behavioral Health Services Cascade 260–261
juvenile justice system: adverse childhood experiences 91–92, 93–94, 96–99; Australia 331, 337; behavioral health interventions 258–264; depression 173–174; Latin America 320, 322; mental health problems 152, 173, 177, 257; occupational therapy 291, 293, 296, 298, 300–301; probation officers 259, 260, 264, 308–309, 310, 344; psychopathic traits 146; qualitative research 305–314; substance use and mental health disorder co-morbidity 169, 177–178, 179; substance use disorders 171; Transformative Justice Initiative 300–301; traumatic brain injury 119, 121, 124–125; *see also* criminal justice system

Kandel, E. 23
Karl, A. 188–189
Keating, D. P. 64
*keepin' it* REAL (*ki*R) program 165
Kentucky Initiatives for Prevention (KIP) Project 249
kidney problems 8, 162
Kilpatrick, D. G. 35
Kingsbury, M. 20–21
Kinner, S. A. 333, 337
Klebold, Dylan 149
Komro, K. A. 251
Kort-Butler, Lisa A. 74–89, 122
Koss, M. P. 204
Kravitz-Wirtz, N. 6
Kremer, P. 334
Krieger, N. 272
Kronenberg, Frank 296–297

La Greca, A. M. 186–187
labels 146
Lahey, B. B. 18–19
Langley, K. 342
Langman, P. 149

Lanziano, C. 316
Latin America 315–328
Latinos/Hispanics: adverse childhood experiences 94; community mobilization 251; depression 172; Head Start 231; health disparities 6, 34–35; high school graduation rates 273; incarceration 36, 37, 105; physical health disorders 344; qualitative research 310; school discipline 275, 283; school dropout 273; school-to-prison pipeline 269; substance use disorders 170; teen dating violence 201; *see also* ethnicity; race
Laub, J. H. 3, 4, 9
Lazarus, R. 125
LCP offenders *see* life-course persistent offenders
lead exposure 24, 40, 53, 210–214
learning disabilities 109, 344
Leech, S. L. 19
legal remedies 205
Lewis, G. J. 65
LGBTQ+ youth 198, 200, 201, 275, 276; *see also* sexuality/sexual orientation
licit drugs 24, 330, 334
life-course criminology 3, 5, 8–11
life-course persistent (LCP) offenders 3–4, 5, 7–8, 65; *see also* serious, violent, and chronic offenders
life expectancy 35, 152, 270
life skills 299
Life Skills Training (LST) 192
lifestyles 11, 330, 336
Lilienfeld, Scott O. 145–159
limbic system 188, 189
limited prosocial emotions (LPE) 145–146
Lin, W.-H. 136
Liu, Jianghong 50–60
liver disease 50, 91, 162, 186
LONGSCAN (Consortium for Longitudinal Studies of Child Abuse and Neglect) 95
Lorber, M. F. 63
Lord, E. E. 211
low birth weight 9, 22–23, 51, 151, 222
Lowe, C. Cory 244–256
LPE *see* limited prosocial emotions
LST *see* Life Skills Training
lung disease 91, 162
Luppescu, S. 282
Lurigio, A. J. 177
Lustick, H. 283
Lynch, M. J. 211
Lyons, J. S. 262

MacKinnon, N. 20–21
Mahedy, L. 20–21
Main, M. 223
Mäki, P. 21
malnutrition 51, 53–57, 68n2, 331
maltreatment 50, 203, 228–229; *see also* abuse; adverse childhood experiences
mandatory reporting 312

Marchbanks, M. P. 277
marijuana 162, 170, 171; community mobilization 249, 250; depression co-morbidity 174, 175; high-school students 244; Latin America 316, 317, 324, 325; lead exposure 211; low self-control 65; prenatal exposure 19, 20; school-based prevention programs 249; traumatic brain injury 122; *see also* cannabis
Marinetti, C. 269
marital conflict 52, 63
marriage 4
mass shootings 149–151
Massoglia, M. 41
mastery 76, 78–79, 81, 84
maternal child health research 341–343
Maternal, Infant, and Early Childhood Home Visiting (MIECHV) program 232
A Matter of Degree (AMOD) 247
mattering 82
maturity gap 4
McGlinchey, E. L. 134–135, 141n1
McKinlay, A. 122
McLeod, J. D. 78
media 150
Medicaid 312
Mediratta, K. 283
Mednick, S. A. 18, 23, 55, 342
Meijer, A. M. 136, 139
Mejía-Trujillo, Juliana 315–328
Meldrum, R. C. 134, 139, 140
memory 123, 224, 226
Mendota Juvenile Treatment Center (MJTC) 152–153
mental health 329, 341, 343–344; adverse childhood experiences 94–95, 227; Australia 330, 332–334; behavioral health interventions 258, 263; deprivation theory 37; homelessness 331; impact of incarceration on families 41, 108, 109, 111; impact of incarceration on the individual 41, 106, 107–108; impact of substance use on 152; malnutrition prevention 57; negative public perceptions 150–151; parental 62, 77, 224–225; patient navigation 262; prenatal alcohol exposure 17; prevalence of mental health disorders in juvenile justice system 152, 173, 177, 257; racial disparities 35, 38; recidivism 174; risk factors 330; self-control theory 38–39; self-esteem 80; social support 81; stress 74, 75, 76, 83, 84, 105; substance use co-morbidity 174–179; temperament 64; victimization 148, 186; *see also* anxiety; depression; psychiatric disorders
metacognitive strategies 126
methamphetamine 20, 171, 250, 318, 335
methylation 190, 222
Mexico 296–297, 320, 321, 322, 324, 325
microbiome-gut-brain axis 57
MIDUS II *see* National Survey of Midlife Development in the United States

migraines 110
Miller, P. G. 335
Mindell, J. A. 136–137
MJTC *see* Mendota Juvenile Treatment Center
Moffitt, T. E. 3–4, 7, 8–9, 16, 63, 66, 68
Mollborn, S. 11
mood: adolescence 172; mood disorders 41, 64, 177, 344; neurotransmitters 175–176; sleep problems 132; teen dating violence 201
Moore, E. 333
morbidity 7, 9
Morris, E. W. 274
Morris, R. E. 344
Morrison, B. E. 278–279, 282
mortality 8, 9, 51; alcohol and drug misuse 164, 171; economic costs of 270–271; impact of incarceration 107, 108; incarceration 7; racial disparities 34; traumatic brain injury 120
MST *see* Multisystemic Therapy
Mueser, K. T. 175
Muller, C. 211
multifinality 222, 229, 234
Multisystemic Therapy (MST) 98, 179, 192, 257–258
Murugan, Vithya 197–208
mutual violence 197–198

Nanda, J. 276
NAS *see* Neonatal Abstinence Syndrome
National Center for Health Statistics 270
National Centers of Excellence in Youth Violence Prevention (YVPC) 253
National Child Abuse and Neglect Data System (NCANDS) 185
National Epidemiologic Survey on Alcohol and Related Conditions 174
National Gang Center (NGC) 248
National Institute of Child Health and Human Development (NICHD) 64
National Institute of Justice (NIJ) 197, 198, 281
National Institute of Mental Health (NIMH) 171–172
National Institutes of Health (NIH) 5, 263, 281, 312
National Intimate Partner and Sexual Violence Survey (NISVS) 200
National Longitudinal Study of Adolescent Health 110, 134–135, 201, 273
National Research Council (NRC) 230, 232
National Resource Center on Domestic Violence (NRCDV) 205
National Survey of American Life (NSAL) 110
National Survey of Children's Exposure to Violence II (NatSCEV) 185
National Survey of Children's Health (NSCH) 109
National Survey of Midlife Development in the United States II (MIDUS II) 65
National Survey of Teen Relationships and Intimate Violence (STRiV) 201

National Survey on Drug Use and Health (NSDUH) 68, 161

Native Americans/American Indians: health disparities 33–35; high school graduation rates 273; incarceration 36; school discipline 275, 276; school dropout 273; school-to-prison pipeline 269; substance use disorders 170; traumatic brain injury 121

NatSCEV *see* National Survey of Children's Exposure to Violence II

NCANDS *see* National Child Abuse and Neglect Data System

Needleman, H. L. 40, 211

negative emotionality 61–68, 69n3, 123; adverse childhood experiences 93, 98; maternal stress during pregnancy 20; stress 77, 82; victimization 185

neglect 40, 67, 99, 226–227; academic performance 228; ACE score 90–91; Australia 331; emotional 227, 228, 229; impact on the brain 188; occupational therapy 297; preventive interventions 230; psychosocial risk factors 52; temperamental deficits 62; two-generation programs 231

Neonatal Abstinence Syndrome (NAS) 226

Netherlands 54, 63–65, 135

Neugebauer, R. 54

neuropsychological deficits 5, 16, 51, 53, 176; lead exposure 210, 211, 212; life-course persistent offenders 3–4; low birth weight 22–23; prenatal alcohol exposure 17

neuroscience 119, 198

neurotransmitters 175–176, 187, 188

New Directions (ND) initiative 249

New Zealand: lead exposure 211; restorative justice 278; temperament 63; traumatic brain injury 121, 122

Newman, D. L. 63

NGC *see* National Gang Center

NICHD *see* National Institute of Child Health and Human Development

NIH *see* National Institutes of Health

NIJ *see* National Institute of Justice

NIMH *see* National Institute of Mental Health

NISVS *see* National Intimate Partner and Sexual Violence Survey

Norway 150

NRC *see* National Research Council

NRCDV *see* National Resource Center on Domestic Violence

NSAL *see* National Survey of American Life

NSCH *see* National Survey of Children's Health

NSDUH *see* National Survey on Drug Use and Health

Nurse-Family Partnership 98, 192, 232

nutrition 50–60, 68n2, 230, 344; prenatal 23–24; self-control theory 38–39; teenage pregnancy 151

Obel, C. 18

obesity: adverse childhood experiences 91; food insecurity 224; impact of incarceration on families 110; low self-control 65; mortality 51; public health model 146; racial disparities 34; socioeconomic disparities 5

O'Brien, E. M. 136–137

obstetric studies 342

occupational deprivation 292

occupational justice 292

occupational therapy 291–304

Ocen, P. 276

Odgers, C. L. 7, 65

Ogilvie, J. M. 122

Ohio State University TBI Identification Method (OSU-TBI-ID) 124–125

Olds, David 192, 341

Omega-3 interventions 55–56

One Vision One Life (OVOL) 247

oppression 202, 270, 272

optimism 82

oral health 334

organized crime 319

Orr, Jessica 315–328

Ouellet-Morin, I. 190

Ousey, Graham C. 33–49

OVOL *see* One Vision One Life

Pacific Islanders 273

Pallotta-Chiarolli, M. 337

Pan American Health Organization (PAHO) 319

Panama 325

pancreatitis 7

Papachristos, A. V. 150

Paraguay 320, 321

*parens patriae* 262

parenting: adverse 3, 4; attachment theory 223; child temperament 69n3; harsh 63, 225; Head Start 231; impact of incarceration 108; occupational therapy 297; parental substance misuse 225–226; parenting programs 230, 233–234; poor 52; racial disparities 39

parents: Child-Parent Psychotherapy 232–233; drug use and delinquency in Latin America 326; early childhood risk factors 222–223; ecological framework 203; impact of incarceration 104; lack of supervision and support 201–202; mental health disorders 224–225; parent training 57, 97, 324; qualitative research with justice-involved youth 307, 309–310, 311; restorative justice 279, 281; self-control theory 38; social support 81; stress 16, 106; substance use 62, 67, 77, 223, 225–226, 322; therapeutic interventions 258; two-generation programs 231–232; *see also* family

Parents as Teachers 232

Paris, Ruth 221–243

Parker, Kenneth 300

partnerships 253, 277, 308

Pathways to Desistance study 123
patient navigation 261–262, 264
Patton, G. C. 175
PBIS *see* Positive Behavioral Interventions and Supports
Peach, H. D. 134, 139
Pearlin, L. I. 106
Pease, C. R. 65
peers 21, 68, 119, 133, 148–149; psychopathic traits 152; school-based prevention programs 248; social learning theory 203; stress 75, 77; substance use 162, 163, 245; support for illicit behavior 82; teen dating violence 199; temperament 64; victimization by 186–187
Peguero, A. A. 277
Pérez-Gómez, Augusto 315–328
Pérez-Trujillo, Mónica 315–328
perinatal health risks 16–17, 21–25, 230, 342; *see also* prenatal health risks
Perry, B. L. 274
Perry, Raymond C. 308, 344
person-in-environment perspective 306
personality 61, 65, 67; adverse childhood experiences 93; general strain theory 82; psychopathic traits 145–159; traumatic brain injury 123; *see also* temperament
personality disorders 54, 203, 343
Peru 317, 320, 321, 325
Peters, R. H. 177, 179
physical health research 343–344, 345
Piquero, A. R. 7–8, 22–23
play 297, 299–300
policing 247–248, 253
policy: drug use in Latin America 318–322, 326; policy research 344–345; teen dating violence 205
Ponsford, J. 126
Porter, L. C. 7
Posick, Chad 185–196
Positive Behavioral Interventions and Supports (PBIS) 283
post-traumatic stress disorder (PTSD) 257, 343; adverse childhood experiences 40; amygdala activation 190; community violence 224; first-responders 150; health care disparities 344; life-course persistent offenders 65; parental substance misuse 225; racial disparities 35; temperament 67; terrorist attacks 150; victimization 148, 185
poverty 52, 191, 224; Brazil 325; child abuse and neglect 227; Colombia 322–323; community mobilization 251; depression 172; deprivation theory 37; occupational therapy 296; parental incarceration 105, 109, 111; person-in-environment perspective 306; school absenteeism 281; social determinants of health 147; stress 78; structural interventions 277; teen dating violence 202; traumatic brain injury 121; two-generation programs 231; violence linked to 223

Pratt, T. C. 38
prefrontal cortex 176, 187, 189; exposure to violence 192; sleep 133; stress 191; traumatic brain injury 120, 122, 125, 126
pregnancy complications 23, 151, 222
prematurity 22–23, 38, 151, 222
prenatal care 53, 97
prenatal health risks 9–10, 16–32, 51, 53; alcohol exposure 17–18, 20, 25, 51, 297; drug exposure 19–20, 24, 51, 53, 226, 297; lead exposure 24, 210–214; maternal smoking 18–19, 20, 23, 24–25, 51, 53, 342–343; maternal stress 20–21, 39–40; nutrition/malnutrition 23–24, 54; pregnancy and birth complications 23, 151, 222, 342; prematurity and low birth weight 9, 22–23, 38, 51, 151, 222; racial disparities 39–40, 42
prevention: adverse childhood experiences 96–97, 98, 99; alcohol and drug misuse 164–165; biosocial life course perspective 164; classification of activities 330; community mobilization 246–247, 248, 251, 253; continuum of health care 338; drug use and delinquency in Latin America 319–320, 324, 326–327; early childhood 230–234; evidence-based 5, 98, 245, 251, 253; health disparities research 8–10; homeless youth 337; integrated approach 11, 336; lead exposure 210; malnutrition 57; occupational therapy 293; positive goals 85; prenatal and perinatal health risks 25; psychopathy 152, 153; public health model 146; school-based prevention programs 248–249, 251; sleep 141; teen dating violence 206; victimization 191–192
Prinstein, M. J. 148
prison *see* incarceration
probation officers 259, 260, 264, 308–309, 310, 344
problem behavior theory 161–162
problem-solving 80, 295, 299
Project Northland 248–249, 251
PROmoting School-community-university Partnerships to Enhance Resilience (PROSPER) 249, 250, 251, 253
prosocial behavior 85, 152–153, 226, 245, 248
protective factors: community mobilization 245, 248, 250, 251–252; early childhood 52–53, 55–56, 229–230, 234; general strain theory 75; maternal nutritional health 54; multiple domains 338; parental depression 225; public health approaches 330, 336; school connectedness 273; sleep 140; social structure 37; substance use 244; teen dating violence 199
psychiatric disorders 152, 188, 221–222, 343–344; *see also* mental health
psychological abuse 199–200, 201
psychopathic traits (PT) 7, 145–159
psychopathology 221–222
psychosis 333
psychosocial risk factors 51, 52
PTSD *see* post-traumatic stress disorder

public health model 146–147, 329–330, 336; drug use in Latin America 318, 319, 326; policy research 344; psychopathy 153
public safety 259, 262, 322
punishment 119, 292, 298, 322, 324; *see also* incarceration

qualitative research 305–314
Quintenz, S. 262

race: adolescent status characteristics 82; adverse childhood experiences 94, 99, 227; behavioral health interventions 258, 263; criminal justice system 36–42, 105; critical race theory 283; depression 172; health disparities 6, 9–10, 33–49; high school graduation rates 273; impact of incarceration on families 105, 111; as moderating factor 4; physical health disorders 344; policy research 344; restorative justice 279, 281, 282–283; school absenteeism 281; school discipline 275–277, 279, 282–283; sleep 140; substance use disorders 170; teen dating violence 201, 202; violent crime 5, 8; *see also* African Americans; Black people; ethnicity; Hispanics/Latinos; Native Americans; White people
racism 37–38, 39, 42, 272, 277, 283, 306
Raine, A. 55, 342
randomized control designs: Circle of Security 234; community mobilization 250, 252, 253; epidemiological research 213; family engagement 263; home visiting 232; sleep 138; *see also* research designs
rape 202, 204
Raphael, S. 41
Rathouz, P. J. 18–19
Rausch, M. K. 283
recidivism: adverse childhood experiences 93, 94, 98; juvenile probation 259; mental health disorders 174, 257; restorative justice 279, 282; substance use and mental health disorder co-morbidity 178, 179; substance use disorders 171, 257; therapeutic interventions 258, 259
recruitment of research participants 309–311, 313
reentry 260, 300, 305, 306, 307–313
rehabilitation 262, 300; cognitive deficits 125; juvenile probation 259; occupational therapy 293, 296; traumatic brain injury 126
Reider, C. 53
Reidy, Dennis E. 145–159
Reingle, J. M. 7–8
relapse prevention 178
relational ecology 278
religiosity 82
Renn, Tanya 119–131
research designs 209–210, 213–214; community mobilization 252, 253; restorative justice 281; sleep 137–138, 141; *see also* data collection; randomized control designs

residential mobility 96
resilience 85, 229, 230, 234, 295
Resnick, S. G. 175
resource deprivation 37, 39
resources 75, 76, 78–82, 83, 84, 105
respiratory disease 244
Restivo, E. 135
restorative justice 269, 278–284, 321–322, 324, 326
Rettew, D. C. 63–64
Reuben, A. 210
Reyes, J. W. 211
Reyes-Rodríguez, M. F. 316
Rice, F. 343
Riggins, T. 19–20
rights 321, 322
risk factors 5; community mobilization 245, 248, 250, 251–252; early childhood 51–52, 221–229, 234; ecological framework 203; environmental 176–177, 209–210, 213–214, 224; multiple domains 338; public health approaches 330, 336; sleep 140; social structure 37; substance use 244, 245; teen dating violence 199, 200, 201–202; *see also* prenatal health risks
risky behaviors 64, 329; abused children 186; adolescence 172; adverse childhood experiences 91; alcohol and drug misuse 161, 163; Australia 330, 335; criminal propensity 82; incarceration 7; psychopathic traits 148, 151, 152; sleep and risk-taking 132, 134–135, 136; stress proliferation 78; teen dating violence 201; temperament 66; victimization 148
Roberts, B. W. 66
Robinson, J. 177
*Roper v. Simmons* (2005) 119, 127
Rothbart, M. K. 67–68
Rothman, K. J. 212–213
routines 295, 298
Royal Australian College of Physicians (RACP) 330, 337
Rumberger, R. W. 273
Runions, K. C. 64

Sacks, S. 179
Salas-Wright, Christopher P. 160–168, 341–346
same-sex teen dating violence 198
SAMHSA *see* Substance Abuse and Mental Health Services Administration
Sampson, R. J. 3, 4, 9, 211
Samson, J. A. 188, 189
Sapolsky, Robert 127
Sareen, J. 177
Sariaslan, A. 214
Sayal, K. 17
Scharrer, E. 150
schizophrenia 35, 214
Schmalleger, F. 316
Scholes-Balog, K. E. 334

schools 269–290; adverse childhood experiences 228; discipline 273–277, 279, 282–283, 284; drug use and delinquency in Latin America 326; ecological framework 203; Life Skills Training 192; occupational therapy 296, 297–298; psychopathic traits 148, 149; restorative justice 269, 278–284; risk factors for substance use 245; school-based prevention programs 248–249, 251; school dropout 37, 68, 152, 273, 274–275, 279, 315, 320; school-to-prison pipeline 36, 269, 284; social support 85; start times 140; stress 77, 83; *see also* academic performance; education
Schwartz, J. A. 123
Schwartz, Katherine 257–268
Schwartz, M. D. 203
Schwartz, S. J. 299
screening: adverse childhood experiences 97, 99; behavioral health treatment 260, 261; developmental 230; intimate partner violence 205–206; juvenile probation 259; needs identification 337; sleep 141; substance use and mental health disorder co-morbidity 178
Sebring, P. B. 282
secondary prisonization 108
Seewald, K. 173
segregation 6, 40, 272, 276–277
SEL *see* Social Emotional Learning
selection bias 212–213
self-advocacy 295
self-control 10, 65, 68; interventions 98; prefrontal cortex 191; self-control theory 38–39; sleep/delinquency relationship 138–139, 140, 141; temperament 64–65, 66; traumatic brain injury 123; youth organizations 191–192; *see also* effortful control
self-directed coalitions 246–247, 251
self-efficacy 78–79, 81
self-esteem: child abuse and neglect 228; community violence 224; stress 76, 78–79, 80–81, 84; teen dating violence 201; WHO principles 337
self-harm 67, 121–122, 228, 329, 332–333; *see also* suicide/suicidality
self-medication hypothesis 176–177
self-regulation: adverse childhood experiences 91; executive functioning 122–123; impact of stress on 74; interventions 98; malnutrition 68n2; occupational therapy 298; parental depression 225; prefrontal cortex 133; prenatal cocaine exposure 19; protective factors 229; temperament 61, 64, 65, 69n3; traumatic brain injury 123; *see also* emotional regulation
self-reports 137, 204, 206
sensation-seeking 133, 134, 161, 172, 330; *see also* thrill-seeking
September 11th 2001 terrorist attacks 150
serious, violent, and chronic (SVC) offenders 93, 187; *see also* life-course persistent offenders
serotonin 175–176, 189, 190

SES *see* Sexual Experiences Survey
sexual abuse 40, 94, 227, 228; amygdala activation 190; Colombia 323; drugs linked to 315; human trafficking 96; impact on mental health 186; impact on the brain 188; teen dating violence 197–198, 200, 201; *see also* abuse
sexual behaviors 51, 329; abused children 186; adverse childhood experiences 91, 228; Australia 330, 335; Fetal Alcohol Spectrum Disorder 18; peer influence 149; psychopathic traits 145, 148, 149, 151; risk-taking 134; temperament 64, 66; victimization 148
Sexual Experiences Survey (SES) 204–205
sexual offenders 92
sexual violence: children's exposure to 185; health consequences 50; psychopathic traits 149, 151; teen dating violence 199, 201
sexuality/sexual orientation 82, 270; *see also* LGBTQ+ youth
sexually transmitted diseases (STDs) 7, 50, 344; alcohol and drug misuse 163; Australia 335; foster care 228; homelessness 331; psychopathic traits 149; racial disparities 34; self-control theory 38–39; teen dating violence 202; victimization 148, 185
Shasha, M. 262
Shaw, D. S. 342
Shepherd, J. 336
shootings 149–151
Short, M. A. 134
Shum, D. H. 122
sickle cell disease 344
Siegel, J. A. 186
SIG *see* State Incentives Grant
Silva, P. A. 63
Simi, Pete 132–144
single parents 66
Skiba, R. J. 283
sleep 11, 132–144; health promotion research 344; impact of incarceration 108; impact of trauma 191; maternal depression 343; parental incarceration 8; peer victimization 187
Slep, A. M. S. 63
Smith, A. 19
Smith, L. M. 20
smoking: adolescence-limited offenders 4; adverse childhood experiences 91, 228; benefits of home visits 341–342; community mobilization 249, 250; educational attainment relationship 270; high-school students 244; incarceration 108; Latin America 318; low self-control 65; lung cancer link 213; maternal depression 343; maternal smoking during pregnancy 18–19, 20, 23, 24–25, 51, 53, 342–343; mortality 51; peak age of 170; residential mobility 96; school-based prevention programs 249; school dropout 68; secondhand smoke 11; sleep 134; teen dating violence 202; temperament 66

social bonds 4, 5, 9
social capital 5, 6
social class 4, 82; *see also* socioeconomic status
social cohesion 245
social contagion 148–149, 150
social context: biosocial life course perspective 164, 165; homelessness 332; occupational therapy 293; personal and social resources 79; social support 82; stress 75, 77, 78; therapeutic interventions 258
social control 9, 10; general strain theory 82; informal 3, 4, 248, 253; restorative justice 283
social determinants of health 147, 151–152, 227, 284, 330, 336
Social Development Model 330
social ecological model 147, 203, 329–330
Social Emotional Learning (SEL) 283
social learning theory 202–203
social privilege 10
social structure 37, 74, 75, 79, 277–278
social support: adverse childhood experiences 98; bolstering 85; impact of incarceration on families 107, 109, 111; parental depression 225; stress 76, 78–79, 81–82, 83, 84, 105, 107; treatment of co-occurring disorders 179
socialization 8–9; personal and social resources 79; psychopathic traits 145; secondary prisonization 108; stress 75
socioeconomic status: depression 172; educational quality 230; health disparities 5–6, 9–10; incarceration 105; Latinos 34; maternal prenatal smoking 19; oppression 270; parental substance misuse 226; policy research 344; risk factors 224, 330; school discipline 275; sleep 140; substance use disorders 170; temperament 66; violence linked to 5, 8, 223
Sohoni, Tracy W. P. 33–49
Solomon, J. 223
Spinrad, T. L. 63
Springer, K. W. 186
stalking 199
State Incentives Grant (SIG) 249, 253
status 82
STDs *see* sexually transmitted diseases
Stevenson, J. 63
Stewart, A. L. 122
stigma: homeless youth 337; incarceration 106, 107; mental illness 150–151; psychopathic traits 146; stress 77, 83
Stone, M. H. 149
strain theory 74, 75–76, 78–79, 82
street children 296–297
stress 74–89, 172; adverse childhood experiences 91, 93, 95; appraisal 76, 78, 80, 82, 84; arrest and incarceration 257; early intervention 97; early life 222; epigenetics 190; general strain theory 74, 75–76, 78–79, 82; impact of incarceration on families 104, 105–107, 108, 111; impact on the brain 188, 189, 191; key stress domains 77–78; maternal 20–21, 39–40, 53; parents 16, 225; personal and social resources 76, 78–82, 83, 84, 105; pregnancy and birth complications 23; proliferation 77–78, 83, 84, 85, 105, 106, 108; racial disparities 40; socioeconomic disparities 6; stress process model 74, 75–76, 78–79, 105–107, 111; substance use and depression co-morbidity 176; teen dating violence 198, 201; teenage pregnancy 95–96; violence linked to 223
Stretesky, P. B. 211
STRiV *see* National Survey of Teen Relationships and Intimate Violence
stroke 110, 186
structural interventions 277–284
Study of Early Child Care and Youth 139
Substance Abuse and Mental Health Services Administration (SAMHSA) 172, 174, 249, 253
substance use 160–168, 170–171, 257, 329; adverse childhood experiences 91, 94, 95, 98, 227; Australia 334–335; behavioral health interventions 258, 263; chronic health conditions 83; community mobilization 244–256; coping styles 80; depression co-morbidity 169, 174–179; ecological framework 203; first-responders 150; general strain theory 75; health care disparities 344; homelessness 331; impact of incarceration on families 109, 110; impact of incarceration on the individual 107, 108; Juvenile Justice Behavioral Health Services Cascade 260; juvenile probation 259; life-course persistent offenders 65; Life Skills Training 192; maternal prenatal smoking 18; occupational therapy 297; parental 62, 67, 77, 223, 225–226, 322; peer influence 148; poor housing 224; pregnancy and birth complications 23; preventive interventions 230; psychopathic traits 148, 151–152; psychosocial risk factors 52; racial disparities 35; school connectedness 273; school discipline 273–274; stress 76, 105; teen dating violence 201, 202; temperament 64, 66, 67; traumatic brain injury 122, 126; victimization 148; *see also* alcohol use; drug use
suicide/suicidality: abused children 186; adverse childhood experiences 91, 94–95, 228; deliberate self-harm 333; health care disparities 344; incarceration 7; life-course persistent offenders 65; residential mobility 96; school connectedness 273; school dropout 68; sleep problems 132; substance use 152, 174–175; teen dating violence 198, 202; teenage pregnancy 151; temperament 66, 67; traumatic brain injury 121–122; victimization 148
Supreme Court 119, 127
suspension from school 274, 275–276, 279, 280, 282–283
SVC offenders *see* serious, violent, and chronic offenders
Sweden 20, 40, 121, 214
systems alignment 98–99

Taiwan 135, 136
TBI *see* traumatic brain injury
technology 137, 200
teen dating violence (TDV) 197–208
teenage pregnancy 52, 53–54, 151, 344; adverse childhood experiences 91, 95–96, 228; drug use linked to 315; poor housing 224
Teicher, M. H. 188, 189
temperament 5, 61–73, 123, 222; life-course persistent offenders 3; maternal stress during pregnancy 20, 21; parental mental illness 225; prenatal health risks 16; protective factors 229
Ten Point Coalition 248
Teplin, L. A. 258
terrorism 150
Teten, A. L. 199–200
TF-CBT *see* Trauma-Focused CBT
TFCO *see* Treatment Foster Care Oregon
therapeutic communities 179
therapeutic interventions 192, 232–234, 257–258, 259; *see also* cognitive-behavioral therapy
Thoits, P. A. 81, 82, 106
Thorsborne, M. 278–279, 282
thrill-seeking 148; *see also* sensation-seeking
Tibbetts, S. G. 22–23
TJI *see* Transformative Justice Initiative
tobacco *see* smoking
Todic, Jelena 269–290
Toumbourou, J. W. 334
Towers, S. 150
toxin exposure 24, 40, 42, 51, 210–214
Tracking Adolescents' Individual Lives Survey (TRAILS) 64–65
tranquillizers 317, 324, 325
Transformative Justice Initiative (TJI) 300–301
transitions: depression 173; informal social control 4; occupational therapy 293, 298, 299
trauma 77, 186, 333–334; adverse childhood experiences 91, 94, 227; alcohol and drug misuse 164, 165; Australia 331; Child-Parent Psychotherapy 232–233; early childhood 221, 229; impact on physical health 187; impact on sleep 139, 191; impact on the brain 189, 190; occupational therapy 297; psychiatric disorders 188; substance use and depression co-morbidity 176; *see also* abuse; post-traumatic stress disorder
Trauma-Focused CBT (TF-CBT) 97
traumatic brain injury (TBI) 7, 40, 119–131; assessment 124–125; interventions 125–126; negative outcomes of 121–123; racial disparities 42; substance use 163
treatment: behavioral 257–268; sexual abuse 186; substance use and mental health disorder co-morbidity 178–179; substance use disorders 171; *see also* interventions
Treatment Foster Care Oregon (TFCO) 257–258
Trombetta, Elise 197–208

tuberculosis 34
Turner, K. A. 65
Turner, R. J. 40
Turney, Kristin 8, 104–115
twin studies 63, 190, 209–210, 213–214
two-generation programs 231–232
Tzoumakis, Stacy 16–32

ulcers 8
Um, Phoebe 50–60
UN Convention on the Rights of the Child 321, 322
unemployment: depression 173; deprivation theory 37; ecological framework 203; occupational therapy 296; parental 52
United Kingdom: antisocial behavior 329, 334; deliberate self-harm 333; maternal stress during pregnancy 20–21; traumatic brain injury 121
United States: alcohol use 244, 316; anger 65; antisocial behavior 329; child abuse and neglect 226; community mobilization 246–253; deliberate self-harm 333; depression 172; drug use as delinquent behavior 315; education and costs of poor health 270–271; health disparities 5; high school graduation rates 273; home visiting 232; incarceration 7, 104, 109, 110; lead exposure 211–212; malnutrition 53; occupational therapy 293, 297–301; oral health 334; prenatal drug exposure 19; qualitative research 307–313; racial disparities 6, 33–49; restorative justice 278–284; *Roper v. Simmons* 119, 127; school discipline 273–277; school-to-prison pipeline 269; sleep problems 132, 140; substance use and depression co-morbidity 174, 175; substance use disorders 170, 171, 174; teen dating violence 197; tobacco use 244; traumatic brain injury 121, 122, 127; victimization 185; "War on Drugs" 319
Uruguay 317, 318, 321, 325–326

Vaandering, D. 278–279, 283
Valente, T. W. 148
values 82
Van den Bergh, B. R. 21
van Den Bulk, B. G. 190
Van der Ende, J. 63–64
Van Hulle, C. A. 18–19
Varela, K. S. 277
Vaughn, Michael G. 3–15, 341–346; maternal health risks 39–40; sleep 135, 136; substance use 161; temperament 61–62, 63, 64, 67, 123; traumatic brain injury 122
Veeh, Christopher A. 119–131
Venables, P. H. 55
Verhulst, F. C. 63–64
victimization 185–196; adolescence 75, 77; alcohol and drug misuse 163, 164, 165; bullying 148; child abuse and neglect 226; depression 173–174; health consequences 148; psychopathic traits 152; Sexual

Experiences Survey 204–205; sleep/delinquency relationship 139, 140; teen dating violence 198, 206

violence 5, 8, 9–10, 11; adverse childhood experiences 40, 91, 92–93; alcohol and drug misuse 161, 163, 165, 334; Colombia 323; community mobilization 247, 248, 250, 251; cycle of 92; desensitization to 150, 151, 152; exposure to family violence 223; health outcomes 7–8; high-school students 244; homeless youth 332, 333, 337; incarceration 107; Latin America 320; lead exposure correlation with 211–212, 214; life-course persistent offenders 65; Life Skills Training 192; malnutrition 54–55; mass shootings 149–151; maternal stress during pregnancy 21; occupational therapy 296; parental 67; prevention 165, 230; psychopathic traits 146, 147–148, 149, 151; as public health issue 50; racial disparities 6, 38; restorative justice 279, 280; schools 273, 274; sleep/delinquency relationship 134–135, 136–137; teen dating violence 197–208; temperament 66, 67, 69n4; traumatic brain injury 40, 121, 123; victims of 185–196; "War on Drugs" 319; *see also* abuse; aggression; domestic violence; intimate partner violence

Wadhwa, A. K. 283
Wakschlag, L. S. 342–343
Wandersman, A. 245
Wang, F. L. 63
Watts, Stephen J. 209–217
Weber, N. 134
Weisburd, D. 253
Wekerle, C. 202
well-being: maternal stress during pregnancy 21; occupational therapy 295; qualitative research 305, 306; restorative justice 279, 281; schools 273; sleep/delinquency relationship 138, 141; social support 81; socioeconomic disparities 6; stress 75–76, 78–79, 84
Wexler, H. K. 177

White, B. A. 65
White, Norman 293
White people: adultification 277; adverse childhood experiences 94; depression 172; health disparities 6, 33–35, 37; high school graduation rates 273; incarceration 36, 99, 105; poverty 37; school discipline 275–276, 283; self-control theory 39; substance use disorders 170; teen dating violence 201; *see also* ethnicity; race
White, S. F. 148
Whiteford, G. 292
WHO *see* World Health Organization
Wildeman, C. 8
Williams, L. M. 186
Williams, W. H. 121
Winkelman, T. N. 344
Winter, A. S. 211
Wolfe, D. A. 202, 204
Wolff, K. T. 62, 93
women: drug use in Latin America 316–318; impact of incarceration on families 108–109, 110; support for pregnant 25; violence against 202, 203; *see also* gender differences; prenatal health risks; teenage pregnancy
working memory 123, 224
World Health Organization (WHO) 50, 197, 203, 270, 293, 337
Wright, J. P. 211

youth organizations 191–192
Youth Risk Behavior Surveillance System (YRBSS) 201, 244
Yücel, M. 64
YVPC *see* National Centers of Excellence in Youth Violence Prevention

Zehr, H. 278
zero-tolerance policies 273, 274–275, 276, 279
Zhang, N. 211
zinc deficiency 54–55